SIN AND MENTAL AILMENTS

SIN AND MENTAL AILMENTS

PASTORAL PSYCHIATRY AND PSYCHOLOGY FOR HEALING PROFESSIONALS, PASTORS AND INQUIRING CHRISTIANS

Paul Ungar MD, Ph.D.

ELM HILL

A Division of
HarperCollins Christian Publishing

www.elmhillbooks.com

SIN and MENTAL AILMENTS

PASTORAL PSYCHIATRY AND PSYCHOLOGY FOR HEALING PROFESSIONALS, PASTORS AND INQUIRING CHRISTIANS

Published in Nashville, Tennessee, by Elm Hill, an imprint of Thomas Nelson. Elm Hill and Thomas Nelson are registered trademarks of HarperCollins Christian Publishing, Inc.

Elm Hill titles may be purchased in bulk for educational, business, fund-raising, or sales promotional use. For information, please e-mail SpecialMarkets@ThomasNelson.com.

Library of Congress Cataloging-in-Publication Data

Library of Congress Control Number: 2019910456

ISBN 978-1-400327270 (Paperback)
ISBN 978-1-400327287 (eBook)

ACKNOWLEDGMENTS

The author acknowledges that the *Sin And Mental Ailments Pastoral Psychiatry And Psychology For Healing Professionals, Pastors And Inquiring Christians* is not an independent book, but is, in part, a compilation of the author's previously published books: *The Mystery of Christian Faith: A Tangible Union with the Invisible God: An Apologetic on the Borderline of Theology, Medicine, and Philosophy* (University Press of America, 2008) and Flawed Institution: *Flawless Church: A Response to Pope John Paul's Appeal for a Critical Self-Evaluation of the Church* (Cambridge Scholars Publishing, 2013). Thanks to Dr. Eva Bezzegh for cover design.

DEDICATION

This book is dedicated to my dear children—
Maria, Julia, Paul, Joseph, Andrew, Marta, and Thomas—
and my wife, Marta, without whose support this book could
not have been completed.

CONTENTS

Part 3: Conditions of Special Pastoral Interest and Their Treatment

PART 4: PERSONALITY TRAITS CORRELATING TO SPECIFIC FAITH PROBLEMS AND THEIR PASTORAL TREATMENT

PART 5: PASTORAL-PSYCHOLOGICAL ASPECTS OF EVANGELIZATION

PREFACE

The Church is in crisis. One of the signs of this crisis is that only about thirty percent of all believers regularly attend Sunday worship in North America. Therefore, a new evangelization focused on reevangelization of already-baptized Christians is dearly needed. It would focus on pastoral care not only for those who consciously and deliberately transgress God's law, but also for people suffering from sickness (i.e., psychological or psychiatric disorders), which facilitate their sinful estrangement from Jesus. Such an approach is substantiated by the fact that despite all differences, there are also numerous connections between sinful behaviors and sickness. For example, the malignant selfishness that we recognize as sin is often tied to unhealthy narcissistic character features. A repeated belligerent acting out might be facilitated by a paranoid mindset. Emotional cruelty may be not freely chosen but tied to antisocial personality traits. Likewise, there is a self-evident connection between sinning against the Sixth Commandment "You shall not commit adultery" (Exodus 20:14) and the illness of peadophilia. The reverse is also true. In peadophilia and most other sick behaviors, an intentional and sinful transgression of Jesus' commands occurs. Thus, sin and sickness are not always mutually exclusive categories, but are often connected; both are a paramount human reality, and their relationship is often comparable to a chicken and the egg paradigm: which caused which?

The mutual causation between sin and sickness makes efforts to cure them complicated. Consider the case of Tammy, a depressed twenty-three-year-old woman. Her father abandoned the family before Tammy's birth, and her mother perceived Tammy as responsible for the loss of her partner. Defending herself from this imposed guilt, Tammy rationalized, "My mother is evil. She chased away my father. But he will come and protect me from her." Since her father never returned, the disillusioned and rebellious Tammy assumed that he must be dead, and then generalized, "Like my earthly father, God does not protect me. He must be dead [nonexistent] too." Therefore, she became a militant atheist. Tammy's depression endorsed her doubts, and her living in a godless world enforced her depression. How to heal the stigma of mental problems, and cure the sufferings caused by the intricate ties between sinful and psychologically distorted behaviors in people like Tammy, and in all fallen descendants of Adam and Eve, is the topic of this book.

As an atheist, Tammy proved to herself through an invalid syllogism to be a futile and worthless "natural event." For her healing, she needed to appreciate that she was a living soul and the object of God's love. Therefore, the first part of this book integrates biblical and scientific anthropology. It also discusses how sin and sickness relate to responsibility in people suffering from psychoses, people suffering from nonpsychotic disorders, and virtually healthy people. Finally, it discusses demonic and medical aspects of psychic ailments and the role of pastoral disciplines in the orchestra of therapies.

The second part of the book compares the professional and pastoral healing of psychic ailments. Tammy could be prescribed antidepressants that would numb her depression but not heal her worldviews. She would continue living a meaningless life and adapt her mood to that gloomy reality. Pastoral healing, however, would help Tammy say something like, "Yes, I lost my biological father, but this helped me find my heavenly Father!"

The third part of the book examines topics of specific pastoral interest, such as early childhood, adolescence, sexuality, eroticism, love, masturbation, pornography, homosexuality, old age, death, grief, suicide, and post-abortion reactions. Unresolved conflicts in these turning points of human life facilitate the risk of sick and/or sinful behavior and estrangement from Jesus, as is evident in the case of Tammy.

The fourth part of the book discusses personality traits that correlate to specific faith problems. The book will discuss scruples, moral laxity, superstition, idolatry, fanaticism, positivism, hypocrisy, and the phenomenon called "the dark night of the soul," which are not psychiatric disorders but still jeopardize a believer's peace of mind and union with Christ.

The fifth part of the book focuses on evangelization. All people are called by God, but we observe that atheists, like the chronically depressed Tammy, are unsuccessful in answering God's call. To understand why this is and how to address it, this book will examine the role that sin and psychological problems play in individuals' ability to experience the trust, love, peace, and joy that faith gives so that they can encounter God.

Since the healing of conditions like depression, anxiety, and atheism does not know man-made denominational boundaries, this book uses an ecumenical approach. This concise but detailed compendium, both a textbook and a Christian self-help book, provides information about pastoral healing of both frequent and rare disorders.

Thank you,
Paul

PART ONE

REVELATION AND KNOWLEDGE

Until 1633 Earth was perceived as the centre of the universe, symbolically demonstrating God's providence for humans. Galileo's discoveries destroyed this security and caused a shift in the collective thinking during the Enlightenment. Scientific astronomy and biblical theology came to be viewed as mutually exclusive. In the last two hundred years, a similar change has occurred in secular anthropology, the perception that humans are nothing more than highly evolved animals. But while astronomy has become generally synchronized with biblical teachings (since the discovery of the Big Bang), Christians, in their anthropological self-understanding, are still contested by other forms of knowledge that seemed to render faith-as-knowledge superfluous or absurd.[1] Consequently, there exists a communications gap between Christians and people like Tammy. For instance, nothing is more evident to believers than being created in God's image, although nothing is *less* evident to atheists. Different ideas about what it means to be human can produce contrasting knowledge, feelings, information, language experiences, behaviors, and lifestyles even for people living in same time and culture. If atheists and believers inhabit such parallel worlds, then how can we help people like Tammy to appreciate being created in God's image and likeness?

To paraphrase philosopher Wayne H. Dyer, if you change the way you look at humanity, then the humanity you look at changes. This section of the book will enable atheists to perceive humanity from a Christian perspective while helping Christians to better understand atheists. After contrasting both paradigms, the compendium will integrate relevant biblical-theological and empirical-scientific facts into a unified system.

CHAPTER ONE

SYNCHRONIZING BIBLICAL AND MEDICAL ANTHROPOLOGY

P sychologically, it is hard to believe one thing while scientifically believing or experiencing the contrary. So it is tough for Tammy and sceptics like her to appreciate the notion that they are living souls if their anthropological beliefs contradict biblical revelations. The first step in resolving such hardships is to clarify what is meant by synchronizing biblical and biological anthropology and then to discuss whether such integration is doable.

1.1 The Rationale of a Biblical-Medical Integration

While the Scriptures are static, "written in stone," theology is dynamic and is integrated with the mental climate of its age. Such an integration process has occurred throughout the whole of church history. For example, it became obvious to Christians in the fourth and fifth centuries that the creeds of the early church could not be successfully formulated by discussing particular questions or defining answers to them in figurative and metaphorical biblical terminology. So, the church, during the first great ecumenical synods, supplemented Semitic biblical vernacular with painfully precise biblical-philosophical definitions in formulating Christological and Trinitarian definitions. This trend of supplementing biblical concepts with philosophical ideas culminated in Middle Age scholasticism. Thomas Aquinas (1225–1274), in his grandiose work *Summa Theologiae*[2], discussed in 3 parts, 38 tracts, 631 questions, 3016 articulations, and approximately 15,000 proofs the possibility of integrating Aristotle's philosophical concepts with Christian theological concepts.

While in the past synchronization between theologians and devout philosophers occurred regularly, today we are required to go a step further than Aquinas. We need to find common ground, not only between theologians and God-friendly philosophers like Aristotle, but also between these and modern scientists who are often agnostic, religiously indifferent, or atheistic in their world views. Also, we Christians and, even more urgently, a skeptical world need a common denominator between empirically known and revealed truths.

My first encounter with a discrepancy between what I believed and what I could observe came when I was a medical resident. I saw how measurable biological functioning made the difference between life and death in my patients. A biblical, ineffable spirit seemed, in my naive medical exuberance, unnecessary for healing and sustaining life. Privately I trusted the Bible, but professionally I had to respect medical facts. I was therefore challenged by the feeling that two mutually exclusive concepts cannot be equally true.

I was not alone in my insecurity. All Christian students, residents, physicians, psychologists, nurses, and virtually all people of faith today have to choose between two paradigms: biblical or scientific, anthropological concepts. That choice is made difficult by the fact that both paradigms have unquestionable merit—one reflecting infallible biblical revelation, the other having been empirically proven. In such a situation, we must acknowledge both paradigms as valid. If it seems hard to integrate them, the problem is not with the concepts themselves but with our ability to synchronize them. We should adopt a paradigm in which religion and science have their appropriate roles and are not mutually exclusive of one another.

The rationale for such a synchronization has been best formulated by the theologian Rudolf Schnackenburg. Humans are, as he notes, "a new lifeform in which existence in the world is united with holiness," which "makes a radically new creation in which the two orders [natural and spiritual]

4

become connected."[3] If humans are, as Schnackenburg states, "natural and spiritual" creatures, then an anthropological model is needed in which both aspects of humanity, the natural and the spiritual, have their place.

In this context, we will introduce the essentials of biblical anthropology and discuss the basic concepts of scientific anthropology.

1.2 A Summary of Biblical Anthropology

St. Paul summarizes his anthropology in 1 Thessalonians 5:23: "May your whole spirit, soul, and body be kept blameless at the coming of our Lord Jesus Christ." Throughout his epistles, the terms *spirit, soul,* and *body* are often synonymous, but in some passages, they are different entities. His purpose was not to define terms with scientific accuracy but to share the Good News. For this purpose, the apostle frequently used metaphors. Concepts such as soul and spirit lie on the edge of human understanding and are difficult to conceptualize in concrete terms.

For example, the spirit—God's life-giving breath—is biblically depicted by a contemporary metaphor. In most oriental civilizations 3,000 years ago, breathing was viewed as an obvious sign of life. For Hebrews, receiving God's breath (*the spirit* in English, *ruah* in Hebrew, *pneume* in Greek, and *spiritus* in Latin) symbolized receiving the mystery we call life. "The same Hebrew word designates the wind and the spirit," and as the wind may be "barely sensible, and as such close to nonmaterial" or powerful and "nonre-sistible,"[4] so is it also with God's life-giving spirit. It is barely perceptible (as in Gen 2:7, 6:17, 7:15; Job 33:4) when God's breath acts as the principle of life, and it is irresistible as Job 34:14–15 establishes: "If it were his intention and he withdrew his spirit and breath, all humankind would perish together and man would return to dust."[5] In death, God takes his creative power back (Ps 104:29). *Spirit is the principle of life and a sign of a basic existential relationship with God manifested by the phenomenon of living.*

The word soul (*nefesh* in *Hebrew,* psyche in Greek, and animus in Latin) has even more diverse metaphorical meanings than spirit. It is described by attributes like throat (Isa 5:14; Hab. 2:5), neck (1 Sam 28:9; Ps 105:18), hunger (Deut. 12:20; 1 Sam 2:16), thirst (Prov 25:25), desires (Prov 23:2), justice (Isa 26:8– 9), evil (Prov 21:10), power (2 Sam 3:21), hate (Isa 1:14), grief (Jer. 13:17), joy (Ps 42:5), unhappiness (1 Sam 1:15), and seeking and yearning for God (Ps 42:1–2). These metaphors reflect the complexity and wholeness of the human person whose task is keeping God's commands (Ecclesiastes 12:13–14).

The New Testament also describes the soul in metaphors. John 3:6 illustrates, "Flesh gives birth to flesh, but the Spirit gives birth to spirit," and John 6:63 says, "The Spirit gives life; the flesh counts for nothing." Romans 8:16 reads, "The Spirit himself testifies with our spirit that we are God's children," and 1 Corinthians 6:17 similarly says, "But he who unites himself with the Lord is one with him in spirit." Despite the fact that the terms *spirit* and *soul* are often used interchangeably, we realize that the soul receives "life" and "birth," is "one" with the Lord, and "testifies" with God. Colloquially, *soul* is *the principle agent of a responsible relationship with God.* As such, the soul has one more important property.

Jesus, in Luke 23:43, promised the repentant sinner, "I tell you the truth, today you will be with me in paradise." He talks not about resurrection but about being with him immediately after death. Taking biblical revelations into account, on January 29, 1336, Pope Benedict XII proclaimed as an infallible dogma in his bull *Benedictus Deus* that the souls of exemplary Christians enjoy an eternal face-to-face relationship with God, beginning immediately after death (i.e., before Jesus' Second Coming and before bodily resurrection happens). In this context, the soul, representing the whole person, is judged immediately after death and is able to receive the benefit of eternal glory with God immediately after death.[6]

The Catechism envisions happenings in and after death.

> In death, the separation of the soul from the body occurs, the human body decays and the soul goes to meet God, while awaiting its reunion with its glorified body. God in his almighty power will definitely grant incorruptible life to our bodies by reuniting them with our souls, through the power of Jesus' resurrection.[7]

Note that the biblical idea of the body (*bassar* in Hebrew, *soma* in Greek, and *corpus* in Latin) is not limited to the biological body. The biblical idea of the body is what enables humans to take their "appropriate place in the universe in the hierarchy of created things."[8] But there is also a resurrected body. What will this body be like?

The resurrection happens "at the last day"—that is, "at the end of the world" (John 6:39–40, 44, 54; 11: 24). "It is closely associated with Christ's Parousia. For the Lord himself will descend from heaven with a cry of command, with the archangels call, and with a sound of a trumpet of God. And the dead in Christ will rise first."[9] John Paul II explains (drawing from Luke 20:27–40) that resurrected bodies "are equal to the angels and, being sons of the resurrection, they are sons of God." This indicates a spiritualization of man after death and a divinization of humanity that is a participation in the inner life of God himself. "The 'natural body' (1 Cor. 15:44) is condemned to death; instead, he should rise as a 'spiritual body,' as the man in whom the spirit will gain its supremacy over the body."[10]

Besides spirit, soul, and body, St. Paul introduces one more essential human aspect:

> Now this is our boast: Our conscience testifies that we have conducted ourselves in the world, and especially in our relationship with you, in the holiness and sincerity that are from God. We have done so not according to worldly wisdom, but according to God's grace (2 Corinthians 1:12).

Where is the place of conscience in St. Paul's anthropology, and how is it related to the body, spirit, and soul—and to God? He does not answer these questions explicitly. Nevertheless, he notes that Gentiles also obey the natural law written in their hearts, "their consciences also bearing witness, and their thoughts now accusing, now even defending them" (Romans 2:14–15). It is hard not to see the parallel: as soul is the spiritual function of responsibly keeping God's law, so is conscience the psychological function "bearing witness" about one's reflecting (or not reflecting) God's love. Conscience is performing a similar task in a psychological area, as soul is performing in a spiritual area. While conscience strives "that [it] may serve the living God" (Romans 9:14), the soul "pants for you, O God" (Psalm 42:1–2). Biblically, as the soul reflects God's nature (Matthew 11:29; Luke 1:47; Philippians 1:23; Luke 23:43), so also does conscience (1 Tim 1:5; 1 Tim 1:19; 2 Tim 1:3; Hebrews 13:18). While other anthropological ideas may seem ineffable, conscience is empirical. By judging human behavior from God's perspective (2 Corinthians 1:12) and using our "thoughts now accusing, now even defending" (Romans 2:14–15), conscience psychologically informs us about God's law of love.

1.3 A Summary of Scientific Anthropology

As medical students, my peers and I had to attend an unpleasant experiment. It began with a frog being put into narcosis. Then the heart of the living frog was carefully extracted. After awakening from his stupor, the frog began to crawl away while its extracted heart continued to beat. Next, the heart muscle was isolated from the frog's heart and placed in an appropriate physiological solution. The heart muscle continued to contract. Our physiology professor then invited us to continue the experiment in our thoughts. She proposed that the living molecules of actine and mysosin could be extracted from the heart muscle and kept alive for a while. But we could go even further, she explained, and extract the living atoms which build the living heart muscle's molecules. Our professor finally concluded her demonstration by describing a reversal of the experiment. We could now, she said, return the living atoms into the living molecules and return the living molecules into the frog's living heart muscle. Next, we could insert the living heart muscle into the living frog's heart, and finally we could put the frog's heart back into the frog. At that point, the frog would once again be a living animal.

"What then is life?" she asked. "Life is a complexity. It is an organization in which every atom, every molecule, every tissue, and every organ is in its place and fulfils its role, so the body becomes that of a living creature." In this description of life, the biblical spirit is replaced with organization and complexity. Living creatures are differentiated from nonliving things by their complex organization, with which every living atom and molecule is organized to function so that it sustains the processes we call the life of the organism, while the organism sustains the living functions in all of its living cells. How does this occur in practice?

The British physician John H. Jackson (1836–1911) recognized a correlation between the principles regulating bodily functions and the sophistication of behaviors in living creatures.[11] For example, in the bodies of the simplest living creatures (like viruses), simple physical-chemical processes (like adhesion, cohesion, osmosis, oxidation, and reductive processes) are linked together, enabling their behavior (living functions). In the simplest multicellular organisms (like sponges or sea stars), the single physical-chemical processes in their cells are biochemically linked in behaviors serving the whole organism. We discern an even more complex hierarchical organization in animals possessing a nervous system. For example, in spiders there are physical-chemical and biochemical processes that are neurologically linked in the performance of their quick, precise reflex movements. In the most highly-developed animals that possess an elemental psychological life (dogs, for example), the physical-chemical-biochemical-neurological regulation principles are linked together in executing psychological commands inside a hierarchical chain of command. When a dog psychologically recognizes its master, its brain sends neurological impulses to its tail muscles, which biochemically regulate the local muscle tissue and the chemical processes in the single muscle cells, enabling the dog to wave its tail.

We finally arrive at the point where we consider humans, the highest and most complex organization of matter in the universe. In the understanding of nonbelievers, they are this and nothing more. As Murphy notes:

> All of the human capacities once attributed to the mind or soul are now fruitfully studied as brain processes. Or, more accurately, I should say, processes involving the brain, the rest of the nervous system and all other bodily systems, all interacting with the sociocultural world…. When I enter most deeply into that, which I call myself, I seem to discover that I am a living animal.[12]

Does reality corroborate Murphy's supposition? We can illustrate the correlation between the complexity of living creatures' bodies and the regulation of their behaviors in chart form, as shown below.[13]

Fig. 1.1. The creatures and their regulation

ORGANISMS   **REGULATION PRINCIPLES**

Viruses & Bacteria	Physical & Chemical				
Sponges or Plants	Physical & Chemical	Bio-chemical			
Insects or Reptiles	Physical & Chemical	Bio-chemical	Neuro-logical		
Primates	Physical & Chemical	Bio-chemical	Neuro-logical	Psycho-logical	
Humans	Physical & Chemical	Bio-chemical	Neuro-logical	Psycho-logical	Spiritual

We can see from the illustration that humans, like primates, are seamlessly linked in physical-chemical-biochemical-neurological-psychological organization. However, are we really only that?

No. The typical difference between humans and animals is not simply our higher intelligence but that we are factually spiritual. Frankl asserts, "The spiritual is what is human in man ... indicating that we are dealing with a specific human phenomenon, in contrast to the phenomenon that we are sharing with other animals."[14] A visible and measurable effect of the phenomenon of human spirituality is that humans are *God-seeking organisms*, building churches, mosques, synagogues, temples, and other places of worship all around the world, in all civilizations and in all moments of history. Thus, we need to add one more level to the chart—spiritual—to finish our description of the human's physical-chemical-biochemical-neurological-psychological dimensions. Only in this way does our model represent the behavioral and factual reality of the human person.

Notes

[1] Lindsay Jones (ed.), *Encyclopedia of Religion*, vol. 5 (Farmington Hills, MI: Thomson Gale, 2005).

[2] Anton C. Pegis, *The Basic Writings of Saint Thomas Aquinas* (New York: Random House, 1945), 683–94.

[3] Rudolph Schnackenburg, *The Gospel According to St. John* (New York: Herder and Herder, 1968), 371.

[4] R. E. Brown, J. J. Castelot, and J. J. McKenzie, *The Jerome Biblical Commentary* (Englewood Cliffs, NJ: Prentice Hall, 1980), 159.

[5] Ibid., 173.

[6] Joseph Weismayer, *Dogmatik, VII Kapitel: Hofnung Auf Vollendung* (Vienna: Fernkurs Fur Theologische Laienbildung, 1985), 24.

[7] Canadian Conference of the Catholic Bishops, *Catechism of the Catholic Church* (Ottawa: Publications Service, Canadian Conference of Catholic Bishops, 1994), 214.

[8] René Le Trocquer, *What Is Man?* (London: Burns & Oates, 1961), 26.

[9] Canadian Conference of the Catholic Bishops, *Catechism of the Catholic Church*, 215.

[10] John Paul II, *Man and Woman He Created Them: A Theology of the Body* (Boston, MA: Pauline Books and Media, 2006), 389.

[11] Srboljub Stojiljkovic, *Psihijatrija sa Medicinskom Psihologijom* (Belgrade: Medicinska Knjiga, 1975), 181–2.

[12] Nancy Murphy, *Bodies and Souls, or Spirited Bodies?* (Cambridge: Cambridge University Press, 2006), 113.

[13] Paul Ungar, *The Mystery of Christian Faith: A Tangible Union with the Invisible God* (Lanham, MD: University Press of America, 2008), 148.

[14] Viktor E. Frankl, *Man's Search for Ultimate Meaning* (New York: Basic Books, 2000), 27.

CHAPTER TWO

THE SPIRIT: INTEGRATING BIBLICAL AND EMPIRICAL PARADIGMS

How the spirit initiates and sustains the gift of life widely surpasses human understanding. God's ultimate creative power—how the spirit enters into the bones of the embryo in the mother's womb (Ecclesiastes 11:5, author's paraphrase)—is a mystery, conceptualized throughout history in different ways.

Pondering this mystery, St. Augustine perceived Plato's writings almost as a supplement to the teachings of St. Paul. Even in the Middle Ages, a commonly-repeated refrain in Thomas Aquinas's *Summa Theologiae* was the phrase, "The Philosopher says." The philosopher St. Thomas refers to is Aristotle, whose wisdom was, alongside the Scriptures, perceived as a criterion of perfection through ensuing centuries. However, in the seventeenth century, a radical turnaround occurred; not ancient philosophers' speculation, but empirical evidence became the criterion of truth. This trend culminated in modern positivism, which appreciates only the visible, touchable, and measurable (positive) facts.

Positivism has not only been a philosophy or methodology; it has been one of those schools of suspicion that the modern era has seen grow and prosper. . . . If we put ourselves in the positivist perspective, concepts such as God or the soul [or the spirit] simply lose meaning. In terms of sensory experience, in fact, nothing corresponds to God or the soul [or the spirit].[1]

The current age represents a paradigm shift. Arguments based on Aristotle's insights about the interaction of matter and form are irrelevant to contemporary believers seeking to substantiate a biblical spirit, and they are even less persuasive to non-believers. Could we, however, deduce by analysing our biological being that it is caused by God's breath of life (Genesis 2:7), that which Thomas Aquinas adequately describes as the "first principle of life,"[2] and phrase biblical concepts in empirical terms cogent to postmodern positivists? Or could we set the bar even higher and synchronize the theological understanding with a modern empirical understanding of life?

As already noted, medical understanding is based on stringent causal principles organized so that they ensure a seamless flow of the physical, chemical, biochemical, neurological, and psychological processes constituting life. We can illustrate these causally occurring processes with a row of dominos. Tipping the first domino (symbolizing conception) tips the one next in line. The successive fall of all of the dominos, until the fall of the last (symbolizing death), illustrates causally-regulated physiological events in living human bodies. However, the causal observation of living processes (like that of atheists) is not the only possible approach to life. Observing the same model can also lead us to the contrary conclusion; that life is ultimately purposeful.

Fig. 2.1. The illustration of causal and final regulation

CONCEPTION   PRESENT   DEATH

The figure illustrates believers' concept of life. In the Christian view, the causally-occurring tipping of the first domino is organized by reason (God) and happens *teleologically*, with a final purpose, which is that the next and all successive dominos tip over until the fall of the last domino in line (symbolizing death). So tipping the last domino is not an aimless end but, by God, the established ultimate purpose of human biological life.

The crucial question is how organisms really function: aimlessly, or purposefully, such that all causally-occurring, single, physiological functions fulfill a common final purpose? In the first case, we are like causally-functioning human machines; in the second, we are teleologically-functioning, purposefully-created spirited beings.

Inanimate objects like dominos behave aimlessly, or causally regulated. On the other hand, animate organisms behave teleologically, or purposefully-regulated. The goal-oriented organization of their biological functions is not an anthropomorphic deduction or simply a teleological theologically-coloured assumption, but a measurable behavioral reality common in all living creatures. Take, for example, the well-known self-regulation principle of homeostasis. All organisms meaningfully correct physical-chemical-biological processes that jeopardize their lives. In all creatures there prevails the "one for all and all for one" principle, with which single physiological processes serve the functioning of the whole organism, and the whole organism works to sustain every single living process. Such purposeful organization of an organism's parts (the somatic and psychic dimensions) and the purposeful functioning of the whole organism indicate that living creatures are purposeful and shaped by a teleological organizing principle, which is, as noted, the breath of life of the living God.

Could life be a product of evolving matter?

The age of the Earth is around 4.5 billion years, while the earliest evidence of life on our planet dates between 3.5 and 3.9 billion years ago. Therefore, atheists suppose that between 3.5 and 3.9 billion years ago, the climate of our planet must have been able first to synthesize amino acids and proteins, which later became the building blocks of the first living creatures. An inverse development "life first-proteins later" could not happen. Since only a relatively few prebiotic synthetized protein molecules have become living organisms, most of them had remained inanimate. Thus, enormous quantities of prebiotic proteins must have already existed before the appearance of the first living creatures. However, paleontology excludes the possibility of such "protein first-life later" model. There is no evidence of the existence of vast quantities of prebiotic proteins before the first living creatures appeared. So, it is highly improbable that a meaninglessly functioning nature, on its own, could employ purposeful organization to produce any living organisms, let alone the very highest order of sentient creatures on earth without the process we identify as creation. In short, we might have developed through evolution, but our evolution *could not happen without ultimate meaning, God, purposefully directing that progression.* In other words, where there is a law which directs evolution there also must be a lawmaker, God.

Why do atheists then fail to recognize spiritual regulation in living creatures?

Recall the earlier thought experiment with the frog. Purposeful organization of every atom, molecule, cell, tissue, and organ into its place by our professor proved that life is not a product of meaningless material changes. She demonstrated that without this teleological life-giving principle, which causes meticulous organization of every organism, as if imitating creation itself, neither the existence of the frog nor of any living creature would be possible. But led by her strong prejudice that God cannot exist even if reality demonstrates the contrary, she failed to recognize that she just imitated (and proved) the action of the spirit, God's creative power.

Finally, let us make a surprising digression here. In his *Republica*, Plato attributed to Socrates the admonition, "We must follow the argument wherever it leads."[3] Let us follow Socrates' advice by appealing to the position of the church. Pope Francis' encyclical *Laudate Si* notes that all human activities participate in, and have a responsibility for, sustaining the God-created natural world.[4] We may expand this line of thought by saying that medical practitioners, by their skills, participate in God's life-creating and sustaining power. The medical practitioner's work sustains the spirit, the principle of life, by organizing and synchronizing the physical, chemical, biochemical, neurological, and psychological functioning of the human body. *Thus, the principle of life, the certainty of the existence of the spirit, replicated in all medical healing practices, is also a reality.* And yet, the contribution of the medical practitioner is only that—replication—and forces us to acknowledge life as the gift of an ultimately more sophisticated, omniscient creator.

Notes

[1] John Paul II, *Crossing the Threshold of Hope* (New York: Alfred A Knopf, 1994), 33.

[2] Louis P. Pojman and Lewis Vaughn, *Philosophy: The Quest for Truth* (New York: Oxford University Press, 2009), 219.

[3] Antony Flew, with Roy Abraham Varghese, *There Is a God: How the World's Most Notorious Atheist Changed His Mind* (New York: Harper Collins, 2007), 22.

[4] Pope Francis, *Laudate Si*, Libreria Editrice Vaticano. 2016

CHAPTER THREE

THE SOUL: INTEGRATING BIBLICAL AND EMPIRICAL PARADIGMS

As *Homo sapiens*, we are also *Homo religiosus*. Can we conclude that we are God-seeking creatures—we, who build churches, mosques, synagogues, and temples—enter into a relationship with a supreme being whom Christians call God? In other words, can we deduce that we are living souls from the fact that humans in all historical periods have sought a relationship with an ineffable God? Before discussing this question, let us first place the soul in its historical context.

3.1 Historical Overview of Theological-Empirical Controversies

As previously noted, until the sixteenth and seventeenth centuries, theologians and philosophers posited a symbiotic relationship when discussing the soul and nature, theology and science. Since the mind (i.e., ideas, will, or intelligence) has no physical, tangible extension, it was universally believed that our intellectual capacities must be nonmaterial, or products of the soul.

Aquinas, in his *Summa Theologiae*, gives an explanation that is still discussed among theologians. He explains.

It must necessarily be allowed that the principle of intellectual operation which we call the soul is both incorporeal and subsistent. For it is clear that by means of the intellect man can have knowledge of all corporeal things. Now whatever knows certain things cannot have any of them in its own nature: because that which is in it naturally would impede the knowledge of anything else ... [If] the intellectual principle contained the nature of a body it would be unable to know all bodies ... it is impossible for the intellectual principle to be a body....[1]

Therefore, the intellectual principle must be a spiritual soul.

Many theologians from the persuasion of neoscholastic Thomism use similar arguments today. For example, René Le Trocquer in *What is Man?* proposes that intelligence serves the understanding of reality, of that which exists. Intelligence distinguishes both the existing and nonexisting. Therefore, intelligence transcends space and time, reality and nonreality, and also discerns the nonsensorial, the universal, and general. At the same time, intelligence is able to withdraw into itself and distinguish the self from the nonself. This unique capacity of the mind is, in Trocquer's explanation, "linked to a deliverance from everything material, to the mind's situation beyond space and time." Humans are "not enclosed" within themselves but able to "step out" of themselves, which "is a sure sign of the immaterial nature of the knowing subject." While "matter, indeed, makes the subject one particular fragment of a species, one part of the universe...," the ability of the human intellect to contact reality outside of the person is a "sure sign of the immaterial nature of the knowing subject [who] in so far as he thinks, must be spiritual." Such "illuminative power in the intelligence" is "like a reflection in us of the divine intelligence" we call God.[2]

Enlightenment philosophers looked at the same topic from a different perspective. René Descartes (1596–1650) "began his philosophy by sweeping away all the errors 'of the past.'"[3] First, he acknowledged as paramount that "I" (the soul) exists ("I think, therefore I am"). But he described the functioning of the body as a mechanical automaton moved by muscles and bones. In such a mechanistic, materialistic concept of the body, a soul seemed redundant. Hence the dualist "Descartes myth" was born.

The essence of Cartesian dualism rests in polar opposition between mind and matter.

> Material objects are situated in a common field, known as "space," and what happens to one body in one part of the space is mechanically connected with what happens to other bodies in other parts of the space. But mental happenings occur in insulated fields, known as "minds," and there is, apart maybe from telepathy, no direct causal connection between what happens in one mind and what happens in another.[4]

Nevertheless, by the eighteenth century it had become obvious that the human mind functions differently from machines. Therefore, ideas of mechanic materialism were replaced with biological materialism. The French physician Pierre J. G. Cabanis[5] (1757–1808), for example, proposed, "The brain is producing thoughts as the liver is producing bile."[6] However, it was obvious that the human brain functions differently than the liver and other organs, so biological materialism was replaced with neurological materialism.

At the end of the nineteenth century, the Russian physician Ivan Mihailovic Secenov (1828–1905)[7] described the "reflexes of the brain." His phrase "the machine replaces the machinist" (meaning that the neurological processes of the brain replace the mind, and indeed the soul) is still popular today. The twentieth-century reflexologist Ivan P. Pavlov (1849–1936), at the institute he headed for fifty years, required everyone who even accidentally mentioned the word *psyche* to pay a fine. He proclaimed that such a thing does not exist, only unconditioned or conditioned reflexes of the brain.[8]

Despite following a different pathway, American behaviorists came to similar conclusions. In the 1920s, John B. Watson "made the radical suggestion that behavior does not have mental causes." In the view of his successors, such as Burrhus S. Skinner, "The problem of explaining the mind-body interaction vanishes; there is no such interaction."[9] The mass media, invigorated in the postmodern culture of scepticism, positivism, and atheism, which is appreciating Christian's relationship with God as nothing more than an illusion (by Freud), a delusion (by Dawkins), or a mental sickness (by Ellis), still propagates such surreal concepts.

Basing their conclusions on new research (advances in neurology, the physical study of the brain, scans of rare cases of localized brain damage, the discovery of genetic causes for a variety of mental illnesses, and research into the effects of drugs on the brain), scientists have offered material, psychological explanations for a variety of states of consciousness. At the same time, innovations in computer technology have generated advanced forms of artificial intelligence. For the first time, humans can create artifacts that appear more intelligent than themselves. This has led to the reexamination of popular concepts of the distinctive essence of humanity.[10] How do Christians react to such reductionist reexaminations of our humanity?

That the reflexes of the brain have an essential role in producing the contents of our mind is an empirical fact. Nevertheless, the hierarchical question is crucial: are reflexes of the brain simply causing the mind, or is the mind regulating the reflexes of the brain? Are thoughts, feelings, will, faith, and even communion with God causal products of the reflexes of the brain, or do thoughts, feelings, will, and faith direct reflexes of the brain to enable communion with God? Colloquially formulated, were the reflexes in Dante's brain responsible for the composition of his poetry to the beloved, or, inversely, did Dante's love to Beatrice also direct the reflexes in his brain for the composition of his poetry to the beloved?

In our effort to integrate revealed truths and empirical facts, we will not discuss outdated mechanical and biological materialistic concepts like those of Descartes and Cabanis. Instead, we will meticulously examine challenges raised by proponents of neurological and psychological materialism. The discussion will be broken into three sections:

(1) Integrating the body and mind
(2) Integrating the mind and soul
(3) Introducing humans as an integrated somatic-psychological-spiritual link

3.2 The Brain: Integrating the Body and Mind

After an event which occurred September 13, 1848, virtually no physician has continued to doubt the body's (i.e. the brain's) role in psychological life.

As Faw[11] notes, it was on that day that railroad construction foreman Phineas Gage "was preparing to blast away a large section of rock. A hole had been drilled in the rock, and Gage was using a steel rod to pack gunpowder into the hole. When the powder exploded unexpectedly, this tamping rod, thicker than a broom handle and nearly as long, became a missile. It was driven into the side of his face and out the top of his head, landing on the ground some distance away." Gage did not lose consciousness, but walked to Dr. John M. Harlow's office, allegedly saying, "Here is business enough for you." Phineas survived, but as Dr. Harlow allegedly wrote, "His friends found him no longer Gage."[12] The questions we have asked ever since are, "How are the brain and mind integrated, and how do they work together?"

Joseph Feigl explains this process as follows: "[If a psychologist would] investigate my brain processes and describe them in full detail, then he could formulate his findings in neuropsychological language and might be even able to produce a complete microphysical account in terms of atomic and subatomic concepts." That would be a "physical" projection of the subject's mental processes. However, as Feigl continues, "I am directly acquainted with the qualia of my own immediate experience. I happen to know (by acquaintance) what the neuropsychologist refers to when he talks about certain configurationally relevant aspects of my cerebral processes." So the physical (that which is registered by the observer) and the mental (that which is experienced by the subject) are two aspects of the same occurrence.[13]

Based upon evidence, it is accepted by contemporary neurologists and psychiatrists that neurological processes in the brain manifest as thinking, feeling, willing, observing, and other functions. They also accept that neurological processes manifest as psychological experiences. In other words, as we psychologically experience heartbeats or breathing, we analogously experience the above neurological processes.

For example, reasoning is performed by nerve cells in the frontal lobe of the brain and occurs in a stimulus-response pattern. From this neurological input, the nerve cells determine the necessary output. Logical reasoning can therefore be described by an oscillating pendulum. The input (stimulus) on the left side of this pendulum must be logically consistent with the output (response) on its right side. In formulations like "1+1=2," "today is a hot day," or Einstein's formula "e=mc²," the left side of the pendulum must equal the right ("2," "hot day," or "mc²"). Knowing one side of the equation, myriad nerve cells predict the values on its other side and exclude false conclusions such as 2+2=5. People experience these neurological processes in their brains as psychological phenomena, namely rational reasoning.

Thus the neurological and psychological are two aspects of one process. But the question remains: by which mechanisms could the causally-occurring reflexes in the brain produce purposeful reasoning (e.g. faith in God)? How might the causally-functioning reflexes of Dante's brain have produced his psychological and spiritual love poems?

There are trillions of possible synaptic connections between nerve cells in the frontal brain, theoretically enabling countless reflexes to produce equal numbers of possible psychological reactions. In order to select from the innumerable contents of the mind, the brain regulates its own activity, fostering those synaptic connections which produce functional (healthy) psychological outcomes. Synaptic connections that produce the desired psychological outcomes will be repeatedly activated, becoming hypertrophic, like the muscles of a well-trained athlete. On the contrary, synaptic connections not producing desired psychological outcomes will therefore become atrophic and will eventually be "pruned."[14]

> There are attempts to explain "pruning" using discoveries in quantum mechanics and in the dynamics of subatomic particles. These efforts seem promising, nevertheless are still based more on assumptions than facts. In our discussions, we will stick to well-known neurological and psychological information.

Neurologically, pruning is a fight for the survival of the fittest between the billions of nerve cells and trillions of synaptic connections in the brain. When they produce psychologically healthy and desirable reactions, they flourish; when they produce psychologically useless neurological

connections, they are eliminated. Their psychological purpose—the production of useful reflexes of the brain—shapes the brain's neurological
functioning. In the case of Dante, while he was writing his love poems, his
brain adjusted its electrochemical activities to achieve the expression of his
love to Beatrice.

For specialized professionals and readers interested in the minuscule
details of where, when, and how the mind hierarchically directs the reflexes
of the brain, let me demonstrate this process by analysing the real neurological-psychological interaction of vision. Vision starts when the eyes receive
photons reflected by observed objects. The photons impact nerve cells of the
retina, triggering an electrochemical discharge—comparable to the negative in photography—which is subsequently transmitted by the optic nerve
to the primary visual area in the occipital brain. The discharge and subsequent effort to restore the previous electrochemical balance of the primary
visual area is perceived as sight.

The next step, recognition, consists of organizing primary visual information into psychologically meaningful information. This happens in
the secondary and tertiary visual area by harmonizing a primary visual
impression (colours, patches, and contours seen like a highly-confusing
impressionist painting) with visual ideas and psychological information
of the mind. We recognize not only what our eyes photograph, but what
the brain and mind "make" and recognize as meaningful from the primary
sensory impression. How this neurological-psychological link works is
illustrated in Fig. 3.1 below.[15]

Fig. 3.1. The neurology and psychology of vision

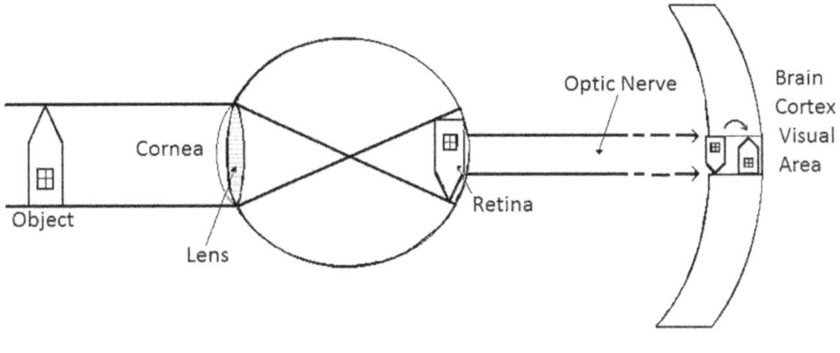

The illustration shows how the eye's lens projects the observed picture of the world onto the retina upside down. This inverted image is subsequently transported through the optic nerve to the visual area. But since we have a firm psychological knowledge that houses stand on their foundations, the brain in the secondary visual area automatically turns the image 180 degrees, and the house is recognized as it ought to be seen. Thus knowledge, visual ideas, logic, perspective, interests, experience, and other psychological factors regulate the reflexes of the brain and shape recognition.

Our brains can therefore recognize psychologically meaningful images. For instance, we know that a horse and rider are separate from one another. However, South American aboriginals with no visual conceptions of a horse recognized Cortez's horse and horseman as one creature. Similarly, while we clearly recognize a driver as distinct from the car, small children recognize car and driver as one object. This principle is exploited by magicians, who carry out their visual illusions by causing us to recognize what they *want* us to see instead of what we *ought* to see. Similarly, military personnel use camouflage, causing the opposition to see only grass and leaves instead of tanks and soldiers. That we recognize what we know illustrates the position of Jesus' disciples on the road to Emmaus. As Luke reports in 24:15-16, "Jesus himself came up and walked along with them; but they were kept from recognizing him." They did not recognize the resurrected Jesus due to their false belief that he was dead. Receiving the gift of faith had corrected their mistaken knowledge and made the recognition of Jesus possible. From the moment of Jesus' intervention, the disciples' renewed faith teleologically synchronized the reflexes of the brain that directed their behaviors.

The brain also performs countless physiological reflex regulations in our body independently of the psyche. To paraphrase Secenov, the machine does not need the machinist. That is, the brain does not need the mind's direction to perform its autonomous reflex regulation (e.g. its regulation of heart rhythm and digestion). But the mind, "the machinist," teleologically directs the brain, "the machine," in making psychological choices. Mind and brain then function in a neurological-psychological link.

A healthy mind, for example, demonstrates the correct functioning of the brain's structures acting as a neurological-psychological link. When disorders in the mind's functioning occur (i.e. behavioral problems), the reflexes of the brain need to be corrected either by psychological treatment (with words) or psychiatric treatment (with medicine). In such cases, psychologists and psychiatrists are, to once more paraphrase Secenov, "replacement machinists," temporarily helping to steer the machine so that the neurological-psychological link produces healthy ideas, thoughts, feelings, and intentions.

3.3 The Conscience: Integrating the Mind and Soul

Browning and Cooper describe how "psychoanalysis helped to create a new type of personality called 'psychological man.'"[16] We are psychological beings in the sense that ideas and information are contained in our minds. We could not even know about God without the psychological functioning of our personality. But what is a human personality?

In theological anthropology, the term *personality* signifies the indivisible unity of the body, soul, and spirit. In psychological jargon, though, the same term refers to the I, the self, or the ego, and is responsible for individual behavioral characteristics. Similarly ambiguous is the meaning of the term *psychology*. The term was first used by the German philosopher Christian Wolff (1679–1754) in his book *Prolegomenon* to distinguish empirical psychology, formulated as the soul's discernment of worldly realities, from rational psychology, focused on the soul's discernment of the spiritual realities.[17] From Wolff's empirical psychology evolved professional psychology, while rational psychology evolved into theological studies. What Wolff named *psychology*, composed of the Greek words *psyche* (soul) and *logos* (science), is literally the science of the soul. In modern vernacular, however, it is the science of the mind.

Let us illustrate the atheistic understanding of personality using Sigmund Freud's concepts, which in this book will represent all other atheistic personality theories.

Many readers may first think of Freud's iceberg analogy, which proposes that the memories, thoughts, and feelings we are aware of (i.e. the visible tip of the iceberg) make up the smaller and less important portion of our minds. In Freud's view, the unconscious mind, corresponding to the submerged portion of the iceberg, consists of hundreds of repressed impulses, memories, and conflicts too painful to contemplate. Although we are not aware of them, they nevertheless powerfully influence our behavior and emotional health.[18]

In Freud's view, the conscious, as well as the suppressed subconscious contents of the mind, spring from three different sources, which we can present through another analogy: a glass half full of water. This is illustrated in Fig. 3.2 below.[19]

Fig. 3.2. Sigmund Freud's personality model

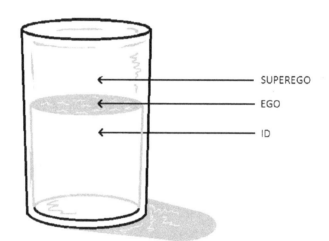

What is below the water's surface represents instinct. Freud called it the *id*, symbolizing the instinct's distance from the rest of the self. What is above the water's surface represents the *superego*, representing overly strict societal norms. Only the thin line of the water's surface represents the *ego* (the self), often called the I, which is analogous to a decision-maker.

Instinct is "the dark side of human personality which does not know space, time, or reality but has only one goal: to direct behavior."[20] It knows how to protect life (the survival instinct) and multiply it (the sexual instinct) and thus is necessary for the survival of the individual and the human race.

Nevertheless, for humans living in a civilized society, the quest to satisfy the id's unrestricted desires would cause havoc.

The ego is the main structure that communicates with reality. It has little power, represented by the thin line of the water's surface, but has a supreme responsibility. It has the task of fulfilling the demands of instinct (id) without colliding with the prohibitions of the superego and, in this effort, it takes into account the objective conditions of external reality.

Instinct is inborn, able to help the self-preservation of infants. The ego starts developing during the first year of life. The superego develops last, typically between eighteen and twenty-four months, facilitated by upbringing—potty training, for example.

Since atheists often point to a superego-like conscience to explain Christian moral functioning, let us discuss its development in detail. When using the term *superego*, we mean the strict, rigid, policeman-like structure solely aimed at worldly survival, developed through socially learned psychological function. This is the opposite of the "Christian conscience."

Until the time of potty training, parents usually give their toddlers everything they need, expecting nothing in return. When potty training begins, though, parents set the first strict expectation for their children: that they control their instinctual need to urinate and defecate. If toddlers succeed in controlling their drive for urination and defecation, the parents applaud, praise, and show love. If toddlers do not, the parents express dissatisfaction and scold them (i.e., deprive them of love). Toddlers feel they cannot exist without the parents' love and care, so this makes them willing to trade the satisfaction of their instincts for the parents' love. During later life, the superego provides security similar to that which children receive from their parents by ensuring social appreciation, support, and approval.[21]

Except for sexual instinct, most other instincts in our culture are relatively easy to govern. A prominent task of the superego in ensuring socially acceptable behavior is controlling the sexual instinct. As Freud describes in *Three Essays on the Theory of Sexuality*, "The production of sexual excitation … produces a store of energy which is employed in a great extent for purposes other than sexual—namely … (through repression) in building up the subsequently developed barriers against sexuality."[22]

Let us now take a critical look at Freud's practice of psychoanalysis. The acid test of every theory is whether it is in harmony with reality. However, the reality of Jesus' unconditional love is inexplicable from a Freudian or worldly perspective since holiness contradicts the demands of the id, the ego, and the superego. Jesus adhered to completely different behavioral standards than what Freud's (or atheists') theories are able to explain. The same is true of Jesus' disciples. They behaved very differently from Freudian personality structures wired for survival of the fittest. Even today, Christians and non-Christian people of goodwill who are obedient to their Christian-like conscience behave in a way that is inexplicable from a Freudian or atheistic perspective. For example, we would expect that the more instincts are controlled by the ego and superego, the greater the chances for a prosperous life. In practice, we see the contrary. Many exemplary disciples and martyrs had poorly-preserved lives, not because they were directed by anti-social instincts or were disobedient to their superegos, but because they were servants of a structure inexplicable from Freud's perspective—that of Christian conscience. How did Freud fail to recognize this?

Freud was a committed atheist, and as Paul Vitz notes, "Nowhere did Freud publish psychoanalysis of the belief in God based on clinical evidence provided by a believing patient."[23] Despite all of the respect he earned, Freud, like his atheist colleagues, was ignorant; he neither experienced nor understood what the Christian conscience is.

Let us summarize some differences between these two types of consciences, namely the superego and the Christian conscience.

(1) The superego serves the world, while the Christian conscience aims at holiness (i.e. being set apart from the world).

(2) The superego promotes biological life, while the Christian conscience serves everlasting life.

(3) One's position in society shapes the superego, while the Father's commands, Jesus' teaching, and the Holy Spirit's guidance shapes the Christian conscience.

(4) The superego is an internal inhibitor of instincts, while the Christian conscience is an internal stimulator of discipleship.

(5) Fear gives power to the superego, while receiving Godly joy gives power to the conscience.

(6) Obedience to the superego is externally (socially) rewarded, while obedience to the Christian conscience is internally rewarded by biblical gifts of the Holy Spirit.

(7) The superego is unforgiving and judgmental, like an internal policeman, while Christian conscience is Jesus like, loving and all-forgiving to repentant sinners.

(8) The superego is concerned with faults (harm to social success), while the Christian conscience is concerned with sinful behaviors (intentional estrangement from God).

(9) The superego enforces laws, while Christian conscience judges integrating justice and mercy.

(10) The superego is a neurological-psychological dimension acting according the cause and effect principle, while conscience is a psychological-spiritual dimension acting teleologically, seeking God as ultimate meaning to live for.

Viktor Frankl characterized the conscience as "irrational…alogical or, better put, prelogical." It is irrational, he says, because "it can never be explained in rational terms," and is prelogical because "the pre-moral understanding of meaning precedes any understanding of values, and therefore is not contingent upon values." He concludes, "Through the conscience of the human person, a transhuman agent [whom Christians call God] is *per-so-nat* [sounding through]."[24]

St. Paul supports this truth, stating that the conscience judges "in the holiness and sincerity that are from God" (2 Cor. 1:12). Indeed, just as the brain functions as a neurological-psychological link, the Christian conscience functions as a psychological-spiritual link. As such, the conscience integrates the mind and soul, linking the believer's psyche to God. Schnackenburg contends that the Christian conscience enables Christians to become "a new life-form in which existence in the world is united with holiness."[25]

3.4 Anthropology as a Spiritual-Psychological-Somatic Link

In his book *Philosophic Classics*, Forrest E. Baird posits:

The I that Descartes found at the end of his methodological doubting was "entirely distinct from the body." This I was an immaterial mind, a "spiritual" thing. The body is an extended "not-thinking thing." As such it is a part of the material world.... This Cartesian distinction leads to a problem about the relationship between body and mind. It addresses questions which we still struggle with today.[26]

As Baird notes, even today many people, including professionals, struggle with Descartes' question: Is my mind "entirely distinct from the body," a "spiritual thing," or is it a product of the brain and, as such, "a part of the material world"?

The contemporary solution to the Cartesian problem can be illustrated as follows. When writing his poems, Dante's love (a psychological-spiritual function) played the role of a colonel instructing officers (his brain and nerves) to command petty officers (biochemical structures in his muscles) to direct soldiers (physical and chemical processes in his muscle cells) to execute the writing of his love poems. But posed this way, the whole chain of command is hanging in the air. An intuitive question emerges: Which general inspired Dante's spiritualized love for Beatrice? It could not have been a nonspiritual, atheist general (superego). In producing this Christian masterpiece of spiritualized love, neither Dante's profane instinct nor his superego could have been the commanding general, but rather his Christian conscience.

We could further ask where the spiritual reflection in his Christian conscience came from. Was Dante's conscience autonomous and self-sufficient or subordinated to a higher command? To answer this question, we need to recall our discussion about the Christian conscience and its biblical and psychological characteristics, and subsequently integrate empirical and revealed truths to observe Dante's activity starting from the basics (the soldiers) and moving up to the supreme commander of his behavior.

Transmissions of impulses from Dante's brain to his muscle tissues, establishing a biochemical-neurological link of command, made the bodily act of writing possible. Ascending further up the chain of command, the neurological function in his brain was directed by his mind, acting as a neurological-psychological link. Additionally, Dante's mind was hierarchically organized; his Christian conscience acted as a psychological-spiritual link connecting his mind and soul. However, his soul could not be the supreme commanding authority. As the Scriptures define, the soul receives "life" (Jn. 6:63) and "birth" (Jn. 3:6), "testifies" with God (Rom. 8:16), and is what "unites us" (1 Cor. 6:17) with God, who is the supreme commander of everything in existence. The chain of command is illustrated in Fig. 3.3. below.

Fig. 3.3. The spiritual-psychological-somatic chain of command

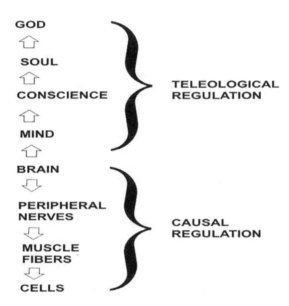

The figure illustrates the proportions of teleological and causal regulations in humans. It also gives an answer to nonbelievers' still-puzzling question, indirectly raised by Descartes and explicitly formulated by Gottfried W. Leibniz in his *Théodicée* of 1710: How could a spiritual God influence the material and causal functioning of human bodies, brains, and behaviors?[28]

First, God forwards a call, which Fritz Rothschild summarized as "Man knows God because God knows man, and man's purpose is to live in such a way that he may be worthy of being known to God."[29] God is not causally commanding. He is not giving a "must" but an "ought to," a teleological call to human souls. The soul, again teleologically, informs the conscience about what one ought to do to live in a responsible relationship with God. The conscience, acting as a spiritual-psychological link, once again teleologically discerns concretely where, when, and how the mind ought to behave and informs it of this. The unique structure of the mind has a chief role in directing behaviors. It has the prerogative of obeying or disobeying the direction of the conscience, soul, and God when executing its choice. When deciding "I will," the mind, the last in the described teleological chain of command, influences the brain as we observed discussing Dante's example when writing his love poem. From the brain downwards, as illustrated by figure 3.3, neurological impulses are transmitted causal-regulated. As such, they reach peripheral nerves, muscle tissues, and virtually all single cells partaking in teleological, spiritual-psychological direction of our causal-functioning bodies.

Everything in the universe is causally regulated, but the only beings able to transgress God's commands are humans. One day, there will be "restoration to the true life of human bodylines, and 'a new submission of the body to the spirit,'" and only then will a "definitively and perfectly 'integrated' state of man" be established.[30] After the resurrection, "the body will return to perfect unity and harmony with the spirit: man will no longer experience the opposition between what is spiritual and what is bodily in him."[31] Living creatures who are not yet angels, however, are still fighting two great obstacles to perfect holiness: sinful and sick behaviors.

Notes

[1] Forrest E. Baird, *Philosophic Classics* vol. 3 (Upper Saddle River, NJ: Prentice Hall, 2003), 362.

[2] René Le Trocquer, *What Is Man?* (London: Burns & Oates, 1961), 27.

[3] Baird, *Philosophic Classics*, 10.

[4] David J. Chalmers: *Philosophy of Mind, Classical and Contemporary Readings* (New York, Oxford: Oxford University Press, 2002), 14.

[5] Jarosevski Mihail, *Istoria Psihologii* (Moscow: Moskva Izadateljstvo Misl, 1966), 63–6.

[6] Ibid.

[7] Ibid.

[8] Ibid.

[9] Louis P. Pojman, *Classics of Philosophy* (New York: Oxford University Press, 2003), 315.

[10] Aviezer Tucker, "The Mind," the New Dictionary of the History of Ideas vol. 2, Marianne Cline Horowitz (ed.) (Farmington Hills, MI: Thomson Gale, 2005), 435.

[11] Harold W. Faw, *Psychology in a Christian Perspective, an Analysis of Key Issues* (Grand Rapids, MI: Baker Books, 1995), 17.

[12] Srboljub Stojiljkovic, *Psihijatrija sa Medicinskom Psihologijom* (Belgrade: Medicinska Knjiga, 1975), 181–2.

[13] David J. Chalmers, *Philosophy of Mind, Classical and Contemporary Readings* (New York, Oxford: Oxford University Press, 2002), 14.

[14] Benjamin James Sadock, Virginia Alcott Sadock, and Pedro Ruiz, *Kaplan and Sadock's Synopsis of Psychiatry: Behavioral Sciences/Clinical Psychiatry* (Philadelphia, PA: Wolters Kluwer, 2015), 19.

[15] Paul Ungar, *Flawed Institution—Flawless Church: A Response to Pope John Paul's Appeal for a Critical Self-Evaluation of the Church* (Newcastle Upon Tyne: Cambridge Scholars Publishing, 2013), 112.

[16] Don S. Browning and Terry D. Cooper, *Religious Thought and the Modern Psychologies* (Minneapolis, MN: Augsburg Fortress Press, 2004), 147.

[17] Joseph Weismayer, *Dogmatik, VII Kapitel: Hofnung Auf Vollendung* (Vienna: Fernkurs Fur Theologische Laienbildung, 1985), 98.

[18] Faw, *Psychology in a Christian Perspective*, 56.

[19] Ungar, *Flawed Institution—Flawless Church*, 96.

[20] Joseph Schwarz, *Durch Psychologie zum Gott, Argumente Fur Gottes Existenz* (Eisenstadt, 1988), 80.

[21] Otto Fenichel, *The Psychoanalytic Theory of Neurosis* (New York: W.W. Norton Company, 1972), 102–7.

[22] Viktor E. Frankl, *Man's Search for Ultimate Meaning* (New York: Basic Books, 2000), 27.

[23] Paul Vitz, *Faith of Fatherless; The Psychology of Atheism* (Dallas TX.: Spence Publishing Company, 1999), 8.

[24] Frankl, *Man's Search for Ultimate Meaning*, 39–60.

[25] Rudolph Schnackenburg, *The Gospel According to St. John* (New York: Herder and Herder, 1968), 371.

[26] Baird, *Philosophic Classics*, 13.

[27] Ungar, *Flawed Institution—Flawless Church*, 117.

[28] Mihail, *Istoria Psihologii*, 186.

[29] Fritz Rothschild in Abraham Heschl, *Between God and Man* (New York: The Free Press, 1959), 16.

[30] John Paul II, *Man and Woman He Created Them: A Theology of the Body* (Boston, MA: Pauline Books and Media, 2006), 390.

[31] Ibid., 391.

CHAPTER FOUR

APPROACHES TO THE MYSTERY OF SIN AND SICKNESS

A ccording to the Scriptures, humans are living souls, created in God's image and likeness. Psychologically, this refers to our possession of a conscience that motivates seeking union with God, and leads us to seek Jesus-like selflessness, love, peace, and joy. Therefore, the picture that the Scriptures paint of our existence is an optimistic one. However, proclaiming biblical optimism in public life, in the mass media, on the streets, in courts, or in hospitals would sound delusional. There are two cardinal reasons for the contrast between Christian optimism and a gloomy world picture: sin and sickness.

4.1 Contemporary Actuality of the Biblical Understanding

Biblically, sin and sickness are the consequences of Satan's persuading Adam and Eve to disobey the Lord's command. Sin and sickness are consequences of our ancestors' tragic estrangement from God. But can this basic biblical truth be also empirically validated?

The unknown author of Genesis 3:1–25, speaking some 500 years before Christ's birth, gave an explanation for the mystery of sin that still touches the hearts and minds of modern people. Its relevance is proven by the reality that Sigmund Freud (who portrayed himself a "completely Godless Jew, rejecting religion in all nuances and dilution"[1]) reiterated it 2,400 years later, rephrasing it in a materialist framework.

In the biblical story, Adam and Eve play roles similar to that of the ego in Freud's model; they are obedient at one time to God (impersonated by the superego) and at another time to Satan (playing a role similar role to instinct). As Celestin Tomic[2] notes, we modern, individualistic Western readers think of Adam as our abstract ancestor with whom we have only a genetic similarity, but to contemporary Hebrew readers, Adam was a human being in the general sense. Therefore, Adam is not only a particular individual but also a "corporate personality"[3] representing the whole human race. This perspective is essential for understanding the Fall because the story perfectly replicates the personal dynamics at work in every sin and sinner, which Freud's model also attempts to account for.

Estrangement from God usually begins quite naively, at first with seemingly harmless or chaste actions, and then successively, step by step, the rupture intensifies. Adam and Eve opened an innocent dialogue with Satan (or, in Freud's terms, a dialogue with illicit demands of the id), the crafty and attractive archenemy of God. Satan next insinuated insecurity and doubt, asking, "Did God really say, 'You must not eat from any tree in the garden?'" (Genesis 3:1). Finally, in verses 4–5, Satan assures Adam and Eve that they will not die as God warned; instead, he tells them, "When you eat of it your eyes will be opened, and you will be *like God, knowing good and evil*" (Gen. 3:5, emphasis added).

At first, submission to the serpent appeared attractive since the apple was "good for food, and pleasing for the eye, and also desirable for gaining wisdom" (Genesis 3:6). However, verse 8 says that when "the man and his wife heard the sound of the Lord God as he was walking in the garden ... they hid from the Lord God among the trees of the garden." In verses 12–13, the couple begins a process of self-justification that is typical of sinners: Adam accuses Eve, while Eve accuses the serpent. Nevertheless, the warning in Gen 2:16–17, "When you eat of it you will surely die," was already unfolding. Adam and Eve did not immediately die, but consequently their close union with God was terminated.

To understand the biblical message, we must keep in mind that the original texts of the Bible were transferred to us in the Greek language. Greek translators used two words to mean "life": *bios* and *zoe*. *Bios* meant biological life, while *zoe* meant the totality of life, in eternal union with God. Sin causes the loss of hope of possessing *zoe* (everlasting life). Adam and Eve continued to live biologically for many years. Their sin jeopardized not *bios*, biological existence, but *zoe*, everlasting life with God. Having eaten the forbidden fruit, Adam and Eve lost *zoe* and died spiritually.

In paradise, where they had a happy life without sin or sickness, what could have motivated Adam and Eve's nonsensical and self-defeating action to rebel against God? C. S. Lewis explains it a follows: "From the moment a created being becomes conscious of God as God, and itself as self, it is faced with 'the terrible alternative of choosing God or self for the center.'"[4] As he further explains, "There was nothing to prompt them to choose themselves in preference to God except the bare fact that the selves they chose were *their selves*."[5] We know from the Scriptures, that it was Satan who manipulated our ancestors to rebel against God. But which psychological functions of Adam and Eve, and of us contemporary people, does Satan use, to achieve his purpose? Utilizing Freud's personality model to answer this question, we presume that Satan could not use Adam's and Eve's ego or superego. Even less could Satan use our ancestor's Christian like conscience. Rather, Satan exploited Adam's and Eve's instinct to access their human nature and vulnerability. His strategy was the following: Before meeting the serpent, Adam and Eve satisfied their normal and innocent instinctual desire to "be like God, knowing good and evil" (Gen. 3:5) by living in union with God. They humbly participated in God's wisdom. But Satan evoked in them, and then manipulated their hubris, deceitfully promising egalitarianism with the Deity should they disobey his commands. However, eating from the forbidden fruit had just the opposite effect, the severing of our ancestor's union with God. Their search for equality with God has become the mother of all sinful behaviors and psychological disorders, occurring first with the fall of Adam and Eve and regularly ever since in our fallen world.

With Adam and Eve representing the human self (ego), they had the freedom to choose between obedience to God (conscience) or the Satan (instinct), just as we do today. We also have an often sinful and sick desire to "be like God, knowing good and evil" (Gen. 3:5). We also are tempted to disobey God's laws and be servants of our illicit instinct (representing Satan), and be the masters of our conscience (representing God), just like our ancestors. So, Freud and the Bible offer to somewhat complementary explanations for understanding the fatal choice of Adam and Eve, and of the postmodern people who turn away from God and strive to determine what good and evil are arbitrarily.

But there are, of course, significant differences between biblical and Freudian perspectives. The biblical author's worldview is theocentric, while Freud's is anthropocentric. While the biblical author observes the problems of evil and sin from a Godly point of view, Freud observed the same from an atheist's perspective. While the biblical author observes the first cause of evil in the serpent (i.e. outside of our ancestors), psychoanalysis perceives the same cause inside human personalities. While fighting sin is the purpose of believers, Freud sees the liberation of Christian morality as a virtue. While for Christians the solution to the fall of Adam and Eve is the restoration of union with God, sceptics see the solution in being equal with God in deciding what good and evil are.

Despite Freud and his proponents' scepticism, the consequences of sin are still occurring today. Biblically, sickness and especially mental disorders are a consequence of original sin (Romans 8:20–22). Empirically, all psychiatric disorders are the consequence of acting out nonbiblical mindsets—attitudinal and behavioral estrangement from God—which can be attributed to one underlying motivation: the intent of being "like God, knowing good and evil" (Gen. 3:5). The biblical view offers hope for redemption from this condition. St. Paul wrote in Rom 5:20, "Despite the increase of sin, grace has far surpassed it." And the Church echoes, "O happy fault ... which gained for us so great a Redeemer."[6]

Factually, Gen. 3:6 fits between metahistory and history with two foci within an ellipse. The metahistorical focus explains the past concretely—why sickness and sin exist in a God-created world. The other historical focus points the reader toward healing, Jesus' having paid the ransom for our redemption. One focus is insufficient without the other. There is no solution to Adam and Eve's fall without the second focus of Jesus' redemption, and Jesus' mission would be unnecessary without Adam and Eve's fall. Denying original sin, atheists deny any need for salvation; they seek to ban Jesus' mission as nonsensical. For their sake, let us make a short apologetic detour here.

Atheists and even some theists, like C. G. Jung, in his *Answer to Job*, perceive the Father as "total justice and also its total opposite,"[7] sending even his own son to unjustly suffer. Pastoral healers are often asked questions such as, "Who demanded Jesus to unjustly suffer?"; "Who determined the quantity of Jesus' suffering needed for our propitiation?"; and "To whom did Jesus pay the satisfaction and ransom price for our redemption?"

In Heb. 9:14 St. Paul says, "How much more, then, will the blood of

Christ who through the eternal Spirit offered himself unblemished to God, cleanse our consciences from acts that lead to death, so that we may serve the living God." In other words, Jesus offered himself unblemished to God to cleanse our consciences. Although we are not unblemished, we faithfully put our hope and trust in God and can therefore offer ourselves to him. On the other hand, sceptics, whose consciences are not cleansed from acts that lead to death (because they submit themselves to the guidance of the superego), are unable to trust in God and offer themselves to him, living instead in denial of their guilt and need for salvation. So Jesus' sacrificial death did not occur because the Father cruelly demanded satisfaction in the form of highest injustice: Jesus died for *our* sake. Jesus' ministry saves both by its transcendental effects of redemption and also by its behavioral model of holy living that it sets for Christians and all enlightened people. Jesus-like willingness to fight the consequences of Adam and Eve's inheritance of sin and sickness offers biblical peace, love, joy, optimism, and hope to all. Among the first to formulate this insight was the scholastic Peter Abelard (1079–1142), who explained that "[Christ] demonstrated to man the full extent of the love of God for him. This was accomplished by Christ's death. So the major effect of Christ's death was upon man rather than upon God."[8]

4.2 Empirical Validation of Biblical Ideas

On the topic of our compulsory inheritance and the relationship between sickness and sin, atheists like Albert Ellis are of the opinion that, "Devout, Orthodox, or dogmatic religion (or what might be called religiosity) is significantly correlated with emotional disturbance."[9] In the sceptic's understanding, "Guilt and self-blame induce the individual to bow nauseatingly low to some external authority which in the last analysis is always some hypothetical deity.... Guilt inevitably leads to the unsupportable sister concept of self-sacrifice for and dependency upon others—which is the antithesis of true mental health." And the guilty individual "tend[s] to focus incessantly on past delinquencies and crimes rather than on present and future constructive behavior.... [He is] obsessively focused on blaming himself for his past and present misdeeds... [and] cannot think clearly of anything, least of all constructive changes in himself."[10] This is how people who do not know God's grace perceive the relationship of sin and psychological disorders. But how do people who know God's grace perceive the same interaction?

The ancient Hebrews understood famine, sickness, and military defeats as God's punishment (Exodus 4:6, Job 16:12, Psalm 39:11). More precisely, they perceived these conditions as the consequences of sin (Gen. 3:16-19, Exodus 9:1-12, Deuteronomy 28:21), which could be forgiven through repentance (Psalms 38:2-6; 39:9-12, 107:17; 1 Kings 17:17-24; 2 Kings 4:18-37). Receiving healing from sickness was perceived as a sign, the proof of having obtained God's forgiveness and benevolence.

The connection between sin and sickness was self-evident to members of the early Church. Jesus often described sickness and suffering as the consequences of Satan's bondage (Luke 13:16), and healing as the forgiveness of sins and returning to his dominion after estrangement from God is resolved (Mark 2:1-12; John 5:1-9, 5:19-26). St. James recommends, "Is anyone among you sick? Let them call the elders of the church to pray over them and anoint them with oil in the name of the Lord." (James 5:15) However, John 9:1-3 recounts Jesus' words that place the relationship of sickness and sin in a fundamentally new context: "As he went along, he saw a man blind from birth. His disciples asked him, 'Rabbi, who sinned, this man or his parents, that he was born blind?' 'Neither this man nor his parents sinned,' said Jesus, 'but this happened so that the work of God might be displayed in his life.'"

What does Jesus' explanation mean? Does it reduce or eliminate the connection between sin and sickness? No. It means that God is not a vengeful deity. We should not imagine a connection between sin and sickness as was assumed in Old Testament times; not every sickness, and especially not every psychological ailment or psychiatric disorder, is a chastisement for a particular sin. Inversely, though, every healing happens with a purpose "so that the work of God might be displayed." Therefore, we can say respectively that in the biblical view *not every sickness is a consequence of sin, but every healing happens with a Godly purpose.* Can Jesus' explanation be empirically validated by contemporary medical healing practices?

As unbelievable as this may sound, all mental problems manifest in dysfunction, in determining what is evil or good, wrong or right, false or true, immoral or moral, existent or nonexistent. We will repeatedly observe in the second part of the book that a dysfunctional, self-fulfilling prophecy occurred in the case of the chronically-depressed Tammy and occurs with virtually all disorders described in the DSM-5 (*Diagnostic and Statistical Manual of Mental Disorders, Fifth Edition*). With only one exception, that of intellectual deficiency, all psychological ailments and psychiatric disorders are characterized by dysfunctional, and certainly non-Christian beliefs and behaviors that facilitate, justify, and fuel responses like desperation, anger, hate, fear, distrust, paranoia, hopelessness, jealousy, suspicion, and agitation. Furthermore, *there is no disorder (psychotic or nonpsychotic) that is not energized by dysfunctional belief systems contradictory to Jesus' basic commands* given in Mark 12: 29-31: "Love the Lord your God with all your heart and all your strength" and "Love your neighbour as yourself" (standing for all Jesus' commands in this book). And conversely, there is no psychological healing without helping patients to become more biblical—loving, forgiving, peaceful, optimistic, and self-critical, with a joyful attitude toward Jesus and neighbours so that evermore "the work of God may be displayed" in healed persons' lives.

4.3 WHO and DSM Categories Compared to Biblical Ideas

Psychiatrists, psychologists, psychotherapists, and counsellors heal sick behaviors. However, if the biblical lines are disregarded, how can professionals distinguish symptoms of mental disorders and sicknesses from healthy but sinful behaviors? How do professionals, for instance, differentiate violence that results from an evil but healthy mind from violence that results from a sick mind?

These decisions are made by professionals relying on WHO (the World Health Organization) and DSM-5 categories that define sick behaviors as they differ from what are classified as healthy behaviors. Such distinctions, however, shift the question from pathology to a broader topic much more difficult to define: What are the psychological characteristics of mentally healthy people?

As Lindsay Jones recognizes, "To a large extent, the history of evolutionary ethics is associated with efforts to find alternatives to religion as a foundation to moral law."[11] In this context—from a mercilessly objective evolutionist perspective—what is defined as healthy behavior is that which contributes to *sustaining and multiplying life.* However, for postmodern Western societies, neither sustaining nor multiplying life seems a satisfactory criterion of health.

The WHO defines health not only as the absence of disease but as a state of complete physical, mental, and social well-being. The DSM, on the contrary, relies on the definition of health as the absence of a psychiatric disorder. Since it is a commonality of all mental health disorders that its symptoms cause "clinically significant distress or impairment in social, occupational, or other important areas of functioning,"[12] it defines mental health as being marked by the absence of the symptoms of distress or impairment. Even these definitions are not satisfactory, though. The presence of "complete physical, mental, and social well-being" is, by real people and in real life, never achievable. On the other hand, since the social ranking of a "clinically significant distress" is historically changeable, DSM criteria are amended every few years. In fact, there is a greater problem that we will later discuss: sinful and sick behaviors are not arbitrarily determined by humans but are actually objective categories. The reliability and validity of the DSM and the WHO categories depend on how closely they approach the objective truth, existing independently of human subjectivity. Reoccurring revisions corroborate the need for perfecting these instruments.

Defining behaviors we call healthy in a pastoral perspective relies on biblical criteria. As John Paul II notes in his *Theology of the Body*[13], "The soul expresses itself in the body." So a healthy psychological state ought to be the expression of humans' spiritual nature, of our being living souls and subsequently living in a "responsible relationship with God." Jesus concretized what such living means in Mark 12:29–31: living with a supreme love for God and a Christlike love for our neighbours.

The behavior that is required by Jesus, regulated by the soul and psychologically experienced through the conscience, can be disrupted by the two agents of sin and sickness. Sin is a deliberate transgression of a law of God. Accordingly, from a pastoral perspective, we speak about sin in cases of a conscious, voluntary, and intentional disobedience of God's commands in mentally healthy people. We speak about sick behaviors, however, in cases of unintentional, or not completely conscious or wilful, but pathological disorders causing rejection of God's command of love. In other words, if we are not dealing with willingly chosen behaviors but physical-chemical, biochemical, neurological, or psychological disorders producing unchristian (unloving, aggressive, distrustful, selfish, or abusive) behaviors, we classify the case as sickness, a mental ailment.

Reducing all wrongdoings and dysfunctional acts to motives that are sinful or sick may seem artificial. As the saying goes, "To err is human." Must even trivial omissions be either sick or sinful? There is a sharp difference between mistakes, and sick or sinful behaviors. Challenges to acknowledge or correct sinful or sick behaviors is always met with resistance. Banal mistakes, on the other hand, *are easy to prevent, acknowledge and correct.* Therefore, unlike sickness or sin, corrected omissions cause neither significant impairment or distress, nor estrangement from Jesus. On the other hand, the greater the negligence or resistance to the prevention or the correction of a mistake (for example in drunk driving), the more it will cause impairment, distress or estrangement from Jesus' commands and morph into sinful or sick behavior.

In practice, spiritual and mental healing are often connected. Only perfect discipleship is able to ensure behavior free of any clinically significant distress to the maximally achievable extent, guaranteeing complete mental well-being. This speculative conclusion is also supported by practical evidence. It was easy to recognize Jesus' disciples by their modesty, simplicity, honesty, good family life, and biblical love, peace, and joy. And yet they enjoyed neither worldly "physical, mental, and social well-being" nor freedom from any "clinically significant distress." Instead, the exemplary disciples had something which neither the WHO nor the DSM describes: a spiritual resilience. Such resilience correlates more significantly to mental health than any WHO or DSM standard.

The question then becomes how, from a pastoral perspective, is it possible to receive such a spiritual gift? To paraphrase the admonition which Frankl borrows from Maria von Ebner Eschenbach, the answer is by "[being] the master of your instinct and servant of your conscience."[14] From here onward, this will serve as our definition of mental health. If the human species were to live and behave in such a conscience-directed, Christlike manner, we would see an almost immediate restoration of paradiselike conditions on our planet and, as they were for Jacob, the "gates of heaven" (Gen. 28:17) would be opened.

Notes

[1] Wilhelm Bitter, *Psychotherapie und Religioise Erfahrung* (Stuttgaret: Ernst Klett, 1965), 63.

[2] Celestin Tomic, *Prapovjet Spasenja* (Zagreb: Provincijalat Hrvatskih Franjevaca Konventualaca, 1977), 120.

[3] Adalbert Rebic, *Biblijska Prapovjest* (Zagreb: Krscanska Sadasnjost, 1972), 74–6.

[4] C. S. Lewis, *The Problem of Pain*, chapter V, quoted in the RCIA, St. Jude's Parish, 2016–17 (Vancouver, BC, Canada), 21.

[5] Ibid., 22.

[6] Thomas Aquinas, *Summa Theologiae* 111, 1, 3, ad 3, and a song in the Easter Exultet, quoted in the RCIA, St. Jude's Parish, 2016–17 (Vancouver, BC, Canada), 28.

[7] Don S. Browning and Terry D. Cooper, *Religious Thought and the Modern Psychologies* (Minneapolis, MN: Augsburg Fortress Press, 2004), 171.

[8] Millar Erickson, *Christian Theology* (Grand Rapids, MI: Baker Book House, 1995), 803.

[9] E. Thomas Dowd and Steven Lars Nielsen, *The Psychologies in Religion: Working with the Religious Client* (New York: Springer, 2006), 9.

[10] Browning and Cooper, *Religious Thought and the Modern Psychologies*, 171.

[11] Lindsay Jones, *Encyclopedia of Religion* vol. 5 (Farmington Hills, MI: Thomson Gale, 2005), 2917.

[12] DSM 5. Diagnostic and Statistical Manual of the American Psychiatric Association (2013).

[13] John Paul II, *Man and Woman He Created Them: A Theology of the Body* (Boston, MA: Pauline Books and Media, 2006), 395.

[14] Viktor E. Frankl, *Man's Search for Ultimate Meaning* (New York: Basic Books, 2000), 59.

CHAPTER FIVE

THE PROFESSIONAL APPROACH TO SICKNESS AND SIN

We concluded the previous chapter by defining mental health as being the master of instinct and the servant of conscience. Objectively it is hard for any of us to be a complete master of our instinct, and it is even harder to be a completely committed servant of conscience. But there is nothing more difficult than drawing a clear line between sickness and sin and explaining how, when, and why persons become the complete opposite of what they ought to be. However, it is of paramount importance to pastoral healers that we find clarity in this maze.

5.1 What Is Normal?

In postmodern times, when many contemporaries view faith as nothing more than a socially-tolerated delusion, the question "Am I normal for believing in an ultimately loving and almighty God?" may occur, at least occasionally, in every Christian's mind. Let us therefore ask: Who and what is normal according to stringent psychiatric criteria?

Normality and mental health are not synonymous. For example, it was normal for many Hebrews to reject the true prophets like Isaiah or Jeremiah and to celebrate false prophets. It was normal for Romans to believe that

Caesar was god, and in the Middle Ages it was normal to burn witches at the stake. Conversely, the reasoning and behavior of those considered abnormal differed from the reasoning and behavior of the rest of society. In the Soviet Union, dissidents and nonconformists were diagnosed as suffering from "sluggish schizophrenia." Respectively, the word "normal" has historically not meant "healthy" but rather "socially appreciated" in beliefs and behavior.

Today, though, we are living in a time of social-psychological turmoil, when traditional, deeply-entrenched social, religious, moral, and familial standards are questioned by many. What is socially appreciated, therefore, is much more difficult to define. Following Benjamin Sadock, Virginia Sadock, and Pedro Ruiz, we could define normality in at least three ways: as health, an average, and an ideal.[1]

Common sense often defines normality as health or the absence of mental disorders. A normal person, for example, does not exhibit symptoms listed in the DSM. However, every revision of the DSM introduces new diagnoses and/or omits conditions deemed as disordered in previous editions. For example, homosexuality was, until 1973, perceived as a disorder, but today it is perceived as normal behavior.

The statistical concepts of normality state that the average (in relation to beliefs and behaviors) is what is normal. However, the most common opinion is seldom synonymous with ultimate truth, as in the trials of Jesus and Galileo Galilei. Society as an arbiter has never been free of social pathology and false beliefs. Our age is no exception.

The normative ideal recognizes normality as the maximum that is personally achievable. Normal in this sense is to strive not for being an average teacher, sprinter, or parent but for being an ideally good one. Striving for ideals has a practical justification: people would want to be served by ideally good pilots, surgeons, or lawyers, not average ones. Also, from a biblical standpoint, Jesus did not set average standards in Matthew 5:1–12 (the Sermon on the Mount) as the statutes of his kingdom; he set ideal standards.

For pastoral disciplines, normality aims to bring about ideal and maximum healing. Pastoral disciplines observe Christians as they biblically ought to be, not as they really or statistically are. That is not to say that pastoral healing closes therapists' eyes to reality or causes them to escape into denial of imperfections; on the contrary, it helps Christians transcend their weaknesses so that they more closely resemble Christ. To paraphrase Proverbs 24:16, a just man falls seven times a day ... but he rises up again.

In a society in which the majority of the population is suffering from some sort of chronic anxiety[2], Sigmund Freud's pessimistic formulation that the "normal ego is like normality in general, an ideal fiction,"[3] may seem justified. This grim reality, however, helps us discern a parallel. In a society where no one is completely healthy mentally, mental ailments ought not be a stigma producing guilt, shame and disconnection from others. On the contrary, from a biblical perspective, mental illness is a challenge to grow in discipleship. Only an ideal disciple would be able to fulfil Jesus' commands in Mark 12:29–31. Thus, normality in a psychiatric sense is in a positive relationship with discipleship in the Christian sense. It is a process. It is not a permanent state of mind but a constant progression toward the ideals advanced by Jesus.

5.2 The Entanglement of Sickness and Sin in Forensic Disciplines

Religion is as old as the *Homo sapiens*, and the idea of sin is as old as religion. However, around the middle of the nineteenth century, the idea of being responsible for transgressing God's commands was too archaic and had to be discarded in the cold, rational light of science and medicine. In short, the baby was thrown out with the bathwater. In forensic psychiatry and psychology, the biblical idea of sin has been replaced with the idea of transgressing the rule of law and of forensic culpability. Consequently, there prevails a dualism in our culture. Sin disappeared from our official vocabulary, but *feeling* guilt has become almost synonymous with feeling sinful. Professional offices are crowded with people who feel sinful but complain about feelings of guilt. Paradoxically, nonbelievers feel guilty as often as believers despite not being forensically culpable. Factually, introspective spiritual-psychological and objective forensic criteria are different. We will here deal with the professional criteria.

In some cases, psychiatric illness and legal culpability mutually exclude each other. This principle was defined in British courts by 1843. The court established that the accused killer Daniel M'Naghten had for many years complained of delusional, persecutory ideas. Finally, he decided he would rectify the situation by killing his alleged persecutor, Robert Peel. When Peel's secretary, Edward Drummond, came out of his employer's home, M'Naghten mistakenly shot the secretary, believing that he was protecting himself from his alleged persecutor. The court accepted M'Naghten's mental illness defence and established the principle that "people are not guilty by reason of insanity if they laboured under a mental disease such that they were unaware of the nature, the quality, and the consequences of their acts, or if they were incapable of realizing that their acts were wrong with respect to the crime committed."[4] In practice, this means that people suffering from psychoses may not be free in differentiating right from wrong regarding their delusions and, accordingly, may be neither forensically culpable nor responsible for behaviors dictated by their disorder.

But what if it is not a psychotic disorder that is the reason for an offensive behavior? We can answer this by examining the case of Jeffery Dahmer who, between 1978 and 1991, killed seventeen boys and young men.

Dahmer would meet his victims in gay bars and then invite them for a drink. "Then he would drug them, strangle them, masturbate on the body, or have sex with the corpse, dismember the body, and dispose of it." After his arrest, Dahmer pleaded not guilty by reason of insanity. "That Dahmer could plan his murders and systematically dispose of the bodies convinced the jury, however, that he was able to control his behavior. All of the testimony bolstered the notion that, as with most serial killers, Dahmer knew what he was doing and knew right from wrong. Finally, the jury did not accept the defence that Dahmer experienced a mental illness to the degree that it had disabled his thinking or behavioral control." He was sentenced to 957 years in jail.[5]

Apparently, Jeffrey Dahmer had psychological problems but not to a degree that made him unable to grasp the nature, quality, and consequences of his acts; differentiate right from wrong; and control his behavior. Therefore, he was forensically responsible for his murderous behavior. In his case, sickness did not exclude responsibility.

Not only in sophisticated forensic cases but also in everyday life we may see bizarre behaviors getting in the way of exact psychological, qualifying responsibility.

Stojiljkovic gives the example of a young lady (let us call her Anne) ailing from histrionic personality disorder. She attended a party and everyone was enjoying the evening's entertainment, paying little notice to the young lady. Disconcerted by not receiving adequate attention, she nervously lit a cigarette and, after drawing a few puffs, slowly and theatrically dropped the burning cigarette in her décolleté—a placement, to be sure, that ensured the attention she craved—and began crying loudly for help. Indeed, all the guests jumped to extinguish the fire and help the little-burned but very satisfied young lady.[6]

Anne was not psychotic, and she was able to differentiate between right and wrong. But she suffered from prominent dysfunctional ideas, low self-esteem, a need to gain attention, and a tendency to dominate, control, and manipulate others, which are symptoms of most serious personality disorders. The motivation to abuse others for her own selfish purposes was so strong that, in particularly challenging situations, it drove her to act out various attention-seeking behaviors. Thus, it would be hard to determine which came first, the symptoms or her dysfunctional beliefs. The salient point is that her shrewd ability to manipulate those around her, though histrionic in the extreme—even lurid and risqué—demonstrated cognizance of her actions, for which she was psychologically responsible, although in a diminished form.

Finally, let us focus on so-called healthy people. Subconscious desires, fantasies, fears, or irrational hopes may take command in unexpected ways in those deemed healthy, as in a patient of mine whom I will call Willard.

Willard was thirty-four years old, living in an exemplary Christian marriage with his wife, age twenty-three, until his widowed mother-in-law, age forty-three, joined the family. After her arrival, raging confrontations spoiled the family's life. Living with one's in-laws, of course, may be occasionally taxing under normal circumstances if one is to appeal to conventional wisdom, but that notwithstanding, Willard's situation entailed serious friction within his home. Willard felt guilty for escalating the animosity with his mother-in-law. He fervently prayed, fasted, and repeatedly went to confession. Finally, the couple looked for professional help. The sessions shed light on a competitive relationship between the mother-in-law and her daughter (Willard's wife). The mother-in-law, closer in age to Willard than his wife, emotionally manipulated the couple to fight with each other, although she did this unconsciously. Willard rejected her intrusion by overprotecting his wife and claimed, "I'm not attracted to my mother-in-law at all. On the contrary, I hate her." Consciously, Willard denied his hate, but he had been affected by the subconscious and expressed ambivalence—sympathy and antipathy—which often influences the judgment and behavior of even the best Christians.

Not every acting-out behavior in healthy people is unconscious in nature, though. Our frustration tolerance is limited, and traces of impulsive, aggressive, and antisocial drives, which are often hard to suppress or control, exist in every one of us. In situations of intense stress, fear, or frustration, they may surface and direct our behavior, as the following case study shows.

Jonathan was an obsessively disciplined driver, to some degree even fearful, who painfully respected all traffic regulations. Hurrying home from an exhausting workday, he was about to stop at a red traffic light when another car unexpectedly swerved in front of him, forcing him to brake suddenly. He stopped less than an inch behind the other vehicle and, displaying a classic case of road rage, rushed to the driver's side of the car. Without saying a word, he slammed his fist against the car's side window, which shattered, hurting Jonathan's hand. The woman behind the wheel looked at him, mortified, as he lifted his fist to hit her again. Fortunately the light turned green and the woman slowly moved forward, leaving him behind. Jonathan returned to his car and continued driving as if nothing had happened. His broken index finger required surgery and took three months to heal. On the insistence of his wife, Jonathan received psychological counselling during that same time.

Given that the number of discourteous acts, gestures, or outright rage one witnesses on streets and highways, it's obvious that Jonathan's aggressive social behavior is manifested more frequently than one would like to admit. And yet Jonathan was considered a healthy person. He had never manifested or received treatment for psychological problems before this incident. His inappropriate sick and sinful behavior shows the inherent form of a fallen human being and that serious disorders often seethe beneath the veneer of the ordinary—that which appears healthy but requires counselling. Such entanglement does not hinder assessing culpability but makes a precise psychological assessment of responsibility hard.

Notes

[1] Benjamin James Sadock, Virginia Alcott Sadock, and Pedro Ruiz, *Kaplan and Sadock's Synopsis of Psychiatry: Behavioral Sciences/Clinical Psychiatry*, 11th ed. (Philadelphia, PA: Wolters Kluwer, 2015), 123–30.

[2] Ronald M. Rape and David H. Barlow, *Chronic Anxiety, Generalized Anxiety Disorder and Mixed Anxiety Disorder* (London New York, The Guilford Press 1991)

[3] Sadock, Sadock, and Ruiz, *Kaplan and Sadock's Synopsis of Psychiatry,* 11th ed. 129.

[4] Benjamin James Sadock, Virginia Alcott Sadock, and Pedro Ruiz, *Kaplan and Sadock's Synopsis of Psychiatry: Behavioral Sciences/Clinical Psychiatry* (Philadelphia, PA: Wolters Kluwer, 2015), 1378.

[5] Ibid., 1379.

[6] Srboljub Stojiljkovic, *Psihijatrija sa Medicinskom Psihologijom* (Belgrade: Medicinska Knjiga, 1975), 81.

CHAPTER SIX

The Pastoral Approach to Sickness and Sin

We have established that sin and sickness have appeared together in metahistory. What, though, are the pastoral implications of the common appearance of these tragic inheritances in contemporary times?

6.1 The Continuum of Sickness and Sin

A. J. Ayer illustrates a virtually unsolvable controversy as follows.

> For a man is not thought to be morally responsible for an action that it was not in his power to avoid. But if human behavior is entirely governed by causal laws, it is not clear how any action that is done could ever have been avoided. It may be said of the agent that he would have acted otherwise if the causes of his action had been different, but they being what they were, it seems that he was bound to act as he did. Now it is commonly assumed both that men are capable of acting freely, in the sense that is required to make them morally responsible, and that human behavior is entirely governed by causal laws; and it is the apparent conflict between these two assumptions that gives rise to the philosophical problem of the freedom of the will.[1]

Christian anthropology perceives humans as the hierarchically organized, causally, and teleologically-functioning physical-chemical-bio-chemical-neuological-psychological-spiritual link previously discussed. Such thought transcends the philosophical dilemmas Ayer speaks of and, despite causal determinism in the functioning of our brains, acknowledges our factual, psychological-spiritual freedom and subsequent responsibility in choosing between good and evil.

In practice, the ability to do good is limited only by two factors: sickness and sin. Following the examples discussed in previous chapters, it appears that most evil behaviors are like a pendulum swinging between sin and sickness. Most sins have psychopathological components facilitated by unintentional dysfunctional behaviors (i.e. psychiatric disorders), and most psychiatric sicknesses have components of intentional unchristlike behaviors (i.e. of sins). We can only conclude that psychiatric disorders and sin are entangled to a greater or lesser degree. We discern both attributes in the behaviors of Tammy, Anne, M'Naghten, Dahmer, Willard, and Jonathan (Ch. 5), behaviors which either lean toward being more sinful or more sick but are not exclusively one or the other. The problem of untangling these complimentary attributes might be likened to unravelling the Gordian knot. It is not impossible to do so, however.

The question of behavior leaning in one direction or the other—to sickness or sin—was dealt with eloquently by the evangelist in his account of the cure of the man born blind (John 9:1-41). After the cure, the outraged Pharisees claim that they are not blind when Jesus (to paraphrase verse 39) says that he came into the world that the blind might see and that the sighted might become blind. Jesus' words are quite telling when he responds that if his critics were truly blind, they would not be guilty of sin. But what does "truly blind" mean in this context? The answer lies in the Pharisees' accusations that the man in question was probably not the person born blind—that a mistake in identity had been made; their accusation that Jesus healed on the Sabbath; and their demands that the parents of the blind man be produced to settle the matter. Throughout the story they demonstrate anger, judgment, lies, sarcasm, rudeness, confrontation, and (perhaps more than anything else) an unwillingness to accept demonstrable reality. Thus, "truly blind" includes all symptoms of their mental ailment causing the Pharisees' estrangement from Jesus. It is a psychological condition facilitating detrimental spiritual effects. But since Pharisees claim to have intact sight, they claim to be mentally healthy. Jesus concludes: "If you were blind, you would be not guilty of sin; but now that you claim you can see, your guilt remains" (verse 41). Their sin persisted, for they consciously and deliberately refused to accept responsibility for their estrangement from God which, in the estimation of the Lord, they have the capacity to acknowledge.

What are we to make of this verbal exchange and Jesus' enigmatic reply? Simply put, Jesus alludes to the continuum we have been discussing. He is clearly willing to excuse the Pharisees' behavior, but only if they are incapable of perceiving it. This, however, isn't the case. In just one verse, Jesus refers to the spectrum that proceeds all the way from total inability to perceive dysfunctional reasoning causing a genuinely sick behavior to a conscious and deliberately angry, judgmental, dishonest, sarcastic, rude, and confrontational behavior that can be recognized as outright sin. As stated above, sin and sickness are not exclusive of one another—not part of an either-or dynamic. In the case of the Pharisees, their psychopathology leaned toward sin. The gospels do not always provide exacting rationales for Jesus' words or actions, but they do state in many passages that he knew what was in men's hearts. In the above passage, we witness Jesus, the master diagnostician, who can see the complex interaction between sin and sickness in very short order.

We imperfect diagnosticians will discuss the complex relationship between sickness and sinful behaviors in three following sections: (1) people suffering from psychoses; (2) people suffering from nonpsychotic disorders; and (3) virtually healthy people.

6.2 Persons Suffering from Psychoses

M'Naghten, the man who had delusional beliefs that he was being persecuted, suffered from paranoia. Grave mental disorders like schizophrenia, paranoia, or schizoaffective disorder are classified as psychoses. Psychoses are caused by a sickness of the mind, expressed in symptoms of distorted reality judgment such as illusions, hallucinations, or delusional, dysfunctional belief systems that result in conduct characterized by distorted emotions, bizarre sensory experiences, and aggressive behaviors.

Note that not every person suffering from psychosis is dangerous, paranoid, or aggressive like M'Naghten. Nevertheless, the most significant characteristic of people suffering from psychoses is distorted reality judgment. The longer a distorted reality judgment is not expressed in behaviors harmful to the well-being of the subject or his neighbour, the longer it remains a private—and potentially dangerous, festering matter. In practice, however, a seriously distorted reality judgment is typically connected to dysfunctional beliefs and behaviors that jeopardize the well-being of the subject or his environment.

People suffering from psychoses may be religious but unable to reflect genuine biblical peace, love, and joy in behaviors affected by their disorder. For example, M'Naghten, long before killing Mr. Drummond, must have suffered from delusional ideas that made him fearful, suspicious, unforgiving, and jealous, among other unchristlike qualities. He did not intentionally choose to do evil but was persuaded by his delusions that he was doing the right thing when murdering his innocent victim. So what was his responsibility?

As A. J. Ayer defines it, "When I am said to have done something of my own free will, it is implied that I could have acted otherwise; and it is only when it is believed that I could have acted otherwise that I am held morally responsible for what I have done."[2] However, M'Naghten's dysfunctional, delusional beliefs disabled him from acting otherwise in the mental area affected by his disorder when killing Mr. Drummond. His cruel non-Christian behavior was not his choice but was facilitated by a mental disorder. Therefore, there is no responsibility for violent or malicious behaviors in people like M'Naghten. In prominent psychoses, where there is delusion, there is no sin. Since no one is completely engulfed by delusions and there always exist some healthy aspects in a person, the exact boundaries between sickness and sin can be determined only by the ultimate psychiatrist, Jesus Christ.

6.3 Persons Suffering from Nonpsychotic Disorders

People such as Tammy, Anne, and Dahmer suffered from ailments such as dissociative, obsessive-compulsive, anxiety, and conduct disorders, as well as antisocial disorder and other similar nonpsychotic conditions. Their general reality judgment is not significantly impaired. With psychoses, the brain and mind are sick. The same is not true for nonpsychotic disorders as can be seen by the following comparison.

The human brain is not like a television, which reproduces good or bad programs with indifference and without damaging the function of the TV set. Rather, a bad program (i.e., a traumatic experience like child abuse) spoils the functionality of the brain's judgmental capacities. A bad program provokes bad behavior. For example, sexually abused children often become abusers themselves. Or to use another analogy, a traumatic experience is like a computer virus. It will reproduce indefinitely until antiviral software (healing) restores the computer to normal functioning without permanent damage to the hard drive (the brain).

We noted that psychotic patients like M'Naghten suffer from delusional ideas, while people with nonpsychotic disorders, like Anne or Dahmer, suffer from overvalued ideas. While delusional ideas are impossible to correct by logical reasoning (only medication can help), overvalued ideas are hard but not completely impossible to correct logically. While psychotic patients abandon reality (i.e., live in the delusional worlds of their minds), people who suffer from nonpsychotic problems fight a relentless battle against the undisputed fabric of reality. Such people frequently come to the conclusion that "something is wrong with me" and attempt to correct their symptoms. They are sometimes capable of self-criticism, but their dysfunctional belief systems, irrational expectations, and self-centredness limit them in this regard. Since they are divided within themselves, they are unlikely to choose discipleship. This painful, dichotomous existence represents a variation on Jesus' admonition that "no man can serve two masters … (Matthew 6:24). How frightening it must be when both masters are part of a single psyche!

In contrast to psychotic disorders, which disable differentiation between right from wrong, nonpsychotic disorders decrease that ability.

As the Catechism formulates: "Responsibility for an action can be diminished or even nullified by ignorance, inadvertence, duress, fear, habit, inordinate attachments, and other psychological or social factors."[3] Note the use of the word "diminished." We are not to regard the statement as offering a "get out of jail free" card, but rather a chance to remain in the game, so to speak. Put another way, we see that grace and mercy can overtake sin.

From a pastoral perspective, people suffering from nonpsychotic ailments are typically of diminished responsibility for unchristian behaviors and feelings (hopelessness, anxiety, selfishness, frustration, fear, anger, rage, hate, jealousy, competitiveness, low self-esteem, pessimism, egocentrism, narcissism, abuse, etc.) influenced by their psychological problems or psychiatric disorders, as such conditions may result in the above factors noted by the Catechism.

6.4 Mentally Healthy People

Only an individual who is holy (spiritually ideal) and mentally healthy to the maximum extent would be able to completely fulfil the aspirational goals Jesus set in Matthew 5:1–12 (the Beatitudes). Traces of psychological problems exist not only in the Pharisees that John 9:1-41 talks about but in every one of us. For that reason, it is difficult to discern whether the non-Christian behavior of seemingly mentally healthy people is a subclinical form of a disorder (a pathology) or a sin (estrangement from God). Christians are paradoxically more resistant to acknowledging sickness than sin. Believers often say, "There is nothing wrong with me. I'm just a bad person."[4] Distinguishing whether the motives and dynamics of unchristlike behaviors are more sinful and less sick or, conversely, more sick and less sinful, is often part of the pastoral healer's task of discernment.

This dissection—unravelling another Gordian knot, if you will—is made even harder because pastoral criteria in distinguishing sickness and sin are much more delicate than those used in forensic psychiatry, such as in M'Naghten's mental illness defence. A pastoral healer called to help

Willard's or Jonathan's self-understanding in order to make the distinction between sinful and sick behavior would first focus on clarifying whether their *understanding of moral requirements in morally challenging situations is adequate.*

In assessing this ability, the pastoral healer looks for not only the right words but also the understanding behind them. For instance, it is well known that for believers, the word "church" (theologically defined) meant "a perfect society" until 1943, "the body of Christ" until 1964, and "the people of God" after Vatican II in 1964. The same word indicated a slightly different reality for Christians in different periods of history. By the same token, "church" can simultaneously mean something quite different to an atheist than to a Christian. This is a trivial example, but in some pastoral situations it is of paramount importance to recognize that the same terms indicate different realities for different people. Understanding matrimonial covenant and its resulting duties, a very relevant topic in marriage tribunal cases, requires that there be a precise correlation between words and ideas. Perhaps in no other social institution is there such a profound disconnect as in marriage, in which civil and Christian ideas of the same word elicit profoundly different definitions. The idea of a quick ceremony in a Las Vegas wedding chapel does not begin to connote the sacramental nature of marriage practiced by Christians.

The next step would be assessing Willard's and Jonathan's discretional judgment. Discretional judgment means not only understanding the moral requirements of a situation but also *having the ability to give a response proportionate to the gravity of the situation.* For the pastoral healer, this means assessing whether the information the patient provides, as well as his judgment in discerning good and evil in a complex situation, is sufficient. Discretional judgment may be sufficient in discerning moral right from wrong in simple, familiar scenarios, but not sufficient for resolving an ethically complicated problem. Determining the state of discretional judgment for Willard and Jonathan would mean assessing whether their judgments were sufficient for responding in a Christlike way despite the gravity of the challenges they were subjected to. Furthermore, was the ethical complexity of their respective situations of such a level that their ability to discern the morally right answer was essentially compromised? Without discernment from the Holy Spirit in ethically complicated situations—and a great deal of professional competence—some scenarios represent a minefield for the pastoral healer.

To behave like Christ, Willard and Jonathan would also need appropriate *appreciative judgment*, which means *the ability to apply and enforce the standards of their consciences to their feelings, thoughts, will, and all other mental functions directing their behaviors.* Appreciative judgment is, accordingly, not only about abstract, theoretical knowing what is morally right and ought to be applied in a frustrating, ethically-complex or ambiguous situation. It also means the ability to behave as Christ's disciple by controlling impulsive or acting-out behaviors and conforming, automatic thoughts, selfish feelings, blind drives, all of which are reactions to the well-informed Christian conscience.

Neither Jesus nor his disciples lived in an ideal world. Nevertheless, the acid test of faith is the ability to preserve a sound discretional and appreciative judgment in fighting sickness and sin when faced with physical, mental, and social predicaments. The Acts of the Apostles describes countless examples of disciples who possessed this ability, calling them "saints." These saints had the courage to act, not wavering between holiness and worldliness, but strictly adhering to Christian moral judgment. This kind of clear-cut yes, a full commitment to Jesus, is also the best and only way to complete mental health and holiness. It is a commitment that, in the words of Jesus, signifies a fully-trained disciple (Luke 6:40).

The fact that we are not yet fully-trained disciples, but mentally compromised sinners ought not to discourage us. Unlike in the business world, where only successes and failures matter, in pastoral work all efforts to fight sin and sickness prove discipleship. Even failures in fighting the sin-sickness continuum should to motivate us to "Love the Lord your God with all your heart and all your strength" and "Love your neighbour as yourself" (Mark 12: 29-31), and heal the irrational pride, shame and nihilism that disconnect us from Jesus, his Church and from each other.

Notes

[1] David J. Chalmers, *Philosophy of Mind, Classical and Contemporary Readings* (New York, Oxford: Oxford University Press, 2002), 662.

[2] Ibid.

[3] Canadian Conference of the Catholic Bishops, *Catechism of the Catholic Church* (Ottawa: Publications Service, Canadian Conference of Catholic Bishops, 1994), 371.

[4] David H. Barlow (ed.), *Clinical Handbook of Psychological Disorders: A Step-by-Step Treatment Manual* (New York: The Guilford Press, 2008), 375.

CHAPTER SEVEN

THE PSYCHOLOGICAL–SPIRITUAL ASPECTS OF CHRISTIAN RESPONSIBILITY

As Joseph Feigl notes, "The enormous differences in behavior and neural processes that exist between e.g. humans and insects indicate equally great differences in their corresponding direct experience."[1] Extrapolating Feigl's observation, we can acknowledge that human reasoning, in comparison to ultimate truth known only by God, has limits. As Isaiah 55:8–9 states, our thoughts are not God's thoughts. Accordingly, Jesus knew the topic of human accountability quite differently than humanity is able to grasp it. Nevertheless, how God reasons has always been a challenging question for philosophers.

While the German philosopher Georg Wilhelm Friedrich Hegel (1730–1841) promoted a universal concept of logic—meaning that angels, cherubs, and even God need to respect the rules of logic if they want to reason in a logical way—the Danish philosopher Søren Kierkegaard (1813–55), instead of Aristotelian "either/or" logic, used an "also/as well" approach called paradoxical logic. Kierkegaard concluded from his analysis of the Scriptures that since God and humans are significantly different, their reasoning is also different.[2] God's reasoning, he found, was paradoxical. These are some examples of God's logic that he observed from Scripture: We need to use logic but are unable to understand God rationally; one must lose life to gain life; some of the first may become the last; God is everywhere and nowhere; the blind gain sight, while those who see lose theirs; Jesus was ultimately glorious and ultimately humble; the smallest one is the greatest; we are responsible for sins but unable to avoid being sinners. These represent the sacred mysteries of the faith.

Notwithstanding the speculations of philosophers, our intellectual and emotional limitations need to be supplemented by revelation. So what does our responsibility look like when seen from a psychological viewpoint synchronised with a more objective, biblically-painted perspective? What colour palette does Scripture provide for the informed pastoral healer?

7.1 Biblical Truths and Christians' Self-Scrutinizing

The Greeks had great mathematicians, philosophers, and physicians, but no great prophets. Unlike the Greeks, the Hebrews had no great mathematicians, philosophers, and physicians, but they had great prophets. The Hebrew mentality was theocentric. They used the terms "sin" and "sickness" almost interchangeably, as two sides of a same coin, both signalling estrangement from God. In this context, St. Paul says of himself in Romans 7:14, "We know that the law is spiritual, but I am unspiritual, sold as a slave to sin." In the next verse, Romans 7:15, he explains, "I do not understand what I do. For what I want to do I do not do, but what I hate I do." He is here not exclusively speaking about sin, which the Catechism describes as being committed with full knowledge and with fully conscious and intentional consent. Rather, he qualifies his prior statement in saying, "I do not understand what I do," which indicates a psychological obstacle limiting his cognition and his will. It facilitated his doing what he hated (i.e., sin). St. Paul was, like every one of us, fighting a sin-sickness continuum on which it is difficult to determine where one component ends and the other begins.

The coexistence of sin and mental ailments is also repeatedly illustrated in the gospels, but quite dramatically in Luke 7:36–50. Jesus, while eating at the home of a Pharisee, was approached by a woman with a bad reputation—a prostitute—who wept upon the Lord's feet and wiped them with her hair. Her choice of a profession certainly resulted from her total life experience—upbringing, education, lack of nurturance, and any number of socioeconomic variables, not to mention possible pathological motivations for her behavior—but she did not attempt to explain her sins away as a psychological weakness, a mistake, or a consequence of an inadequate social structure. On the contrary she was keenly aware that she had transgressed God's law and was genuinely repentant. For this reason, Jesus forgave her many sins (v. 47). The reader is to infer that Jesus, the divine healer, cleansed her of both sin and sickness simultaneously, and differentiating between these two aspects of Adam and Eve's inheritance in her behavior was for Jesus almost irrelevant. If it was so unimportant for Jesus, why is differentiating between the two so relevant for us?

Jesus did not use clinical terminology in the gospels as he talked with farmers, fishermen, and the repeatedly emphasize in many passages that Jesus knew what was in people's hearts. However, twenty-first century pastoral healers are infinitely far from his supranatural diagnostic and therapeutic skills, and our patients' mentality is different from Jesus' listeners'. Distinctions such as "was my behavior sinful or sick?" are substantial in contemporary believers' self-scrutinizing and healing. If pastoral healers would like to help people like Daniel M'Naghten, Jeffrey Dahmer, Anne, Willard, or Jonathan, marginalized. Neither did he talk in forensic terminology but in a manner that helped his Hebrew listeners to understand his message. Therefore, despite addressing the topic of being "truly blind" in John 9:1–41, he did not permanently and explicitly insist on precisely differentiating between sin and sickness. The gospels, as noted, seldom explain the rationale for his words and actions, but they do repeatedly emphasize in many passages that Jesus knew what was in people's hearts. However, twenty-first century pastoral healers are infinitely far from his supranatural diagnostic and therapeutic skills, and our patients' mentality is different from Jesus' listeners'. Distinctions such as "was my behavior sinful or sick?" are substantial in contemporary believers' self-scrutinizing and healing. If pastoral healers would like to help people like Daniel M'Naughten, Jeffrey Dahmer, Anne, Willard, or Jonathan, then they need to be able to distinguish between their sick and their sinful behaviors. Pastoral healers need to help their clients discern whether their unwanted behaviors are sick or sinful. The effectiveness of pastoral healing depends on such distinctions. Attempting to heal sinful behaviors committed by an epileptic psychopath by solely pastoral methods would be futile. Inversely, the same distinction is often needed; selfish and predatory behaviors cannot be healed by Machiavellian professionals perceiving themselves as useful, necessary, or even mandatory for a successful life.

Jesus warned about the reality of sin in stern words. In Mark 9:43–47, he says:

> If your hand causes you to sin, cut it off. It is better for you to enter life maimed than with two hands go to hell, where fire never goes out. And if your foot causes you to sin, cut it off. It is better for you to enter life crippled than to have two feet and be thrown into hell. And if your eye causes you to sin, pluck it out. It is better for you to enter the Kingdom of God with one eye than to have two eyes and be thrown into hell.

The reality of sin, as the Catechism warns, is a paramount human reality "present in human history; any attempt to ignore it or to give this dark reality other names would be futile."[3] Any temptation "to explain it as merely a developmental flaw, a psychological weakness, a mistake, or the necessary consequence of an inadequate social structure, etc."[4] would be a self-deception. On the other hand, sin is a deliberate transgression of the law of God. Thus, "to choose deliberately—that is, both knowing and willing it—something gravely contrary to the divine law and to the ultimate end of man, is to commit a mortal sin."[5] The crucial task for pastoral healers is not only to prevent the classification of mentally ailing peoples' behaviors as solely sinful, but to determine how much a particular transgression of God's law is a deliberate choice and how much it is an expression of a clinical or subclinical disorder eventually modifying people's responsibility for full knowledge and complete consent.

Our aid in this delicate task is a well-informed Christian conscience inspired by the Holy Spirit, shaped by correctly interpreted Scriptures and supplemented by tools like the *Catechism*. Thus, in assessing responsibility, let us first quote the Catechism's directives.

> A human being must always obey the certain judgment of his conscience. If he were deliberately to act against it, he would condemn himself. Yet it can happen that moral conscience remains in ignorance and makes erroneous judgments about acts to be performed or already committed.[6]
>
> This ignorance can often be imputed to personal responsibility. This is the case when a man "takes little trouble to find out what is true and good, or when conscience is by degrees almost blinded through the habit of committing sin." In such cases the person is culpable for the evil he commits.[7]
>
> Ignorance of Christ and his gospel, bad examples given by others, enslavement to one's passions, assertion of a mistaken notion of autonomy of conscience, rejection of the Church's authority and her teaching, lack of conversion and of charity; these can be the source of errors of judgment in moral conduct.[8]
>
> If, on the contrary, the ignorance is invincible, or the moral subject is not responsible for his erroneous judgment, the evil committed by the person cannot be imputed to him. It remains no less an evil, a privation, a disorder. One must therefore work to correct the errors of moral conscience.[9]

For a sin to be mortal, as noted, it must be seriously wrong and committed deliberately, with full consent and with the full knowledge that it is seriously wrong. Sins that are not grave enough to be mortal are called "venial," meaning "light" or "less serious." They do not kill the relationship with Jesus, but "if deliberate and unrepented, can lead us into mortal sin."[10] In John 15:5, Jesus proclaims, "I am the vine; you are the branches...." To what extent does sin compromise our connection to the vine or even sever it completely?

These principles are based on Jesus' revelation, so we must ask, "How does he apply the above principles in his judgment?"

7.2 God's Justice and Mercy

To answer the above raised question, consider the following biblical example.

> The teachers of the law and the Pharisees brought in a woman caught in adultery. They made her stand before the group and said to Jesus, "Teacher, this woman was caught in the act of adultery. In the Law Moses commanded us to stone such women. Now what do you say?" They were using this question as a trap, in order to have a basis for accusing him. But Jesus bent down and started to write on the ground with his finger. When they kept on questioning him, he straightened up and said to them, "If any one of you is without sin, let him be the first to throw a stone at her." Again he stooped down and wrote on the ground. At this those who heard began to go away one at the time, the older ones first until only Jesus was left, with the women still standing there. Jesus straightened up and said, "Woman, where are they? Has no one condemned you?" "No one," she said. "Then neither do I condemn you," Jesus declared. "Go now and leave your life of sin."
>
> (JOHN 8:3–11)

The Hebrews perceived prostitution as a paramount transgression of the law. Lev. 19:29 and Deuteronomy 22:21 prescribe stoning as a possible punishment for prostitutes, while Leviticus 21:9 recommends burning them to death. Why, then, did Jesus not condemn this woman?

One can discern Jesus' unimaginable mercy in this story. Mercy means God doesn't punish but blesses repentant sinners. As we can reconstruct from John 1:14-18 and 4:8, Titus 2:11, Matthew 21:37 and 26:28, and 2 Corinthians 8:9 and 8:1, mercy is a two-way street. It consists of God's free giving and the subject's responsible accepting of his ultimate mercy. Mercy without responsible reception would enable sin rather than healing. Because the prostitute dearly accepted it, the merciful Jesus was ready to forgive her. A popular cliché says that it is better to give than to receive. An equally important maxim states, "Have humility and gratitude, and know how to receive a gift graciously."

One can also see Jesus' sense of justice in this account. In determining what the woman deserved, Jesus might have taken into account not only her transgression of the law but also its alleviating conditions. For example, she would not have engaged in promiscuous behavior without a compelling reason. Jesus might have also taken into account her possible pathology. Prostitution, for example, correlates with child abuse, neglect, drug use, mood disorders, intellectual disability, and borderline personality disorder, all of which would have contributed to judgments disproportionate to the gravity of the choices involved in her profession. Her sin certainly didn't merit that she be stoned to death in conformity with Mosaic law. We see in this story another example of Jesus emphasis that the heart of the law is mercy (Matthew 12:7) and that the joint consideration of justice and mercy is how the law (never to be ignored, of course) is to be fulfilled in the New Covenant.

One could therefore acknowledge both biblical realities, mercy and justice, in Jesus' verdict, "Go now and leave your life of sin." Even though Jesus did not use clinical terminology in the gospels, he was always able to look at the aggregate of a person's behavior (or of a situation). He operated holistically, not in the New-Age sense of the term, but in a spiritual sense that could understand the thoughts and intents of the mysterious, elusive human heart.

The same realities of God's ultimate mercy and justice appear in other biblical examples, as in the parable of the prodigal son (Luke 15:11–30). The parable demonstrates the unimaginable mercy of the father but also shows that, despite mercy, justice cannot be completely disregarded. In Jesus' words in verse 17 ("when he came to his senses"), we see that the younger son's state of mind at the time of his acting-out behavior was not impeccable. We discern that his mental functioning was limiting his sound discretional and appreciative judgment as he exhibited his selfish and self-defeating behaviors. Thus, in Jesus' narrative he was not only sinful but also suffering from psychological problems that limited his judgment and subsequent responsibility for his behaviors. (Today, traces of adjustment disorder, conduct disorder, or even borderline personality disorder would be noted in his psychology tests.) Besides Jesus' ultimate mercy, his ultimate justice requiring that everyone receives what he or she deserves motivated the father to take his son's mental conditions into account and extend forgiveness. The law must be fulfilled, but mercy is possible when we have "come to our senses."

God's ultimate mercy is inseparable from his ultimate justice. Nevertheless, while Christians almost always universally appreciate mercy, our attitude toward God's justice is often ambivalent. We sometimes perceive God's justice as a counterweight to Jesus' mercy, or in extreme cases, a horrifying threat to salvation, giving us "what we really deserve." Nevertheless, members of the early church collectively sang "*Maranatha*" ("Come, O Lord"), impatiently expecting Jesus' Second Coming and Judgment Day. What was different about them? Such a perspective comes to Christians who view their relationship to God not from a self-centred, salvation-seeking standpoint, but from one of personal association with him, following the Virgin Mary's example of saying, "Here I am, the servant of the Lord; let it be with me according to your word" (Luke 1:38). The Lord's judgment and punishment are appreciated by such Christians, who struggle against the dark sides of their own personalities and are able join the Lord in condemning themselves while at same time hoping in Jesus' forgiving grace. But is "condemning" too strong of a word here? No, for the prodigal son freely confessed that he had sinned against heaven and against his father (Luke 15:21).

Jesus did not give explicit clarification of how he would use his logic to judge humankind justly and mercifully, but he implicitly spoke about this issue at a turning point of human history: his crucifixion. In human understanding, the people crucifying the Messiah were the worst sinners. Rather, Luke 23:34 conveys the weary but heartfelt words of Jesus from the cross: "Father forgive them; for they do not know what are they doing." Jesus did not specify whether the people crucifying him did not know what they were doing because of their sickness (an impairment of their discretional and appreciative judgment), their sin (prompted, as the Catechism notes, by ignorance, erroneous moral judgment, blindness, or enslavement to passions), or both. Neither did he distinguish between the need for mercy and justice with pedantic, hair-splitting precision as Christians often do. Instead, he demonstrated the integration of God's ultimate justice and mercy in the context of his unconditional love. Despite the reality of sin, punishment, and hell, repentant sinners may wholeheartedly trust in God's infinite justice and mercy. It is the essence of our faith!

Talking about the essence of our faith, it is interesting to consider one more fact. The Old Testament Hebrews had difficulty distinguishing true and false prophets. According to an anecdotal story, a false prophet would declare on a rainy day, "People, see how wet it is outside," and everyone would agree. A true prophet, on the other hand, would exclaim, "People, see how dry it is outside," and nobody would agree with him. Why is then the first prophet false and the other true? Because the first one prophesised what everyone already knew, while the other prophesised what people would only realize a hundred or thousand years later. So it is also with Jesus' words as quoted by St. Luke. Forensic psychiatry was completely unknown in the ancient world. As discussed, it was not until 1843 that the first British court realized that mental ailments may influence responsibility. That Jesus assessed the moral responsibility of the people crucifying him eighteen centuries earlier, evaluating their mental ailments more precisely than any contemporary forensic expert, proves his divine prerogatives. Acknowledging this is also the essence of our faith.

With this understanding, let us return to our original topic and ask how clerics, as leaders, and Christian professionals and pastoral healers working in a team with them, when confronted with the convoluted relationship of sin and sickness, may make themselves useful to those tormented with the psychological-spiritual aspects of Christian responsibility.

7.3 The Proportions of Sickness and Sin in Evil Deeds

We previously illustrated the relationship between sickness and sin with a swinging pendulum, a continuum between the extremes of sin and sickness. From this comparison it appears that the relationship between sickness of the mind and sin in evil behaviors does not always demonstrate exacting uniformity and is not written in stone. Indeed, the proportions of psychological problems and sin are variable in every kind of unchristlike behavior. We can visualize that relationship as in Fig. 7.1 below.

Fig. 7.1. The "proportions" of sin and sickness

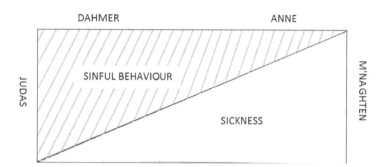

Fig. 7.1 illustrates the variable distribution of sickness and sinful behavior in different forms and nuances. Sinful behavior like that of Judas (i.e., deceitful, greedy, abusive, or unloving behaviors in healthy people) is placed at the far left. Sick behavior like that of M'Naghten (i.e., sick beliefs promoting distrusting, revengeful, paranoid, and other non-Christian behaviors) is placed at the far right. From left to right on the scale, the proportion of sin decreases while the proportion of psychiatric disorders increases. Jeffrey Dahmer, for example, would be placed closer to sin, while the histrionic acting out of Anne would be placed closer to sickness. This figure also illustrates that virtually every sinful behavior involves a psychopathological component, and reciprocally, most mentally sick behaviors imply a transgression against God's basic command of love.

So, acknowledging our condition as sick sinners does not mean explaining away sins with sicknesses (the latter an all too prevalent tendency among the cold rationalism of the New Atheism). Excluding extreme cases (e.g., Judas's or M'Naghten's), sin and sickness are not mutually exclusive but are *mutually inclusive and occurring on the same continuum.* Most sinful, deliberate transgression of God's law of love is also motivated by varying degrees of pathological personality traits. The reverse is also true. Most psychiatric conditions are typically accompanied by at least a semi-conscious or partially deliberate transgression of Jesus' commands given in Mark 12:29–31, "Love the Lord your God with all your heart and all your strength" and "Love your neighbor as yourself." We can visualize that dynamic as in Fig. 7.2 below.

Fig. 7.2. The dynamics of sin and sickness

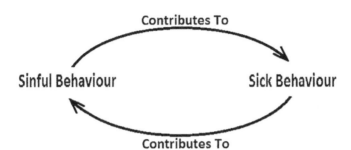

Fig. 7.2 illustrates the dynamics of sinful and sick behaviors. Sinful choices decrease the control over or even empower the expression of sick personality traits, while unhealthy personality traits assist in making sinful choices. In extreme cases (like Judas's and M'Nagthen's), one focus in this ellipse dictates all the dynamics, while most often both sinful and sick motives play a certain role.

As the Catechism also notes, it would be a great mistake to explain away sin as merely a psychological weakness or a mental ailment. On the contrary, all psychiatric sicknesses are a manifest and flagrant transgression of Jesus' commands of love and, except in extreme cases, all mental ailments contain at least some traces of consciousness and will. In other words, as we will repeatedly observe in our study of psychopathology, virtually all psychiatric sicknesses facilitate and are enhanced by distrust in the biblical God. As noted, sin and sickness are intricately tied; their relationship is often like that of the chicken and the egg. Such a mutually inclusive relationship causes us to feel responsible not only for deliberately committed sinful behaviors, but also for our psychologically inappropriate behaviors.

But where is human love, goodness, freedom, and responsibility in our model?

We are not implying a pessimistic or Augustinian anthropological concept, as if fallen humankind were only sick or only sinful. As already noted, this either-or logic cannot accomplish the synchronised approach we seek as caring pastoral healers. We are all created in God's image and likeness and as such possess a Christian or Christian-like conscience that facilitates a plethora of unselfish, loving, Christlike behaviors. Our focus, though, is on healing the ties of sin and sickness of the mind. The illustration above is an abstraction. It is a two-dimensional transection of the human personality, illustrating the proportionality between psychiatric disorders and sin. Nevertheless, we should not, in Frankl's words, "destroy the unified whole of the human person,"[11] which is factually multidimensional.

It is easy to take a stand concerning responsibility in a clear-cut murder case like M'Naghten's. But as we have observed, not only psychotic people but also people deemed healthy like Jonathan may lose their temper, regress into a furious rage, and act in ways that disrespect God and their neighbours. And people like Willard, tormented by his subconscious ambivalence toward his mother-in-law, or Anne, driven by her attention-seeking motives, may exhibit sick and/or sinful behaviors. In cases like these, even the best pastoral psychiatrist, psychologist, confessor, or priest is not able to fully answer all moral and pastoral questions concerning freedom and responsibility. The individual's informed conscience is the best source of this information, but only Jesus, adept at comforting, healing, and even confronting all he encountered in his public ministry, knows the full truth. Because of the fragility of our human knowledge, a loving and trusting submission to Jesus is the best counterweight to our healthy angst of our responsibility and of his judgment.

7.4 Sin and Sickness as Objective Categories

To most sceptics it seems absurd to talk about sin and sickness as objective categories. As Jean Paul Sartre says in *L'existentialisme est un humanism*, "It is extremely unpleasant that God does not exist, because with the disappearance of God disappears also the possibility of finding any eternal values on the 'meaningful painted sky.'"[12] It is true that without God, not only eternal values but all basic virtues of humanity become insignificant. If God did not exist, then Christianity and all religious practices would be, as Albert Ellis in his *Case Against Christianity* puts it, "essentially masochism" and "mental sickness."[13] This is a position that is readily evident in the arguments of New Atheists such as Richard Dawkins and Neil deGrasse Tyson. To them, Christianity is a superstition that has already been disproven, a malignancy that causes needless pain and suffering.

However, it is not only agnostics and atheists who perceive sin and mental sickness as purely human-shaped categories. Adam and Eve did not deny God's existence, but they did falsify his image, nature, and commands as if there were no objective values. That misconstrued image of God resulted in an arbitrary decision of what was good and evil. We continue to live with this legacy of self-centredness today, for sinful and sick people deny the objective, God-given classifications of good and evil, right and wrong, true and false, and sinful and sick.

Sick sinners would like to be "like God, knowing good and evil" (Gen. 3:5), which is the hubris of original sin. Consequently, as the Latin saying implies, "Changing times change humans," and even our comprehension of biblical passages and Jesus' words have changed. Each era perceives sin from its own perspective. Even Jesus' basic command, "Love your neighbor as yourself" is understood differently today than it was a few hundred years ago, when slavery was accepted. But Jesus' commands have not changed; rather, our understanding of them has improved. If masters had genuinely loved their slaves as themselves, history would have evolved differently, no doubt for the better. This has an unpleasant implication: the morality of every historical period ought to be assessed from its own perspective. Today, we pride ourselves, too generously perhaps, as generally living up to biblical standards. In a few hundred years, however, as God's kingdom progresses, Christians will look at the injustices, abuse, greed, and hunger for power in our times as critically as we now view slavery. Thus, when talking about eternal biblical values, we mean Jesus' ultimate truth, which transcends space, time, and social and cultural bias. On this basis, our understanding of Jesus' eternal values in our rapidly changing world should be empirically validated. Such validation would ensure that the words of the Gospel are also written, on men's hearts, where the Spirit can facilitate understanding in any historical time period. Let me explain what I mean by the idea of empirical validation of sin and sickness. As we observed when discussing the murderous M'Naghten and Dahmer, the manipulative Anne, the assaultive Willard, and the enraged Jonathan, the root of all of their distress was their disobedience of Jesus' commands given in Mark 12:29–31 ("Love the Lord your God with all your heart and all your strength" and "Love your neighbour as yourself"). The sufferings caused by paranoid, greedy, abusive, and all other forms of sinful and/or sick behaviors are all touchable, visible, and even quantifiable consequences of estrangement from Jesus' laws of love. Only adherence to genuine biblical standards remedies such suffering, but sick sinners live, intentionally or unintentionally, with self-made gods—their own sources of truth—which permit or even encourage the unchristlike behaviors they exhibit. The consequences of such behaviors are destructive not only for the individuals but also the whole human race. All social injustice, abuse, and bloody wars can be traced back to this problem, in which we forever hear echoes of Adam and Eve's intention to become self-made gods. Simply formulated, *there is very little distress, disappointment, or anguish in human life that is not related to estrangement from Jesus' two basic commands to love God and neighbour.*

An atheist would counter, "But let's be rational! How could a transcendental deity impose any objective categories of sin and sickness on autonomous enlightened humans?" As Fritz Rothschild describes, religion answers the ultimate questions of life that "arise under the impact of the elemental forces of reality confronting man."[14] Persons estranged from God challenged by these elemental forces are unable to give an optimistic and psychologically satisfactory answer to life's ultimate questions since their arbitrary, nonexistent gods neither demand discipleship nor give the spiritual gifts that God gives. Sick sinners justify their self-centredness with a self-deceptive regression to, as Nancy Murphy describes, being a "living animal,"[15] integrating sin and sickness into their behaviors and lifestyles derived from popular culture that provides no meaningful direction, purpose, or understanding. It is a vicious circle in which the blind leads the blind.

Christians inherit Adam and Eve's legacy of sin and sickness like all people, but their attitudes in dealing with it are radically different. St. Paul's life, for example, was not painless. He lived in a society much more hostile toward biblical living than we do today. He survived a shipwreck, imprisonment, and countless challenges and threats from Jews and fellow Christians—even narrowly averting death on several occasions. However, his most painful experience was probably none of these but what he reveals in 2 Corinthians 12:7—his "thorn in the flesh." Drawing from Galatians 1:10, where St. Paul pathetically asks, "Am I now trying to win the approval of men, or of God? Or am I trying to please men? If I were still trying to please men, I would not be servant of God," Lindsay Jones interprets this thorn in the flesh to mean that Paul's self-consciousness was bruised by despairing self-humiliation: "His will is divided; his body does not obey him; his urgent convictions are challenged by adversaries, his life's work overthrown."[16] Nevertheless, these inner pains helped him to place his self's importance in a Christlike context and realize that, as noted in Psalm 34:18, "the Lord is near to the broken-hearted, and saves the crushed in spirit." Consequently, while "In Romans, conscience the accuser caught up in an eschatological drama always convicts (3:9, 7:15–20), a good conscience before God means surrender of what men call good conscience."[17]

Notes

[1] David J. Chalmers, *Philosophy of Mind, Classical and Contemporary Readings* (New York, Oxford: Oxford University Press, 2002), 71.

[2] Millard Erickson, *Christian Theology* (Grand Rapids, MI: Baker Book House, 1995), 315.

[3] Canadian Conference of the Catholic Bishops, *Catechism of the Catholic Church* (Ottawa: Publications Service, Canadian Conference of Catholic Bishops, 1994), 87.

[4] Ibid.

[5] Ibid., 393

[6] Ibid., 379

[7] Ibid.

[8] Ibid., 380.

[9] Ibid., 381.

[10] RCIA, St. Jude's Parish, Vancouver, BC (2016–17), 500.

[11] Viktor E. Frankl, *Man's Search for Ultimate Meaning* (New York: Basic Books, 2000), 27.

[12] Ferenc Szabo, *Ember es Vilaga* (Roma, 1988), 183–4.

[13] E. Thomas Dowd and Steven Lars Nielsen, *The Psychologies in Religion, Working with the Religious Client* (New York: Springer, 2006), 8.

[14] Fritz Rothschild in Abaraham Heschl, *Between God and Man* (New York: The Free Press, 1959), 9–10.

[15] Nancy Murphy, *Bodies and Souls, or Spirited Bodies?* (Cambridge: Cambridge University Press, 2006), 113.

[16] Lindsay Jones (ed.), *Encyclopedia of Religion* 3 (Farmington Hills, MI: Thomson Gale, 2005) 1940.

[17] Ibid, 1940

CHAPTER EIGHT

SICKNESS AND SIN: A NATURAL OR DEMONIC CAUSE?

In biblical times it was collectively believed that sin and sickness were caused diabolically. Jesus, as we see in John 9:1–3, warned that not every hardship is caused by sin (i.e. Luciferian input). Nevertheless, he "did not put a lot of effort into differentiating naturally-caused sickness from demonic possession."[1] His purpose was rather practical: establishing the kingdom of God. The pastoral healer's purpose too is rather practical, concentrated on preventing and healing sin and mental sickness. The devil and his power are for Christians an unquestionable reality but in some situations, it is crucial to differentiate between demonic and natural causes.

A middle-aged, anxious, and distressed lady—a committed believer—experienced what she perceived to be repeated attacks by Satan. A demonic force, she alleged, was seizing control of her body and behaviors, causing her to twitch and move her extremities unstoppably and unintentionally. She turned to her priest for help. Touched by her faith and intensive complaints, the priest recognized a demonic possession and helped her to receive deliverance. Subsequently, the lady felt better and travelled overseas for a holiday. When her condition returned and worsened, however, she was referred to a local hospital. Unfortunately, her final diagnosis was Huntingon's disease, a neurological disorder with involuntary movements. The ultimate reason for her disorder was Satanic, but today there are more effective ways to curb Satan's influence in a malignant and neglected case of Huntington's disease than deliverance rituals. The consequences were catastrophic for her health.

But what are the pastoral psychiatric criteria? When is a professional or pastoral healing necessary, and when is an exorcism indicated?

8.1 Indications for Medical Healing and Exorcism

The *Oxford American Dictionary* depicts the devil as "the supreme spirit of evil and the enemy of God."[2] He is, in biblical reports, described as the ultimate liar, deceiving postmodern humans exactly as he did our ancestors, Adam and Eve, by making them distrust God and luring them into the ultimate self-deception of being their own God.

Neal Lozano,[3] an expert in spiritual warfare, illustrates demonic influences with James Wheeler's division of six levels of demonic bondage. Listed from the most benign to the most malignant, these levels are as follows: negative emotions, bondage from possessive relationships, harassment from outside spirits, obsession, oppression, and possession.

The mildest level of demonic influence is characterized by negative emotions like guilt, resentment, and jealousy. As Lozano describes, in this case evil spirits work within the heart to exaggerate the negative emotion that is present as a result of "a long pattern of sin or self-negation that is often unconscious for the person that needs to be released."

The middle level of demonic influence, called obsession, occurs when "some person or evil has seized control over an area of the personality, causing an extreme affliction and deep temptation, or where several areas of the personality have been affected."

The third and worst level of slavery to demons is naturally possession, which occurs "when a force not identifiable as the person's own will has taken total control of the personality." Such a person becomes the tool of the devil in performing his Luciferian goals. Demonic possession is characterized by losing personal identity, freedom, will, and the power to resist the devil's influence. As Lozano explains, "Possession is one in which there are signs that an evil spirit has gained access, not simply to aspects of thinking and will, but also to the actual person's body. In such cases, the demon at specific moments can speak and move through [the body] without the person being able to prevent this."[4] From a psychological-psychiatric perspective, observed demonic possession may also have other signs. People truly possessed by the supreme prince of evil will fight and hate God, not only theatrically but with cunning, premeditated, intelligent, and genuinely callous methods. They replicate under contemporary conditions the serpent's behavioral patterns seen in Genesis 3:1–25. When possessed people are behaviorally contravening Jesus' basic commands, they are genuinely unloving, cruel, abusive, and hostile toward family, neighbours, the whole of human society, and especially against the body of Christ and all Christians building the kingdom of God.

In numerous biblical quotations, such as Mathew 10:8 and Mark 16:17, Jesus gives his Church the power to expel the supreme evil we call the devil. Catholics, despite seldom using exorcism, renewed in 1999 the rite of exorcism after 400 years. Exorcism is "a liturgical rite of the Church, a sacramental provided for those cases where spiritual bondage has grown into possession."[5] Exorcism is accordingly not a sacrament ordered by Jesus but a sacramental. It has no exactly prescribed rubrics and words but may be adapted to particular situations as needed. In the Catholic understanding, only people possessed by the devil need exorcism. In this context, Lozano notes the continued relevance of the 1983 warning of Cardinal Leon Suenens: "Cases of genuine possession, which only the bishop or his delegate may deal with, are rare. But everything that falls short of the strict sense remains a blurred, ill-defined area where confusion and ambiguity prevail."[6]

Who needs exorcism? Lozano answers that "a person who has been introduced to demons as a child, through abuse, occult practice, or even by being dedicated to the Devil by his parents, may continue through ignorance, sliding down the road towards possession."[7] With this clarification, the confusion Cardinal Sueness warned about becomes apparent. All forms of unloving, inappropriate nourishments of a child—and also intellectual, ritual, verbal, and emotional abuse, alongside exposure to demons and occult practices—may cause not only demonic but also psychiatric problems. Indeed, those who are abused, neglected, or exposed/dedicated to the devil are not always sliding "down the road towards possession" but are often suffering from psychiatric disorders and psychological problems. It is a practical, empirical dilemma as to whether verbally, emotionally, or intellectually abused children (and those who have been introduced to demons or occult practices) could be better helped by professional healing and appropriate pastoral care or by exorcism. Only evidence-based research can answer this question. The current ecclesial view is that even believers who feel themselves to be possessed by demons seldom need exorcism according to their bishop's adjudication, but more often need pastoral care combined with professional healing. This is important because, as modelled in the case of the middle-aged woman with Huntington's disease, any mistake in exercising this delicate task may be of grave consequence, especially for the intellectually, emotionally, or verbally abused people Lozano talks about and those suffering from psychiatric, neurological, or somatic disorders!

Quite different is the situation with people not possessed but tempted, challenged, or even oppressed by the devil. They do not need exorcism; instead, they need what is in charismatic vocabulary called "deliverance." Lozano defines deliverance as "the effort—through prayer counsel, or spiritual direction—to help someone take hold of the authority he has been given in Christ."[8] Deliverance accordingly includes a wide range of sacramental and nonsacramental activities—baptism, confirmation, prayer, pastoral care, liturgy, fasting, reconciliation, evangelization, healing ministry, and pastoral healing. The fact that these core activities of the Church are so undervalued, even denigrated by contemporary society, highlights the need for such deliverance.

8.2 Synchronizing the Demonic and Empirical Paradigms

As the Catechism states, "The reason the Son of God appeared was to destroy the works of the Devil."[12] However, if Jesus succeeded in his mission of destroying his works, can Christians experience the devil's influence to the same degree that they experience God's peace, love, and joy?

C. G. Jung notes in his book *A Psychological Approach to the Dogma of the Trinity*, "As psychological experience shows, 'good' and 'evil' are opposite poles of moral judgment which, as such, originates in man. A judgment can be made about a thing only if its opposite is equally real and possible. The opposite of a seeming evil can be seeming good, and an evil that lacks substance can only be contracted with a good that is equally nonsubstantive…. There is no getting around the fact that if you allow substantiality to good, you must also allow it to evil." In Jung's opinion, "The Christian doctrine of the trinity needs to be revised and enlarged."

Jung pondered changing the trinity to a quaternary. In addition to the Father, the Son, and the Holy Spirit, Jung wanted to include the devil, or Satan, in our psychological representation of the godhead because "it is no exaggeration to assume that in this world good and evil more or less balance each other, like day and night."[9] Clearly, Jung went too far here. God and the devil are neither biblically nor in Christian experience equal partners, and Lucifer definitely is not a counterbalance to God.

Jung's contention was the same position embraced in *The Marriage of Heaven and Hell* by English poet William Blake. Years later, C. S. Lewis responded to Blake's collection of poems in his novel *The Great Divorce*, in which he argued that there can never be a marriage between good and evil. Such an attempt will always result in a Faustian bargain that allows evil to masquerade as goodness.

To conceptualize the devil's evil power from an experiential perspective, we need a more empirical and less speculative approach. However, Satan, like God, is invisible. While people of faith certainly experience God, the first empirical question is how and through which psychological functions oppressed, obsessed and possessed people feel, sense, know, and experience the devil's influence. We've noted that antisocial, destructive, or sadistic instincts are the dark sides of the human personality, the tragic kind of behaviors that wreak havoc in families and communities and are even featured on the evening news. If uncontrolled, these instincts play a similar role to that of the serpent in the biblical account of Adam and Eve; that is, slavery to instinct physically presents as demonic bondage. Instincts are produced in the brain stem area called the diencephalon. This structure weighs only a few grams and is no larger than a fingernail. Nevertheless, this generator of the dark side of the human personality is metaphorically controlled by 1,250 grams of inhibition, equal in weight to the cerebral cortex. Neurologically, the spiritual warfare Lozano talks about occurs between the diencephalon and the brain cortex, where neurologically supreme intellectual functions controlling responsibility (and the conscience) are located. Psychologically, the metaphorical warfare between God and Lucifer occurs in the self—the personality—which, paraphrasing Frankl, in a healthy person is the master of instinct and servant of conscience. People experiencing demonic possession exhibit the contrary: the self is master of the consciences and servant of the dark side of the personality (i.e. of instinct). Before the scientific era, during which reasoning and behavioral studies started, the collective consciousness was impregnated with devils, witches, and werewolves, and there was a plethora of alleged encounters with Satan, investigated through horrifying trials wherein victims allegedly did things they could never actually do. Accounts of the Inquisition and the Salem witch trials are replete with tales that now make Christian and non-Christian healers cringe.

During the witch trials in both Salem and England, women accused of witchcraft were weighted with rocks and thrown into drowning pools. If the woman drowned, she was exonerated. If she was possessed, her judges believed that demons would tear the body apart to be free of death by water. It was a lose-lose situation for the accused, and one can say with veracity that the cure was worse than the disease.

Another example is that of Magdalena de la Cruz who, in 1546 in Cordoba, was tried by the Inquisitional tribunal for making a pact with a demon and taking him as her lover.[10] It is an absurd accusation, but such cases were not an exception but rather a pattern. Paintings from those times vividly depict the contemporary artists' common experiences of permeating horror wrought by demons. Robert Fossier writes, "No artist rendered this madness and hideous fear better than Hieronymus Bosch. His *Last Judgment* mingles prehistoric phantasms, pagan myths, and witchcraft in a hallucinatory swarm of monsters, hybrid shapes or delirious half-macabre and half-erotic scenes of tortured, grimacing, infirm beings—sinister caricatures of all-human anguish."[11]

Similar beliefs in occult powers, witches, and demons today flourish in the postmodern collective consciousness. With disorders facilitating theatrical, mythical, magical, or allegorical thinking (as in most prepsychotic, borderline, dissociative, histrionic, narcissistic, and epileptic conditions), people may verbalize these experiences exactly as Wheeler described. Our contemporaries may also describe experiencing the uncontrollable influence of evil motives, negative emotions, bondage to possessive relationships, harassment from outside spirits, obsession with the devil, and oppression—or even possession—by the devil. In such people, however, unconscious fears, rage, desperation, helplessness, hate, horror, and other contents of mind may have produced obsessive internal evidence that evil seized control of their thoughts, feelings, and behaviors.

Let us conclude this section focused on synchronizing the demonic and empirical paradigms by raising a hard question. Clearly, in cases of genuine demonic possession, the facilitator of the subject's evil behavior is the devil. In all other situations, though, is it the devil's power or the individual's sin and sickness that takes control of thoughts, feelings, and behaviors and leads to estrangement from God?

An anecdotal story helps lead us to the answer. The devil is carrying a man on his shoulders. A neighbour passing by asks, "Where is the devil carrying you?" The man answers, "He is carrying me to hell." The neighbour says, "Oh, how sad!" But the man responds, "Oh no, it would be much worse if I had to carry him on my shoulders."

From a practical perspective, it is not as important whether, metaphorically, the devil is carrying sick sinners on his shoulder (as in sickness) or the sinner is carrying the Devil on his shoulder (as in sin). The effects are virtually the same: an estrangement from God. But what is essential is that, *although we are unable to influence the Devil's intentions, we are responsible for and able to fight our own sinful and sick motives and behaviors.* For that reason, pastoral psychiatry and psychology are focused not so much on demonology, as much as on personal sins and sickness, which no person is immune from.

8.3 Distinctions Between Genuine and Fake Demonic Influences

In the 1920s, Sigmund Freud described his analysing and healing in the case of the painter Christopher Heinemann, who suffered from a so-called "demonological neurosis."[13] It may seem peculiar that an atheist like Freud would deal in religious territory, but demonological neurosis can be understood and healed differently from the psychoanalytic approach. When an authoritarian exorcist pronounces powerful words like "In the name of Jesus, I command the spirit of oppression to leave you," one's self may be empowered to serve the conscience and master the instinct. Such subjects may, in fact, experience their emotional bondage in one moment as being broken even in the absence of demonic possession. How then does one decide what healing practice fits a particular person's best interests?

In harmony with the practice of the Church, before exorcism is performed, a potential psychiatric illness ought first to be excluded. This is important because many psychiatric disorders may symptomatically mimic demonic possession. It is equally imperative to note the behavioral signs that indicate genuine demonic possession. Besides the behavioral signs noted by Lozano, there are two more criteria that can help with the differentiation between psychiatric disorders and demonic possession.

Usually, it is less important what individuals say than how they behave. The behavior of those not actually possessed by demons is often grotesque, mythomanic, bizarre, theatrical, or histrionic, but not genuinely evil. Those really obsessed with or possessed by the supreme spirit of evil are more likely people like Nero, Hitler, Stalin, or Pol Pot, all of whom never complained about being oppressed, obsessed, or possessed, but freely and responsively demonstrated their hatred of Christlike behaviors.

The worst enemies of God are not those who, in Lozano's words, experience that "a force not identifiable as the person's own will has taken total control." As history proves, people with distorted belief systems like Saul and Diocletian (who killed Christians) and ideologists like Marx and Engels (who killed believers' minds) were actually much greater enemies of God than any who theatrically complained about being possessed by Lucifer. In our own times, the number of those complaining of being obsessed with or influenced/possessed by Satan are definitely less oppressed by the devil than those torturing, killing, and beheading Christians on a large scale. A cursory glance at daily headlines reveals what C. S. Lewis called (from the title of one of his books) "that hideous strength" that affects world populations. From a pastoral psychiatric/psychological perspective, it is not only those complaining of being possessed but those sadistically murdering the body of Christ who are really possessed by the spirit of "supreme evil."

There is no medicine able to give or take away faith, which is a spiritual-psychological phenomenon beyond the reach of psychotropic drugs. Inversely, we can state that Satanic possession controllable with antipsychotic or sedative medication is a DSM-5 category rather than a genuine demonic possession. As Pope Francis notes, "True enough, the biblical authors had limited conceptual resources for expressing certain realities, and in Jesus' time epilepsy, for example, could easily be confused with demonic possession."[14] However, to heal epilepsy (or any other medical disorder) with exorcism today would be a grave mistake, although it is regularly attempted by less informed pastoral healers of a fundamentalist persuasion—those not grounded in sound exegesis. Disorders that can be medically and psychologically healed are not caused by a demonic possession.

With this criteria in place, what explains the controversy that those in whom "the demon at specific moments can speak and move through [the body] without the person being able to prevent this"[15] are saintly in comparison to those who never seek exorcism but actually attempt to kill God's kingdom in the hearts, minds, and souls of millions of Christians and people? The paradox can best be explained by Jung's example in *Man and His Symbol*.[16]

Ancient magicians and shamans resolved the conflict between instinct and conscience in a ritual of regression in order to achieve what might be loosely termed therapeutic results. They would adopt the behavior and anthropomorphic persona of an animal, regress to its instinct-directed behaviors, and exclude conscience from consciousness. This seemingly negated the conscience and thus alleviated the tension between it and instinct. In reality, what the magicians effected with help of the ritual dance and music was nothing more than a trancelike state perceived as part of a healing process. Granted, suggestibility effected short-term results, validating less than orthodox methods. A similar psychological mechanism may direct theatrical and regressive behaviors of allegedly possessed persons, who identify not with animals but with Lucifer. As Lindsay Jones notes, "Exorcisms have been regarded as having therapeutic value in part because they are couched in the same idiom as the patient's own expression of neurosis while nonetheless orchestrating the same kind of emotional buildup and catharsis that underlay in Freud's early psychoanalysis."[17]

People of faith acknowledge the existence of Lucifer, his role in temptation, and the possibility of being possessed despite having never had a significant encounter with him. Nevertheless, postmodern Christians (contrary to those in the Middle Ages) are more focused on Jesus and their responsibility in fighting deliberately-committed sins than on discerning demonic influence. Postmodern Christians trust biblical revelations such as "Submit yourself therefore to God. Resist the Devil and he will flee from you" (Jas 4:7). For them, the reasons for sickness or sin instigated by the devil seem less important than focusing on imperfections that lead to sin and estrangement from God. They are aware that "neither death nor life, neither angels nor demons, neither the present not the future, nor any powers, neither heights nor depth, nor anything else in all creation, will be able to separate us from the love of God that is in Christ Jesus our Lord" (Rom. 8:38–39).

Notes

[1] Xavier Leon Duffour, *Rijecnik Biblijske Teologije,* Josip Turcinovic (ed.) (Zagreb: Krscanska Sadasnjost, 1988), 126.

[2] Eugene Ehrlich, Stuart Berg Flexner, Gorton Carruth, and Joyce M. Hawkins, *Oxford American Dictionary* (New York: Avon Books, 1979).

[3] Neal Lozano, *Resisting the Devil: A Catholic Perspective on Deliverance* (Huntington, Indiana: Our Sunday Visitor Publishing Division. Our Sunday Visitor Inc. 2010), 210.

[4] Ibid., 29.

[5] Ibid., 15.

[6] Ibid., 29.

[7] Ibid., 59.

[8] Ibid., 16.

[9] Don S. Browning and Terry D. Cooper, *Religious Thought and the Modern Psychologies* (Mineapolis, MN: Augsburg Fortress Press, 2004), 171.

[10] Susan E. Schreiner, *Are You Alone Wise? The Search for Certainty in the Early Modern Era* (New York: Oxford University Press, 2016), 397.

[11] Robert Fossier, *The Cambridge Illustrated History of the Middle Ages* vol. III (Cambridge, MA: Cambridge University Press, 2006), 511–12.

[12] Canadian Conference of the Catholic Bishops, *Catechism of the Catholic Church* (Ottawa: Publications Service, Canadian Conference of Catholic Bishops, 1994), 89.

[13] Lindsay Jones (ed.), *Encyclopedia of Religion* vol. 5 (Farmington Hills, MI: Thomson Gale, 2005), 2935.

[14] Pope Francis, *Gaudate et Exsultate* (Libreria Editrice Vaticano. 2018), 33-34

[15] Lozano, *Resisting the Devil: A Catholic Perspective on Deliverance*, 210.

[16] Carl Gustav Jung, *Man and His Symbols* (London, Amsterdam: Aldus Books, 1964).

[17] Jones, *Encyclopedia of Religion* vol. 5, 2935.

CHAPTER NINE

THE PLACE OF PASTORAL HEALING IN THE ORCHESTRA OF THERAPIES

As is known from the history of medicine, physicians in the Middle Ages were powerless in healing mental ailments. Patients suffering from mental disorders were kept in chains like criminals until the year 1793, when during the French Revolution the physician Philippe Pinel (1745–1826) freed them. Soon after that turnaround, a gradual rise of a scientific and empirically validated healing of mental ailments started. This trend of scientism continues today in a methodical healing of all people (believers and atheists) exactly the same way and expecting the same outcome. Self-evidently, such healing methods often propose Christian, religious, and moral values and treatments either useless or harmful. We classify them in this book with the common term "professional healings." On the contrary, pastoral healing assists an individual discipleship that fosters Jesus-centered healing. Every healing is as good as its effects. But how effective is pastoral healing?

9.1 The Healing Power of Faith

Patients often perceive psychiatric and psychological ailments like destiny, the escape from which is nearly impossible. However, they suffer not only because of their depression, anxiety, or compulsions. The perceived meaninglessness of their sufferings causes their worst distress. Friedrich Nietzsche experienced this. Frankl says of him, "What worried him most was not that he had to suffer, but that he did not know why."[1] However, biblical examples (1 Peter 1:3–9, Hebrews 10:34, Philippians 2:17, and James 1:2) show that Jesus' disciples, when confronted with suffering, were courageous and optimistic. Acts 5:41 reports, "The apostles left the Sanhedrin, rejoicing because they had been counted worthy of suffering disgrace for the Name." What does the enigmatic phrase "counted worthy of suffering," unknown to Nietzsche and his sceptic followers, mean?

During Jesus' Galilean ministry, he performed miracles, preached, taught, and healed. Jesus left Galilee, however, and "began to teach them that the Son of Man must suffer many things and be rejected by the elders, chief priests and teachers of the law, and that He must be killed and after three days, rise again" (Mk. 8:31). Immediately after these words, he added the warning, "If anyone would come after me, he must deny himself and take up his cross and follow me" (Mk. 8:34). He also predicted, "No servant is greater than his master. If they persecute me, they will persecute you also" (Jn. 15:20). This information was unacceptable to the disciples. Presumably, they thought to themselves, "This is not the Messiah we hoped for." They were yet "unworthy of suffering."

After Jesus' death, resurrection, and ascension, however, the situation changed substantially. The quoted example in Acts 5:41 describes the disciples becoming "worthy of suffering." The disciples identified with the "suffering servant" described in Isaiah, but at the same time were confident in finally being one with the "glorious Messiah," experiencing and realizing a biblical purpose that supersedes pain, a hope that supersedes suffering, and a joy that supersedes distress. Therefore, people worthy of suffering are not afraid (as people normally are) of having to suffer or being humiliated or abused. Everything that postmodern culture has internalized as healthy— fear of servitude, poverty, injustice, abuse, sickness, and death—is somehow missing from those counted "worthy of suffering."

Noteworthy in this context are the observations of Viktor Frankl, a religious Jew who survived three concentration camps during the Second World War.

> The way a man accepts his fate and all the suffering it entails, in which he takes up his cross, gives him ample opportunity—even under the most difficult circumstances—to add a deeper meaning to his life. It may remain brave, dignified, and unselfish. Or in the bitter fight for self-preservation he may forget his human dignity and become no more than an animal. Here lies a chance for a man either to make use of or to forgo the opportunities of attaining the moral values that a difficult situation may afford him. And this decides whether he is worthy of suffering or not.[2]

It is faith, trust, and complete security in identifying with the suffering Messiah that open the gate for union with the glorious Jesus. These are the preconditions of being worthy of suffering.

I often hear from patients receiving strong painkillers for excruciating pain that, "I feel the pain, but it does not hurt me." This is a good way to describe the condition of disciples who are worthy of suffering. They feel the pain, but it neither frightens nor breaks them. The more a genuine disciple suffers, the closer they feel to Jesus' presence. Is faith therefore an "opium for the masses," as Karl Marx described it? No. Faith is rather an endorphin, an internal, brain-produced painkiller. A believer's joy, peace, hope, optimism never decrease, but permanently increase. Indeed, medicine and psychology can only dream about such healing power!

Now we can answer the previous question: how effective is pastoral healing? Is it only effective in answering philosophical questions? In answering those ultimate questions of life that heal the pain of meaninglessness in suffering incurable diseases? Paraphrasing Frankl, we could say that pastoral healing cannot heal all disorders, but as the reader will realize when studying the healing of DSM-5-listed disorders, *no mental ailment can be genuinely cured without pastoral healing.*

9.2 The Empirical and Theological Basics of Pastoral Healing

The RCIA manual states that if you want valid information, you need the opinion of experts. For example, if you want a true account of your heart problems, you do not seek help from patients but a physician, and if you want true information about love, you ought not seek it from lovers but from a psychologist. Analogously, in atheists' understanding, if you seek a true account of Christian faith, you must not go to the believers but to anthropologists or sociologists. The paradox is that laymen perceive a phenomenon experientially, "from the inside," while professionals perceive it "from the outside," objectively.[3] But pastoral healers ought to know the problems they are healing both from the outside (an objective medical-psychological perspective) and also from the inside (a practicing believer's perspective). For the same reason, they need professional knowledge and personal faith.

Pastoral psychiatry and psychology therefore stand on two legs. One leg stands on the empirical ground in standard professional textbooks. In discussing psychiatric and psychological disorders, we will rely most heavily on the tenth and eleventh editions of Kaplan and Sadock's textbook *Synopsis of Psychiatry: Behavioral Sciences/Clinical Psychiatry*[4] as well as on the DSM-5.[5] Standing on empirical ground is necessary for recognizing symptoms, knowing causes, understanding dynamics, and providing prognoses and professional treatment—or, in one word, for gaining a "feeling" for particular disorders.

The other leg of the pastoral approach requires discipleship: a lasting personal commitment to the Father, the Son, and the Holy Spirit; the Scriptures; the tradition, the Church; and the Christian form of living as well as relevant theology. This means, firstly, personally bearing witness to the Christian truth with one's whole life, words, and deeds. Secondly, it means helping affected Christians to take hold of the authority received from Christ in fighting sin and sickness (paraphrasing Lozano's formulation). In other words, it is about encouraging patients to accept sacramental and nonsacramental help which foster a union with Jesus.

9.3 Similarities Between Professional Healing and Pastoral Healing

A non-Christian's unloving, hateful, reckless, or murderous behavior can be caused either by sin or a psychological disorder. So, mental problems and sin often produce similar effects. Consequently, pastoral and professional healing sometimes treat the same kinds of problems and strive to achieve the same purpose: Jesus-like behavior. Frankl[6] illustrates the relationship between faith and mental health as in Fig. 9.1 below.

Fig. 9.1. The commonalities of professional and spiritual healing

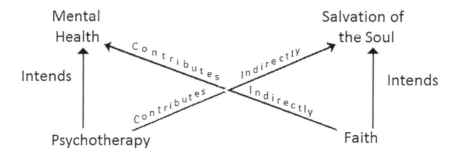

Fig. 9.1 illustrates that the purpose of professional healing is mental health. Improving mental health decreases hate, anger, jealousy, and other non-Christian attitudes. Indirectly, mental healing contributes to Christlike behaviors and the salvation of the soul. A similar change occurs in pastoral healing. Directly it aims at the salvation of the soul, but indirectly it resolves hate, suspicion, anxiety, and anger. It helps with the restoration of mental health.[7] Such a mutually inclusive relationship of professional and spiritual healing causes Christians to feel responsibility not only for their sins but also for their psychologically-distorted behaviors. This removes all doubt that we need psychological-spiritual healing. Spiritual help without psychological help may be insufficient, as is psychological help without spiritual healing.

On the topic of commonalities, we need also to clarify how far inclusiveness extends between pastoral and professional healers. Cardinal Ratzinger illustrates theologian Karl Rahner's concepts, saying, "Christianity is present in all religions, or (putting it another way) all religions, without knowing this, are moving towards Christianity. It is from this inner direction that they derive their power to save: they lead to salvation insofar as they carry the mystery of Christ hidden within them."[8] We can rephrase Rahner's ideas to apply to counselling practices and state that all therapists of goodwill are able to heal sickness and sin insofar as they unconsciously carry the mystery of Christ hidden within them when resolving various afflictions. Respectively, professional and pastoral psychotherapists also derive their ability to heal from an inner connection with truth, or more precisely, with some aspect of the ultimate truth of Jesus Christ. As Frankl implies, even in the minds of agnostic and nonbelieving therapists there is an unconscious God.[9]

Therefore, pastoral healers ought not to be exclusive toward professional therapists. As the *Lumen gentium* of Vatican 2[10] discerns that some basic elements of the Church exist not only in the Catholic faith but also in other Christian denominations (Orthodox and Protestant) and non-Christian faiths (Hebrew and Muslim), so there are elements of truth and Jesus' love not only in pastoral healing but also in most professional healing practices. Freud's psychoanalytic healing (representing all other non-Christian psychotherapies) could produce fruit if it helped to discern forgiveness, peace, love, hope, and other genuinely-Christian values and decrease the Luciferian inheritance of fear, anger, desperation, jealousy, paranoia, and animosity.

On the other hand, sinful, selfish, and unloving—in one-word, unchristian—behaviors cannot be healed by professionals ignorant of faith but irrationally proclaiming Christianity an emotional disturbance, a masochism or a mental sickness. There is no egalitarianism between the healing of genuine Christian and nonbelieving therapists. Healing on the sin-sickness continuum requires a psychological-spiritual approach; one approach without the other is often insufficient. Therefore, when being treated by agnostic or atheistic therapists, Christian patients may consider filtering and supplementing their psychological healing with an adequate and well-informed spiritual counterbalance, an awareness that the more Christ-centred their healing is, the more it is able to approach the ultimate truth of Jesus Christ, the preeminent healer.

Even some Christian healers may be tempted to disregard the above truth. After completing my residency in neuropsychiatry, I earned an MS in Freudian psychodynamics and a PhD in Viktor Frankl's existential psychotherapy. I was surprised to find that my fellow students in both disciplines almost literally gave up their critical minds and accepted our truly great teachers' (Freud and Frankl) conclusions uncritically, respecting them as if they were gods. Yes, all pastoral healers stand on the shoulders of great teachers, but they ought to be critical of them as well so that their techniques may point in a Godly direction. So, although pastoral healers may apply an array of techniques—psychodynamic, cognitive behavioral, cognitive dialectical, solution-focused, transactional, existential-oriented, or many others—for psychological healing, they need to be critical of their atheistic and agnostic teachers and their therapeutic backgrounds while being aware that Jesus is the best and ultimate healer. One cannot take the splinter out of someone else's eye if there is a plank in one's own (Matthew 7:5).

Christian clients need to be aware of their responsibility too. It is their prerogative to discern, assess, and monitor how the progression toward imitating Christ really occurs in every concrete pastoral session and through the whole course of healing. It is not only patients who learn in the patient-therapist relationship; therapists also learn from their patients. Christian patients have an opportunity to awaken unbelieving or lukewarm therapists' awareness of and interest in biblical values, perhaps even helping them progress toward the same. It is the Christian equivalent, gently and humbly tendered as always, of "physician, heal thyself."

9.4 Differences Between Professional Healing and Pastoral Healing

Besides the differences between professional and pastoral healing already mentioned, there is one more important dissimilarity. The efficiency of professional treatment, especially medical, is based on two criteria: validity (it fulfils what it promises) and reliability (it produces repeatable results).

For example, a surgical method is considered valid if it factually heals appendicitis and also reliable if it heals everyone with equal effectiveness. Professional healing ought to heal almost every patient with equal validity and reliability.

Pastoral healing, on the contrary, is not applicable to everyone in the same way. Consider the story in Matthew 17:14–20:

> When they came to the crowd, a man came to him, knelt before him, and said "Lord, have mercy on my son, for he is an epileptic and he suffers terribly; he often falls in the fire and often into the water. And I brought him to your disciples, but they could not cure him." Jesus answered, "You faithless and perverse generation, how much longer must I be with you? Bring him here to me." And Jesus rebuked the demon, and it came out of him, and the boy was cured instantly. Then the disciples came to Jesus privately and said, "Why could we not cast it out?" He said to them: "Because of your little faith."

Disciples with little faith could not perform miracles. In a similar way, pastoral healing is often powerless if applied by people who have no faith or oppose Christian principles. Unlike the universal reliability of professional healing, the efficiency of pastoral healing often hinges on the faith of the practitioner.

On the other hand, pastoral healing aims to achieve what no professional healing is able to do. An example from Frankl demonstrates this.

> A depressed young lady suffered from inoperable cancer and complained to Freud that her life had no meaning since she would soon die. Freud however allegedly answered: "Ah my dear, your life never had a meaning!... You should not concern yourself with such matters." Later, in a letter to Princess Bonaparte, Freud remarked: "The moment one inquires about the meaning of life, one is ill."[11]

The young lady's angst and fear of death are genuine human experiences that cannot simply be explained away. The only real help available to her would be discerning a hope stronger than the threat of approaching death. Only Jesus could help her joyfully anticipate her passing from human existence into Godly transcendence.

One might label pastoral healing as a cure that has real effects only in ideal disciples and in an ideal but nonexistent biblical world. As noted, pastoral healing factually produces paramount healing in people with exemplary faith. However, a version of the ideal biblical world exists internally in all Christians, and not only in Christians but in all humans directed by their "synderesis" (conscience) to seek good. A striving for genuine ideals exists in every human being. As "the wind blows where it chooses" (John 3:8), so the Spirit evokes faith in people it chooses—people fighting sins and psychological problems. And because "faith the size of a mustard seed moves mountains" (Matthew 17:20), pastoral healing should be made available to all believers and nonbelievers who require it.

9.5 The Cautions, Limits, and Boundaries of Pastoral Healing

The ideal candidates for pastoral healing, including children participating with their parents' consent, have consciously and deliberately decided to follow Christ. But doubtful cunctators, sceptics, and atheists may also seek theological information or help. This makes the healers' role complex. Not only is every pastoral healing a learning experience, and every learning experience is hard, but it is not easy to be a student—a recipient. So the pastoral healer may need to help patients become receptive to treatment, which is much harder than just giving them what they originally required. As Guilmartin notes, people tend to "shut down the 'intimate' connection by trying to return the favour right away, rather than graciously accepting what has been given."[12]

Therefore, the common precondition for pastoral healing, besides motivation, is willingness to be helped, which emerges from biblical humility, meekness, self-criticism, and brokenheartedness. It presumes openness in considering one's own mistakes, faults, sins, and sicknesses, and entails the courage to rely on God's mercy. For this reason, notably psychotic, uncritical, antisocial, rigid, and self-righteous people are difficult to heal by pastoral psychotherapy. How then can we help Christians who are not appropriate candidates for pastoral healing?

All pastoral healing focuses on encouraging participation in the Church's sacraments, so these and a plethora of nonsacramental aids are helpful to believers unable to receive other forms of pastoral counselling. We should not perceive these methods as being less efficient! They are, for believers and patients disposed to such pastoral service, much more efficient than any human word or medicine.

For instance, my personal interest in pastoral healing started when, as a resident, I observed two physicians desperately but unsuccessfully attempting to calm a patient suffering from a heart attack and horrified by death. When, however, pastoral help arrived in the form of a priest, the patient, a firm believer, miraculously regained his peace, hope, and optimism.

Like all people, pastoral healers have their own biases which Corey summarizes are "the need for control and power; the need to be nurturing and be helpful; the need to change others in the direction of our own values; the need to persuade; the need for feeling adequate, particularly when it becomes overly important that the client conform to our competence; and the need to be respected and appreciated." As he says, "The crux of the issue is that ethically it is essential that we do not meet our needs at the expense of our clients."[13]

By the same token, pastoral healers need to also be aware of other limits and boundaries.

Pastoral healing, to paraphrase Guilmartin, is not always about curing sicknesses but about "understanding why certain aches and pains are in our life and learning from them anyway." It is about realizing that "our pain isn't really our pain. It's part of a continuum of life that connects us to other people" and to Jesus.[14] And above all, it is about accepting life as an opportunity for seeking Jesus' healing by appreciating St. Peter's advice: "Rejoice that you participate in the sufferings of Christ, so that you may be overjoyed when his glory is revealed" (1 Pt. 4:12–13).

We need to be painfully aware of one exemption. Pastoral healers need to be cautious when applying St. Peter's advice in their efforts to heal Christians suffering of depression, schizophrenia or paranoia, anxiety disorders, scrupulousness, and suicidal thoughts. These suffering people often feel socially labelled, ashamed and isolated. Pastoral healers may unintentionally reinforce their fear that all their mental health challenges are caused by lack of faith. Thus, they may unwittingly contribute to their moral stigmatization.

Stigma was originally a sign burnt into the skin of slaves in ancient Greece making them easy to distinguish from free men and women. Many Christians seeking pastoral help carry an even worse internal stigma. They feel responsible to God, themselves, and society for their mentally disordered or sinful behaviors. Attempting to improve themselves, they pray, fast and repent with no quick or spectacular impact on their mental health. They fear that their behavioral problems are caused by lack of true discipleship. The dread of lacking true discipleship is the greatest fear of Christians. The more we fuel the client's guilt feelings, the more their irrational fears increase.

Like their clients, pastoral healers may also feel insecure when confronted with irrational guilt caused by lack of improvement in mental functioning despite earnest spiritual practices. The basic tool of pastoral healing is to evoke true contrition and sorrow for one's sinful behaviors. No one is without sin. Christians suffering of depression, anxiety disorders, scrupulousness or suicidal thoughts, or those recovering from schizophrenia or paranoia feel an extremely painful gap between how they are and how they ought to be. Sound self-criticism is the precondition of healing sinful behaviors as well as mental illness. But stigmatized patients already feel excessively responsible for lacking discipleship and willpower to direct their behaviors. How can we resolve such controversial situations?

As the Latin saying goes, "Justice applied overly strictly is the highest form of injustice." The flagrant mistake a pastoral healer can make in healing extremely anxious, scrupulous, depressed or suicidal people is applying justice "overly strictly," by being harsh and judgemental, not Christlike just and merciful. Sin and mental illness are connected. But in situations where mentally ill Christians feel stigmatized because of irrational self-accusations, pastoral healers should to *disregard the intricate connection between sin and sickness, and initially focus solely on supporting depressed, severely anxious, hopeless or suicidal people.*

How can we discern the right balance between evoking self-criticism and giving unconditional support in cases where we are uncertain whether a behaviour is deliberately sinful or directed by mental illness?

The principles of pastoral healing ought to be applied holistically. In practice, this means that, in answering hard questions, we should rely on a combination of empathy (or "feeling the feelings of the client"), a well-formed conscience, as well as the principles of Christian accountability. For example, when practice calls healers to take a stand in delicate moral and therapeutic situations, they should ponder the criteria of sound discretional and appreciative judgment. Thus, our conclusions from Chapters Six and Seven discussing biblical-psychological criteria for making correct moral judgments may help find the right balance between evoking healthy self-criticism in our clients, versus providing them with unconditional support.

With the understanding of these basic principles, we will nevertheless repeatedly detect in our case studies a pattern: that pastoral healers "can do all things through him who strengthens [them]" (Philippians 4:13). In the second part of this book, we will review where, when, and how to apply that paramount healing power, as well as specific healing methods available to pastoral healers and the people of God for easing pain and suffering.

Notes

[1] Viktor E. Frankl, *Anthropologische Grundlagen der Psychotherapie* (Bern, Stuttgart, Vienna: Hans Huber, 1976), 243.

[2] Maria Marshall and Edward Marshall, *Spiritual Psychotherapy: The Search for Lasting Meaning* (Canada, Ont.: Ottawa Institute of Logotherapy, 2015), 81.

[3] Quoted in the RCIA (Roman Catholic Initiation of Adults), St. Jude's Parish 2016–17 (Vancouver, BC, Canada), 148.

[4] DSM-5. Diagnostic and Statistical Manual of the American Psychiatric Association (2013).

[5] Benjamin James Sadock and Virginia Alcott Sadock, *Kaplan and Sadock's Synopsis of Psychiatry: Behavioral Sciences/Clinical Psychiatry*, 10th ed. (Philadelphia, PA: Wolters Kluwer, 2007); Sadock, Sadock, and Ruiz, *Kaplan and Sadock's Synopsis of Psychiatry*. 11th ed., 2015.

[6] Paul Ungar, *Flawed Institution—Flawless Church: A Response to Pope John Paul's Appeal for a Critical Self-Evaluation of the Church* (Newcastle Upon Tyne: Cambridge Scholars Publishing, 2013), 108.

[7] Maria Mendez, *A Life with Meaning: A Guide to the Fundamental Principles of Viktor E. Frankl's Logotherapy* (Victoria: Trafford, 2004), 77.

[8] Joseph Ratzinger, *Truth and Tolerance; Christian Belief and World Religions* (San Francisco: Ignatius Press, 2004), 49–52.

[9] Viktor Frankl, *The Unconscious God: Psychotherapy and Theology* (New York: Simon Shuster, 1975).

[10] Austin Flanery. Vatican Collection, vol. I. Vatican Council II; the Conciliar and Post-conciliar Documents (Northport, NY: Costello, 1992), 799–812.

[11] Marshall and Marshall, *Spiritual Psychotherapy*, 162.

[12] Nance Guilmartin, *Healing Conversations: What to Say When You Don't Know What to Say* (San Francisco: Jossey-Bass, 2002), 13.

[13] Gerald Corey, *Theory and Practice of Counseling and Psychotherapy* (Thomson Brooks/Cole. Thomson Learning Academic Resource Center, 2005), 38.

[14] Guilmartin, *Healing Conversations: What to Say When You Don't Know What to Say*, 87.

PART TWO

PSYCHIATRIC DISORDERS

This second part of the book addresses professional and semiprofessional interests. It will therefore address primarily those clinicians who are committed to taking a role in the psychological-spiritual healing of patients belonging to the flock of Jesus' disciples, numbering almost 300 million in North America. Since the purpose of this compendium is to discuss most clinical conditions that Christian healers may encounter, we will in the following sections discuss both common and rare challenges in pastoral healing.

Secondly, this part of the book addresses Christian pastors. If their congregations are reflective of the average demographic data, then approximately 20 out of every 1,000 believers suffer from some kind of intellectual disability, 60 from persistent depression, 26 from bipolar disorder, 180 from anxiety problems, 11 from schizophrenia, 50 from hypochondriasis, 40 from anorexia, almost 450 from periodic insomnia, and so on. Pastors can therefore acquire basic psychiatric and psychological information to enhance their pastoral skills in dealing with these psychological disorders that facilitate sinful behaviors in their flocks.

Thirdly, this compendium represents a valuable Christian self-help resource. No one among us is free from the need for self-scrutiny and healing behaviors. Permanent self-reflection and self-perfection are the essence of Christian being. The people of God ought to be vehicles for bringing up to date (or *aggiornamento*, the motto of Vatican II) the ancient saying "Christians are another Christ." Since, for Christians, the world's pains are our pains, no one among us ought to be ignorant in helping the world transcend weaknesses so as to resemble Christ. In this effort, to paraphrase John Donne, no cleric, believer, or professional is an island. In fighting sin and sickness, we need to work as a team.

CHAPTER TEN

Disorders Usually First Diagnosed in Childhood and Their Pastoral Treatment

Adults' relationships with Jesus are significantly influenced by their early impressions about the world, God, and the Church, all of which shaped their infant brains, minds, personalities, and behaviors. It is therefore important to discuss disorders that occur early in life not only from the perspective of the help that children may need but also from that of the pastoral help that parents, teachers, and pastors may need in support of children joining the kingdom of God.

10.1 Intellectual Disabilities

Intelligence is the ability to resolve problems. Intellectual disability is the nondevelopment of intellectual capacities. The DSM-5 sets three criteria for diagnosing intellectual disability: (1) confirmation by assessment and intelligence tests; (2) a deficit in adaptive functioning causing a failure to fulfil expectations; and (3) symptoms occurring in the developmental period.[1]

From Sadock, Sadock, and Ruiz's description, we could summarize that the first symptoms of intellectual disability are often unrecognized until school age, while the peak in diagnosis occurs between the ages of ten and fourteen. Some 1–3 percent of the population has some form of intellectual disability, and it is 1.5 times more prevalent in males. Its aetiology can be genetic, environmental, or sociocultural. There are thirty-three designated genetic causes of intellectual disability. In some cases the disability is definite (like Down syndrome), and in others it is preventable (phenylketonuria). Environmental causes can be prenatal in nature (rubella), perinatal (premature birth), and postnatal (head injuries). An environmentally-caused intellectual disability is often preventable, but when occurring is usually not curable. The sociocultural causes of intellectual disability are mostly preventable and treatable. They are caused by lack of care, security, cognitive stimulation, and nutrition, among other factors. Maternal care is essential. Babies born in jail (nourished by their imprisoned mothers) cognitively progress better than babies brought up by absent or working mothers.[2]

For orientation, below are the levels of intelligence ranked from highest to lowest.

Very high level of intelligence	120–140
High level of intelligence	110–120
Average level of intelligence	90–110
Below average level of intelligence	70–90
Mild intellectual disability	50–70
Moderate intellectual disability	35–50
Severe intellectual disability	20–35
Profound intellectual disability	0–20

Mild intellectual disability, categorized as "educable," encompasses almost 58 percent of all intellectually-challenged people. Such people function at the level of schoolchildren ages seven to twelve and are able to finish the grade six level of education. They can successfully communicate, read, write, and perform simple mathematical operations and are able to manage work tasks, but they may need help in resolving new, complicated, or unexpected challenges. Their functioning depends on the support they receive.

With the right resources, they are able to live independently, raise families, and even perform skilled jobs.

Moderate intellectual disability includes "trainable" people. This accounts for approximately 10% of the intellectually-disabled population. These people function at the level of preschool children. They are able to communicate verbally but not at an abstract level, are able to complete educational grade one, are able to be trained to perform semiskilled jobs, and are able to dress, nourish, and protect themselves from elemental threats such falling, fire, or water. They need guidance in their private lives.

Severe intellectual disability constitutes approximately 3–4 percent of the intellectually disabled population. Individuals with this level of disability are unable to complete any academic grades, and their intelligence is comparable to that of small children. They are essentially limited in motor, sensorial, cognitive, and social functioning but are able to eat, drink, and protect themselves from simple threats like falling, water, or fire. Without help, such people do not attend to their personal hygiene, dress, or grooming and are unable to negotiate traffic. They are able to perform simple work-related tasks but do not know the value of money, are suggestible, and can be easily manipulated or scared. If properly taken care of, however, they are able to emotionally compensate for their intellectual deficits to some degree and understand messages and basic communication.

Profound intellectual disability constitutes 1–2 percent of the intellectually-disabled population. This level of functioning does not surpass that of a two-year-old child. People with profound intellectual disability have a need for special care that is apparent at first sight. They are profoundly limited in motor, communication, and sensory functioning; can communicate only with signs or unarticulated voices; can walk only with help; are unable to independently eat, drink, or nourish themselves; are often unable to control their urination and defecation; and are unable to protect themselves from fire, falling, injuries, or drowning. Their coordination is poor, and they need permanent care.

Pastoral Considerations

Until the eighteenth century, intellectually-disabled people were often jailed with criminals. During the Enlightenment, the collective attitudes moved to the opposite extreme. It was believed that, with the right education, intellectual disability could be corrected. Even until the middle of the twentieth century, intellectually-disabled people were placed in boarding schools with considerable education but insufficient love.[3] Deinstitutionalization started around 1950. Since the 1990s, education "within the least restrictive environment" has been guaranteed, and a "child who demonstrates significant underachievement (more than two standard deviations below the measured ability) may be eligible for special education."[4] Pastoral care is focused not only on providing rights (not necessarily equal rights), but on providing Christian love to disabled children based on the following principles.

(1) From a professional perspective, "the same perceptual difficulties that impair academic learning can interfere with a child's comprehension of social information and may result in inappropriate social behaviors.... Social skills training programs teach behaviors creating a personal approach to communication skills and understanding the nature of social interactions and personal space."[5] On the other hand, intellectually-disabled individuals are not emotionally handicapped and may emotionally compensate for their missing intellectual capacities in astute ways.

A forty-two-year-old moderately intellectually disabled person dying of inoperable cancer repeatedly crossed his hands in prayer on his deathbed. Seeing that he was aware of his oncoming death and was praying, his mother asked curiously, "What is Jesus telling you?" He answered, "He tells me that everything is okay." He emotionally appreciated Jesus' closeness more profoundly than many highly intelligent philosophers do.

(2) Despite all deficiencies, the intellectually disabled can build God's kingdom efficiently. For example, in one municipal parish, the priest often evaded hearing confessions because of alleged other duties. One day, though, a severely intellectually-disabled boy, motivated by his feelings of guilt, walked with big, determined steps into the sacristy immediately after

holy mass, took the priest by his hand, and pulled him into the confessional room. The ice was broken. The priest overlooked the disabled boy's forwardness and, after that, the boy regularly confessed his sins.

(3) The saying that "children are the mirror of the family" fits nowhere better than in intellectually disabled people. If the environment is loving and caring, they reflect the same values exponentially. However, even harmless situations evoke fear and stubborn resistance. Taking a soft, mothering approach often creates happiness in disabled children, diffusing fierce opposition from the child when help is offered.

(4) Even children with profound intellectual disabilities emotionally grasp the ideas of love and attachment and can exhibit biblical unselfishness. They also feel closeness or estrangement from Jesus intensely and often have an emotional knowledge of confession, repentance, forgiveness, and restored union with Jesus. Even severely intellectually disabled people participate (on their level of functioning) in the sacramental life of the Church. The Church has always taught that the sacraments are outwards signs of inner grace and allow the indwelling of the Holy Spirit, and the Spirit's work in anyone can *never* be underestimated. Indeed, it is through the work of the Spirit that the least among us becomes the greatest.

(5) The general principle in helping such children to accept their intellectual disability is to help them discern value in their lives and conditions.

A sixteen-year-old severely mentally disabled Down syndrome boy asked his mom why he was not like others. In response, she explained to him that it was because he was an angel. This not only helped him accept his difference but also overcome low self-esteem and feel appreciated and worthy.

(6) Because of their humility and noncompetitiveness, the intellectually disabled are sometimes the only people who are uniformly loved by the whole community. In this way they may have a "special authority." Consider, for instance, the following story.

A small rural congregation was bitterly divided, with a small group threatening to abandon the community. After a lengthy and unproductive discussion, a person with Down syndrome spontaneously stood up and, with a poorly well-articulated but loud and desperate cry of "Brother!" he hugged the speaker of the opposing party. Everyone understood his message, and the schism was terminated.

(7) Intellectually disabled people are often good as greeters, ushers, gift carriers, or altar boys and girls. Through their naiveté, defencelessness, and understanding of the need to protect, they perform a definite community-building role.

10.2 Autism Spectrum Disorder and Other Pervasive Developmental Disorders

The DSM-5[6] sets three specific indicators of autism spectrum disorder: (1) persistent deficits in social communication; (2) restricted, repetitive behavior patterns, interests, and activities; and (3) symptoms emerging (despite not always being registered) in early childhood. According to Kaplan and Sadock, around 8,000–10,000 children suffer from this disorder, but the numbers are gradually increasing. It is five times more common in boys, and its cause is unknown. Usually the disorder starts before the age of three, but it can sometimes begin later, around the age of seven. Babies with the disorder are less common but often do not smile when nourished, do not maintain eye contact with the mother, and don't respond to affection. In all children with the disorder come early difficulties in verbal communication skills, which may develop to some degree, but in 25 percent of cases, these skills gradually decrease later, something that parents are seriously alarmed by. These children are not able to infer the feelings, reactions, or mental states of other people, and their emotional communication remains poor. This hinders their ability to develop empathy and leads to emotional isolation. They occupy themselves by playing with their own bodies or toys, vigorously resisting any changes in their accustomed habits. Acting out, temper tantrums, and unpredictable aggression are signs of confusion, frustration, and fear because of their inability to understand others and not being understood by their environment. Around 80 percent of children with autism spectrum disorder are first diagnosed as intellectually disabled, and "about 30 percent of such children function in a mild to moderate range, and about 45 to 50 percent are moderate to severely [mentally disabled]."

They may have splinter functions, like exceptional memory or mechanic, computer, or mathematical skills.[7]

Pastoral Considerations

(1) The most important treatment goals for children with autism spectrum disorder are developing integrative and social skills, attachments, peer relationships, proper social behaviors, and improving communication skills by using structured programs.[8] Treatment should start early because "early intervention appears to be the most important factor related to positive outcomes." Since there is no efficient cure, "Treatment for children and their families requires a lifespan developmental approach."[9] Supplementing these professional goals, the pastoral healer's role lies in promoting the spiritual courage, determination, peace, love, and hope that only faith can give.

(2) While establishing an exact diagnosis occurs in specialized institutions, "parents are the people who ensure continuity across the lifespan of the child." Because of this, "parents need education, advocacy, training, and support" to become "co-therapists, attending meetings to assist in the development of individual treatment plans and belonging to the support groups."[10] Families may be supported by "networking resources such as the Autism Society of America, the Rett's Syndrome Association, and the Online Asperger Syndrome Information Support (OASIS)."[11] Pastoral healers may help in mutually connecting such families supporting each other to run a marathon of love, to share pain, and encourage hope.

(3) The parents of children with autism spectrum disorder sometimes suffer feelings of irrational guilt. Healing in such cases starts with helping the parents to realize that their children's living in an "emotional refrigerator" is not their fault. Believers need encouragement to persist in being "worthy of suffering" (Acts 5:41) and not giving up trust in Jesus but perceiving their unique mission as an opportunity to grow in discipleship. Replacing guilt with a sense of mission and purpose is, in itself, a palpable form of healing. Guilt is called for in a myriad of situation, but Christ never wants us to bear *unnecessary* guilt. One of the most comforting passages in the New Testament says, "Come to me, all you who are weary and burdened,

and I will give you rest. Take my yoke upon you and learn from me, for I am gentle and humble in heart, and you will find rest for your souls. For my yoke is easy and my burden is light" (Matthew 11:28–30). The burdens Jesus asks us to carry can free the human spirit to develop deeper discipleship.

(4) Especially painful is the suffering of a mother crying out desperately, "I am unable to love him!" Parents, however, must be brought to the understanding that love is not only a feeling but, above all, a behavior. Parents' feelings will follow their loving commitment and behaviors.

> In 2011, Ms. Olga P. requested urgent counselling after having a dream that she was repeatedly putting her autistic daughter, Roxana, into a deep freezer to cause recurrent pneumonia and gradually kill her. Pastoral counselling focused on helping the family get past the perspective that they were being tested by God, like Job. After three months of counselling, the family accepted Roxana not as a punishment but as a gift. The mother described that "Roxana's 'unavailability' provoked an irresistible need to fix her." The "need to fix" gradually evolved into a "mystery of acceptance," that is, accepting Roxana as a unique creature of God. The family went on to have three more children, but nevertheless, as paradoxical as it may seem, Roxana remained "the heart of the family." Despite being autistic, she reflected God's love to the family. If she could by some miracle freely choose, her mother would now wholeheartedly choose Roxana as she is.

(5) It is a widespread belief that caring for a sick child often destroys family harmony. What I have witnessed is the contrary. Nothing keeps Christian families united in love as much as caring about a child with special needs. It integrates the deepest parenting instincts with the most sophisticated gifts of the Holy Spirit in a supremely unselfish way of living.

(6) Autistic children live in almost permanent anxiety. Such children have feelings but do not display them as socially expected. They do not understand the world and feel that, in turn, they are not understood by *it*. Pastoral healers help children with autism spectrum disorder discover their unique purpose, which gives them self-esteem and empowerment and helps foster their faith.

If and when they grasp their place and role, they can be surprisingly firm in pursuing their purposes, often with more determination than those without disabilities. Perhaps this is why they are so close, literally and metaphorically, to the Kingdom of God.

> For instance, a family with an autistic child and a healthy child went boating on a small yacht. The motor exploded, both parents were injured, and the children decided to row the damaged yacht to port. The eighteen-year-old son gave up rowing after an hour. The twenty-one-year-old autistic son, however, rowed silently and nonstop like a machine for more than seven hours, bringing the boat home to the family dock.

(7) Autistic children feel more uncomfortable when dealing with unpredictable situations than predictable ones. Teachers and parents therefore frequently help with autistic children's behaviors because they function in a predictably nurturing way, almost like warm, loving "mechanical automatons." Visual cues such as standard signs, gestures, and body language are preferred to words, and an overdose of praise and approval as a predictable consequence of performing skills is helpful for reducing anxiety. In short, imitating Jesus less by words and more by deeds is the productive healing approach with autistic children.

(8) Helping autistic children to appreciate an abstract God is often easier than introducing the warm and emotionally-charged God-man mystery of Jesus. In religious education (preparing for first communion, for example), stereotypical and repetitive phrases and techniques are most effective because they organize information so that it is predictable, down to the smallest details. Stereotypical and repetitive prayers may be especially appreciated too. Such an approach might seem routine, almost monotonous, but it is nevertheless inventive and creative artwork, because what works for one autistic child does not always work for another. So there is need to experiment with unique approaches to every child. Just as God treats us as unique individuals, so we too must treat each other with special and individual pastoral concern and creativity.

(9) Children with autism spectrum disorder need a safe area where they

feel protected and secure. A relationship with God may represent one such place for them. Contrary to their emotional indifference toward other people, they may develop attachments with religious pictures, symbols, statues of saints, smells, colours, and sounds of the church community.

(10) First religious interests are, in healthy children, usually shaped by the emotions. Philosophical concepts about God appear in teenage years. In autistic children, however, this pattern is reversed. Their concept of God is often factual and rational rather than emotional, and they are more directed by the law than by love. However, in my experience, mature people with autism may give very self-reflective descriptions of their hidden, often emotionally warm, spiritual experiences as children.

(11) Although autistic children sometimes seem uninterested in religion, their external coldness is often disproportionate to their internal warmth toward Jesus. While they do not express their attachment in words, faith is, for them, a fortress into which they repeatedly withdraw for protection from frustrations. In general, such children may relate to the transcendental God more warmly than other humans. Paradoxically, their emotional alienation from the world may facilitate a close attachment to Jesus.

10.3 Attention Deficit and Attention Deficit Hyperactivity Disorder

The DSM-5[11] characterizes ADHD as "A persistent pattern of inattention and/or hyperactivity-impulsivity that interferes with functioning or development." Inattention is marked with failing to give attention to detail, making careless mistakes, having difficulties in sustaining attention, not listening when spoken to, not following through on instructions, experiencing difficulties in organizing activities, avoiding tasks requiring sustained attention, losing things, being easily distracted from tasks, and being forgetful in daily activities. Impulsivity is characterized by fidgeting, inability to sit still (in schoolchildren), inability to stay quiet, running away, being on the go as if "driven by a motor," excessive talking, answering before a question is asked, having difficulty waiting in line, and interrupting others.[12] At least six symptoms lasting at least six months before the age of twelve are needed to make a diagnosis.

Between 2 percent and 20 percent of schoolchildren suffer from ADHD, with boys making up four times more cases than girls. Its aetiology is unknown. The triad of inattention, hyperactivity, and impulsiveness often begins before the age of seven and, of these, hyperactivity is usually the most alarming to parents. Often, ADHD children are depressed, have low self-esteem, experience feelings of guilt, and are full of self-accusations. After puberty, the disorder is less prominent or a spontaneous healing occurs in approximately half of the cases, while the other half of patients may suffer from impulsivity, social adaptability problems, depression, drug use, or antisocial acting out.[13]

Pastoral Considerations

(1) Working with parents is often more important than working with children since negative behavior traits found in children with ADHD can disrupt the whole family system. Therefore, treatment should include a parental management training component to help reduce parent-child conflict.[14] Pastoral help often starts with making parents aware of the strong medicine they possess: that of forgiveness. ADHD children are able to forgive themselves only if they feel forgiven by their families. Advancing hope, love, encouragement, and optimism, but also setting and enforcing strict boundaries, comprise a method of choice in healing such children.

(2) Children are usually most inattentive in boring situations (at school), while attention problems are less prominent in challenging situations like sports. Accordingly, school is one of the main areas where the battle with ADHD has to be fought. Usually, children with ADHD are bad students and are teased and humiliated by their schoolmates. On the whole, "ADHD is seen as a disorder of performance, rather than of knowledge or skills. Treatment is most often designed to improve attention and enhance motivation for these children to display their knowledge."[15] Not only coaching and tutoring, but also increasing Christian self-esteem, motivation, and

courage help to improve school performance and turn self-perceived losers into winners.

(3) If an episode of impulsive behavior in children with ADHD is recognized early, it can often be controlled with a loving, forgiving, but firm response. When impulsive behavior becomes uncontrollable, though, it means the caregiver's reaction has come too late. At that point, only strictness can restore the right behaviors. Strictness has positive short-term but negative long-term effects in disciplining these children.

(4) Parents of children with ADHD may have difficulty striking the right balance between strictness and spoiling. In their effort to avoid being too strict, they try to give their children almost everything they want. Spoiled ADHD children are conditioned to demand receiving without giving back—that is, they become selfish. Such children permanently demand more and more, and their desires can never be met. As a result, they feel permanently frustrated and discontent. Bringing up such children requires a balance of discipline and love, justice and mercy.

(5) Often, ADHD behavior is combined with attention-seeking behavior in the context of striving to be equal with others. Being involved in the scouts, sports teams, and similar groups that don't require specials skills—and where ADHD children can be like their peers—is often helpful. Participating in competitive sports, however, may be counterproductive. Instead, sports that involve competition with oneself—overcoming one's own limits—and that have no winners and losers (mountain climbing, for example) are often the best choice for ADHD youngsters.

(6) Fathers consciously or unconsciously represent the "ideal Father," or God. When they offer love, emotional closeness, and benevolence, they give their children a foretaste of God's personality. When, however, they are overly cold, demanding, strict, or legalist, they not only play a counterproductive role in ADHD children's behavior control but also spoil their relationship with God. Firmness does not exclude love. On the contrary, identification with order and a "benevolent strictness" provides extra security and a sense of achievement for children.

(7) ADHD children feel inferior, so increasing their feelings of guilt is counterproductive. Instead, they should be coached to grow, to compete

against and challenge themselves, to make sacrifices, and to demonstrate to themselves the power they have (supported by their consciences) in fighting their impulsive needs for power, domination, and selfishness. The internally-experienced truth of the saying "no pain, no gain" motivates ADHD children in this effort. Progress made despite the pain ought to prove to them that Christlike living has greater power than their despair, resistance, and pessimism.

(8) ADHD is often accompanied by other behavioral problems like noncompliance, stubbornness, and aggression, and ADHD children are thus more frequently disciplined than others. This reality creates a feeling of being picked on and ostracized, which leads the children to perceive themselves as being unwanted and unlovable, and worsens the existing behavioral problems. Because of this, ADHD children are often naturally inclined to establish a relationship with Jesus. They intuitively feel that only God gives the attention, love, forgiveness, and care they need. And we must recall that Christ was able to calm a storm on the lake. He can help children with these chaotic, aggressive tendencies to control their inner storms when the church community and families use the power of prayer for those with ADHD.

> In one case, the parents of an ADHD boy divorced, after which his father became his caregiver but soon died. The boy was then placed in foster care, where he was verbally, emotionally, and physically abused. Because of his ADHD and accompanying behavioral problems, he was subsequently placed in a group home, where, in his words, "no one looked at [him]." When I asked him, "So, you are completely alone?" he responded, "No, I am never alone. I am always with Jesus."

Like this particular boy, ADHD children are often worthy of their sufferings. Faith is able to give them a resilience, courage, and determination to make the best of their negative circumstances.

(9) As Linda Seligman and Laurie W. Reichenberg formulate in cognitive-behavioral language:

Counselors can model such traits as self-confidence, empathy, flexibility, resilience and being nonjudgmental, which can become a part of the child's repertoire of coping skills.... Due to deficits of executive functioning, children and adolescents with ADHD benefit from learning skills that help with improving daily functioning, such as time management, anger management, and impulse control.[16]

Pastoral terminology defines these same behavioral goals as coaching children to become Christlike. Christian self-criticism, humility, and meekness help with self-forgiveness, self-acceptance, self-discipline, and self-control. Becoming Christlike correlates with becoming well-behaved. In fact, the internal strength, hope, and courage that suffering for God's glory gives (which these young patients yet do not grasp but already feel) can be more therapeutic than any external behavioral conditioning.

(10) Involving ADHD children in church activities is sometimes a demanding but highly fruitful pursuit. For the most success, they ought to be given undemanding tasks that are not pass-fail and do not require long stretches of concentration, teamwork, or competitiveness. Simple, short, individual tasks (like being gift carriers) may be appropriate. Only after establishing a basic trust in themselves, their parents, their peers, their pastors, and their community can a gradual involvement in collective chores begin, such as being altar boys and girls. Public appreciation increases ADHD children's self-confidence, impulse control, and general success in the body of Christ exponentially increases their trust in Jesus. Helping ADHD children relate with Christ not only helps in regard to their salvation but also has visible and measurable effects in improving their psychological-spiritual well-being.

(11) In few other childhood disorders are irrational sin and resulting sickness so obviously connected. Children who are inattentive and hyperactive yet ambitious and motivated perceive themselves as being sinful and bad. The more they are ostracized from their families, their schools, and society, the more they lose self-esteem, optimism, and trust in themselves, parents, friends, and teachers. This acts as a self-fulfilling prophecy. Inattention, impulsivity, and repeated failures cause feelings of being a

loser, deepening inattention, impulsivity, and acting-out behaviors, while impatient parents and teachers often make the situation worse. Therefore, focusing the pastoral curing of irrational sins and self-accusations is the best healing of the noted self-fulfilling prophecy. As in other childhood problems, parents who trust Jesus heal their children's behavioral problems.

10.4 Aggressive Disorders in Children

In no other childhood disorder are sickness and non-Christian behavior patterns as dramatically connected as in aggressive disorders. Aggressive disorders in children are often precursors of antisocial personality disorders. They are therefore of significant social and pastoral concern. The DSM-5 lists in this category disorders such as oppositional defiant disorder, intermittent explosive disorder, and conduct disorder.

Oppositional defiant disorder (ODD) is characterized by irritable mood swings (losing one's temper often and being resentful), argumentative and defiant behaviors (arguing, actively rebelling against authority figures, and blaming others for one's own misbehavior), and vindictiveness.[17] Kaplan and Sadock estimate that its prevalence in children varies from 2–16 percent, and it is more common in boys. Children with ODD are strong-willed, assertive, temperamental, argumentative, socially deviant, short-tempered, deliberately annoying, uncritical, and easily provoked, and they blame others for their own mistakes and take no responsibility. The typical parenting style applied to children suffering from ODD is harsh and punitive, and there is often parental conflict in the background in which children are used as pawns.[18]

Intermittent explosive disorder is the inability, after the age of six, to control verbal or physical aggressive outbursts that frequently result in property damage or injury to animals and humans. Its prevalence is difficult to assess because cases are underreported, but the disorder is more prevalent in families suffering from relational, behavioral, or legal problems.

Conduct disorder is a recurring pattern of behavior violating the basic rights of others and manifested in aggression (threatening, bullying, fighting, stealing, extorting, or raping), destruction of property, deceitfulness, theft, and the serious violation of rules (running away from home or staying out at night before the age of thirteen). A lack of remorse, guilt, and empathy, and having no concern about behavioral consequences are other characteristics. Children with conduct disorder do not express feelings but act like machines, able to quickly turn emotions on and off.[9] The frequency of conduct disorder is estimated to be between 1–10 percent, and it appears more often in children whose parents themselves have a history of the following: antisocial behaviors; family discord; hateful fights; a lack of parental supervision; physical, emotional, and sexual abuse; and other problems. Divorce in itself is a factor promoting conduct disorder; however, "the persistence of hostility, resentment and bitterness between divorced parents may be the more important contributor to maladaptive behavior" conditioning, whereby "children unconsciously act out their parents' antisocial wishes."[20] Children with conduct disorder are prone to alcohol and drug use, sexually acting out, glorifying selfishness, violence in fighting society, and are not concerned about consequences, only quick and easy gratification. They frequently suffer from delinquency, depression, and suicidal temptations.

Pastoral Considerations

(1) For cases of aggressive disorders in children, professional textbooks recommend the following:

> (a) "Therapists should have a solid understanding of the multiple causal factors that lead to the development of these disorders and should have the ability to assess and treat comorbid disorders."[21]
> (b) "Early interventions for children with conduct problems are more effective, easier, and have a protective element for children who might otherwise escalate into increased problem behavior, peer-rejection, self-esteem deficits, conduct disorder, and academic failure."[22]
> (c) "The use of trans-diagnostic treatment approaches that work to alleviate one, or a cluster, of symptoms" improves such children's

"emotional dysregulation, impulsivity, anger management, learning deficits, and deficits in social skills" and helps them "define the problem, identify goals, generate options, choose the best option, and evaluate the outcome."[23]

Pastoral healers approach this same topic in a less scientific, more personal way.

(2) The pastoral healing of aggressive children starts in the family. Christian parents may be helped to grasp that their children's aggressive behavior is not a free choice but rather their reaction to an "experiential catastrophe" causing a "belief catastrophe" expressed in a "behavior catastrophe." The parents' humility, meekness, brokenheartedness, and selflessness is the best healing for the multiplicity of these catastrophes since young children consciously or unconsciously imitate their parents' beliefs and behaviors.

(3) Aggression is the opposite of love and inevitably provokes feelings of guilt. Violent children alleviate their guilt by submitting to antisocial idols. Proclaiming in their self-talk that "good is bad, and bad is good," they feel justified or even obliged to be evil. On the contrary, Christian love takes the wind from the sails of such destructive beliefs.

(4) In cases of aggressive children, Jesus-like love means, above all, forgiveness. Forgiveness redirects conflict resolution strategies from primitive flight-or-fight patterns to the motivation to fix one's behaviors. Jesus-like love (formulated in age-appropriate vernacular and exemplified through parents' and healers' personal examples) increases frustration tolerance, enabling sacrificial behavior, selflessness, and even acceptance of mental pain for the sake of spiritual gain in imitating Jesus. It is the only tool that empowers aggressive children's consciences and helps them to feel, understand, and experience living in the world but being not of it (Jn. 17:11; 17:17). The invulnerability resulting from being in the world but not belonging to it is the most effective defence mechanism in preventing acting-out aggression. It enhances the experience of being the object of God's love. The realization that they are loved and lovable facilitates aggressive children's efforts to be worthy of that gift. Such young children are not yet

mature enough to think this abstractly; however, their parental and church attachments help them feel and experientially appreciate these theological-psychological truths and mature in becoming the masters of their instincts and servants of their consciences.

(5) Treatment of aggressive children is marked by many ups and downs, mainly because aggressive children desire, like everyone else, to live in biblical love, peace, joy, and optimism, but this seems unachievable for them. These children defend themselves from the fear of being unfit for Christian ideals by fighting the ideals they are attracted to. It is thus imperative to emotionally convince such children that they fit in and have a place among the people of God. Advancing such trust acts as a self-fulfilling prophecy. It helps biblical self-criticism, self-forgiveness, self-acceptance, self-discipline, and self-control.

(6) New self-esteem, aspirations, and optimism help aggressive children find new friends. Joining cadets, scouts, or sport clubs and finding hobbies helps them find new identification models. Joining prayer groups and youth groups enhances their identification with Jesus Christ and his Church.

(7) Children suffering from aggressive behavior patterns may seem unapproachable because their feelings tend to boil over. Their behavior, however, is often a cry for help and an opportunity. Suffering like theirs propelled many canonized and noncanonized saints to discover God's peace and love that surpasses all human understanding. As pastoral healers' experience demonstrates, faith can produce paramount outcomes in such children if they gain a foretaste of the biblical, Godly joy achievable as early as the teenage years. In no other childhood disorder is receiving biblical peace, love, and forgiveness as important as in children with aggressive disorders.

10.5 Separation Anxiety Disorder, Reactive Attachment Disorder, and Disinhibited Social Engagement Disorders

The DSM-5 defines separation anxiety disorder as "fear or anxiety concerning separation from those to whom the individual is attached." The disorder is characterized by excessive distress and worry when separating from or losing attachment figures; excessive worry about getting lost, being kidnapped, or having an accident; reluctance to leave the house (e.g., to go to school); fear of being alone or sleeping alone; and the occurrence of nightmares, headaches, and nausea when attachment figures are absent.[24]

The fear of separation already occurs in newborns and is expressed in crying, rejecting food, and delayed thriving. In children it emerges before the age of 1 year, peaks between 9 and 18 months, and decreases at around 2 1/2 years. When starting school, some 15 percent of children experience uneasiness, fear, and a gradually-increasing anxiety that can reach the level of panic. Symptoms also include "irritability, difficulty eating, staying in a room alone, clinging to parents, and following a parent everywhere." [25] Such children are sensitive, vulnerable, introverted, and unpredictable, and they often exhibit physical symptoms including headaches, nausea, vertigo, vomiting, and gastrointestinal pains. The prognosis improves if children are motivated to attend school.

Reactive attachment disorder is mostly characterized by angst and is expressed, according to the DSM-5, by a pattern of withdrawn behavior. They are hard to comfort and emotionally introverted, distanced, enigmatic, and unresponsive. They may exhibit unexpected fearfulness, depression, irritability, and anger.[26] In some cases, reactive attachment evolves into paradoxical attachment, which causes children to desperately cling to and seek an attachment relationship with a distant, cool, or indifferent parent.

Disinhibited social engagement disorder is caused by a lack of attachment to parents in children younger than five. The resulting isolation and anxiety is overcompensated for with a lack of natural caution. These children are overly-familiar and trusting, and even venture away from their parents to go with strangers. Poor parental attachment later translates into poor peer relationships and partner relationships.[27] Attachment disorders are mostly transitory. Nevertheless, "research has demonstrated a connection between insecure attachment and subsequent behavioral and impulse-control problems, low self-esteem, poor peer relationships, psychiatric syndromes, criminal behavior, and substance abuse."[28]

Pastoral Considerations

(1) Children experience more anxiety if they see their parents' fears. Therefore, "anxious parents are at increased risk of having children with anxiety disorders."[29] Fearful parents, however, may be coached to prevent transferring anxiety to their children. Children need to see optimism, trust, and hope in their parents in order to feel the same in themselves.

(2) Children's anxiety often first significantly manifests in their relationship to school; it is like a barometer indicating the children's psychological stability. In regard to treating school-related anxiety, Kaplan and Sadock state, "If school attendance is an issue and the symptoms are of brief duration, a return to school may be a sufficient treatment." If, however, absenteeism persists or if children's school attendance is marked by "many visits to the school clinic, or significant problems at school," family treatment is the recommended approach.[30]

(3) Nothing is more fear-evoking in children than experiencing abandonment, emotional indifference, coldness, unavailability, or distance from a parent. There are two different approaches for healing such fears. The first is the following: "Fears and phobia are acquired through classical conditioning. Such fears can be unlearned through the use of behavioral techniques of exposure therapy, in which the child systematically confronts the feared situation through graded exposure"[31] and so gradually becomes deconditioned and immunized against fears. The second recognizes that fear of parental abandonment is always paired with a cry for help and is thus treatable by talking openly about personal problems and making life choices together with children, and is "more effective in younger children (age 7–10) and girls."[32]

(4) Pastoral healers always insist on enhancing emotional, intellectual, and, above all, spiritual attachments between parents and children. Like love in general, parent-child attachment is psychologically a multifaceted mystery of paramount importance. If the parent-child attachment is once extinguished, it is very hard to reestablish. If, however, the attachment remains strong and parents convey a strong and genuine Christian message,

most socially-induced sins and sicknesses in their children's behaviors are minimized.

(5) In uncomplicated cases of separation anxiety in the context of healthy parent-child attachment, healers may use paradox intention. Its rationale is giving to children too much security—that is, more than they require.

> A five-year-old boy developed a persistent pattern of fearful crying and clinging to his parents before leaving for kindergarten, as well as withdrawn, anxious behavior during his time apart from them. Most of his time in the classroom was spent sitting in a chair, rarely seeking contact with other children and responding minimally to the nanny's comforting. He exhibited irritability, sadness, emotional apathy, and unresponsiveness; rejected food; and behaved fearfully when involved in activities. To treat the boy's condition, his parents were coached to permanently demonstrate their love. They were to hug and kiss him, offer him food and drinks, dress and undress him, and cuddle and embrace him more than usual. The purpose was to make him certain of being loved. After ten days of receiving "too much love," the boy blew up, saying, "No hugs!"—after which he started to like kindergarten, and his anxiety virtually disappeared.

(6) Treating reactive attachment disorder is often hard. Professionals describe how it is of utmost importance that the child has a caregiver who is emotionally available, sensitive, and responsible, one to whom the child can develop attachment. With this condition met, there are two primary approaches. Psychoeducation is the first, which is usually a shorter, superficial therapeutic intervention for parents, permanent caregivers, and children. This approach is aimed at enhancing their communication and problem-solving skills, empathy, and mutual cooperation. Play therapy is one example. Observing the parent and child's spontaneous behaviors while playing together, the therapist models positive interactions and fosters their mutual attachment.

The other method, infant-parent psychotherapy, contains a plethora of longer and deeper therapeutic approaches, starting from psychodynamic and extending to cognitive behavioral and to existential methods which aim to understand the relevance of the parent's current and past experiences that are shaping their perceptions, feelings, purposes, values, and attitudes toward their infant. These psychotherapeutic interventions seek to resolve problems that transpire between infants and parent and "to improve the emotional communication between the child and caregiver."[33]

(7) While all of these measures are important, a genuine trust in God is the most powerful anti-anxiety and attachment-mending medicine.

A nine-year-old boy was the shortest child in his class. He was also the only one who cried when his mother brought him to school. The situation turned from bad to worse when other children realized his weakness and bullied and ostracized him. On one occasion, the bigger boys even beat him up. Subsequently, he avoided his peers and hid in the washroom, waiting for an opportunity to go home. His mother was an introverted, emotionally cool, and enigmatic person with schizoid personality disorder who, despite her best efforts, had difficulty establishing warm relationships with anyone, including her son. However, the diligent mother discerned an effective healing method: she coached her son to seek God's help whenever he felt threatened. The boy's main support in his frustrating situation became turning to Jesus for consolation. His faith did not initially help to improve his status among his peers, but it gave him the courage and strength to carry his cross. Gradually, with help of his trust in Jesus he learned to overcompensate for his anxiety by excelling in studies and sports—he became a star of martial arts—and at thirty-two years old he became the director of a prominent bank and a deacon in the Episcopalian church. His attachment to Jesus helped with his attachment to his emotionally-distant biological parents and helped him turn a disadvantage into an advantage.

(8) In healing so-called disinhibited social engagement disorder, professional psychological or psychiatric help (or even ministry for children and families) needs to be involved. Often, the reasons for this disorder in children are parental attitudes facilitated by a lack of commitment to loving,

unselfish, self-sacrificial parental behavior or by neglect, abandonment, or abuse. Unfortunately, for children with disinhibited social engagement disorder and their parents, pastoral healing is not always able to help, and in the worst cases children need to be placed in foster care.

(9) The most unpleasant task for pastoral healers is dealing with children suffering from disinhibited social engagement disorder. The pastoral healer is often confronted with the unpleasant duty of reporting any doubt about neglected or physically, verbally, emotionally, or sexually abused children to social services. No certainty is needed to file a report as doubts regarding neglect or abuse constitute a moral and legal duty to report such cases for investigation.

10.6 Elimination Disorders (Encopresis and Enuresis)

As Sadock, Sadock, and Ruiz note, bladder and bowel control develops between one and three years of age. Therefore, a diagnosis can be given only after age four for encopresis (soiling underwear or inappropriate areas areas) and five years for enuresis. Encopresis affects around 3 percent of children aged four, and affects 0.75 percent between ages ten and twelve. Enuresis (involuntary urination or bed-wetting) occurs 5–10 percent of the time in five-year-old children, and 1.5 to 5 percent in children ages nine to ten. The most frequent cause of encopresis is functional, that is, holding and suppressing the need for defecation until soiling occurs. A variety of emotional reasons can cause the intentional or unconscious depositing of feces in inappropriate places. It is most often provoked by children's rebellion, anger, or passive-aggressive bahaviour against harsh parenting styles. In other cases, it is part of an attention-seeking behavior, or it can signify stressful situations such as the birth of a new sibling or a passive resistance of the child against the environment. Most patients have significantly low-self-esteem, feel isolated, unlovable, ostracized, and humiliated.[34]

Nighttime and diurnal enuresis occurs more often in boys. As Sadock, Sadock, and Ruiz note, most patients are not bed-wetting intentionally and are not aware of it until they find themselves wet. Stressors facilitating the disorder can be different, such as the birth of a sibling, hospitalization, fighting, travel, harsh punishments, the beginning of a school year, divorce, moving to a new environment, and other stressors within the family. Bed-wetting is often connected to low self-esteem, loneliness, isolation, attention-seeking behaviors, poor self-image, a cry for help, attention seeking, intra-familial conflicts, estrangement, and abandonment.[35] Both enuresis and encopresis usually spontaneously disappear in adolescence.

Pastoral Considerations

(1) Alarmed parents ought to be coached not to reinforce enuresis and encopresis by giving too much attention to the disorder or by spoiling children, fulfilling inappropriate requests, or allowing children to blackmail them. Feelings of neglect, jealousy, envy, being unloved, and suffering from low-self-esteem should be addressed in the family. There needs to be a fine line between parental spoiling and strictness.

(2) The next step in professional healing is assessing whether the child received appropriate toilet training. Parents ought to be coached to be patient, persistent, and forgiving, but also to set firm boundaries in toilet training.

(3) In professional treatment of enuresis and encopresis, all concurrent disorders like the child's intellectual capacity, urinary and bowel infections, or neurological disorders ought to be checked out. Also, psychological reasons (anxiety, frustration, passive-aggressive behaviors, negativism, rebellion, and other acting-out behaviors) ought to be addressed before specific treatment starts. The same is valid for anxiety and impatient attitudes in parents, but also neglect, indifference, emotional abuse, and conflicted family relationships worsen the prognosis.

(4) As the most effective way to treat enuresis, Seligman and Reichenberg proposed the enuresis alarm, which helps significantly in some 10 percent to 30 percent of cases. It works by training the child to "make an inhibitory pelvic floor response during sleep that stops the flow of urine." This alerts the child that the bathroom needs to be used. In the authors' opinion, "the recent trend toward overnight diapers or pant liners, which actually have the effect of habituating the child to being wet at night," is not helpful.[36]

(5) Professional healing of encopresis consists of energetic behavioral conditioning in toilet training. An imperative urge to use the washroom may be first induced with laxatives. Next, children are coached in gaining mastery in psychologically controlling neurological regulation mechanisms, located in the cortical area and in the sacral spine.

(6) Pastoral healing of enuresis and encopresis disorders should first focus on resolving resistance. Elimination control is a highly private act, and therefore talking about it appears to some believers as especially liberating, but to others embarrassing, disgusting, or shameful. The pastoral healer's first role often is demystifying elimination functions. This facilitates parents and children talking freely about elimination problems.

(7) Pastoral therapists heal by placing the past, present, and future of such young patients into a biblical context. A cathartic discussion of past traumas and frustrations often results in processing distressing memories and increasing the willingness to forgive and restore trust in parents, which decreases the emotional reasons for enuresis or encopresis. Current problems are mostly expressed in unconsciously using elimination problems as a cry for help, attention- seeking, or rebellious behaviors, signaling ongoing personal, family, sibling, school, or environmental conflicts. Children burdened by guilt and fears concerning their future often use regression as defense mechanisms. Such children behaviorally return to passive-receptive behavior, imitating patterns used before bladder and bowel control was established. The panacea in such children is Jesus' love since abundant love is the best healing for regressive behaviors. It enables children abandoning unsuccessful defense mechanisms to reciprocate love by eagerness to psychologically and spiritually grow and transcend.

(8) A unique advantage of pastoral healing is its ability to discern a sacral meaning in healing and defeating elimination problems. Children can learn to discern not only a problem but also the solution, a call to participate in God's healing power "so that the work of God might be displayed in [their] life" (John 9:1–3). This effort converts high distress into high attachment to God.

Notes

[1] DSM-5. *Diagnostic and Statistical Manual of the American Psychiatric Association* (2013), 16.

[2] Benjamin James Sadock, Virginia Alcott Sadock, and Pedro Ruiz, *Kaplan and Sadock's Synopsis of Psychiatry: Behavioral Sciences/Clinical Psychiatry*, 11th ed. (Philadelphia, PA: Wolters Kluwer, 2015), 1118–36.

[3] Ibid., 1136

[4] Linda Seligman and Laurie W. Reichenberg, *Selecting Effective Treatments* (Hoboken, NJ: John Wiley & Sons, 2014), 55.

[5] Ibid., 56.

[6] DSM-5, 27.

[7] Sadock, Sadock, and Ruiz, *Kaplan and Sadock's Synopsis of Psychiatry*, 11th ed. 1152–68.

[8] Benjamin James Sadock and Virginia Alcott Sadock, *Kaplan and Sadock's Synopsis of Psychiatry: Behavioral Sciences/Clinical Psychiatry*, 10th ed. (Philadelphia, PA: Wolters Kluwer, 2007), 197.

[9] DSM-5, 219.

[10] Seligman and Reichenberg, *Selecting Effective Treatments*, 58.

[11] Ibid., 64.

[12] Sadock and Sadock, *Kaplan and Sadock's Synopsis of Psychiatry*, 10th ed. 197.

[13] Sadock, Sadock, and Ruiz, *Kaplan and Sadock's Synopsis of Psychiatry*, 11th ed. 1116–81.

[14] Seligman and Reichenberg, *Selecting Effective Treatments*, 68.

[15] Ibid., 68.

[16] Ibid., 70

[17] DSM-5, 219–24.

[18] Sadock, Sadock, and Ruiz, *Kaplan and Sadock's Synopsis of Psychiatry*, 11th ed. 1244–7.

[19] DSM-5, 24.

[20] Sadock, Sadock, and Ruiz, *Kaplan and Sadock's Synopsis of Psychiatry*, 11th ed. 608–15.

[21] Seligman and Reichenberg, *Selecting Effective Treatments*, 78.

[22] Ibid., 78.

[23] Ibid., 80.

[24] DSM-5, 115.

[25] Sadock, Sadock, and Ruiz, *Kaplan and Sadock's Synopsis of Psychiatry*, 11th ed. 1253–4.

[26] DSM-5, 141.

[27] Sadock, Sadock, and Ruiz, *Kaplan and Sadock's Synopsis of Psychiatry*, 11th ed. 1217–21.

[28] Seligman and Reichenberg, *Selecting Effective Treatments*, 106.

[29] Sadock and Sadock, *Kaplan and Sadock's Synopsis of Psychiatry*, 10th ed. 1277.

[30] Seligman and Reichenberg, *Selecting Effective Treatments*, 99.

[31] Ibid., 98.

[33] Ibid., 100.

[34] Ibid., 105.

[35] Sadock, Sadock, and Ruiz, *Kaplan and Sadock's Synopsis of Psychiatry*, 11th ed. 1211–14.

[36] Sadock, Sadock, and Ruiz, *Kaplan and Sadock's Synopsis of Psychiatry*, 11th ed. 1214.

[37] Seligman and Reichenberg, *Selecting Effective Treatments*, 93–96.

CHAPTER ELEVEN

PSYCHOSES AND THEIR PASTORAL TREATMENT

T he first distinction in professional and pastoral practice is determining whether a subject is suffering from a psychotic or nonpsychotic disorder. Psychoses are characterized by a withdrawal from objective reality into sick beliefs and hallucinations. Nonpsychotic disorders, previously known as neuroses, are characterized by fighting of external reality instigated by dysfunctional internal beliefs.

11.1 Schizophrenia and Schizophrenic Spectrum Disorders

As the most typical signs of schizophrenia, the DSM-5 recognizes delusions, hallucinations, disorganised speech, disorganized or catatonic behavior, and diminished emotional expression.[1] This disorder affects men and women equally. Genetic factors apparently have a role in aetiology. If one parent has schizophrenia, the prevalence of the disorder in their children is 12 percent, while if both parents have the disorder, the prevalence rises to 40 percent. Other biochemical, neurological, and psychological explanations indicate that schizophrenia is a multi-aetiological disorder.[2]

The disorder often has a gradual onset and a slow evolution, with remissions and relapses. Premorbid signs may exist for years before the disorder is diagnosed. Children developing the disorder later were usually seen as withdrawn, quiet, passive, enigmatic, and introverted. As adolescents, they are often loners, with no close friends, social life, or referent groups, and they may avoid team sports. One of the first signs of schizophrenia is isolation: becoming gradually disconnected from the tasks, goals, problems, and pleasures of everyday life; from family, friends, and colleagues; and from workplace duties. Schizophrenic individuals live in a separate world with unusual rules, bizarre principles, and standards of behavior that are difficult for others to understand. For example, one patient woke a cloistered nun at 3:00 a.m., saying, "Pray for me because I will die." Besides hallucinations, delusional ideas are the most common characteristic of schizophrenia. Patients may believe that others control their minds or behavior or that they are able to control outside events in extraordinary ways. Other patients "may have an intense and consuming preoccupation with esoteric, abstract, symbolic, psychological, or philosophical ideas" or worry about nonexistent and bizarre, life-threatening somatic conditions, such as the "presence of aliens inside the patient's testicles affecting his ability to father children." Patients lose ego boundaries and have no clear sense of "where [their] own body, mind and influence end and where those of other animate and inmate objects begin."[4] Associations are loose, and patients talk about nonreal connections and nonexistent things, and they discuss events in neologisms (made-up words or expressions). Kaplan and Sadock give the following example of a psychotic delusion, which other people do not understand.

> Mental health in the blessed Trinity, and as man cannot be without God, it is futile to deny His son. For the Creation understand germ-any in Voice new Order, not lie in chained reaction, spawning mark in temple Cain with Babel graven' image to wanton V day "Israel." Lucifer fell Jew prostitute and Lambeth walks by roam to sex ritual, in Bible six million of the Babylon woman, infer-no Salvation.[5]

Communication with schizophrenic patients is often characterized by "idea affective dissociation," that is, a split between the emotional and mental contents of the mind. Patient may laugh when talking about sad things, or talk with a sad voice about happy events, or they may have the same emotional expression independently of talking about happy or sad events, a phenomenon called "flat affect." Because reasoning and feelings are disconnected, it is hard for patients to emotionally connect with others. They do not experience the feelings of other people. It is as if they are talking to a computer because their feelings are dissociated from their thoughts.

Another prominent symptom is the gradual disappearing of instinct-regulated vital dynamisms, causing total passivity and loss of interest in self-image, nourishment, and even the sustaining of life. Such a person may not react appropriately to hazards. Their whole attitude toward life changes, and delusions have a greater influence over their behavior than reality. Suicides are bizarre and brutal, such as hanging with barbed wire or putting one's head in a burning oven. Additionally, the sexual drive becomes grotesque and unusual, and patients repeat gestures that have meanings known only to them.

While a healthy person's mental functions are "synthym," that is, mutually synchronized, the mental functions of a schizophrenic patient are "katathym," or desynchronized and dissociated. A patient feels one thing, thinks another, perceives a third, and intends to do a fourth. The personality disintegrates, and there is a discrepancy between memories, thoughts, feelings, will, and the senses.

In schizophrenic people, logical causality disappears. Delusions are distortions in reasoning about nonexistent people, happenings, connections, and problems that cannot be logically corrected. Another typical symptom is hallucinations, most often auditory and seldom visual. Auditory hallucinations may echo one's disturbing thoughts or present as other voices (known or unknown) that command the individual to carry out unpleasant tasks. Especially tormenting are hallucinated commands that the patient does not know how to carry out. Visual hallucinations are unusual, bizarre, and frightening. In so-called cenesthopathic hallucinations, for example, individuals may observe their own bodies from the inside, seeing heir organs, or get the impression that their bodies are not the same anymore, feeling that they are not the same people any longer. Patients sometimes stand in front of a mirror for hours, analysing themselves and trying to determine their own identities. This is illustrated with a paraphrased version of Stojiljkovic's study.

N.N., a twenty-three-year-old student, was brought to a clinic by his friends. They described that his recent behavior had changed. He had started avoiding his friends, always finding some reason to excuse himself and abandon their company. He was no longer going to university but staying in bed all morning, covering his head and remaining in the apartment alone. When he studied, he read the same page repeatedly. He neglected himself, avoided grooming, and didn't change his clothes. He stood for many hours in front of a mirror, moving his hands as though touching and exploring himself. He would not share food, and if he received a cookie (a food which he loved), he would put it in paper and hide it. He demanded that the windows be permanently open and didn't respond to telephone calls. He would not even respond to his parents' letters and when asked why, he stated that it was because it was now clear to him that the letters were not really from his father but from unknown offices. He was also getting into fights with friends because he believed they were torturing him.

By the time of his admission to hospital, he was silent, distrustful, and responded only with short, angry answers. He was unshaven and had long nails. He did not want to sit but suspiciously examined the room and, without asking, opened the window. When asked why he was doing this, he explained that "You are accustomed to this, and probably it does not harm you ... maybe you have contra venom, but I have not." He would not cooperate because he was "quite well" in his own estimation. "What do you want from me?" he asked.

When his father arrived, he was quite cold with him, as though he was meeting him for the first time, and he did not ask for his mother. Additionally, he was uninterested in anything happening within his family. It was as if he did not recognize the tears of his father. When asked if he heard voices, he explained, "Those are my problems. Nevertheless, you can hear them as well if you will." Asked about his thoughts, he returned permanently to the topic of "transformation of the material energy." He wondered why his statements were unclear to others. On departure, he was isolated and did not communicate with anyone, and at home he lay in bed for hours, keeping his hands in his pyjama pockets because "they are also a matter prone to transformation."[6]

The DSM-5 has removed the categorization of different subtypes of schizophrenia. However, the following distinctions are still used in professional and nonprofessional reports.

(1) The undefined type is characterized by a gradual onset and slow progression, with delusions, hallucinations, and, if not treated, disintegration of the personality into dementia. Typical signs are passivity, emotional coldness, and loss of interest. Patients sit passively in their rooms, deep in thought, searching for nonexistent answers from other people who do not understand their problems.

(2) *Disorganized schizophrenia* is characterized by early onset, before the age of twenty-five, and polymorphic symptoms characterized by extremes, such as extreme laughing that turns unexpectedly to extreme sobbing. The onset can be severe and unexpected (like an acute psychosis), with acoustic hallucinations, agitation, general suspicion, paranoid interpretations, hypochondria, histrionic-like seizures, bizarre rage, introverted passivity, bursts of laughter without any apparent reason, and incongruous grinning and grimacing.

(3) *Catatonic schizophrenia* involves negativism, rigidity, or unexpected excitement or aggression with periods of stupor. Stupor is a disorder of the will, causing an inability to perform intentional movements. Patients resemble a sculpture; they may hold the same, often bizarre, body posture for hours or even days without moving, eating, or drinking, or repeat stereotypical, meaningless questions and thoughts (perseveration), repeat the words of other people meaninglessly (verbigeration), or repeat meaningless movements (echopraxia).

(4) *Paranoid schizophrenia* is characterized by paranoid delusional ideas and hallucinations. The paranoid ideas are unconvincing, impossible, and bizarre. Patients may feel that their thoughts are being stolen or that enemies can read their thoughts or direct their thinking. They might hear the dialogue of their enemies threatening to kill them, change their food

and drink tastes, or believe they can smell poison or gas. The disorder has a progressive tendency, but it seldom ends in the complete disintegration of the personality. The external image remains relatively preserved.

(5) *Residual schizophrenia* occurs after completing antipsychotic treatment, when the positive symptoms of schizophrenia (hallucinations, delusions, disorganized behavior, and catatonia) usually improve. Nevertheless, negative symptoms, such as odd beliefs and practices, emotional coldness, and flat affect may remain even in remission. The prognosis of the listed subtypes of schizophrenia is better the later it appears, and acute forms, in general, have better prognoses. Disorganized schizophrenia has a worse prognosis, while catatonic and paranoid schizophrenia have better chances for improvement.[7]

(6) *Brief psychotic disorder* is distinguished from schizophrenia in the DSM-5 classification by brief (lasting at least one day and no longer than one month) psychotic symptoms, delusions, hallucinations, disorganized speech, and disorganized or catatonic behavior. The prognosis is good, and an "eventual full return to the premorbid level of functioning" is possible.[8]

(7) *Schizophreniform disorder* is characterized by delusions, hallucinations, disorganized speech, disorganized behavior, and negative symptoms such as decreased emotionality that last no longer than one month. The prognosis of the disorder is worse than for brief psychotic disorder but better than for schizophrenia.[9]

(8) *Schizoaffective disorder* includes signs of schizophrenia and mood disorder.[10] It almost represents a continuum between mood and thought disorders. Therefore, schizophrenics with a mood disorder, as well as those with mood disorders suffering from schizophrenia, receive this diagnosis. Its lifetime prevalence is around 1 percent, with equal numbers of males and females. Its prognosis is better than that of schizophrenia and worse than that in mood disorders. Mood incongruent psychotic features (i.e., delusions contradicting feelings) significantly worsen the prognosis.[11]

As David Barlow notes, "Among the most remarkable advances in the last decade is the direct treatment of 'positive' symptoms of schizophrenia with psychological treatments."[12] Despite that optimistic note, in everyday practice the method of choice in the treatment of schizophrenia and other psychotic disorders is still neuroleptic medicines, supplemented with psychological counselling and, in the case of believers, pastoral counselling.

Pastoral Considerations

(1) Those most exposed to this disorder are socially awkward, isolated, eccentric, impulsive youngsters who are absorbed with fantasies, use drugs and alcohol, and have a positive heredity. "Recent research shows that certain drugs (amphetamines and cocaine) may actually promote the onset of psychotic symptoms in vulnerable individuals. Especially if used early in life, cannabis use increases the risk [of the disorder]."[13] Also, despite the good prognosis of brief and schizophreniform disorders, 50 percent of patients relapse.[14] Schizophrenia cannot be prevented, but professional and pastoral attention may focus on preventing drug use and treating personality problems that cause the fragmentation of the personality to begin with. Enhancing social communications, discerning a fulfilling purpose in life, boosting school performance, occupational and vocational counselling, and support in resolving relational and family problems all have a certain stabilizing and preventive effect.

(2) Schizophrenia is a chronic disorder with remissions and relapses. The kind of pastoral help one needs depends on whether one is in remission or has relapsed. In relapses, pastoral care consists of helping families and patients to receive medical care and remain in treatment.

(3) Even deeply religious patients in periods of relapse suffer from bizarre and delusional ideas, and despite their relationship with God, they can be uncritical. In one case, a religious patient was attempting to cut out "atheist thoughts" from his roommate's brain with a fork. When asked, "Are you not sorry for making him to suffer?" he explained coldly, "No, he enjoys it. It helps him to get rid of his godless ideas." Relatives are therefore understandably cautious in engaging schizophrenic patients when their logic is so hard to fathom. But a delusional motivation for violence is relatively rare[15] and has to be individually assessed.

(4) Reality judgment in patients with a schizophrenic relapse is often delusional in one area of mental functioning but healthy in other areas. One

patient illustrated his experience of a psychotic relapse with a highly abstract comparison, saying, "I feel in relapse as if my mind stays human but my body has suddenly converted to a fly. As a fly, I cannot grasp my place and role nor relate to other flies, who look like me but are desperately strange to me. As a human I am unable to think, feel, communicate, or even eat like a fly. A permeating fear of being hopelessly alone and lost in a strange world of insects is all I can experience." In such conditions, any rational approach is useless. However, pastoral healers are specialized in providing exactly what patients with schizophrenic relapse need, which is love. When Jesus healed, whether his action involved a physical healing or driving out "unclean spirits" (psychiatric disorders), his motivation (one might even say method) was unconditional love. It was his love that was able to reach those who the general population were afraid of or had alienated.

(5) When pastoral healers approach patients in relapse, they first let the patients direct communication. The healer may speak in nonchallenging, small, conversational sentences that include polite, cautious, and respectful language but that always reveal a compassionate willingness to help. Establishing communication (sometimes using gestures, mimicry, gifts, kindness, smiles, and half-sentences) decreases fears and increases trust, which is needed for establishing a therapeutic relationship later.

(6) Delusional ideas may provoke interpersonal conflicts, social estrangement, and create "evidence for persecution, whereas withdrawal and isolation probably result in confirmatory rumination and resentment, with a lack of opportunity to disconfirm these paranoid beliefs."[16] Pastoral healers may seek communication with the "healthy parts" of the patient's self while avoiding topics affected or produced by the "sick parts" of their personalities.

(7) Despite the fact that medicine plays the primary role in healing schizophrenia, faith, even in periods of relapse, is of enormous help. Even passive participation in religious activities such as liturgy and prayer may serve as a powerful support for the healthy aspects of the self. As one patient described, "The church is the only place where I feel equal to others." The Mystical Body of Christ, represented by the church, is a great equalizer and

continues to offer the unconditional love that can cut through even complex diagnoses such as schizophrenia.

(8) Pastoral help becomes especially important in remission. In recuperating patients, a decrease in emotional and mental functioning, a decrease in life satisfaction, and an increase in stress, frustration, depression, and suicidal ideation are common.[17] Pastoral help may focus on support in reality testing, establishing realistic goals, avoiding demoralization and blame, developing interpersonal (and other) skills, and empowering the patient by reminding them that, as Christ did through all aspects of his public ministry, they are not alone.

(9) The best way to deal with lingering bizarre and awkward ideas and fantasies in periods of relapse is with a combination of curiosity and politeness. The healer should be nonconfrontational, show interest, and help to gradually distinguish and label irrational creations and daydreams as "tricks of the mind."[18]

(10) Often, patients feel a mixture of shame, embarrassment, and fear about how they will be accepted by their families, friends, and the Church. Behaving as though nothing happened, with a friendly, supportive attitude and without asking too many questions is the most helpful approach. Skill training, self-management of symptoms, self-scheduling of recreation and leisure activities, self-management medication, job searching, casual coaching of basic conversation skills, friendship, dating, and family activities are areas in which the body of Christ can help empower the self of recuperating patients. These pastoral approaches use the gifts and fruits of the Spirit, such as kindness, gentleness, and patience. Such virtues can often help patients to not arbitrarily stop consuming their prescribed medication.

(11) Barlow recommends the following behavioral steps in healing schizophrenic patients' self-esteem: (a) request that patients list ten positive qualities about themselves; (b) rate each quality from 0 to 100 depending how much they really believe it to be a true quality; (c) ask patients to produce concrete examples of the listed qualities; (d) monitor the frequency of the occurring qualities (for example, during the previous week); (e) ask patients to coach and self-monitor the weekly increase of their qualities; (f) the therapist should provide feedback demonstrating the patients'

values; (g) patients should monitor whether their self-esteem correlates to the result on their chart; (h) a gradual progression in the quantity and qualities as well as the self-esteem of patients is the purpose of this self testing.[19] I have used a similar plan to help patients self-assess the progress of their behavior in becoming more Christlike and have found that patients are frequently encouraged by their self-assured progress. Even though the religious life of schizophrenic patients is usually very guarded and enigmatic, using the above plan may open a window for pastoral healers to receive more insight into schizophrenic patients' intimate relationships and communications with Jesus. In recuperating patients, such a plan may also facilitate their spiritual healing and even provide future spiritual direction. In this regard, the power of the Holy Spirit cannot be underrated, for "The wind blows wherever it pleases. You hear its sound, but you cannot tell where it comes from or where it is going. So it is with everyone born of the Spirit" (John 3:8).

(12) An important pastoral purpose is to help resolve what Frankl calls "passivization." Passivization refers to patients perceiving themselves not as subjects but as objects.

> While the normal person experiences himself thinking, watching, observing, influencing, listening, eavesdropping, seeking and persecuting, taking still or moving pictures, etc., the schizophrenic experiences all these acts and these psychic functions as if they were being rendered in the passive; they "are being" observed, "are being" thought about, etc. In other words, in schizophrenia experiences an experiential passivizing of the psychic functions.[20]

Consequently, instead of spontaneously talking, moving, and behaving, they analyse and reflect on their voice, words, and behaviors, silently asking, "Should I say 'Hello' or 'Good day'?" or "Should I smile or show a serious face?" or "Should I keep my hands in my pockets, crossed on my chest, or beside my body?" Such constant self-reflective scrutiny may spoil the patients' security, creating a feeling of being observed or judged. A pastoral healer may encourage such overly-reflective patients to observe themselves not from a human perspective, but a Godly perspective, where judgment for such tendencies simply doesn't exist. Consider the following case.

> A twenty-six-year-old man in remission was suffering intense self-scrutiny because he perceived himself to be "behaving strangely." When instructed not to attempt to hide but to intentionally demonstrate his bizarre behaviors, he jokingly compared his own strange image with John the Baptist's appearance and said that God was "testing the strength of his faith" by forcing on him a behavior that jeopardized his social prestige. By applying his passivization to his understanding of God's perspective, this exceptionally religious man was able to accept his behavior. This exchange of perspectives became a daily routine which made it possible for him to function in an optimistic and self-confident way in everyday life. He now perceives himself as being watched by God and no longer cares about being watched by the world. God's perspective always allows rest for the weary soul (Matthew 11:28–30).

(13) As the religious person in remission becomes more acquainted with everyday functioning, he may express a desire to take a more active role in the church community. A brotherly welcoming of such a person's striving may give a big boost to their remission. Passive activities (i.e., prayer groups) in which one may remain anonymous are ideal at first. Later, activities demanding no emotional initiative or exposure may be appropriate, such as counting money. The patient remains engaged, but in an unthreatening manner. The welcoming arms of Christ are always open for those who feel scrutinized or marginalized in any way.

(14) As Seligman and Reichenberg note, some 50 percent of those hospitalized for schizophrenia are readmitted within two years. Those who relapse within five years have a 78 percent chance of relapsing again.[20] In no other psychiatric disorder is family support so important as in schizophrenia (which includes the support of the larger family, namely the Church).

> As a student, John was the best mathematician in his school, repeatedly winning competitions. After completing his studies, he graduated from

a reformed theology school and became a priest. At the age of twenty-four, he started taking mission trips, first to the Soviet Union and later to Russia, during which he "travelled like Jesus"—without money, food, or water. He was repeatedly caught by the police and hospitalized, one time in Kazan and another time in Moscow. In Moscow, he was diagnosed as a paranoid schizophrenic with delusional religious ideas. As such, he was brought back to Canada unshaven, emaciated, and squalid. On his next trip in 1990, John fell in love with a Russian psychiatrist and married her. Soon after, he got a permanent placement in the reformed church, and he and his wife adopted two children. His wife took exemplary care of him, and he preached and served actively in his congregation until he retired in 2016.

(15) Studies have shown that more than 55 percent of people with schizophrenia do not follow treatment recommendations.[22] The church community has the opportunity to take on the role of family for such sick members. Supporting such patients is probably one of the best ways to extend the reach of the body of Christ. Accordingly, people suffering from schizophrenia may be a gift in that they present an opportunity for the church community to imitate Christ in compassion, empathy, care, and love.

11.2 Delusional Disorder and Other Paranoid Conditions

Besides paranoid schizophrenia, there are three other paranoid conditions.

(1) *Delusional disorder*, or paranoia, is characterized by delusional ideas lasting, according to the DSM-5, for at least one month. Hallucinations are not prominent, and the disorder does not cause disintegration of the personality.[23]

(2) *Paranoid personality disorder* is characterized by overvalued ideas that, according to the DSM-5, cause pervasive distrust and suspicion about being exploited, harmed, and deceived; being doubtful of others' loyalty, with a reluctance to confide; bearing grudges; perceiving persecution; and having suspicions about the fidelity of one's partner.[24]

(3) *Paranoid reactions* are not included as nosological entities in the DSM-5's[31] and Kaplan and Sadock's textbook's[32] classification of adjustment disorders. In my clinical experience, and in some European textbooks, however, paranoid reactions (absent of paranoia or a paranoid personality disorder) occur commonly in normal people, so we will also consider them when considering paranoid conditions.

Delusional disorder is characterized by the DSM-5 as the experiencing of delusional ideas in people who are otherwise not markedly impaired.[25] This rare disorder's incidence is "estimated to be 0.025 to 0.03 percent."[26] Its aetiology is unknown. Paranoia appears mostly in males over fifty, but it can sometimes appear much earlier.

People with paranoia are often secretive people, isolated and enigmatic loners who do not feel well when they are close to anyone because of their recurring insecurity and suspicions. They interpret words and mimic the gestures of others in a paranoid context, finding hidden meanings and messages (e.g., disguised threats in television programs, newspapers, or church sermons). They like conspiracy theories and perceive various happenings as animosity or attempts to harm or kill them. The reasons they give for the alleged threats have to do with their morality, perfection, innovations, or extraordinary intelligence, such as an imagined close friendship with a great philosopher or politician. They believe that everyone is jealous of them, as their messianic, world-redeeming ideas challenge the powers of the evil world. These individuals distance themselves from family and friends and obsess about their grandiose ideas of persecution, keeping a diary and noting and perusing suspicious remarks. Their personal image is relatively well-preserved. "Patients are usually well-groomed and well-dressed, without evidence of a gross disintegration of their personality or daily activities, yet they may seem eccentric, odd, suspicious, and hostile."[27] Their emotions are "consistent with delusions. A patient with grandiose delusions is euphoric; one with persecutory delusions is suspicious."[28] Hallucinations, except for auditory ones, are not prominent, while illusions frequently occur. It is often hard to recognize delusional ideations, which often perfectly resemble conspiracy theories since they seem quite convincing to nonprofessionals. Even as medical students, we were sometimes tempted to believe the stories told by patients suffering from paranoia. Typically, patients develop a deceptive, seemingly rational and logical system of thought in which only the primary idea ("I am persecuted") is clearly irrational and the rest are convincing. This gives rise to the saying, "It would take one paranoid person to convince one hundred normal people, rather than one hundred normal people to convince one paranoid person about the falsity of their paranoid ideas."

The paranoid systems can be distinguished by their different delusional ideas. The persecutory type is characterized by querulousness, irritability, anger, and even homicidal behavior. The jealous type, or "conjugal paranoia," is marked by "delusions of infidelity," which sometimes only divorce or the death of a spouse may resolve (ensuring the partner's safety is essential). The erothomanic type is characterized by delusional ideas of others being in love with the patient or of the patient being sexually abused by famous people. Individuals with this form of paranoia may be vengeful if their love objects do not reciprocate affection. They are so-called stalkers, who "persistently follow their alleged lovers." The somatic type is characterized by hypochondriac delusions. The grandiose type is characterized by delusional ideas of ostentatiousness, like enormous achievements and merits (such as having invented a world-saving device). Those with paranoia of extraordinary heritage believe that they have extraordinary ancestors or were even created by God to save the world. Those experiencing paranoia of entitlement believe they have enormous and extraordinary rights that are not acknowledged by society.[29]

Paranoid personality disorder is a nonpsychotic paranoid disorder. The prevalence of this disorder is around 0.5–2.5 percent in the general population. It starts in adolescence and is characterized by overvalued ideas of being persecuted, exploited, harmed, deceived, or abused. Sufferers experience permanent suspiciousness, jealousy, and mistrust. As Kaplan and Sadock's textbook notes, "Bigots, pathologically jealous spouses, and litigious cranks often have a paranoid personality disorder." Such people are excessively suspicious even of their family members, children, and friends. They are prone to interpreting the innocent actions of others as abusive, malevolent, dangerous, threatening, manipulative, or deceitful. They also question and scrutinize the loyalty or trustworthiness of their family members, coworkers, and friends. Such people are often extremely jealous and scrutinize the fidelity of their spouses or sexual partners. "People with this disorder externalize their own emotions and use the defense of projection; they attribute to others the impulses and thoughts that they cannot accept in themselves."[30] Paranoid suspicions work together as a self-fulfilling prophecy; distrust and animosity cause others to feel threatened. Coworkers, colleagues, friends, and even family members ridicule the individual suffering from paranoid personality disorder, while the individual feels nearly able to read the unconscious thoughts of others. People with this disorder may be vengeful and bear grudges. In contrast to paranoia, however, their lifestyles are not delusional. Rational and logical reasoning and reality judgment are preserved, and they make attempts to restore relationships. Heart-to-heart talks may help to ease their paranoid attitudes.

Paranoid reactions are provoked by conflict, confrontation, or stress, facilitating affected people to interpret events in an exaggerated, malicious, confrontational, suspicious, slandering, or insulting way and attack not the arguments of the opponent but their personalities. Subsequently, these people perceive animosity even in harmless gestures and react in an irrationally defensive, hyperemotional way. Paranoid reactions occurring in otherwise mentally healthy people most often do not need healing. Nevertheless, they may present a grave problem if they escalate to violence. They are seen virtually everywhere, such as in paranoid domestic and religious discussions, foreign and domestic politics, street and gang fighting, road rage, and fighting among sport fans.

Pastoral Considerations

(1) There is a wide range between normal socially-required paranoid interpretations and the genuine delusional ones. Distorted ideologies (like fascism or communism) often play a paramount role in producing such interpretations. Uncritical identification with extreme ideologies empowers the paranoid self of such people in justifying almost any act of deception, cruelty, violence, abuse, or murder. Even prominent political leaders (like

Stalin, for example) had such personality traits. Significant parts of populations in previous communist dictatorships were empowered by a collective paranoid mental climate and ideology. Hodi describes that after the collapse of communism, many ex-communists in Eastern European countries were not only unable to accept the new political situation but were "losing their personalities," which were conditioned in a paranoid manner by the previous communist regime. [33]

(2) It is the task of professionals to make a differential diagnosis between paranoia (a psychosis), paranoid behaviors (a personality disorder), and paranoid reactions (in normal people). Differentiation is difficult because all three conditions may be provoked by insecurities, fears, traumatic events, or other stressors and include persecutory symptoms and the use of defensive denial, projection, and reactive formation.[34] Exact diagnosing is important because the pastoral healing of nonpsychotic paranoid conditions may start immediately, but the healing of psychotic paranoid disorders must only begin after the psychotic features are, to some degree, controlled with antipsychotic medicines. Let us in our overview focus on approaching patients suffering from paranoia since the principles involved in their healing can be applied also in healing nonpsychotic paranoid conditions.

(3) Because of persistent delusions, pastoral help in paranoia often starts with assuring family members that there is no need for them to self-rectify the patients' accusations (since the pastoral healer knows the disorder) and encouraging the family not to give up on demonstrating their love for and commitment to the paranoid member. Providing security for the family members of the people suffering from paranoia is of paramount importance.

(4) A pastoral healer should never attempt to rationally correct delusional belief systems. Such an attempt is not only futile but may cause the pastoral healer to become a part of the delusional system of the patient. In confrontational patients, contact can be sustained by focusing on secondary symptoms (insomnia or occupational and family issues) rather than the paranoid contents.[35]

(5) Paranoia is a delusional defence against frustrations, fears, irritability, dysphonia, and anxiety caused by perceiving "the world as an unfriendly

place."[36] Pastoral healing addresses these root issues after patients regain at least some reality judgment. Healers focus initially on resembling Christ through a peaceful, loving, and empowering attitude, attempting in this way to decrease patients' delusional fears. Such an attitude cannot heal paranoia but is the precondition for establishing a therapeutic alliance with the patient.

(6) In the early stages of healing, liturgy, sacraments, and prayer do not have the power to correct delusional or overvalued ideas. Nevertheless, trusting God may help to ease paranoid conditions in many ways. Firstly, discipleship and paranoia are mutually exclusive in the sense that the Christian way of living is a direct and supreme antidote to paranoia, decreasing aggression even in delusional believers. Secondly, faith is often the only safe haven for distressed, paranoid people who allegedly receive no loyalty, love, security, or support from their families or the rest of the world. And thirdly, people of faith suffering delusional ideas tend to be more self-critical, humble, and repentant and more agreeable to medical treatment than those with no faith.

(7) The healer needs to be aware that even people suffering nonpsychotic paranoid conditions believe they are threatened. They defend themselves, and in so doing they perceive exactly "what they have feared—the nevertheless invited animosity of others."[37] Paranoid subjects may even "take pride in what they perceive as their independence and objectivity." They externalize blame for conflict and behave rigidly, attempting to impose discipline. They fear being shamed or criticized; isolate themselves, avoiding intimacy; and experience difficulty in handling stress.[38] Their behaviors are shaped not only by patients' actual sickness, but also by their unforgiving, revengeful, distrusting, proud, self-righteous, and jealous—in sum, sinful—attitudes and behaviors. In such cases, an "antivenom" in Socratic dialogues is emphasizing the biblical duty to forgive seven times seventy-seven times. In promoting forgiveness, pastoral healers need to be nonintrusive, careful to avoid discussing particular paranoid interpretations, and to speak only in terms of generalities (like "forgive us our trespasses, as we forgive those who trespass against us" or "those who forgive receive forgiveness"). The internal reward of resembling Jesus when forgiving is for committed believers

an uplifting reward, especially if their forgiveness is reciprocated by love, appreciation, and gratitude. Patients' readiness to make peace with alleged persecutors usually marks the turning point in their healing process.

(8) In nonpsychotic patients, therapy may also be focused on problem-solving, compromising with alleged enemies, and giving the paranoid person assurances about being accepted, appreciated, respected, and loved—or at least fairly treated—even by their alleged enemies. In nonpsychotic paranoid conditions, it often helps to strike a *quid pro quo* deal, such as "if you forgive me this, then I will forgive you that." Since paranoid reasoning is an extremely unpleasant and painful mental condition, many believers feel a peak experience, almost a theophany, when they are internally released from their tormenting paranoid suspicions.

(9) In recuperating psychotic patients and people with nonpsychotic paranoid conditions, their ability to observe their alleged enemies in a biblical, loving, nonjudgmental, and forgiving perspective is a test of their faith. Therefore, their strength of faith (measurable in the ability to overcome suspicions) positively correlates to their healing. Analysing biblical examples of individuals like Jesus' disciples, who suffered even more injustice than the patient allegedly suffered, may help demonstrate the power of Christian faith and love. Resolving conflict in a biblical spirit often heals better than medicines, demonstrating the previously-discussed correlation between mental healing and spiritual healing.

(10) It is usually difficult for guarded, enigmatic, and introverted people healed of delusional contents of mind, and also patients with nondelusional ideas, to acknowledge their previous delusional or overvalued ideas. After their treatment is completed, they typically need time, sometimes years, to process their distress. This ought to be made as painless for them as possible. So long as they are uncomfortable talking about their previous paranoid condition, ex-patients ought not be challenged, examined, or tested by nonprofessionals.

(11) The reintegration of people with paranoid reactions into the community is simple. Taking an attitude that nothing happened while avoiding reviewing or renewing previous confrontations is sufficient. This is similarly the case with people suffering from a paranoid personality disorder, who

nevertheless may project their suspicions onto innocent situations; for their integration into the church community, annoying, upsetting, or provoking situations ought to be minimized as much as possible. In people suffering from paranoia or paranoid schizophrenia, integration is only possible if their conditions are well-controlled by medication. If they are not taking medication regularly (which becomes evident through their behaviors), some paranoid ideas may resurface, making integration into the community possible at a formal level only. The focus in these cases is then on including them in prayer, liturgy, and the sacraments, which are of paramount help. When relapse occurs, it is in the best interest of the patients and the church community to seek professional help. Relapse hinders integration, but in such cases, patients, even delusional believers, still find refuge in Jesus, who accepts and loves them as they are.

Notes

[1] DSM-5. *Diagnostic and Statistical Manual of the American Psychiatric Association* (2013), 50.

[2] Benjamin James Sadock, Virginia Alcott Sadock, and Pedro Ruiz, *Kaplan and Sadock's Synopsis of Psychiatry: Behavioral Sciences/Clinical Psychiatry*, 11th ed. (Philadelphia, PA: Wolters Kluwer, 2015), 301–23.

[3] Ibid., 311.

[4] Benjamin James Sadock and Virginia Alcott Sadock, *Kaplan and Sadock's Synopsis of Psychiatry: Behavioral Sciences/Clinical Psychiatry*, 10th ed. (Philadelphia, PA: Wolters Kluwer, 2007), 483.

[5] Ibid., 483.

[6] Srboljub Stojiljkovic, *Psihijatrija sa Medicinskom Psihologijom* (Belgrade: Medicinska Knjiga, 1975), 244.

[7] Sadock, Sadock, and Ruiz, *Kaplan and Sadock's Synopsis of Psychiatry*, 11th ed. 307–9.

[8] DSM-5, 47.

[9] Sadock, Sadock, and Ruiz, *Kaplan and Sadock's Synopsis of Psychiatry*, 11th ed. 327–9

[10] Ibid., 323.

[11] Linda Seligman and Laurie W. Reichenberg, *Selecting Effective Treatments* (Hoboken, NJ: John Wiley & Sons, 2014), 425.

[12] David H. Barlow (ed.), *Clinical Handbook of Psychological Disorders: A Step-by-Step Treatment Manual* (New York: The Guilford Press, 2008), 463.

[13] Seligman and Reichenberg, *Selecting Effective Treatments*, 410.

[14] Ibid., 418.

[15] Ibid., 412.

[16] Barlow, *Clinical Handbook of Psychological Disorders*, 470.

[17] Seligman and Reichenberg, *Selecting Effective Treatments*, 426.

[18] Ibid., 418.

[19] Barlow, *Clinical Handbook of Psychological Disorders*, 470.

[20] Viktor E. Frankl, *The Doctor and the Soul, From Psychotherapy to Logotherapy* (New York: Vintage Books, 1973), 208–9.

[21] Seligman and Reichenberg, *Selecting Effective Treatments*, 417.

[22] Ibid., 411.

[23] DSM-5, 45.

[24] DSM-5, 322.

[25] DSM-5, 155.

[26] Sadock, Sadock, and Ruiz, *Kaplan and Sadock's Synopsis of Psychiatry*, 11th ed. 330–6.

[27] Sadock and Sadock, *Kaplan and Sadock's Synopsis of Psychiatry*, 10th ed. 506.

[28] Ibid. 506

[29] Sadock, Sadock, and Ruiz, *Kaplan and Sadock's Synopsis of Psychiatry*, 11th ed. 332–6.

[30] Ibid., 744–6.

[31] DSM-5, 151–2.

[32] Sadock, Sadock, and Ruiz, *Kaplan and Sadock's Synopsis of Psychiatry*, 11th ed. 446–50.

[33] Sandor Hodi, *Kongresszus Abbaziaban, A Titokzatos EN nyomaban* (Ada, Serbia, Szechenyi Istvan Strategiakutato Tarsasag, 2014) 229.

[34] Seligman and Reichenberg, *Selecting Effective Treatments*, 423.

[35] Ibid., 423.

[36] Ibid.

[37] Ibid., 354.

[38] Ibid., 356.

CHAPTER TWELVE

MOOD DISORDERS AND
THEIR PASTORAL TREATMENT

The mind is like an orchestra of many instruments, all with their role in playing the symphony of consciousness. In mood disorders, mania and depression—one emotional instrument—overwhelms all other instruments. Mania is not—as often used in popular terminology—a state of mind characterized by "too high" a level of mood, nor is depression a state of mind characterized by "too low" a level of mood. Rather, in mania as well as depression, there is an excess of mental energy. In mania, the overwhelming emotions are polarized toward euphoria, while in depression they are inclined toward sadness.

In healthy people, emotions occasionally influence judgment. However, in individuals with mood disorders, emotions pathologically (i.e., almost irresistibly) overpower the executive functions needed for sound appreciative and discretional judgment. While psychotic people violate Jesus' main commands given in Mark 12:29–31 because of sick cognitions, manic and depressed patients do so because of uncontrollable, sick emotions.

12.1 Manic and Hippomanic Disorders

The DSM-5[1] characterizes mania with increased energy, inflated self-esteem, grandiosity, a decreased need to sleep, talkativeness, fast-moving ideas, distractibility, and increased activity lasting at least one week. Hippomania has the same but less prominent signs. There is only a quantitative difference between mania and hippomania.

Euphoria, the main characteristic of mania, can be defined as happiness without sufficient reason. It dominates mental functioning, causing inappropriate laughing, joking, and singing as well as nonstop, fast-paced talking with frequent topic changes and fragmented thoughts. As mania increases, speech becomes louder, less articulated, faster, and less coherent. However, as Sadock, Sadock, and Ruiz's description notes,[2] manic people are not happy; they have a feeling that objects and people are "running away from them" and they cannot capture them. This makes them irritable, with a low tolerance for frustration, leading to anger and hostility. For this reason, around 75 percent of manic patients are threatening or violent. Their judgment is distorted by powerful emotions. They break laws and can be sexually provocative, aggressive, and uncontrolled. They are in a permanent state of action, organizing activities and proposing radical changes, looking for avenues in which to invest their surplus of energy. They are often seen with their clothing neglected and dirty, their hands full of things, and their mouths filling with food faster than they can chew and swallow. Their thinking is quick, their memory vivid, and their attention span short.

There are different levels of mania. Hippomania can be an introduction to mania or a form of functioning for a hyperactive person who often overvalues their abilities and has significant ego inflation. In delirious mania, the emotions are elevated to extreme levels, and confusion, extreme agitation, threatening illusions, and defensiveness against imagined dangers are also present. However, manic episodes, after a rapid onset, often evolve toward depression. In contemporary understanding, manic episodes most often occur in the context of bipolar disorder, periodically giving way to depressive episodes, with or without periods of well-balanced emotional functioning between extreme mood swings. In this context, it is especially hard to treat bipolar disorder with quick and intensive changes in mood regulation.

Pastoral Considerations

(1) Except for counselling, hypomania most often does not require strenuous healing. On the contrary, in people suffering from mania (and especially agitated or delirious mania), the first task of pastoral care is to assist the patient in finding adequate psychiatric help as soon as possible. Family members may initially be uncooperative, mostly because of their perceived loyalty to the patient or because of "the discomfort of talking about family or couple issues in front of a stranger."[3] This usually improves, however, as the manic symptoms progress.

(2) Patients often resist treatment, especially "interventions that require them to take more responsibility for their behavior."[4] Since their self-criticism is decreased and the ego is inflated, they feel powerful, successful, and competent and therefore often deny any need for help. They may even reject necessary medication since they prefer feeling manic to euthymic. In such cases, therapists may "use therapeutic alliance as a mood stabilizer"[5] to sustain the cooperation of the patient.

(3) Meaningful counselling in periods when "euphoria and grandiosity increase resistance to the idea that treatment is necessary"[6] is not possible. In such periods, medication plays the main role in healing, and the role of the pastoral healer is rather passive, nondirective, and inclined to listening rather than talking, giving the patient an opportunity to express and ventilate their overwhelming emotionality.

(4) The purposes of pastoral and professional healing in cases of mania are often similar—aimed at evoking patients' self-criticism and self-discipline, which are preconditions of a sound reality judgment. They are also both concerned with convincing patients who are directed by their emotional exuberance and feelings of omniscience and omnipotence about the limits and boundaries of their freedom and competence. The ways that professional and pastoral healing achieve these goals, however, are different.

(5) While the goals of professional therapy include "treatment

compliance: alleviating acute symptoms; remedying any occupational, interpersonal, or other lifestyle problems that have resulted from the disorder; and preventing or minimizing future episodes,"[7] pastoral healing, in context of a Socratic dialogue, aims to help Christian patients move from a mind-set of "I feel good about myself" to "God and my neighbours feel good with me." Pastoral healing facilitates a shift from the perception of being "like God, knowing good and evil" (Gen. 3:5), a common symptom of manic disorder, to accepting the feedback of Jesus, family members, and neighbours about the subject's behavior as accurate. This effort emphasizes the words of Mark 12:29–31: "Love the Lord your God with all your heart and all your strength," and "Love your neighbour as yourself."

(6) In the church community, hippomanic and recuperating manic people are often full of energy, initiative, and ideas, inspiring, mobilizing, and leading others in a variety of activities. They are seldom tired but can make others tired through their expectations of them. Pastoral healers ought to be aware that other members of the congregations rarely have the energy to follow such hyperactive people's pace. It may help to give such people an opportunity to apply their energy in meaningful ways (doing physically demanding activities, starting with tasks like mowing the lawn and making small repairs). Conscious, intentional, and diligent critical self-monitoring can achieve grandiose effects.

> A young priest in a village community with a small population was renting a warehouse adapted to worship. The ambitious young priest, tirelessly lobbying, succeeded in mobilizing not only his parishioners but also schools, sporting clubs, and local businesses to help build a church for the village. He worked endlessly, outperforming other volunteers in building the church. His hands were calloused, his posture was hunched, and his back hurt, but in three years the village church was completed, and it was a spectacular structure. People came from neighbouring cities just to see it. However, his unconventional behavior had gained the priest a lot of enemies. He was accused by the local bishop of "spending sprees." When summoned to an internal examination, the young priest revealed that he had been diagnosed as hypomanic and "prone to hyperactivity" and had

decided to intentionally use his energy surplus for meaningful purposes. The local bishop commended him for "using his psychological disadvantage for a spiritual advantage."

(7) Recuperated manic people often go to the opposite extreme and feel embarrassed by their previous acting out, spending sprees, sexualized behaviors, foolish business enterprises, and boastful and arrogant behaviors. Pastoral healing may help patients in this position to clarify their mania as sickness and not a sin—not a reason for shame for people of faith. However, a sudden shift toward sadness and self-accusations, low self-esteem, guilt, and passivity may be an indication of the patient's mood evolving toward depression, which indicates the need for an urgent professional consultation.

(8) From a pastoral perspective, the behavior of people suffering from prominent mood disorders is sick rather than sinful. Patients therefore have little or no responsibility for their acting-out behaviors. As in psychoses, to assess the responsibility of such people is the prerogative of God.

In latent or subclinical forms of mood disorders, however, as the previous example demonstrates, the healthy aspects of the personality are able to efficiently direct, control, and supervise excessive emotions.

(9) Effective preventive counselling has not yet been fully developed and proven in practice. The best method of prevention for reoccurring mania is being monitored by professionals, family members, or friends; taking preventive medication; and, above all, in people of faith, self-monitoring "how God and neighbours perceive me." This latter method may be akin to "dying to one's self" in certain patients since such self-reflective behavior may be painful.

(10) While manic and hippomanic disorders (e.g., bipolar disorder, formerly called manic-depression) may pose unique and significant challenges to professional and pastoral healers, we should remember that Jesus dealt with both extremes in his public ministry when he healed disease and behavioral disorders. He healed those who lived in the shadows and those with dropsy, hopelessness, and despair, and even raised people from the dead. On the other hand, he healed those who were possessed or suffered from mental disorders on our continuum of sin and sickness, such as the

wild Gadarene demoniacs chained to tombs (Matthew 8:28–34). There is no part of the continuum that is beyond the reach of pastoral healers trying to follow Jesus in his compassionate love.

12.2 Depressive Disorders

As noted, depressive disorders are characterized by intensified emotionality that is polarized toward sadness. With an understanding of the cause, treatment, duration, and outcome of episodes, it is possible to differentiate between three types of depression: major depression, persistent depressive disorder (dysthymia), and adjustment disorder with depressed mood.

Major depressive disorder is characterized, according to the DSM-5,[8] by sadness, diminished interest, weight loss, sleeplessness, slower psychomotor (or restlessness), fatigue, loss of energy, feelings of guilt, decreased concentration, and suicidal ideation almost every day for two-week durations.

Persistent depressive disorder (also called dysthymia and neurotic depression) is characterized by durations of at least two years, with most days seeing a depressed mood, poor appetite (or overeating), sleeplessness (or too much sleep), low energy, tiredness, low self-esteem, poor concentration, and hopelessness.

Adjustment disorder with depressive mood is characterized by out-of-proportion sadness, fearfulness, and hopelessness, causing a significant impairment in functioning and appearing within three months of trauma.[9]

Let us discuss the clinical features of these types of depression in detail.

(1) Major depression occurs, in Sadock and Sadock's[10] description, in some 12 percent of the population and is more common in women. It can start as early as age five and does not begin after the age of fifty. Genetics play a role. If one parent is depressed, the likelihood of their children suffering depression is 25 percent. If, however, both parents suffer from depression, the likelihood is 50 percent. Major depression mostly occurs, though, because of endogenous reasons—that is, a lack of norepinephrine, serotonin, or dopamine needed for mood regulation. According to Kaplan and Sadock's textbook, "About 10–15 percent of all depressed patients commit suicide, and about two thirds have suicidal ideation."[11] Living as single or in

a noncommitted relationship increases the risk of depression. Individuals with major depression feel sad, see no purpose in life, and suffer irrational guilt. Accordingly, they lack motivation, feel powerless, and withdraw from their work and everyday activities. They may talk slowly, in a low voice, or in short sentences, gradually sinking into silence because they see themselves as "not worthy of even talking." Their demeanour reflects their inward experience of unworthiness, guilt, and remorse; they have no initiative, strength, or will to even to live. They seldom laugh, and their faces appear sad, with deep wrinkles. They cry easily or have no energy to cry; have a decreased appetite and frequently reject food and water, causing them to become undernourished; and complain of sleeplessness. They are not interested in their own destinies, and they neglect their hygiene, grooming, and clothing because they "do not deserve it." Delusions are seldom "mood-congruent delusions." Patients might call attention to their own sinfulness, unworthiness, and alleged evil deeds, or accuse themselves of starting world wars, disasters, or all the problems of the world. Their thinking is slow and fixated on painful memories of their own "loss, guilt, suicide and death."[12] They perceive their whole lives as having been full of suffering; or have no energy to reason at all (which is called depressive pseudodementia). Paradoxically, risk of self-harm increases as patients begin their recovery and regain the energy to carry out suicide. Major depressive episodes last for a few weeks or months and then either gradually improve or give way to a new depressive period or hypomanic or manic episode. Psychotherapy is insufficient for treating major depression, and medical help and hospitalization are often needed.

(2) As Kaplan and Sadock's textbook notes,[13] persistent depressive disorder, or dysthymia, affects some 5–6 percent of all people. A typical patient is a younger, unmarried single woman with low income. Dysthymia is an almost constant state of mind, and patients have the feeling that they have always been depressed. The disorder often begins in adolescence. Its most prominent characteristics are not so much sadness as much as guilt, frustration, irritability, disquietude, anger, and a general loss of pleasure in life. In contrast to major depression, in persistent depression in which "the symptoms outnumber the signs," it is a more subjective than objective

depression. There is no psychomotor retardation (as in major depression), and there is no loss of sexual interest or appetite. There may, however, be psychological complaints about them. The person suffering from persistent depressive disorder is angry, hates him- or herself, and is disappointed and full of resentment. This form of depression lasts for years, with ups and downs, resembling "a long-standing, fluctuating, low-grade depression, experienced as a part of the habitual self."[14] It is treatable with medicines and psychotherapy. If dysthymia is combined with major depression, it is considered "double depression."

(3) Reactive depression, or adjustment disorder with depressed mood, is caused by a precisely definable external stressor. For example, if someone were to receive a telephone call informing them that all their family members had died in a traffic accident, then the individual would react to the bad news with reactive depression. The depression is, however, not always congruent with the gravity of the stress. It is a kind of overreaction that, after a certain time period that depends on the kind of trauma (usually nine months), spontaneously recuperates. Accepting and adjusting to the outcome of the incident and discerning new goals, tasks, and purposes to live for helps, even without clinical help; time is the best healer of reactive depression.[15]

Pastoral Considerations

(1) Since ancient times, the first principle in healing has been to "do no harm." It is especially important to heed this warning in treating depression. People with endogenous depression, like all those suffering of mental ailments caused by disordered brain functioning, have little or no control, or responsibility for their symptoms. It would be a mistake to tell a depressed person, "Come on, have fun, enjoy your life!" They try to do this but are unable to. Requests to do impossible tasks deepen their pain. Initially, it may be more helpful to accept the depression. This does not lead to fatalism; it means realizing that depression is a sickness occurring with God's permission that must be endured and with God's help defeated. As St. Paul said,

we may be knocked down, persecuted, and tormented, but we are never abandoned by Jesus (2 Corinthians: 4–9).

(2) We need to note one more caution. As previously mentioned, a basic principle of pastoral healing is evoking meekness, biblical self-criticism, humility, and genuine sorrow for one's sins. The treatment of depression, however, is an exception to this rule. Even mildly depressed people have an increased sensitivity to guilt, and those suffering from major depression always suffer irrational and intense self-accusations and feelings of guilt. Depressed believers are unable to trust God's forgiveness or surrender their feelings of guilt to his mercy. Note that the pastoral healer should never reinforce the false belief or overvalued idea present in most depressive individuals that their mental health challenges are solely caused by lack of discipleship. Efforts to evoke remorse are necessary when faced with genuine sin, but they are counterproductive when addressing the irrational self-accusations of gravely depressed, anxious, or scrupulous people. Therefore, rather than seek to humble the patient, the pastoral healer ought to be Jesus-like and unconditionally supportive. Such a self-esteem-boosting attitude may help depressed people to at least cognitively appreciate that they are objects of God's love just as they are. Jesus' ire was reserved for the Pharisees in his sevenfold indictment of their hypocrisy (Matthew 23:13–16). For most others, his approach was accepting and gentle without losing sight of the justice demanded by the Father.

(3) Interestingly, as Seligman and Reichenberg found, "The therapeutic alliance seems far more important than the intervention strategy in determining the outcomes of treatment for depression." In their study, even the placebo group "demonstrated the significant alleviation of depression, apparently because of the power of a positive therapeutic alliance."[16] Thus, a good personal contact that offers genuine warmth and compassion is often equally important as applied counselling techniques.

(4) Another peculiarity in treating depressive patients is that, since depressed people are passive, therapy should be moderately to highly directive. However, to avoid building up an overvalued dependence in the patient, directedness should be gradually decreased as treatment progresses.[17]

(5) The Socratic dialogue usually used in pastoral healing may take

unexpected directions. All humans, and especially depressed patients, as Corey notes, are "relational beings."[18] The extent to which empathy helps severely depressed people is illustrated by the following anecdotal story.

A depressed lady treated from early summer to November could see from her hospital window the leaves falling from an old oak tree. Every day, one by one, the leaves worsened her depression. She predicted that the last leaf would signal her death. Soon, there were only four, then three, then two, then finally one leaf left. The next day at dawn, she looked with trepidation to find out whether the last leaf had fallen. However, it was still in place. This was a turning point, and her depression rapidly improved. On the day of her discharge, her nurse told her that, on the doctor's order, she had glued a painted paper leaf to the tree. The nurse was quite surprised when the patient revealed that she already knew the trickery. In her file were noted the patient's words: "Since my healing was important to so many people [the staff], I fought to not disappoint them." Here and in other cases, a small act of kindness—a small idea or intervention—can have surprising consequences.

(6) As Seligman and Reichenberg observe, "People who are depressed often have partners with emotional disorders." This "raises the question whether difficult marriages contribute to the incidence of depression or whether people who are depressed select partners with similar traits."[19] Regardless of how one answers this question, a good family life generally helps with healing depression. But as noted, not every family, and not every family treatment, is equal. Emphasizing less the sexual and erotic aspects of love (what depressed people are disabled from) and focusing more on the psychological and spiritual aspects of love (partner relational issues) is the approach of choice in the family treatment of depressed Christians.

(7) People with severe depression, as the saying goes, "suffer tearlessly." In other words, they are unable to cry or express their feelings. In dealing with such inexpressible sadness in depressed people, Barlow suggests "provoking these emotions with the goal of your being able to let the emotion wash over you, to stand beside it, and act out these emotion-driven

behaviors, stripping away those procedures that prevent you from experiencing emotions."[20] In my experience, this method works when used in conjunction with a Socratic dialogue, but only if patients see a purpose to live and suffer for beyond their depressive symptoms. What hurts depressed patients the most is the seeming meaninglessness of their suffering. Viewing their depression as having a purpose they ought to fulfil helps them to imitate Jesus and gives them courage, hope, and joy stronger than depression.

(8) To discern a purpose in depression, patients need to allow the Master (Jesus) to heal in the way he knows is best even if it is not instantaneous or does not conform to their own timetables. In this context, let us recall that even St. Paul had a "thorn in his flesh" and as he noted in 2 Cor. 12:8–10, "Three times I pleaded with the Lord to take it away from me. But he said to me, 'My grace is sufficient for you, for my power is made perfect in weakness'" The thorn in his flesh helped St. Paul, (similar to depression and depressed Christians) to recognize that "When I am weak, then I am strong." The next case study illustrates this.

> A twenty-eight-year-old Orthodox priest was suffering from major depression. The patient was functioning on an almost vegetative level because of his grave suffering. The only activity he could perform was prayer. He then recalled a saying he learned during his theology studies: "Jesus is the closest when you suffer the most." He prayed even more diligently and was surprised when he experienced exactly what the saying predicted. While depressed and completely deprived of every pleasurable experience, he could pray and rely on Jesus more deeply than when he was healthy but distracted from God. He then started to ask Jesus to deepen his depression so he could be closer to him. Paradoxically, by praying to become even more depressed, his depression vanished.

(9) Religious people recuperate from depression more easily if their suffering is placed in a biblical context, such as that of Job 3:19–21: "He throws me into the mud and I am reduced to dust and ashes. I cry out to you, God, but you do not answer; I stand up, but you merely look at me. You turn on me ruthlessly; with the might of your hand you attack me." The experience

Job describes is common to all severely depressed people. However, Job continues to trust his God, and, as verse 33:26 says, "He prays to God and finds favour with him, he sees God's face and shouts for joy; he is restored by God to his righteous state."

As noted, biblical stories did not happen only once in time but are happening again and again in every person's life. Depressed and suffering believers may be encouraged to imitate Job in trusting God and praying with the certainty that they will see God's face.

(10) Believers recuperating from depression may be helped to understand that guilt regularly occurring in depression is, in reality, only an illusion of guilt. It is exaggerated by enslavement to an unforgiving, internal, policeman-like superego instead of a Jesus-like, forgiving, Christian conscience. From a pastoral perspective, depression itself is a call for replacing the worldly "internal punisher" superego with a genuine loving Christian conscience. Such a transition helps the patient to focus on everlasting life lived in union with God, *zoe*, instead of only on *bios*, worldly duties. Shifting perspectives from *bios* to *zoe*, gaining a foretaste of eternal life with God, is for believers the ultimate healer of depression.

(11) It is difficult to imagine any situation in which God would remain silent in response to the prayers of depressed people asking for his help. This is illustrated in Frankl's case study.

> "Sister Michaela suffered from severe depression and had considered suicide. She particularly suffered from guilt based on her belief that as a good Christian her faith should be strong enough to conquer her sickness." Frankl prescribed her medicines and explained, "This kind of depression has a primarily organic cause in the dimension of her body (a biochemical imbalance) a dimension which she has no direct control over and thus bears no responsibility for." After processing this message, she remarked, "I feel at peace with myself and grateful. I have accepted this cross."[21]

Too often, modern Christianity tries to factor out pain and suffering, but the suffering, death, and resurrection of Jesus remain the crux of the faith. It is a paradoxical but empirical truth that healing major depression always correlates with the acceptance of it as one's cross, which faith does not always abolish but always makes easier to carry. Faith allows patients to feel a biblical value in carrying the cross of depression despite all worldly unease.

(12) In persistent depression, and reactive depression, pastoral treatment is focused on healing conscious or unconscious conflicts, frustrations, and traumas by discarding traditional values of the world and identifying a biblical purpose. In this there is a significant difference between healers' approach with believers and their approach with nonbelievers. For example, following Corey's advice, "Perhaps the task of the therapeutic process is to help clients create a value system based on a way of living that is consistent with their way of being."[22] But what, in the context of healing depression, is the authentic human "way of being" that Correy talks about?

> The Dominican friar Jirolamo Savonarola was walking the streets of Florence when, through a window, he unexpectedly spotted a painting of the Virgin Mary standing and crying below the cross of her dead son. Savonarola immediately went to the artist and told him in an angry voice, "Take down and correct your painting immediately!" Yes, the Virgin stood below the cross, but she did not cry. On the contrary, despite all her motherly pain, she was joyful in her heart that Jesus' glory was finally achieving humankind's salvation.[23]

One can agree or disagree with Savonarola's psychological assessment of the Virgin and his theological explanation. Nevertheless, if in our "way of being" we could all firmly trust in God's providence like the Virgin according to Savonarola's understanding, who then would be depressed?

(13) The commonality in all aspects of pastoral healing is encouraging people of faith to use prayer, liturgy, sacraments, and other resources to foster their union with God. Receiving internal encouragement, hope, trust, and optimism that surpasses all human understanding is—to many committed people of faith—as powerful a pastoral medicine as all those previously listed. In a period of severe depression, patients may be coached to participate in church activities, even passively. Even an inactive attendance

in the life of the church often helps with bearing hopeless, helpless, and pessimistic, dysfunctional, depressive beliefs. As long as people belong to the body of Christ, its many parts can silently but synergistically heal. Involvement in activities, from ushering to prayer groups and Bible study groups, helps recuperating patients to experience the collective solidarity of believers, which acts as an antidepressive boost and measure of reality that contrasts with their internal experiences of isolation, helplessness, and hopelessness. As Henry Lubac wrote, in the Church, "Each one in his very being receives of all, and of his very being must give back to all."[24] If it is powerful to demonstrate that depressed believers are appreciated, loved, and lovable, then such a church community is a powerful pastoral healing tool able to give more help than any individual. This is the body of Christ in action.

(14) The church community is the best environment for people of faith suffering from depression. It is the greatest pity that clerics, believers, and the body of Christ in general do not play a more prominent role in healing depressed believers and nonbelievers today. Jesus said that disciples were the light and salt of the earth (Matthew 5:13–16). Disciples are meant to season the world and let their light shine for all men, not hide it under a bushel basket. When believers fail to do this, they overlook countless opportunities to heal others by simply participating in their faith or demonstrating virtues such as kindness, mercy, and understanding.

Notes

[1] DSM-5, *Diagnostic and Statistical Manual of the American Psychiatric Association* (2013), 65–7.

[2] Benjamin James Sadock, Virginia Alcott Sadock, and Pedro Ruiz, *Kaplan and Sadock's Synopsis of Psychiatry: Behavioral Sciences/Clinical Psychiatry*, 11th ed. (Philadelphia, PA: Wolters Kluwer, 2015), 347–86.

[3] David H. Barlow (ed.), *Clinical Handbook of Psychological Disorders: A Step-by-Step Treatment Manual* (New York: The Guilford Press, 2008), 456.

[4] Ibid.

[5] Linda Seligman and Laurie W. Reichenberg, *Selecting Effective Treatments* (Hoboken, NJ: John Wiley & Sons, 2014), 176.

[6] Ibid., 177.

[7] Ibid., 182.

[8] DSM-5, 73.

[9] DSM-5, 97.

[10] Benjamin James Sadock and Virginia Alcott Sadock, *Kaplan and Sadock's Synopsis of Psychiatry: Behavioral Sciences/Clinical Psychiatry*, 10th ed. (Philadelphia, PA: Wolters Kluwer, 2007), 545.

[11] Ibid.

[12] Ibid.

[13] Ibid., 565.

[14] Ibid., 562.

[15] Sadock, Sadock, and Ruiz, *Kaplan and Sadock's Synopsis of Psychiatry*, 11th ed. 446–50.

[16] Seligman and Reichenberg, *Selecting Effective Treatments*, 154.

[17] Ibid., 155.

[18] Gerald Corey, *Theory and Practice of Counseling and Psychotherapy* (Belmont, CA: Thomson/ Brooks/Cole, 2005), 139.

[19] Seligman and Reichenberg, *Selecting Effective Treatments*, 167.

[20] Corey, *Theory and Practice of Counseling and Psychotherapy*, 141.

[21] Maria Marshall and Edward Marshall, *Spiritual Psychotherapy, the Search for Lasting Meaning* (Canada, Ont.: Ottawa Institute of Logotherapy, 2015), 58–9.

[22] Corey, *Theory and Practice of Counseling and Psychotherapy*, 141.

[23] Janos Erdody, *Requiem Firenzeert* (Budapest: Szepmuveszeti Kiado,1977), 107.

[24] Henri De Lubac, *Catholicism, Christ and the Common Destiny of Man* (San Francisco: Ignatius Press, 1988), 333.

CHAPTER THIRTEEN

Anxiety Disorders and Their Pastoral Treatment

In the large group of anxiety disorders, the DSM-5[1] lists ten distinct disorders. We will overview only the most relevant ones and discuss the treatment commonalities at the end of the chapter.

13.1 Panic Disorder and Agoraphobia

The most typical sign of *panic disorder* is reoccurring panic attacks. The DSM-5 defines a *panic attack* as "an abrupt surge of intense fear or intense discomfort that reaches a peak within minutes." Panic attacks are associated with symptoms like pounding and racing of the heart, sweating, trembling, shaking, shortness of breath, a fear of choking, chest pain, nausea, dizziness, chills or numbness, feelings of unreality (as if being lost in space and time), depersonalization (experiencing being detached from oneself), a fear of going crazy, and a fear of dying. After receiving medical help or experiencing a spontaneous recovery the horror vanishes, but there is permanent concern about future panic attacks and losing control.[2] Between 3 percent and 5.65 percent of the general population suffer panic attacks. A panic attack begins as "a ten-minute period of rapidly increasing symptoms" and "generally lasts twenty to thirty minutes and rarely more than an hour."

13.2 Specific Phobia and Social Phobia

A *specific phobia* is characterized in the DSM-5[3] by irrational, out-of-proportion anxiety, fear, or horror and avoiding the precisely definable fear-provoking situations for at least six months. As its name denotes, it signifies an excessive, almost constant fear of reoccurring panic attacks, occasionally evolving into horror and appearing in specific harmless situations, such as open spaces or certain social situations. As Kaplan and Sadock's textbook describes, phobic terror is most often connected to a panicky fear (escalating to a level of horror) caused by a feeling of imminent fainting, collapsing, losing control, dying, or complete annihilation; it affects between 10–25 percent of the population. Social phobia is characterized by fear and avoidance of social situations in which one could be scrutinized or tested. A panicky fear of embarrassment in such social situations affects between 3–13 percent of the population. Its aetiology is unknown. The other most common forms of specific phobias are agoraphobia (fear of open places), acrophobia (fear of heights), aichmophobia (fear of sharp objects), ailurophobia (fear of cats), hydrophobia (fear of water), claustrophobia (fear of enclosed spaces), mysophobia (fear of dirt), pyrophobia (fear of fire), thanatophobia (fear of death), xenophobia (fear of strangers), and zoophobia (fear of animals). The most common form of phobic disorder is agoraphobia, affecting some 2–6 percent of the population, marked with anxiety (lasting for at least six months) about using mass transportation, being in open spaces, being in crowds, and being outside of the home alone. Fear is triggered by a perceived impossibility of escape or getting help.[4]

In contrast to panic attacks, which appear unexpectedly, specific phobias are always connected to a precisely definable thing or situation. Thus, when the reason for the fear is unknown and its appearance unpredictable, we assume we are dealing with a panic disorder. Conversely, when the reasons for the fear are known and predictable, then we are talking about a specific phobia. What is common to all phobias is a lasting anxiety (as a permanent personality characteristic). People suffering from phobic disorders are aware of the irrational quality of their fear or that their fear is out of proportion to the danger the situation may pose, but it is experienced as such an imminent, life-threatening disaster (in the case of specific phobias) or a feeling of being scrutinized, assessed, judged, and finally humiliated (in the case of a social phobia) that the fear threatens to evolve into debilitating and paralyzing horror. Patients therefore avoid particular situations in which the panic will strike. Those suffering agoraphobia avoid open places, for example, while those suffering social phobia avoid communicating with unknown people. If the person escapes the cause of the phobic reaction, the fear disappears, but the anxiety remains as a constant warning.[5]

13.3 Generalized Anxiety Disorder

The DSM-5 defines *generalized anxiety disorder* as worrying, present for more days in the preceding six months than not, connected to a multiplicity of activities (in personal life, school, leisure, vocational, relational, work, choices, making decisions, taking responsibility, and moral or religious issues) and manifesting in restlessness, fatigue, concentration problems, irritability, muscle tension, and sleep problems.[6] As Kaplan and Sadock note, we may suspect generalized anxiety disorder in people "who seem to be anxious about almost everything." They also specify that "the disorder is more common in women, and it affects approximately 3 to 8 percent of population. Often the disorder coexists with other forms of phobic disorders.... Ninety percent of patients suffering from generalized anxiety disorder also suffer from some other mental condition." People with generalized anxiety disorder are in a permanent "flight or fight" mode, without bursts of panic (as in phobic disorder). Their anxiety is sustained, seamlessly flowing throughout all of their life events, and is periodically excessive. Their worrisome behavior is "difficult to control and is associated with somatic symptoms, such as muscle tension, irritability, difficulty sleeping and restlessness, and essentially interferes with the person's functioning. Common problems are cardiac and gastrointestinal problems, and headache and cognitive problems (like forgetfulness), which often motivate people suffering from this disorder to seek medical help."[7] Deeper psychological analysis of people suffering from generalized anxiety disorder most often uncovers specific causes such as unresolved or tormenting problems, conflicting responsibilities, unfulfilled duties, procrastinated tasks, ambivalent attitudes, insecurities, division and fighting, tension between how they live and how they ought to live, a feeling of guilt, moral conflicts, or existential suffering because of the perception of meaningless living.

The perception of a meaningless mindset in patients is not an easy hurdle for pastoral healers to surmount. But the meaning of the Incarnation is that Christ entered human history to show us that every life has meaning, purpose, and a destiny, both now and in the world to come.

13.4 Obsessive Compulsive Disorder (OCD)

The DSM-5[8] defines *obsessive compulsive disorder* by the presence of obsessions and compulsions. Obsessions are recurring and compelling thoughts, urges, and images that are intrusive and unwanted, causing anxiety and distress. Compulsions are repetitive behaviors which an individual feels driven to perform (for example, repeated handwashing). Patients are aware of the irrational nature of their unwanted thoughts, fears, and behaviors. Around 2–3 percent of the population suffers from this disorder. Its aetiology is unknown. Empirically, it is known that dysfunctional families, conflict, and interpersonal difficulties increase patients' OCD symptoms.

In the psychodynamic understanding, like everything in nature, anxiety disorders are the product of a cause and effect process. The symptoms may seem senseless but nevertheless have a purpose. They are symbolic, mystical, or allegorical expressions of an unconscious desire and the compulsive defence against it. That is, symptoms such as in OCD are an expression of a compromise between the satisfaction of forbidden (disgusting, shameful, or sinful) desires and their symbolic rejection. This kind of simultaneous occurrence of mutually exclusive feelings (like the unconscious desire and its conscious rejection) is called ambivalence. For example, in the compulsion to wash one's hands fifty to one hundred times a day, the dirty hands symbolize a sinful behavior, which is unconsciously desired. However, the sinful behavior is rejected, and its rejection is consciously demonstrated by symbolic cleansing. The more a sinful behavior is unconsciously desired, the more compulsory its symbolic rejection in the obsessive washing of hands will be. The compulsory action of washing hands therefore expresses the need for a clean conscience. One could therefore ask why such a person does not "wash their conscience," that is, go to confession. The reason is that illicit desires are suppressed in the subconscious mind. The person is not aware of the desires, so they are unable to confess them. Acknowledgement of the need to confess would require acknowledgement of guilt, which the ritual of handwashing is protecting the individual from. It is a vicious circle which calls for compassion and understanding from those around them.

OCD patients maintain an ambivalent and compromising attitude in almost every area of behavior. They are often, however, uncooperative with treatment because they "become invested in maintaining the symptomatology because of secondary gains." People suffering OCD receive countless secondary gains thanks to their disorder. Their family, friends, and even coworkers may change their routines to accommodate them.[9]

People suffering from OCD sometimes first feel a need to resist their compulsions and obsessions. However, with the passing of time they rationalize their obsessions and compulsions, even making a virtue of washing their hands countless times a day.[10] Intentional refraining from fulfilling obsessions and compulsions causes a paniclike fear or paralyzing horror. In general, resisting obsessions (i.e., thoughts) is less tormenting than resisting compulsions (i.e., deeds).

Pastoral Considerations

(1) Not every anxiety ought to be healed. As Corey explains, anxiety is not always the sign of a disorder but sometimes of an opportunity to grow. "We experience this anxiety as we become increasingly aware of our freedom and the consequences of accepting or rejecting that freedom."[11]

(2) Anxious patients are usually hesitant to start treatment since they have a history of unsuccessful professional contact in attempting to heal their disorder. Sometimes they are resistant to or even angry at being referred for psychological treatment because they are convinced it is a medical disorder. Professionals must therefore first communicate to patients

that treatment outcomes are often promising, especially with early intervention and patients' commitment to treatment. The purpose of professional treatment is to convince patients that their disorder is not life-threatening and help them realize their mistaken beliefs about the alarming signs of the physical sensations they experience (like fear of fainting, heart attack, or imminent dying.)[12] Patients' motivation in treatment is often dependent on their grasping the cause of their irrational anxiety, which is not always easy to explain.

(3) Accordingly, let us focus on understanding psychological dynamics in anxiety disorders. In what is probably the best-known case study in literature, William Shakespeare (1564–1616) described the counterproductive effects of anxious insecurity (which we would today diagnose as a generalized anxiety disorder) in Hamlet's story. As the story goes, after receiving the message from a ghost about his father's assassination, Hamlet spends his life in doubt about whether the received information is credible. He explains the reasons for his insecurity with following:

> The spirit I have seen
> May be a (devil,)
> and the (devil) hath power
> To assume a pleasing shape; yea, and perhaps,
> Out of my weakness and my melancholy,
> As he is very potent with such spirits,
> Abuses me to damn me. (2.2.627–32)[13]

In short, Hamlet is not sure whether it was his father's ghost or the devil who approached him. If it was his father's ghost, then Hamlet is obliged to undertake bloody revenge, but if it was the devil, then giving in to the request will cause his doom. Namely, in the popular beliefs of the sixteenth and seventeenth centuries, purgatorial ghosts occasionally returned to the world of the living, asking for prayers to be released from purgatory. If the ghost that Hamlet encountered were really the purgatorial ghost of his father, it definitely would not have demanded a bloody revenge. For Christians the answer is clear—the ghost requiring a bloody revenge must have been Luciferian—but not so for Hamlet, whose anxiety reflects the religious, philosophical, moral, and political ambivalences of his times. Hamlet is therefore ambivalent. His Christian conscience does not permit revenge, but the devil's message, void of any scruples, motivates him to do just that. He experiences doubt, insecurity, and hesitation over whether he should behave according to his Christian conscience or worldly behavior patterns. The conflict between his Christian conscience and his superego-type conscience is the source of Hamlet's mental condition so masterfully depicted by Shakespeare.

(4) Like Hamlet, contemporary anxious patients hesitate. Their "insight into the senselessness of their beliefs, doubts and panicky fears often fluctuates ... [so] patients readily acknowledge that their beliefs are irrational, but they still cause a marked distress."[14] They also experience anxious insecurity similar to Hamlet's. Of course, instead of the ghost of Shakespeare's narrative, a policeman-like conscience is what spoils contemporary patients' peace of mind. For the anxious person's strict, unforgiving conscience, "Having a thought about an action is like performing the action"[15] in that it results in guilt, anxiety, panic, obsessions, and compulsions. Other symptoms are consequences of the intrapersonal conflict caused by such irrational guilt. In my clinical experience, guilty feelings promoted not by a Christian conscience but a strict and unforgiving "internal inhibitor" causes anxiety problems more often than genuine sinful estrangement from God, for which forgiveness is always readily available by repentance.

(6) Barlow gives the account of a real patient suffering from paralyzing anxiety attacks.

My husband really does not understand. He thinks it is all in my head. He gets angry at me for not being able to cope. He resents having to drive me around and doing things for the kids that I used to do. We argue a lot, because he comes home tired and frustrated from work, only to be frustrated more by the problems I'm having. But I can't do anything without him. I'm so afraid that I will collapse into a helpless wreck without him, or that I will be alone for the rest of my life. As cruel as he can be, I feel sage around him because he always has everything under control. He always knows what to do.[16]

Professional treatment in this case would be focused on alleviating the symptoms of the lady's anxiety with sedatives, processing her anxiety either by focusing on childhood experiences (psychoanalytic therapy), recent mal-adaptive behaviors (cognitive behavioral therapy), or establishing a future purpose for her to strive for (existential therapies). Pastoral healers would be focused on family therapy, using a Socratic dialogue in helping the couple in imitating Christ. This would specifically mean supporting their Christian consciences to bring them to a place of offering each other biblical forgive-ness, respect, appreciation, encouragement, praise, hope, and other gifts reflecting Godly love. Success in this would resolve the cause of the woman's paralyzing anxiety and the consequent symptoms of her OCD and phobic or panic attacks, which all express in symbolic language, gestures, drives, and behaviors. The couple's basic problem: mutual estrangement from Jesus.

(7) There are also shortcuts to defeating anxiety. In healing anxiety dis-orders, Frankl often used "paradox intention" (the intentional evoking of fear to paradoxically defeat it), which is illustrated by one of his case studies.

One day a patient "happened to meet his chief on the street and, as he extended his hand in greeting, he noticed that he was perspiring more than usual. The next time he was in a similar situation he expected to perspire again, and this anticipatory anxiety precipitated excessive sweat-ing. It was a vicious circle; hyperhidrosis provoked hidrophobia and hidrosis, in turn producing hyperhydrosis." Frankl advised his patient to challenge his fear, and "in the event that his anticipatory anxiety should recur, to resolve deliberately to show those whom he was with at the time how much he could really sweat." A week later he returned to report that whenever he met anyone who triggered his anticipatory anxiety, he said to himself, "I sweat only a quart before, but now I am going to pour out at least ten quarts!" And his anxiety was healed.

As Frankl comments, "I do not wish to convey the impression that paradoxical intention is a panacea."[17] Not every patient in every situation has the courage to challenge their fear. The paradox intention can be successful only in patients who have the courage and determination to do exactly what they are uncomfortable with. It is the ultimate expression of human freedom which gives one the ability to conquer the fear of even fear itself.

(8) As Seligman and Reichenberg note, exposure to fear is the most efficient way to resolve phobic fears. In this context, some authors recommend a treatment in which fears are aroused and defeated in a single session.[18] However, paradox intention in a pastoral context is infinitely more than a simple behavioral intervention; it is also concerned about a fundamental change in attitude. It calls on the patient to trust God, who enables them to take a new stand—a courageous and self-confident posture toward anxiety based on biblical courage. People of faith releasing themselves from the bondage of anxiety may even forge a virtue from seeking and playing with anxiety, not avoiding but provoking it, proving to themselves that if "God is with me, nothing can hurt me." Take the following case, for example.

> A thirty-eight-year-old lady suffering from anxiety about committing suicide challenged her fear, saying to herself, "Yes, I am going to kill myself. I will jump from a bridge into the ocean. But to be sure I die, before jumping I shall drink poison. And to be even more sure, I will hang myself from the bridge, to be strangled before being poisoned and drowned. And to be even surer still, I will spill gasoline on myself and set myself on fire before I hang myself." As the lady rehearsed the sequence in her mind, she began laughing, gaining self-confidence. Soon, she was no longer afraid of suicidal ideas but instead able to manipulate and ridicule them. She said to herself, "Come anxiety, come fear, come horror—let me see whether you can disturb my peace from God!"

Such paradoxical provoking of fear with the purpose of defeating it can be done while sitting comfortably in an armchair for a duration of four to five minutes, five to six times a day. When courageously challenging anxiety, panicking will not occur. On the contrary, patients find "the more I challenge fear, the less it can hurt me." If one wholeheartedly trusts in God, then their attitude toward the anxiety changes. A Christian's surrendering to God and trusting his providence mobilizes courage and generates biblical security stronger than anxiety. As Scripture notes, "But perfect love drives out fear" (1 John 4:18).

(9) Concerning OCD, a similar approach may help.

Consider the case of a twelve-year-old boy who was obsessed with lighting and throwing away matches. He had already caused three fires, and his treatment was ordered by the medical health officer. The healing did not progress well. His obsession with fire seemed unstoppable. Finally, his mother was asked to bring a thousand matches to the next session. In the backyard of the office, the boy was told, "Here are the matches. Now you can light them as much as you want." The boy lit about forty matches and then slowed down. After a few more, he stopped, about to cry. He was no longer enjoying himself and wanted to stop. At this point he was told, "Okay, you can stop now. But your mom will take home the remaining matches, and if you light even one more match, you will have to light all of the rest." This was a turning point. His mom took home the matches and put them on the fireplace, but the young patient never again obsessively lit and threw away another match.

What psychologically happened in the young patient's heart and mind?

Just as eating the forbidden apple was desirable for Adam and Eve, so too was lighting the matches for the young boy. The more it was forbidden, the more it became desirable. However, when the young patient got what he wanted, he realized that burning matches was not so desirable, and its attractiveness was then gone. The evil lost its allure, and with the devil gone, so to speak, the angel could come forth in the young patient's behaviors and journeying further in his discipleship.

(10) As Barlow notes, "The suffering associated with social anxiety disorder is often minimized as a common trait in the population that does not require a heavy artillery of formalized treatment interventions."[19] However, "People suffering from social phobia—especially those staying permanently

in their comfort zones—tend to significantly decrease their personal, professional, occupational and vocational opportunities: they are frequently unemployed or underemployed and often unmarried."[20] Pastoral help focuses on healing the concurrent symptoms (most often depressive) by restructuring social attitudes and through assertiveness training and other interventions. All these, however, are means to one fundamental change: growth in discipleship, a shift in focus from social outcomes to God.

(11) Pastoral healers typically heal the tormenting fear and powerlessness of anxiety disorders by evoking what we could call (paraphrasing Stefanic and Henrion's book title) "the defiant power of the human spirit."[21] Although the patient's mind is enslaved by anxiety, their soul is not. The soul-inspired Christian conscience can ensure the patient, "If God is for us, who is against us?" (Rom. 8:31). Let me illustrate what I mean with a biblical example we repeatedly use.

Around the year AD 67, imprisoned and aware of his coming execution, St. Paul was not fearful, anxious, or depressed, but wrote to his disciples, "Rejoice in the Lord always. I will say again: Rejoice! Let your gentleness be evident to all. The Lord is near. Do not be anxious about anything, but in everything, by prayer and petition, with thanksgiving, present your requests to God" (Phil. 4:4). St. Paul's ego, his personality committed to his Christian conscience, gave him the courage and optimism, despite the hopelessness and helplessness of his situation, to overcome all traces of hesitation, insecurity, anxiety, panic, or obsessive horror. This is what only a genuine commitment to the Christian conscience and Jesus can give. This is what Hamlet needed and what real people like him still need.

(12) Pastoral healers need to help their patients realize that building the kingdom of God is associated with their anxieties, problems, and pain. To paraphrase and supplement Barlow's observation, a "respectful, understanding, encouraging, explicit, and challenging therapist [who helps Christians to be worthy of suffering for the sake of God's kingdom] is more likely to achieve a successful outcome than a permissive, tolerant therapist."[22] Thus, pastoral healers must be biblically courageous, confident, optimistic, and unselfish in order to be able to help anxious patients become the same in defeating fears and anxieties.

Notes

1. DSM-5. *Diagnostic and Statistical Manual of the American Psychiatric Association* (2013), 119–20.

2. Ibid., 119.

3. Ibid., 116.

4. Linda Seligman and Laurie W. Reichenberg, *Selecting Effective Treatments* (Hoboken, NJ: John Wiley & Sons, 2014), 202.

5. Benjamin James Sadock, Virginia Alcott Sadock, and Pedro Ruiz, *Kaplan and Sadock's Synopsis of Psychiatry: Behavioral Sciences/Clinical Psychiatry*, 11th ed. (Philadelphia, PA: Wolters Kluwer, 2015), 387–417

6. DSM-5, 122.

7. Sadock, Sadock, and Ruiz, *Kaplan and Sadock's Synopsis of Psychiatry*, 11th ed. 622.

8. DSM-5, 129.

9. Sadock, Sadock, and Ruiz, *Kaplan and Sadock's Synopsis of Psychiatry*, 11th ed. 604.

10. Ibid., 604.

11. Gerald Corey, *Theory and Practice of Counseling and Psychotherapy* (Belmont, CA: Thomson/Brooks/Cole, 2005), 145.

12. Seligman and Reichenberg, *Selecting Effective Treatments*, 198–201.

13. William Shakespeare, *Hamlet*. Coles Notes *Total Study Edition Hamlet*, (Missisauga, Ontario, John Willey & Sons, 2012) 93.

14. Ibid., 181.

15. David H. Barlow (ed.), *Clinical Handbook of Psychological Disorders: A Step-by-Step Treatment Manual* (New York: The Guilford Press, 2008), 169.

16. Ibid., 202.

17. Viktor E. Frankl, *The Doctor and the Soul, From Psychotherapy to Logotherapy* (New York: Vintage, 1973), 221–9.

18. Seligman and Reichenberg, *Selecting Effective Treatments*, 209–11.

[19] Barlow, *Clinical Handbook of Psychological Disorders*, 123.

[20] Seligman and Reichenberg, *Selecting Effective Treatments*, 213.

[21] Charlotte Stefanic and Rosemary Henrion, *The Power of the Human Spirit* (Kettering, OH: Joseph Publishing Company, 2002).

[22] Barlow, *Clinical Handbook of Psychological Disorders*, 191.

CHAPTER FOURTEEN

Trauma and Stress-Related Disorders and Their Pastoral Treatment

The latest edition of the DSM-5[1] (2013) introduced a new category of trauma and stress-related disorders. The DSM-5 lists reactive attachment disorder and disinhibited social engagement disorder (occurring in children, which we have already discussed) and posttraumatic stress disorder, acute stress disorder, and adjustment disorder, which we will discuss in this section.

14.1 Posttraumatic Stress Disorder and Acute Stress Disorder

The DSM-5 describes *posttraumatic stress disorder* (PTSD) as being caused by directly witnessing or experiencing traumatic events, learning that a traumatic event happened to a close relative, or being repeatedly exposed to traumatic events. Its signs include repeated, involuntary, and intrusive, distressing recollections; dreams, flashbacks, and psychological distress or reactions when exposed to cues that resemble the traumatic event; and efforts to avoid internal or external reminders of the distressing event. Further signs are irritability, anger, recklessness and self-destructiveness, hypervigilance, startling easily, and concentration and sleep problems lasting for at least one month.[2]

The symptoms of *acute stress disorder* are similar but usually milder. The difference between acute stress disorder and posttraumatic stress disorder is their duration. While PTSD lasts for more than one month (sometimes for years or even for life), the duration of acute stress disorder is at least three days but no longer than one month. The incidence of PTSD syndrome is 9–15 percent and its lifelong prevalence around 8 percent in the general population. However, it is 15.5–30 percent in subclinical forms among Vietnam veterans. Also, acute traumatic stress disorder and PTSD are processing dysfunctions. In healthy people unessential memories are forgotten, but with trauma-related disorders the opposite occurs: forgetting is an impossibility. Despite attempts to forget traumatic recollections, they intrusively dominate the consciousness, causing patients to relive the events and subsequently feel immense fear, helplessness, and hopelessness that threaten to evolve into horror. Both acute traumatic stress disorder and PTSD patients react to unremarkable events that resemble the past traumatic events with horror, intense sweating, a racing heart, trembling, or even dissociative symptoms, such as disorientation, confusion, and memory gaps. They avoid activities, places, and people that resemble the traumatic event or evoke memories of it. They are permanently hyperalert and have difficulty sustaining their attention while their vigilance increases (i.e., shifting their attention from one topic to the next), as if expecting the repetition of life-threatening challenges.

Subsequently, people suffering from PTSD become exhausted, numb, distant, and uninterested in everyday activities while their emotional lives become limited to sadness, anger, and depression, often accompanied by suicidal ideas. Acute traumatic stress disorder is often accompanied by a nihilistic, pessimistic, and withdrawn worldview; almost constant arousal; and overreaction to external and internal stimuli. Difficulties in relaxing and feeling rested are common symptoms. Patients' demeanour is irritable, tense, angry, and grumpy, with inexplicable and unexpected acting-out behaviors. Patients may also describe dissociative states and panic attacks, and illusions and hallucinations may be prominent. In contrast to acute stress disorder, PTSD is always evolving, with ups and downs, and psychotherapy and medical treatments are often not fully effective. Associated symptoms may include aggression, violence, poor impulse control, depression, and substance-related disorders. An early onset of PTSD symptoms improves the prognosis, while a late onset has the opposite effect.[3]

14.2 Adjustment Disorders

According to the DSM-5 definition, *adjustment disorders* are always caused by an identifiable stressor which causes significant distress that is disproportionate to the severity of the stressor. The functional impairment, however, does not match the intensity and extensity of acute stress disorder or PTSD. Adjustment disorders can be expressed by a depressed mood, anxiety, and conduct disturbance, or a mixture of these symptoms.[4]

Kaplan and Sadock's textbook notes that a variety of stressful events, such as financial catastrophes, traffic accidents, and relational or occupational problems can provoke adjustment disorders. These disorders are found in 2–8 percent of the contemporary American population, and women are diagnosed twice as often as men. In general, three criteria are indicative of the appearance and severity of adjustment disorders: the nature of the stressor, its conscious and unconscious importance, and especially the affected person's preexisting stability and vulnerability (early childhood experiences, recent support systems, and family and relational background). Besides the already-noted characterization of depression, adjustment disorders can also show signs of anxiety and conduct disturbance or a mixture of these symptoms, and can be expressed in irritability, aggression, reckless driving, drinking habits, and withdrawal from social contact.[5] Nevertheless, the disorder does not last longer than six months, after which time the subjects are usually able to process and deal with the stressful event causing the adjustment disorder.

Pastoral Considerations

(1) The trauma and the symptoms in adjustment disorders occur as a cause and effect connection. The healing of adjustment disorders therefore

takes place in two interconnected and inseparable areas. The first is healing symptoms such as depressive, anxious, or paranoid reactions. The second is the healing of the traumatic experience itself, which will be our current topic.

(2) In addition to the trauma's intensity, the kind of trauma often determines the severity of disorders. The impact of human-caused traumas (like murders) is more severe than that of natural disasters (like an earthquake). And the impact of traumas perceived as being deserved (like those caused by high-risk behavior (e.g., road racing) is more severe than those perceived as being undeserved[6] (e.g., being an innocent victim of a traffic accident). Aggravating factors are feelings of guilt, either stemming from responsibility for a disastrous event or (irrationally) from surviving an ordeal in which others perished (survival guilt). As human beings, we have all survived trauma, dysfunction, and sin to one degree or another. As Christians, we lay our trauma and sins at the foot of the cross and accept God's mercy and forgiveness, for by his wounds we are healed (Isaiah 53:5). As in healing all other conditions, pastoral healers use a Socratic dialogue to empathetically and knowledgeably help, step by step, realizing this purpose in healing trauma and stress-related disorders.

(3) The treatment of trauma-related disorders ought to begin as soon as possible, preferably after the patient has established a safe environment and been disconnected from the traumatic event.[7] This principle applies to both professional and pastoral help.

(4) Healing people, especially those suffering from PTSD, "can be notoriously difficult due to their ambivalence about therapy. They want help, but they fear confronting their memories and have difficulties trusting others, including therapists."[8] In believers, this initial resistance may be mitigated by involving religious professionals, especially pastoral healers, and members of the clergy to whom Christian victims more easily invest trust.

(5) The patient initially needs "only to survive," that is, maintain their basic physiological functioning, rest, and especially get good, nightly sleep. Sleep helps with processing traumatic experiences and the reconstruction of the brain's wiring distorted by stress hormones. New challenges, and especially stress, ought to be avoided as much as possible. Pastoral healers may

help injured people to realize their God-given duty to exclude themselves from activities in favour of rest. Sleep is a gift from God too little appreciated, for it allows our minds and brains to rest—to reset and grow strong again.

(6) In the next step, pastoral healers help to gradually recall, relive, and talk about the traumatic incident. Like children who listen to the same story ten, twenty, or more times, in patients with trauma- and stress-related disorders, their brains learn to process information, find new ways to deal with the trauma, and discern new resolutions to stress when retelling the incident. As Seligman and Reichenberg state, "Exposure therapy is a behavioral intervention that involves exposure to the feared stimuli until the client's anxiety is extinguished."⁹ A version of this process occurs when patients recall and relive traumatic incidents. Processing fears, flashbacks, and intrusive memories may be helped with drawing, painting, role playing and enacting, and writing poems, novels, or newspaper articles about the events. Such activities may temporarily increase a productive anxiety, though, since "we experience anxiety when we use our freedom to move out of the known into the realm of the unknown."¹⁰ Exposure to unknown (i.e., feared) contents of the mind ought to be done cautiously, gradually, and progressively. The subject's increasing courage to confront and challenge anxiety and fear is an indicator of progress. Even when progressing well in healing, however, some questions remain to be considered.

(7) For example, it has been clinically observed that synchronized group and individual therapy may be helpful in healing many forms of suffering from stress-related disorders. Group therapy may have advantages in "reducing the isolation felt by most survivors, who withdraw from interactions and believe that others cannot understand their feelings." However, in patients with severe PTSD, "groups may elicit strong effect and memories that can overwhelm an unprepared client."¹³

(8) Maria and Edward Marshall recount the case of a lady called Jana who migrated from a war-torn country. She continually asked herself, "How can I go on when have I lost so much?"

M. "I am very sorry to hear about the loss of your parents, your close friends, and your older brother.... I am sure that you miss them a lot." [Jana sobs]

"However, I am glad to see that the legacy of your loved ones was entrusted to someone who was able to carry their courageous example with her into a beautiful and free land." (She looks at me) "Now I'd like to ask you, can anyone take this spirit and snatch it away from you? Can anyone erase the legacy of your loved ones once it is written in your heart?"

J. "No, no one could do this...."

M. "What they have accomplished, can it ever be erased, taken away, or destroyed?"

J. "No...."

M. "What your loved ones built up and accomplished, even how they suffered and they died, can that ever be erased from the world?"

J. "No...."

M. "So what you are saying is that what your loved ones have accomplished, no one can remove from the world. No one can really annihilate their legacy. For in your heart their legacy remains. Right?"

J. (Thoughtfully) "Yes, I can see what you mean...."[11]

As the authors note, "Her will to meaning can no longer affect the past, but it can shape the future." In this context, the authors note Frankl's saying that "in the granaries of our past everything is preserved and safely stored."[12] From a pastoral perspective, without an ultimate meaning (God), no real meaning exists, neither in sustaining a meaningless existence nor in past accomplishments or sufferings. On the contrary, though, trusting God helps to discern a purpose stronger than stress-related disorders can harm.

(9) Whether we are living in more dangerous times than 1,000, 2,000, or 3,000 years ago is an open question. Nevertheless, the number of stress-related disorders in our times is rapidly increasing. One may discern from this that losing trust in God correlates to losing resilience against stress. This is especially the case in treating the hardest symptom of trauma- and stress-related disorders: irrational guilt. In this context, Barlow recounts the

words of a military man who had killed an Iraqi family who, because of a misunderstanding, did not stop their car at a military checkpoint:

> The reason that this traumatic event happened is because I was friggin' stupid and made a bad decision. I killed an innocent family, without thinking, I murdered a man's wife and child, I can't believe that I did it, I took that man's wife and child, and oh yeah, his unborn child too. I feel like I do not deserve to live let alone have a wife and a child on the way... I always fail and let others down. I'm not sure what other-esteem is, but I do love my wife. In fact I don't think she deserves to have to deal with me, and I think they would be better without me around.[14]

In psychiatric terms, under the effect of stress hormones which alter the synaptic connections of the brain, a disintegration of the mature psychological defences occurs. In such conditions, regression to and repetition of feelings of guilt and helpless horror occur, which in PTSD patients may evolve into depression or even suicidal ideation. In my experience, in such situations "sharing responsibility" may sometimes help by encouraging patients not to obey their own self-judgment but temporarily accept the moral judgments of the therapist's conscience. In cases of strong Christian therapeutic alliance, such a delegated responsibility lasting until the patient's personality is able to accept its own Christian conscience's "not guilty" verdict may help in easing the self-imposed sufferings of irrational guilt. This alliance mirrors our relationship with God, who took upon himself our sins though he himself was blameless. Once God has helped to carry our load and, in doing so, forgiven us, who are we not to forgive ourselves?

(10) A prominent pastoral task is diverting patients' attention from thinking, "What have I done wrong?" or "If only I had done differently!" Pastoral healers help believers to reevaluate their self-blame in the light of the words of John 9:1–3: "'Neither this man nor his parents sinned' said Jesus, 'but this happened so that the work of God might be displayed in his life.'" The more committed, zealous, and diligent patients are in living so that the "works of God might be displayed" in their lives, the more their irrational self-accusations decrease. That is, the more self-blame is replaced

with a new purpose, that of building the kingdom of God, the more the subjective and objective signs (and measureable psychological tests) show progress in healing.

(11) The progression toward healing sometimes does not happen as the patient and therapist would like, and some outcomes of stress disorders are hard or seemingly impossible to process. In such cases, it may help to follow Jesus' admonition of Mark 8:34: "If anyone would come after me, he must deny himself and take up his cross and follow me." Discerning a sacred purpose in suffering and doing one's best despite suffering eases pain. In this context, praying, listening to Christian music (gospel songs or hymns), and participating in the liturgical life and sacraments (especially confession and holy communion) opens up new perspectives and empowers patients to proportionately seek the depth of their faith. The intentional, conscious, and determinate denial of self, carrying one's cross, and following Jesus despite all pains is an endogenously produced painkiller (like an endorphin), which may in people of faith be more powerful than suffering caused by stress or trauma.

(12) Establishing community (e.g., church groups, occupational groups, workshops) among people suffering from trauma- and stress-related disorders brings promising results and may be commonplace in the future. Accordingly, more pastoral healers with psychological knowledge will be needed, along with professionals with theological knowledge, to heal the ever-increasing number of patients with trauma- and stress-related disorders.

(13) Agnostic and atheist healers may have doubts about the healing effects of faith discussed here and the reliability of our conclusions. Faith, as noted, can have almost miraculous healing effects, but such effects unfortunately do not apply in cases absent of faith.

Notes

[1] DSM-5. *Diagnostic and Statistical Manual of the American Psychiatric Association* (2013), 143.

[2] Ibid.

[3] Benjamin James Sadock, Virginia Alcott Sadock, and Pedro Ruiz, *Kaplan and Sadock's Synopsis of Psychiatry: Behavioral Sciences/Clinical Psychiatry*, 11th ed. (Philadelphia, PA: Wolters Kluwer, 2015), 436–7.

[4] DSM-5, 151–2.

[5] Sadock, Sadock, and Ruiz, *Kaplan and Sadock's Synopsis of Psychiatry*, 11th ed. 446–7.

[6] Linda Seligman and Laurie W. Reichenberg, *Selecting Effective Treatments* (Hoboken, NJ: John Wiley & Sons, 2014), 224–9.

[7] Ibid., 224.

[8] David H. Barlow (ed.), *Clinical Handbook of Psychological Disorders: A Step-by-Step Treatment Manual* (New York: The Guilford Press, 2008), 86.

[9] Linda Seligman and Laurie W. Reichenberg, *Selecting Effective Treatments* (Hoboken, NJ: John Wiley & Sons, 2014), 226.

[10] Gerald Corey, *Theory and Practice of Counseling and Psychotherapy* (Belmont, CA: Thomson/ Brooks/Cole, 2005), 141.

[11] Maria Marshall and Edward Marshall, *Spiritual Psychotherapy, the Search for Lasting Meaning* (Canada, Ont.: Ottawa Institute of Logotherapy, 2015), 216–18.

[12] Ibid., 218–22.

[13] Barlow, *Clinical Handbook of Psychological Disorders*, 87.

[14] Ibid., 91.

CHAPTER FIFTEEN

DISSOCIATIVE DISORDERS AND THEIR PASTORAL TREATMENT

The DSM-5 lists six disorders under the umbrella of dissociative disorders.[1] However, since dissociative states of mind have less pastoral than medical import, we will focus only on three diagnostic entities from this group.

15.1 Depersonalization/Derealization Disorder

Depersonalization/Derealization disorder is characterized by the DSM-5 as a dreamlike state in which space and time, happenings, and people seem unreal, or in which the self is observed like a detached vessel, like a puppet. Reality judgment, however, remains preserved (unlike with psychotic hallucinations or illusions).[2] Patients may feel detached, like automatons, or as if they were watching themselves in a movie. The disorder is widespread; it is the third most common disorder after depression and anxiety disorders. "One survey found a yearly prevalence of nineteen percent in the general population." It is common in people suffering from psychological conflicts, migraines, and epilepsy and appears in psychoses, histrionic personality disorder, and drug use. Often, it is a defence against traumatic experiences.[3]

15.2 Dissociative Amnesia Disorder

Dissociative amnesia disorder is marked by the inability to recall personal information inconsistent with forgetfulness.[4] According to Kaplan and Sadock, around 6 percent of the general population suffer from this disorder. It is facilitated by grave psychological problems like guilt, shame, disgust, despair, helplessness, rage, and depression, but is also associated with psychotic symptoms, drug use, and histrionic and convulsive disorders. Abuse and childhood trauma are often predisposing elements. The prognosis of dissociative amnesia depends on the success in the treatment of its causes. However, in some cases irreparable damage in recollection remains, although it seldom causes a need for permanent care and supervision. It is important to recover lost memories as soon as possible because "the repressed memories may form a nucleus in the unconscious mind around which future amnestic episodes may develop."[5]

15.3 Dissociative Identity Disorder

Dissociative identity disorder, previously called multiple personality disorder, is characterized in the DSM-5 by the disruption of the identity in connection with changes in attention, thinking, emotionality, memory, perception, and sensory and motor functioning, causing gaps in the recollection of events and continuity of consciousness.[6] It is also, according to Kaplan and Sadock, characterized by perceiving at least two quite different personalities (or alters). Until about 1800, the disorder was understood as demonic possession. In around 85–97 percent of cases, severe childhood mistreatment, abuse, or neglect can be detected.[7] Although half of all cases report no more than ten identities, there are dramatic cases with more than one hundred distinct identities alternating in some way to control the same person. Each identity may claim a different name, gender, image, and personal history.[8] The exact prevalence of the disorder is not known, and it appears significantly more often in women in a ratio between 5:1 and 9:1. Most often, the cause of the disorder is physical and sexual abuse. Other symptoms are "blackouts, or time loss, unremembered behavior, fugues, unexplained possession, inexplicable changes in relationships, fluctuations in skills, habits, and knowledge, fragmentary recall of the entire life history, chronic mistaken identity experiences, and micro dissociations." Communication is vague, and patients often talk in the third person about themselves. Comorbidity, depression, anxiety disorders, OCD, substance abuse, suicidal behaviors, eating, and somatization disorders are common.[9]

Pastoral Considerations

(1) Dissociation is not a yes or no process but rather a continuum between the extremes of integration and disintegration in a functioning mind. Thus, forms of dissociation may appear in healthy people. For example, for concentration camp prisoners it was normal to be dissociated from abnormal reality. Similarly, a commitment to Christian ideals may cause a constructive dissociation from the rules and laws of the world.

> St. Francis was born in 1182 to a wealthy merchant family. As a youngster, he was systematically groomed to succeed his father's enterprise. Originally, Francis lived a lavish lifestyle and fulfilled his parent's expectations, but after 1205, a transformation started unexpectedly and he "began to seek in prayer and solitude the answer to his call." Suddenly, "he went into his father's shop, impulsively bundled together a load of coloured drapery, and mounting his horse hastened to Foligno, then a market of some importance, and there sold both horse and drapes to procure the money needed for the restoration of St. Damian's church." When his father accused him of irresponsibility, he ran away and hid in a cave. After a month he reappeared but was "emaciated with hunger and squalid with dirt." Consequently, "Francis was followed by a hooting rabble, who pelted him with mud and stones, and otherwise mocked him as a madman." Next, the young Francis stripped himself of his clothes and wandered in the countryside singing hymns. When robbers threatened him, he cried to them, "I am of the great King!"[10]

Many exemplary Christians are "strangers in the world." In St. Francis' case, he behaved strangely (from a worldly perspective) not because of a sickness but because he escaped from worldly reality in a state of, as Kazimierz Dabrowski would call it, "positive disintegration."[11]

(2) The cause of genuine dissociate disorders is the significant "inability to integrate memories and experiences into awareness."[12] It is a defence against stress, loss, disaster, conscious or unconscious conflicts, guilt, or fear that patients believe they are incapable of procession. It is not helpful to strip away a person from that last defence before adequate protection is established.

(3) Clinical forms of dissociative disorders (despite often being grotesque and bizarre) are not a psychotic process. People suffering from them do not abandon the world as in psychoses but temporarily escape the unpleasant reality and then subsequently return to it. Professional and pastoral healing aim to make the return faster and easier by helping with the processing of the causes of dissociation.

(4) Before starting any professional or pastoral intervention, it is essential to gain the trust of the affected patients, usually timid and insecure. To some degree, they usually expect rejection, so their complaints ought to be taken at face value; the healer's response should never reveal doubt. Regardless of how unrealistic their experiences may seem, they are a reality for the subject.

(5) Sudden and unexpected but usually short-lived dissociation (as in dissociative amnesia disorder) is often provoked by financial, marital, occupational, vocational stress, or other personal catastrophes. In some cases, previously healthy people without apparent problems rebel against their problems by "suddenly walking away."[13] In other cases, as Seligman and Reichenberg describe, patients might experience a feeling of being changed and observe themselves as if outside of their bodies (as if watching themselves in a dream or a movie). This is especially widespread in young people.[14] Following episodes of dissociation, patients are confused and cannot explain how they came to the strange situation. A similar phenomenon occurred "after the September 11th attacks on the World Trade Center, where several people who had been reported missing were later found alive but had apparently developed dissociative amnesia."[15] In pastoral healing of such transitory forms of dissociation, it helps not only to know but to feel

that God has given every human being a marvellous resilience. While it may be difficult to find at times, almost all things are possible through faith, and this internal evidence comes almost spontaneously with the passage of time. For such people, time spent with Jesus is the best healer.

(6) More serious and longer-lasting forms of dissociative amnesia, depersonalization/derealization disorder, and especially dissociative identity disorder are facilitated by ongoing and helpless protesting against stress, depression, abuse, disappointment, abandonment, and frustration. Such protesting serves as a defence in dealing with self-blame, low self-esteem, rage, fear, helplessness, and guilt, from which subjects escape into dissociation. Often, their inability to adjust to an unpleasant reality is caused, fully or partially, by another psychological problem or psychiatric disorder.

(7) If dissociative "escaping from the world" has a psychiatric reason (like borderline personality disorder, schizophrenia, epilepsy, migraine, or drug use), then before starting psychological healing, the patient should be helped in managing it. By healing the basic disorder, the symptoms of dissociation usually disappear. If, on the other hand, dissociative reactions are caused by experiential catastrophes (like natural disasters, traffic accidents, rape or criminal assaults), then the primary task is helping the patient feel secure. Only after restoring physical and psychological security can specific healing of the dissociation itself begin.

(8) In healing dissociation, professional therapists strive to restore the affected person's psychological stability, trust, optimism, meaning, values, and purpose for living. Corey, for example, notes how "existential therapy helps clients come to terms with the paradoxes of existence—life and death, success and failure, freedom and limitations, and certainty and doubt."[16] In healing these existential challenges, most professional treatments attempt to help patients live in a Christlike way—courageously, purposefully, and optimistically—despite the perceptions of sceptical therapists and patients of an ultimately meaningless existence. They propose Christlike living, but without Christ. This, of course, is impossible. If Christ is the way, truth, and life (John 14:6), courage, purpose, and optimism have their source in him.

(9) In a Socratic dialogue, pastoral healers clarify that dissociated believers' internal conflicts occur on a continuum of sickness (in this case by the

trauma-caused distress) and lack of trusting God (which causes in them a deficiency of biblical courage, trust, optimism, and hope). Thus, pastoral healing for dissociation is based on the recognition that no worldly healing gives resilience like faith. Nothing but faith is able to bridge the gap between certainty and doubt, freedom and its limitations, success and failure, and death and life. Healing dissociate disorders is often an opportunity and call for a change to one's whole understanding of being and meaning. It may be an opportunity to discern, like St. Augustine, that "restless are our hearts without you, O Lord." The English language uses a plethora of words (fear, worry, concern, uneasiness, awareness, sadness, worry, sorrow, torment, and restlessness) to articulate adverse emotional reaction to stressors of the world. Only one word, however, is sufficient to control these anxieties: faith.

(10) Pastoral healing helps people understand that genuine Christians, as described in the Acts of the Apostles, are holy; they are "set apart" from the world. All Christians have at least some elements of holiness. As many biblical saints (as described in Acts 5:41, 1 Peter 4:13–14, and Philippians 4:4–7) demonstrate, a genuine closeness to Jesus decreases dissociation—the horror of a tormenting reality or the attempt to run from it. Psychologically, being set apart from the world facilitates a commitment to being "worthy of suffering" (Acts 5:41), helps to place adverse worldly happenings in a sec-ondary perspective, provides an armour against trauma, and helps to build a psychological-spiritual immunity against psychiatric dissociation from the Luciferian world. Indeed, Christians are "in the world—but not of it" (Jn. 17:11; 17:17). It is precisely this that helps them to persist in "being in the world" and not dissociating from it. Living in the world often looks like being in a "valley of tears," but the awareness of being "not of it" is what the suffering world needs today.

Notes

[1] DSM-5. *Diagnostic and Statistical Manual of the American Psychiatric Association* (2013), 155.

[2] Ibid., 157.

[3] Benjamin James Sadock, Virginia Alcott Sadock, and Pedro Ruiz,

Kaplan and Sadock's Synopsis of Psychiatry: Behavioral Sciences/Clinical Psychiatry, 11th ed. (Philadelphia, PA: Wolters Kluwer, 2015), 454–6.

4 DSM-5, 143.

5 Sadock, Alcott Sadock, and Ruiz, *Kaplan and Sadock's Synopsis of Psychiatry*, 451–4.

6 DSM-5, 155.

7 Sadock, Alcott Sadock, and Ruiz, *Kaplan and Sadock's Synopsis of Psychiatry*, 458–62.

8 Ibid., 462.

9 Ibid., 463.

10 Pascal Robinson, "St. Francis of Assisi," *Catholic Encyclopedia* vol. 6 (New York: Robert Appleton com, 1909), 221.

11 Sal Mendaglio, *Dabrowski's Theory of Positive of Positive Disintegration* (Scotsdale, AZ: Great Potential Press, 2008).

12 Linda Seligman and Laurie W. Reichenberg, *Selecting Effective Treatments* (Hoboken, NJ: John Wiley & Sons, 2014), 226.

13 Ibid., 431.

14 Seligman and Reichenberg, *Selecting Effective Treatments*, 432.

15 Ibid., 432.

16 Gerald Corey, *Theory and Practice of Counseling and Psychotherapy* (Belmont, CA: Thomson/ Brooks/Cole, 2005), 144.

CHAPTER SIXTEEN

SOMATIC SYMPTOM AND RELATED DISORDERS AND THEIR PASTORAL TREATMENT

In the group we are going to discuss, the DSM-5 lists somatic symptom disorder, illness anxiety disorder, and conversion disorder among others.[1] The commonality of these disorders is that they "encompass mind-body interactions in which the brain, in ways still not well-understood, sends various signals that impinge on the patient's awareness, indicating a serious problem in the body."[2] Like in all other DSM-5 categories, they are distressing and cause a marked disruption in functioning for at least a six-month period. Let us discuss the components of these disorders, which are hard to treat and even more painful to suffer from.

16.1 Somatic Symptom Disorder

The DSM-5[3] defines *somatic symptom disorder* as overreacting with excessive and exaggerated thoughts, feelings, or behaviors relating to objectively-existing, genuinely distressing somatic symptoms. These concerns cause constant anxiety, and excessive time and energy are devoted to them. As Kaplan and Sadock's textbook notes, somatic symptom disorder is characterized by nondelusional fears and ideas about suffering a serious disease based on the affected person's misinterpretation of their bodily symptoms and feelings. It constitutes 4–15 percent of patients attending a family physicians' offices. Men and women are equally exposed, and it starts between the ages of twenty and thirty. People suffering from somatic symptom disorder "have low thresholds for, and low tolerance of, physical discomfort." What an average person perceives as normal sensations, they interpret as pain. They look for alarming signs of serious disorders, focusing on and scrutinizing their body's functioning, discovering and misinterpreting its functioning before tirelessly seeking medical help, which they are never satisfied with. They become frustrated with physicians allegedly not recognizing their serious and life-threatening disorders and demand renewed proof confirming their health concerns. In reality, somatic symptom disorder is a kind of defence against guilt, "a sense of innate badness," and its resulting low self-esteem and overvalued self-concern. Thus, fear, pain, and suffering are "means of atonement and expiation (undoing) and can be experienced as deserved punishment for a past wrongdoing (either real or imaginary) and a sense of the person's wickedness and sinfulness."[4]

16.2 Illness Anxiety Disorder or Hypochondriasis

Contrary to patients with somatic symptom disorder who factually have one or more distressing physical symptoms, the DSM-5 characterizes *illness anxiety disorder* as a preoccupation with suffering a serious illness while objectively having no appropriate signs of it.[5] Such people are anxious about their health and are excessively concerned with avoiding, preventing, or checking on signs of medically nonverifiable disorders for at least a six-month period. According to Sadock, Sadock, and Ruiz, somatic complaints in people suffering from this disorder are primarily caused by psychological problems.[6] The disorder occurs more often in women, and its lifetime prevalence "is estimated to be 0.2 to 2 percent in women and 0.2 percent in men." The disorder is characterized by a triad: "(1) The involvement of multiple organ systems, (2) an early onset and chronic course without the development of physical signs or structural abnormalities, and (3) the absence of laboratory abnormalities that are characteristic of the suggested medical condition." Despite multiple visits to the doctor's office, other symptoms of the perceived illness do not appear, and "although patients with this disorder consider themselves medically ill, the evidence is that they are no more likely to develop another medical illness in the next twenty years than people without illness anxiety disorder."

Illness anxiety disorder is not a benign psychiatric condition. On one occasion while I was in medical school, my peers and I discussed what we believed the most horrific disease to be. Some voted for cancer, others for strokes, and others for leprosy. Our teacher, though, voted for illness anxiety disorder, saying, "Imagine that you experience daily signs of dangerous disorders but neither physicians nor relatives take you seriously. They ridicule and humiliate you, yet you feel the relentless progression of the disorder."

16.3 Conversion Disorder

The DSM-5 characterizes *conversion disorder* as having "symptoms of altered voluntary, motor or sensory function," expressed in weakness or paralysis, swallowing difficulties, unusual body movements, speech difficulties, seizures, aesthesia or sensory problems, or symptoms related to the senses (blindness, hearing disturbances, or similar).[7] Conversion disorder is widespread. Some symptoms may occur in up to one third of the population at some time during their lives. The measured rates of conversion disorder vary between 11 of 100,000 to 300 of 100,000 in statistical samples.[8]

The idea of "conversion," introduced by Sigmund Freud to explain unconscious psychological conflicts, translates into somatic symptoms. Accordingly, conversion means the expression of psychological conflicts in a somatic language; its symptoms are symbolically disguised theatrical expressions of psychological conflicts. Patients suffering from conversion disorder unconsciously express suppressed conflicts, which helps to release psychic tension but still enables the avoidance of confrontation with the environment. Conversion also aids in manipulating the environment to bring about special treatment and other secondary gains.

People suffering from conversion disorder accept their conversive symptoms (paralysis or blindness) with a kind of fearless indifference, without worry, sorrow, or fear, called in French *la belle indifference* ("bland indifference"). In Sadock, Sadock, and Ruiz's description,[9] it is an "inappropriately cavalier attitude towards serious symptoms; that is, the patients seem to be unconcerned about what appears to be a major impairment." However, conversion disorder is not synonymous with factitious (malingering) disorder, which the DSM-5 defines as a "falsification of physical or psychological signs or symptoms, or induction of an injury or disease."[10] People suffering from factitious disorders intentionally present themselves as ill (they are consciously feigning a disorder) for reasons known only to them. Conversive symptoms are, on the contrary, always dramatically exhibited as the particular person imagines the disorder. To paraphrase a German saying, people malingering with a disorder are not "willing to be able" to be healthy, while people suffering from a conversion disorder are "not able to will" themselves to function as healthy people. The disorder may be expressed in older psychiatric textbooks' descriptions[11] as having sensory or sensitive symptoms (like hemiaesthesia, with the line between healthy and sick parts of the body following a straight line, which is inconsistent with central and peripheral neurological lesions). The disorder is sometimes expressed in mutism (wherein the subject is able to cough, which mute people generally cannot do, but unable to whistle, which mute people generally can do) or blindness (wherein the subject can walk around freely without colliding with objects and whose pupils react normally to light). The motor symptoms include paralysis (but with normal reflexes unlike in stroke). When the allegedly paralyzed person leans forward, their hands do not swing forward as gravity requires, but remain parallel and beside the body. Other symptoms are abnormal movements, tremors, tics, and jerks, which are inconsistent with any neurological damage but reflect the subject's understanding and theatrical exaggeration of particular disorders. All described symptoms are generally worse if attention is paid to their demonstration and, in general, all of them convey a symbolical and theatrical message. Patients, despite unintentionally enacting serious neurological problems, seldom fall; if they do, they do not injure themselves. Conversion pseudoseizures (with an absence of injuries and without tongue-biting and urinary incontinence, as in epileptic seizures) are typical. After conversion pseudoseizures, a content mood often occurs, as if the patient were enjoying the effect they have produced. A secondary gain is in receiving attention and compassion.

Pastoral Considerations

(1) Before healing any of the disorders listed in this group, depression needs to be excluded as it may sometimes produce symptoms similar to somatic symptom disorders. Because some depressed patients have difficulty expressing emotions, they may channel their worries into physical complaints. They are also powerless to resolve anxiety, which promotes the need for dependence, and such helpless subjects want others to take care of them.[12] Additionally, "somatic appeal," a cry for help of suicidal people, may be expressed in inexplicable somatic complaints. If the patient is in fact depressed, conversive symptoms may be exacerbated by stress, anxiety, low self-esteem, and frustration.

(2) In conversion disorders, symptoms occur in the motoric, sensitive, or sensorial functioning of the body. These symptoms are caused by unconscious dynamics and are a symbolical expression of repressed instinctual drives. Because the conflicts causing the disorder are unconscious, healing of the conversion symptoms (for example of paralyses or blindness) often requires a psychodynamic approach. Such healing starts with decoding, or retranslating, the symbolically-expressed symptoms into words. After symptoms are translated into words, a rational and emotional resolution of the unconscious conflicts causing the symptoms begins, which is then supplemented with pastoral methods. While discussing the details of psychodynamic healing is beyond the scope of this book, in supplemental pastoral healing of conversion disorders, therapists may adapt and use the therapeutic methods described in healing other somatic symptom and related disorders.

(3) In explaining dynamics in other somatic symptoms disorders listed in this group, we will climb on Viktor Frankl's shoulders. In this context, it is notable that, according the pontifical document "Charter for Health Care

Workers" of 1995,[12] Frankl's logotherapy is recommended as the approach of choice in Catholic pastoral settings.

(4) Medicine distinguishes two different regulations. One is conscious and intentional (handshaking), while the other involves autonomous, regulating somatic processes (breathing). If a person attempts to direct their breathing intentionally (for example, deeply and rhythmically), after a few minutes they will experience discomfort. As Frankl observes, subjects "hyperintending" to regulate body functions consequently suffer "hyperreflection," reflecting (i.e., experiencing) unpleasant sensations otherwise disregarded by nonconcerned subjects.

In this context, Frankl describes the case of a violinist.

[He] tried to play as consciously as possible. From putting his violin in place on his shoulder to the most trifling technical detail, he wanted to do everything consciously, to perform in full self-reflection. This led to a complete artistic breakdown. Treatment had to give back to the patient his trust in the unconscious by having him realize how much more musical his unconscious was than his conscious ... dereflection liberated the creative powers from the inhibiting effects of any unnecessary reflection.[13]

The crucial question is this: What facilitates the hyperintention, the overfocusing on bodily functions that results in hyperreflection in patients with somatic disorders?

(5) In 1944, the philosopher Karl R. Popper published his book *The Open Society and Its Enemies*.[14] Popper maintained that the ideal of the open society is an almost "absolute freedom" in the sense of possibly having fewer obligations. In such a society, people would have only lucrative, professional, or business-related commitments, but no lasting loyalties—marital, familial, religious, patriotic, or otherwise. Even the innate mother-child attachment ought to be minimized as much as possible in an open-ended society. Individuals in a society based on the premise "in business with everyone but belonging to no one" focus solely on two goals: making money and seeking pleasure.

Western individualism has in many aspects realized Popper's vision, and the consequences of it are apparent. On September 30, 2014, the Canadian TV station CBC introduced an otherwise healthy man in his sixties who elected to die because he had "nothing more to expect from life."[15] Many patients suffering from somatic symptom and related disorders, despite having a great deal of social communication, suffer from a loneliness, egotism, and disregard for their families, loved ones, friends, and society, counting not what they can give but only what they can receive from others. Such malignant individualism and self-centeredness causes hyperintention of health, performance, fun, and unavoidable hyperreflection, which unconsciously asks, "Am I healthy enough? Do I enjoy life as I ought to? [Or is my existence becoming worthless?]" Having no other purpose to live for than their own well-being, subjects hyperintend, overfocusing on only one task to protect their own health, and by this they unintentionally provoke the hyperreflection of their anxieties, worries, and fear of sickness.

(6) Because physicians are unable to discern the organic reasons why patients are dissatisfied and feel misunderstood,[16] sensations sourcing from a normally-functioning body become ever more interpreted by patients as alarming signs of diseases, further fuelling the attempt to consciously supervise the autonomously regulated somatic processes. Therefore, the process turns into an increasingly vicious cycle—hyperreflection aiming to disprove fears about sickness increases hyperintention of health, while hyperintention of health further increases fears of sickness.

Frankl compares the human mind to the eye. The eye is permanently focused on observing objects outside of itself. If it does not see objects in the external world but a cloudy image of itself, this is a sign of a problem—a cataract, for example. "Equally, by virtue of the self-transcendent quality of the human reality," Frankl says, "the humanness of man is most tangible when he forgets himself—and overlooks himself."[17] Like the eye suffering from a cataract sees what should not normally be perceived, so people suffering from somatization perceive their bodies' functioning as a sign of sickness.

(7) To stop this destructive trend, a commonsense idea would be proving to patients that everything in their somatic functioning is okay. However, gaining the patient's trust with a simple logical demonstration of health is most often not quite so easy.[18] A patient of mine was suffering from the

hypochondriacal fear that she had a brain tumour. After lab examinations excluded her fears, I optimistically confronted her with the fact that she was healthy, but she looked at me and said, "Yes, this was yesterday. But didn't the tumour start to grow in my head today?" There must, therefore, be other methods for treating these patients.

(8) With this said, the healing of somatic disorders ought never start before the possible somatic sources of the patients' complaints are excluded. Demonstrating patience and understanding for patients who explain their problems at great lengths and in minuscule detail is essential. As Seligman and Reichenberg note, therapists who proceed too quickly and are too directive, confrontational, or unsympathetic are unsuccessful.[19]

(9) Professionals heal patients suffering from somatic disorders with medicines and different types of cognitive-behavioral, psychodynamic, and existential therapies that aim to counter the deepest and most pressing fear, that of death, which is expressed in somatic symptoms. Pastoral healing often continues where professional healing stops, is powerless, or gives up. Very often, the preoccupation with bodily symptoms serves to distract from psychological-spiritual problems, which are the real causes of the disorder.

(10) We noted that Frankl compared the functioning of the human mind to the eye. Pastoral healers go a step farther than Frankl, quoting Jesus' words from Matthew 6:22–23: "The eye is the lamp of the body. If your eyes are healthy, your whole body will be full of light. But if your eyes are unhealthy, your whole body will be full of darkness. If then the light within you is darkness, how great is that darkness!" If the inner eye cannot see accurately, then behavior, understanding, and self-reflection will be compromised. Thus, pastoral healers treat somatic disorders connected to a disproportionate "self- and body-centeredness" caused by a lack of a committed, zealous, and wholehearted Christ-centeredness.

(11) As previously quoted biblical examples prove (Acts 5:41, 1 Peter 4:12–13, Hebrews 10:34, Philippians 2:17, James 1:2), Christ-centeredness excludes self-centeredness and excessive health- or body-centeredness. For that reason, pastoral healing is focused in context of a Socratic dialogue on helping patients to see goals and values (namely living for God and neighbours as ordered by Jesus) as purposes to live for. Only striving for

an ultimate meaning that is, in Pope Benedict XVI's words, "worthy to die for"[20] and even more worthy to live for is able to provide a purpose more important than preserving health. Only this stops the brain from "sending various signals that impinge on the patient's awareness, indicating a serious problem in the body." As noted, fully deliberate rejection of God, as well as halfhearted commitment to him and halfhearted belief in his providence, causes one to feel significant psychological distress and seek a mirage of biological security instead of available spiritual safety.

(12) In Corey's words, "an essential aim of existential therapy is not to make life seem easier or safer but to encourage clients to recognize and deal with the sources of their insecurity."[21] However, existential insecurity of sickness and death is hardly resolvable without making a decision of faith. It is a call for throwing all mental, physical, and spiritual energy into God's hands, as St. Paul explains in Hebrews 11:1: "being sure of what we hope for and certain of what we do not see."

(13) For Christians to be sure of what they hope for and certain of what they do not see, the use of behavioral methods may be facilitated during their healing. For example, pastoral healers use the previously discussed paradoxical intention. With all somatic disorders excluded, Christians may be instructed not to be afraid of fear but, on the contrary, to challenge and intentionally provoke symptoms of the imagined disorder. People of strong faith courageously confront and ridicule somatic disorders, aware that, as St. Paul noted in Romans 8:38–39, "neither death nor life, neither angels nor demons, neither the present not the future, nor any powers, neither heights nor depth, nor anything else in all creation, will be able to separate us from the love of God that is in Christ Jesus our Lord." Using spiritual-behavioral exercises such as not running away but rather challenging and ridiculing fears for four to five minutes four to five times daily may defeat even the psychiatric disorder called hypochondriasis. This helps "becoming like the eye" in Frankl's example, focusing less on one's own somatic well-being than on wholeheartedly seeking and trusting in their union with God and receiving the healing power of faith.

Notes

[1] DSM-5. *Diagnostic and Statistical Manual of the American Psychiatric Association* (2013), 161.

[2] Benjamin James Sadock, Virginia Alcott Sadock, and Pedro Ruiz, *Kaplan and Sadock's Synopsis of Psychiatry: Behavioral Sciences/Clinical Psychiatry*, 11th ed. (Philadelphia, PA: Wolters Kluwer, 2015), 468–71.

[3] DSM-5, 161.

[4] Sadock, Sadock, and Ruiz, *Kaplan and Sadock's Synopsis of Psychiatry*, 11th ed. 468–71.

[5] DSM-5, 162.

[6] Sadock, Sadock, and Ruiz, *Kaplan and Sadock's Synopsis of Psychiatry*, 11th ed. 471–3.

[7] DSM-5, 163.

[8] Sadock, Sadock, and Ruiz, *Kaplan and Sadock's Synopsis of Psychiatry*, 11th ed. 477–83.

[9] Ibid, 640.

[10] DSM-5, 155.

[11] Sadock, Sadock, and Ruiz, *Kaplan and Sadock's Synopsis of Psychiatry*, 11th ed. 640.

[12] The Pontifical Council for Pastoral Assistance to Healthcare Workers, "Charter for Health Care Workers" (Vatican City, 1995).

[13] Viktor E. Frankl, *The Doctor and the Soul, From Psychotherapy to Logotherapy* (New York: Vintage Books, 1973), 160–4.

[14] Karl Popper (with a new introduction by Alan Ryan and essay by E. H. Gombich,) *The Open Society and Its Enemies* (Princeton, Princeton University Press, New Jersey, 2013).

[15] Canadian TV station CBC (September 30, 2014).

[16] Linda Seligman and Laurie W. Reichenberg, *Selecting Effective Treatments* (Hoboken, NJ: John Wiley & Sons, 2014), 320.

[17] Viktor E. Frankl, *Man's Search for Ultimate Meaning* (New York: Basic Books, 2000), 85.

[18] Linda Seligman and Laurie W. Reichenberg, *Selecting Effective Treatments* (Hoboken, NJ: John Wiley & Sons, 2014), 321.

[19] Ibid.

[20] Benedict XVI, *Benedictus, Day by Day with Pope Benedict XVI*, edited by Rev. Peter Cameron (New York: Magnificat, 2006), 79.

[21] Gerald Corey, *Theory and Practice of Counseling and Psychotherapy* (Belmont, CA: Thomson/ Brooks/Cole, 2005), 144.

CHAPTER SEVENTEEN

EATING DISORDERS AND THEIR PASTORAL TREATMENT

T he DSM-5[1] lists eight disorders in the category of eating disorders. We will discuss only the most important ones from a pastoral perspective.

17.1 Anorexia Nervosa

Anorexia nervosa is characterized as a restriction of food intake causing a less than normal body weight, triggered by an irrational fear of weight gain or body shape. The disorder is instigated, according to Kaplan and Sadock's textbook, by relentlessly pursued thinness and a morbid fear of fatness. Half of anorexic patients suffer the voluntary reduction of food intake, and the other half eat regularly or sometimes excessively but then induce vomiting, or purge. Anorexia nervosa is a relatively widespread disorder, occurring ten to twenty times more often in females, so that some 4 percent of girls and women suffer from it. The onset of the disorder is between ages ten and thirty. Patients with anorexia nervosa find support for their practices in society's emphasis on thinness and exercise. According to Sadock, Sadock, and Ruiz, participation in demanding programs like ballet increases the likelihood of later suffering from anorexia nervosa more than sevenfold. A similar phenomenon is observed in high school boys, in whom symptoms indicating eating disorders increase around 17 percent during wrestling season. Girls suffering from eating disorders are usually overly attached to their parents but experience conflict with them. Families, especially with children exhibiting binge eating and induced vomiting, often show patterns of marital conflict, animosity, estrangement, indifference, and isolation without genuine care or empathy. People suffering from anorexia nervosa do not lose their appetite, as is the case with some cancer patients. They crave food, sometimes gathering recipes or preparing food for others. Those who cannot resist hunger will binge eat (usually secretively, during the night) and induce vomiting or use laxatives or diuretics to lose weight. When eating in public, they make a significant effort to postpone putting food into their mouths, often hiding food in their pockets. Personality-wise, they are rigid, permanently scrutinizing and judging themselves, as well as secretive, and "poor sexual adjustment is frequently described in patients with the disorder." Often, sexual interest is decreased. Anorexic people who used drugs or lived in promiscuity before the onset of the disorder, however, are seldom sexually inhibited. Depression, anxiety, and OCD are frequently seen in anorexic patients, and prolonged starvation causes a multiplicity of somatic problems, including lack of energy, low strength, pale skin, hypothermia, oedema, low blood pressure, and menstrual irregularity.[3]

17.2 Bulimia Nervosa

Bulimia nervosa is characterized in the DSM-5 by spells of eating extra-large amounts of food in a short time frame and subsequent attempts to control weight gain through several means: self-induced vomiting; laxatives, enemas, and diuretics; fasting; or excessive exercising. These occur at least once a week for three months.[4] The prevalence of the disorder is 2–4 percent, and its onset occurs later in adolescence than anorexia. Additionally, people suffering from bulimia, like those suffering from anorexia, tend to respond to social and fashionable pressures to be thin, but bulimia more often occurs "in an individual less able to sustain prolonged semistarvation or severe hunger." Unlike anorexia, subjects more frequently live in families with conflict, with parents who are more often neglectful, indifferent, or rejecting. Psychologically, bulimic patients are more confrontational, rebellious, angry, impulsive, and prone to acting out with families and society than anorexic patients. Many of them feel inadequate and suffer from low self-esteem and anxiety. They eat fast and secretively, and their self-induced vomiting, usually by putting a finger down the throat, brings only short relief and is often followed with anguish. This, in turn, is sometimes treated with alcohol and drug use. Depression, anxiety, impulsiveness, acting-out behaviors, suicidal behaviors, and dissociative disorders may accompany bulimia nervosa. Bulimic people are seldom sexually shy and are concerned about their sexual attractiveness and appearance.[5]

17.3 Binge Eating Disorder

Binge eating disorder consists of eating enormous quantities of food on average for two days to a week over a period of at least six months.[6] After binge eating, what is popularly called "wolf hunger" often occurs, wherein people feel uncomfortably full, guilty, and embarrassed, yet continue to eat alone, isolated from their families and friends. As Kaplan notes, binge eating is usually connected to mood changes like anxiety, dysphoria, and frustration, and feelings are significantly released by the disorder. Accordingly, binge eating serves as the self-healing of a mood dysregulation. Often, the disorder is accompanied by mood disorders, substance use disorders, and borderline personality disorder. Also, child abuse may appear in the patient's history.[7]

Pastoral Considerations

(1) The instinct regulation of eating is a strong and critical drive. Hungry people kill for food. Thus, the fact that in eating disorders subjects willingly reject food illustrates how powerful is their "judging their self-worth largely or even exclusively in terms of their shape and weight and their ability to control them"[8]. Their overvalued ideas overrule even the strongest instincts.

(2) These dysfunctional belief systems usually begin in adolescence with emotional estrangement from family and the imitation of peers in musical groups, sporting groups, or, in the worst cases, gangs. The new loyalties are

expressed in accepting the dictates of fashionable, sexual, and erotic idols, opening the door to a neverending effort to become popular.

(3) Sensing signs of the described estrangement in their children, parents often hide their disapproval and feign indifference, saying, "It's their choice." It is a crucial task of the pastoral healer to coach such parents to realize that Christian families are a community. A family unit has love, care, and responsibility for everyone or it isn't a genuine family at all. Let me demonstrate what the parents' responsibility and love in such cases mean.

A sixteen-year-old gravely anorexic, newly-immigrated girl, also struggling with academic problems, ran away from her family. Such behavior was completely at odds with her upbringing and culture. Day and night her parents searched for her but could not find her. Neither the school nor the police helped. The only support the parents had was their faith and church community. The words of the priest (functioning in this case as a pastoral healer) were, "Do not worry! She can run but cannot erase from her heart the love you have invested in her. She will come back!" This gave them courage and hope that their daughter would be back. In their effort to locate her, they first found out who her best friends were and then organized a network of parents who gathered information from their children. After three months of hard work, with the help of friends and parents, they learned their daughter's whereabouts. The parents then sent her food, clothes, and money. Finally, after eight months, the daughter came home, enrolled in school, and started treatment for anorexia. Today, she is a radiologist and a pillar of her family. Without the faith of her family and support from the local priest, however, this happy outcome might never have happened. In virtually all cases of healing, pastoral and otherwise, people are merely the vessels for the workings of the Holy Spirit.

The priest demonstrated the kind of faith alluded to in Mark 11:23–24, which says that we are to believe that we have already received what we are praying for or expecting, even if it is the movement of a mountain. Faith produces courage and hope that can produce healing in even desperate situations such as in the one described above.

(4) People suffering from eating disorders need not only a special kind of therapy but also a special kind of therapist. Seligman and Reichenberg note that less than one third of people suffering from eating disorders enter treatment. To balance patients' lack of motivation, therapists need the ability to extend long-term empathy and patience. They should not attempt to control patients' behavior but should make compromises and balance nurturing with authoritativeness to ensure that the patients' goals can be attained.[9]

(5) The first task of the professional healer and pastoral therapist is ensuring the somatic health and safety of the patient, often jeopardized by prolonged starvation. Only then can the pastoral healer broach the subject, through long-term therapy, of heavenly food. Christians, of course, have the great advantage of optimism, hope, trust, and courage sourcing from knowing that the ultimate source of nourishment is the body of Jesus himself (John 6:54–56).

(6) The next task is focusing on concurrent psychopathology. Barlow notes that "most patients with an eating disorder have secondary depressive features, but a subgroup has an independent but interacting clinical depression" expressed in pervasive and extreme negative thinking, hopelessness in general, recurrent thoughts about death and dying, suicidal thoughts, irrational guilt over events in the past, isolation, loneliness, loss of interest in activities and hobbies, and a decrease of drive and initiative.[10] There is an increased risk of substance abuse and psychiatric disorders such as borderline personality disorder, histrionic personality disorder, anxiety disorder, and conversion disorder, which ought to be monitored before focusing on eating disorders. When registering concurrent disorders, if the pastoral healer is not professionally competent, then, as in all other similar situations, a team approach using both professional and pastoral healers is needed.

(7) Despite many differences, professional and pastoral practices have certain commonalities in approaching eating disorders. The basic motor of eating disorders is a special fear that Corey summarizes as "Only when I am perfectly skinny can I be secure."[11] For professionals' and pastoral healers, the first step in healing an eating disorder is usually attempting to establish new eating habits while respecting the patients' wishes and needs. Barlow

states, "Patients should be allowed to choose what they eat in their meals and snacks. The only condition is that the meals and snacks must not be followed by vomiting, laxative misuse, or any other compensatory behavior."[12] This approach helps patients realize that healing is within their control, understand the adverse consequences of eating disorders, and commit to healing and, by doing so, gain a crucial existential security. Among Christians it is common knowledge that complete security does not exist without God. "Replacement security," based only on patients' self-discipline, does not give sufficient security to overcome the feeling of irrational fears. Most believers and nonbelievers need a stronger self-confidence, optimism, and security than what the described behavioral methods can provide. In such cases, more profound and thoroughgoing psychodynamic, cognitive behavioral, or existential therapeutic interventions are used to psychologically and spiritually resolve the cause (the dysfunctional beliefs bringing about low self-esteem, fears of unfitness, retroflexed anger, self-hate, depression, and other self-defeating attitudes) of the patients' insecurity and motivation to find security by becoming thin. In healing such irrational beliefs and fears, pastoral healers go a step further than professionals.

(8) The pastoral healer's imminent task is to understand what is really happening in the affected individual's heart, mind, and soul. Corey explains that "humans set goals for themselves, and behavior becomes unified in the context of these goals." Eating disorders occur in the context of a particular kind of "fictional finalism" or a "guiding self-ideal,"[13] which, in people choosing self-defeating patterns of fasting, vomiting, or purging, aims at resolving the irrational fear "Only when I am perfectly skinny can I be secure." These overvalued ideas reflect a basic problem of belief and faith that we described previously as a form of estrangement from God, a half-hearted trust and reliance on Jesus' love, care, and providence in seeking existential security. This basic belief problem (common in all eating disorders) is addressed by pastoral healers in two steps: coming to an understanding of the real reasons behind patients' fear and resistance against trusting God and then giving them biblical truths that reveal the existential security found in Jesus.

(9) In understanding the patients' fears and resistance, let us quote Corey again: "Courage develops when people become aware of their

strength, when they feel they belong and are not alone, and when they have a sense of hope and can see new possibilities for themselves and their daily living."[14] Patients with eating disorders would ask, though, what could bring about stronger courage than being skinny, successful, attractive, popular, powerful, and desired, admired, and envied by everyone? How could trusting an invisible and sensorially nonexistent God provide a greater security than the visible, touchable, and measurable triumphal jubilation of countless admirers? What could be more rewarding than being a venerated social idol? Thus, the crucial task of the pastoral healer is to help patients discern the right answers to these hard questions.

(10) People suffering from eating disorders are convinced of their distorted views to the point of almost seeing themselves as "like God, knowing good and evil" (Gen. 3:5). The pastoral approach is correcting this mirage or, in professional terms, replacing the patient's "goals of perfection" (success, admiration, superiority, and desirability) with biblical humility, simplicity, and modesty, thus replacing worldly idolatry with biblical ideals. Pastoral healing occurs in the context of a Socratic dialogue aiming at practically demonstrating St. Paul's truths: "Therefore I am content with weaknesses, insults, hardships, persecutions and calamities for the sake of Christ; for whenever I am weak, I am strong" (2 Cor. 12:10). Only choosing worldly weakness and becoming biblically strong brings about a courage stronger than the false lures and rewards of social idolatry. Feeling, knowing, and experiencing this eternal truth enables its practice and proves that good discipleship correlates to excellent mental health.

(11) In treating eating disorders in which sexuality and eroticism play a significant role, the pastoral healer can also clarify that sexual attraction is not synonymous with erotic attraction, that erotic attraction is even less synonymous with love, and that love is not synonymous with Christian love—the crescendo of a lasting, joyful relationship unavailable even to the most popular idols. The relevant aspects of relational issues will be discussed in the third part of this book.

(12) Replacing a "bad addiction" of narcissistic idolatry of worshipping one's own body with a "good addiction" of belonging to the kingdom of God is probably the most effective treatment for people with eating disorders.

But it has one precondition: the wholehearted commitment to discipleship. From people suffering from eating disorders, Jesus requires a genuine commitment to discipleship, for which success, social appreciation, superiority, and an erotic body image are the least relevant preconditions. Appreciating the spiritual and psychological components of discipleship and Christian love (instead of sex appeal) is, for people with eating disorders, an acid test of faith.

Notes

[1] DSM-5. *Diagnostic and Statistical Manual of the American Psychiatric Association* (2013), 169.

[2] Ibid., 170.

[3] Benjamin James Sadock, Virginia Alcott Sadock, and Pedro Ruiz, *Kaplan and Sadock's Synopsis of Psychiatry: Behavioral Sciences/Clinical Psychiatry*, 11th ed. (Philadelphia, PA: Wolters Kluwer, 2015), 509–15.

[4] DSM-5, 172.

[5] Sadock, Sadock, and Ruiz, *Kaplan and Sadock's Synopsis of Psychiatry*, 11th ed. 519–20.

[6] DSM-5, 174–6.

[7] Sadock, Sadock, and Ruiz, *Kaplan and Sadock's Synopsis of Psychiatry*, 11th ed. 519–20.

[8] David H. Barlow (ed.), *Clinical Handbook of Psychological Disorders: A Step-by-Step Treatment Manual* (New York: The Guilford Press, 2008), 578.

[9] Linda Seligman and Laurie W. Reichenberg, *Selecting Effective Treatments* (Hoboken, NJ: John Wiley & Sons, 2014), 281.

[10] Barlow, *Clinical Handbook of Psychological Disorders*, 578.

[11] Gerald Corey, *Theory and Practice of Counseling and Psychotherapy* (Belmont, CA: Thomson/ Brooks/Cole, 2005), 96.

[12] Barlow, *Clinical Handbook of Psychological Disorders*, 596.

[13] Corey, *Theory and Practice of Counseling and Psychotherapy*, 96.

[14] Ibid., 101.

CHAPTER EIGHTEEN

SLEEP DISORDERS AND THEIR PASTORAL TREATMENT

From a medical and pastoral perspective, two categories of sleep disorders can be distinguished: insomnia and parasomnia.

18.1 Insomnia Disorder

Insomnia disorder is characterized by the DSM-5[1] as dissatisfaction with either the quantity or quality of sleep due to difficulty falling or staying asleep or early awakening from sleep, occurring at least three nights per week for three months. Insomnia is often associated with anxiety disorders, depression, manic disorder, and different somatization disorders. Insomnia is the most widespread psychological problem, found in 30–45 percent of adults. It can be transient or persistent. The most common reason for the first type is stress, anxiety, or life changes, and in this case a normal sleep pattern often spontaneously re-establishes itself. In persistent sleep problems, tension and anxiety are most often the reasons for insomnia. People "discharge the anxiety through physiological channels" and they "may complain chiefly of apprehensive feelings or ruminative thoughts that appear to keep them from falling asleep." As noted, insomnia may cause first mild, then serious, emotional and behavioral problems. Its first signs are tiredness and an inability to focus, sustain attention, and perform complicated mental operations. Its more prominent signs are losing emotional balance, irritability, restlessness, impulsivity, aggression, depression, and even dissociative states of mind.[2]

18.2 Parasomnia

Parasomnia concerns a large group of disorders. From the pastoral perspective, let us focus only on nightmares. According to the DSM-5, these are "occurrences of repeated, extremely dysphoric, and well-remembered dreams that usually involve an effort to avoid threats to survival, security, or physical integrity." However, after "awakening the individual rapidly becomes oriented and alert."[3] Sadock, Sadock, and Ruiz characterize nightmares as vivid dreams that, as they progress, become more anxiety-producing, ultimately resulting in awakening and sometimes trouble or anxiety about falling back to sleep. Around 50 percent of the adult population have occasional nightmares, especially in situations of stress, anxiety, or other illnesses. Occasionally, a dissociated state of mind may accompany nightmares, causing the person to act automatically (i.e., sleepwalk) without being able to recall their activities.[4]

Pastoral Considerations

(1) Treating sleep disorders is not easy for three reasons. Firstly, as Seligman and Reichenberg observe, insomnia complaints are often trivialized and undervalued by professionals. Secondly, patients are reluctant to consider a correlation between sleeping problems and life-management problems.[5] And thirdly, the fact that it is easier to sleep beside a waterfall than beside a dripping tap proves the complex nature of this delicate neurological-psychological-spiritual problem. Nevertheless, healing usually starts with trying the simplest approaches.

(2) Clarifying that with aging the need for sleep declines or taking hygienic and dietetic measures like exercising and avoiding overeating before going to bed may be sufficient to ease sleeping problems.

(3) Seligman and Reichenberg recommend the following simple steps

for resolving both simple and complicated sleeping problems (the latter not related to medical reasons): (a) go to bed only when tired, (b) use the bedroom for sleeping only (not for work, watching television, or eating), (c) do not nap during the day, (d) get up and do something after 15–20 minutes of sleeplessness, (e) wake up in the morning at the same time every day as if you have slept well.[6]

(4) There is a plurality of cognitive behavioral approaches, relaxation techniques, stimulus controls, and biofeedback approaches in healing insomnia. For treatment of light, occasional insomnia, Frankl advocates "dereflection." Patients suffering from sleeplessness often complain that they become especially concerned with falling asleep at bedtime. It appears that this concern inhibits their falling asleep. Asking "Why can't I sleep?" acts as a self-fulfilling prophecy; it stops the body (especially the muscles) from relaxing and the mind from falling asleep. Such hyperintention to sleep, in Frankl's recommendation, "must be replaced by the paradoxical intention to stay awake."[7] This vicious cycle is stopped by intentionally keeping the eyes open and "not being willing to fall asleep." This takes away the expectation that anxiety causes through the "duty to fall asleep" and makes sleeping easier.

(5) If all of the simple methods have been tried and the noted disorders and psychological reasons excluded, a professional may consider prescribing medication. Sleeping medications are a double-edged sword, however. They quickly and easily resolve sleeplessness in many cases, but their side effects and the possibility for addiction limit their efficiency as a long-term solution. Benzodiazepine use has reached alarming proportions. It is easier to get a prescription for Ambien (Zolpidem) than it is to discover through therapy the underlying cause of anxiety or insomnia.

(6) Borderline, histrionic, and narcissistic personality disorders, PTSD, and especially mood disorders (hypomanic, manic, and depression) may be the cause of insomnia. In these cases, psychiatric treatment may be necessary. Resolving personal, family, occupational, or vocational conflicts, frustrations, and ambivalence may require psychotherapy.

(7) Insomnia is obviously a sign of stress in most cases. Stress is an unintended response to worldly tasks, insecurities, and responsibilities,

among other things. For Christians, though, stress may rather be understood as a sign of overvaluing and overly worrying about biological being rather the spiritual meaning. In this context, stress is a call for entering into the kingdom of God more deeply. Thus, if all other reasons for insomnia are excluded, then insomnia may be a sign of a special kind of stress coming from the tension between Christians' God-given purpose and the realities of their worldliness—a gap between comfy living and God's call for sainthood.

(8) Jesus and his disciples also lived hectic and stressful lives, but there are no biblical reports about them suffering from exaggerated worry, burnout, angst, irritability, depression, insomnia, or other symptoms of prolonged stress. Western Christians today are not living in fear of persecution as in the early church, so their stress exposure ought to be lower. This suggests that the problem may not be that Christians today have too much stress but that they have too little resilience. The crucial question then is what the difference is between our postmodern Western stress management and that of Jesus Christ, his disciples, and the early church.

(9) Many contemporary Christians suffering from insomnia do not perceive themselves as being exemplary saints, but since they work hard, live satisfactory family lives, pay taxes, and bring up their children, they often do not see a reason to change anything in their lives. Nevertheless, virtually all of us live in stress like the rich young man described in Mark 10:17–31, who kept all the commandments but still felt called upon to do something more to inherit eternal life. On the other hand, we observe that Jesus' closest disciples were not ambivalent in their efforts to inherit eternal life and did not suffer from stress-related irritability, insomnia, or dysphoria. Thus, faith helps disciples to bear any and every worldly stress: the greater one's submission to Jesus, the less their vulnerability to stress. Based upon this understanding, the crucial purpose of the pastoral healing of stress-related insomnia is to help affected Christians grow in discipleship and confidently hope in Jesus' words promising the security of eternal life.

(10) Resolving stress requires that the patient and healer work together in discerning what Jesus requires for one to have "treasures in heaven" and bringing the patient to trust Jesus' words about already having eternal life. This, as the ancient saying puts it, enables "Christians being another Christ"

even in paradoxically accepting suffering but not being stressed out by it. This psychological-spiritual condition enabled Jesus, who suffered more than any human (as Mark 4:35–41 and Matthew 8:23–27 report), able to sleep even in a small boat on the stormy Sea of Galilee. Following Jesus also enables a disciple to follow his sleep patterns.

(11) In my practice, I was repeatedly surprised by the paramount power of faith in healing stress (including stress arising from insomnia). However, the effect of biblical peace, relaxation, trust, and optimism in countering stress and as a treatment for insomnia depends on the believer's commitment to Jesus. Peace brings relaxation, and relaxation brings healthy, restful sleep.

(12) Let us ask a question that many readers may ask: do dreams enable information beyond rational and empirical knowledge?

According to Carl Gustav Jung, "Many dreams contain messages from the deepest layers of the unconscious, which he describes as the source of creativity." They "reflect an individual's personal unconscious and the collective unconscious of all humanity." The collective unconscious is "the deepest part of the psyche containing the accumulation of inherited experiences of the human and prehuman species," which Jung calls "archetypes." Archetypes contain "thoughts, feelings, and actions," and "in a dream all of these parts can be considered manifestations of who and what we are."[8]

In his dream analysis, Freud was focused on discerning the suppressed and unconscious aspects of the human personality. Also, Frankl notes that, "after all, dreams are the true creations of the unconscious, and therefore we may expect that not only elements of the instinctual unconscious will come to the fore, but elements of the spiritual unconscious as well." He gives an example.

"A woman dreamed that, along with her dirty washing, she took a dirty cat to the laundry. When she came to pick up the laundry she found the cat was dead." As she said, she loved her cat "above all," equal to how she described loving her daughter. "From this we may infer that the cat stands for 'child.' But why was the cat 'dirty'?... [Because] she had been worrying about gossip surrounding her daughter's love life—her 'dirty linen' was being washed in public. That was the reason why the patient, as she admitted, was constantly watching and hounding her daughter. The dream therefore expressed a warning to the patient to not torment her daughter with exaggerated demands of moral 'cleanness' or she might lose her child."[9]

In ancient times, the apperception of reality was different than in contemporary times; our ancestors wondered whether dreams were the reality, or the inverse, was reality a dream. No wonder there are countless descriptions of people receiving messages in dreams. Additionally, the Scriptures describe visions and dreams as a form of communication with God. Examples include Jacob's dream described in Genesis 28:10–17 and Solomon's dream described in 1 Kings 3:5–15. Also, St. Joseph received many angelic visitations in the form of divinely inspired dreams. In dreams he was instructed to take Mary, already with child, as his spouse. Likewise, dreams instructed him to take Mary and Jesus to Egypt and later to return the Holy Family to Israel. Faw gives the following advice to Christians who "wish to make wise use of the gift of dreams."

(a) Recognize that while God may speak to us through a particular dream, this is not the norm.

(b) Write them [dreams] down immediately upon awakening and take time to reflect on what they may indicate.

(c) Adopt an expectant attitude. Dreams may provide useful keys to self-understanding if one is teachable.

(d) Share your dreams with someone else and ask that person to help you understand its message.

(e) Do not be overly concerned about whether a dream is predicting the future.

(f) Since we know God is interested in our growth, we can ask him as often as needed for wisdom to learn from our dreams.[10]

Christians may approach dreams with both common sense and the discernment of the Holy Spirit.

Notes

[1] DSM-5. *Diagnostic and Statistical Manual of the American Psychiatric Association* (2013), 181.

[2] Benjamin James Sadock, Virginia Alcott Sadock, and Pedro Ruiz, *Kaplan and Sadock's Synopsis of Psychiatry: Behavioral Sciences/Clinical Psychiatry*, 11th ed. (Philadelphia, PA: Wolters Kluwer, 2015), 532–44.

[3] DSM-5, 191.

[4] Sadock, Sadock, and Ruiz, *Kaplan and Sadock's Synopsis of Psychiatry*, 11th ed. 556–7.

[5] Linda Seligman and Laurie W. Reichenberg, *Selecting Effective Treatments* (Hoboken, NJ: John Wiley & Sons, 2014), 308.

[6] Ibid., 313.

[7] Viktor E. Frankl, *The Doctor and the Soul, From Psychotherapy to Logotherapy* (New York: Vintage Books, 1973), 253–4.

[8] Gerald Corey, *Theory and Practice of Counseling and Psychotherapy* (Belmont, CA: Thomson/ Brooks/Cole, 2005), 96.

[9] Viktor E. Frankl, *Man's Search for Ultimate Meaning* (New York: Basic Books, 2000), 47–8.

[10] Harold W. Faw, *Psychology in a Christian Perspective, an Analysis of Key Issues* (Grand Rapids, MI: Baker Books, 1995), 66.

CHAPTER NINETEEN

SEXUAL DYSFUNCTIONS AND THEIR PASTORAL TREATMENT

The DSM-5[1] lists the following conditions within the category of sexual dysfunctions: delayed ejaculation, erectile disorder, female orgasmic disorder, female sexual interest/arousal disorder, genito-pelvic penetration disorder, male hypoactive sexual disorder, and premature (early) ejaculation disorder. From a pastoral perspective we will discuss those that are sexual desire disorders, sexual excitement disorders, and orgasm disorders.

19.1 Sexual Desire Disorders

Male hypoactive sexual disorder and *female sexual interest disorder* are, according to the DSM-5, characterized by a deficit in (or absence of) sexual/erotic thoughts, fantasies, and desires for a duration of at least six months.[2] According to Kaplan and Sadock's textbook, "an estimated twenty percent of people have hypoactive sexual desire disorder." Such people "often use the inhibition of desire defensively, to protect against unconscious fears about sex." However, "Loss of desire may also be an expression to a partner or the sign of deteriorating relationship," and in other cases marital discord is also a significant consequence of the disorder. Associated problems are low self-esteem, depression, not accepting one's own sexual nature, and feelings of guilt, all of which may exacerbate the disorder.[3] In other words, what are altered sexual behaviors trying to tell partners, spouses, therapists, and pastoral healers? Changes in behavior and libido can be symptoms of dysfunctional relationships or other disorders altogether, some serious, that present as sexual symptoms.

19.2 Sexual Excitement Disorders

Erectile disorder is characterized according the DSM-5[4] as a significant difficulty in obtaining or maintaining an erection during sexual activity or a significant decrease in erectile rigidity (in 75–100 percent of occasions) for at least six months. Female sexual arousal disorder is, in Sadock, Sadock, and Ruiz's definition, characterized by reduced initiation of, unreceptiveness to, and reduced pleasure in sexual activities, sexual cues, and genital or nongenital sensations (in 75–100 percent of occasions). The disorder in both sexes can be temporary (which is the case for about 10–20 percent of males) or persistent (for about 1 percent of males). The cause of erectile disorder can be organic (hormonal) or psychological. The presence of sexual fantasies, genital arousal, and especially interest in masturbation indicates a psychological reason.[5]

19.3 Orgasm Disorders

Premature ejaculation is characterized according to the DSM-5 by a persistent or temporary pattern of ejaculation within approximately one minute of vaginal penetration and more often occurring before the person wishes it to (in 75–100 percent of occasions) for at least six months. *Delayed ejaculation* is characterized by a significant delay in (or infrequency or absence of) ejaculation for approximately six months (in 75–100 percent of occasions). *Female orgasmic disorder* is characterized as a significant delay in or infrequency, absence, or reduced intensity of orgasmic feelings (in 75–100 percent of occasions) for a duration of approximately six months.[6]

Orgasmic disorders have a prevalence of about 5 percent in both men and women. Their frequency is to some degree age-related. While the orgasmic potential in men decreases with age, in women it shows the opposite trend. In the last few decades, an increase in delayed ejaculation has been observed. "This has been attributed to the increased use of antidepressants, which can have the side effects of delayed ejaculation, as well as a high use of internet pornography sites,"[7] which, as we will later discuss, decrease the arousing effect of real partners. Another common reason for orgasmic disorders is perceiving sex as dirty, sinful, or an aversion to the partner. In women, fear of pregnancy may also have a role.

Pastoral Considerations

(1) There are significant differences between medical and pastoral approaches to sexual dysfunctions. Medicine analyses human sexuality from a biological-psychological-sociological perspective, while the pastoral perspective takes a theological-psychological-spiritual view. For a professional therapist, the central question is whether a particular sexual behavior causes clinically significant distress or impairment in social, occupational, or other areas of functioning. For a pastoral healer, the crucial question is whether one's sexual behaviors contribute to a fruitful spiritual-psychological relationship with God as well as family members and neighbours. From a medical perspective, the purpose of sexual behaviors is to satisfy one's own sexual needs in a way that does not collide with legal, social, academic, occupational, and other areas of functioning, while from the pastoral perspective sexuality has the purpose of promoting Christlike love and procreation. While Christian moral standards are not a primary focus for professionals, the pastoral perspective is holistic and focused on Jesus' teachings on the acceptable and correct use of sexuality—its place in the divine order—and the well-being of all parties.

(2) The medical approach is focused on sexuality but not on love, which St. Paul tells us in 1 Corinthians 13 is the highest attainment of all the virtues. The lack of love in a relationship is neither a medical problem nor a medical diagnosis despite it being the possible reason for countless behavioral disorders, such as sexual desire, excitement, or orgasmic dysfunctions as well as other psychological, legal, and criminal behaviors occurring in

loveless relationships. On the contrary, pastoral healing is primarily focused on facilitating Christian love, which heals almost any relational problem.

(3) While the medical understanding of sexuality is regulated by instinct adjusted to social standards, in the Christian understanding, even sexual pleasure is a function, sign, and expression of Jesus' love. This has a practical importance since Christlike love supersedes DSM-5 categories and may flourish in Christian relationships despite all distressing conditions. For example, mutual affection may flourish even if an absolute sexual gratification is missing in a relationship. Although healing DSM-5-listed medical disorders is important from the pastoral perspective, it is nevertheless even more important to foster the giving and receiving of biblical trust, appreciation, respect, peace, joy, empathy, and spiritual support. If God is genuinely present in a relationship, almost all relational problems, sexual and otherwise, can be much more easily resolved.

(4) Numerous sexual dysfunctions listed in the DSM-5 are characterized, as Seligman and Reichenberg note, by anxiety, insecurity, fantasies, and disinformation about sexual life. Negative information about sex is typical for both sexes. "Once a sexual dysfunction develops, it is more likely to continue and permeate all phases of sexual functioning, negatively impacting desire arousal and orgasm,"[8] provoking performance anxiety or other medical conditions.

(5) Performance anxiety, the most common problem in sexual life, is rooted in seeking sexual pleasure according to prescribed pass/fail standards. As Viktor Frankl describes it:

> Pleasure and happiness are by-products. Happiness must ensue. It cannot be pursued. It is the very pursuit of happiness that thwarts happiness. The more one makes happiness an aim, the more he misses the aim. And this is most conspicuous in cases of sexual neurosis such as frigidity and impotence. Sexual performance or experience is strangled to the extent to which it is made either an object of attention or an objective of intention. I have called this first one "hyperreflection" and the second "hyperintention."[9]

Respectively, measuring sexual life according to socially-indoctrinated criteria evokes the hyperintention "to enjoy sex as it ought to be enjoyed" and facilitates hyperreflection, that is, a self-scrutinizing "Am I enjoying sex with him/her sufficiently?" (This can often become a shallow quantitative rather than a qualitative judgment.) This becomes a vicious cycle. A hyperintention of sexual pleasure facilitates subjects' hyperreflection and shifts their attention from their partners onto themselves, whether their sexual enjoyment is as it is required. Since their attention is not focused on their partners anymore (but on scrutinizing themselves), the partners' sexual attractiveness decreases, contributing to countless desire, arousal, and orgasmic disorders. Anytime the focus is shifted from the partner to the self, the sacramental nature of marriage and its attendant sexual union is lost.

(7) In cases of dysfunctions brought on by hyperreflection, sensate focusing is helpful. Couples can enjoy closeness and intimacy but without the duty of having intercourse, reducing the feeling of being pressured and judged.[10] Viktor Frankl recommends that the pastoral healer set a (virtual) prohibition: "You may hug, kiss, fondle, and do anything you'd like—except one thing: seek intercourse." (The healer does not reveal that this prohibition is set with only the purpose of it being transgressed). As partners hug and kiss, they stimulate each other erotically (but without hyperintending intercourse). Overwhelming erotic stimulation helps partners to transgress the prohibition and spontaneously have sexual intercourse.[11] This happens in a manner not unlike the previous instance in which prohibition yielded positive results. We earlier saw that a cure for insomnia is for someone to forbid himself to fall asleep, resulting in the opposite effect. In the same way, two people (assuming that they are a loving, committed Christian couple) may find the desired result by attempting to force themselves away from that which is desired.

(8) The pastoral healer's purpose in healing all relational problems is to coach partners in their mutual reflection on God's love. All forms of love (sexual, erotic, psychological, and spiritual) are by-products of replicating God's love. Sexual gratification, erotic attraction, and psychological and spiritual unity are, for Christians, expressions of their union with Jesus.

Sexuality is found not only in "being one flesh" but also in being of one mind and being one in God's glory. Some couples pray after having intercourse, appreciating sex as God's gift, bringing married couples closer to each other and God. Without a genuine psychological and spiritual oneness and unity in God—expressed also in giving and receiving biblical trust, optimism, joy, peace, purpose, and unselfishness—erotic and sexual attraction will quickly vanish. Metaphorically, erotic and sexual heaven turns unavoidably into hell.

(9) Procreation of new life is also a foretaste of union with God. In it, Christians experience participating in a mystery that surpasses their understanding, a mystery that enables them to participate in the creation of life according to the means by which God wisely established procreation in the human species. It is a union with and a participation in the God who continually pours forth himself in ongoing acts of creation in order to add to the Mystical Body of Christ. Accordingly, sexuality—contrary to the DSM-5 perspective—is, for Christians, a tool that enables them to know and feel their participation in a union not only with each other but primarily with God. Such love has eternal meaning, importance, and consequences which are unfortunately out of the reach and attention of the DSM-5 categories. It substantiates that pastoral healing can give what even medicine, despite all its performances, is unable to.

Notes

[1] DSM-5. *Diagnostic and Statistical Manual of the American Psychiatric Association* (2013), 201.

[2] Ibid.

[3] Benjamin James Sadock, Virginia Alcott Sadock, and Pedro Ruiz, *Kaplan and Sadock's Synopsis of Psychiatry: Behavioral Sciences/Clinical Psychiatry*, 11th ed. (Philadelphia, PA: Wolters Kluwer, 2015), 525–77.

[4] DSM-5, 202.

[5] Sadock, Sadock, and Ruiz, *Kaplan and Sadock's Synopsis of Psychiatry*, 11th ed. 576.

[6] DSM-5, 201.

[7] Linda Seligman and Laurie W. Reichenberg, *Selecting Effective Treatments* (Hoboken, NJ: John Wiley & Sons, 2014), 289.

[8] Ibid., 287.

[9] Viktor E. Frankl, *Man's Search for Ultimate Meaning* (New York: Basic Books, 2000), 89–91.

[10] Seligman and Reichenberg, *Selecting Effective Treatments*, 290.

[11] Viktor E. Frankl, *Aerztliche Seelsorge* (Vienna: Franz Deuticke, 1965), 168–70.

CHAPTER TWENTY

PARAPHILIC DISORDERS AND THEIR PASTORAL TREATMENT

The DSM-5 distinguishes the following forms of paraphilia disorder: voyeuristic disorder (seeking sexual excitement by observing non-consenting people naked or engaged in sexual intercourse), exhibitionistic disorder (sexual arousal by exposing one's genitals to a nonconsenting person), frotteuristic disorder (sexual arousal by touching or rubbing against a nonconsenting person), sexual masochism disorder (seeking sexual arousal by being humiliated, bound, or made to suffer), sexual sadism disorder (sexual arousal by making other nonconsenting people suffer), paedophilic disorder (sexual arousal and behaviors with children aged thirteen or younger), fetishist disorder (seeking sexual arousal from things or nongenital body parts), transvestic disorder (seeking sexual arousal from cross-dressing), zoophilia (sexual arousal through animals), necrophilia (sexual arousal through corpses), coprophilia (sexual arousal through faeces), urophilia (sexual arousal through urine), and klismaphila (sexual arousal through enemas).[1] All these conditions can be diagnosed after a duration of at least six months. Kaplan and Sadock's textbook offers an effective summary of paraphilia:

The major functions of human sexual behavior assist in bonding, to create mutual pleasure in cooperation with the partner, to enhance love between two people, and to procreate. Paraphilic disorders are divergent behaviors in that these acts involve aggression, victimization, and extreme one-sidedness. The behaviors exclude or harm others and disrupt the potential for bonding between people.[2]

As in other disorders, paraphilia is regarded as pathological only if it causes a significant impairment in personal, occupational, social, or academic functioning of the person. Despite this, paraphilia is practiced by a relatively small proportion of people, but because of the nature of the disorder, it nevertheless victimizes the general population. For example, an estimated 10–20 percent of children are exposed to abuse by people suffering from paedophilia by the age of eighteen, and about 20 percent of adult women have been exposed to exhibitionism and voyeurism. Paraphilia comprises disorders that have a multi-aetiological cause, including endogenous, neurological-endocrinal, and psychologically-learned components.[3] Seligman and Reichenberg report that among sexually abused children, 41 percent have school problems and 25 percent have been patients in psychiatric hospitals. Furthermore, "Molestation as a child can predispose a person to accept continued abuse as an adult, or conversely, to become an abuser of others."[4]

The pernicious side of such disorders is that they cause a ripple effect. They spread through families and communities, usually in secret or via the Internet, causing considerable medical, psychological, and spiritual harm.

Pastoral Considerations

(1) As Seligman and Reichenberg note, paraphilic disorders are probably much more common than statistics indicate, mostly because only a small number of affected people seek help. On the other hand, many sexualized behaviors are "below the diagnostic line." Respectively, "Such 'paraphilia-related disorders' may include compulsive masturbation, telephone sex,

dependence on pornography, cybersex and protracted promiscuity, among others."[5]

(2) Mild or soft paraphilic disorders may include occupations that arouse fantasies, perhaps followed by masturbation. The criterion between mild and malignant forms of paraphilic disorders is whether the subject's eliciting is composed of sufficient engagement in sexual fantasies or whether, in severe cases, physical coercion, victimization, or even murder are necessary.[6]

(3) The behavioral endorsement of sexual fantasies in paraphilic disorders usually follows guilt, sorrow, and fear. With passing time, tension that is otherwise impossible to release builds up again and can be released only by a repeated act of paraphilia.[7] In general, paraphilic disorders appear less often in females. Sadistic and masochistic impulses appear in a ratio of 20:1 in favour of male perpetrators. Although half of all people engaged in paraphilic disorders are married, most have some impairment in their married lives and most complain of distress, frustration, and angst in their personal and social functioning. Usually, the partner, a family member, or a friend encourages patients to commit to healing, but in most cases the negative consequences of the paraphilic behaviors (moral, personal, relational, and legal conflict) are sufficient for motivating patients to get treatment.[8]

(4) While the professional criteria of sexual normality (in discerning what is paraphilia and what is not) are based on changeable social standards, the pastoral criteria of sexual morality are based on biblical standards, natural law, and the interests of society as a whole.

(5) Although orthodox evolutionist schools of thought are (like the fight for survival itself) mercilessly realistic, while the Christian worldview is extremely loving, forgiving, and meek, the two are in unison in their understandings of the basic purposes of sexuality. Sexuality from these standpoints serves to express mutual love, joy, commitment, fidelity, and to multiply life. The DSM-5, however, is based mostly on the current Western mental climate (preferring abundant sex with no pregnancy) and accordingly differs from both the biological natural law and Godly perspectives.

(6) Let us next analyse a well-known paraphilia labelled as such from the biological, legal, social, medical, and pastoral perspectives, like that of

paedophilia, sexual arousal from and behaviors with children aged thirteen or under. Such a "philia" (attraction) is contrary to genuine love. In healing affected subjects, one question usually comes up: why is paedophilia excluded from genuine love if seduced victims allegedly, as some perpetrators state, "willingly participate"?

It is excluded because coercion, seduction, brainwashing, or a defence mechanism called "identification with the aggressor," not love, motivate victims' alleged willing participation. In such relationships, the victim's personality is "taken away." Losing one's personality (as noted with schizophrenia) is accompanied by extreme fear and horror, but there is only one situation in which giving up one's personality does not cause distress: in genuine trusting, committed, and blissful love, in establishing that "my *I* and your *you* are one common *we.*" However, children are not able to experience this; they are too immature to lovingly give their personalities in sexual intercourse and regain their self after the sexual act occurs, which is what happens in mature people. On the contrary, children are emotionally overwhelmed by sexual stimulation. They are unable to intentionally and rationally control their behaviors and accordingly feel as if they are losing their personalities or that their personalities are being taken away. This causes sexually abused children to see themselves as annihilated individuals and react with shame, disgust, guilt, humiliation, and panic paired with feelings of worthlessness, self-hate, and depression. Such feelings result in the eruption of pathology, starting from acting-out behaviors and extending to suicidal behavior, drug use, borderline personality disorder, and countless other pathologies. Since, in the subconscious phantasms of abused children, it is often "better to be the abuser than the abused," they identify with the aggressor and may willingly participate in their own abuse out of fear or may themselves become abusers. A pandemic of pathology therefore spreads through time, from generation to generation.

(7) From a forensic perspective, people with paraphilia have no freedom in choosing their sexual preferences but do have the freedom to choose to abstain from or practice their inverted sexual preferences. Most people suffering from paraphilia engage in their sexual activities (with corpses, children, animals, or things) because they feel inferior or are afraid of

rejection in relationships with adult partners. Thus, healing is focused on the one hand on helping subjects to resolve their fears relating to partners appropriate in age, sex, and psychological and spiritual aspects, and on the other hand helping them to develop strong moral inhibitions against abusive, sadistic, and predatory sexual behaviors.

(8) Unfortunately, many "paraphilic disorders seem to be treatment-resistant, and behaviors tend to increase when the person is under stress." Modern medicine has not yet developed satisfying treatment methods for all kinds of paraphilic disorders. Nevertheless, the prognosis, from a professional perspective, is better with subjects possessing great moral strength and intrinsic motivation for treatment and sexual relationships with appropriate adult partners.[9]

(9) In pastoral healing of victims of sexual abuse, the first task in healing is to ensure the abuse victim's safety. Next is to avoid the contamination of the victim's recollections. Only after investigations are completed should victims talk to third parties (including pastoral healers) about the details of their abuse. The pastoral healing of abused children consists of giving age-appropriate explanations about sexuality and what really happened to them, clarifying that they are victims and not perpetrators. A further purpose is increasing victims' self-esteem, demonstrating that they are lovable and loved by God and their families and then coaching them in protecting themselves from future abuse. It seeks to include such children in church activities, scouts, and sports and especially to foster their school performance by helping them to become commendable students. It is essential to promote closeness to Jesus, which helps victims process their feelings of guilt and humiliation and place their traumatic experiences into a meaningful context by eventually forgiving their perpetrators. Modern culture fails to understand that forgiveness has a cleansing property that few other acts can duplicate. While modern medicine may fall short, a Christian perspective forever relies on the undeniable truth that perfect love casts out all fears (1 John 4:18).

(10) The perpetrators of sexual abuse also need professional help, and if they are believers they might also seek pastoral healing. The pastoral healer may help in acknowledging the gravity of the damage done, encouraging

the abuser to voluntarily take the appropriate steps and measures to avoid the possibility of future incidents, motivating the abuser to get professional healing and coaching the abuser in becoming a "master of instinct and servant of conscience." This is the pathway to healing their grave inferiority; helping them to fulfil their family role; easing their feelings of being unloved and unlovable, lonely, incompetent, abandoned, and unworthy; and fuelling their determination to heal alcohol, drug addictions, and concurrent psychological problems.

(11) Pastoral healers encourage repentance, discipleship, trust in Jesus' mercy, and rebirth through the Spirit, which is the ultimate antidote for all forms and nuances of paraphilic and sexually abusive behaviors. The perpetrators may be helped to realize that the more they seek a deep and committed relationship with God, the more they will change, grow, and progress in fulfilling their Christian family role and the more they will achieve what all humans desire: genuine biblical peace, love, joy, and other gifts of the Holy Spirit.

(12) Rape is not a paraphilia but a power struggle in which sexuality is used with a sadistic purpose. Victims of rape are harmed physically but much more so psychologically. Being treated as a sexual object and being cruelly coerced into giving up their personalities in serving rapists' sexual desires causes extreme panic, humiliation, pain, helplessness, and feelings of worthlessness and guilt, facilitating in victims the impression that all sexuality is awful and horrifying. Pastoral care for rape victims is similar to that for victims of posttraumatic stress disorder. It aims to help them regain their self-esteem, peace, and courage to grasp that they are still temples of the Holy Spirit, able to control their sexualized "will to power" in the face of sinful and sick rapists.

(13) As noted, from a professional perspective, paraphilic disorders often seem to be treatment-resistant. This is not the case in God's perspective, however. Living in and with God does not make paraphilic sexual drives disappear, but genuine faith gives patients the power to control them more effectively. Are we irrationally optimistic? No. As Matthew 17:20–21 says, "For truly I tell you, if you have faith the size of a mustard seed, you

will say to this mountain 'Move from here to there' and it will move; and nothing will be impossible for you."

Notes

[1] DSM-5. *Diagnostic and Statistical Manual of the American Psychiatric Association* (2013), 333–9.

[2] Benjamin James Sadock, Virginia Alcott Sadock, and Pedro Ruiz, *Kaplan and Sadock's Synopsis of Psychiatry: Behavioral Sciences/Clinical Psychiatry*, 11th ed. (Philadelphia, PA: Wolters Kluwer, 2015), 593–600.

[3] Ibid., 595

[4] Linda Seligman and Laurie W. Reichenberg, *Selecting Effective Treatments* (Hoboken, NJ: John Wiley & Sons, 2014), 292.

[5] Ibid., 292.

[6] Ibid., 293.

[7] Ibid., 294–5.

[8] Ibid., 297.

[9] Ibid., 297.

CHAPTER TWENTY-ONE

GENDER DYSPHORIA AND ITS PASTORAL HANDLING

In discussing *gender dysphoria*, let us first define the terms we use. As Kaplan and Sadock's textbook defines it, *gender* means a sense of being a male or a female. *Dysphoria* is a mood disorder signalling dissatisfaction or discomfort. The term *transgender* describes identification with a different gender than that assigned, while the term *transsexual* refers to the desire to have the body of a different gender than that assigned. People describing themselves as "gender queer" feel themselves as being between genders, or being both male and female. So a transgender man who has an assigned female body may identify as heterosexual, homosexual, or gender queer.[1]

Usually, children start to understand themselves as being male or female around the age of three. However, according to Kaplan and Sadock's textbook, some 10% of boys below age twelve and 5% of girls below age twelve show some signs of dilemma in this area. Transgender adults (around 0.005–0.012% of males and 0.002–0.003% of females) may request medical interventions to synchronize their assigned and desired genders.[2]

The aetiology of gender dysphoria is polymorph and often unknown. When accompanying other medical conditions it may be attributed to prenatal reasons, like genetic factors (as in Turner syndrome, wherein an individual possesses only one X chromosome and appears female at birth, or Klinefelter syndrome, wherein one possesses XXY chromosomes and appears as male at birth). Hormonal factors, which determine anatomy, the wiring of the brain, and the proportion of masculinity to femininity in a person, also play a role (as in congenital adrenal hyperplasia, which causes androgenisation at birth, and the 5-alpha reductase deficiency, which is responsible for feminization at birth). Postnatal contributors include psychological problems (like attachment/individuation problems and those resulting from hostile mothering, parental rejection, abuse, and parent-child estrangement) and adverse social influences.

The DSM-5 criteria for diagnosing gender dysphoria in children include a marked incongruence between the expressed and assigned gender for six months and at least six of the following indicators: a strong desire to be the other gender; an interest in cross-dressing; an interest in cross-gender roles; an interest in toys, games, or activities used by the other gender; an interest in playmates of the other gender; a rejection of same-gender toys, games, and activities; a strong dislike of one's own sexual anatomy; a desire to match the desired gender's secondary sex characteristics; and significant distress or impairment in school or social functioning. However, most children with gender dysphoria as adults do not need surgical or other medical intervention.[3]

As Seligman and Reichenberg note, "Treatment for children with GID is controversial. Some suggest early intervention in the hopes of changing GID behavior." However, "it is not yet known how often childhood complaints about gender identity dysphoria extend to the teenage years and adulthood.[4] So treatment goals initially ought rather to focus on improving adjustment and life satisfaction than radical pharmacological or surgical interventions.

The DSM-5 criteria for adults include a marked incongruence between the expressed and assigned gender for six months and at least two of the following signs: incongruence between assigned and desired sexual characteristics; a strong desire to get rid of primary or secondary sexual characteristics; a desire for the sexual characteristics of the other gender; a desire to be the other (or an alternative) gender; a desire to be treated as the other (or an alternative) gender; the conviction of the feelings and reactions of the other (or an alternative) gender; and significant distress or impairment in work or social functioning. From a professional perspective, no so-called "reparative" or "conversion" therapy is recommended.[5]

Pastoral Considerations

(1) The pastoral approach is not primarily a debate of these criteria, but a healing. Nevertheless, pastoral healers ought to be prepared for debates, especially in healing persons suffering of gender dysphoria. As in every debate, Christian supporters of the LGBT lifestyle put forward arguments mostly based on the fact that every single human is created in God's image and likeness and that it would be unreasonable not to use technical knowledge, skills, and freedom of choice to achieve a spiritual-psycho-sexual contentment and well-being as intended by God. In answering such viewpoints, pastoral healers need to be familiar with the Scriptures and Church teachings and appreciate moral theological doctrines, but they also need to know *what is happening in the hearts, minds, and souls of their patients* (the kind of assessment that Jesus made of all people who approached him during his public ministry). They must always remember that the purpose in healing believers suffering of gender dysphoria, as in all pastoral interventions, is facilitating growth in union with God, who is love (1 Jn. 4, 8:16).

(2) Classically, the terms *gender* and *sex* meant one of the two God-created forms of the human being. In the contemporary vernacular, *sex* remains reserved to male or female, while *gender* means one's self-decided sexual role in society. Accordingly, in the mind of those suffering from gender dysphoria, natural anatomic, hormonal, and genetic factors do not determine their psychosexual characteristics because they believe that the gender-role they play in society should be their personal choice. For them, sex signifies a binary, male or female category, while gender signifies one among seventy-two self-decided social-behavioral categories. But do such concepts of gender really contribute to a more fulfilled, joyful, and contented life?

Just as our faces are slightly different, so the gender roles we exhibit in society are personal and unique. Everyone among billions of people who appreciate and carry out their natural male or female sexual roles in society does so in an idiosyncratic way. There are many billions of unique and personal gender roles that are consistent with the sex assigned by God. Only seventy-two types of newly valued gender roles cause significant suffering, impairment or distress. None of these seventy-two types are God-given gender roles. They are all self-chosen by people suffering from gender dysphoria.

(3) From a professional perspective, gender dysphoria is a diagnosable condition and a psychiatric disorder, but it can be assigned only if it causes clinically significant distress or impairment in social, vocational, occupational, or other important areas of functioning. However, as Seligman and Reichenberg note, affected people more often seek help because of anxiety, depression, drug use, low self-esteem, peer-related problems, and suicidal tendencies than the gender dysphoria itself.[6] In some cases the described distress and impairments are the consequences of social stigmata; in others they are intrinsic consequences of the chosen lifestyle. Most often they are both. A case study illustrates this.

> I treated my first case of what we call gender dysphoria today some forty years ago while living in a communist country where military service was obligatory. The patient was a twenty-three-year-old electro engineer assigned as male but perceiving herself as female. She was treated for two years because of persistent depression mostly caused by her inability to conceive. Suddenly, however, she was recruited for military service and, despite all objections, was drafted into the male infantry. Simply put, she could not identify herself with her assigned military role, and in the fourth month she ended her military career. During a war game with rifle, ammunition, helmet, and full military gear, she marched straight into the icy River Danube, where she drowned in front of her battalion.

(4) For the purpose of helping people suffering from gender dysphoria, pastoral psychiatrists and psychologists first follow the lead of Christ and understand the dynamics occurring in their patients' hearts and minds. Humans are psychological beings in the sense that they perceive

and process all spiritual and worldly information psychologically. As history proves, humans die or kill for their (true or false) social, political, or personal beliefs. While a great majority of people adjust their gender beliefs to their genetic, anatomical, and physiological realities, in people suffering from gender dysphoria, their beliefs determine their self-perceived gender more prominently than their visible, touchable, and measurable sexual characteristics.

(5) Orthodox Christians may also suffer from gender dysphoria. As Marsha Wiggins Frame reports, "Many GLB people value their faith and the beliefs of their religion more than their gender. Some, mostly those associated with fundamentalist groups, enrol in conversion or reparative programs designed to cure them of their homosexuality or bisexuality."[7] However, treatments using aversive stimuli to effect a change in sexual orientation are of questionable value, and prohibited by many professional colleges.

(6) A significant majority of Christians propose the integration of gender self-experience and assigned sexuality, which seems to them to be a much less distressing choice than other options. Christians substantiate this position by biblical directives, noted in Genesis 1:27 and 2:21–24, Deuteronomy 22:5 and 23:1, 1 Corinthians 6:9, and Romans 1:26–27.

The first official reaction of the Catholic Church came from Pope Benedict XVI in 2008, emphasizing God as the creator of male or female for every individual. Human individuals, he said, ought to therefore accept their personal, God-given sexual identities and make a purpose of it.[8] Around fifty years ago, Simon de Beauvoir proclaimed, "One is not born a woman, one becomes so." However, in the words of Pope John Paul II, when becoming what one chooses to be, hormonally or surgically, "the freedom to be creative becomes a freedom to create oneself, then necessarily the Maker himself is denied and ultimately man too is stripped of his dignity as a creature of God, as the image of God at the core of his being."[9]

A 2017 publication of the American College of Pediatricians asserts, "Human sexuality is an objective biological binary trait... [its] obvious purpose being the reproduction and flourishing of our species... a person's belief that he or she is something they are not is, at best, a sign of confused thinking." In those cases, "an objective psychological problem exists that lies in the mind, not in the body, and it should be treated as such." Accordingly, gender dysphoria, in the most recent edition of the DSM-5, is recognized as a mental disorder. Its healing ought not be a sex change since "Rates of suicide are nearly twenty times greater among adults who use cross-sex and undergo sex reassignment surgery, even in Sweden, which is among the most LGBT-affirming countries." Therefore, "Conditioning children into believing a lifetime of chemical and surgical impersonation of the opposite sex is normal and healthful is child abuse."[10]

Indeed, Bailey and Blanchard confirm that "There is no persuasive evidence that gender transition reduces gender dysphonic children's likelihood of killing themselves."[11] The president of the American College of Pediatricians further note, "twin studies prove no one is born 'trapped in the body of the opposite sex,' and that 'Gender identity is malleable, especially in young children.'" Since some "75 to 95 percent of pre-pubertal children who were distressed by their biological sex eventually outgrow the distress,"[12] the current social climate often creates more harm than good in this maturing process.

(7) It is self-evident that pastoral healers ought to be extremely non-judgemental, practically demonstrating that no gender dysphoria can exclude a patient from being a recipient of God's love. They need to continually focus on listening to the Holy Spirit's guidance as to where, when, and how to best apply the Father's law and Jesus' love for the benefit of God's kingdom. But how to apply these basic principles in practice?

(8) In treating children, the pastoral healer may first focus on comforting the religious parents who do not understand what is really going on. They may encourage parents to neither underestimate nor overestimate the importance of early impressions, taking into account that definite gender roles are established much later than at age three, or even ten. Encouraging parents' biblical optimism, hope, trust, and love, along with giving age-appropriate, Scripture-based sexual information to children, helps committed Christian families to surrender everything except submission to God. The treatment of children includes biblical, medical-psychological, individual,

family, and group counselling, as well as psychological support to explore and resolve gender identity questions in an age-appropriate context.

There is wriggle room in maleness and femaleness. As there are female sexual hormones in the blood of all males and male sexual hormones in the blood of all females, there are traditionally feminine psychological characteristics in males and traditionally masculine psychological characteristics in females. This biological fact alone could shed light on much of the confusion and misinformation surrounding the issues of gender dysphoria. Let us repeat, gender roles are not like a strait jacket. Each Christian who appreciates his or her male or female sexuality executes his or her gender role in a unique and individual way. Most often they accomplish this by avoiding the seventy-two types of gender roles that are not God-given, but self-chosen; they avoid gender dysphoria, which the DSM-5 defines as a diagnosable condition causing significant impairment and distress. Obsessive fantasizing about how it would feel to be some other sex or gender is harmful to adults. And the compulsive manipulation of immature children by encouraging them explore how it would feel to be some other sex or gender is even more harmful. Even school aged children are highly vulnerable since they do not possess the information, experience, defence mechanisms, or a stable sexual-erotic-psychological-spiritual connection with a spouse (which helps fortify and corroborate gender orientation) that adults have. A compulsive deconstructive school curriculum may provoke confusion, insecurity, doubt, anxiety, fear, and dysphoria in children concerning their sexuality and gender. The duty to prevent gender dysphoria properly rests with parents. This role cannot be delegated to or usurped by educational institutions without severe negative consequences in the long run.

Pastoral healers should counsel parents and children about the risk they take before signing the informed consent documents at so called paediatric "gender clinics." According to Michelle Cretella, the transition-affirming protocol used in these clinics is as follows.

[The clinic] tells parents to treat their children as the gender they desire, and to place them on puberty blockers around the age 11 or 12 if they are gender dysphoric. If, by age 16, the children insist that they are trapped in the wrong body, they are placed on cross-sex hormones, and biological girls may obtain a double mastectomy. So-called "bottom surgeries," or genital reassignment surgeries, are not recommended before age 18, though some surgeons have recently argued against this restriction.[13]

Cretella warns, "There is an obvious self-fulfilling effect in helping children impersonate the opposite sex both biologically and socially. This is far from benign since taking puberty blockers at the age of twelve or younger, followed by cross-sex hormones, sterilizes a child."[14] Such an approach furthermore causes turmoil in the hormonal regulation of young bodies and psychological crises paired with a reported significant risk of suicide despite gender adjustments even many years after these interventions.

(9) In working with adult patients, pastoral healers need to be aware, as Marsha Wiggins Frame says, "Many GLB people come to counselling with misinformation about sexual orientation."[15] Healers need first to assess their clients' Christian (or non-Christian) beliefs influencing their judgements. Quickly or abruptly setting the highest Christian standards for someone with extremely immature discretional and appreciative judgement may damage rather than benefit their union with Christ, which goes against the ultimate purpose of the Church – to be a sacramental, visible sign of the "intimate union with God"[16] and a visible continuum of Christ's ministry.[17]

(10) All adult clients can be divided into three categories: committed Christians, ambivalent believers, and atheists opposing faith in any dilution.

The pastoral healing of committed Christian clients determined to stick to biblical standards and Church teaching should be focused on helping them to assess God's guidance in dealing with transgender challenges. In the Christian experience, God's presence gives the fullness of peace, optimism, joy, purpose, value, fidelity, sincerity, trust, and other spiritual attributes to Christian marriages. In such marriages, sexuality is the most adaptable, flexible, and plastic among all instinct-directed behaviors. If gender is a choice, if one can arbitrary decide their sexual role in society (as some in favour of gender change propose), then the choice of gender can also be made in harmony with assigned genetic, hormonal, and anatomic sexual characteristics.

(11) Pastoral help for people with lukewarm or weak faith requires focusing on healing the concurrent depression, anxiety, low self-esteem, drug use, helplessness, suicidal ideations, and other complaints, which is usually more helpful than directly addressing their gender problems or apologetic insecurities. If there is any shadow of resistance against biblical teachings, there must also be a light of attraction to God. This gives the Church an opportunity to demonstrate experiential evidence that biblical peace, joy, optimism, hope, forgiveness, love, and other spiritual gifts infinitely surpass the level of uneasiness in unconditionally submitting to Jesus. Pastoral healers ought never to miss the opportunity to demonstrate that they are not a barricade against "the pillar and foundation of the truth" (I Tim. 3:15) but that the Church is the "gateway to Jesus" (Jn. 10:1–10) and his grace, and mercy.

(12) Extreme liberalism does coach people to rebel against faith, God and even against basic facts of reality. Gender dysphoria is sometimes an aspect of such rebellion, causing not only impairment and distress, but also a helpless rage. Therefore, in dealing with people rejecting the Christian approach, pastoral healers, despite all their compassionate love, need to be prepared for belligerent reactions. An anecdotal story illustrates how to deal with such challenges.

> According to the story, the soul of a sinner arrives at the heavenly court to be judged. The judges are humans; the witness, since he knows everything, is Jesus. The presiding judge asks, "Is it true that this sinner stole bread in the Walmart?" Jesus responds, "Yes, he was jobless, had no money, his children were hungry—" But the judge interrupts, "Did he steal or not?" Jesus confirms, "Yes, he did." The judge continues listing the sinner's sins, insisting only on facts and disregarding his motives. Finally, the judges leave the room to make their verdict, and the sinner turns to Jesus. "I learned all my life that you would judge me?" And Jesus responds, "The one who knows everything about you finds it not easy to condemn you."

In general, belligerent reactions are provoked by suffering. If none is closer to the suffering person than God, then Jesus may be closer to LGBT people than they, or "objective observers" may realize. This insight may inform the pastoral healer's approach to argumentative or aggressive LGBT clients. Acknowledging God's closeness to, and love for them, will invite them toward the kingdom of God more powerfully than merely presenting Church teachings and brushing off their resistance.

Notes

[1] Benjamin James Sadock, Virginia Alcott Sadock, and Pedro Ruiz, *Kaplan and Sadock's Synopsis of Psychiatry: Behavioral Sciences/Clinical Psychiatry*, 11th ed. (Philadelphia, PA: Wolters Kluwer, 2015), 600.

[2] Ibid.

[3] DSM-5. Diagnostic and Statistical manual of the American Psychiatric Association (2013), 215–18.

[4] Linda Seligman and Laurie W. Reichenberg, *Selecting Effective Treatments* (Hoboken, NJ: John Wiley & Sons, 2014), 298.

[5] DSM-5, 215.

[6] Seligman and Reichenberg, *Selecting Effective Treatments*, 296.

[7] Marsha Wiggins Frame, *Integrating Religion and Spirituality in Counseling: a Comprehensive Approach* (Pacific Grove, CA: Thomson/Brooks/Cole, 2003), 252.

[8] Pope Benedict XVI. *Christmas Address to the Curia, December 22, 2008.* www.vatican.vaholy father/benedictxvispeeches/2008/documents/hf_ben-xvi_spe_20081222_curia-romana_en.html.

[9] John Paul II, *Man and Woman He Created Them: A Theology of the Body* (Boston, MA: Pauline Books and Media, 2006), 460.

[10] American College of Pediatricians, "Gender Identity Harms Children." www.acpeds.org/the-college-speaks/position-statements/gender-ideology-harms-children.

[11] Michel J. Bailey and Ray Blanchard, "Suicide or Transition: the Only Options for Gender Dysphoric Kids?" 4th Wave Web Publication. www.4thwavenow.com/tag/5michael-bailey.

[12] Michelle Cretella, "Society Commentary: I'm a Pediatrician. How

Transgender Ideology Has Infiltrated My Field and Produced Large Scale Child Abuse." *The Daily Signal*, (July 3, 2017). www.dailysignal. com.

[13] Ibid.

[14] Ibid.

[15] Wiggins Frame, *Integrating Religion and Spirituality in Counseling.*

[16] F. L. Cross and F. A. Livingstone, *The Oxford Dictionary of the Christian Church* (London: Oxford University Press, 1974), 288.

[17] M. J. Havran, "The Church," New Catholic Encyclopedia vol. 3, edited by Bernard L. Martheler (Farmington Hills, MI: Thomson Gale, 2003), 577.

CHAPTER TWENTY-TWO

PERSONALITY DISORDERS AND THEIR PASTORAL TREATMENT

According to the DSM-5, *personality disorders* are enduring and pervasive behavior patterns manifested in cognitive, affective, interpersonal, and impulse control.[1] According to Kaplan and Sadock's textbook, the prevalence of personality disorders is around 10–20 percent in the general population. What is common for all people suffering from these disorders is "enduring subjective experiences and behavior that deviate from cultural standards, are rigidly pervasive, have an onset in adolescence or early adulthood, are stable through time, and lead to unhappiness and impairment."[2] Because of the intricacies and delicateness of these disorders, the pastoral approach will be discussed separately for each disorder.

22.1 Schizoid Personality Disorder

The DSM-5 characterizes *schizoid personality disorder* as a "pervasive pattern of detachment from social relationships and a restricted range of expression of emotions."[3] According to Kaplan and Sadock's textbook, the disorder affects an estimated 7.5 percent of the population. Individuals with this disorder choose solitary pursuits; have only moderate sexual interests; lack friends, close family, and other relationships; appear uninterested in others' opinions; are emotionally cold and detached; and exhibit a constant pattern of social alienation. They are often perceived "as eccentric, isolated, or lonely." They seem shy, avoiding eye contact and revealing with their body language how uncomfortable they are or that they are preparing to leave. Schizoid people do not talk about themselves, and even less about their personal lives. They are formal, participate in only small talk, use general phrases, and are mostly serious. They neither understand nor use humour, and can be unexpectedly obsequious and eager to prove their point. Schizoid people show little empathy to individuals but love humankind and may be committed to ideological systems striving to save the world. They may be fascinated by abstract, philosophical, and metaphysical constructs. As people they seem mysterious, controversial, and enigmatic. In their professional activities they are in some areas precise and conscientious, while in others (which they perceive as unessential) they may procrastinate and be sloppy and unreliable. They choose "solitary jobs that involve little or no contact with others. Many prefer night work to day work so that they need not deal with many people." They often go their own way without taking into account others' opinions. They do not care about fashion and have their own personal style. The sexual life of schizoid people "may exist exclusively in fantasy." Accordingly, "men may not marry because they are unable to achieve intimacy; women may passively agree to marry an aggressive man who wants the marriage." Schizoid personality disorder is not a psychosis. Such people have no delusions or hallucinations, and their personalities are not disintegrating, as in schizophrenia. On the contrary, schizoid personalities may be successful in abstract sciences like philosophy, physics, engineering, mathematics and astronomy, and they may be active in occult, religious, or environmentalist matters. Also, "dietary and health fads, philosophical movements, and social improvement schemes, especially those that require no personal involvement, often engross them." They provide humankind with genuinely original, innovative, and creative ideas.[4]

Pastoral Considerations

(1) To make it easier to approach schizoid people, let us illustrate the condition with a well-known example. Isaac Newton (1642–1727) was a deeply religious scientist and genius who used mathematics to attempt to understand God's logic when creating the world. In his famous book *Philosophiae Naturalis Principia Mathematica* (published in 1687), he explained mathematically, using his universal gravitational theory, virtually every occurrence in the known universe. His personal life, however, sharply contrasted with his glorious scientific career. Newton the genius was a deeply introverted, enigmatic, insecure, suspicious loner. He never married or had friends, and he suffered numerous nervous breakdowns accompanied by violent temper tantrums and acting-out spells. While he was nationally and internationally adored, he remained anxious and paranoid. For example, Newton discovered calculus but left it unpublished. When Leibniz rediscovered and published calculus some ten years later, Newton was convinced that Leibniz had somehow stolen his ideas. Until the end of his life he was engaged in fanatically fighting Leibniz, attempting to destroy his reputation.[5]

Thus, having extremely high intelligence and even a formal religious commitment does not always correlate to biblical love, peace, and joy, but they can be used for biblical purposes if wisely channelled. In modern times, it is the job of the pastoral healer to use a patient's intelligence and religious inclinations to create both health and discipleship. As Jesus said, from the person to whom much is given, much will be expected (Luke 12:48). Such patients have indeed been given much, but they must be taught to appreciate their own qualities.

(2) What makes schizoid people like Newton so desperately unhappy? As Seligman and Reichenberg demonstrate, they avoid relationships and escape into their private lives. They fantasize a lot but never lose contact with reality. They are afraid of emotions. Any confutative scrutinizing of their emotional lives makes them resistant.[6] The motor of their personal dynamics is introverted shame, distrust, anxiety, fearfulness, and low self-esteem. They are loners who feel unfit to socially communicate, but they do not

enjoy isolation. They seldom wish to change the world and would rather retreat from it.[7] If we can characterize them in one phrase, it is that schizoid personalities are like "a glass of hot wine in a barrel of ice," meaning that strong feelings boil in them, but their emotions are deeply suppressed below an icy facade. Professional and pastoral healing strive to ease schizoid people's social isolationism and break them out of their self-imposed jail. It is the job of the pastoral healer, in the words of Jesus, to set free those who are captive (Luke 4:17).

(3) How is it possible to even talk to such introverted people? Communication may be initiated by an objective, almost scientific measuring of the advantages and disadvantages of their treatment. This can then be followed by the development of an achievable and systematized, hierarchical, organized system of goals and, finally, coaching in the gradual fulfilment of these goals.[8] Professional treatment is usually focused on decreasing social isolation and resolving family, vocational, and occupational conflicts. Professional healers in general do not expect great emotional turnarounds or that schizoid people will become socially warm communicators. In general, they have well-established careers, relatively stable ways of living, and are not overly motivated for treatment. Their basic personality traits often remain unchanged by any kind of treatment.[9]

(4) Typical pastoral healing usually supplements professional approaches, raising more personal and less standardized issues like patients' often unique and "hand-woven" worldviews, which they may protect with a surprising vehemence and emotional charge. Such personal communication enables pastoral healers to access the metaphorical hot wine boiling below the icy facade in schizoid people. Cautiously discussing the pastoral healer's own dilemmas and even requesting patients' opinions regarding sensitive questions may help clients to project themselves and reveal the hidden aspects of their personalities.

(5) Schizoid people are internally sensitive, self-reflective, analytical, and self-critical, while externally they are categorical, defensive, and "non-psychologizing." Internal meekness, sensitivity, and insecurity are paired with external defensiveness and strictly enforced moral infallibility. Pastoral healers ought to therefore avoid any unnecessary critique or disagreement

that would have counterproductive effects. They need to be aware that, as in all other psychiatric disorders (except mania), schizoid people would like to be different (warm, communicative, and trusting) although they feel unable to change. They are unable to synchronize intellectual self-expectations with their emotional and behavioral performance, their self-judgmental natures acting as a self-fulfilling prophecy, and deepening their introverted isolation even more. Accordingly, pastoral healing may start by identifying a virtue in the self-perceived weakness of such people, appreciating their internal meekness, self-criticism, and brokenheartedness as genuine Christian qualities. The virtue may seem small and as seemingly insignificant as a mustard seed, but a mustard seed can grow into the biggest of branches (Matthew 13:31–32).

Patients ought to be thankful for, not ashamed of, themselves. Internal self-forgiveness may help to propel external social openness.

(6) Special attention in the pastoral healing of believers is given to the family life of schizoid people, which can compensate for all other social frustrations. In this area, the healing power of the spouse is often more important than that of the pastoral healer. And in practically demonstrating that "no man is an island," pastoral healers have one more powerful tool: the church community. Realizing that the people of God are their referent group and support system is a great, uplifting experience for schizoid people of faith and just seeing that they are not alone can represent an emotional breakthrough.

(7) Inviting schizoid people to prayer groups that they can attend silently and anonymously as observers before becoming participants or leaders may be advantageous in their integration into the church community. As they progress through making connections, acquaintances, and friends, they can be encouraged to play a more prominent communicative role in the community, such as giving presentations, which may help their social affirmation.

(8) People with schizoid personality disorder most often think in metaphysical terms and thus tend to have paramount religious interests. Their distancing themselves from the world has the potential to be a gift that pushes them nearer to God, but they nevertheless often have a self-created

image of God as distant, cool, withdrawn, unfriendly, strict, and judgmental. They seek a God who instead demonstrates attributes opposite their emotional coldness, distance, and suspicion.

One's image of external, objective reality is most often a reflection of their internal experiences. One who is internally fearful will find a thousand external reasons to be cautious. Since schizoid individuals' socially-alienated world picture is a reflection of their image of God, changing their image of God correlates to changing their image of the world. Appreciating a loving God causes them to perceive a more loving world. Thus, improving relational and family issues often acts almost as a theophany, and internally encountering a loving God helps soften external schizoid isolation, suspicion, and doubts.

(9) Living in union with a loving and living God is a progressive process that, as noted, helps to melt the metaphorical ice in the patient's social environment. Despite continuing to be speculative, introverted, and cold, as if not caring about others, such people are often prominently gifted in and committed to building the heavenly kingdom on earth. They may genuinely surprise others with quite unexpected and remarkable deeds of unselfishness and self-sacrifice in social areas and activities, which compensate for their frugal interpersonal communications.

(10) Despite their loneliness, schizoid people usually grow accustomed to living in their own introverted world. Many of them establish a relationship with God that is more rewarding than any human relationship can be for them, including with family members and friends. God is their ultimate refuge, as he was for Newton. Often, this is the ultimate goal for healing schizoid persons. Establishing a warm, close, and rewarding relationship with the invisible, mystical, but experienced God may compensate for missing human relationships.

22.2 Schizotypal Personality Disorder

The DSM-5[10] characterizes *schizotypal personality disorder* as discomfort with and reduced capacity for social and interpersonal relationships and five or more of the following symptoms: eccentric behavior, cognitive distortions, ideas of reference, odd beliefs, magical thinking, unusual perceptions (mainly illusions), odd thinking and speech, suspiciousness, lack of friendships, paranoid fears, and social anxiety. The disorder, according to Kaplan and Sadock's textbook, occurs in 5 percent of the population and is easy to recognize as patients seldom tolerate eye contact, often feel uncomfortable during exchanges, and attempt to shorten them if possible. They also appear aloof or rigidly serious, give short answers, and avoid offering deeper revelations about themselves. Such patients use unusual figures of speech, odd metaphors, and are attracted to metaphysical questions. They have little information about everyday happenings or the concerns of others. They appear harmless, quiet, distanced, and unsociable. Their sex lives exist more as fantasy than reality. Men may never marry because they are unable to achieve intimacy, while women may marry if pressured by the opposite sex. They invest enormous interest in abstract constructs and dehumanized activities (such astronomy and mathematics), philosophical movements, social justice, and dietary movements, and may be absorbed in daydreams without displaying any psychotic features.[11]

Pastoral Considerations

(1) People suffering from schizotypal personality disorder may be approached like those with paranoid conditions. Patients reveal a plethora of unusual, bizarre, mythical, and magical fantasies, events, and fears.[12] The task to keep communication open until a therapeutic relationship is cemented is not easy to accomplish since such people are often not motivated and easily give up.

(2) Patients with schizotypal personality disorder often have family members with schizophrenia and mood disorders.[13] They often perceive themselves as odd and seldom marry, living with their parents. They are also frequently involved in cults and groups with unusual beliefs. They are suspicious and often paranoid and awkward, employing magical thinking. They are eccentric, superstitious, bizarre, socially odd, and isolated, and they feel estranged from the world. However, it would be unfair to attribute all their characteristics to genetic factors. Schizotypal patients often report being

humiliated, bullied, and abused as children. They received as children, and show as adults, little love, affection, and attachment. They often suffer from depression and dysthymia with paranoid ideation.[14]

(3) Professional and pastoral healers ought to be extraordinarily empathetic, warm, and nonjudgmental with schizotypal patients. Even then, though, it is often not easy to maintain a productive therapeutic relationship. Pastoral healers may feel they are not getting through to patients even after unusually strenuous and lengthy periods of working together.[15] The therapeutic relationship is often focused on giving patients advice in taking care of themselves, along with coaching in basic hygiene skills, self-care, and grooming. Helping patients build the security they need in social relationships and bridge their isolation from society encourages them to discern sound and achievable vocational, occupational, and professional goals. Their achievements in these areas substantially help to ease their basic anxiety, fears, insecurities, and low self-esteem, opening the way to deeper and more personal communication about their personal issues.

(4) It is especially beneficial if pastoral healers address patients' relationships with their parents, siblings, extended family members, spouses, and children. Pastoral healers can help reconstruct Christian family relationships and bring families to accept their schizotypal members as they are. Family therapy often opens old wounds but also breaks the silence and introversion. Unusual emotional reactions and illusions may come to the surface and be resolved, and unexpected attachment reactions to patients' spouses may emerge. Families are the first and most basic communities that we are born into. When they reflect genuine Christian values, discernible healing can take place among its members.

(5) A unique focus of pastoral healing in helping people of faith suffering from schizotypal personality disorder is rephrasing their relationship with God. Because they are explicitly prone to idolatry, bizarre and odd biblical interpretations, superstitions, and magical thinking, the nonbiblical ideas about God in schizotypal people are hard to correct logically, philosophically, or theologically. Instead, helping such people to appreciate Jesus' love and forgiveness will help in the progression to emotional qualities of faith and their commitment to God.

(6) Schizotypal individuals adjust more easily to groups in which they may remain anonymous. Therefore, their integration into the body of Christ ought to be very gradual and nondemanding. In coaching church groups and services in how to include such people, pastoral healers should focus on simple, short-term, easily-achievable goals. Despite all disturbing elements in schizotypal people's appearance and communication, for empathetic pastoral healers, even one small step of the patient in this integration process demonstrates that, with Jesus-like love and care, their social integration is achievable, which is often also a reward for the pastoral healer.

22.3 Histrionic Personality Disorder

According to the DSM-5,[16] *histrionic personality disorder* is characterized by a pattern of "emotionality and attention seeking." People with this disorder are uncomfortable if they are not the centre of attention. Their emotions are shallow and quickly shift from one extreme to the other, and they are sexually seductive in order to attract attention and, as such, are theatrical, overdramatically emotional, and easy to manipulate. They present themselves as being closer and more intimate in relationships than they really are. The prevalence of histrionic personality disorder is about 2–3 percent. Patients are easy to recognize. They are constantly excited, hyperemotional, theatrical, extroverted, and flamboyant. Only on the surface do histrionic people seem warm and cooperative; "when pressed to acknowledge certain feelings (e.g. anger, sadness, and sexual wishes) they may respond with surprise, indignation or denial." And if they are not the centre of attention, they exhibit short but intensive temper tantrums—theatrical scenes with inappropriate anger, tears, and laughter—or become almost paranoid, accusing their families, friends, and coworkers of not giving them sufficient praise, admiration, or approval. They have highly seductive behaviors, which are prominent in both sexes in a specific way. Histrionic people "may be coy or flirtatious rather than sexually aggressive." They often suffer from "a psychosexual dysfunction; women may be anorgasmic, and men impotent." Consequently, they are permanently seeking reassurance about their sex appeal.[17] As is known from the history of medicine, such conspicuous sexualized behavior was recognized early on, and the Greek physician Hippocrates believed that histrionic behavior in women was the result of a frustrated uterus wandering through the patient's body. This belief was probably based on the observation that people with this disorder behave as if endlessly playing a sexualized role. Occasional melodramatic semisexualized acting-out in histrionic personality disorder is classically described as a histrionic seizure, most often provoked by emotional frustration. Typically, with a dramatic cry the subject falls to the ground (always avoiding self-injuries), crying, yelling, screaming, and tearing at their hair and clothes. Sometimes the body takes on a theatrical arc, with only the head and heals touching the ground. Such attacks happen in front of observers and are enacted for them. After a few minutes, subjects awaken from the seizure, relieved and smiling as though nothing happened.

Pastoral Considerations

(1) Corey notes that "we can only think, feel and act in relation to our perception of our goal."[18] Accordingly, histrionic personalities and behaviors can be understood only by understanding patients' goals, which are often polarized in the opposite direction than in schizoid personalities. For people suffering from histrionic personality disorder, emotional and social communication, as well as being popular and appreciated, is of the utmost importance.

(2) According to an anecdotal story, the German emperor Friedrich the Great ordered his soldiers to love him. Those who did not fulfil the command were flogged. People suffering from histrionic behaviors resemble the emperor's behavior; they force their family members, friends, and coworkers to give them attention, protection, love, and care. In their attention-seeking behavior, histrionic people can enact almost any disorder with one purpose: to receive attention. We already illustrated such behavior with Anne's example; however, let me give another from my own practice:

> As a young physician, I had to work with paramedics. One time, we got an
> urgent call about a person on her deathbed. Despite running through the

city, we arrived too late; surrounded by a few crying people, the deceased person was dressed for her funeral in a solemnly decorated darkened room lit only by burning candles. My duty was to provide the death certificate. When I attempted, as the protocol required, to open her eyes to check corneal and pupil reflexes, the corpse resisted and did not let me open her eye. I gasped, for the lady was alive. I commanded her to open her eyes, but she continued to feign death. I then closed her nostrils and, after a minute, she finally opened her mouth and angrily sat up in bed. The mourners screamed, and she yelled in anger, "I wanted to see who would cry and who would laugh when I die."

(3) As Seligman and Reichenberg describe, initial contact with histrionic people—charming, attractive, and eager to please but in reality abusive and manipulative—may seem easygoing, but patients quickly become frustrated that the therapist has not rescued them. Subsequently, they become unpredictable, capricious, and moody,[19] warm outside but cold inside.

(4) The way histrionic patients are approached initially determines the outcome of their professional and pastoral healing. Taking a polite, cautious, respectful, distanced, benevolent attitude is the most promising approach. Communication ought to be kept on a logical, rational, and non-emotional level. Engaging in any sexualized flirtation is extremely risky and counterproductive. The best way to respond to histrionic, sexualized attention-seeking behaviors is to not react—to ignore it, behave phlegmatically, and, as one of my colleagues formulated, act as a "genderless collaborator."

(5) After the histrionic patient acknowledges that the therapist is resistant to participating in any of the offered flirtatious exchanges, they usually change their strategy. For example, they might act as if they are insulted, as if they are no longer interested in therapy, or as if therapy is more important to the healer than them. In such cases, it is essential for pastoral healers not to accept the role of saviour. Benevolently making the patient aware of their responsibility (making them aware that their healing is also in their hands) is probably the best strategy for resolving such challenging situations.

(6) The phrase "silence is your best ally" is valid in dealing with histrionic people. In this context, it is noteworthy to listen to Guilmartin's advice.

> In the early stages of a difficult situation, the kind of listening they want at this time is not for us to feel that we have to say a lot. However, if we sit there in a pained silence, afraid to say anything, that won't be helpful either. It can be helpful to let them tell us what they are worried about.... We don't have to provide the answer. Instead, we can reflect back to them what it sounds like they are feeling through the words they are saying.

The purpose of silence is letting the patient know that you sympathize with them even though you don't know their distress firsthand. "By making it safe for them to feel whatever they are feeling and by letting them know that they don't need to chase those feelings away, they may then go on to tell you the hopes they have."[20]

(7) People suffering from histrionic personalities are not aware of their role-playing but perceive their theatrical struggle for admiration, superiority, and power as legitimate. Receiving respect is a "to be or not to be" task for them. Taking into account their vulnerability, pastoral healers need to exercise special care not to mobilize often brutal, paranoid, and defensive interpretations in histrionic subjects, which may escalate to furious theatrical aggression.

(8) Let us now shift from discussing therapists' attitudes to pastoral healing. Histrionic people have a need to talk about themselves. Often, the subjects spontaneously reveal their frustrating childhood attachments. Since histrionic patients unconsciously regress and reenact their childhood conflicts, therapy is focused on resolving their feelings of being unloved, unappreciated, and abused; on addressing their low self-esteem, feelings of guilt, and ambivalent, love-hate attachments; and on helping to resolve any recent emotional, familial, occupational, or vocational conflicts. Following this, pastoral healers focus on analysing their patients' relationship with God.

(9) Seligman and Reichenberg note that "the histrionic personality disorder shares some traits with the paranoid personality disorder. People with the histrionic personality disorder are particularly likely to develop paranoid traits under conditions of extreme stress."[21] Therefore, such patients find it hard to see themselves from a self-critical perspective or with biblical modesty. At first, pastoral healing ought to be focused on the merciful and

forgiving attributes of God, and then on justice. Realizing their own imperfection in front of a forgiving and loving God helps patients' self-forgiveness and biblical transformation. We saw such a realization earlier in the parable of the prodigal son, who realized and acknowledged his transgressions before his just but loving father.

(10) The pastoral healer may cautiously direct Socratic dialogue toward agreement that what the histrionic person really needs surpasses all human resources. Only God can satisfy such a subject's needs for appreciation, love, peace, forgiveness, attention, and providence. The rationale in the pastoral healing of Christian histrionic personalities is to help subjects to acknowledge that their cry for human attention is in reality a cry for God's attention.

(11) The shift from seeking a relationship with humans to emphasizing a relationship with God often provokes emotionally turbulent, cathartic acting-out behaviors. These emotional reactions signal a decrease in the often competitive, envious, jealous, vengeful, and ambivalent attachment to the father figure in boys and the mother figure in girls, which enhances attachment to the ideal father figure—God. In shifting from ambivalent human attachments to attachment to God, histrionic people may be surprisingly docile. The originally flirtatious, expansive, domineering, power-hungry, and sexualized personality traits gradually disappear and a warm, authentic, empathetic, emotional, and personal structure often appears.

(12) If successfully healed, formally histrionic people are rarely lukewarm Christians. Usually, it is easy to integrate them into church communities. After committing themselves to seeking "to be known by God" (instead of being admired by humans), they radiate their abundant spiritual gifts to their families, churches, neighbours, and to the whole of society.

22.4 Narcissistic Personality Disorder

Narcissistic personality disorder is characterized in the DSM-5 by a behavioral pattern of grandiosity, a need for admiration, and a lack of compassion. People with this disorder have overvalued, grandiose ideas of self-importance, power, success, intelligence, beauty, morality, love, unselfishness, and uniqueness, making them feel especially entitled to respect and admiration. In reality, such people lack empathy and are selfish, egocentric, exploitive, and jealous.[22]

According to Sadock, Sadock, and Ruiz, the prevalence of the disorder is around 1 percent in the general population. However, "people with the disorder may impart an unrealistic sense of omnipotence, grandiosity, beauty, and talent to their children" and put their children at risk for developing the disorder. Accordingly, "the number of cases of narcissistic personality disorder reported is increasing steadily." Narcissistic people "consider themselves special and expect special treatment." Consequently playing up to the image of perfection, they bluntly reject any criticism and usually become either defensive and aggressive or put on a mask of complete ignorance and indifference at any observation they perceive as derogatory. Without compromise, they enforce their own will, and on the surface they are self-confident and ambitious, perceiving themselves as predestined for fame, success, admiration, and fortune. Their social relationships are dictatorial but fragile since they often, even unintentionally, make others furious by their behavioral superiority. They have no genuine friends. Narcissistic people "feign sympathy only to achieve their own selfish ends" and are prone to depression and hypochondriasis disorders that they often hide while accusing others of making them suffer. Usually, their "interpersonal difficulties, occupational problems, rejection, and loss are among the stresses that narcissists commonly produce by their behavior—stresses they are least able to handle." Such patients "must constantly deal with blows to their narcissism, resulting from their own behavior or from life experience." They give special attention to their image and "value beauty, strength, and youthful attributes, to which they cling inappropriately."[23] Respectively, one can safely conclude that that they are the antithesis of the ideal Christian disciple who, showing meekness and humility, is willing to die to the self and become last that he might become first.

Pastoral Considerations

(1) Like histrionic personality disorder, narcissistic personality disorder also has a purpose. It is, as Corey describes, a "striving for significance and

superiority," compensating for a basic inferiority complex. "Inferiority is not a negative factor in life" if it motivates a person to grow and "cope with feelings of helplessness by striving for competence, mastery, and perfection in other areas."[24] However, narcissistic people strive for perfection in all their activities, outperforming everyone and proving their superiority in all areas of life. Jesus said that we must become perfect as the heavenly Father is perfect (Matthew 5:48). This perfection is diametrically at odds with the superficial superiority sought after by narcissists.

(2) The behavior of people suffering from narcissistic personality disorder is in many aspects similar to histrionic personality disorder, except that the flirtatious behavior is missing. They have a sense of a much higher entitlement than cheap sexuality and behave like glorious and unapproachable kings or queens. Superior knowledge, desirability, perfection, and charming beauty are used to demonstrate their unapproachable nobility and perfection. However, as Seligman and Reichenberg note, although such people maintain a cool facade, they react with furious aggression, rage, or depression to any criticism. Their extensive use of rationalization, projection, and denial limits self-criticism.[25] They deny any imperfection but blame others for the mishaps in their lives.

(3) How does a healer approach people with narcissistic personality disorder? Intellectualizing (discussing arts, music, philosophy, history, or theology) and acknowledging and appreciating patients' information, knowledge, tastes, and sophistication may help open communication with them. The purpose of their healing, however, is exactly the opposite: to decrease perfection-oriented defensiveness and increase self-criticism. Their healing, in the long run, requires not only intellectual schmoozing but also hard discussions.

(4) The behavior of narcissistic people is far more predictable than histrionic people. However, because of their image of perfection, reaching the core of their problems—that is, their deeply entrenched dysfunctional beliefs promoting malignant egocentrism—is difficult. Their ambivalent need to be challenged in order to prove their superiority encourages such people to engage in a Socratic dialogue, in which personal problems may also surface.

(5) Their endless quest for respect makes narcissistic people feel like both victorious achievers and hopeless losers. They are "externally strong but internally weak." They appreciate help in resolving familial, professional, or vocational problems, but this does not change the unconscious fear and denial of their imperfections, even in therapy. Their allegedly unspoiled childhood and their parents' alleged perfection are often better left unquestioned initially because they often serve as the last and only safe haven for narcissistic people. The same is the case for their personal (almost sinless) rightness; to correct these overvalued ideas early on would disintegrate their defensive mechanisms of entrenchment in their hypocritical excellence and would cause more harm than good.

(6) A narcissistic patient's disclosures about their personal history often reveal a less-than-perfect picture in which both extreme parental approaches of cruelty and spoiling were present in their upbringing. They were simultaneously coached to undervalue and overvalue themselves. Therefore, narcissistic people anxiously and obsessively press for special rights with their therapists as they once did with their parents. They may become contentious if they do not receive what they believe they deserve.[26]

(7) The initial focus in the healing of narcissistic believers ought to be on the ultimately merciful attributes of God and his ultimate justice, which helps patients process the feeling of guilt they are so resistant to. Promoting biblical self-criticism, which is the essence of pastoral healing, is achievable in narcissistic people after empowering them internally. Biblical humility takes away the need to demonstrate competence externally. Appreciating one's own weakness helps to welcome Jesus' forgiveness and mercy in place of narcissistic perfectionism, excellence, and righteousness.

(8) Focusing on becoming like Jesus helps a narcissistic person deal with the perceived "unjust world" in a new way: as being "worthy of suffering." If perceived or real humiliation is received as a sign of discipleship, patients can find the courage to endure it. A Socratic dialogue may help them interpret their pain, suffering, and disappointments as proof of exceptional discipleship. Then, in turn, they may gradually come to appreciate and practice biblical humility, meekness, and brokenheartedness and rely solely on Jesus as their authority instead of themselves.

(9) Paradoxically, patients' narcissism may make it easy for them to identify with biblical saints (who were not appreciated by the world, as is the case with narcissistic subjects). Their previously deeply-entrenched narcissism may be the exact thing that propels them to identify with exemplary Christians and Jesus Christ. That new identification may help them take a new, more self-critical and humble look at themselves, enhancing their growth in discipleship. To identify with a saint shows that there is a different path to greatness, albeit it is a greatness characterized by service rather than dictatorship.

(10) Every human being is to some degree narcissistic, desiring to be Godlike, omniscient and omnipotent, and relying on the illusion of their own of perfection instead of trusting in Jesus. However, with progressing pastoral healing, narcissistic subjects grasp that those who boast are "strong outside but weak inside," but that those who boast in the Lord may be "weak outside but strong inside." When this insight is reached, pastoral healing has achieved its purpose.

22.5 Avoidant and Dependent Personality Disorders

Avoidant personality disorder is, according to the DSM-5,[27] characterized by a "pervasive pattern of social inhibition, feelings of inadequacy, and hypersensitivity to negative evaluation." Sadock, Sadock, and Ruiz describe avoidant patients as having "extreme sensitivity to rejection" but at the same time "a great desire for companionship." This conflict leads to a socially withdrawn lifestyle and public anxiety because such people need "unusually strong guaranties of uncritical acceptance" but seldom receive them. They are perceived by others as suffering from an inferiority complex. This disorder is widespread, its prevalence around 1–10 percent in the general population. People with avoidant personality disorder desire the warmth and security of human affiliations but justify their avoidance of relationships by their alleged fear of rejection. They are eager to please but seldom receive requests and are uncertain, shy, unconfident, self-effacing, and hesitant to appear in public. They are also defensive and prone to misinterpreting other people's feedback as disrespectful, derogatory, or ridiculing, and so they often withdraw into themselves, feeling frustrated and hurt. "These people are generally unwilling to enter relationships unless they are given an unusually strong guarantee of uncritical acceptance. They have no close friends or confidants." Some of them establish families and feel content surrounded by children and relatives. "Should their support system fail, however, they are subject to depression, anxiety, and anger."[28]

Dependent personality disorder is characterized in the DSM-5[29] by an "excessive need to be taken care of that leads to submissive and clinging behavior and fears of separation." People with dependent personality disorder are submissive, self-conscious, uncomfortable when alone, and inclined to let others make choices for them. The disorder is more common in women and comprises almost 2.5 percent of all personality disorders. It is easy to recognize through subjects' indecision, deflected responsibility, and refusal to take leadership roles. People with the disorder prefer to be submissive and may seem altruistic; they "find it difficult to persevere at tasks, but may find it easy to perform these tasks for someone else." They permanently seek the company of others and prefer people on whom they can count. Dependence may go to extremes in the so-called shared psychotic disorder, wherein "the submissive partner takes on the delusional system of the more aggressive, assertive partner on whom he or she depends."[30]

Pastoral Considerations

(1) A commonality between avoidant and dependent personality disorders is dysfunctional beliefs that make it hard to relate to other people. While people suffering from avoidant personality disorder appear shy and distance themselves from others, those suffering from dependant personality disorder stick to powerful protectors and appear submissive. Both disorders indicate problems in the separation-individuation process that occurs at around four to five years of age. At this age, toddlers abandon symbiotic relating and "experience separation from significant others yet turn to them for a sense of conformation and comfort. The child may demonstrate ambivalence, torn between enjoying separate states of independence and dependence."[31]

(2) Ambivalent early attachments become imprinted in toddlers' brains and minds and cause repeating love-hate behaviors in adults. Repeated disappointments source from such behaviors and act as self-fulfilling prophecies, convincing subjects that they do not have the courage to even try a socially adaptable behavior pattern. Such people either retreat into the security of an ivory tower of isolation (in avoidant personality disorder) or seek protection by submitting to powerful individuals (in dependent personality disorder).

(3) The shyness and low self-esteem in both cases has a peculiar characteristic seldom described in other disorders. Discouraged from fighting for their own interests, avoidant and dependent people may surprise with courage and persistence in fulfilling altruistic purposes. The following case study illustrates this.

> A seventeen-year-old girl with dependent personality disorder went with schoolmates to work in a cornfield to earn money for a school excursion. One of her schoolmates took his younger brother, who suffered from Down syndrome. The cornfield was enormous (7,700 acres), and the boy with Down syndrome got lost. The children desperately looked for him all morning and then, since their cell phones did not work, they ran to the farm for help. It was work time, so the farmhouse was locked and empty. The girl, however, found a Harley-Davidson motorcycle in the yard and rode it down side roads to the next farmhouse to get help.

The problem in avoidant and dependent personality disorders is not genuine social incompetence (as in intellectually disabled people) but the inability for patients to will themselves to be competent, a kind of learned helplessness deriving from the experience of being a failure after repeated unsuccessful attempts.

(4) Seligman and Reichenberg note that while avoidant people avoid talking about unpleasant things, dependent personalities resolve their unpleasant immobility by mobilizing others.[32] Both groups reveal anxiety, depression, and fear. Usually, they come from strict petite bourgeoisie families to whom the image of social perfection is important but unachievable.

They feel unworthy in social interactions. Therefore, the first step in their healing is helping them to accept themselves as they are—a temple of the Holy Spirit—and not to counterproductively despise, push, and punish themselves for not being able to socially act as they should. Decreasing feelings of guilt improves their chances of changing.

(5) Avoidant and dependent personality traits may correlate to particular gender beliefs. Seligman and Reichenberg note that females suffering from these disorders are often very conservative in their gender role identity; they are passive, insecure, and dependent, seldom assertive and never violent. Such women seldom seek help. They are people-pleasers, playing a subservient role, and are extremely tolerant, submissive, accepting of abuse, filled with self-doubt, and avoidant of competitive situations. Autonomy was discouraged in them as children, and loyalty to their parents was appreciated.[33] Often, such people have a strong desire for community activities, but their learned helplessness inhibits their active participation in broader family and social engagements. Gradual involvement in parish activities can produce turnarounds. Activating these previously isolated people to overcompensate for their submissive attitudes by passionately and fervently participating in generous and charitable activities helps increase their societal competence and self-esteem.

(6) Especially in family therapy, promoting a fulfilling and happy Christian married life can lead to a complete turnaround in avoidant and dependent patients. Unhappy marriages, on the other hand, often have the opposite effect, deepening their dysfunctions. After living for many years in content Christian relationships, such individuals overcompensate for their previous frustrations and inhibitions and become self-confident, competent, and autonomous.

(7) Similar to depressive patients, the superego-type conscience in avoidant and dependent people is irrationally judgmental, strict, and unforgiving. Consequently, these individuals are often timid, self-accusatory, and self-judgmental. Pastoral healing in these cases ought seldom (or never) focus on increasing humility or meekness or on identifying sins since subjects already despise themselves and feel powerless and brokenhearted. Rather, pastoral healing encourages such people to perceive themselves as

recipients of God's special graces listed in Matthew 5:1–12 (Jesus' blessings). The commonality in the eight groups of different people Jesus lists in this story is biblical humility, a gift avoidant and dependent people feel they receive abundantly. Therefore, healers can identify value in their meekness, which may ease their feelings of incompetence and also empower them, increasing self-esteem and enabling growth in discipleship.

(8) Patients' new purpose-driven attitudes in familial, educational, occupational, and vocational settings are, in believers, supplemented with a new, unambivalent, open, wholehearted, and submissive attitude toward God. God, the almighty, eternal, and ultimately loving partner, gives them strength, courage, and security that avoidance of or submission to other people cannot.

(9) Both of these personality traits may function as strong motivators, calling for deeper discipleship. Only complete surrender to Jesus gives these patients a sense of freedom grounded in biblical dignity and self-esteem sourced from increasing competence and decreasing fear of existential incompetence. There is a rule noted many times in our discussions: the stronger the biblical faith, the stronger its healing power will be.

22.6 Obsessive-Compulsive Personality Disorder

The DSM-5[34] characterizes *obsessive compulsive personality disorder* as a "pervasive pattern of orderliness, perfectionism, and mental and interpersonal control, at the expense of flexibility." According to Sadock, Sadock, and Ruiz, the disorder may or may not manifest with symptoms of OCD. Its prevalence is unknown, but it is found more often in males. It is more common in families in which obsessive-compulsive personality patterns are dominant. Usually, patients report strict, punitive, military-type childhoods with a lack of emotionality. Patients are recognizable by their "emotional constriction, orderliness, perseverance, stubbornness, and infectiveness," supplemented by a pervasive perfectionism. Their perfectionism helps them control challenging, everyday situations. Because of their internal insecurity, subjects seek security in organization and structure, preferring predictability, regulation, and rules over improvisation. In general, they are rigid and lack spontaneity. They are often enigmatic, cool, distanced, serious, and strict, lacking a sense of humour and neatly attending to even small, inessential details. They have a "stiff, formal, and rigid demeanour. Their affect is not blunted or flat, but can be constricted." Such people tend to be hardworking personalities who like routines and do not like changes or innovations. They demand respect from subordinates but may be submissive to those standing higher in the hierarchical order and therefore fit into authoritarian structures. Their basic anxiety and fear of mistakes makes them hesitant. They are reliable in their interpersonal relationships, in general living in stable marriages, but have only a few superficial friends. "Anything that threatens to upset their perceived stability or the routine of their lives can precipitate much anxiety otherwise bound up in rituals that they impose on their lives and try to impose on others."[35]

Pastoral Considerations

(1) It is sometimes hard to draw a clear line between OCD and obsessive-compulsive personality disorder. In differential diagnosis it helps, as Seligman and Reichenberg summarize, that OCD is an unpleasant anxiety disorder with obsessions and compulsions, while people with obsessive-compulsive personality disorder envision themselves as powerful, comfortable, well-defended individuals in their fortress of perfectionism and require others to adjust to their rigid rules and ways of living.

(2) People suffering from obsessive-compulsive personality disorder seem on the surface unapproachable. Some professionals characterize them as difficult clients in the sense that they are nonflexible and rigid and do not like giving up control over their behavior. They are not reflective and do not psychologize but they would like to change others but not themselves. A nonintrusive, friendly, polite approach that respects formalities (like hierarchical relationships) makes engaging such people in communication easier. Establishing a deeper relationship is more difficult because they may become defensive. As Seligman and Reichenberg recommend, the main approach for therapists is to not engage in power struggles or arguments[37] but rather remain benevolent listeners.

(3) Those suffering from obsessive-compulsive personality disorder are often authoritarian, perceiving the world and society in an overly hierarchical way. They are more interested in "who said it" than the truth of any information. Their spouses, children, colleagues, and society as a whole need to resemble a well-oiled machine. Their obsessive construct gives them a security and armour which is not helpful to question since the purpose of their healing is most often not "fixing" their obsessive nature but rather making it easier for them to live with it.

(4) Despite being socially communicative, such individuals internally feel lonely, isolated, and misunderstood by others. As Corey notes, "One of the greatest fears of clients is that they will discover that there is no core, no self, no substance, and that they are merely reflections of everyone's expectation of them." So they escape in ritualistic behaviors, sometimes becoming trapped "in a doing mood to avoid the experience of being."[38] Professional and pastoral healing aims at decreasing their slavery to a rigid policeman superego that forces them to monomaniacally fulfil self-imposed duties.

(5) From a pastoral perspective, obsessive-compulsive personalities may resemble Old Testament Pharisees in their rigorous, stringent, letter-by-letter fulfilment of the law. Obsessive personality traits are also a defence system serving to decrease lingering angst and insecurity. Therefore, providing such people with security, predictability, openness, and correctness decreases their defensive and obsessive personality traits and helps the authentic personality to surface.

(6) The first task of the pastoral healer is replacing patients' image of a strict, judgmental, and fear-inducing God with the biblical image that 1 John 4 and 8:16 reveals: "God is love." The acknowledgement that God is love should not only be rational but also experiential; unselfishness correlates to deepening internal peace, forgiveness, and joy, which in turn increases trust in God's love. The turning of this "angelic circle," as we might call it, necessarily correlates to the activation of a Jesus-like, loving, Christian conscience and the decrease of the Freudian internal policeman's power. Judging themselves from the perspective of a loving and forgiving God increases patients' freedom from obsessively adhering to duties, orders, rules, regulations, and being judgmental, strict, and uncompromising with themselves and others.

(7) The method for healing obsessive-compulsive personality disorder is Socratic dialogue that coaches patients in living in a free, Augustinian-like "love and do whatever you will" attitude. This is more powerful than any theoretical argumentation, yielding biblical peace, simplicity, and joy. In general, emphasizing the role of the Holy Spirit—encouraging patients to trust its guidance in where, when, and how to freely and competently apply the Ten Commandments and Jesus' law of love instead of Pharisaically obeying principles written in stone—has an effect comparable to opening "the eyes that are blind, to [freeing] captives from prison and ... [releasing] from the dungeon those who sit in darkness" (Isa. 42:7).

(8) Believers with obsessive-compulsive personality traits fit in well with the church community. They tend to be strictly organized, polite, respectful, reliable, persistent, disciplined, and conscientious and they seldom cross boundaries. In such cases, they may behave like the "church police," demanding from others the same rigid discipline that they prefer. However, this happens rarely since they vigorously respect others' boundaries just as they prefer their own personal choices to be respected. Most often, they become a genuine blessing for church communities.

(9) Jesus' purpose was never to change the personalities of his disciples. Each of the Four Evangelists maintained his unique personality after his conversion (which is evident from their individual reports of the same events from Jesus' life). Likewise, the purpose of pastoral healing is not to literally change patients' personalities but to perfect them. Thus, obsessive people will remain introverted and will seldom demonstrate their feelings externally, but peace, love, and joy will nevertheless be evermore a part of their lives.

(10) Obsessive people are often strongly motivated to take an active role in perfecting their strict, rigid, and judgmental superego and supplementing it with a Jesus-like, loving, Christian conscience. They have enormous potential to be exemplary disciples by synchronizing their personal gifts with a Christian conscience, reflecting that "God is love." By doing so, they demonstrate that God works for the good in all things with those who love him (Romans 8:28).

22.7 Antisocial Personality Disorder

The DSM-5[39] characterizes antisocial personality disorder as a "pervasive pattern of disregard for and violation of the rights of others" in people over the age of fifteen. It is, according to Kaplan and Sadock's textbook, "an inability to conform to the social norms that ordinarily govern many aspects of a person's adolescent and adult behavior." Its prevalence is 3 percent in men and 1 percent in women. People suffering from antisocial personality disorder can fool those around them. They may appear to be honest, competent, and credible idealists, but beneath "the mask of sanity lurks tension, hostility, irritability, and rage." Nevertheless, "these patients often impress opposite-sex clinicians with the colourful, seductive aspects of their personalities, but same-sex clinicians may regard them as manipulative and demanding."[40] Their personal history is filled with reports of lying, stealing, deception, theft, cruelty, alcohol and drug use, street and gang fights, convictions, police incidents, and jail time, usually beginning in the teenage years. They present themselves as people without anxiety or fear and, as Robin Hood-like fighters for social justice, are eloquent in advocating their parasitic and abusive lifestyles. Antisocial people are extremely seductive and manipulative, frequently acting out sexually and behaving deceptively and promiscuously. They may also be abusive to their spouses or children. Joblessness, drug addiction, and drunkenness are common. Patients almost never show remorse and "appear to lack a conscience." Despite that, antisocial personality disorder is not a mental disorder (it does not essentially decrease responsibility), but a behavior pattern manifesting in problems of character, affect, will, and ways of thinking that are channelled into resistance against ethical and social norms and that therefore result in repeated conflicts with society. Classically, psychiatrists distinguish five types of antisocial people.

(1) Schizoid antisocial people are characterized by rigidity, introversion, unpredictability, and bizarre cruelty. They live in an ideal world distanced from reality, and their behavior is characterized by extreme impracticability.

(2) Cycloid antisocial people are characterized by their abundance of ideas, frenzied activity, incessant talking, and imperative desire to lead

others. This hippomanic mood is then followed by a subdepressive withdrawal from reality, with the subject becoming uninterested in things that are happening, their personal image, and their environment.

(3) Epileptoid antisocial people often appear in the context of epileptic personality changes and are characterized by sticking behavior (unable to change topics or ideas they have started to talk about) and attacks of unprovoked and uncontrollable anger during which they blindly destroy everything around them, followed by intense feelings of guilt and servile behavior.

(4) Histrionic antisocial people are characterized by childlike behavior, emotional lability, immaturity, an imbalanced lifestyle, egocentrism, theatrical behavior, and furious expressions of their will to power. They attempt to gain the attention of everyone and to remain in the middle of events.

(5) Sexual antisocial people are characterized by a multitude of sexually inappropriate behavior patterns, aggression, and rage. Sexuality is used as a tool in the antisocial person's power struggle, demonstrating the physical superiority of the subject. The quality of sexual relationships is compensated by quantity, while love is reduced to brute sexuality.

Pastoral Considerations

(1) As Seligman and Reichenberg emphasize, antisocial personality disorder is the only personality disorder that cannot be diagnosed before the age of eighteen. Despite the personal histories of people with antisocial personality disorder, a conduct disorder—expressed through cruelty to animals, vandalism, fighting, stealing, a lack of empathy, and senseless aggression—usually persists. Such people are unable to sustain employment or a balanced monogamist lifestyle and in general live a parasitic lifestyle despite sometimes finding a place for themselves in banking, business, politics, or other lucrative enterprises.[41] The most common and most surprising impression is, however, their "moral insanity," which makes it seem as though they have no conscience.

(2) To better understand the hearts of people with antisocial personality

disorder, let us make a digression into delicate scholastic distinctions to clarify what we are talking about.

To refer to the conscience, St. Paul used the Greek term *suneidesis*, which was misspelled by Medieval scholars as *synderesis*. The Franciscan scholars understood *synderesis* as an emotional quality—in Latin called *pottentia affective*, a "disposition of the heart"—while the term *synderesis* meant in Dominican scholastic terminology "the faculty that knows the moral law." This "knowledge"—that is, differentiating between good and evil—"remained unaffected by the fall." Thomas Aquinas went even further in making fine distinctions. He described two attributes of the conscience. The aspect called *synderesis* has the task of deciding to do good, while *conscientia* has the task of distinguishing right from wrong. *Synderesis* cannot be silenced but can be set aside by *conscientia*, and "while *synderesis* cannot err, *conscientia* is a sort of decree of the mind, which is fallible."[42]

Observing antisocial personalities' behaviors from the perspective discussed here, we could say that their *synderesis* (knowledge of the moral law) is overpowered by instincts imbued with malignant selfishness. Formulated in Thomist terminology, although their *synderesis* instructs them to always do good and their *conscientia* witnesses and morally justifies what they have done, their *conscientia* is a false witness, proclaiming evil deeds as good. Forensically, as noted, antisocial behaviors are perceived as a chosen behavior pattern rather than a disorder. Therefore, their responsibility is usually not significantly diminished.

(3) For children who have irresponsible and abusive parents or who witness many family tragedies, pastoral work starts whenever possible to prevent antisocial personality disorder. In situations such as these, children become resistant, insensitive, and almost immune to punishment. They escape into substance abuse and violence, practicing what they have learned in their families.[43] Prevention starts with helping dysfunctional families extend love, forgiveness, acceptance, support, encouragement, and peace, which are antivenoms to antisocial beliefs and behaviors. The outcome of early family treatment often determines the outlook of the young patients' lives.

(4) In the families of people with antisocial personality disorders, discipline is usually inconsistent, overly strict, and punitive as well as spoiling.

Children receive the double message of "be good but also not [good]," which creates unbearable frustration because they feel unable to fulfil conflicting demands. For example, a strictly raised fourteen-year-old girl was greeted by her grandfather, who said, "Oh, how sexy you look!" This short but spontaneous sentence had a profound impact on the girl. It justified her subsequent sexual acting-out behaviors that started three years later. Without realizing it, the grandfather provided what the Church calls "the occasion of sin." It was a random remark, but Jesus made it clear that small things (such as a mustard seed) can grow into larger things. In some cases, the magnified result is not holy or intended.

Youngsters with the disorder feel victimized by their parents, school, church, or society. This usually starts in late adolescence, when their conduct disorder signals the start of their destructive cycles characterized by the phrase "good is bad, and bad is good." It is a turning point when subjects experience impulsivity and low frustration tolerance. They actively despise their consciences and everything that is, in their perception, weak, loving, humble, gentle, or Christian. They act out a moral insanity.

(5) The first practical task of professional and pastoral healers is attracting antisocial personalities to treatment. As Seligman and Reichenberg note, such people seldom seek help on their own. They are usually court-ordered to attend therapy; "therapy may be a condition of their parole or probation, or they may be treated while incarcerated."[44] To some professionals, this "suggests that therapists initially empathize and join with the client in his or her hostility, then proceed toward a collaborative relationship." This "may afford therapists an initial honeymoon phase, but their opposition to treatment is likely to surface once therapy progresses beyond superficial interactions."[45] Pastoral healers seek a different approach, but let us first review what else should be avoided by the pastoral healer.

(6) People with antisocial personality disorder will often challenge healers. The most counterproductive thing to do when this happens is to show fear, even to raging antisocial personalities. A therapist who is scared is behaving exactly as subjects would like their victims to behave. Seeing fear, submissiveness, schmoozing, or unreasonable humility unleashes antisocial people's instinctual recklessness. It increases their will to exert power

and their temptation to repeatedly dominate the therapeutic alliance by repeated attempts to dominate the process. Jesus was frequently challenged during his ministry, such as when people asked whether he should pay taxes to Caesar (Matthew 22:15–22). He answered them directly but without fear. He was gentle but would not be manipulated. Pastoral healers ought to imitate his attitude when challenged by antisocial people.

(7) People suffering from antisocial personality disorder have a history of unsuccessful attempts to fit into society. They consequently perceive themselves as underachievers and failures, and their angry and aggressive behaviors originate from the pain and disappointment resulting from their failures.[46] Accordingly, what is common in antisocial patients is that they respond to real or imagined challenges like a punisher or avenger. They believe they have a right, almost a duty, to teach others a lesson and, in such instances, think not of the punishment they will receive but of the pain they can inflict. The pastoral healer's best response is to adopt a benevolent, forgiving, and almost mothering, Christlike posture, a firm, resolute, and unwavering attitude in helping antisocial people grasp the consequences of their behaviors.

(8) Antisocial people mask their moral insanity with their own concept of morality. In their estimation, they are fighting for social justice. They generally like to think of themselves as victims—morally above society—incorruptibly just and without any character blemishes. However, the elemental factors of reality (i.e., families, friends, and society as well as occupational, vocational, and everyday life situations) do not tolerate their counterproductive antisocial behavior. Repeated confrontations and disappointments caused by adverse consequences to their behaviors gradually compel even hardcore sociopaths to realize their need for change. This is the right moment to start pastoral healing.

(9) The pastoral healer's strategy may be summarized as the following: Christians and antisocial people equally seek peace, joy, and love. However, while distress typically motivates people to change, in individuals with antisocial personality disorder, distress enforces accustomed dysfunctional behaviors. Patients exclude themselves ever more from their underlying desire to be lovable and loved. Demonstrating that Christian love offers the

desired biblical gifts therefore substantiates the attractiveness of (and is the motivator for) pastoral healing.

(10) This raises two questions. What does love concretely mean and how does a healer demonstrate it to antisocial people who do not know Christian love? Love involves a plurality of behaviors that may at times seem paradoxical. For example, antisocial people often expect or even provoke rejection. To prevent it, they enact an attractive but also frightening seductive charm. In such cases, love means ignoring, or at least refusing to accept, their manipulation. Love also means a subtle, inconspicuous, but persistent channelling of the sociopath's energy toward finding a purpose, hobby, or activity that makes him or her feel appreciated, respected, and needed.

> A private sanatorium bought a sailboat for recreational purposes. On one occasion, people with antisocial personality disorder were invited to sail. The patients enjoyed the outing, competing with each other in sabotaging the activity until a strong wind unexpectedly struck. At that point, the behavior of the patients, who had never before endured a stormy lake, changed. They worked together like clockwork for the common goal: reaching shore. Following this, sailing excursions were repeatedly organized in intentionally rough water for the same group. Sailing helped to channel the patients' destructive impulsive energy toward a common, prosocial purpose.

Help with the practical realization of occupational, professional, and vocational goals is also a demonstration of love toward antisocial individuals. A healer may support a subject in becoming a good student, doing meaningful work, and striving to achieve a worthy purpose, which may in turn help reverse their learned helplessness. Above all, though, love in the healing of antisocial personality disorder means proving that, despite enacting a Luciferian role, patients are still temples of the Holy Spirit. Advancing reasonable trust (despite all risk factors) and treating them as people of God empowers their self-esteem. An increased self-worth then helps them to take a stance of forgiveness toward alleged abusers, learn from their mistakes in order to adjust and fit into the social environment, and discover a hidden striving for a Christlike life. Antisocial people intensively use the defence mechanism called reactive formation against biblical values. However, when they embrace faith and come to believe that God is their true Lord and friend, their evangelization (which we discuss in the fifth part of this book) may start. The healer can help such people realize where, when, how, and through which psychological functions they genuinely and experientially communicate with the living God. And with the Spirit's help, as happened with many saints, the smallest may become the greatest, and the last may become the first in the kingdom of God.

(11) The healer's persistent, enthusiastic, Don Bosco-like pastoral zeal can often evoke in antisocial patients what seems to be impossible from a professional perspective: an interest in the spiritual-psychological blessings of Christlike living. Thus, parallel to giving them hope for establishing a place in society, pastoral healing helps patients exchange their accumulated and helpless spiritual defeatism for St. Peter-like optimism: "Although you have not seen him you love him; and although you do not see him now, you believe in him and rejoice with an indescribable and glorious joy, for you are rejoicing the outcome of your faith, the salvation of your souls" (1 Pt. 1:8–9). Such antisocial personalities awakened to faith may surprise by unexpectedly pursuing the very Christian ideals they previously opposed. Such is the power of the Holy Spirit.

(12) Working with antisocial people is never an easy task. There are countless unexpected setbacks and challenges, but there are also unexpected opportunities. The therapist's persistence therefore represents a great advantage. Pastoral healers set goals in their efforts that may seem unrealistically optimistic, but they do so in striving, not for a statistically mediocre or average outcome of healing, but an ideal one based upon Jesus' words, "If you have faith … nothing will be impossible for you" (Mt. 17:20).

22.8 Borderline Personality Disorder

Borderline personality disorder is characterized by the DSM-5[47] as a "permanent pattern of instability of interpersonal relationships, self-image and affects, and marked impulsivity." According to Sadock, Sadock, and

Ruiz, the prevalence of the disorder is 1–2 percent in the general population, and it is twice as common in women as in men. People with borderline personality disorder are easy to recognize, as they appear to be in a state of a permanent crisis with extreme mood swings. They are argumentative one moment, depressed the next, and then paranoid. Later, they may complain of having no feelings at all. Such patients can have transitory psychotic episodes (so-called micropsychotic episodes) and can be impulsive and easily agitated, and these intermittent changes can sabotage their mental functioning. They often talk about suicide and undertake abundant self-destructive actions "to elicit help from others, to express anger, or to numb themselves to overwhelming affect." They are ambivalent, both dependent and hostile at the same time, and can be extremely friendly one moment but raging the next. Patients with borderline personality disorder cannot tolerate abandonment or loneliness and thus make quick, transitory, hyperemotional friendships and may also behave promiscuously. They often feel empty and bored as though in a vacuum, lack consistency in their mental functioning, suffer from "identity diffusion," and complain of persistent depression despite being euphoric. The engine of the disorder is patients' projecting their own hated characteristics onto other people. Those people are subsequently manipulated by the patient to act out the projected role. For example, driven by their emotional ambivalence, patients set up others (even their therapists) to play the role of someone jealous, overprotective, impatient, aggressive, or cordial. Patients with borderline personality disorder distort their relationships by maximization or minimization, (i.e., going to extremes and perceiving each person they deal with to be either all good or all bad). They classify acquaintances as either irrational benevolent attachment figures or hateful, sadistic abusers. The alleged good people are deified, while the bad are hatefully devalued. Shifts of allegiance from one group to another and reevaluations of previous allegiances are frequent. These personality traits are fairly stable, and patients change little over time.[48]

Pastoral Consideration

(1) As Barlow notes, "Few therapists are willing to undertake the overwhelmingly difficult and wrenching task of treating individuals with 'borderline' characteristics, yet these people are among the neediest encountered in any therapeutic setting."[49] Their reasoning, will, and mood swings fluctuate between wide parameters, causing unexpected and unpredictable behavioral extremes. For these reasons, before discussing methods of pastoral treating borderline personalities, we will look at a series of warnings.

(2) The term *borderline* was originally invented to indicate that a disorder's symptomatology was on the border between psychosis and neurosis. Borderline personality disorder has no psychotic or delusional symptoms, but its treatment, like the treatment of psychoses, requires extreme patience and caution and special personal skills, mainly because of patients' ambivalence. Borderline patients may exhibit both positive and negative emotions and create ambivalent love-hate relationships, barely manageable, in pastoral settings as they do in the other areas of their lives. Healers need to be prepared for unexpected challenges.[50] They will likely encounter patients' high sensitivity to emotional stimuli; unexpected, intense, and conflicting emotional responses; and a slow return to the baseline, which renders them unable to perceive personal interactions realistically. They interpret healers' responses as malicious, intended to harm or manipulate them.[51]

(3) Among the causes of borderline personality disorder, Corey states the following.

> People with borderline personality disorder have moved into the separation process but have been thwarted by the maternal rejection of their individuation. In other words, a crisis ensues when the child does develop beyond the stage of symbiosis but the mother (or mothering figure) is unable to tolerate this beginning individuation and withdraws emotional support.[52]

Borderline people are repeatedly reliving and reenacting this turbulent period of infancy. Their emotional instability, irritability, self-destructive behavior, impulsive anger, extreme mood shifts, desperate search for support, and manipulative search for companionship are reflections of ambivalent childhood experiences. In short, they are grown-up people with childish behavior.

(4) Since borderline patients are disappointed in their previous relationships, they seek a saviour. Pastoral healers are easily "caught" (i.e., manipulated) by borderline patients who wish to be dependent on their "paid friends," which is a trap to the patients as well. As the therapeutic relationship progresses, patients transfer both positive and negative feelings onto their therapists, who risk becoming enablers. Therefore, the aim in healing borderline people is increasing their self-reliance, competence, and responsibility while avoiding engaging in a counterproductive, mutually dependent relationship. Let us discuss how to avoid the noted traps lying in wait for both parties.

(5) The behaviors of borderline personalities "have an external locus of control" (such people believe that events in their lives are caused by factors they are unable to influence, control, or direct), and because they are scared of therapists' rejection, they are often unable to explain what or how they feel.[53] Pastoral interventions, communication, and relationships (and the whole emotional dynamic in general) ought therefore be slowed down (healers should speak in a low voice, slowly, and with pauses) and kept on a maximally rational level. This also provides the opportunity for the client and healer to establish limits and boundaries, guaranteeing mutual security.

(6) Before starting genuine pastoral treatment, exploring and healing the physical, emotional, and sexual abuse that borderline patients are still intensively suffering from is necessary. The healer can trace current conflicts, disappointments, frustrations, self-esteem issues, feelings of guilt, depression, acting out, and aggressive behaviors back to ambivalent early childhood attachments.[54] In discussing, clarifying, and, if possible, processing these love-hate attachments, pastoral healers need to be painfully aware of the possibility of their own misleading impressions.

(7) Barlow calls attention to borderline patients' "active passivity" and "apparent competence," referring to "a tendency of other individuals [including therapists] to overestimate the capabilities of the individual with BPD." Patients seem assertive, determined, and skilled in resolving strangers' problems but are surprisingly incapable of resolving their own.

Consequently, "not only do they not get the help they need, but also their emotional pain and difficulties may easily be invalidated, leading to a further sense of being misunderstood."[55] Trusting patients' words but never being completely sure of their underlying meaning causes ongoing uncertainty in most therapists.

(8) Special attention ought to be focused on decreasing suicidal risks, especially with patients in adolescence and early adulthood, when emotional dysregulation is at its height. In borderline people, there may be evidence of self-injuring behaviors with or without the serious intent to die. They cause themselves physical pain (mostly by cutting or burning) to distract themselves from psychological pain. They act out to prevent abandonment, boredom, and depression. In these situations, pastoral healers, as noted, should not become rescuers, as giving too much attention provokes irrational attachment and even servility. Conversely, though, too little attention provokes aggression and a self-destructive drive for revenge. The best approach is for the healer to consult with colleagues about countertransferential reactions useful for understanding the emotional dynamics in the patient.[55] However, even after consultations it is often hard for pastoral healers to find a strategy for manoeuvring on such insecure ground.

(9) As noted, the basic professional purpose in healing borderline people is increasing self-reliance. The difficulty in their professional healing, however, is that they have no stable self they can rely on. As such, they permanently feel and fear abandonment. To heal their loneliness, they need attachment figures. Borderline people with attachment problems are naturally inclined to seek an ultimate "replacement authority" to identify with—one who can compensate for all previous backfired attachments. The more trustworthy, reliable, and consistently loving an attachment figure is, the greater peace, trust, optimism, and courage they are able to evoke in borderline people's hearts. Trust in Jesus' almighty and eternal love is what borderline people ultimately need to resolve their malignant emotional oscillations and aggressive and autoaggressive behaviors. Establishing a trusting relationship with Jesus also helps them come to a place of forgiveness, acceptance, peace, and loving their neighbour as themselves. It also gives them the optimism and courage to accept that other believers trust

Jesus as they do. Faith becomes a common denominator that assists bonding and decreases fears of abandonment.

(10) As Barlow notes, the "primary task is stabilizing the client and achieving behavioral control."[56] In helping patients achieve behavioral control, pastoral healing takes an approach different from any worldly type of counselling based on "giving-receiving relationships." It facilitates personal freedom obtainable only by stepping into a biblical reality in which the most important consideration is "not what I can receive, but what I can give." It is an emotional, intellectual, and intentional living with a loving God who does not take away worldly suffering but makes his people "worthy of suffering." The transition to and validity of this new lifestyle is proven by patients' biblical peace, hope, trust, and joy that supersede their previous behavior.

(11) Behavioral methods, in my experience, help heal borderline personalities when supplemented with other pastoral approaches. Suitable and willing patients may be instructed to "model," that is, to attempt to feel and behave like an all-forgiving saint. This new attitude can be at first coached by the pastoral healer and later monitored by the patient. Borderline individuals may also use paradox intention—intentionally seeking challenging situations and, in them, attempt to behave like Jesus by radiating forgiveness, peace, and love.

(12) The final goal of these methods is to help patients find a spiritual purpose wherein the modelled attitude (of behaving like a saint) becomes an authentic personality trait or, in other words, the personality of the borderline patient becomes identified with the modelled behavior. Such a transformation indeed requires titanic effort from the pastoral healer as well as the patient, and it will not happen without setbacks. Nevertheless, it pays off for the patient, the Church, and society.

(13) A significant help in this journey is the Church's being an open-hearted and welcoming Christian community. Accepting borderline people and including them in the community, giving them the opportunity to receive and share the faith and biblical experiences of others proves to them that they are not alone or abandoned. Belonging to Christ becomes a visible community experience for cured believers. To be grafted onto the vine of true life—to become part of the body of Christ—is to experience the deepest and truest form of healing.

Notes

[1] DSM-5. *Diagnostic and Statistical Manual of the American Psychiatric Association* (2013), 321.

[2] Benjamin James Sadock, Virginia Alcott Sadock, and Pedro Ruiz, *Kaplan and Sadock's Synopsis of Psychiatry: Behavioral Sciences/Clinical Psychiatry*, 11th ed. (Philadelphia, PA: Wolters Kluwer, 2015), 742–62.

[3] DSM-5, 321.

[4] Sadock, Sadock, and Ruiz, *Kaplan and Sadock's Synopsis of Psychiatry*, 11th ed. 746.

[5] Vladimir Stanojevic, *Tragedija Genija* (Belgrade: Nolit, 1976), 104–7.

[6] Linda Seligman and Laurie W. Reichenberg, *Selecting Effective Treatments* (Hoboken, NJ: John Wiley & Sons, 2014), 358.

[7] Ibid., 361.

[8] Ibid., 362.

[9] Ibid., 361.

[10] DSM-5, 323–4.

[11] Sadock, Sadock, and Ruiz, *Kaplan and Sadock's Synopsis of Psychiatry*, 11th ed. 747.

[12] Ibid., 748.

[13] Seligman and Reichenberg, *Selecting Effective Treatments*, 362.

[14] Ibid., 363.

[15] Ibid.

[16] DSM-5, 326.

[17] Sadock, Sadock, and Ruiz, *Kaplan and Sadock's Synopsis of Psychiatry*, 11th ed. 747.

[18] Gerald Corey, *Theory and Practice of Counseling and Psychotherapy* (Belmont, CA: Thomson/ Brooks/Cole, 2005), 96.

[19] Seligman and Reichenberg, *Selecting Effective Treatments*, 376–8.

[20] Nance Guilmartin, *Healing Conversations: What to Say When You Don't Know What to Say* (San Francisco: Jossey-Bass, 2002), 15.

[21] Seligman and Reichenberg, *Selecting Effective Treatments*, 378.

[22] DSM-5, 327.

[23] Sadock, Sadock, and Ruiz, *Kaplan and Sadock's Synopsis of Psychiatry*, 11ᵗʰ ed. 751–3.

[24] Corey, *Theory and Practice of Counseling and Psychotherapy*, 97.

[25] Seligman and Reichenberg, *Selecting Effective Treatments*, 382.

[26] Ibid.

[27] DSM-5, 328.

[28] Sadock, Sadock, and Ruiz, *Kaplan and Sadock's Synopsis of Psychiatry*, 11ᵗʰ ed. 753–5.

[29] DSM-5, 328–9.

[30] Ibid., 754–6.

[31] Corey, *Theory and Practice of Counseling and Psychotherapy*, 77.

[32] Seligman and Reichenberg, *Selecting Effective Treatments*, 380.

[33] Ibid., 390.

[34] DSM-5, 329–30.

[35] Sadock, Sadock, and Ruiz, *Kaplan and Sadock's Synopsis of Psychiatry*, 11ᵗʰ ed. 756–7.

[36] Seligman and Reichenberg, *Selecting Effective Treatments*, 394–5.

[37] Ibid., 395.

[38] Corey, *Theory and Practice of Counseling and Psychotherapy*, 141.

[39] DSM-5, 324.

[40] Sadock, Sadock, and Ruiz, *Kaplan and Sadock's Synopsis of Psychiatry*, 11ᵗʰ ed. 748–50.

[41] Seligman and Reichenberg, *Selecting Effective Treatments*, 361.

[42] Lindsay Jones (ed.), *Encyclopedia of Religion* vol. 5 (Farmington Hills, MI: Thomson Gale, 2005), 1941.

[43] Seligman and Reichenberg, *Selecting Effective Treatments*, 365.

[44] Ibid.

[45] Ibid., 366.

[46] Ibid.

[47] DSM-5, 325.

[48] Sadock, Sadock, and Ruiz, *Kaplan and Sadock's Synopsis of Psychiatry*, 11th ed. 750–1.

[49] David H. Barlow (ed.), *Clinical Handbook of Psychological Disorders: A Step-by-Step Treatment Manual* (New York: The Guilford Press, 2008), 365.

[50] Seligman and Reichenberg, *Selecting Effective Treatments*, 370.

[51] Barlow, *Clinical Handbook of Psychological Disorders*, 373.

[52] Ibid., 78.

[53] Seligman and Reichenberg, *Selecting Effective Treatments*, 370–1.

[54] Ibid., 370.

[55] Barlow, *Clinical Handbook of Psychological Disorders*, 375.

[56] Ibid.

CHAPTER TWENTY-THREE

IMPULSE-CONTROL DISORDERS AND THEIR PASTORAL TREATMENT

Among impulse-control disorders mostly occurring in adults, the DSM-5 lists kleptomania, pyromania, and pathological gambling. *Kleptomania* "is a recurrent failure to resist impulses to steal objects not needed for personal use or monetary value."[1] More than 60 percent of patients are women. The disorder usually appears in mildly depressed, rebellious, dissatisfied, and frustrated people suffering from social injustice, anxiety, shame, and guilt. It may also be a reactive formation countering depression by risk-taking behaviors, and it often coincides with eating disorders (bulimia nervosa), OCD, mood disorders, paranoia, histrionic personality disorder, and hoarding behaviors. Approximately 5 percent of those who shoplift suffer from kleptomania.[2]

Pyromania is the starting of fires for pleasure or, more precisely, a relief of tension not for revenge or financial gain.[3] People suffering from pyromania are often fascinated with fire, are associated with fire fighters, and like setting off fire alarms. The disorder often occurs alongside intellectual disability; histrionic, narcissistic, and borderline personality disorders; psychoses; and depression. Subjects often have dysfunctional families, poor social skills, interpersonal difficulties, low self-esteem, problems with alcohol and drugs, sexual dysfunctions, and enuresis.[4]

Pathological gambling "is characterized by persistent and recurring maladaptive gambling that causes economic problems and significant disturbance in personal, social, or occupational functioning."[5] Gambling is characterized by spending increasing amounts of money and repeated and unsuccessful attempts to control the habit. It serves as an escape from other problems, a method to recoup previous losses, and/or a source of excitement. Gamblers often disguise their addiction, commit illegal actions to finance it, lose their occupational or vocational interests, and rely on others to pay their debts. This addiction is often associated with substance abuse, alcoholism, a history of child abuse, dissociative disorder, mania, and depression. Narcissistic and antisocial personality disorders (with grandiose ideas), feelings of guilt, family problems, divorce, and a harsh upbringing are common in gamblers. Seligman and Reichenberg describe four periods in gamblers' lives: (1) the winning phase, which causes the addiction to gambling; (2) the losing phase, characterized by feelings of guilt and hope, borrowing money, and focusing on self-rehabilitation; (3) the desperate phase, in which addicts enslaved by the addiction become involved in illegal activities to make money for gambling; and (4) the hapless stage, wherein gamblers seek arousal and excitement despite the awareness of their unavoidable and complete deterioration.[6] Typical gamblers are intelligent, overconfident, energetic, extroverted, competitive, restless, and prone to taking risks. They often simultaneously suffer from depression, from which gambling serves to reduce the negative effects. The disorder is often connected to overeating and alcohol abuse, and it usually causes grave family, financial, and occupational problems.

Pastoral Considerations

(1) People suffering from impulse-control disorders abundantly use defence mechanisms of regression, and in seeking thrills, excitement, and adrenalin rushes, they virtually refuse to acknowledge reality. They balance on the edge of the possible and impossible, often seeking empowerment through a mixture of irrationalism, occultism, and esoteric interests. Even

in therapy, patients are prone to risk-taking attitudes. They may give healing a chance but not fully commit to it.

(2) Beside preventing the patient's engaging in gambling, professional therapy is usually focused on reducing the boredom, meaninglessness, and frustrations that cause patients' risk-taking behaviors and on helping them find new socially acceptable interests and goals. If simple cognitive-behavioral or existential-oriented therapies are not sufficiently helpful, and if subjects are willing and appropriate candidates, then psychodynamic approaches may be used. These methods are focused on resolving unconscious dynamics symbolically expressed in self-defeating and risk-taking behaviors like pyromania, kleptomania, or gambling disorders.

(3) Some healers report that reducing exposure to risky behaviors (with the hope that those who accept reduction will later accept abstinence more easily) is often more productive than enforcing complete abstinence up front. In the worst cases of gambling addiction, abstinence from gambling is strictly (and institutionally, if needed) enforced, and professional healing is started after three months of abstinence.[7] However, restrictive measures may have a counterproductive effect. Frustrated subjects are even more attracted to the idea of "outsmarting reality" and often "play with and challenge destiny."

(4) It is well documented that "children with multiple risk factors, an earlier onset of symptoms, severely aggressive behavior, and family adversity"[8] have the poorest treatment outcomes. "Multimodality treatment programs that use all available family and community resources are likely to bring out the best results in an effort to control conduct-disordered behavior,"[9] but even these methods are often incapable of changing the inclination toward impulsive behaviors, especially gambling.

(5) Patients suffering from impulse-control dynamics often have similar attitudes toward their families, responsibilities, and even God in regards to their own treatment. They are not committed ("great in words but small in deeds"), often experimenting and testing God rather than being fully committed Christians.

(6) Even strongly committed Christians with impulse-control disorders can be hard to attract to the healing process. Therefore, pastoral help is

often not initially focused on directly addressing their sick and sinful habits but on the weak points in their self-image, such as low self-esteem, the feeling of being unloved and unlovable, the feeling that life is meaningless, depression, boredom, disappointments in love and family relationships, attachment problems, and the fears and anxiety associated with incurable sickness. Other concurrent disorders, from hypomania to borderline personality disorder, are also considered as these may be the problems patients are attempting to heal with their infatuations.

(7) At the root of impulse-control disorders and any concurrent disorders are most often relational issues, so Christian family therapy is frequently a substantial part of patients' pastoral treatment. Family therapy empowers patients. It motivates them to make a firm commitment, especially for the sake of their children, which is the most essential precondition in healing impulse-control disorders. Strongly-committed patients are often able to withstand their temptations by combining family healing with behavioral methods. This is illustrated by the following case study.

> Peter M., a thirty-four-year-old truck driver, escaped, as he described it, from his dominant wife into a rebellious gambling habit. When his wife threatened to divorce him, the committed Christian family made a deal. Peter decided to sacrifice his "hobby" (as he called his impulsive gambling) for his wife's sake, while she pursued a radical behavioral change to better foster her husband's self-esteem, competence, and responsibility and help him to feel like a "biblical patriarch." The family prayed together whenever Peter felt an impulsive need to gamble (often during a phone call), and as Peter grew more confident, he used paradox intention to provoke and challenge his previously uncontrollable impulses, defeating them by meditating, praying, and reading the Bible. Gradually, he went closer and closer to the casino where he had often gambled. Finally, overjoyed at his victory over gambling, Peter had the courage and stamina to enter the casino while remaining firmly focused on the love of Jesus and his wife. At the successful conclusion of his treatment, he no longer felt that his wife

was a detriment to him. Rather, he felt that Jesus was using her as tool in healing his addiction.

Not every pastoral healing has such a positive outcome, however. As repeatedly noted, the power of pastoral healing depends on the patient's commitment to faith.

(8) The purpose of pastoral healing in cases of impulse-control disorders could be summarized as replacing the sick need behind kleptomania, pyromania, gambling, and other addictive, fun-seeking behaviors with a "holy addiction" to Jesus. While treatment for impulse-control behavior may not always be effective, faith always gives what it promises: biblical love, joy, and purpose. The crucial task of the pastoral healer is helping patients experience this basic Christian truth for themselves, which they can only do by demonstrating it to others.

(9) Spiritual healing helps believers understand their suffering from impulse-control behaviors as a call for the conversion of their hearts. A heart conversion for them means transforming from unsuccessful pursuers of the mirage of worldly gratification into successful providers of biblical optimism, courage, hope, and trust for their family and neighbours. Providing these biblical gifts to others helps believers in their healing because they receive the same spiritual gifts they offer. In biblical terms, you reap what you sow.

(10) Accordingly, pastoral healing for impulse-control disorders aims to establish a virtual receiving-giving relationship between the patient and Jesus, their family members, and their neighbours. Just as people continuously inhale and exhale, so pastoral healers coach the giving and receiving of biblical gifts. The one who breathes out biblical hope, optimism, and courage to neighbours will breathe in the same from Jesus. An addiction to such a lifestyle is the best cure for impulse-control disorders. Such a lifestyle is the best prevention and cure for impulse-control disorders.

(11) When former impulse-control addicts witness the healing power of faith, they frequently find a new purpose in becoming co-therapists for those suffering as they once suffered. Seeing living examples of the healing

power of faith helps other patients in their seemingly hopeless situation to "fight the good fight of faith" (1. Tim. 6:12), which is empirically measurable in their healing.

(12) While the number of people suffering classical forms of impulse-control disorder is increasing slowly, the numbers of those suffering new forms of impulse-control problems (such as addictions to cell phones, computer games, social media, and thrilling but risky sports) are increasing explosively. Both teens and adults have become addicted to activities and materials in virtual reality and cyberspace. Twenty years ago, spending more than an hour on the Internet was considered serious, and nightly news stories featured "addicts" who spent up to three hours on their computers. With the advent of smart phones and tablets, the bahaviour is mistakenly accepted as normal. Cyber addiction can blur the line between what is real and what is not. Such addiction also causes people to withdraw from normal interactions and conversation with people.

Despite the concerns and recommendations of the World Health Organization, these behaviors are not yet categorized as a distinct psychiatric nozological entity. Since, however, the pastoral healing of these new forms of impulse-control behaviors is in many aspects similar to the methods used in healing classical forms, the discussed methods can be adapted and applied in those cases.

Notes

[1] Benjamin James Sadock, Virginia Alcott Sadock, and Pedro Ruiz, *Kaplan and Sadock's Synopsis of Psychiatry: Behavioral Sciences/Clinical Psychiatry*, 11th ed. (Philadelphia, PA: Wolters Kluwer, 2015), 611.

[2] Linda Seligman and Laurie W. Reichenberg, *Selecting Effective Treatments* (Hoboken, NJ: John Wiley & Sons, 2014), 300.

[3] Sadock, Sadock, and Ruiz, *Kaplan and Sadock's Synopsis of Psychiatry*, 11th ed. 612–14.

[4] Seligman and Reichenberg, *Selecting Effective Treatments*, 301.

[5] Sadock, Sadock, and Ruiz, *Kaplan and Sadock's Synopsis of Psychiatry*, 11th ed. 609–13.

[6] Seligman and Reichenberg, *Selecting Effective Treatments*, 302.

[7] Ibid., 81.

[8] Ibid., 80.

[9] Sadock, Sadock, and Ruiz, *Kaplan and Sadock's Synopsis of Psychiatry*, 11th ed. 1245.

CHAPTER TWENTY-FOUR

Disorders Connected to Addictions and Abuse and Their Pastoral Treatment

In the fourteenth century, the population of the world was decimated by the Black Death. In the eight years between 1345 and 1353, it killed between 75 and 200 million people. Today, we are confronted with a global challenge of comparable dimensions in alcohol and drug abuse, which kills not only the bodies but also the souls of millions of people. To fight this modern plague, let us first focus on its psychological dynamics.

24.1 Alcohol-Related Disorders

The DSM-5[1] characterizes alcohol-related disorders by "a problematic pattern of alcohol use leading to clinically significant impairment or distress." Patients consume large amounts of alcohol despite efforts to reduce and control their drinking habit and spend a great deal of time, money, and energy on obtaining alcohol and satisfying the craving. They consume alcohol even in hazardous situations, causing impairment in fulfilling important social, occupational, and family roles. There is a significant need to increase the quantity of consumed alcohol to achieve the desired effects, while consumption reduction results in significant withdrawal effects. We may distinguish three levels of alcohol consumption: alcohol use, alcohol abuse, and alcohol addiction. Sadock, Sadock, and Ruiz report the gravity of the contemporary situation with the following statistical information: "About 51 percent of all US adults are current users of alcohol." Approximately 30–40 percent of all adults have had at least one episode of alcohol-related problems, with around 10 percent of women and 20 percent of men suffering from alcohol abuse and 3–5 percent of women and 10 percent of men suffering from of alcohol dependence during their lifetimes. About 200,000 deaths per year are connected to alcohol abuse. Unfortunately, alcohol abuse is involved in about 50 percent of all automobile fatalities, and this rate increases to 75 percent when only accidents occurring during night are counted. Alcohol consumption occurs in about 50 percent of homicides and 25 percent of suicides. It also decreases life expectancy by about 10 years.[2] In our times (after heart disease and malignant cancers), alcohol-related disorders constitute the third largest health problem in the United States. But what makes alcoholics sacrifice their jobs, health, and family for a drink?

Alcohol has a gradual paralyzing effect on the brain. If the alcohol level reaches 0.5–1.5 promille (the lower level of alcohol intoxication), most subjects' functions of conscience and self-criticism are inhibited. Such people are happy and euphoric, often singing, laughing, and joking, and their shyness and caution disappear. Like the Latin saying *in vino veritas* ("in wine, truth"), the intoxicated person reveals their secrets, and their ethical and mental control mechanisms decrease. All problems are minimized, and the person feels almost omnipotent.

The middle level of alcohol intoxication, between 1.5 and 3.5 promille, is characterized by paralysis of the deeper brain functions regulating balance, vision, and motor coordination. The person is unable to talk fluently, has double vision, difficulty standing upright or walking, and vomits. Executive functions are reduced, logic and cognitive functioning are extinguished, and the person uncritically accepts suggestions, not defending themselves in life-threatening situations but gradually sinking into a deep sleep.

If the alcohol level in the blood reaches 3.5–4.5 promille, the highest level of alcohol intoxication, the deepest and most basic brain functions are inhibited and the person slips into a coma. Death occurs without medical help because of paralysis of the lungs' breathing centre in the brain stem.

People drink because consuming alcohol eases their feelings of guilt, self-criticism, fears, worries, low self-esteem, anxiety, and moral responsibility. However, upon sobering up, all these feelings exponentially return, so the alcoholic attempts to heal their problems with renewed drunkenness, causing even greater problems. Not everyone who drinks alcohol becomes dependent upon it, however. There are many known and unknown personal, psychological, neurological, social, and genetic factors in alcoholism, but above all, the choice to drink is a personal one.

The adverse effects of alcohol consumption start with a repeated pattern of heavy drinking, at first limited to weekends and interrupted by long periods of sobriety and later with binges of heavy drinking lasting for days, weeks, or even months. As the saying goes, "First the alcoholic takes the alcohol, and then alcohol takes the alcoholic." Losing control happens when tolerance increases (and alcohol does not cause pleasurable or euphoric feelings anymore), but alcoholics need to drink to reduce the symptoms of abstinence, including hangovers, fears, tremors, sweating, and hallucinations. Losing control occurs parallel to decreasing psychological, physical, mental, and social functioning. In this stage, self-esteem, honesty, feelings of duty, and responsible behavior decrease. Patients neglect their families, jobs, and image; sell their property; lose interest in future responsibilities and duties; and spend all of their money on securing their alcohol supply. Without an income and with increasing neglect and aggression, their families fall apart. As Kaplan and Sadock's textbook describes it, "Such people feel well only in the company of comrades with similar problems, to whom they confess and complain about the cruelty of the society which has abandoned them. Quite unexpectedly, they get into fights and often physical aggression with them; such people become untrustworthy … and deceitful. Exposed to repeated police interventions, they live on or without social help starving on the periphery of the society."[3] These individuals are dirty and unkempt; are unable to concentrate; experience difficulty in thinking; are uncritical; are unable to predict the consequences of their actions; and accuse partners, parents, children, or society as being the source of their problems, never themselves. Somatic changes include a specific alcoholic voice, a swollen red face, pale skin, yellowish sclera, and signs of polyneuropathy (inflammation and damage of the sensitive nerves that cause pain in the legs, resulting in walking with a wide gate), and are alarming signs of advanced alcoholism. Sleeplessness, sweating, tremors, and hallucinations of small people and animals are the introductory signs of delirium. Alcoholics often seek help in this phase.[4]

24.2 Drug-Related Disorders

Kaplan and Sadock's textbook[5] lists the following drugs that are relevant from a pastoral perspective:

Amphetamines have a medical use (in treating ADHD and some forms of depression). Their generic names are Ritalin, Adderall, Dexosyn, and Dexedrine, while their street names are speed, methamphetamine, ice, crystal, and others. They mainly have stimulating effects that cause euphoria. Some three out of every ten people abuse this drug, and lifetime dependence is around 1.5 percent in the general population. Intoxication is characterized by euphoria, increased activity, a short attention span, anger, anxiety, grossly impaired judgment, psychomotor agitation, and aggression. After the short-term stimulating effects have abated, exhaustion occurs, with delirium and psychotic episodes, racing heart, sweating, chills, sexual dysfunction, seizures, confusion, and eventually coma. In chronic use and despite an increased dose, lethargic mental exhaustion, tiredness, powerlessness, changes in blood pressure, loss of weight, and chest pains occur. The withdrawal symptoms are tiredness, anger, headaches, insomnia, and sometimes suicidal ideation.[6]

Cannabis derivatives are obtained from Indian hemp (*Cannabis sativa varietas indica*) and have been in use for some 8,000 years. Hashish is extracted from the dried leaves, while marijuana is produced by drying the plant and smoking it in "joints." The street names of marijuana include weed, pot, and grass. Collective poisoning by the drug, caused by massive intoxication, is called "St. Anton's fever." As Kaplan and Sadock's textbook notes, "An estimated 90.8 million adults (42.9 percent) aged twelve years or older have used marijuana at least once in their lifetime." When smoking marijuana, euphoria appears within minutes, peaks at half an hour, and lasts for not longer than four hours. The cognitive and motoric effects may last for 5–12 hours. Cannabis is "2–3 times less potent if digested in the form of cakes and cookies."[7] Cannabis intoxication causes euphoria and increased reactivity to external stimuli, while colours seem more vivid and accentuated, and time seems to slow down. Cannabis intoxication also includes the following: geometrical illusions; derealisation; depersonalization; compromised reality judgment; delirium; decreased memory, perception, and coordination; disorientation; and substantially decreased cognitive skills. On rare occasions, cannabis may cause paranoid and psychotic reactions. There is no physical dependence, but there may be psychological dependence, bringing about impairment of memory, attention, and the integration of complex information. The so-called avolitional syndrome consists of the inability to perform tasks requiring mental concentration (at school or the workplace). "People are described as becoming apathetic and lacking energy, usually gaining weight and appearing slothful."[8] Smoking marijuana poses the same risks of lung cancer as smoking tobacco, a fact that is almost totally ignored in the growing movement to legalize marijuana in the United States and elsewhere.

Cocaine is extracted from the leaves of the South American plant Erytroxylon coca. It has been chewed by native Indians for centuries and increases muscular strength. "In 2002 and 2003, 5.9 million (2.5 percent) people aged twelve or older used cocaine." Males are twice as likely to use it.[9] Cocaine is extremely addictive, and even one use may cause addiction. Since the effects are short (lasting up to one hour), tolerance is quickly increased. The drug is inhaled, smoked (in the form of crack cocaine), swallowed, or injected. Intoxication causes euphoria, with a feeling of enormous power and increased mental and physical abilities. Later come paranoid hallucinations of being followed, observed, and persecuted; haptic hallucinations, such as feeling worms underneath the skin; and Lilliputian hallucinations, or seeing the world in small dimensions. Further symptoms are irritability, aggression, acting out sexually, impaired reality judgment, manic agitation, personality changes, an inability to focus, insomnia, weight loss, delusions, homicidal drives, and self-mutilation. Long-term use of high dosages causes multiple brain and heart muscle lesions, which may eventually cause death.

Hallucinogenic drugs such as psilocybin (extracted from mushrooms) or mescaline (extracted from peyote cactus) were used for many thousands of years in social and religious rituals, while synthetic hallucinogenic drugs like LSD were synthesized in 1938. There were peaks in using hallucinogenic drugs between 1965 and 1969 (LSD) and in 1992 and 2000. Designer drugs of unique and often hard-to-distinguish compositions are currently fuelling a third peak. Kaplan and Sadock's textbook reports that around 10 percent of the population have used hallucinogenic drugs at least once.[10] These drugs cause perceptual changes (geometric, spatial, and temporal hallucinations, as well as hallucinations of noises and voices) that intensify to delirium and bizarre behaviors (e.g., running around naked outside or fleeing a hallucinated attack) that can be aggressive in nature. Psilocybin often causes psychotic episodes, dimethyltryptamine provokes toxic delirium, and LSD causes severe panic and psychotic symptoms. These drugs may provoke schizophreniform or genuine schizophrenic episodes, mood and anxiety disorders, and disintegration of the personality.

Inhalant drugs encompass relatively cheap and easily accessible chemicals like gasoline, spray paints, solvents, glues, and thinners. Approximately 6 percent of the population have used such drugs at least once in their lives, and about 1 percent are continual users. About fifteen to twenty deep breaths of 1 percent gasoline vapour may cause intoxication, with an onset in five minutes and lasting for several hours.[11] Abuse is characterized by apathy, diminished social and occupational functioning, impaired judgment, anxiety, and impulsive or aggressive behavior, along with neurological symptoms like nystagmus, depressed reflexes, and diplopia. Prolonged use brings seizures and unconsciousness, delirium, persisting dementia, and psychotic symptoms, while delusions, hallucinations, and mood and anxiety disorders may also appear.

Opioid-related drugs have been well known and used for millennia. Morphine, opium, and codeine can be extracted from poppies and were chemically isolated in the nineteenth century. In the twentieth century, opioids like meperidine and methadone were synthesized and also used for the treatment of morphine addiction. This group also encompasses medicines containing opioids (like OxyContin) used for nonmedical purposes. Kaplan and Sadock's textbook estimates that in the United States some 600–800,000 people use heroin.[12] Opioid drugs can be used through injection, smoking, or snorting. They have a strong analgesic effect and cause pleasant feelings of relaxation and unorganized but pleasant hallucinations that cause euphoria and gradually evolve into pleasant sedation. The side effects are vomiting, dry mouth, and itchy nose. Patients suffering from great pain tolerate larger amounts of morphine. Terminally ill cancer patients can tolerate even five times the dose that would be lethal for an average person. The tolerance increases over prolonged use, so drug addicts need to increase their doses significantly to achieve the desired relaxation, the cessation of all problems and worries, euphoria, and ecstasy. This increases the risk of overdosing, characterized by losing interest in reality, withdrawal, slurred speech, slow and impaired thinking, drowsiness, delirium, psychotic behaviors, intense mood disorders, and sleep and sexual dysfunctions. Intoxication causes papillary constriction, decreased blood pressure, respiratory depression, and eventually coma. Death occurs because of respiratory paralysis. Dependence on opioids is characterized by losing social contacts; withdrawing from any mental or physical activity; abandoning interest in family, work, and friends; selling property; and deceitfulness since the user is focused solely on ensuring the next drug supply. Addicts live in euphoric daydreams, and returning to reality is painful because of the following: intense cravings; a long-lasting irritable, depressed, and hopeless mood; tremors; muscle pain; diarrhoea; abdominal pains; cold sweats; intense lacrimation; feverish hypothermia; and pupil dilatation. Withdrawal symptoms may be complicated by delirium, schizophreniform psychotic disorders, panic and mood disorders (manic, depressed, and mixed episodes), sleeplessness, sexual dysfunctions, and parkinsonism.

PCP (Phencyclidine), as Kaplan and Sadock's textbook notes, concerns the group of medicines synthesized after 1950 and introduced as dissociative anaesthetics. Such drugs make it possible to keep patients awake during surgery without feeling pain. PCP became popular in the 1970s and is used today as a designer drug as it is easily synthesized in underground laboratories. The exact number of PCP addicts is unknown. About 3 percent of deaths are caused by PCP overdoses. The drug is smoked or injected, and its effects appear within five minutes and plateau in less than an hour.[13] Users are often oblivious to reality and experience fantasies, euphoria, body warmth, tingling, peaceful floating sensations, and occasionally depersonalization, auditory and visual hallucinations, alterations of body image, distortions of space and time perceptions, and delusions. Users may be sociable and talkative at one moment and negative, hostile, and paranoid the next. They may also become irritable, paranoid, assaultive, suicidal, or homicidal. Behavioral disturbances may be severe (public masturbation, removal of clothes, violence, and urinary incontinence). Approximately 25 percent of PCP users suffer from delirium, characterized by bizarre, agitated, and aggressive behavior. PCP causes psychotic disorders that may last for thirty days and include delusions and hallucinations and that are often complicated by injuries accidentally acquired during the psychotic period (in some 40–50 percent of subjects). Mood disorders also occur, mainly with manic, agitated, and aggressive behavior.

Concerning sedative, hypnotic, and anxiolytic abuse, *barbiturates* like veronal, nesdonal, kemital, baytinal, and luminal were introduced around 1903 and are used for inducing sleep, sedation, and treating epilepsy. *Benzodiazepines* like Librium, Valium, and Serax were introduced in the 1960s and are used for sedation, relaxation, and anxiolytic effects. The effects of both groups overlap in many aspects. Some 15 percent of all Americans have been prescribed benzodiazepines by physicians, and around 6 percent use these drugs illicitly.[14] Intoxication with barbiturates is characterized by psychomotor slowdown; coordination, balance, memory, thinking, and comprehension problems; disinhibited behavior; sexual aggression; paranoid interpretations; and suicidal behaviors. Barbiturate poisoning paralyzes the brain's respiratory centre. Typical for intoxication with benzodiazepines are psychomotor agitation, aggression, vertigo, sluggishness, and incoordination. The symptoms resemble those of alcohol intoxication. If taken in greater doses, drowsiness, psychomotor slowdown, disorientation, confusion, and the depression of vital functions (blood pressure and breathing) occurs. Lethal outcomes are relatively rare. Symptoms caused by barbiturate withdrawal range from mild (anxiety, sweating, and insomnia) to severe (seizures, delirium, psychotic disorders, and death). The psychotic symptoms resemble those of alcohol abuse, including delirium, agitation, delusions, and auditory and visual hallucinations. Withdrawal symptoms of benzodiazepine use are milder than those of barbiturates and consist of anxiety, dysphoria (a bad mood), insomnia, agitation, sweating, nausea, intolerance of bright lights and noises, and seizures. There is also a risk of dementia and memory problems, which increases the longer withdrawal symptoms are present.

Pastoral Considerations

(1) In the case of addiction, professional and pastoral healers are fighting a challenge that may, in the future, surpass all other threats to the mental health of the human species. The reasons behind the relative inefficiency of professional postmodern treatment methods, as Seligman and Reichenberg note, are patients' denial of symptoms, refusal of treatment, and relapses most often fuelled by "negative emotional states of mind," "interpersonal conflicts," and "social pressure."[15] The efficiency of pastoral interventions in healing the integration of sickness and sin in addictions is hard to gauge accurately. Since its effectiveness depends on commitment to Jesus, in some cases it is the most effective treatment and in others it is completely powerless.

(2) Prevention starts with the family. Beginning in the first few years of their children's lives, fathers have a special role of providing a Christlike loving strictness that fosters optimistic and resilient self-esteem and self-confidence that prevent drug usage. A report written by a twelve-year-old immigrant boy illustrates the importance of fathers fulfilling this role.

> My father is old, he is sick, he is poor, he does not work, and he does not speak English. My mom said he is an alcoholic and a burden to the family. However, I never feel so safe, so secure, so protected as when he is sober and hugs me. When he does, I feel that my father is satisfied with me.

It seems that the approval of parents, and especially of respected and morally strong father figures, is still a strong source of empowerment in our culture. As we will later discuss, experiencing the heavenly Father's support gives an even stronger resilience against alcohol and drug abuse.

(3) The broader family also has a role. Nagging a family member to end their problematic drinking or to take control of their drinking habit by curtailing their finances or liquor supply can have either a productive or negative effect. Alcohol is, however, frequently served at family celebrations, and this can become an antecedent for addiction.[16] In such cases, the broader family needs to be involved in preventing and healing their loved one's addiction by maintaining an antialcoholic- and antidrug-centred family climate, facilitating abstinence and the referral of addicted members to institutions specialized in therapy for alcoholics.

(4) Spouses of alcoholics and drug-addicted people sometimes give up, having no more energy to fight, accepting the social, financial, occupational, moral, and spiritual demise of their loved ones. They accept addiction almost as fate. The phrase "to kill God in someone," used in Slavic languages to describe the worst thing that can happen to a human being, applies here. Addicts' spouses and other family members who act as enablers help addicts "kill God" (extinguish all optimism, self-respect, hope, meaning in life, courage, and values) in their personalities.

(5) Addicts are motivated for treatment when the perceived costs of their addictive behaviors outweigh the perceived benefits. We may imagine the process of treatment as a continuum, which consists of precontemplation (in which a behavior is not yet perceived as problematic), contemplation (in which a behavior is perceived as potentially problematic), determination or preparation (in which the decision to change is made), and action (in which behavioral changes are initiated). Following this is maintenance (maintaining the behavioral changes) or relapse (in which a return to the problem behavior occurs).[17]

(6) In practice, the common symptom of alcohol and drug abuse is reflected in the refrain I heard from one addict: "Stop the world, I wanna get off." Stepping off the frustrating world is easy. However, when the inevitable

return to the world becomes so tormenting that addicts perceive that things cannot possibly be any worse, the motivation for change starts.

> The best results I personally saw in the professional treatment of addicted patients were achieved in an institutional setting that required patients to run a distance akin to a marathon as a precondition for admittance for treatment. At first, most people weren't able to run more than a few hundred yards. However, with the help of skilled motivators, diligent training, coaching, and singing "no pain, no gain," the participants were eventually able to run the distance. This showed them that the impossible is achievable and gave them the determination, stamina, self-confidence, courage, and self-esteem to overcome their addictions.

(7) The purposes of pastoral and professional healing in cases of disorders connected to addictions and substance abuse are to some degree similar and are aimed at evoking the patient's self-criticism and self-discipline. Since addictive disorders are facilitated by ongoing, counterproductive, and self-defeating protests against perceived injustice, hopelessness, stress or abandonment, the methods of both professional and pastoral therapy include alleviating the lifestyle problems that have contributed to these disorders. Both professional and pastoral therapy are focused on resolving the patient's feelings of being unloved, unappreciated, and abused; on addressing their ultimate sense of meaninglessness and the ensuing low self-esteem, feelings of guilt, and love-hate attachments; and on resolving frustrating childhood experiences, family and relational conflicts, and any recent emotional, occupational, or vocational conflicts. Family therapy often helps resolve couples' self-defeating conflicts that inevitably cause mutual estrangement and diminished commitment and love, which promote the escape into addictive behaviors. If the patient's alcohol or drug problem has a psychiatric reason (such as anxiety disorders, schizoid or borderline personality disorder, mood disorders, or antisocial personality disorder), the disorder needs to be managed. The healing of substance abuse disorders can begin only after at least a partial restoration of the affected person's psychological stability, as well as discretional and appreciative judgment.

(8) Healing addicts always requires implementing abstinence. The degree of abstinence is, however, a wide-open question. In the traditional medical view, total abstinence is the only option because it regards alcohol and drug addictions as progressive diseases that can only be defeated with complete avoidance. Others state that giving the treated addicts the opportunity to choose between total abstinence and the reduction of alcohol or drug intake increases their cooperation in treatment.[18] In practice, though, neither approach is able to eradicate addictions. Addicts are treated in expensive clinics with expensive medicines and even more expensive psychotherapies that attempt to mobilize their determination for healing, but unfortunately the results are very mixed. The role of the pastoral healer in using the orchestra of therapies starts when the addict's psychiatric, neurological, and somatic symptoms are under control.

(9) Initially, addicts' perception of God fits their defeatist world picture.[19] So long as they seek the consolation of a "hashish paradise" (to quote a poem by Charles Baudelaire), talking to them about a biblical God of love may cause the healer to feel like "the voice of one calling in the wilderness" (Mk. 1:3). Nevertheless, the Spirit "blows where it chooses" (Jn. 3:8). I witnessed this truth as a resident in psychiatry.

> As I was speaking with one of my older colleagues in the hospital hallway, he turned and greeted a man with a notable amount of respect. "Who was that man?" I asked. He explained, "He was a heavy drug addict whom I treated for six years—unsuccessfully. Then he joined a strict denomination, and since that time he has never come back to me."

(10) As the well-known saying of St. Basil the Great goes, "A spark of divine love exists in every human being." The rationale behind all pastoral work with alcoholics and drug-addicted people is to coax from this metaphorical spark a God-inspired fire of love, unselfishness, and determination to fight addiction. In practice, this means escaping the living hell of a hashish paradise through the gates of heaven or, more concretely, replacing a bad addiction to alcohol or drugs with a good addiction to Jesus.

(11) The prototypes of pastoral healing methods are found in principles

of the well-known twelve-step program. This famous AA program originated from unsuccessful analytic healing.

As Marsha Wiggins Frame notes, Carl Gustav Jung treated a person known as Rowland H. After many unsuccessful attempts, Jung "purportedly told his client that he could not help him and declared that only a religious or spiritual experience could rescue him from his condition." Jung's encouragement motivated Rowland to join the Anglican Oxford Group, which helped him to overcome his addiction. Thanks to Rowland's continued networking after his healing, the well-known twelve steps of AA were born. The twelve-step program is summarized as follows.

(1) We admit we are powerless over alcohol and that our lives have become unmanageable.

(2) We believe that a power greater than ourselves can restore us to sanity.

(3) We have made a decision to turn our will and our lives to the care of God as we understand Him.

(4) We have made a searching and fearless moral inventory of ourselves.

(5) We have admitted to God, to ourselves, and to another human being the exact nature of our wrongs.

(6) We are entirely ready to have God remove all these defects of character.

(7) We humbly ask Him to remove our shortcomings.

(8) We have listed all the people we have harmed and are willing to make amends with all of them.

(9) We have made direct amends with the listed people wherever possible, except when to do so would injure them or others.

(10) We continue to take a personal inventory and promptly admit it whenever we're wrong.

(11) We seek through prayer and meditation to improve our conscious contact with God as we understand Him, praying only for the knowledge of His will and the power to carry it out.

(12) Having had a spiritual awakening as a result of these steps, we try to carry this message to alcoholics and to practice these principles in all our affairs.[20]

Different Narcotics Anonymous programs have similar missions. These self-help groups, as Barlow states, "can be an effective way to develop a new network of associates that supports a sober lifestyle."[21] However, as with all faith-based treatments, they are only effective in proportion to one's faith.

(12) In only a few Christian communities are serious attempts made to not only exercise charity toward, but also evangelize and heal, people suffering from addiction problems. Additionally, there is a common perception that alcohol- and drug-dependent people are unapproachable concerning the happy news of the Bible. Hopefully, though, as the number of affected cases exponentially increases, so too will the collective awareness that turning to Christ is both the most cost-effective and efficient way to resolve the perception of meaningless existence that so many of our contemporaries are suffering from, facilitating the pandemic of alcoholism and drug abuse. Working out new, innovative pastoral methods for treating addiction would have an effect comparable to that of antibiotics in fighting the Black Death. Indeed, addiction to "other gods" such as drugs and alcohol is conquerable only with Jesus' help. Recalling Frankl's paraphrase, we could say that *pastoral healing cannot cure all disorders which are connected to abuse and addiction, but no disorder connected to abuse and addiction can be cured without pastoral healing.*

Notes

[1] DSM-5. *Diagnostic and Statistical Manual of the American Psychiatric Association* (2013), 233.

[2] Benjamin James Sadock, Virginia Alcott Sadock, and Pedro Ruiz, *Kaplan and Sadock's Synopsis of Psychiatry: Behavioral Sciences/Clinical Psychiatry*, 11th ed. (Philadelphia, PA: Wolters Kluwer, 2015), 624–625.

[3] Srboljub Stojiljkovic, *Psihijatrija sa Medicinskom Psihologijom* (Belgrade: Medicinska Knjiga, 1975), 122.

[4] Benjamin James Sadock and Virginia Alcott Sadock, *Kaplan and Sadock's Synopsis of Psychiatry: Behavioral Sciences/Clinical Psychiatry*, 10th ed. (Philadelphia, PA: Wolters Kluwer, 2007), 407–66.

[5] Ibid., 408.

[6] Ibid., 416.

[7] Ibid., 419.

[8] Ibid., 420.

[9] Ibid., 435.

[10] Ibid., 436.

[11] Ibid., 656

[12] Ibid., 444.

[13] Ibid., 435.

[14] Ibid., 454.

[15] Linda Seligman and Laurie W. Reichenberg, *Selecting Effective Treatments* (Hoboken, NJ: John Wiley & Sons, 2014), 246.

[16] David H. Barlow (ed.), *Clinical Handbook of Psychological Disorders: A Step-by-Step Treatment Manual* (New York: The Guilford Press, 2008), 492.

[17] Ibid.

[18] Ibid., 200.

[19] Gerald Corey, *Theory and Practice of Counseling and Psychotherapy* (Thomson Brooks/Cole. Thomson Learning Academic Resource Center, 2005), 520.

[20] Marsha Wiggins Frame, *Integrating Religion and Spirituality in Counseling: A Comprehensive Approach* (Pacific Grove, CA: Thomson/ Brooks/Cole, 2003), 107.

[21] Barlow, *Clinical Handbook of Psychological Disorders*, 588.

PART THREE

CONDITIONS OF SPECIAL PASTORAL INTEREST AND THEIR TREATMENT

The DSM 5, in the section "Other Conditions that may be a Focus of Clinical Attention," lists issues related to medical, social, and environmental problems. These conditions are not "disorders" in a medical sense, but they modify or contribute to psychiatric morbidity and psychological problems. A similar purpose is served by discussing conditions of special pastoral interest. They do not signal sick or sinful behaviors but conditions that affect the risk of estrangement from God in a specific way and therefore have a special importance in new evangelization and in pastoral healing.

CHAPTER TWENTY-FIVE

EARLY CHILDHOOD FROM A PROFESSIONAL AND PASTORAL PERSPECTIVE

The DSM-5 does not recommend giving diagnoses in the early years of life. All babies are deemed to be mentally healthy.[1] Babies do, however, learn quickly; their brains are "plastic," meaning mistakes in their upbringing may be imprinted in their brains and minds and cause lasting adverse consequences. This is where pastoral healing comes in: aiming to be especially helpful in the delicate process of raising young generations that will determine humankind's future.

25.1 The Newborn Period

Reflexes enabling breathing, sucking, and swallowing are present from birth. Although the sensory organs are still incompletely developed, "three-day-old newborn babies can distinguish their mother's voice." Infants' mental development is rapid. Three-week-old babies begin mimicking, two-month-old babies begin smiling, and four-month-old babies begin responding with smiles to stimulation.[2] Responding to a mother's stimulation by producing voices begins around the second month, and it facilitates an emotional attachment to the mother. Attachment quality is one of the substantial factors ensuring or harming later development. In toddlers, it reduces anxiety, enabling the child to occasionally move away from the mother and explore the environment on its own. Abrupt separation from the mother, especially during the second six months of life, can lead to permanent personality changes. Even worse is maternal rejection or neglect, which causes developmental retardation at a severe level. Babies usually receive care from their mothers, while fathers play with them. Therefore, when looking for security, infants usually seek it from their mothers. Only if mothers are unavailable do infants turn to the father. These first learned "patterns of infant attachment affect future adult emotional relationships,"[3] and they also significantly influence social interests, behaviors, and personal functioning that develop later in life. The ability to resist, process, and defeat virtually all mental ailments discussed in DSM-5, and especially those of alcohol and drug addiction, in many aspects depends on the basic security acquired in these first months of life.

25.2 Forming the Personality in the Toddler Period

Babies are best characterized by "primary narcissism," that is, their inability to differentiate between I and "not I." Since to them everything is "I" (i.e., there is no "not I"), every impulse seems easy to satisfy. Except when they seek nourishment, signalling hunger or thirst by crying, babies are resting in peace or sleeping. Toddlers, however, start differentiating between I—the internal world—and not I—the external reality. In this transition, they first attempt to control the external world directly by crying, screaming, and protesting. Around the age of nine to eleven months, they learn to adjust their behaviors to reality (e.g., learning when to comply and where, when, and how to say no). Thus, while babies are solely impulse-regulated (motivated by their internal world), toddlers gradually establish their personalities, enabling them to take a stand for or against the requirements of their internal world (their needs and impulses) and the external world (represented by their parents).

The "parental task in the toddler stage requires firmness about the boundaries of acceptable behavior and encouragement of the child's progressive emancipation" while protecting the child's security.[4] This process involves integrating the instincts under the self's command, expedited by the parents' teaching and their training toddlers where, when, and how they may successfully approach others (the external world) to satisfy their needs. The parents' tools in this process are giving love and, if needed, triggering fear or the loss of love. Fear of losing parental love as a consequence of disobeying commands evokes a feeling of existential threat in toddlers, while obeying the parental commands arouses a basic trust and security.

The conflict between complying and rebelling against parental authority is manifest in toddlers' behaviors. These generally swing between two extremes: attachment, expressed in affectionate body language like hugging and kissing, and dissatisfaction, expressed in crying, running away, or even biting and hitting. The worst form of dissatisfaction is expressed in children's detachment from parents, manifested in behaviors of turning away, coldness, and apathy. In all cases, however, parents, and especially fathers, are perceived as essentially protective and virtually omnipotent figures. Thus, these first experiences shape not only basic trust or distrust toward the father, who represents the external world, but also the ideal father image, or God. God and the Christian conscience gradually come to be the most important "internally experienced external reality" in religious toddlers.

25.3 The Concept of the Difficult Child

The same upbringing has different effects on different children. This is because each newborn has innate physiological characteristics, collectively known as the temperament. Therefore, every child needs a unique approach to his or her upbringing. This is especially true of so-called "difficult children who make up ten percent of all children." Such children "have a hyperalert psychological makeup. They react intensely to stimuli (cry easily at loud noises), sleep poorly, eat at unpredictable times, and are difficult to comfort." These children need a greater emotional investment from parents than infants who seem more phlegmatic.[5]

Pastoral Considerations

(1) The parents of difficult children are often anxious about not parenting well enough or being unfit to manage their children's eating, sleeping, and behavioral habits. The first task in pastoral help is reassuring them that their children are like diamonds: they just need polishing in the form of extra patience, care, and love. Jesus said, "Truly I tell you, unless you change and become like little children, you will never enter the kingdom of heaven" (Matthew 18:3). Being human, Jesus knew, of course, that all children can be difficult, and yet he knew how special children are because of the innocence and faith that resides in all of them even if these traits are temporarily hidden for a time.

(2) The saying "anxious mothers produce anxious babies" holds true. Difficult children's excessive and loud crying, angry and acting-out behaviors, and eating and sleeping problems are more frightening for anxious patients who may overact by spoiling such children. Meanwhile, children learn quickly to manipulate their anxious parents. Such children accept suffering (for example rejecting food), aware that their parents will suffer even more than they will. Parents should allow their children to experience the consequences of their adverse behaviors. If this approach remains ineffective, professionals may be consulted.

(3) Some instincts are formed at birth and therefore cannot be changed, modified, or redirected. Only control and censorship of them through the self, the superego-type conscience, and later the Christian conscience, are achievable. These learned control functions are like clay shaped by parents' love, which in time becomes written in stone. The greater the invested love that difficult children receive, the greater the return in their attachment. They first appear to be high-maintenance children, but later they often become high achievers in love and loyalty to their parents and other family members.

(4) Pastoral help is aimed at establishing and supporting a metaphorical symbiotic relationship between high-maintenance children and their parents. Parents receive help from their difficult children by becoming Christlike themselves. Their role of parenting gives their lives a strong

meaning that permeates deep into their hearts, minds, and souls. In turn, they express parental love, which is experientially the kind of human love that comes closest to God's love and shapes the foundation of their children's relationship with Jesus.

(5) Being a difficult child is not a disorder. Therefore, besides giving an extra dose of empathy, love, and support, no other specific intervention is usually needed. If, on the contrary, symptoms of stubbornness, anger, communication problems, stuttering, or enuresis, formerly called childhood neuroses, occur that do not fit the difficult child's profile, early professional interventions may be needed.

25.4 Moral, Religious, and Spiritual Development in Children

Lawrence Kohlberg describes moral development in three levels.

(1) *The Preconventional Level* is common in children younger than nine. It includes stage one, moral behavior driven by obedience and fear of punishment, and stage two, moral behavior driven by self-interest. For people of preconventional moral maturity, lying and stealing, for example, are perceived as morally wrong if there is a likelihood of being caught and punished, or if such behaviors are not profitable.

(2) *The Conventional Level*, common to adolescents, includes stage three, moral behavior driven by social expectations, and stage four, moral behavior directed by obedience to the law and social standards. For people of conventional moral maturity, violence is wrong because collective, legislative regulations disapprove of such behaviors.

(3) *The Postconventional Level* is common to abstract thinking in late adolescents and adults. It includes stage five, morality directed by a social contract, and stage six, morality directed by universal ethical standards. A person of postconventional moral maturity would refrain from cheating because it contradicts one's commitment to honesty and justice and also opposes God's love.[6]

Influenced by Kohlberg's model, and after interweaving 359 individuals, James Fowler published his faith development theory, distinguishing seven levels of faith.

(1) *Primal Faith* occurs during infancy and consists of trust and attachment bonds.

(2) *Intuitive-Projective Faith* occurs in prelogically reasoning children ages three to seven as a projection of their relationships with their parents.

(3) *Mythic-Literal Faith* occurs between ages eight and twelve and is marked by the ability to think logically and distinguish fantasy from reality. God is perceived as being anthropomorphic, punishing evil and rewarding goodness.

(4) *Synthetic-Conventional Faith* appears until the end of adolescence and is characterized by abstractions of universal values (for example, the need to respect authorities) and a need for a close personal relationship with God.

(5) *Individuative-Reflective Faith* emerges in young adults and is connected to the critical evaluation of myths and rituals and demythologizing them, taking a critical attitude toward religion but deepening personal faith.

(6) *Conjunctive Faith* appears in midlife and beyond, but only one in every six adults achieves this stage. God is imagined as dialectical, as personal and abstract, close and distant.

(7) *Universalizing Faith* appears in mature people and is limited to a few people per thousand who strive for universal values and live as if complete love, peace, justice, and the kingdom of God are already a reality.[7]

How applicable are Kohlberg's and Fowler's models in a pastoral setting?

In the development of his model, Kohlberg devised a test of "short stories known as moral dilemmas"—stories that depicted a hypothetical character facing a particular moral choice—for which people of various ages were asked to decide the right course of action. The test, however, was standardized for young male subjects living in the Chicago area. Consequently, "the reasoning Kohlberg describes is more characteristic of men than women."[8] In the case of Fowler's model, it is questionable whether the samples used represent all Christian denominations.

Also neglected by both models is the observable truth that moral reasoning and faith choices are not a static but a dynamic quality. Even mature Christians occasionally regress to lower levels of moral functioning (as in "road rage"). Children especially, though, can progress to higher levels of faith maturity than is age-appropriate according to the models of Kohlberg and Fowler or occasionally regress to lower levels.

As is widely known, when Jacinta Marto, one of the children who saw the Virgin Mary at Fatima, heard about Jesus' crucifixion at age five, she bitterly cried and resolved "not to make our Lord suffer any more." Such highly empathetic moral reasoning definitely supersedes Jacinta's age-appropriate preconventional level of morality in Kohlberg's model. Thus, union with God is clearly achievable in children despite their immature mentality. For example, when the Virgin Mary appeared to Jacinta Marto in 1917, Jacinta, seven years old at the time, reacted in an intellectually age-appropriate and childlike way, offering the Virgin Mary cheese and bread. But at the same time she understood the context and ultimately the holy, uplifting meaning of the situation, proving that Jacinta had a very different conscience than would be appropriate in Kohlberg's concept. Her conscience in that particular moment superseded the functioning of many adults (like the Bishop of Antigonish, whom we will observe in our next case study).

While even the highest ethical standards in Kohlberg's model are socially learned, Christian conscience, known as "synderesis" in scholastic terminology, is written on human hearts (Rom. 2:14–15). Faith written by the conscience, even in children's hearts, may be more discerning than in Kohlberg's six-stage morality or Fowler's universalizing faith. Even early experiences of God's grace may surpass all socially learned universal ethical standards. Faith is God's gift, given according to his judgment and not always according to human standards.

On the other hand, the moral and faith qualities of a person are like a mosaic, composed of morally good and false motives filtered by their discretional and appreciative judgment. Just as toddlers can surprise with very high ethical standards in one situation and very childlike behaviors in another, so can adults generally adhere to universal standards of morality and faith or surprise with extremely sick and sinful behavioral patterns. In other words, sickness and sin in one area of functioning may spoil the otherwise perfect functioning in other areas.

The Bishop of Antigonish, Nova Scotia, Canada, was respected as an exemplary successor of the apostles, being especially skilled in resolving delicate moral matters. However, in 2009 he was apprehended by police because of his involvement in paedophilia. In some situations he must have seemed exceptionally moral, but in this and perhaps others, he was clearly exceptionally immoral.[9] A similar case occurred in Cardinal Theodore McCarrick's case in June, 2018.

For these reasons, an objective and scientific assessment of one's morality and faith is hardly possible. From a pastoral perspective, it seems that a broader and less categorical approach is one like that of Benedict J. Groeschel, who distinguishes religious development from faith development. Religious dynamics are in children (and some adults) mostly focused on a desire to control God's behaviors by good works, prayer, and formal adherence to expectations of their confessional belonging, maintaining a kind of giving-receiving relationship with God. The "entire external fabric of religion is founded upon this impulse; it reaches from St. Peters' Basilica to the Taj Mahal, from Boys' Town to Care passages."[10] In adolescents capable of abstract thinking, God may be conceptualized in spiritual terms (being everywhere and nowhere), while dialectical thinking usually opens the Pandora's Box of theological speculation. During the whole of adolescence, religiosity is intellectualized with speculations and hypotheses; biblical texts are explained or supplemented with often naive, personal, and invented explanations that reflect the adolescent's experiences of life, family, community, and church. Also, crises, scepticism, and doubts occur during this period, offering a chance for further maturing in both religious views and in faith. Mature faith is characterized by accepting one's own powerlessness and need for Christ's grace and being awakened to the need to grow in holiness, humility, and a combination of "holy fear" and ultimate trust that surpasses all human understanding and logic.

Notes

[1] DSM 5. *Diagnostic and Statistical Manual of the American Psychiatric Association* (2013), 355–75.

[2] Benjamin James Sadock and Virginia Alcott Sadock, *Kaplan and Sadock's Synopsis of Psychiatry: Behavioral Sciences/Clinical Psychiatry*, 10th ed. (Philadelphia, PA: Wolters Kluwer, 2007), 23–4.

3 Ibid., 27.

4 Ibid., 30.

5 Ibid., 29.

6 Harold W. Faw, *Psychology in a Christian Perspective, an Analysis of Key Issues* (Grand Rapids, MI: Baker Books, 1995), 117.

7 Marsha Wiggins Frame, *Integrating Religion and Spirituality in Counseling: A Comprehensive Approach* (Pacific Grove, CA: Thomson/Brooks/Cole, 2003), 39.

8 Faw, *Psychology in a Christian Perspective*, 117.

9 Paul Ungar, *Flawed Institution—Flawless Church: A Response to Pope John Paul's Appeal for a Critical Self-Evaluation of the Church* (Newcastle Upon Tyne: Cambridge Scholars Publishing, 2013), 99.

10 Benedict J. Groeschel, *For Those Who Seek Spiritual Passages: The Psychology of Spiritual Development* (New York: Crossroad Publishing Company, 1996), 67–88.

CHAPTER TWENTY-SIX

THE CHALLENGE OF ADOLESCENCE

P arents often feel as though their sweet, caring, and kind children become different people in adolescence. Adolescents lose their previous loyalty to their families and even their attachment to God. Before discussing how parents and pastoral healers may help in this turbulent period, let us consider the behavioral changes in adolescents.

Following Kaplan and Sadock's textbook, we can divide this period into four stages:

(1) *Preadolescence* (ten to twelve years of age) is characterized by a distancing from the family and a growing interest in actors, athletes, politicians, or other celebrities. The new interests and sympathy with a new, overly free-thinking subculture are marked by a slavery to fashion, modernity, freedom, swear words, and toilet humour, demonstrating power, courage, and rebellion against conventional standards.

(2) Early adolescence (twelve to fourteen years of age) is characterized by intense growth, forming primary and secondary sexual characteristics, an increased need for competence and power, and impulsiveness. A new awareness of the opposite gender emerges, with idealized or vulgar sexualized fantasies. A challenging of the parents often occurs, and if childhood attachment was insufficient, then a definite turning away from them occurs.

(3) Middle adolescence (between fourteen and sixteen years of age) is characterized by increased sexual interests, oscillations in self-esteem, striving for independence and self-affirmation expressed in risk-taking behaviors, a desire to belong to avant-garde groups, experimenting with new lifestyles, and sharp opposition to outdated social idols. Religious adolescents establishing themselves as different from their families join church groups.

(4) Late adolescence (between seventeen and nineteen years of age) is characterized by the exploration of academic, vocational, musical, artistic, or sporting pursuits and striving for ideals that speak to the challenges of mature life. Such consideration of mature life also applies to relational issues. Loveless sex, unavoidably ending in short-term and shallow relationships, evolves into seeking of mutual hopes, ideas, feelings, and fears, and practicing unselfishness and love.[1] This is the theory, but how does adolescence fulfil this purpose in practice?

If we compare statistical data of the tenth edition of Kaplan and Sadock's *Synopsis of Psychiatry*[2] with the eleventh edition,[3] we can discern some improvements in adolescents' psychological functioning. The eleventh edition reports that some 47 percent of ninth- to twelfth-grade students have had sexual intercourse, while the number was 53 percent in 1993, as the tenth edition of the same textbook reported. The median age of first engaging in sexual intercourse was, according the tenth edition, 16.9 years for boys and 17.4 years for girls, and these numbers have dropped slightly to sixteen and seventeen years of age respectively according to the latest edition. However, other reports estimate that "currently 98 percent of teenagers aged fifteen to nineteen are using at least one method of birth control," suggesting that the numbers are possibly higher. Unfortunately, an alarming 750,000–850,000 girls under the age of nineteen get pregnant every year, 418,000 of whom choose to receive abortions (a 19 percent increase since 1991). This number amounts to 3 percent of all girls in the Unites States aborting a pregnancy at some point in their adolescence, while this rate is 6.8 percent in Germany, 6.3 percent in Italy, and 4.5 percent in Spain. One of the lowest teenage pregnancy rates in the world is found in Holland, "where contraceptives are freely available in schools." When young couples do have children together, they seldom marry; "the fathers, usually teenagers, cannot care for themselves, much less the mothers of their children." If they marry, they often divorce later and end up on welfare.

Adolescents exhibit more risk-taking behaviors than any other age group. In one study, nearly 30 percent of twelfth graders reported having had five or more drinks in a row, and this within a two-week period. The statistics on drug use, although slowly declining, are likewise staggering. An estimated 9.7 million teenagers use marijuana, with 5.6 percent of twelfth graders reporting daily use (compared to 6 percent in 1999). As Kaplan and Sadock's textbook notes, "Once teenagers are dependent on marijuana, they often tumble into truancy, crime, and depression." Cocaine use is seen in around 13.1 percent of twelfth graders, which is a slight drop from 14 percent in 2003's figure, but is still significantly higher than the national average of 3.6 percent. Some 2 percent of twelfth graders admit to the use of heroin, and almost 0.7 percent admit to the use of phencyclidine (PCP). The exception to the downward trend of drug use is prescription pain relievers, the use of which for nonmedical reasons has increased to around 15 percent. Violence has also increased so that homicide is the second leading cause of death among people ages fifteen to twenty-five. Kaplan and Sadock's textbook reports that every day nearly ten American children are killed in "handgun suicides, homicides, and accidents."[4]

Pastoral Considerations

(1) Working with youngsters is like building a three-legged stool, for which the legs are adolescents' cognitive, sexual, and spiritual development.

Let us illustrate adolescents' challenges in discerning and fulfilling their vocational, occupational, and professional goals and the importance of a Christian parental approach to them with an example.

In a company team-building meeting, a well-respected member complained about an untenable situation in his family. His daughter wanted to major in astronomy, his wife preferred she pursue the arts, and he insisted she choose to become a lawyer like him. After furious fights, his daughter took off for Papua New Guinea, allegedly to rescue sea turtles. She stopped communicating with her parents, and even the local police were unable to locate her address. Like a spreading bushfire, all participants in the meeting then started to recount similar fiery discussions and conflicts in their families. Finally, they turned to a mother of four young daughters and said, "Do you see what is awaiting you?" She responded, "Oh, this is no real problem at all. It is not what professions my daughters choose that matters most but that they be humble and modest in their demands, disciplined in their studies, and conscientious and diligent in their work. The rest will follow."

The second metaphorical leg is Christian restraint, caution, and behavioral prudence, without which sexuality, as the next example illustrates, is a double-edged sword.

At the very beginning of my medical career, I worked as an emergency physician. One evening we got an emergency call about a boy threatening to commit suicide, but our ambulance arrived too late. The seventeen-year-old had hanged himself on the doorknob in his room. His body was still warm while I read his suicide note describing his sentimental disappointment. In this moment I realized that sexuality can be an extremely dangerous drive. Indeed, helping adolescents progress toward a happy and blessed marriage is a titanic but most dignified parental and pastoral task.

The third leg is the most important: adolescents' relationship with God. A committed and genuine discipleship guarantees efficiency in assembling the other two legs. This can be done in the home by augmenting church attendance and formal religious education with model Christian behavior and discussion of Scriptures.

Before discussing how pastoral healers can help in the noted three areas, let us first summarize what *not* to do in dealing with adolescents.

(2) Adolescents are sensitive to criticism. They are overcritical and

easily disappointed with pastoral healers who attempt to play an authoritarian role. This happens especially if they feel closer to God than their pastors, families, or church communities. Thus, the biggest challenge for pastoral healers in working with adolescents is proving the authenticity of their own faith. The pastoral healer ought to be genuinely Christlike and loving.

One of the most influential television personalities of the twentieth century was Fred Rogers, host of *Mr. Rogers' Neighborhood*. In addition to hosting his show, he was also a minister. He was far from what young people might call "cool," but he was determined to be himself and let the authenticity of his personality, beliefs, and values shine through his presentations. He was a loving man who also told his young audience that he liked them "just the way they were." While he was dealing with preadolescents, his combination of honesty and acceptance worked wonders for two generations of viewers, thousands of whom thanked him when they were grown men and women with families. Professionals should not underestimate what a warm, friendly, accepting personality, one imbued with faith, can do for young people of all ages.

(3) What does love mean in practice with adolescents? Adolescents are "half strong"—they are "half child, half adult," emotionally exuberant but lacking skills and persistence in realizing their often overrated goals. They claim power, competence, and experience that they apparently lack. Therefore, the pastoral healer can show them love by appreciating them as if they have the qualities they believe they have. (This was exactly the approach taken by Fred Rogers.) Advancing confidence in them in turn motivates them to strive to be worthy of it. The most counterproductive approach is being overly directive. However, all counselling is learning, and all learning is hard, so pastoral healers must find a balance in the therapeutic alliance with adolescents.

(4) The method of choice in the counselling of adolescents is the Socratic dialogue, or asking questions requiring answers that help subjects recognize and resolve their problems. When unwilling adolescents realize the solution they are being directed toward, they often become resistant, argumentative, and emotional. To avoid such pitfalls, pastoral healers should keep the pace of communication slow, refrain from correcting the naive social, moral,

or theological concepts of adolescents, and take a few moments of silence before responding. The Socratic method allows adolescents (and many other patients mentioned in this book) to believe that they have discovered the answers themselves. This is the goal of many therapeutic approaches, if not most, but it is even more effective and applicable for teens who want the satisfaction of believing that they came up with the answers themselves.

(5) There are two extreme types of adolescents who are hard to work with: introverted and extroverted types. It is hard to work with mostly silent, seemingly indifferent adolescents who are masking their cries for help with apathy. They are overly self-reflective and self-critical, insecure and timid, and they overcompensate for their frustrations with enacted indolence and passivity. In other words, silence is their stock in trade as talking warmly and outwardly might violate the behavior expected of them by their counsellors. It is a posturing that makes both parents and pastoral healers want to pull their hair out. Beside extraordinary patience, the pastoral healer's tool in approaching such adolescents is giving them an opportunity to externalize their frustrations. An example would be to ask questions such as "If you were a parent, teacher, the Pope, or even if you would be Jesus, what would you do differently?"

Extroverted adolescents, on the other hand, are difficult to work with because they are more bold, intolerant, arrogant, and verbally aggressive. In short, teens in this category believe they know everything and monopolize the conversation with swagger, making it hard for others to get a word in edgewise. Despite their being generally unpleasant, though, they make it easier than do introverted types for the pastoral healer to identify their troubles, doubts, and anxieties. Calming fears, genuinely praising personal qualities, increasing self-esteem, and helping patients see themselves more from Jesus' perspective than the world's perspective are effective approaches for both behavioral extremes.

(6) Adolescents' often competitive attitude (their aiming to prove "I am greater") is not a narcissistic but defensive attitude that can often be turned around. An anecdotal story illustrates how the pastoral healer can best accomplish this.

The sun and the wind made a bet about who could take off the winter coat of a man who was walking on the road. The wind started blowing, attempting to take the coat from him, but the man wrapped it even more firmly around himself. Then the sun said, "Let me do the job" and started shining so that it became warmer. Finally, the man took off the coat and threw it angrily on the ground.

Being like the sun in this story (i.e., nonconfrontational, seeking compromise, or even allowing adolescents to win less important arguments) may make them receptive to more substantial truths. Such a giving and receiving attitude from the pastoral healer will decrease anxiety and increase young patients' willingness to cooperate. It is the nature of adolescents to run the other way or grow silent if they perceive they are being harshly confronted. Warming up to them is truly the best path to take when possible.

(7) As Sigmund Freud proclaimed, "Even the smallest thing is not so meaningless that it can be taken as if it never happened." Pastoral healers can achieve much more than they usually realize in contributing to adolescents' still-evolving discretional judgment (their rational distinguishing good from evil) and appreciative judgment (their ability to apply the standards of their conscience to their behaviors). Good examples are imprinted in adolescents' personalities so that they might never be erased. Even short, seemingly superficial relationships with people of God—exemplary Christians, priests, ministers, pastoral healers, and all people of goodwill— have an anonymous but lasting effect in adolescents' hearts and minds.

In Luke 24:1–4, Jesus observed a widow putting two pennies into the Temple treasury while wealthier people put in much larger sums. Jesus commented that the widow had put in far more since she had little to give in the first place. Sometimes it's not the amount or quantity that counts, but rather the attempt itself or the small, seemingly insignificant gifts we can give others, even if it is a smile, a word of reassurance, of just taking the time to notice someone. Adolescents are shrewd, observant, and notice such attempts.

(8) Adolescents' behaviors may be hypocritical, but hypocrisy is an attitude that is diametrically opposite to adolescents' ideals. They are extremely

sensitive to and deplore manipulation of any kind. The worst mistake a pastoral healer can make is twisting the truth (for example, in discussing the touchy topics of church history). On the contrary, a self-critical approach from the pastoral healer often evokes a similarly self-critical posture in adolescents. Pastoral healers should not try to score points or prove psychological theorems, but focus on effecting the desired behavioral outcomes. The proof is in the pudding, not in how the pudding is made.

(9) Adolescents' early educational (and their later vocational and occupational) conflicts are only the tip of the iceberg. They are anxious because they are fighting opposing motives within themselves. The real struggle occurs between two options: being the master of conscience and servant of instinct, or being the master of instinct and servant of conscience. Choosing the second option facilitates a behavioral dichotomy of simplicity, modesty, and meekness paired with a biblically self-confident, trusting, and optimistic attitude, which is important for following Jesus. In his ministry, Jesus' ultimate humility, modesty, and meekness went hand-in-hand with his ultimate splendour, magnificence, and grandeur. Identifying with Jesus in humility is therefore a way of also participating in his glory. This dichotomy prepares young people to deal with greater challenges that culminate in middle and late adolescence. It facilitates the attitude of "being in the world but not of it" (John 17:11; 17:17), which is a precondition of psychological-spiritual resilience. Adolescents are inherently concerned because of their biology and peer pressure with being "in the world." When they become servants of conscience, they can more easily distance themselves from the illusory demands of the world that they falsely deem so essential to their growth.

(10) Pastoral interventions with adolescents frequently deal with sexual matters since an important purpose of adolescence is preparing for psychosexual maturity. Psychosexual maturity means a hierarchical integration of sexuality, erotic, and psychological attraction under a spiritual "supreme command." Setbacks in this process of maturation often cause the loss of ideals and the regression to more immature ways of relating to the opposite sex.

Frankl describes a neglected and sexually abused youngster falling in love with a psychosexually mature girl. After a fight with her, the boy "plunged back into his former life of crude pleasure-seeking, sexual behavior. His social and sexual behavior retrogressed." He wrote to the girl, "Do you want me to be again what I once was, to go back to my former life, sitting around in dives, drinking and whoring?"[5]

Every disappointing experience relating to the opposite sex increases the risk of a return to more instinct-regulated forms of sexual behavior. But how can disappointments, which necessarily occur in adolescents who are too immature to deal with complicated relational issues, be prevented? Put another way, how can they find maturity when immaturity, hardwired into their current stage of development, is holding them back?

(11) In our culture, there is a discrepancy between reaching sexual maturity (the ability to have sex) and social maturity (the ability to establish a family). The frustration caused by this maturation gap allegedly forces adolescents into having sex before being mature enough for a genuine marital relationship and all the richness and depth that accompanies it. In this context, pastoral healers may focus on coaching adolescents in dating. The purpose of such coaching is to help young patients to understand that dating is not an introduction to sex but rather an exercise in communication— mutually revealing hopes, concerns, and fears while discerning common goals, ideals, purposes, and values—with the other sex. In other words, the purpose of dating is learning to establish a psychological and spiritual connection. Initially in this kind of biblically-oriented dating relationship, there occurs a shift of attention from sexual unity to personal and spiritual unity, called by Frankl "accent displacement." This shift enables abstinence until the conditions for genuine love and marriage are met. When these are achieved, an "accent reversion" occurs and interests switch back to eroticism and sex, which are at that time integrated with the spiritual and psychological components of love.[6]

(12) Religious adolescents are under pressure from modern sexual propaganda, which is more widespread than ever before because of the Internet and social media. They need encouragement to trust their own worldviews, reality judgments, and consciences. Gaining security in their biblical lifestyle helps them bear good fruit, as Matthew 7:20 describes, and by doing

so, they recognize that they are growing into a "good tree." In practice, this means getting confirmation that their behaviors are good by experiencing the biblical peace, courage, optimism, trust, joy, and purpose they receive from such behaviors and sharing these Godly gifts with neighbours. These help adolescent know that Christian ideals are a reality; only faith gives a purpose and power stronger than the world that so relentlessly tries to claim their attention and their souls.

(13) As the saying goes, "Everyone is as strong as their ideals." Adolescence is a period for finding one's own ideals. If Christian ideals are not discerned during adolescence, they may never be found in later life. Teenagers frequently rebel against what they regard as outdated morality, distance themselves from their parents and society, and criticize the Church and orthodoxy. These are, in fact, all attempts to discern an ultimate purpose that will provide them with the strength and courage to live the Christian ethic throughout their entire lifetimes. Pastoral healers may use some of the same principles of evangelizing adults (discussed in the fifth part of this book) when approaching adolescents.

(14) As noted, adolescents are "half child, half adult." As "half child" they are docile inquirers who may at first be attracted to the body of Christ through personal examples. Next, emotional evangelization may follow (evoking reasons of the heart such as hope, optimism, courage, desire, and passion for personal salvation). Finally comes rational evangelization (giving adolescents realistic, logical support for their decision to believe in the faith). The essence of their evangelization nevertheless occurs in their taking a new stand in resisting sin. In the context of pastoral healing, treatment of adolescents' psychological problems (inferiority, rational and irrational self-accusation, low self-esteem, the feeling of being unloved and unlovable, frustration, angst, anxiety, and fear) can be a motor that drives the search for the almighty, eternal, and ultimate love of God. Resolving challenges gives patients a boost in ascending the progressive spiral leading to the ultimate truth of Jesus Christ. The victory that adolescents can experience at this time is not a victory of the world, but a triumph of seeing through its illusions to genuine maturity, love, and commitment to a Christian lifestyle. As already noted, however, if this process is not started early enough,

adolescents are likely to rebel against any kind of ascension to the holy life at all.

(15) Maturing in faith comes with ups and downs. This is illustrated in the life of St. Augustine.

In the fourth book of *Confessions*, the teenaged Augustine "almost deprived a dying friend of the grace of baptism and salvation." For the remainder of his life, the man who later became the Doctor of Grace frequently pondered this incident from his adolescence and drew from it further repentance and gratitude to God.[7] Indeed, crises and setbacks often produce later success in finding a strong purpose to live for. Indeed, Augustine lived a fairly dissolute life in general until he converted to Christianity at age thirty-one, but he is now considered to be one of the most brilliant doctors of the Catholic faith. His initial setbacks produced grace for himself as well as countless generations that have followed.

(16) Adolescents seek the "guidelines and values that they appropriate for the newly discovered facets of themselves, and yet for a time they are without them."[8] They often feel inferior, frustrated, unworthy, or challenged in interactions with others. That personal insecurity is, however, often productive if it is countered by their establishing a strong alliance with Jesus, who is able to convince adolescents that "disgrace for the sake of Christ [is] of greater value than the treasures of Egypt" (Heb. 11:26). Once deeply ingrained, this pattern protects disciples all their lives from the Luciferian challenges they have to face.

Notes

[1] Benjamin James Sadock and Virginia Alcott Sadock, *Kaplan and Sadock's Synopsis of Psychiatry: Behavioral Sciences/Clinical Psychiatry*, 10th ed. (Philadelphia, PA: Wolters Kluwer, 2007), 40–4.

[2] Ibid., 45–7.

[3] Benjamin James Sadock, Virginia Alcott Sadock, and Pedro Ruiz, *Kaplan and Sadock's Synopsis of Psychiatry: Behavioral Sciences/ Clinical Psychiatry*, 11th ed. (Philadelphia, PA: Wolters Kluwer, 2015), 1099–1107.

[4] Sadock and Sadock, *Kaplan and Sadock's Synopsis of Psychiatry*, 10th ed. 40–4; Sadock, Sadock, and Ruiz, *Kaplan and Sadock's Synopsis of Psychiatry*, 11th ed. 1099–1107.

[5] Viktor E. Frankl, *The Doctor and the Soul, From Psychotherapy to Logotherapy* (New York: Vintage, 1973), 169–71.

[6] Ibid., 160–4.

[7] Benedict J. Groeschel, *For Those Who Seek Spiritual Passages: The Psychology of Spiritual Development* (New York: Crossroad Publishing Company, 1996), 68.

[8] Gerald Corey, *Theory and Practice of Counseling and Psychotherapy* (Thomson Brooks/Cole. Thomson Learning Academic Resource Center, 2005), 117.

CHAPTER TWENTY-SEVEN

END OF LIFE DILEMMAS IN
THE MEDICAL AND PASTORAL
PERSPECTIVES

Instead of aging and dying with dignity among caring family members, the contemporary mental climate appreciates models of successful aging in luxurious nursing homes and imagining passing away as an almost Elysium-like pleasant exit from life by choosing physician-assisted suicide. However, are the psychological-spiritual challenges concerning aging, dying, and death really that trivial, or are they far more complex and worthy of pastoral and professional consideration? If our journey as Christians is toward the kingdom of God, then how we age and die is as important as how we live, for aging and death represent leaving behind our temporary clothes in order to put on those which are eternal and incorruptible (1 Corinthians 15:53).

27.1 Empirical Facts

According to Kaplan and Sadock's textbook, the average life expectancy in the United States increased from around 48 years in 1904 to 73.5 years for men and 80.4 years for women by the end of the twentieth century. While 4 percent of the population was older than 65 in 1904, by 2003 it was 12.4 percent, and that number is expected to be 20 percent by 2030. The segment of those older than 85 is increasing most rapidly. Accordingly, care for elderly people will be an ever-increasing challenge for pastoral healers in the years to come.

27.2 Aging: Its Healthy and Sick Aspects

Aging is invariably characterized by a decrease of interest in challenges and new information, a decline in the body's performance, and a decrease of sexual interest. People in high positions, realizing they cannot progress any further in their careers, become introverted and focus more on maintaining what they have already achieved. Some people demonstrate superiority to younger people, while others boast of their sporting abilities (skydiving, running a half-marathon, or mountaineering) and of enjoying life to the fullest, undertaking unexpected travels, risky adventures, or dating younger people. Retirement gives a new boost to self-examination. Instead of a period of relaxed, leisurely enjoyment, some experience retirement as a time of losing all competence, power, financial well-being, and competitive edge, on which self-esteem is often based. When spouses, friends, and former coworkers die, it causes social isolation and loneliness.

Personal health becomes a primary concern in later life. Many problems occur, both small and large. They are often easily manageable but herald concerns for the future.[2] Selfishness, worrying about fulfilling needs, hoarding food and meaningless things, trouble memorizing new information, thinking more slowly, difficulties in focusing on and understanding current happenings, the inability to find solutions to unexpected challenges, walking with small steps, the onset of tremors, and decreased strength are often precursors of senile dementia. People suffering from dementia sometimes regress to childish levels of functioning (believing their parents to still be alive), are unable to care for themselves, neglect their image, do not care about feeding and grooming themselves, and live in disarray. Nevertheless, they reject any support, care, or supervision, maintaining the semblance of self-sufficiency. They sometimes behave oversubmissively (like a child with a parent) or relate with physicians, priests, or caregivers like they do with their children. According to Kaplan and Sadock's textbook, "Although only 5 percent are institutionalized in nursing homes at any time, about 35 percent of older people require care in a long-term facility at some time during their lives. Older nursing home residents are mainly widowed women, and about 85 percent are over age 85."[3]

Even for very active elderly people, aging is a time when they consciously or unconsciously confront the reality of death and dying. Elisabeth Kűbler-Ross describes five stages in reacting to impending death: (1) Shock and denial, characterized by refusing to acknowledge the unfavourable outcome; (2) Anger, often directed toward others (such as family members, caregivers, physicians, or even God); (3) Bargaining with physicians or God for a miraculous healing in exchange for things like large donations or fundamental life changes; (4) Depression, which may be caused by the reality of death or worrying about loved ones' destinies; and (5) Acceptance of imminent death, which may bring relief or even euphoria. "Under ideal circumstances," Kűbler-Ross says, "patients resolve their feelings about the inevitability of death and can talk about facing the unknown."[4] This ideal circumstance can be only faith!

27.3 The Death of Loved Ones: Grief and Mourning

Grief is the internal experience caused by the death of a beloved person. An individual's first response in grief, summarizing Sadock, Sadock, and Ruiz's description, is a protest—a painful "Why?" This is followed by a longer period of searching and asking, "What did I do wrong?" Both reactions are conditioned by a need to reestablish the relationship with the deceased person. The greater the attachment, the more painful the grief. Psychologically, grief helps survivors to place their relationship with the deceased person in a new and meaningful context by forming enduring ties able to resolve or mitigate even the worst long-lasting consequence of the death of a loved one, which is loneliness. Other effects of grief are more short-term and may reoccur (for example, when handling items that belonged to the deceased person), but these experiences have a tendency to become less frequent with the passage of time. The so-called anticipatory grief that sometimes precedes the death of a loved one may have an adverse role. It may decrease the pain immediately following the death, but not later grief. Reactions on anniversaries may also have a counterproductive effect if they precipitate an intensive reliving of the separation. The term "mourning" encompasses the processes, customs, and rituals used in resolving grief. Mourning enables people in grief to return to normal life in a few weeks or months. Burials, for example, have a healing purpose. They help mourners to "acknowledge the real and final nature of death, countering denial; they also garner support for the bereaved, encouraging tributes to the dead, uniting families and facilitating community expressions of sorrow."[5] Visits to the gravesite, family gatherings, anniversaries, prayers, and other ceremonies ensure continuing support to mourners and help them accept the reality of losing their connection with the deceased. Certain cultural and religious rituals also serve the purpose of protecting the mourners from isolation and vulnerability and setting reasonable limits on grieving.[6]

If grieving does not fulfil its purpose, complications can occur, such as the following. *Chronic grief* occurs after the death of a very close, irreplaceable, and important person or, conversely, of a hated person or a person whose death evokes feelings of guilt in one who lives on. *Hypertrophic grief* occurs after the sudden death of loved one when the survivor's coping strategies are insufficient for absorbing grief. *Delayed grief* is the consequence of a long-lasting denial, not enabling the acknowledgment of the loss of the deceased person, for which significant signs of grieving emerge long after acute grief ought to have been resolved. *Traumatic bereavement* signifies grief that is chronic and hypertrophic. It is "characterized by recurrent, intense pangs of grief with persistent yearning, pining and longing for the deceased" as well as intrusive memories and recollections that disrupt everyday functioning.[7]

Pastoral Considerations

(1) There is a Latin saying, "Seniors cannot do what they could do but can do what they could not do." They are unable to study, work, and excel as before, but they may have patience, experience, and wisdom like never before. Whether this saying will actually be realized in one's life depends on accepting aging optimistically, with hope and trust in Jesus.

(2) Chronological age does not correlate with psychophysical age. Even very old people are able to maintain their social and emotional contacts and stay physically, intellectually, and sometimes even professionally active. Even the popular notion that the elderly are essentially asexual is often a self-fulfilling prophecy rather than a reality. Accordingly, even older people of faith ought to be vigorously active in spreading God's kingdom according to their ambitions and abilities. It is not uncommon for older segments of the population (even some who are widowed) to start new careers or families or join different faith communities. Many give their time to charity and volunteer work and devote more time to prayer and attending liturgy and receiving the sacraments.

(3) A much greater puzzle is how to help people unprepared for the challenges of their old age. Aging is invariably connected to an increased awareness of the transitory nature of life, provoking in nonbelievers a sense of frustration, meaninglessness, and hopelessness. All people, but especially the elderly, are caught in a paradox between the instinctual drive to protect life and the awareness of unavoidable death. This paradox causes angst, which is manageable during the adolescent, generative, and productive years, but which often becomes harder in the later years of life.

Viktor Frankl compares the nonbeliever to a person standing in front of his calendar, every day tearing one page from it and throwing it away, one after the other, realizing how the future is becoming thinner and thinner. The person of faith, however, is like someone who stands in front of the same calendar but saves the torn-out pages, saying, "I completed this and that purpose in my life, what I achieved is fortunately growing, and what I still have to accomplish is fortunately declining."[8]

While people of faith wait for the greatest adventure in their lives—meeting Jesus—with hope, trust, and even impatient joy, atheists react with growing fear of approaching the end. Old age is the last moment when, for atheists, a turnaround is still possible. Pastoral healers ought not confront atheists with their hopeless situation since they are most often aware of it. It is, self-evidently, more productive to demonstrate the solution: turning to the merciful and all-forgiving Jesus.

(4) The hardest task for a pastoral healer is helping a dying person find hope. We may illustrate a possible solution to this difficulty with the following paraphrased exchange between Frankl and a depressed woman, which took place in front of an auditorium of students attending his presentation.

> Ms. Linek is an eighty-year-year-old impoverished single lady who worked all her life as a servant and is now suffering from inoperable cancer and depressed because she is aware that her death is close.

> Frankl: Ms. Linek, how do you perceive your life? Was it a happy life?

> Ms. Linek: Ah, I must acknowledge my past life was good. I must be satisfied with it….

> Frankl (thinking): *Yes, that's good. But I have to bring her current suppressed desperation concerning the unstoppable approaching of her death into her conscious mind.*

> Frank: Your past life was good, but will all this come to an end soon?

> Ms. Linek: Yes, sadly this will all end soon.

> Frankl: But do you think that all the good things you experienced will somehow be erased from history?

> Ms. Linek (talking to herself): Ah, my nice experiences…. They are all gone now….

Frankl: But tell me, Ms. Linek, is anyone able to simply blot out all these nice things you experienced?

Ms. Linek: You are right; nobody can make them not have happened.

Frankl: Is anyone able to make the things you did during your long life invalid?

Ms. Linek: You are right; nobody can erase them from history.

Frankl: Is someone able to change the history that you vigorously and courageously endured? Is someone able to erase from reality everything you did and heroically suffered?

Ms. Linek (moved to tears): Nobody can do this! Nobody.... Yes, I had to suffer a lot—all my life was suffering—but I stood my ground with God's help.

Frankl: But tell me, Ms. Linek, isn't it possible that life is like an exam? Isn't it possible that God wanted to see how you would bear suffering? And must even God at the end not acknowledge that, yes, Ms. Linek fought the good fight and fought it hard? Can anyone or anything erase such performances?

Ms. Linek: No, nobody and nothing can erase this!

Frankl: This remains forever, doesn't it?

Ms. Linek: Yes, this remains for sure!

Frankl: You know, Ms. Linek, you not only performed through your life, but you did your best despite your suffering. And you are an example to our patients. I congratulate you in the name of your fellow patients that they may take you as an example.

(In this moment, something happened that nobody could have predicted. The students listening to this presentation broke into spontaneous standing applause.)

Frankl: Do you see, Ms. Linek? This applause is directed at you and your whole life. How few people can be proud of their lives at the end! Your life is like a monument that no man and no sickness can delete from the world!

Slowly, the old lady left the auditorium. A week later she died, but during the last week of her life she was not depressed. On the contrary, she was proud and faithful, trusting in God's appreciation of her life.[9]

This case study is not the only possible approach to depression in elderly people. It may, though, serve as a pattern for how to resolve similar pastoral situations and be adapted to the pastoral healer's taste, skills, and preferences.

(5) Aging is, for Christians, a period in which the importance of worldly tasks decreases and spiritual freedom increases; it is "the moment of total freedom, and total responsibility."[10] Death in the pastoral understanding has a privileged and central position in human life. It is a unique opportunity to be totally free of all worldly influences, duties, and tasks and, in such total freedom, definitively choose between God and the devil, heaven and hell, biblical life and death.

(6) St. Paul summarizes the committed Christian's attitude to death in Philippians 1:21 and 1:23: "For me to live is Christ, and to die is gain ... I am torn between the two: I desire to depart and be with Christ which is better by far." We may be perplexed and ask what gave St. Paul such courage in dealing with the challenge that very few are able to deal with. Apparently he perceived the mystery of death very differently from turning into nothingness. We are prone to perceiving our existence in terms of our relationships to different things and people, distinguishable by their particular kinds of physical characteristics (size, weight, appearance, texture), psychological traits (likable or dislikeable), and forms of being. Death opens the door to

a different form of existence, not as a particular kind of being but as a pure, abstract, genuine being—sheer existence—a pure "is" unrelated to any sensorial quality but related to the absolute "Is"—God. Let me clarify this with Pojman's thought experiment.

If we take a person and subtract all of his natural physicality (height, weight, colour, smell, and all other sensorial properties), then what is left of that person is bare existence—that the person "is," that he exists. Such a pure being is, however, a pure sensorial nothingness and a pure spiritual form of being, relating to a quite different reality than that of the world, one whom Christians call God. It is for human beings, trapped or absorbed in the material and sensorial form of existence, an escape. Death is a passing from existence into transcendence.[11]

Faith like that of St. Paul is a mystical experience, a gift from God. A believer like St. Paul is able, through faith, to appreciate biblical revelation, trust Jesus' message, and impatiently wait for the greatest and most attractive adventure in every believer's life: the moment of transition from existence to transcendence.

In meditating about human life and death, believers are comparable to astronomers considering the universe. Astronomers know that the sensorial universe (representing humans' sensorial existence for our purposes) is only 5 percent of the whole universe, while 95 percent of it (representing humans' nonsensorial being after death) is antimatter, dark energy, and other nonsensorial, mathematical, transcendental components. But while scientists do not know what to expect on the other side of the transcendence of the universe, people of faith know what is beyond death because Jesus revealed it: God's ultimate love!

(7) In my experience with people at the end of their lives, dying looks terrible for observers but not for the dying person. And in talking numerous times with people who have awakened from a coma (such as a deep diabetic coma) or even what we call clinical death, I have received the report, "I felt quite well until I was forcefully brought back to life." Returning to life, seeing lights and worried faces, hearing incomprehensible commands, and being unable to grasp happenings in a meaningful context were much more frightening to such patients than the experience of dying itself. Some even

described a wish to return to the peace and tranquillity of being disconnected from the world and resisted being brought back to life by refusing to come to their senses and open their eyes.

(8) As Kotesky notes, "Since Moody's (1976) popular book about the experiences of people who have been close to dying, many people have reported these near-death experiences....Are these visions? Are they hallucinations? Are they the actual way to heaven?"[12] What we know for sure is that there is no return from death. In other words, clinically dead people who were resuscitated were not dead but alive. From the medical perspective, there are possible signs of death (the cessation of breathing and a heartbeat), probable signs of death (complete coldness and rigor), and certain signs of death (intensive stench and the decomposition of the body). In clinical death, signs of death may be present but not probable, or certain signs of death are present, while in actual death all signs of mortification are evidently present. It is almost impossible to determine when the exact moment of death occurs (i.e., when the soul and spirit leave the body). The stopping of all electrical activity of the brain measured by an EEG is the most probable indicator of the exact moment of death.

(9) Grieving evolves through successive phases. Pastoral help depends on the personality of the grieving subject and the current period of grief. The pastoral healer should be aware that, as Faw describes, "almost everyone experiences shock" after receiving the sad news of the death of a loved one. "This involves a sense of unreality and a vague hope that one will awaken to find it was all a bad dream." Even committed Christians may feel some initial guilt "since none of us have done all we could for others" and the opportunity to do so has been lost forever. Usually, one of the first reactions is anger directed at oneself, people who treated the deceased person, relatives, or even God, who permitted the circumstances. As the grieving period progresses, feelings of loss, loneliness, isolation, sleeplessness, and fatigue follow, which end with processing the loss and gaining hope, optimism, and trust despite the pain that often remains forever. Faw gives the following advice that pastoral healers may consider.

(a) Not talking but sitting in silence, partaking in pain "says more than words."

(b) Don't imply "I know how you feel," but rather give an opportunity to the grieving person to talk about their pain.

(c) Call the deceased person by their name and mention what struck you about his life.

(d) Accept and encourage the expression of sadness in words, gestures, and crying.

(e) Do not hurry to terminate the grieving process by saying that they are "in a better place now."

(f) Physical assistance, like shopping for groceries, preparing meals, and maintaining the household is helpful in the early stages of grief.

(g) Contact the grieving person repeatedly as it helps him to feel protected and cared for.

(h) Visiting the grave, bringing flowers, or sharing memories helps the grieving person process his pain.

(i) General patience, compassion, and participation in the tasks of mourning may also help.

(j) Encourage professional help if the mourning process is stalled.

(k) Attend common prayers, liturgy, and other religious activities.

(l) The most powerful healing for many Christians is confession and holy communion.[13]

The pastoral healer's role gradually changes from being a passive listener to an ever more active partner in dialogue with the mourning person. Dialogue is aimed at fostering his activity in his church community, participation in building God's kingdom, and helping them find peace in his spiritual oneness with the deceased person in the body of Christ. An experience of spiritual unity with the deceased person, despite the temporary physical separation, is for Christians the most powerful tool for resolving suffering from grief. We will resume this topic in the fifth part of the book.

(10) Perhaps the worst form of suffering caused by old age is the lone-liness of the widowed person. For this situation, pastoral healers may apply the following paraphrased dialogue by Frankl.

> After a widower described his suffering and loneliness, Frankl asked him, "But what would have happened if you had died and your wife had sur-vived? Would your wife not have suffered just as you are suffering?" The depressed widower acknowledged, "Yes, she would indeed have, and she probably would have suffered even more than I do." Frankl then said, "So shouldn't you then be happy that you can in some way take away the suf-fering from your wife and suffer instead of her?"[14]

Such a perspective of vicarious suffering may help patients find a value in their pain. This is especially true in people of faith eagerly waiting to be united with their loved ones in a final commonality of the union with and in God.

(11) Must pastoral healers acknowledge that atheists automatically condemn themselves to exist without closeness to God after their death, or can they help survivors (spouses, children, and other family members) to place even nonbelieving relatives' deaths in a more hopeful context? As the great theologian Karl Rahner explains, "There is no such thing as being totally apart from grace. Grace is present even within nature itself. Man experiences grace as part of his own self." Every honest, loving, and unself-ish nonbeliever of goodwill can perhaps be an "anonymous Christian," not being entirely "apart from the grace of God" since "Christ died for them as well."[15] No human being is able to grasp the conditions, circumstances, perspectives, or sins of others, and no human is able to assess others' lives. Only God is competent in those things. Let us therefore hope that Rahner is right. In the words of a former theology professor of mine, as believers "we know that hell exists, but we may hope it is empty." Many theologians, and even popes, have postulated that God's love is so powerful and overwhelm-ing that at the moment of death, virtually all human beings surrender to his grace and unconditional love.

(12) I spent my residency training in psychiatry in an Eastern European communist country. A part of our education included a course offering a materialist understanding of religion. In one of the sessions, the question was raised of why, even after decades of fighting, does religion still flourish in atheist countries? Our otherwise very politically correct lecturer answered by saying, "As long as fear, suffering, and death exist, striving for God will exist." Truly, only trust in God is able to answer the challenge of fear, suffering, and death. Helping patients to experientially grasp this basic fact is the purpose of pastoral healing in the case of sick and dying elderly believers and nonbelievers.

(13) Despite their declining physical and psychological capacities, all elderly people have a unique task and purpose that they can fulfil. Most humans, even children and youngsters, are horrified by death. Therefore, when confronting the unavoidable end of life, elderly people have the opportunity to send a message of optimism, trust, and confidence sustained by counting on Jesus in this most solemn moment of their existence. This last message, which has a lasting impact, is perhaps the most important one they can convey to their loved ones.

Notes

[1] Benjamin James Sadock and Virginia Alcott Sadock, *Kaplan and Sadock's Synopsis of Psychiatry: Behavioral Sciences/Clinical Psychiatry*, 10th ed. (Philadelphia, PA: Wolters Kluwer, 2007), 53.

[2] Ibid., 59.

[3] Ibid., 61.

[4] Ibid., 60.

[5] Ibid., 64.

[6] Ibid., 66.

[7] Ibid., 66.

[8] Viktor E. Frankl, *Aerztliche Seelsorge* (Vienna: Franz Deuticke, 1965), 158.

[9] Ibid.

[10] Ferenc Szabo, *Ember es Vilaga* (Roma, 1988), 183–4.

[11] Adrian Tomer, Grafton T. Eliason, and Paul T. P. Wong (eds.), *Existential and Spiritual Issues in Death Attitudes* (New York: Lawrence Erlbaum Associates, 2008), 18.

[12] Ronald L. Koteesky, *Psychology from a Christian Perspective* Langham, ML: University Press of America, 1991), 40.

[13] Harold W. Faw, *Psychology in a Christian Perspective, an Analysis of Key Issues* (Grand Rapids, MI: Baker Books, 1995), 122.

[14] Viktor E. Frankl, *Aerztliche Seelsorge* (Vienna: Franz Deuticke, 1965), 158.

[15] Millard J. Erickson, *Christian Theology* (Grand Rapids, MI: Baker Book House, 1995), 315.

CHAPTER TWENTY-EIGHT

THE MEDICAL AND PASTORAL ASPECTS OF SEXUALITY

I t is not an overstatement to say that issues connected to the area we are going to discuss are present in the great majority of conditions pastoral healers treat. Sexuality is one of the motors in the human personality that significantly influences, consciously or unconsciously, all mental functions, even appreciative judgment and, through it, discretional judgment and behavior. The resolution of related issues requires extraordinary patience, information, experience, empathy, and courage. We will therefore discuss these topics with special attention.

28.1 Immature and Mature Sexuality

Sexual behaviors in children were more or less unknown before Freud's appearance. In his time, he was often accused of promoting a sexualized anthropology, as if human anatomy consisted of genitals and only a few other organs. However, this picture does not exactly reflect Freud's concepts. As in his *Three Essays on the Theory of Sexuality*, Freud stated that he understood sexuality as all dynamics (regardless of their being genital or not) keeping the balance between two opposing factors: excitation and relaxation. Any activity resolving or decreasing excitation is, in his understanding, sexual.1 Thus, any pleasurable activity decreasing tension or frustration and increasing its pleasurable resolution is, in Freud's wording, synonymous with a kind of a sexual pleasure. Neither the earliest sources of excitation nor the most efficient forms of relaxation are connected to the genital area. The infant's first experiences are excitation in the form of hunger and relaxation in the form of sucking milk, the pleasurable experience of which marks the so-called "oral stadium" in sexual development. Traces of that early oral sexual excitement, in Freud's view, never completely disappear but become surpassed or suppressed. In situations of stress, tension, or frustration, however, they may resurface or regress. Drinking, smoking, oral sex, or vampiric preoccupations are, in psychodynamic concepts, partially based on a regression to oral gratification entrenched in early childhood. Thumb-sucking in adults is a search for a pleasurable relaxation from any kind of excitation, tension, or frustration.

We discussed the second stage of sexual development, the "anal stadium," in Chapter Three. We noted that this period occurs in the second year of life, when potty training starts. This is an ambivalent period, a tug-of-war between compliance with the parents' requests for controlling elimination (promoted by the just-forming superego) and refusal to obey in controlling urination and defecation (promoted by instinct), making toddlers aware of their power to manipulate or even blackmail their parents. Regression to the anal level in mental functioning is connected to countless examples of, in Freudian terminology, neurotic problems.

The third stage of sexual development, the so-called "urethral stadium," occurs in the third year, when children are becoming aware of gender differences through different ways of urinating. Enuresis (bed-wetting) occurs as a regression in this period for one of two reasons: the child is giving in to a kind of pleasant instinct (i.e., uncontrolled urination), or the child is seeking the parents' attention by virtually becoming a baby again. The ureteral period is relatively short and is usually soon replaced by genital eroticism.

Genital eroticism occurs around the fifth or sixth year and is characterized by an ability to achieve relaxation from excitation generated in any part of the body or mind through genital stimulation and discharge. Genitals become the primary focus in discharging tension. They become a locus, able to resolve tensions caused by many kinds of excitements and frustrations.2

From this information, we can surmise that maturing from oral to genital sexuality is not an irreversible process. Freud compares maturation to the progression of an army into the enemy's territory. During the progression, the enemy may counter, in which case the army retreats to well-defendable positions. In the same way, in cases of frustration, trauma, or disappointment, maturation may regress, returning to previously well-entrenched behavior patterns. As noted, a genital dominance does not mean the complete disappearance of all previous elements of infantile sexuality, but rather a suppression. Instead of vanishing, the previous elements are, in a more or less latent form, integrated under genital supremacy. The latently present infantile, pregenital sexual contents shape the uniqueness of every person's sexual desires, fantasies, and behaviors.[3]

28.2 The Physiology of Sexual Functioning

Sexual behavior is a complex psycho-physiological process propelled by the sexual instinct and controlled first by the ego, then a superego-type conscience, and finally, the Christian conscience. Sexual instincts are biochemically mobilized; a structure in the brainstem, the diencephalon (a neurological-biochemical link), receives neurological stimulation from the cortex and produces TSH (testosterone-stimulating hormones) in males and ESH (estrogen-stimulating hormones) in females. The testes and ovaries react to these hormones by producing testosterone and estrogen, which are transferred through the blood in a feedback system to the diencephalon. The diencephalon neurologically stimulates the brain cortex, which subjects experience as sexual feelings, thoughts, fantasies, desires, excitement, and ever-growing tension that can be psychologically controlled but only completely resolved by genital sexual activity.

As well known, the first step in initiating sexual behaviors is arousal. Most males respond sexually to seeing nude or barely dressed females; women respond more often to romantic stories in which the passion of an idealized hero is motivated by a lifetime commitment to the heroine. Sexual arousal is triggered by both sensorial and psychological stimuli. The second step, the excitement phase, lasts for several minutes to several hours. Its peak level, preceding orgasm, lasts from 30 seconds to 3 minutes. The third phase, the orgasmic phase, lasts equally in males and females for between 15–33 seconds. The fourth phase, resolution, lasts for 10–15 minutes after reaching orgasm or 12–24 hours without reaching orgasm. However, "Sexuality and personality are so entwined that to speak about sexuality as a separate entity is virtually impossible."4 Therefore, the physiological aspects of sexuality discussed here need to be supplemented with the psychological and spiritual aspects of humanity and the previously discussed material, as well as the topic of relational issues among partners that will be introduced later.

Pastoral Considerations

(1) In some situations it is normal to be impotent or frigid. Having sex on first sight (such as what happens in some movies) with any partner and in any situation would mean a pathology rather than a high libidinous potential. It would mean a lack of normal inhibitions caused by disregarding the psychological and spiritual aspects of a person, reducing love to a mere satisfaction of instinct—reducing one of the most blissful human experiences to a subhuman, animal level. Sadly, this lack of inhibition is no longer seen just in the movies. Modern culture is frequently characterized as the age of the hookup (casual sex soon after meeting someone), and "friends with benefits" is a dynamic of many relationships.

(2) As Kaplan and Sadock's textbook notes, because of the cultural myths prevalent in our times, it is expected that a marriage be consummated at the first possible opportunity, even if inappropriate. Easy mastery of intercourse is also expected despite any lack of preparation or stimulation and the overwhelming nature of new experiences.[5] However, for a couple not to be excited would degrade their new bond and their marriage itself. It is quite normal to be pleasantly anxious and profound pleasure, happiness, and joy ought to be manifest in behavior, or else genuine love does not exist.

(3) Sexuality and having sexual intercourse need not be learned. Sexual

instincts are born at the end of puberty, as are sexual drives and behaviors. What needs to be learned is how to direct, control, and adapt sexual behaviors in line with biological, psychological, and spiritual reality.

(4) Being overly anxious about intercourse is counterproductive as well. Inappropriate and paralyzing performance anxiety is provoked by often asking, "Will I enjoy sex sufficiently?" or "Am I able to make my partner enjoy it sufficiently?" Because of such insecurities, allow us to ask, "What makes the psychological experience of sexual intercourse satisfactory?"

The self (the ego) is extremely important to every human being. It guarantees our ability to study, work, earn money, pay taxes, give and receive love—in one word, function. Conversely, to lose one's personality would jeopardize one's ability to exist. People suffering from schizophrenia, for example, feel they are losing their personalities and that fear is a forewarning of the annihilation of their existence as a human being. Therefore, humans defend their personalities vigorously in all situations, even more so than their bodies. As previously noted, there is only one situation in which giving up one's self is not frightening, and that is in sexual love. In this case, disabling all personal defences and giving one's self to the loving partner in absolute trust, confidence, and unselfishness is a most blissful experience. A desire for a deep, mutual commitment and love consisting of sexual, erotic, psychological, and spiritual unity (which provides security, trust, and confidence) enables freely and joyfully giving one's personality to a partner and receiving it again. This is enforced and enriched by the partner's love, courage, optimism, and appreciation. If such a sexual, erotic, psychological, and spiritual union in a relationship is missing, then desire will also be missing.

This explanation correlates to empirical evidence. As Barlow reports, "Low desire may be a primary problem or it may be secondary to another sexual dysfunction (e.g., a man may lose interest in sex because he is frustrated)."[6] Indeed, the same is true in females. In the Christian understanding, sexual intercourse is never the ultimate goal; it is a somatic expression of "I am, in body, mind, and soul, one with you." What makes sexual intercourse blissful is that it is a catalyst for and expression of the psychological and spiritual unity we call love. Without these components, it is only an impoverished experience of a physiological sexual discharge.

347

(5) Consequently, the focus of sexual intercourse in Christian couples is not only on sexual pleasure but on expressing commitment, love, and appreciation of a psychological and spiritual unity in body language. Asking questions like "Do I enjoy sex sufficiently?" or "Am I satisfying my partner sufficiently?" are counterproductive. In sexual intercourse, there is a trust expressed as "Independently of how I perform sexually, my partner fully loves me because we psychologically and spiritually fit together."

(6) We previously discussed how to behaviorally help couples suffering from sexual performance anxiety. Some Christian couples regularly say a short prayer after sexual intercourse. This demonstrates trust in the idea that, independently of the quality of sex, the couple's commitment, loyalty, and love is maximal—that their unity is guaranteed in God.

(7) As noted, sexual drives in a psychodynamic understanding are the "dark side of our personality, which do not know space, time, or reality, but have only one goal: to direct behavior."[7] What we call mature sexuality is integrating that dark side with the rest of the personality. The Christian conscience censors and supervises the selfish, hedonistic, immoral, or counterproductive instinctual demands seeking pure sexual gratification without achieving also a psychological-spiritual unity. Sexual maturity means an ability to release the sexual drive from restraint and control of the Christian conscience only if appropriate psychological-spiritual unity is present.

(8) As Barlow notes, "The messages and information that patients receive as children or adolescents may have a significant impact on their attitudes as adults."[8] We live in times of mass sexual propaganda, which was probably never as destructive in history as it is today. Therefore, sceptics may believe that Christian sexual morality is an illusion. It is the responsibility of Christians to visibly, tangibly, and measurably prove to the world that mutual attraction does not decrease with time, as is often believed, but that relationships are a lasting crescendo of love, peace, joy, purpose, and values—in sum, a foretaste of a heaven on earth. Living in a happy marriage is often a test of mutually belonging to Christ and the best defence of Christian sexual morality.

28.3 Masturbation and Pornography

According to Kaplan and Sadock's textbook, "No other form of sexual activity has been more frequently discussed, more roundly condemned, and more universally practiced than masturbation."[9] A similar ambiguity is also reported in the body of professional literature on pornography. For example, Kirsten Weir reports, "Various international studies have put porn consumption rates at 50 percent to 99 percent among men, and 30 percent to 86 percent among women,"[10] while Kaplan and Sadock's textbook reports, "Nearly all men and three fourths of all women masturbate sometime during their lives...[and] about 15 to 19 months of age, both sexes begin self-stimulation."[11] Pornography, says Weir

> is practically ubiquitous...the Internet has made it easier than ever to get an erotic fix.... The accessibility, affordability and anonymity provided by the Web have put adult content right at our fingertips.... In a 2002 survey conducted for PBS/Frontline by the Kinsey Institute for Research in Sex, Gender and Reproduction at Indiana University, 86 percent of respondents said porn can educate people, and 72 percent said it provides a harmless outlet for fantasies. Among those who reported using pornography, 80 percent said they felt "fine" about it.[12]

Sadock, Sadock, and Ruiz state, "Masturbation is abnormal when it is the only type of sexual activity performed in adulthood if a partner is or might be available, when its frequency indicates compulsion or sexual dysfunction, or when it is consistently preferred to sex with the partner."[13] It is not yet clear whether the neuropsychological aspects of both sexual addictions are the same as alcohol and drug addiction. However, some researchers, according to Weir, have found that the same brain centres stimulated when drug and alcohol addicts use their respective substances of addiction are stimulated when pornography-addicted people observe provocative pictures. These results indicate that "porn of the brain" is a factor of pornography and sexual addiction.[14]

Pastoral Considerations

(1) Since healing addiction to masturbation and pornography is about controlling an extremely powerful instinctual drive, it is one of the most difficult tasks in pastoral healing. Some research findings make it seem a Sisyphean task, implying that masturbation and pornography have to be accepted as normal. However, note that truths, half-truths, and untruths can be extracted from virtually all studies. The testing of people addicted to pornography in the mentioned studies was carried out in a way similar to relying on alcoholics or drug addicts to quantify the advantages and disadvantages of drinking or drug use. Healers and the healed need to therefore be critical, neither underestimating nor overestimating the publicized findings, and use critical judgement to recognize the right tree by its good fruits (Mt. 7:20).

(2) Indeed, there is a porn of the brain (presented by sexual instinct) as well as a holiness of the brain (brain centres executing Godlike behaviors). These facts decrease neither freedom nor responsibility; the brain, as previously discussed, does not causally and deterministically produce the contents of the mind, but teleologically realizes the supreme psychological and spiritual commands in our Christlike behaviors.

(3) On the other hand, as Kaplan and Sadock's textbook notes, "Moral taboos against masturbation have generated myths that masturbation causes mental illness or decreased sexual potency. No scientific evidence supports such claims." Claims like these are counterproductive, producing irrational fears and beliefs, such as masturbation causes blindness or drying of the spinal cord.

(4) The first task of the pastoral healer is usually to answer the question all people addicted to masturbation and pornography ask: If such behaviors are carried out individually, secretively, and pleasurably and hurt nobody, why are they pastoral issues? Neither masturbation nor pornography can be practiced secretively. The partners of those with paraphilia-related disorders (such as compulsive masturbation, obsession with erotically provocative clothing, addiction to telephone sex or cybersex, addiction to prostitutes, dependence on pornography, and protracted promiscuity)

experience loss of affection, commitment, and love, which gradually creates mutual estrangement. Additionally, sexuality ought to assist in mutual pleasure, bonding, cooperation, love, and procreation. None of the previously discussed behaviors helps in achieving these purposes.

(5) Viktor Frankl notes that:

> Masturbation is, to be sure, neither a disease nor a cause of disease; rather it is the sign of a disturbed developmentally misguided attitude towards the love life. Hypochondriac ideas about its morbid consequences are unjustified. But the hangover that generally follows the act of masturbation has a reason, quite aside from these hypochondriac theories. The underlying reason is the feeling of guilt which comes upon one whenever one flees from active, directional experience to passive, non-directional experience.[16]

Frankl uses terms like "hangover" to call to mind the image of drunkenness because, in the same way that drunkenness is an attempt to escape from existential frustration, masturbation is an attempt escape from sexual frustration.

(6) In general, pornography is more destructive than masturbation. It is also more addictive. There are described cases of jobs being lost due to pornography being obsessively watched in the workplace. It also causes friction in marriage when a spouse discovers pornography on the computer of his or her partner.

(7) The purpose of masturbation and pornography is to achieve orgasm. However, in masturbation and pornography, one gives his personality not to a genuine partner but, in a hallucinatory shortcut, to an "illusion of an orgasm." A physiological orgasm can be reached, but the experience of "my I and your you build a common we" cannot be replicated. Despite not causing any physical sickness, both masturbation and pornography degrade sexuality from a catalyst for genuine union in love into a catalyst for egotism and loneliness.

(8) Finally, the most destructive aspect of pornography is that, as Kaplan and Sadock's textbook notes, pornography websites offer such a

level of stimulation and variety of sexual acts that they immunize users to the stimulation of typical partnered activities. Research shows that the brains of teens addicted to pornography do not develop the neuronal connections "that will enable them to respond to arousal partnered interactions with sufficient pleasure to allow them to achieve climax."[17] Thus, addiction to pornography is a vicious cycle disabling the escape from its snares by desensitizing users' brains to real attraction (to normal flesh-and-blood partners) and making them receptive only to fanciful, bizarre, grotesque, and nonexistent sexual stimuli.

(9) Addiction to pornography is not equally damaging for males and females in a marriage. While males more often seek anonymous idols, females are more attracted to romantically engaged couples. A husband's fantasizing about other women hurts his wife more than a wife's addiction to pornography hurts her husband. In both cases, however, the failure to focus desire on one's partner weakens the value of the relationship,[18] playing a counterproductive role and deepening unresolved conflicts.

(10) Even very committed Christians have a sexual instinct, which, as noted, does not know space or time and does not care for reality but has only one goal—to direct behaviors. Instinct demands from the ego uncontrolled sexual gratification despite all moral considerations of the Christian conscience. The fight between conscience and instinct may be tremendous, creating a significant distress. Let us illustrate this with an example.

> The wife of a thirty-three-year-old man unexpectedly had to leave for a long trip. Upon her leaving, the husband said, "Sexuality is not like a faucet which you can open or close as you will. I'm missing my wife so dearly that I am unable to function even at my workplace." He masturbated, fantasizing about having intercourse with his wife, and described, "Despite her not being here, I felt and experienced a union with my wife as if she were. It strengthened my commitment and love to her. At the same time, though, I questioned whether my behavior was morally correct."

In sexual morality, things are not always black and white. Therefore, when pastoral healers are called on to answer hard questions, they should take into account not only professional information and the patient's personal makeup, life situation, and discretional and appreciative judgment, but also biblical teaching and their informed Christian consciences' judgment. Answers often need to be uniquely and individually tailored.

(11) The previous atypical but nevertheless instructive case also illustrates an issue that often comes up in healing masturbation and pornography: whether gradual or complete abstinence is a more realistic therapeutic purpose. In my experience, healing which advises gradually reducing masturbation and pornography and intentionally fixating on one's partner when engaging in such acts (as in in the case noted above) and finally ends with exclusively practicing sexual fantasies with the flesh-and-blood partner is often more successful than healing that completely prohibits the satisfaction of the sexual instinct. Healing masturbation and pornography addicts comes with ups and downs. However, not only one's failures but also his efforts in progressing toward biblical standards are relevant in Jesus' eyes.

(12) Most nonpsychotic psychiatric disorders are connected to self-perceived unfitness in establishing personal relationships, fear of accepting personal responsibility, or inability to establish lasting, fulfilling, and genuinely happy, loving relationships, and they are connected to sick and/or sinful behaviors. The general aspects of pastoral healing in such cases are focused on resolving the psychiatric and psychological reasons for insecurity, anxiety, selfishness, angst, low self-esteem, shyness, and introversion that cause patients to perceive themselves as unlovable and unworthy and thus escape into a fantasy world of masturbation or pornography. Family therapy helps to resolve couples' self-defeating conflicts that inevitably cause mutual estrangement in sex, commitment, and love. Always, though, the primary purpose of healing is to strengthen faith, which acts like oil in a machine in couples' relationships, helping husbands and wives reflect Jesus' love. The personal experience of Christlike loving and being loved is probably the most powerful healer of both addictive masturbation and pornography.

(13) Making a determined decision using the sacramental and nonsacramental help of the Church helps in achieving the ultimate goal of giving and receiving Christian love in a Christ-centred relationship. Fervent faith may often achieve what is hard for even the most effective psychological and

psychiatric healing: the spontaneous self-healing of addicted people. Indeed, for some sceptical professionals, such goal-setting may seem irrational. However, as Jesus said, "All things can be done for the one who believes" (Mk. 9:23).

28.4 Medical and Pastoral Aspects of Homosexuality

Medical and psychological criteria of sick and healthy depend on social understandings. While homosexuality is perceived as a variant of healthy human sexual behavior for many Western societies with low fertility rates, aging populations, and declining birth rates, homosexuality is less-welcomed in mostly African and Asian countries with young and growing populations. As Sadock, Sadock, and Ruiz note, "in 1973 homosexuality was eliminated as a diagnostic category by the American Psychiatric Association, and in 1980 it was removed from the Diagnostic and Statistical Manual of Mental Disorders." It is, from a medical perspective, currently perceived as a variant of human sexual behavior, but not a disorder. The rate of homosexuality is around 2–4%; however, only approximately 1% of both sexes are exclusively homosexual. For males and females, the first homosexual attractions appear in early adolescence, but sexual orientation does not become definite until late adolescence or adulthood[19] According to Kaplan and Sadock's textbook, "Approximately fifty-six percent of lesbians have had heterosexual relationships before their first homosexual genital experience, while the same percentage is around nineteen percent in male homosexuals." It is also worth noting that, according to the same source, "The range of psychopathology that may be found among distressed lesbians and gay men parallels to that found among heterosexuals; some studies have reported a high suicide rate, however."[20] Although homosexual couples do not have "the biological capacity for childbearing that bonds some otherwise incompatible heterosexual couples," they often form stable relationships, though, in general, gay relationships are less stable than lesbian relationships.[21]

Pastoral Considerations

(1) Homosexual attraction is not a choice, but dealing with it is a decision, which can be made in accordance with God's love or against it. Since

God's biblical directives are neither arbitrary nor changeable, the intentional transgression of them has detrimental consequences. These consequences are not about the biological, economic, or political impact of the homosexual population (comprising a maximum of 5% of the whole population), but about sexual hedonism, which excludes biblical love that sexuality ought to serve. Some heterosexual or gay peoples' selfish, pleasure-seeking non-love is of pastoral relevance. Before discussing the practical details of the pastoral approach, let us summarize what we are alluding to and focus on the distressing effects of ultimate sexual selfishness and the rationale of the pastoral approach to it.

(2) Rearing children is a hard task. Nevertheless, one often hears in psychotherapy sessions self-revelations like, "If I didn't have children, I would not work so hard," "I would divorce," or even "I would have committed suicide." Responsible procreation and child-rearing provides a powerful bonding experience for couples and also gives paramount responsibility, goal, courage, strength, value, and meaning to their lives. Procreating and bringing up children is not only a matter of a mothering or fathering instinct but also a biological, economical, psychological, and, above all, spiritual need – an objective societal necessity and source of enormous accomplishment, purpose, and joy. Gay and lesbian clients, just like heterosexual clients who lack this essential purpose, need more than a mere "replacement meaning" (a kind of a reimbursement for missing children). Pastoral healers can help those who are open to Jesus find an ultimate meaning to live for, which no biology, psychology, or society—only God—can give. The ultimate purpose of the pastoral approach for gay people of faith is to help them say of themselves, like Tammy in the book's preface, "Yes, I have no ability to be a parent, but this helped me to find my special way to my heavenly parents – the Father, Son, and the Holy Spirit!" How the pastoral healer will accomplish this depends on the specific client's profile, interests, attitudes, and worldviews.

(3) When professionally approaching problems connected to gay lifestyle, psychiatrists and psychologists most often give help, and patients accept it. In many cases of pastoral healing, though, the healer's efforts are focused less on giving help and much more on assisting the client in

accepting help. This is especially so in approaching deeply-committed Christian gay and lesbian people who fervently seek pastoral help but are prejudiced or resistant against the kind of support pastoral healers offer.

(4) The scope of the pastoral approach always depends on a variable – the needs of the clients – and a constant – the pastoral counsellor promoting Christlike love and compassion that infinitely surpass all worldly justice and respects biblical teaching and the biological, psychological, social, and spiritual interests of humankind. Since the needs of heterosexual and homosexual clients differ, pastoral help likewise differs depending on whether the client is a committed Christian, a lukewarm Christian, or an adamant nonbeliever.

(5) Like all humans, zealous Christians also consider "what if?" questions. So heterosexual Christians' occasional questioning, "How would I feel having homosexual attractions?" is neither sick nor sinful. Nevertheless, even such Christians need information, encouragement and support with adhering to the biblical guidance of Leviticus 18:22, Leviticus 20:13, 1 Corinthians 6:9–10, 1 Timothy 1:10, and Romans 1:24–28. A topic of discussion in sessions with such believers may also be the so-called natural law encompassing the principles that constitute the very nature of human biological-psychological-social-economic functioning that necessarily includes responsible procreation and childrearing as a precondition of the well-being of the human society. Counselling may also be focused on providing psychological and practical help in resolving their relational issues, and using their spiritual and often abundant intellectual gifts in unique ways to build God's kingdom. The New Testament (for example in Matthew 27:52, Acts of the Apostles 9:13 and 26:10, and Romans 1:7 and 15:23–33) calls diligent Christian disciples "saints." Committed Christians adhering to biblical teachings in sexual matters are, in many aspects, saints of our time. They prove that sexuality is neither the supreme motivator of their choices, nor the supreme commander of human behaviors. Thus, the task of harmonizing this instinct with the highest psychological and spiritual values of the whole personality is achievable for everyone.

(6) Heterosexual, religiously lukewarm believers may raise hard personal or family issues concerning homosexuality. A strict, non-empathetic,

dogmatic, or judgmental attitude will cause them to drift away from the faith, but giving unbiblical advice will have an even worse outcome. Their pastoral counselling focuses on possibly clarifying the noted practical consequences of a gay lifestyle (as noted under point 2), explaining biblical, theological, and moral aspects of homosexuality while resolving potential personal problems (like low self-esteem, loneliness, or feeling unlovable to the opposite sex). Pastoral counselling of such individuals should also be focused on fostering a genuine, meaningful, and joyful Christian relationship with their spouses. As we will discuss, in Christian dating, love is constituted by spiritual, psychological, erotic, and sexual components. The spiritual and psychological connection of two people may facilitate the resurfacing of the erotic and sexual aspects of love. Regardless of the outcome of pastoral counselling, it is essential for the Church not to lose such people; pastoral healers should take every opportunity to foster God's love, hope, courage, and joy in them. No matter how clients respond to the counsellor, neither lukewarm religiosity or sexual problems can diminish their need for deepening their union with God. Only responding positively to the Father's calls, receive Jesus' love, and follow the guidance of the Holy Spirit can resolve their philosophical, personal, or family problems.

(7) Dealing with gay people who absolutely resist the biblical message is the most difficult task for pastoral therapists. In such encounters, unfortunately, the situation is much like the one we read of in Matthew 17:14–20, which records the story of the disciples who were unable to heal because of their little faith. If a client has little faith, a Bible-oriented pastoral counsellor often cannot help them gain biblical courage, optimism, peace, joy, or love. Instead, the counsellor can help them to not perceive themselves as being ignored by the Church but to empirically feel, know, and experience being recipients of God's love. A genuine, professional, loving, empathetic, and Jesus-like attitude can make an impression even in people currently resisting pastoral help and can possibly facilitate their conversion to Jesus in the future.

Notes

[1] Otto Fenichel, *The Psychoanalytic Theory of Neurosis* (New York: W.W. Norton & Company, 1972), 48–50.

[2] Ibid., 53–60.

[3] Ibid., 60.

[4] Benjamin James Sadock, Virginia Alcott Sadock, and Pedro Ruiz, *Kaplan and Sadock's Synopsis of Psychiatry: Behavioral Sciences/Clinical Psychiatry*, 11th ed. (Philadelphia, PA: Wolters Kluwer, 2015), 568.

[5] Ibid., 570.

[6] David H. Barlow (ed.), *Clinical Handbook of Psychological Disorders: A Step-by-step Treatment Manual* (New York: The Guilford Press, 2008), 616.

[7] Joseph Schwarz, *Durch Psychologie zum Gott, Argumente Fur Gottes Existenz* (Eisenstadt 1988), 80.

[8] Barlow, *Clinical Handbook of Psychological Disorders*, 616.

[9] Sadock, Sadock, and Ruiz, *Kaplan and Sadock's Synopsis of Psychiatry*, 11th ed. 570.

[10] Kirsten Weir, "Is Pornography Addictive?" *American Psychological Association* 45 (4) (2014): 46.

[11] Sadock, Sadock, and Ruiz, *Kaplan and Sadock's Synopsis of Psychiatry*, 11th ed. 570.

[12] Weir, "Is Pornography Addictive?" 46.

[13] Sadock, Sadock, and Ruiz, *Kaplan and Sadock's Synopsis of Psychiatry*, 11th ed. 572.

[14] Weir, "Is Pornography Addictive?" 46.

[15] Sadock, Sadock, and Ruiz, *Kaplan and Sadock's Synopsis of Psychiatry*, 11th ed. 570.

[16] Viktor E. Frankl, *The Doctor and the Soul, From Psychotherapy to Logotherapy* (New York: Vintage, 1973), 169.

[17] Sadock, Sadock, and Ruiz, *Kaplan and Sadock's Synopsis of Psychiatry*, 11th ed. 578.

[18] Ibid., 579.

[19] Ibid., 571.

[20] Ibid., 572.

[21] Ibid.

CHAPTER TWENTY-NINE

PARTNER RELATIONAL ISSUES

P artner relations addresses the area where humans' earthly lives are perhaps metaphorically closest to heaven or hell. Helping couples turn their self-made versions of hell into heaven is pastoral healers' most common task.

29.1 Healing Partner Relational Problems

According the DSM-5, partner relational problems are

> associated with impaired functioning in behavioral, cognitive and affectionate domains. Examples of behavioral problems include conflict resolution difficulty, withdrawal, and overinvolvement. Cognitive problems can manifest in chronic negative attributions of the others' intentions or dismissals of the partner's positive behaviors. Affective problems would include chronic sadness, apathy, and/or anger about the other partner.[1]

Summarizing the information of Kaplan and Sadock's textbook, we could list the following reasons for impaired family functioning: communication problems between the partners, a maladaptive approach to conflict resolution, one spouse being intimidated by the other, discriminating behaviors in child-bearing or child-rearing, conflicting relationships with in-laws, differences in attitudes towards social life, adverse handling of finances, and problems in sexual interaction. A lifelong anorgasmia, or impotence, often indicates intrapsychic conflicts; however, sexual dissatisfaction is involved in many cases of marital maladjustment.[2]

Accordingly, such issues cause more pain in civilized societies today than hunger, sickness, and even natural disasters. Instead of being among the most blissful experiences, family and partner relationships, when dysfunctional, are often among the most dangerous, destructive, and distressing phenomena, facilitating frustration, aggression, and sometimes even violence. These are the reasons why we focus on this topic with special attention.

Pastoral Considerations

(1) Humans are created in God's image and likeness as living souls. They are not a body that has a soul but rather a soul that possesses a body. Despite being invisible, the nonsensorial qualities of human beings—soul, personality, and conscience—factually, objectively exist. They are seen in lovers, empirically enabling their psychological-spiritual attraction—their chemistry—which substantiates the mystery of love. Thus, people in love communicate not only with their bodies but also with their psychological-spiritual essence. That this communication is crucial is proven by the observable fact that even a partner's attractive body becomes highly aversive if psychological-spiritual unity is deteriorating.

(2) From a pastoral perspective, all partner relational problems originate from just one issue: a shortage of love. What exactly is love in marriage, though? Summarizing Viktor Frankl's ideas from *The Doctor and the Soul* and *Man's Search for Ultimate Meaning*, we can distinguish four categories of what, in the popular vernacular, is called love.

(a) Sexual attraction is focused on satisfying instincts. People defining love in this way demand nothing more than the quick and easy satisfaction of their sexual drive. Subsequently, "The result is an inflation of sex; and like inflation on the money market, it is associated with a devaluation. More specifically, sex is devalued because it is dehumanized."[3] The object of love in such cases is not the personality but the physical body, which can be quickly and easily discarded after use. Such love therefore lasts only a short while.

(b) Erotic appeal has to do with passion about and fascination with certain erotic qualities of a partner's body and appearance, mobilizing the sexual drive. There are always particular erotic qualities lauded by the taste of the sexual marketplace. For example, female erotic idols in our time ought to be skinny and have long hair, red nails, and sexually appealing makeup, while males need strong muscles and fashionable clothing. No real uniqueness in appearance is sought. Every person, with a bit of effort, can take on such an image. Having a unique personality is also not desirable. On the contrary, being erotically attractive to everyone requires hiding one's individuality. By hiding their personalities, erotic idols belong to everybody and nobody. TV and movies form the collective erotic taste, and actors and actresses fulfil it. Since it is not easy to find and replace partners who have the preferred erotic qualities, relationships built on erotic attraction tend to last longer than those built on only sexual attraction. Nevertheless, erotic attractiveness declines with age, so those fixated on it often turn to younger partners who fit a more current sexual taste.

(c) The psychological aspect of love is characterized by interest in and attraction to the personality of another. The personality in humans is a stable and permanent characteristic, so partners with compatible personalities that fit like a key in its lock can find lasting mutual attraction. What makes a person psychologically attractive? Psychological attraction is based on mutually giving and receiving the gifts that a person needs to grow and resolve frustrations, conflicts, low self-esteem, anxieties, fears, depression, and other defects in themselves. No upbringing is perfect; every young adult has unresolved personal problems that originated in their childhood. But the love of a complementary partner completes one's upbringing and heals the wounds that prevents him from becoming happy, content, and optimistic. To be able to achieve this purpose, the partner's personality must therefore have the exact qualities that are healing to the other's existing problems. Simply illustrated, for a healthy person, if 100 percent self-esteem is needed but he only has 80 percent, his partner ought to have a surplus of 20 percent. When metaphorically integrating "my *I* and your *you* into a common *we*," 80 percent self-esteem of one partner and 120 percent of the other make it possible for both to have 100 percent. As Frankl says, "Human sex is always more than mere sex. And it is more than mere sex to the extent that it serves the physical expression of something metasexual"[4]—that is, psychological love and, in Christians, even more prominently, spiritual love.

(d) Christian love is spiritual. All loving couples share the same purpose in realizing many different goals—purchasing a house, sailing around the world, bringing up children, etc.—but in people of faith, the *I* and *you* are eminently connected in mutually building a relationship with Jesus and ultimate striving to achieve union with God. Since God is love, Christian marriage ought to reflect Godly love. Both partners serve as incarnations of his love to each other, "sacral mediators," or as Pope John Paul II formulates it, "a sacrament,"[5] a visible sign of a sacral reality, making it possible for them to experience God's closeness, love, power, and support. One partner's *I* acts as a tool for God to help the other's *you* grow and incline more toward Jesus. As the beloved partner's personality that radiates God's love remains a mystery (since spiritual components of the beloved person transcend what is psychologically explicable), so Christian love itself is a mystery but nevertheless is profoundly experienced. One's personality remains a permanent mystery, entrenched in an ever-progressing and deepening relationship with Jesus. Such a marriage never becomes boring. On the contrary, new qualities, surprises, and gifts always appear.

Christian love is not an illusion or self-deception. It is not possible to arbitrarily imagine or fantasize about the love of God or the presence of his gifts presented through a spouse's love. If this were possible, everyone would do it. God is experientially present, acting and setting an angelic circle in motion. Love causes biblical peace, joy, and purpose, while joy proves Christian love. Such love creates the experience of God's presence, exactly as Jesus said, "For where two or three gather in my name, there am I with them" (Matthew 18:20). Although the meaning of the passage is not exclusive to the sacramental union of man and wife, Jesus is the third party present in marriage, and the experience of his gifts proves and empowers the Christian couple's relationship and mutual commitment,

All this does not mean that love is only some esoteric or platonic relationship in Christian marriage; it is also constituted by sexual, erotic, and psychological components. However, while for nonbelievers sexual and erotic attraction are of the greatest importance, psychological unity is of secondary importance, and spiritual unity seems unnecessary and redundant, for Christians the ranking is reversed. For them, spiritual union is of the utmost importance, psychological unity is essential, and erotic and sexual qualities are almost natural consequences of spiritual and psychological attraction. Such love evolves in developmental steps. Erotic love includes sexuality, psychological love includes erotic and sexual attraction, and Christian love incorporates the psychological, erotic, and sexual components of love.

(3) In a Christian marriage, sexuality serves a purpose. As Pope John Paul II notes, it happens "through our ability to possess ourselves and then give ourselves to another person in love, thus forming an image of communion of people in the Holy Trinity."[6] How can the pastoral healer enhance such Godlike communion in conflicted or mutually estranged Christian families?

Some professional therapists prefer to conceptualize and heal family problems using the so-called systems approach. As Marsha Wiggins Frame describes, "Within the systematic perspective, several schools of family therapy have emerged, [like] transgenerational, structural, strategic, brief therapy and others."[7] Pastoral healers either integrate their spiritual approach with the family systems they use or are eclectic in their healing practices, supplementing their method of healing with Christian principles. Before discussing healing, let us first explore the aetiology of marriage estrangement.

(4) Barlow plainly and scientifically summarizes two reasons for marital distress: "reinforcement erosion and the emergence of incompatibilities." The first factor, reinforcement erosion, refers to a couple's once mutual love-enforcing behaviors becoming less reinforcing. The sexual and erotic attraction that initially generated significant pleasure for the couple, after many years, becomes boring, unattractive, or even aversive. In the second case, incompatibilities such as different purposes, values, goals, interests, habits, and belief systems gradually emerge and become ever more divisive and frustrating, causing estrangement, anger, and hate.[8] This may be the usual or even unavoidable dynamic in worldly families, but in families where Jesus himself inspires love, the dynamic is not the same. The presence of Christ and his pervasive, inclusive love does not admit to such estrangement. Problems may arise, but they do not cause alienation or division.

(5) Christian couples are encouraged to take hold of the authority given by Christ through prayer, liturgy, scriptures, and sacraments. Through faith, Jesus ought to be empirically included in families, facilitating their ability to visibly, physically, and measurably imitate the loving communion of the three divine persons in the Holy Trinity. But what does this mean in everyday practice? It means a neverending crescendo of growth in mutual love. A Christian husband or wife can never come to a place of boredom, distaste, or aversion with a spouse who genuinely acts as a sacrament, a visible sign of that sacral reality that can never be completely reached but always mutually approached.

(6) How do Christian families deal with ever-increasing incompatibles? They do so by adhering to the recommendation of Matthew's (7:5), paraphrased as, "first take the plank out of your own eye, and then you will see clearly to remove the speck from your spouse's eye." Christian husbands and wives tend to first look at their own mistakes. This helps them to appreciate their spouses' merits, actions, and qualities. Psychologically, love lasts as

long as partners respect, cherish, adore, and glorify each other. Examining first the plank in one's own eye helps to not only maintain these conditions permanently but also to enhance a committed progression in mutual love. This helps avoid "he said, she said" arguments, which are tantamount to the blind leading the blind.

(7) To enhance forgiveness seven times seventy-seven times, some Christian families practice a type of confession to God with each other. Every week at the same time, couples ritually visit a special place—a park, restaurant, or somewhere they feel comfortable. There they pray, asking Jesus to preside, and then both partners confess selfish, jealous, envious, and vengeful thoughts, paranoia, or other unloving attitudes or actions over the previous week. As Christ is absolutely forgiving, so the partner, imitating Christ's love, not only forgives but even absolves the confessed faults to a degree, saying, "No, you were not selfish, unloving, or aggressive, but frustrated because I made you behave like that. I am guiltier of your imperfection than you are." While in confrontational discussions the aim is proving "I am right, you are wrong," Christian partners' self-critical discussions set an angelic circle into motion: "You are right, I was wrong." The discussion is moved by each partner in a direction of recognizing conflicts more as their own problem than the partner's, and this attitude makes mutual forgiveness possible. Mutual confession ends in thanksgiving to Jesus, whose presence empirically validated for such couples. This is admittedly not the way of the world, which is concerned with blame and finger pointing. It is, however, the path prescribed by the Gospel.

(8) Almost regularly in worldly families, reinforcement erosion and the emergence of incompatibilities facilitate what Barlow calls polarization. He says, "'Polarization process' refers to the destructive interaction that ensues when a distressed couple enters into a theme-related conflict." Naturally, confronted and conflicted partners attempt to resolve their distress by mutually trying to change the other. These attempts are futile. The couple's differences become even more exacerbated and partners become "polarized in their conflicting positions." What results is a "mutual trap," which "typically leaves the partners feeling 'stuck,' or 'trapped' in their conflict." Couples in this situation feel hopeless. They "feel they have done everything they can

to change the other and nothing seems to work" but are "reluctant to give up their efforts to change each other, because this would mean resigning themselves to a dissatisfying relationship."[10] How can pastoral healers help to resolve such unresolvable traps?

(9) A pastoral healer helps heal the no-win situation of dying mutual attraction and skyrocketing incompatibilities by reshaping the couple's personalities. Love is a process, a permanent giving and receiving. It imitates breathing—exhaling (giving) and inhaling (receiving) gestures, deeds, and symbols of love. Christian giving and receiving creates and sustains mutual attraction. In this breathing of love, Christians factually change each other's personalities and behaviours.

> A couple married for forty-nine years owned an expensive car. Their Bentley was treated almost like an idol, kept clean, tidy, and in the best possible condition. The husband drove his idol to work daily. In fact, he was so familiar with it that he could drive the car with eyes closed from the street into the garage (he proved this in winning a bet), which was in the backyard of the house. Arriving home one day, tired from his work, he realized that his wife was drying the bedsheets in front of the garage door in the sun. He thought, "Since I know where the garage door is and the car is clean and the bed sheets are dry, I will drive through the bedsheets into the garage." He opened the garage door and drove into the garage. In doing so, however, he misjudged the space by a few inches and badly scratched the car. In this moment he thought, "I could scratch out my eyes! I could kill myself! How could I be such an idiot—too lazy to stop for a minute to clear the garage door?" His wife saw exactly what happened. She said only three sentences: "Oh, my dear, I do not love you because you can drive through the bedsheets into the garage but because you are a good husband. We will fix the car. It's not a big issue." She said exactly the three sentences he needed to hear to calm down and realize she was right.

Wives and husbands know each other's personalities, and they also know better than anyone else which three sentences the other needs to hear to calm down and experience peace, forgiveness, hope, and optimism. A person has the immense power to change and improve his or her partner's personality by saying those things the partner needs to hear and, in doing so, make the partner grateful and eager to reciprocate the life-giving words, opening a dialogue that serves their joint psychological-spiritual well-being and union. Through this mutual giving and receiving of love, praise, and appreciation, couples make each other not only lovable but also irreplaceably important in giving Godly optimism, self-esteem, peace, and joy.

(10) A sign of being Christlike is selflessness. The paramount power of selflessness in every Christian marriage is demonstrated by the following story.

A twenty-seven-year-old husband's addiction to motorcycles started when he was a teenager. First he was a motorcycle racer, and later he biked hundreds of thousands of miles. His wife took up his hobby when they were dating, and when they married they started going on daily rides. However, when his wife got pregnant she could not go with him. He planned to go on daily rides alone during this time, but his wife asked him to stay at home with her during his free time instead. This was an unexpected shock for the young husband; biking was his hobby, his life, and his "form of being." The couple therefore started negotiating to resolve the discord. They reached a first compromise: three days a week the husband would go riding, and the next three days he would stay at home. However, this compromise made the situation even worse. The husband found himself thinking, "If I go today, I cannot bike tomorrow," and, as he explained, this frustrating awareness spoiled his enjoyment on his days out. He felt like he was in kindergarten, losing his autonomy and competence. So he started deliberating as to what was expected of him as a Catholic husband and future father. In his internal dialogue, he resolved, "Okay, she deserves to be happy. I'll do as she says. I won't ever sit on a motorcycle again. I'll sell all my bikes. But then I'll be depressed and she'll ask me to buy back my bikes." However, after selling his motorcycles the young husband was not unhappy or depressed. On the contrary, he said, "This may have been the first time in my life I felt really worthy. I proved that I am a good husband and a mature person."

Every loving relationship consists of unselfish giving and receiving. The more selflessness one invests in a relationship, the greater the return will be. This helps in turning marriages that are like hell into marriages that are like heaven on earth.

(11) In discussing DSM-5 disorders and difficult pastoral situations, it may seem to sceptics that we are painting an idealistic but unachievable illusion. However, just as Christ always pointed toward ultimate ideals, pastoral healing is always focused not on average results but on the results which those living like Christ can achieve. Living like Christ makes the impossible possible (Matthew 19:26).

29.2 Healing Divorce Traumas

In America 40 to 50 per cent of all marriage end in divorce. Even prominent Christians are not immune from that plaque, causing first one-sided and later mutual spousal estrangement. The process starts when partners discover that their mate "is not the same person anymore" and is not equally attractive as when mutual falling in love. By losing attraction, usually first spiritual, then psychological, and finally erotic and sexual attraction becomes irreparable lost. Most often one partner blames the other. In reality, however, both partners have lost their Christian zeal, they both resist adhering to Christian standards of marriage love, and both are blaming each other. They are mutually stepping on the escalator moving them toward the hell of divorce.

Their first steps on the "highway of tears" are usually marked by one or both spouses feeling manipulated. As Sagi[11] describes, they have a vague feeling of inequality in their relationship. They feel overpowered and forced into defensive and submissive roles. But, because manipulation is invisible and hard to prove, and because their paramount desire is to sustain love, partners initially silence and suppress their doubts.

One husband illustrated this dynamic: "We bought tickets for a show starting at 8PM. My wife went to a hair-dresser but emphatically promised she will be home not later than 7 PM to leave for the theatre. At 6:30 PM, I was already prepared to leave. It was 6:45 she was nowhere. At 7PM, she was not yet home. At 7:15 I got nervous, at 7:30 I was frustrated. At 7:45, I was panicking and phoned the police and hospitals to see if she had an accident. At 8PM, I was desperate. Finally, she arrived at 8:10 with a great smile on her face and said 'Oh, how nice, now we can spend an evening at home together.' The husband reported, 'My feelings were boiling.... But she just asked "Aren't you happy that we can stay together at home?" She forced me to agree with her wholeheartedly.'

Such internal divisions fuel ambivalence, in which the fear of powerless-ness and loss of competence and personal integrity is paired with disregard of one's own feelings, doubts, suspicions and angst. As Sagi[12] describes, the manipulative partner(s) will skilfully take advantage of the ambivalence and insecurity of their spouse. They "lovingly" paralyze the partner's defences, and banalize, deny, or explain away their complaints. They will seek out the other's Achilles' heel, and evoke shame, disgust, fears or guilt feelings to compel the other to retreat into a defensive, submissive and obedient position.

However, these strategies act as a two-edged sword. Sooner or later, the victims either retaliate with similarly sophisticated forms of covert aggres-sion, or even by physical acting out. On the other hand, covert or overt aggression inevitably leads to an intuitive or deliberate mutual withdrawal from each other.

Fantasizing about "what if" distancing from the spouse, or decreas-ing mutual dependence, is usually the next step. This follows a period of ambivalent hesitation consisting of mutual threatening with separation but also seeking reconciliation, since neither of the partner has yet the cour-age to make the fatal choice. Next follows a definite giving up loving the previously adored person, anticipatory grief about ending the relationship, paired with frustration, anger, and hate. The fifth step consists of seeking autonomy, organizing one's life without mutual depending on each other, and having often fiery discussion about division of mutual children and property. The sixth stage encompasses finalizing the legal, economic, and community divorce. Its most painful aspects are custody battles against the court-ordered joint, split, or single custody of children, and negotiating visitation rights. This final stage ends either in a permanent cold war between estranged spouses, or a more or less mutually workable compromise in final resolution of the conflict.

Most people, and especially Christians, report feelings of stress, sadness, depression, anxiety, anger, helpless rage, and mood swings. According to Kaplan and Sadock's textbook, "Studies indicate that recovery from divorce takes about two years; by then the ex-spouse may be viewed neutrally, and each spouse accepts his or her new identity as a single person." [13]

Pastoral Considerations

(1) I never in my practice saw a genuine happy or even an amicable divorce. It is always a bitter disappointment. But pastoral healers need to think positively. They focus on how a divorce ought to be managed (if it happens) in people knowing that with Jesus' help, the impossible in human relationships is achievable.

(2) Christian denominations stand on two legs in dealing with here discussed issues. In more lenient or more strict ways they all oppose divorcing and remarrying, but their purpose is to provide pastoral care for the people of God who fail to fulfil the marriage obligations or transgress biblical commands. Their purpose is not condemning but helping to heal the residual spiritual-psychological wounds.

(3) Beside adhering to church teachings, the pastoral healer's role in healing Christians' sufferings of divorce problems is like sitting on a three-legged chair. They need to focus on current psychological, psychiatric, and spiritual problems occurring during and after a divorce,

(4) Recognizing manipulation is hard, even for seasoned pastoral healers. It may be masked as a loving care or unselfish support of a partner. Moreover, it is hard to expose disguised manipulative strategies, which involve cunning, skilled and relentless but hidden efforts to force the partner

to become a tool in achieving the manipulative partner's goals. Divorcing partners often use a sophisticated arsenal of strategies that are quite logical and financially, socially and legally sensible, in order to force their ex-partner into submission.

These sophisticated methods aimed at dissolving the opponent's resistance can be just as powerful as physically violent behaviors. Professional psychology is unable to heal these "civilised" methods of aggression. Only people of faith have a better tool: promoting Christian forgiveness, helping to adhere to Jesus' command in Matthew 7:3 about paying attention "to the plank in the own eyes." By relying on Jesus' teaching, pastoral healers have a powerful tool in healing the wounds of divorce that often persist even after all psychological, social, financial, legal problems between ex-spouses have been resolved.

(5) The challenges pastoral healers are most hard to deal with are the psychiatric problems; especially anger, hate, and helpless rage often facilitating homicidal or suicidal behaviors in divorcing people. If signs or even threats of outwardly aggressive, or suicidal behaviors are suspected, it is imperative to reach out for professional help (e.g., medical practitioners or law enforcement personnel), as well as to involve the social contacts of the dangerously dysregulated person.

(6) A significant psychological problem after a divorce is losing the personal sense of identity. By losing their partner's support and their children's closeness, people almost "divorce from their previous personality" of being a good spouse, or a good parent. Such experience causes angst and anxiety comparable to that of losing personality in other traumatic experiences, resulting in a kind of derealization and depersonalization. The only safe haven for believers in such cases is faith. Pastoral healers may help to experience "I can lose everything, except my relationship with God."

(7) An almost unavoidable psychological consequence of divorce is decreased life satisfaction. Immediately after a divorce, some divorcees attempt healing themselves by starting a new relationship. They are neglecting spiritual and psychological components of love and focus on sexual and erotic (or sometimes on lucrative) qualities of a new partner. Pastoral healers need to clarify the futility of such attempts and encourage their clients

to pick up their cross and seek consolation by Jesus, trusting that he always responds to his people willing to listen him.

(8) An exception from the general rule of decreased life satisfaction after a divorce is only in families where a grave physical, emotional, or sexual abuse were the cause of the divorce. For Christians leaving such relationships, divorce may be a new opportunity, especially if it means a better chance for their children's future upbringing. Discerning a meaning and ultimate meaning to live for with Jesus after the divorce has a supreme healing power, reserved only for committed Christians.

(9) A unique pastoral task after a divorce, and especially for zealous Christians living in a biblically unacceptable relationship, is providing help in resolving guilt feelings. Pastoral healers may alleviate that distress by two ways:

(10) Resolving guilt feelings not solely by logically acknowledging Jesus' mercy but much more: by counting on the client's judgment and reasons of heart, a rational and emotional identification with the biblical protagonists, almost reliving Jesus' justice and mercy illustrated in the story of the adulterous woman (John 8:3–11) and the prodigal son (Luke 15:11–30). Such rational and emotional appreciation facilitates a spiritual-psychological experience of Jesus's giving and the subject's responsible acceptance of his justice and mercy, expressed also in atonement. A penitent lifestyle facilitates a fundamental qualitative change in one's behavior by making from a past moral disadvantage a spiritual advantage.

(11) A visible sign of that new form of being is also adhering to the Church teachings. All Christian denominations have their more lenient or strict requirements helping reconciliation with Jesus after a divorce and eventual remarrying. For example, annulment of a marriage in the Catholic Church proclaims a marriage as invalid and thus never existing if the basic suppositions of a valid marriage were never met. There are also conditions when and how marriage can be dissolved in Orthodox and Protestant denominations. Adhering to doctrinal standards of their faith and to sacramental and nonsacramental means of salvation is of extraordinary importance. They make to experience what John 3:6 notes: that Spirit gives birth (to the repentant sinners') spirit.

(12) Such spiritual rebirth we talk about enables divorced Christian parents to genuinely forgive themselves and their estranged partners. Christian forgiveness empowers a wholeheartedly committed mutual participation in their children's upbringing. A not mutually competing but helping attitude in achieving that common purpose enables divorced Christian parents to consciously, unselfishly, and self-confidently build the kingdom of God despite all past disappointments.

(13) Finally, only such spiritual rebirth makes divorced Christians fit to pray and receive God's help in eventual establishing new Christian marriages. For them, divorce is not only a tragedy but also an opportunity.

Notes

[1] DSM-5. *Diagnostic and Statistical Manual of the American Psychiatric Association* (2013), 357.

[2] Benjamin James Sadock, Virginia Alcott Sadock, and Pedro Ruiz, *Kaplan and Sadock's Synopsis of Psychiatry: Behavioral Sciences/Clinical Psychiatry*, 11th ed. (Philadelphia, PA: Wolters Kluwer, 2015), 863–894.

[3] Viktor E. Frankl, *The Doctor and the Soul, From Psychotherapy to Logotherapy* (New York: Vintage, 1973), 163.

[4] Ibid., 162–70.

[5] Peter Bristow, *Christian Ethics and the Human Person* (Herefordshire: Gracewing, 2013), 9.

[6] John Paul II, *Man and Woman He Created Them: A Theology of the Body* (Boston, MA: Pauline Books and Media, 2006), 460.

[7] Marsha Wiggins Frame, *Integrating Religion and Spirituality in Counseling: A Comprehensive Approach* (Pacific Grove, CA: Thomson/Brooks/Cole, 2003), 212.

[8] David H. Barlow (ed.), *Clinical Handbook of Psychological Disorders: A Step-by-Step Treatment Manual* (New York: The Guilford Press, 2008), 616.

[9] Ibid., 668.

[10] Ibid., 669.

[11] Zoltan Sagi, *Kotelekeink, Massagunk Szorongasai* (Szabadka; Eletjel Konyvek, 2015), 39-41

[12] Ibid., 41.

[13] Sadock, Sadock, and Ruiz, *Kaplan and Sadock's Synopsis of Psychiatry*, 11th ed. 1132.

CHAPTER THIRTY

MEDICAL AND PASTORAL ASPECTS
OF SUICIDAL BEHAVIORS

I t is a mystery why successful social idols like Marilyn Monroe and Nobel laureates like Ernest Hemingway kill themselves and why, in most developing countries, the suicide rates are low while in affluent Western societies, the will to live decreases. Recent celebrity suicides include Robin Williams, Philip Seymour Hoffman, and Anthony Bourdain. What do professional textbooks say about the mystery of suicide?

According to Kaplan and Sadock, suicide is the eighth leading cause of death in the United States, and its rate is around 12.5 in every 100,000 people, remaining relatively stable. However, the suicide rate among young people ages 15–24 has increased significantly. In comparison, the suicide rate is high (more than 25 in 100,000 people) in Lithuania, South Korea, Scandinavia, Sri Lanka, Russia, Belarus, Austria, Hungary, and Japan, while it is low (fewer than 10 in every 100,000 people) in Australia, the Netherlands, Spain, Italy, Ireland, Albania, Israel, South Africa, and Egypt. Among men, suicide peaks after the age of 45, while among women it does so after 55. In men 65 years of age and older, the rate is 44 in every 100,000 people.[1] Here are some other demographic parameters.

- Gender: suicide is seen four times more often in males than in females.
- Method: aggressive methods like hanging and shooting are more common in males, while women most often choose poison or medicine.
- Race: white people commit suicide approximately two to three times more often than African Americans.
- Religion: suicide rates among Roman Catholics are lower than among Protestants and Jews. However, "the degree of orthodoxy and integration may be a more accurate measure of risk in this category than simple institutional religious affiliation."
- Marriage: marriage decreases suicidal risk, especially if children are in the home. Single people commit suicide almost twice as often as married people.
- Occupation: in general, a higher social status correlates to a higher risk of suicide.
- Health: health problems significantly increase suicidal risk.
- Mental illness: almost 95 percent of all people who commit or attempt suicide have a diagnosed mental disorder, which amounts to a risk of suicide among psychiatric patients that is 3–12 times higher than for the rest of the population. Those most at risk suffer from mood disorders (around 400 in every 100,000 people for males and 180 in every 100,000 people for females). Some 60–70 percent of suicide victims suffer from depression, and instances of suicide among patients suffering from schizophrenia are around 10 percent, antisocial personality disorder around 5 percent, alcohol dependency around 15 percent, and panic disorder or social phobia around 20 percent.

The aetiology of suicidal behaviors is multidimensional. Emil Durkheim distinguishes three types of suicide: egoistic, altruistic, and anomic. Egoistic suicide applies to people not integrated into any social group and therefore not receiving support and not caring about the pain they cause to the people attached to them. Altruistic suicide applies to people excessively integrated

SIN AND MENTAL AILMENTS

with a particular group, such as war veterans. Anomic suicide applies to people with disturbed integration who "cannot follow customary norms of behavior," such as people suffering from psychological problems. Freud explained suicidal behavior as "the self-directed death instinct [Freud's concept of Thanatos] plus three components of hostility and suicide: the wish to kill, the wish to be killed, and the wish to die." Karl Meninnger also used the concept of retroflexed anger and in *Man Against Himself* conceived of suicide as inverted homicide because of the patient's anger toward other people. Modern explanations include motives such as the following: "revenge, power, control, or punishment; atonement, sacrifice, or restitution; escape or sleep; rescue, rebirth, reunion with the dead; or a new life." Depressed people may be suicidal "just as they appear to improve from depression."[4]

Failed attempts at suicide outnumber successful suicides 25 to 1 and are more common in women as well as those suffering from histrionic personal disorders, impulse-control disorders, and antisocial personality disorders. There is a popular but mistaken misconception that "suicide succeeds or it is feigned." As noted, suicidal ideation is never a yes/no choice. Suicidal people do not want to die but rather to live differently. Even people committed to carrying out suicide seldom choose absolutely sure methods; they leave themselves a chance to be saved.

30.1 Presuicidal Syndrome

In every frustrated, angry, depressed suicidal person, the motives for death gradually overtake the motives for life. These motives are almost never absolute. Around 80 percent of suicidal people send out messages to other people, indirectly and vaguely asking for help before committing suicide (saying things like "I will not need my car anymore" or "I'm going to a better place"). Their calls for help are often not understood by others because of their enigmatic nature. These warnings signal indecisiveness and the internal fight between motives for and against committing suicide, referred to as *presuicidal syndrome*, which is often accompanied by depression, pessimism, impatience, irritability, dysphoria, and aggression. However, when a choice is made, the suicidal person calms down or becomes relaxed. Such a mood change, from anxiety to relaxation, often signals the last opportunity when suicidal people can be saved. Presuicidal syndrome is a warning sign. If a person with increased risk (someone who is older, chronically sick, depressed, divorced, widowed, drug-addicted, alcohol-addicted, or fighting with emotional, mental, familial, or financial problems, or who has a history of suicide attempts) implicitly indicates suicidal ideation, he deserves special attention from pastoral caregivers.

30.2 Parasuicidal Behavior

The term *parasuicidal* refers to patients who "injure themselves by self-mutilation (e.g., cutting the skin) but who usually do not wish to die." Most cut themselves delicately, using a razor blade, knife, broken glass, or mirror. Their extremities (wrists, arms, thighs, and legs) are often injured and display scars from previous cuts. Such people typically experience no pain but only a relief of tension, frustration, or aggressive impulses. Risky hobbies with an element of danger also imply parasuicidal behavior.[5]

30.3 "Death with Dignity" and Physician-Assisted Suicide

The idea of so-called death with dignity and physician-assisted suicide has provoked a still-ongoing debate. As Kaplan and Sadock note:

> Despite the abhorrence that many physicians and medical ethicists express regarding physician-assisted suicide, poll after poll shows that as many as two thirds of Americans favour the legalization of physician-assisted suicide in certain conditions, and evidence even indicates that the formerly unified opposition to physician-assisted suicide has eroded.

Nevertheless, the AMA, the APA, and the American Bar Association continue to vehemently oppose physician-assisted suicide. The American College of Physicians-American College of Internal Medicine (ACP-ASIM) recommends improving palliative care while also opposing the legalization of physician-assisted suicide. In this context, the ACP-ASM raised serious ethical concerns about undermining "the physician-patient relationship and the trust necessary to sustain it, which alters the medical professions' role in society and endangers the values the American society places on life, especially on the life of disabled, incompetent, and vulnerable individuals."[6]

Additionally, making a suicidal choice is easy for people in acute emotional distress or mental confusion, but hard for mentally healthy people, as the following illustrates.

There is a Latin saying, "Where I am there is no death, and where is death there I am not." The psychological experience in physician-assisted death with dignity says the opposite "Where I am there is death, and where death is, there I am." The dread caused by choosing death is a daily encounter of those seeking physician assisted suicide. The fight between hope and desperation, courage and despondency, guilt and denial, becomes expressed in a protracted self-destructive, suicidal state of mind, a fight between the motives to live and motives to die. Truly sickness may cause life to seem utterly painful, hopeless, and meaningless. Under its pressure, the personalities of those seeking physician assisted suicide implode. One could say, paraphrasing Acts 5:4, that *counting themselves "unworthy of suffering" for the sake of God, their families, friends and neighbours induces in them a feeling of life "unworthy of living."*

Pastoral Considerations

(1) It is a commonality in professional and pastoral approaches to suicidal behavior to focus on the security of the people at risk. Healing is focused on decreasing motives for dying and increasing motives for living. In this context, healing all concurrent DSM-5 disorders and conditions, including relational, occupational, and vocational problems, as well as applying individual, group, and especially family therapy, are of importance. At this time, however, let us focus mostly on the unique pastoral purpose in preventing and healing sociality.

(2) The societal climate substantially influences suicidal behaviors. For example, listening to the Hungarian song "Gloomy Sunday," also known as the "Hungarian Suicide Song," induced massive numbers of suicides not only in Hungary but all around Europe and America after it was released in

1933. Finally, the song had to be prohibited from broadcast. Thus, pastoral healers' role in suicide prevention starts with sustaining a counter-suicidal mental climate, facilitating an optimistic, hopeful, and trusting social attitude. In this context, the Christian faith is the preventative factor *par excellence*.

(3) We noted a plurality of psychiatric-psychological explanations for suicidal behaviors. Could we also summarize these dynamics in a simple pastoral model?

Let us conceptualize the mental functioning of a suicidal person with an illustration. Suicidal individuals perceive pain, suffering, disappointments, financial disasters, unhealable sickness, and other troubles as a slap in the face from destiny. The first reaction of every subject would be to retaliate. For suicidal people, though, retaliating is impossible because the cause of their frustration (sickness, bankruptcy, a natural disaster, disappointment in love, loneliness, injustice, abuse, incurable sickness, personal mistakes, abandonment, death of a beloved person, loss of a job, financial catastrophe, or alcoholism) cannot be simply attacked, beaten or annihilated. When retaliation is unsuccessful, most people would then react with anger. But for those who are suicidal, anger expressed as depression, loneliness, poverty, addiction, or abuse appears day after day, repeating its painful attack and punishing them without giving them the possibility to escape from their frustration. And when anger is unproductive, a helpless rage emerges. Helpless rage against factors that cause unbearable suffering can be provoked by many different situations, but with one common characteristic: they cannot be rectified, healed, compensated for, or revenged. Humans can endure many feelings but not helpless rage. It is the most destructive emotion, causing the impression that it is better to die, to not exist at all, than to live in such unbearable misery. Because the conflict cannot be resolved by an explosion (aggressive acting out), implosion (introverted aggression) remains the only possible way to get rid of the tormenting, helpless rage. The imploding suicidal person will start fantasizing: "Life [other people, society, physicians, relatives, perpetrators, or even God] can slap me, hurt, and humiliate me, but I will kill myself and reveal that these perpetrators are guilty for my death, and they will never receive forgiveness but suffer incurable sorrow, guilt, and pain after my death!" As noted, helpless rage can be directed against a particular person or many people, society, culture, politics, imagined enemies, a company, physicians, destiny, reality, the human form of being, and even God. The reasons are many; the healing is one: helping suicidal people to biblically resolve and process their helpless rage.

(4) Simply instructing a suicidal person to forget, accept, or forgive the source of their distress may make their helpless rage even worse. It increases their guilt since they feel the need to process their emotions but are unable to do so. Instead, demonstrating empathy and compassion—that is, helping the individual to grasp that their assailants (if they are people) are more miserable than they and are deserving of pity helps with processing rage.

(5) Forgiveness may be fostered by the victim's recognition of his or her own contribution to the conflict. In an anecdotal story, a woman complains to her sister about her rage that was caused by a conflict with a milkmaid. The sister says, "You know, I think that the milkmaid was right," to which the woman responds, "Exactly. That is what's making me angry." Acknowledging one's own faults and genuine sorrow for one's own selfishness and abusive or aggressive behavior helps to resolve helpless rage.

(6) Even the best psychiatrists and theologians are unable to determine how much a particular suicide is the expression of a psychological disorder and how much is sinful behavior. We can, however, draw a deep truth from this anecdotal story about Father Pio.

> A desperate mother ran crying to Father Pio, saying, "Father, my son is now in hell. He committed suicide jumping from the bridge into the river." However, Father Pio answered in a calm voice, "Oh, do not worry. He repented ten times as he fell from the bridge into the river!"

In every suicidal person, the motive for living and dying is fighting. The suicidal person's discretional and appreciative judgment makes a fatal mistake when overwhelmed by helpless rage, and he chooses death. In my professional experience, however, all suicidal people change their minds and judgments in moments of total freedom when confronting self-imposed death, as the story implies.

(7) We have noted in previous chapters that the worst part of suffering is its perceived meaninglessness. It is hard to resolve helpless rage caused by stressors like invalidity, unhealable sickness, loss of a beloved spouse, financial catastrophe, or the perceived senselessness of suffering. In this context, it is beneficial to keep in mind the thoughts of concentration camp prisoner 119104, Viktor E. Frankl.

> Any attempt to restore a man's inner strength in the camp had first to succeed in showing him some future goal. Woe to him who saw no more sense in his life, no aim, no purpose, and therefore no point in carrying on. He was soon lost. The typical reply with which such a man rejected all encouraging arguments was "I have nothing to expect from life anymore." What sort of answer can one give to that?
>
> What was really needed was a fundamental change in our attitude towards life. We had to learn ourselves, and furthermore we had to teach the despairing man that it did not matter what we expected from life but rather what life expected from us. We need to stop asking about the meaning of life and instead think of ourselves as those who were being questioned by life—daily and hourly.[7]

The healing of suicidal people rests in discerning what life is asking from them.

(8) In answering patients' questions of what life is asking from them, we first recognize that, for postmodern disciples to whom it is relevant, "no servant is greater than his master" (Jn. 15:20). Realizing that, for Christians, unselfish and self-sacrificing suffering is a corollary of following Jesus changes one's attitude toward suffering. For example, Jesus' apostles were handed the greatest slap in the face by life, but their reaction to frustration, humiliation, abuse, pain, and persecution are reflected in the words of St. Peter.

> Beloved, do not be surprised at the fiery ordeal that is taking place among you, as though something strange were happening to you. But rejoice that

you participate in the sufferings of Christ, so that you may be overjoyed when his glory is revealed. If you are insulted because of the name of Christ, you are blessed, for the Spirit of glory and of God rests on you." (1 Pt. 4:13–14)

Pastoral healers' purpose is to facilitate a similar resilience in their patients.

(9) Accordingly, the main tool in Christian healing and prevention of suicide is what we call discipleship. As previously noted, discipleship enables one to become worthy of suffering. Those worthy of suffering are not raging helplessly because of injustices, pain, and suffering; rather, as Acts 5:41 describes, they grasp abuse, abandonment, loneliness, sickness, tragedies, and catastrophes as normal, expected, and unavoidable parts of their worldly pilgrimage. Identified with the abused and glorified Jesus, they are resilient (1 Peter 4:13–14). Resilience means the ability to bounce back, like a compressed spring. Those blessed with a biblical hope that supersedes desperation and enables them to process their helpless rage and forgive seven times seventy-seven times are resilient. In short, while helpless rage kills God in worldly people's hearts, in resilient disciples it deepens their union with Jesus.

(10) Faith, or surrendering to Jesus, is the panacea for healing all suicidal behaviors. No psychiatrist or psychologist, and no medical, psychotherapeutic, psychoanalytical, or cognitive behavioral treatment can imitate what genuine faith can do in preventing and healing suicidal behaviors. Jesus mentioned the power of faith 111 times in the four gospels. All of his references to belief put faith in the context of a deep, powerful, life-affirming context that superseded all worldly approaches. The world will only know and appreciate this fact if Christians bear witness to it.

(11) In general, the culture of death that Pope John Paul II spoke about is gradually penetrating Western culture and societies. The legalizing of euthanasia or physician-assisted suicide is a sideshow of this zeitgeist. We do not yet know how far this trend will escalate, but we know Christians' role in this moment of history: it is to glorify God, appreciating Francois Mauriac's well-known observation that "nothing is closer to man than God,

and nothing is stranger to man than living in a Godless world." Current dilemmas regarding euthanasia and physician-assisted suicide demonstrate the truth of the second part of Mauriac's statement. Factually, there is nothing stranger to humans than living an ultimately meaningless life, and hence the need for a dependence on an almighty, eternal, and ultimately loving deity. Christians therefore ought to demonstrate the truth of the first part of Mauriac's observation that such a world picture is not wishful thinking, but that for the one who lives in God's glory "neither death nor life, neither angels nor demons, neither the present nor the future, not any powers, neither heights nor depths, nor anything else in all creation will be able to separate us from the love of God that is in Jesus Christ our Lord" (Rom. 38–39).

(12) The principles noted in Chapter Twenty-seven, discussing end of life dilemmas, apply to the pastoral care of people considering physician assisted suicide. As noted, incurable and terminal illness may cause life to seem utterly painful and worthless. Therefore, providing hospice care, assisting dying people with adequate pain killers and other medication are of supreme importance. In this last but most important period of human life, only the granting of psychological-spiritual help has greater importance than pain management. In their transition from worldliness into eternity, terminally ill people need to be helped to discern a purpose. For some, it is the last opportunity to turn to Jesus. To others strongly connected to Jesus, witnessing their faith, optimism and courage to their loved ones and neighbors is the last, and probably most important act of love they can provide. Their confident trust, like that of St. Paul, for whom to live was Christ, and to die was a gain (Philippians 1:21), is the best proof that they are "worthy of suffering" (Acts 5:41). The family, relatives and friends may reciprocate that supreme act of love by making the dying person sure they are blessed, honoured and empowered by having such an exemplary forerunner on their own way toward Jesus. Dying becomes this way as noted, a solemn act mystically connecting existence and transcendence.

(13) The other contemporary phenomenon that is hard to define as more of a sickness or sin is that of so-called murder-suicide. In contrast to people of faith who seek peace, forgiveness, joy, empathy, mercy, and the

love of God's kingdom despite all injustices, inequities, and abuse, those unwilling or unable (because of organized manipulation, brainwashing, or coaching) to process and forgive real or imagined insults, humiliation, and frustrations experience intense anger and hatred. The pain and suffering caused by the experience that they or their loved ones have repeatedly been slapped in the face gradually escalate, reaching a level of almost insatiable, helpless rage. Such helpless rage forces them to metaphorically explode and implode at the same time. Their suicidal and homicidal revenge helps to decrease their helpless rage; it is the symbolic slapping back at the alleged perpetrator that gives a taste of triumph and, for people of certain religions, hope of their spoils in the afterlife. Since suicidal-homicidal behaviors are facilitated by an unbearable impulsivity, the struggle against them can be won only in the hearts, souls, consciences, and minds of the affected people. The tool is a Jesus-like approach to sin and sickness—conjoint building of the kingdom of Godly love, forgiveness, justice, peace, and joy, in which everyone has his or her place. Today, this may seem an unachievable dream, but nevertheless Jesus' commands given in Mark 12:29–31 force us to consider, strive, and work for it.

Notes

[1] Benjamin James Sadock, Virginia Alcott Sadock, and Pedro Ruiz, *Kaplan and Sadock's Synopsis of Psychiatry: Behavioral Sciences/Clinical Psychiatry*, 11th ed. (Philadelphia, PA: Wolters Kluwer, 2015), 763.

[2] Ibid., 764.

[3] Ibid., 765.

[4] Ibid., 867.

[5] Ibid., 868.

[6] Ibid., 1372.

[7] Maria Marshall and Edward Marshall, *Spiritual Psychotherapy: The Search for Lasting Meaning* (Canada, Ont.: Ottawa Institute of Logotherapy, 2015), 79–80.

CHAPTER THIRTY-ONE

SOME MEDICAL AND PASTORAL
ASPECTS OF WOMEN'S ISSUES

Despite increased social concern for women's psychological needs, their unique challenges are often disregarded. These include workplace bias, significant hormonal and emotional changes, menopause, and pregnancy, birth, and postabortion reactions. Discussing all of these problems at length is not possible given the broad scope of this book, so we will focus primarily on medical and psychological conditions for which pastoral healers' help may play a significant role.

We will not discuss in detail the divisive issue of women's spirituality. As Lindsay Jones accurately notes, "A disproportionate amount of research was devoted to the men and elite males who had shaped religions. Those aspects of religion that were singled out as characteristic, significant, and worthy of study were often male dominated, with females less prominent and portrayed as occupying inferior or only supporting roles."[1] On the other hand, as Marsha Wiggins Frame observes, "Many women feel totally comfortable and secure as members of established religions and spiritual paths and are not especially interested in the issues of gender and feminism. Moreover, some women vehemently oppose the feminist movement and its impact on traditional religious and spiritual practices."[2] On the topic of feminism, as always, we may follow Jesus' advice in Matthew 7:20 and use a conscientious judgment to discern the right tree by its good fruits. Accordingly, as far as particular aspects of feminist movements promote biblical justice, unselfishness, peace, joy, optimism, forgiveness, and courage—which can all be summed up as Christlike love—they are praised in the pastoral perspective. Every believer may consider assessing whether and how much, in their informed consciences, the adherence to ideas of feminist spirituality helps the fulfilment of Christ's main commands given in Mark12:28–31: "Love the Lord your God with all your heart and all your strength" and "Love your neighbour as yourself."

31.1 Postpartum Depression and Psychosis

Postpartum depression should be not confused with the so-called "baby blues." Depression is characterized by intense sadness, weight change, anxiety, and insomnia and generally starts within twelve weeks of giving birth, while baby blues are characterized by emotional fluctuations, anxiety, fearfulness, and insecurity appearing earlier, during the first four to six weeks after delivery. If depression is combined with confusion, restlessness, anxiety, suicidal and delusional ideas, agitation, and hallucinations (like voices commanding the mother to kill the baby or commit suicide), then postpartum psychosis should be suspected. Often, the disorder appears immediately after birth, but not later than eight weeks after delivery,[3] and its incidence and prevalence is greater in women who have a history of psychosis.

Pastoral Considerations

(1) Neither postpartum depression nor postpartum psychosis is a matter for a pastoral healer to treat on his or her own. Most often, depressive or psychotic features are relatively short-lasting but intensive and require a thorough professional, often requiring hospitalization. In the phase of recuperation, however, for committed people of faith, the pastoral healer's participation is of irreplaceable importance.

(2) In working with patients recovering from postpartum depression, the pastoral healer needs to be aware that there is significant emotional and cognitive stress in patients with residual symptoms often hidden below a

well-preserved personality facade since patients are still under enormous hormonal turmoil. Such patients need to be approached with a similar caution to those suffering from major depressive disorders. The early involvement of supportive husbands and family members is helpful.

(3) Although labour pains may appear to be at the limit of humanly endurable pain, they are physiological pains and, as such, are easily and quickly processed and then virtually forgotten. The mystery of participating in God's plans for new life allows mothers to discern new values, goals, and purposes that influence the whole of their future lives. The newborn baby provides them with a paramount new purpose to live for and extraordinary strength and courage, and experiencing child-rearing as a personal mission supports their self-valuation. Such a meaning-oriented attitude immediately after delivery helps in the prevention of mild depressive reactions and also of postpartum depression. The common experience of "We did it!" brings the family hope, joy, peace, cohesion, and optimism in trusting God and brings the opportunity to glorify God for his gift of being a mother.

(4) Severe postpartum depression and psychoses are symptomatic disorders in the sense that they are mental symptoms of biochemical disturbances in patients' brains and minds. Nevertheless, the misperception of the meaninglessness of their suffering is one of the significant facilitators of the distressing contents in the patients' self-reflections. Religious people, and also nonbelievers, recuperate more easily if, besides appropriate medication, they are helped to realize that their sufferings have a purpose. Therefore, the approaches pastoral healers may consider using in healing severe forms of postpartum disorders are similar to those discussed in healing major depression and psychoses.

(5) As in many other disorders, reintegration into the church community is very important in cases of believers' postpartum complications. An empathetic, celebratory response from the community is often as important as individual healing. Including recovered people in church activities helps them focus on the holy purpose of bringing up new members in the body of Christ.

31.2 Postabortion Psychological Reactions

In the United States, abortions have been legal since 1970. According to Kaplan and Sadock's textbook, approximately 246 abortions are performed in every 1,000 pregnancies. Abortions, however, decreased by 15 percent in the last ten years. Abortion has become a religious, political, and philosophical issue. The United States is now divided between the pro-choice and pro-life fractions. Some studies show that most women undergoing abortion "were satisfied with their decision, with few, if any, psychological repercussions" and that only "about ten percent of women who have an induced abortion regret the procedure."[4]

Research referenced by a pro-life organization, however, contradicts those results, showing that there is a significantly increased risk of psychological complaints in people who have abortions compared to those who give birth. The organization also reports the following.

> A 2010 study, which was published in the *Canadian Journal of Psychiatry* and examined a nationally representative sample of more than 3,000 women in the United States, found that women who underwent an abortion had an 89 percent increased risk of mental health disorders compared to women who did not have an abortion. Women who had abortions also had a 59 percent increased risk of suicidal thoughts, a 61 percent increased risk of mood disorders, a 61 percent increased risk of social anxiety disorders, a 261 percent increased risk of alcohol abuse, and a 280 percent increased risk of substance use disorder. Approximately 6 percent of suicidal ideation cases among women nationwide and 25 percent of cases of drug use could be related to abortion, the researchers found.[5]

Postabortion psychological reactions often start with temporary relief in that the intervention is over and the threat of the unwanted pregnancy has been resolved. Most people, after the abortion, attempt to return to their previous level of functioning as soon as possible. In cases of unwanted psychological reactions, however, PTSD-like numbness, involuntary and intrusive recollections, insomnia, and feelings of guilt appear. Other diverse symptoms may also appear, such as flashbacks and distress (when exposed to cues that resemble the abortion), increased anxiety, irritability, anger, insecurity, reactive depression, heavy alcohol and drug use, suicidal ideation, dissociative reactions, and psychotic reactions. Treatment of post-abortion reactions depends on the type and intensity of the reactions. In general, late-term and unwanted (spontaneous) abortions have more traumatic repercussions.

Pastoral Considerations

(1) Pastoral healing of postabortion reactions may start as soon the medical condition permits such help and depressive, autoaggressive, reactive, or other pathological contents of mind are under medical control.

(2) Based upon my own experience, it seems that the number of psychological reactions caused by abortions is higher in Christians than in atheists. However, healing in believers is more favourable.

(3) Using sacramental and nonsacramental tools like prayer, confession, charity, and attending liturgy may be a great help for believers dealing with the psychological consequences of abortion. Postabortion symptoms can often be understood as an internal sign of a need to change, and such change may mark the beginning of a new lifestyle of turning to God.

(4) An essential task of the pastoral healer, in cooperation with pastors, is easing patients' feelings of guilt. Unresolved guilt may activate the defence mechanisms of minimizing, suppressing, or even purposefully forgetting the abortion and acting as if nothing happened. Suppressed feelings of guilt regularly cause indefinable insecurity, angst, low self-esteem, and defensiveness, which are overcompensated for by a moral perfectionism. Persistent depression-like reactions are also present and, left untreated, they escalate into other psychiatric and psychological problems in many areas of functioning.

(5) Pastoral healing in the postabortion period ought to be focused on two fronts. One is healing the specific postabortion symptoms (like guilt, regret, self-accusation, grief, anger, irritability, anxiety, and insomnia), and the other is healing unspecific symptoms (like alcohol and drug use,

depression, suicidal ideation, and dissociative or psychotic reactions). The treatment of postabortion psychiatric complications in believers involves teamwork. A pastor ought to work alongside a professional.

(6) After having an abortion, believers often suffer silently; they do not want to reveal or talk about their pain. They should be encouraged to do just that, though. Talking about and repeatedly reliving their traumatic experience may be painful, but it will help them find answers to their problems and process their painful memories. It may help some people to express their suffering through drawing or painting, while others may write essays, newspaper articles, or even books about their distressing experiences.

(7) Joining in the church community's social activities, participating in the pro-life movement, and helping others fighting with similar problems may substantially help patients ease their psychological pains. Volunteering in humanitarian institutions may lessen their feelings of guilt.

(8) The pillars of the Christian faith include not only culpability but also forgiveness. It may help believing patients to remember that Jesus is an ultimately just judge (knowing the causes of a behavior) and also an ultimately merciful judge (abundantly blessing repentant sinners). As Jesus himself said, "Her sins, which were many, were forgiven; hence she has shown great love" (Luke 7:47). Indeed, even sinful behavior can be used by God to strengthen the faith of the recuperating sinner.

(9) Christ-centred group therapy may help to break the withdrawal, guilt, introversion, depression, psychological numbness, and isolation of people suffering from postabortion psychological symptoms. Groups ought to be homogenous, comprised of people suffering the same distressing traumatic experience and using the same medicine for healing—that of faith. As with some other disorders, group treatment is efficient for treating postabortion reactions through its provision of compassion, support, hope, optimism, and trust for recovery that no individual professional or pastor, only the people of God as a community, can give.

Notes

[1] Lindsay Jones (ed.), *Encyclopedia of Religion*, vol. 14 (Farmington Hills, MI: Thomson Gale, 2005), 9786.

[2] Marsha Wiggins Frame, *Integrating Religion and Spirituality in Counseling: A Comprehensive Approach* (Pacific Grove, CA: Thomson/Brooks/Cole, 2003), 240.

[3] Benjamin James Sadock, Virginia Alcott Sadock, and Pedro Ruiz, *Kaplan and Sadock's Synopsis of Psychiatry: Behavioral Sciences/Clinical Psychiatry*, 11th ed. (Philadelphia, PA: Wolters Kluwer, 2015), 839.

[4] Ibid., 836.

[5] N. P. Mota, M. Burnett, and J. Sareen, "Associations Between Abortion, Mental Disorders and Suicidal Behavior in a Nationally Representative Sample," *The Canadian Journal of Psychiatry* 55 (4): 239–46.

PART FOUR

PERSONALITY TRAITS CORRELATING TO SPECIFIC FAITH PROBLEMS AND THEIR PASTORAL TREATMENT

All Christians have certain personal, "neither sick nor healthy" behavioral patterns. These are not disorders listed in the DSM-5 but are a peculiar compromise in a virtual "continuity between health and disorder."[1] All, however, have one commonality: they always jeopardize a believers' peace of mind and union with Christ in a unique way. So for Christians suffering of scruples, it is easier to acknowledge sins than distressing mental problems. They seek healing for their underlying psychological issues by atoning for nonexisting sins. On the contrary, people suffering of moral laxity, idolatry, positivism, or hypocrisy attempt to justify their estrangement from God under the pretext of psychological or philosophical claims.

How can pastoral healers help such "neither sick nor healthy" people of God?

It is important to acknowledge sin as a real problem and not to "pathologize," i.e., not to assume that a particular faith problem is due to a mental ailment. It is well known that on psychological tests (like the MMPI), sometimes a healthy person can show tendencies toward a psychiatric disorder. For example, they may show depressed, paranoid, or antisocial personality traits. However, healthy individuals are able to suppress, resist, or correct their undesirable tendencies; their Christian conscience is able to direct their Christian behavior patterns. On the other hand, it is equally important to address underlying psychological issues, which may spoil one's relationship with God. Probably it is the most common experience for all Christians that despite the fact that they may pray fervently for holiness, they do not always succeed; they may feel estranged from Jesus, are impatient, frustrated, aggressive, selfish, or jealous despite their best efforts. In such cases, undesired behaviors are often connected not only to sinful motives, but also to psychological problems. Their pastoral healing is focused on helping Christians to continuously pray and use their personal freedom and responsibility to become the master of their instinct and a servant of their conscience. If these pastoral efforts are futile, professional support such as Christian psychotherapy and less frequently, medical treatment, may be needed.

CHAPTER THIRTY-TWO

SCRUPULOUS BELIEVERS

S crupulous believers are easy to recognize. They tirelessly accuse themselves of committing new, grotesque, bizarre-sounding, and often irrational sins that persist or even gradually worsen despite countless confessions. Their overvalued ideas of guilt are most often resistant to any logical, biblical, or moral-theological reasoning or consolation, and they do not trust their Jesus-like loving and forgiving Christian consciences but are enslaved by their superego's irrational accusations. Scrupulous believers are therefore not concerned with genuine perfection but with an *image* of perfection, and not with love but law, striving for worldly perfection rather than genuine holiness. They are obedient to a legalistic "internal inhibitor," an internal punisher instead of a Christian conscience that acts as an internal stimulator in discipleship. In these people's behaviors, there is a plethora of religion but a lack of faith. They fear God instead of trusting in his infinite justice and mercy; they seek proof instead of practicing biblical trust. They spend a lot of time in counterproductive self-analysis, making judgments of themselves based on a worldly perspective instead of God's standpoint of love and forgiveness, which defeats them and makes their often pharisaic, overvalued need for perfection unachievable. Such a dynamic is a no-win battle. The more guilt the superego lays on a scrupulous believer's self, the more threat and fear his self projects on his allegedly immoral and sinful lifestyle. For this reason, the prognosis of scrupulousness is unpredictable.

With the passing of time, a self-healing may occur. When it does, it is usually after the scrupulous person comes to appreciate that he is, despite everything, a lovable person, which can be proven by a functional Christian marriage, for example. At other times, though, scrupulousness becomes a form of living with periodic ups and downs. In the worst cases, scrupulousness evolves toward the opposite extreme: moral laxity.

Pastoral Considerations

(1) The rational and irrational self-accusations of scrupulous people ought to be taken seriously, and their feelings of guilt should never be simply proclaimed as invalid. The subject ought to feel and know that sin is a reality for the pastoral healer and that he is not minimizing it. Giving such people biblical and theological assurance about the irrational character of their self-accusations from a strict, rigorist perspective has a greater impact than doing so from a liberal one.

If, however, the scrupulous resistance is significant, pastoral healing should be focused not on futile, counterproductive attempts to logically prove the irrational character of the patient's self-accusations, but on discerning and resolving the real, often subconscious reasons for his distress.

(2) Pastoral healers may seek a single, genuine, but unacknowledged (and unconfessed) sin hidden behind all of the patient's repeatedly confessed irrational sins. Suppressed or denied sin cannot be simply blotted out or made nonexistent, as though it never happened, so people who preventively punish themselves for meaningless occurrences may be unconsciously punishing themselves for suppressed but real transgressions of God's law of love. The following example demonstrates this.

> A forty-seven-year-old male suffered from a plurality of reoccurring bizarre self-accusations, such as revealing the confessional secrets of saints unknown to him. During pastoral healing, however, he gradually recalled driving his car at around fifty miles per hour in area limited to twenty-five when an older lady crossing the street just barely escaped being hit by him. He then drove even faster to leave the scene. A few miles later, he hit a sick

bird that was unable to fly. This time he stopped and cried out, "What have I done? I ran over this poor raven." Only after acknowledging his reckless driving and apologizing to the frightened old lady did his scruples disappear. In some cases, such a detective-like investigation may bear fruit.

(3) As noted, sin and sickness are objective categories. However, the human perception of them is often subjective. This happens if the Christian conscience is overruled by too strict or too lax forms of conscience-like structures (like the superego or the internal inhibitor), as in scrupulous people. A worldly conscience in Western culture tends to reflect one's father (though increasingly so, one's mother), while the Christian conscience reflects the ideal Father figure—God. A crucial task in the pastoral healing of scrupulous people is abolishing the internal policeman-like father or mother image. Initially, there is often an intense resistance by the patient to acknowledge any imperfection in his ambivalent identification with an overly-strict parental image. The process of dethroning the authority figure, however, evokes an intense emotional reaction called catharsis. Catharsis helps patients forgive themselves and grab on to the ideal, all-forgiving, and loving Father figure; it gives uplifting peace and hope, which were previously unachievable for scrupulous people.

(4) The next step in healing is to practice the gained insights, sharply distinguishing between the superego's dictate, manifested in the form of irrational guilt, and the Christian conscience's standards. Scrupulous people may be trained to meticulously differentiate between the two by analysing their own behaviors daily or as often as the healer deems necessary, across a short period of time or over an entire lifetime. They are coached to be able to pinpoint that "this interpretation is an irrational self-accusation" (i.e., a sick behavior) and "that interpretation is a rational self-accusation" (i.e., a genuinely sinful behavior). In doing so, the scrupulous person may be surprised by how many of their perceived sins are irrational and how few are genuine.

(5) Behavioral methods can be used to further empower self-distancing from scrupulous self-accusations in people already differentiating irrational from rational sins. Self-distancing, as Marshall and Marshall formulate it, is

an "ability to distance ourselves in spirit from our current circumstances."[2] In scrupulous people it means trying to observe themselves from God's perspective rather than that of a policeman. Perceiving themselves as the objects of God's unconditional love is the ultimate form of self-distancing from irrational self-criticism; it helps them to achieve what they previously fought for unsuccessfully: closeness to Jesus in holiness. Holiness, in this case, means being set apart from the world's superego conscience and identifying with a loving, forgiving, and easygoing Christian conscience.

(6) Another spiritual-behavioral approach is paradoxical intention. Barlow describes, "With this strategy the therapist presents a proportional statement that is an extreme version of the clients' own dysfunctional beliefs, and then plays the role of Devil's advocate to counter the clients' attempts to disprove the extreme statement or rule."[3] The pastoral healer exaggerates the scrupulous self-accusations to absurdity and initiates a psychological reaction comparable to the immune reaction of the body. In the example Marshall and Marshall give, the client may state, "It would be better for sinful people like me not to be at all," to which therapist can reply, "If this is true for you, it must be true for all sinners, so then it would be better if even people who commit the smallest sins never existed."[4] Such a paradoxical approach may help scrupulous people come to see elements of value in themselves despite their real or invented imperfections. Feeling and knowing that they are the temples of the Holy Spirit, the greatest of all believers' qualities, stimulates them to act in biblical hope, trust, and joy, which is the best medicine against scrupulous self-harassment.

(7) Improvement in scrupulous behavior can be sustained through repeated self-awareness: "I must not unconditionally submit myself to my judgmental superego. I can rebel against it!" A patient can use humour, make light of or ridicule self-accusations, or intentionally behave imperfectly by making small and meaningless mistakes that nobody can see but them. Such actions demonstrate the power of the self over the superego and the freedom from scruples in Jesus-like living.

One of my theology instructors always had loose shoelaces. One day it would be the laces of his right shoe, the next his left. In a private conversation, he revealed the reason for this. Through this intentional, self-imposed imperfection, he was rebelling against his need for perfection and demonstrating to himself that "I am the stronger one. I can resist my superego." Meaningless, inconspicuous, intentional disobedience to the commands of the strict internal policeman may give substantial freedom to people suffering from scruples.

(8) Scrupulousness has some commonalities with OCD and hypochondria, as well as borderline and histrionic behaviors. If these concurrent disorders appear to seriously hinder the healing of scruples, consultation with a professional therapist may be necessary. Because suffering of scruples is a delicate faith problem, it would be important to choose a sensitive and well-grounded Christian professional.

(9) Scrupulousness may be a collective issue as well as an individual issue. Just as the seasons change between summer and winter, so the whole of human culture swings between extreme periods of scrupulousness and moral laxity. Usually these changes are slow and gradual, but they may also occur suddenly on a large scale, almost as an explosion.

After the decline of the Scholasticism of the Middle Ages, the Renaissance was characterized by moral laxity. Initially, the powerful city-state of Florence, and successively the whole of Italy and gradually Europe, was engulfed with a new kind of spirituality that glorified sensuality, luxury, pomp, power, greed, and even cruelty while maintaining the image of morality. However, in the Lenten season of 1495, the Dominican Friar Girolamo Savonarola started preaching at the San Marco church in Florence about Judgment Day. Anxious crowds listened, mesmerized by his apocalyptic warnings. A mortifying horror of the oncoming Judgment Day spread like brushfire among the population. So, as Erdody notes, luxurious, artistic, and beautiful things, among them erotic clothes, refined food, expensive wine, toys, jewellery, board games, dice, perfumes, playing cards, paintings, books, and fashionable wigs were thrown into a communal bonfire in a ritual frenzy of destruction. Interestingly, Savonarola's most committed followers were children between six and sixteen years of age, called "the friar's kids." In large crowds they harassed citizens, seeking and then investigating, judging, condemning, and destroying on the spot everything they found to be ethically inappropriate, frivolous, or superfluous.[5] This frenzy ended in

1498 when Savonarola was tortured into admitting his cooperation with the devil, after which he was burned to death. A few months after Savonarola's demise, what often happens in scrupulous individuals happened to the population collectively: the mental climate quickly turned in the opposite direction; lavishness euphorically and exponentially returned to Florentine streets.

(10) In social and political jargon, the oscillations between scrupulousness and moral laxity are classified as the ongoing rivalry between conservatism and liberalism. Christian purpose is, however, neither conservative nor liberal, but rather a persistent, unselfish, biblical, and Church-oriented building of the kingdom of God. Accordingly, most Christians are conservative in some aspects of public life and liberal in others.

Notes

[1] David H. Barlow (ed.), *Clinical Handbook of Psychological Disorders: A Step-by-Step Treatment Manual* (New York: The Guilford Press, 2008), 371.

[2] Maria Marshall and Edward Marshall, *Spiritual Psychotherapy: The Search for Lasting Meaning* (Canada, Ont.: Ottawa Institute of Logotherapy, 2015), 82.

[3] Barlow, *Clinical Handbook of Psychological Disorders*, 391.

[4] Marschal and Marschal, 82

[5] Janos Erdody, *Requiem Firenzeert* 9 (Budapest: Szepmuveszeti Kiado, 1977), 139–41. See also Paul Ungar, *Flawed Institution—Flawless Church: A Response to Pope John Paul's Appeal for a Critical Self-Evaluation of the Church* (Newcastle Upon Tyne: Cambridge Scholars Publishing, 2013), 97–8.

CHAPTER THIRTY-THREE

MORALLY LAX BELIEVERS

Benedict Groeschel writes, "Spiritual development relates primarily to persons' willingness to respond openly to God, and an equal willingness to embrace truth, at least as one knows it."[1] In making these decisions, the human self is autonomous. It not only has the freedom to choose loyalty to instinct or a strict, rigid conscience, but also to choose between obeying the superego or the Christian conscience. Morally lax believers seek the ultimate truth of Jesus Christ but interpret their Christian consciences as able to compromise or sympathize with the dark sides of their personalities (i.e., their instincts).

Lax believers, like all other people, have synderesis, which in Scholastic terminology is the aspect of the conscience that requires them to do good. Their laxity, however, affects the other aspect of conscience that Aquinas called *conscientia*, which has the task to discern what is morally good and appropriate in a particular situation. As he describes in *Summa Theologiae* 1.79.12–13, "*Conscientia* is a witness, it says what we have done or not done, it binds or motivates: it says what we should or should not do. Finally, it excuses or accuses: it tells us whether what we have done was well or not well done."[2] This aspect of the conscience is fallible in every one of us. Lax believers noncritically reconcile their *conscientia* and its witnessing with the instinct's demands.

Respectively, behaviorally lax believers are virtually the flipside of scrupulous believers. While scrupulous people are enslaved by a strict super-ego, the lax believer's self is overly sympathetic with hedonism, instinctual egotism, and selfishness. Consequently, unlike scrupulous believers who experience a great deal of irrational guilt, lax believers mitigate or deny many sins. They are students of Protagoras (490–420 BC) who, some 400 years after the story of Adam and Eve's fall was written, proclaimed, "Man is the measure of all things, of existing that they exist, and not-existing that they do not exist." Behaviorally, despite being committed to God, lax believers sometimes critically challenge the crucial points of biblical and Church teachings, striving for holiness but proclaiming worldliness in the name of freedom and empathy. Often they are educated in religious matters, have significant theological, historical, or philosophical knowledge, and integrate true, half-true, and untrue ideas into a self-made and often controversial moral context. (People who proclaim themselves to be "spiritual but not religious" often fall into this category.) There is a permanently reoccurring error in their judgment motivated by a defensive denial of guilt or sin of any kind. While scrupulous believers' mentality sometimes tends to evolve toward laxity, lax believers' psychological functioning often evolves toward positivism or agnosticism.

Pastoral Considerations

(1) As noted, religious laxity is the opposite of scrupulousness. Nevertheless, there is a parallel between the two: both personality traits include prominent feelings of guilt. But while scrupulous people consciously perceive themselves as unhealable sinners, lax believers only subconsciously feel this way. They defend themselves from feelings of guilt by denying them. Thus, they are apathetic only on the surface, and they fear God unconsciously, almost like scrupulous believers. On the other hand, lax, compromising attitudes to narcissism, hedonism, and egotism unavoidably cause patients frustration in dealing with not only the spiritual but also the biological, social, and psychological realities of life constituting the elemental forces of reality that Rothschild talks about (Ch. 3). Lax believers are consequently often rebellious and irritable even when they are not

being challenged, and they strive to liberate themselves and others from an alleged plurality of occupational, vocational, relational, and familial oppression. Paradoxically, the greater their internally-suppressed insecurity, angst, frustration, anger, and hate, the more vehement their rebellion against the Church and God, which in their eyes epitomize an alleged repressive and unjust society. The best initial approach of the pastoral healers to such accusations is not a futile reaction by discussing or arguing, but listening in a tolerant and encouraging manner.

(2) Groeschel explains morally lax individuals by saying, "In order to avoid direct confrontation with the Gospel, those who think of themselves as practicing Christians, when faced with a conflict between self-fulfilment and the higher order of Christian values, will generally adopt the rationalization: 'I can't do it.' It sounds better then saying 'I won't do it.'"[3] However, being lax in faith excludes them from receiving biblical gifts and erodes their genuine closeness to the biblical God. Before any healing starts, this condition needs to be countered by a pastoral approach that is nonjudgmental and characterized by Christlike inclusivity that demonstrates to patients that they are fully-appreciated members of the body of Christ.

(3) In this context, even the patients' often irrational criticisms of the Church or its ethical teachings ought to be taken respectfully. Their overemphasis on God's mercy and desire to receive his forgiveness effortlessly without being a disciple ought not to be proclaimed *ex cathedra* invalid. The same is true of their hedonism and indirect adherence to the Renaissance motto: "On the Judgment Day, you will have to justify all the pleasures you missed enjoying in your life." Only when an alliance of mutual trust between the patient and therapist is established may the focus shift to the essential pastoral topics addressing laxity. Before we discuss that, though, let us focus on one more "do not do" in the pastoral approach to lax believers.

(4) Exposing patients to challenging biblical teachings without appropriate explanation may be counterproductive. For example, radical exposure to the advantages of obeying the constitution of Jesus' kingdom, given in Matthew 5:1–12 (known as Jesus' eight blessings), may increase resistance rather than help the individual properly process biblical information. Accordingly, pastoral healers need to initially provide lax clients not with

arguments but with reasons of the heart in order to soften their ambivalent attitude toward faith.

(5) The rebelliousness of lax believers' attitudes often conspicuously resembles adolescents' behaviors. Lax believers, like adolescents, are confronted with the hard choice between two mutually exclusive options: being the master of conscience and servant of instinct, or being the master of instinct and servant of conscience. They are also in a position where they are called to appreciate a Christlike behavioral dichotomy of humility and modesty in a self-confident, powerful, meaning-oriented, and unselfish lifestyle, which is a significant part of adolescence. For lax believers, only committed discipleship may facilitate being worthy of suffering and, in turn, psychological-spiritual resilience. However, like adolescents, lax believers are divided within themselves between preferring worldliness and holiness. That internal division causes defensiveness, vulnerability, and pessimistic defeatism. As with most adolescents, lax believers' healing centres on encouragement, not criticism; it aims to equip their personalities with the courage to live St. Paul's maxim: "Whenever I am weak, I am strong" (2. Cor. 12:10).

(6) Moral laxity most often stands on three legs. The first is substantiated by adverse childhood, family, and relational experiences (a lack of unselfish love, commitment, peace, joy, care, and attachment in marriage) and is reinforced by the second leg, the *Zeitgeist* of socially-accepted egotism and selfishness. Pastoral healers may address both by helping lax believers realize that their lax giving of love facilitates their lax receiving of love from the allegedly lax-loving entities in their lives: the Church, their families, and society. The third leg may be supported by traces of hypomanic, manic, borderline, narcissistic, histrionic, or antisocial personality traits. These personality features often remain suppressed and therefore unrecognizable in daily functioning. However, they may surface in challenging situations (like moral discussions) and take control of one's behaviors. As long as moral laxity does not significantly impair social functioning, pastoral interventions are usually helpful. On the other hand, when distress is prominent, a Christian professional should be involved in the healing team.

(7) Sufferings caused by living in a lax-loving world may help believers

unmask the false social idols of non-Christian lifestyles and turn to Jesus. Thus, examining such suffering and noting how it illuminates the superiority of the Jesus-like love, unselfishness, mercy, and grace that lax believers are attracted to is the focus in healing moral laxity. In other words, healing is geared toward bringing patients to emotionally and intellectually grasp that disrespecting Jesus' main commandments of Mark 12:29–3 is the cause of most frustrations that they and the lax world are suffering from. This recognition propels them toward discipleship.

(8) Progress in the pastoral healing of lax believers is marked by their courage to talk about their denied or suppressed (often irrational) feelings of guilt and their learned helplessness in fighting Adam and Eve's poisonous inheritance. When this emerges, the pastoral healer needs to be genuinely Christlike in not excusing the sins away but taking into account the contributing circumstances, mitigating factors, and sickness-facilitating sinful behaviors. As patients put forth effort to follow Christ, they find that the spiritual gains they receive from doing so greatly supersede all the pains of discipleship. This is usually the turning point at which laxity starts moving in a biblical direction.

(9) Lax believers progress in their healing similarly to scrupulous believers. They may be coached in routinely analysing their experiences, thoughts, and behaviors, pinpointing adverse psychological-spiritual effects of laxity in their lives and the lives of their loved ones. Such self-scrutiny may have a supremely meaningful effect. While religious laxity in general is a form of philosophical self-justification compensating for the lost spiritual gifts of genuine discipleship, the kind of critical self-assessment we are talking about helps revive biblical optimism, courage, and enthusiasm about being one with Jesus. It is an experience similar to what the prodigal son (Luke 15:11–30) likely experienced after returning to his father.

(10) A wide range of sacramental and nonsacramental activities, including prayer, liturgy, reconciliation, evangelization, and healing ministry are certainly helpful in resolving conscious or suppressed problems of low self-esteem, religious hopelessness and disillusionment, and feelings of guilt, which, as noted, are the primary motors of rebellious moral laxity. Confession has a paramount role among all other sacraments in this process

since it assists the patient in scrutinizing behaviors not only from a self-centred standpoint but also from a God-centred one. In deciding to build the kingdom of God more biblically and self-critically, lax believers often evolve into committed believers. The energy they once invested in fighting and suppressing feelings of guilt converts into zealous activity as they realize that what they previously despised, Christlike living, was what they truly desired all along.

Notes

[1] Benedict J. Groeshel, "For Those Who Seek Spiritual Passages, The Spirituality of Spiritual Development" (New York NY: Crossroad) 94

[2] Lindsay Jones (ed.), *Encyclopedia of Religion*, vol. 14 (Farmington Hills, MI: Thomson Gale, 2005), 2958–9.

[3] Benedict Groeschel, 94

CHAPTER THIRTY-FOUR

Superstitious Believers

Superstitious behavior is almost as old as history itself. Our Stone Age (Palaeolithic) ancestors who lived some 200,000 years ago in the security of deep caves enacted magic rituals, and by misunderstanding cause and effect principles they gained the false impression that magical rituals are effective in controlling worldly events. As Arnold Hauzer notes, our ancestors had limited verbal communication. However, they had to hunt, which greatly benefited from organized planning. By performing the planned hunt in front of images of animals painted on cave walls, hunters could better coordinate and grasp their roles in hunting. When hunts were successful, they believed this was due to their performance rituals rather than their synchronized action. So the belief that enacting or role playing could influence real events was born. With the repetition of these magical rituals through hundreds of millennia, they became so deeply wired in the human brain that even twenty-first century people regress and use ritual curses and swearwords, such as when experiencing road rage, to attempt to magically hurt their enemies.

In the Neolithic Period, around 40,000 years ago, our ancestors became agriculturists. They realized that their survival depended on powers greater than humans and conceived of gods and spirits directing conditions of nature, such as storms, fertility, and the sun. They constructed a two-world picture: the invisible upper world of gods, spirits, and half-gods, and the sensorial lower world inhabited by humans. The mythical beings from the upper world were the masters of famine and prosperity, health and sickness, and life and death. Sicknesses were seen as spiritual matters, so expelling demons by magic or animistic exorcisms and bribing the humanlike corrupt, greedy, and jealous gods and spirits with sacrifices were accepted healing methods among most Near East nations.[1] Despite Scriptural warnings against sorcery, divination, and magical spells (Deuteronomy 18:9–12 and Isaiah 47:12–15), the tradition flourished through the Middle Ages and persists in contemporary astrologists and fortune tellers.

The trend continues today with the growing popularity of so-called earth religions such as Wicca or other cults that profess to worship Gaia, or Mother Earth. The roots of such beliefs can be traced back thousands of years to agrarian civilizations that linked the yearly harvest to deities of the land, sky, sun, and rain. In the nineteenth century, similar pantheistic beliefs were held by Transcendentalists such as Ralph Waldo Emerson. In today's post-Christian world, these beliefs have gained new converts in large part thanks to the New Age movement.

Today we also observe superstitious behavior in the form of three extrasensory perceptions that are not explicit hallucinations, illusions, figments of the imagination, or superstitions, but a mixture of all four: telepathy, clairvoyance, and precognition. Telepathy involves transmitting thoughts from one subject to another without the use of the usual channels of communication. Clairvoyance refers to an awareness of extrasensory information not accessible to other people. And precognition is predicting an event that has not yet occurred.[2] Such phenomena occur when the appreciation of reality is blurred (as in schizophrenia, dissociative disorders, alcohol and drug use disorders, and narcissistic, borderline, and histrionic personality disorders). They also appear as the consequences of indoctrination, suggestion, and intensive imagining and may appear quite accidentally by simply guessing.

Superstition of a special kind, called paganism, may appear in quite cogently functioning institutions. As Noonan and Feaster report, an article in January 2010 announced that since the Air Force had been previously accused of allowing evangelical officers to openly propagate their faith, "in 2005 the Air Force issued new guidelines pledging to accommodate free exercise of pagan religion and other personal beliefs."[3] While, despite all distortions, the civilised way of living is based on biblical principles of freedom, compassion, love, solidarity, peace, brotherhood, and equality, Stone Age paganism reflects a precivilised mentality. Returning to it (instead progressing toward completing God's kingdom) seems, from a Christian perspective, regressive and counterproductive.

Before addressing the question that naturally follows from this discussion—why evangelization is not a superstitious or false belief while paganism is—let us answer another obvious question: Why do twenty-first century people regress to prehistoric, prelogical, childlike, or pagan, superstitious reasoning?

The immediate answer is that, as we have already established, neurological-psychological traces of ancient experiences still exist even in postmodern people's brains. The brain's functions are hierarchically structured like the layers of an onion. The more recently-developed and most complex cortical centres, which produce abstract and logical ideas, are the most vulnerable. Trauma, stress, frustration, disappointment, fear, or pain may cause a functional disintegration of rational reasoning and a regression to primitive, archaic patterns entrenched through hundreds of thousands of years of prehistory. Summarizing Carl Jung's book *The Man and His Symbols*, we could say that the ideas of past generations are present in modern people's minds. Metaphorically, in every one of us, besides a postmodern person there also exists an Enlightenment philosopher, a Middle Age Scholastic, an Old Testament Pharisee, a younger Stone Age animist, and an older Stone Age magical thinker.[4] Superstitious people regress to precivilized and prelogical forms of reasoning aimed at becoming Godlike, actualizing behavior similar to Adam and Eve's that attempted to be "like God, knowing good and evil" (Gen. 3:5), which is appealing to every human being.

Pastoral Considerations

(1) Superstitious reasoning often appears in persons suffering from the following: anxiety; dissociative, schizoid, schizotypal, borderline, narcissistic, and histrionic personality disorders; and alcohol and drug abuse.

These conditions, as well as the irrational and superstitious thinking often resulting from them, are almost impossible to logically correct, so there is nothing more irrational than trying to address overvalued superstitious ideas with rational arguments.

For example, the extremely narcissistic Roman emperor Caligula was attached to his horses, so much so that he ordered his favoured horse to be brought into the Roman Senate and proclaimed a senator. Despite the horse's obvious inability to perform as a senator, the emperor simply could not give up his nonpsychotic (but overvalued) belief. As we will discuss later, preserving beliefs, regardless of whether they are true or false, is often more important to humans than preserving life itself. This is especially true for superstitious beliefs. Respectively, we need a different approach to healing than directly countering superstitions with logic or reasoning.

(2) If psychiatric disorders (psychotic or nonpsychotic) are behind superstitious believers' delusional or overvalued ideas of occult powers, those should, of course, be addressed before pastoral healing starts.

(3) When it comes to understanding healthy believers' overvalued superstitious ideas, the first important consideration is that faith, contrary to self-deception, imagination, or wishful thinking, is a radical choice. It is a choice, as we have said many times now, to be "in the world but not of it" (Jn. 17:11; 17:17). Without making that choice, nobody can know God or receive the gifts of faith. Superstitious people, though, are attempting to take a shortcut; they want to establish communication with and gain the support of the "upper world" without becoming a disciple.

(4) Superstition is the strength of the weak. It receives its life from powerlessness, pessimism, anxiety, hopelessness, frustration, insecurity, angst, and fear. To people feeling weak, powerless, or unworthy, inciting the help of the "upper world" seems to be a chance to rule the "lower world." Pastoral healing therefore consists of empowering such patients to resolve their feelings of powerlessness, fear, and desperation by dealing with social, occupational, vocational, and familial matters, which facilitates their personal integrity and resolves the self-perceived weak points in their psychological functioning.

(5) Pastoral healing gives superstitious people what no professional

healing is able to: biblical courage, hope, and optimism. In Philippians 4:4–6, St. Paul alludes to this as he boldly charges us to "Rejoice in the Lord always. I will say again: Rejoice! Let your gentleness be evident to all. The Lord is near. Do not be anxious about anything, but in everything, by prayer and petition, with thanksgiving, present your requests to God." These verses demonstrate the power of faith. Genuine healing is assistance in progressing from superstition to discipleship.

(6) Superstitious believers, despite being Christians, are seeking an unknown God, like the Greeks in Acts 17:23. When they genuinely find Jesus, whom they were always looking for, they realize that their superstitions were promising everything but giving nothing, and they often rapidly switch from superstition to discipleship.

(7) As Lindsay Jones notes, "Voltaire's *Philosophical Dictionary* asserts that superstition was born in paganism, adopted by Judaism and infested the Christian Church from the beginning."[5] Let us, to address the reasoning of atheists and agnostics like Voltaire, briefly summarize the main differences between superstition and faith.

- Faith requires discipleship, while superstition requires no life changes.
- Faith requires holiness, while superstition serves worldliness.
- Faith serves what the Greek Bible calls *zoe* (everlasting life with God), while superstition serves *bios* (worldly futilities).
- The gifts of faith are invisibly and internally experienced, while the alleged gains from superstition are external and visible, touchable, and measurable.
- Faith gives spiritual gifts (like biblical hope, trust, peace, love, and joy), while superstition is focused on gaining worldly treasures (good luck, health, fortune, power, and protection from calamities).
- Faith makes one worthy of suffering (Acts 5:41), while superstition aims at avoiding suffering.
- Faith gives what it promises (spiritual gifts), while superstition does not give what it promises (worldly advantages).

The final point is the greatest distinction between faith and superstition. Pastoral healers may echo the saying, "You can be disappointed in everything except in God" because the biblical God gives everything he promises. Precisely because God gives what he promises, faith is not self-deception but a realistic understanding of the world and its operations.

(8) There is no such thing as a perfect disciple. Despite every one of us perceiving our theology as perfect, we all have faults when it comes to knowing God. For superstitious Christians, their actual spiritual position is vitally important: steadily-deepening union with Jesus as the best antidote to superstition.

Notes

[1] Arnold Hauzer, *Socijalna Istorija Umetnosti I Knjizevnosti* (Belgrade: Kultura, 1966), 9.

[2] Harold W. Faw, *Psychology in a Christian Perspective, an Analysis of Key Issues* (Grand Rapids, MI: Baker Books, 1995), 45.

[3] Moira Noonan and Anne Feaster, *Spiritual Dceptions in the Church and the Culture, A Comprehensive Guide to Discernment*, (Niagara Falls, NY, USA and Station U, Toronto, Canada, 2015), 196

[4] Carl Gustav Jung, *Man and His Symbols* (New York: Bantam, 1968).

[5] Lindsay Jones (ed.), *Encyclopedia of Religion*, vol. 5 (Farmington Hills, MI: Thomson Gale, 2005), 8866.

CHAPTER THIRTY-FIVE

BELIEVERS WHO SEEK MIRACLES

Each of the Four Evangelists records Jesus' miracles. However, biblical authors understood miracles very differently than people like self-proclaimed psychic Uri Geller. Likewise, they did not regard as miracles the harvesting of health, wealth, prosperity, and success of every kind like televangelist Peter Popoff. Therefore, let us first clarify what kind of miracles Jesus really performed and what the Scriptures understand as miracles in contrast to the grandiose, theatrical, or astonishing shows that miracle-seeking believers expect.

In Jesus' time, there were miracle workers, illusionists, and magicians at every great holiday celebration in Palestinian cities. They could surprise their naive public with inexplicable "supernatural" performances, but no one was ever judged and punished for such displays. Jesus, however, was, so apparently his miracles conveyed a different meaning. The distinctive characteristic of Jesus' miracles was not their inexplicability but that they were signs of God's presence in the person of Jesus, signs and revelations of God's kingdom, conveying one principal message: universal love. So the noted story in John 9:1–3 about the disciples seeing a blind man and asking Jesus, "Rabbi who sinned, this man or his parents, that he was born blind?" illustrates the Hebrew's steadfast conviction that sickness is a consequence of sin. Consequently, healing sickness proved Jesus' ability to release sins, which only God could do, which then proves his Messianic prerogatives and the beginning of the new era of the kingdom of God. Different biblical miracles illustrate this same essence in different ways, forms, and shapes. But the Hebrew/Roman alliance did not want a Messiah-God proclaiming a universal love for everyone (more than just for certain elect people) and so executed Jesus. Paradoxically, however, in doing so it proved that Jesus really did perform divinely-empowered miracles and not only inexplicable, grandiose, theatrical, or astonishing shows and other meaningless performances as the miracle workers of his time performed. In other words, Jesus' enemies demonstrated that they recognized something unique in his miracles by hastily prompting his execution before the approaching Sabbath day, which then led to his greatest miracle: resurrection.

Now, since his ascension, Jesus lives with his people and performs signs of God's presence, genuine miracles, through them. For example, Christian altruism, peace, love, and joy are miracles; they contradict all biological, psychological, sociological, and natural rules. But miracle-seeking believers look for assurances of a different kind. They seek supernatural happenings that prove God's existence. Miracle seekers are not satisfied by what St. Paul talks about in Hebrews 11:1: "Now faith is being sure of what we hope for and certain of what we do not see." They would instead like to see what they believe actually materialised. Therefore, they often uncritically appreciate every seemingly strange, inexplicable vision or event as a miracle and attempt to convince others of the same. However, as Benedict Groeshel says, "The identification of faith with accounts of miracles and similar wondrous events that a later generation has found to be, quite literarily, incredible has undermined the authority of faith itself."[1] Through miracle seekers' sometimes bizarre attempts to showcase miracles, the body of Christ becomes an object of disappointment for those unsuccessfully praying for miraculous healings, and sceptics are given a reason to doubt and ridicule the Church.

Pastoral Considerations

(1) Miracle-seeking attitudes may be connected to various psychotic conditions: (often schizophrenia, with religious-delusional ideas or paranoia); nonpsychotic histrionic, borderline, narcissistic, and dissociative disorders; or hallucinogenic drug use in religious people. If caused by any of these conditions, then healing miracle-seeking mental conditions requires a professional approach, which also resolves miracle-seeking tendencies. Such behaviors, though, also appear in otherwise mentally healthy and well-functioning, so-called mythomanic people who are prone to interpreting everyday happenings in a mystical or miraculous context. New Age practitioners are particularly susceptible to these kinds of interpretations, some of which are little more than magical thinking.

(2) The pastoral healing of miracle-seeking believers requires a cautious approach. If their miraculous experiences, beliefs, and proofs are simply bulldozed, they will not progress toward healing. On the contrary, such an approach may cause their faith to decline. Benevolent and empathetic listening is most often the best initial pastoral approach. When healing begins, the focus should first be on resolving personal, psychological, or pathological reasons for miracle-seeking behaviors and then on providing emotional and rational counterpoints to correct miracle-seeking behaviors.

(3) Genuine miracles may be differentiated from profane illusions of a miracle with the help of examples and stories provided in the Bible. In John 20:24–29, for instance, a typical miracle seeker is portrayed in Thomas, who asks for tangible proof of Jesus' resurrection. The occurrence of a real miracle, though, is marked by Jesus' command in John 20:28: "Stop doubting and believe." As a result of his command, Thomas exclaims, "My Lord and God," which signals a turning point in his faith. In the next verse, John 20:29, Jesus tells him, "Because you have seen me [i.e., because you were my disciple] you have believed; blessed are those who have not seen and yet have believed."

(4) The psychological dynamics involved in miracle-seeking are a resistance to believing without seeing. Miracle seekers feel they must see God and his miracles with their external eyes unlike billions of other believers

who are satisfied by seeing God with the internal eyes of faith. They react like Thomas, who needed to put his hand in Jesus' wounds in order to believe. This is ultimately due to internal insecurity. Thomas, after Jesus' intervention, did not require sensorial-scientific knowledge (the evidence of Jesus' wounded hands) but had sufficient internal proof with his faith. In miracle-seeking believers, though, an internal derealization occurs, which causes them to doubt their own experiences of living in and with God. Pastoral healing may address this internal insecurity by identifying and resolving its psychological-spiritual reasons.

(5) Doubting the validity of one's own internal evidence is a consequence of psychological divisions and intrapersonal fights—experiencing one thing, willing a second, knowing a third, feeling a fourth, and doing a fifth. Resolving such internal conflict and psychological division requires the restructuring of one's personality to know, feel, and will to be Jesus' disciple, which involves addressing conscious and unconscious ambivalence toward the Church, faith, and God. Accordingly, the primary focus in pastoral healing for miracle-seeking believers is not the miracle-seeking behavior itself but the cause of it, the internal fight between doubt and belief in an almighty, eternal, and ultimately loving but sensorially invisible deity. Pastoral healing ought to be focused on resolving the patient's lack of being one with Jesus and his lack of trust in him that is caused by an insecurity in discipleship.

Socratic dialogue is an effective method for resolving ambivalence. It increases the strength, power, and evidence of the internal experience of God that constitutes the kind of faith that eliminated Thomas' need to touch Jesus. Having sufficient internal and, as we will discuss, so-called meta-empirical proof of living with God reduces the need for external, measurable proof. Thus, fostering a genuine kind of communication with the invisible God that is like breathing, exhaling (giving) oneself to God and inhaling (receiving) his gifts of joy, love, hope, and peace is, for believers, a stronger proof of God's existence and closeness than seeing grandiose miracles.

(7) The ultimate goal in the pastoral healing of miracle seekers is a paradigm shift: the miracle-seeking believer's faith may be nourished to transform him from a sceptic like Thomas into a committed Christian able

to cry out, "My God and Lord!" This evolution enables the search for God's presence, not externally (in naturally inexplicable occurrences), but internally (in the heart), and for gift of faith. "Instead of being tentative [such faith] is certain because the author of this faith is God."[2]

(8) One's perception of external, objective reality is a projection of their internal experiences. Just as the one who is internally, endogenously depressed will find a thousand external and allegedly objective reasons to be depressed, a Thomas-like doubter will find plentiful external evidence of personally knowing and trusting God by becoming an optimistic, hopeful, trusting, and joyful believer. Dramatic, visible miracles for such a believer will be welcomed but not required as pillars of his faith.

(9) C. S. Lewis pointed out that "historical Christianity sees the incarnation of God in the world as the greatest miracle that culminates in the crucifixion and resurrection."[3] For nonbelievers, even this greatest miracle is insufficient for belief. But for Christians who also experience miraculous communication with Jesus introspectively, this ultimate miracle provides sufficient security for substantiating faith. Such Christians genuinely live in a miraculous world. For them, every happening is a theophany, a message from God in his loving communication with them.

Notes

[1] Benedict J. Groeshel, "For Those Who Seek Spiritual Passages, The Spirituality of Spiritual Development" (New York NY: Crossroad), 121

[2] Lindsay Jones (ed.), *Encyclopedia of Religion*, vol. 9 (Farmington Hills, MI: Thomson Gale, 2005), 6056.

[3] Ibid., 2958–9.

CHAPTER THIRTY-SIX

RELIGIOUS FANATICISM

God is a mystery, impossible to completely grasp for humans, but every believer seeks to know whether his concept of God is true. When, however, in the words of Groeshel, a believer "denies the individual's underlying uncertainty," proclaiming his concept to be the correct one, that person is what we refer to as a religious fanatic. Religious fanaticism is "a very threatened paranoid condition of belief." A fanatic is insecure in his or her discipleship and attempts to resolve that internal insecurity externally by "project[ing] his or her inner conflicts onto others."[1] Such a person's beliefs are not shaped by Christ but are rather self-made tools for bringing about power or wealth.

According to historical data and the popular Russian ethos, the emperor Ivan Vasiljevich (1530–1584) was one of the greatest of conquerors. On the western front he defeated the Teutons and the powerful Swedish, Danish, and Polish armies. On the eastern front he began conquering Siberia and spread his power toward the Pacific, creating the foundations of the greatest empire on earth. His policy was to centralize power and modernize Russia, bringing a plethora of Western ideas and influences through German and Italian architects, scientists, artists, and craftsmen while promoting trade with England and Holland. He started his day with one holy mass before dawn and a second at 8:00 a.m., followed by prayer, Bible study, and silent meditation. The emperor's routine, after a short breakfast, continued in the hall where he tortured and killed his real and imagined enemies, sometimes with his bare hands. Entire noble families were exterminated, like the well-known Adashev family. The emperor perfected a ritual of physical and psychological torture: the wife witnessed the execution of her husband and sons before she herself was executed. The religious emperor, whose people called Grozni (meaning "terrible"), once kept some 12,000 people in freezing waters while the church bells rang for their souls. In short, Ivan was both a deeply religious and cruel ruler in the same person, executing his allegedly God-given duty to make Russia a great power.[2]

In our times, faith, or belonging to the body of Christ, is less advantageous in achieving political, social, or financial goals than in Ivan the Terrible's times, so the number of religious fanatics has decreased in the Western world (this is not the case in some Eastern countries). Nevertheless, the presence of "mini Ivan the Terribles" justifying their will to power through pseudoreligious buzzwords in our postmodern culture persists. For that reason, the psychological-spiritual profile of bigoted religious fanatics and pseudoreligious mini-dictators is worth discussing.

Pastoral Considerations

(1) Because faith and fanaticism are mutually exclusive traits, our first question is "Why can't religious fanaticism be healed by sacramental or nonsacramental gifts of Jesus and the Church, such as confession, Eucharist, liturgy, prayer, and the Scriptures?" However, in Matthew 7:21, Jesus tells us, "[Not] everyone who says to Me, 'Lord, Lord' will enter the kingdom of heaven." Sins, mental disorders, and psychological problems create a blind spot that limits the healing power of faith. Thus, for fanatics' healing we need to first grasp the psychological drama occurring in their minds.

(2) As with Ivan the Terrible, the basic motor in modern religious fanatics is their will to power, justified by the overvalued idea of "I represent ultimate godly truth." Fanatics attempt to prove their Godlike characteristics of omniscience and omnipotence through cruelty. This strategy unavoidably incites in them a fear of revenge from their self-made enemies, which turns into paranoia—"Everyone is my enemy! To protect the godly

truth my duty is to be cruel!" It is a vicious cycle that turns with ever greater vehemence into increased brutality.

This tendency to appropriate the truth and claim Godlike characteristics—a form of idolatry—can be seen in the rise of cults and their fanatical leaders who exert an almost hypnotic spell on naive believers, who are vulnerable to almost any ideology that, at least at its inception, uses Christian scripture in a perverted way to radicalize its "disciples."

(3) Religious bigotry and fanaticism are often paired with concurrent psychiatric disorders, such as schizoid, paranoid, histrionic, narcissistic, borderline, and epileptic personality disorders. Thus, before starting pastoral intervention, these concurrent disorders, if present, need to be adequately addressed.

(4) As Groeschel notes, in approaching a fanatic believer, "It is necessary to enter his or her somewhat distorted world vision and try to allay his or her fears."[3] It is counterproductive to logically or theologically challenge their last defence (i.e., their maladaptive religious convictions). Instead, aiming to resolve fears, insecurities, low self-esteem, and self-doubt may be the most effective initial approach.

(5) Pastoral interventions may first be focused on healing issues that the subject seems to be quite unaware of (such as selfishness, greed, low self-esteem, sexual frustration, feelings of abandonment, jealousy, revenge, disappointment, and feeling oneself to be unsuccessful and meaningless). These secondary problems often assist fanaticism in making religion a tool for proving superiority, being "like God, knowing good and evil" (Gen. 3:5). Decreasing the need to prove preeminence decreases the need for power.

(6) As we will discuss in the fifth part of this book, progressing (or regressing) in receiving biblical gifts is an internal psychological-spiritual measure and criterion of one's closeness to Jesus. Thus, pastoral healing ought to help patients to focus on receiving, not so much worldly power, prestige, and success, but genuine spiritual gifts such as proof of their close relationship with Jesus. This, however, requires self-criticism and being meek and brokenhearted.

(7) Groschel talks about a "false certitude of fanaticism,"[4] which is often enforced by noted schizoid, paranoid, or narcissistic personality traits in

people deemed mentally healthy. Therefore, in pastoral healing, crucial self-questioning must emerge when the time is appropriate. The patient must ask, "Is my behavior genuinely Christlike or is it a conscious or unconscious self-deception in seeking power, fame, respect, or other worldly gains?" Using biblical and moral criteria in answering this question may be unfruitful because of fanatic people's distortions of logic, so healers often use an introspective approach.

(8) A pastoral healer may encourage self-scrutiny as to whether the fanatical subject personally experiences a crescendo of biblical peace, love, and joy and whether his attitude helps his neighbours, family members, and colleagues experience biblical gifts of faith. This is much like what Nathan did for King David in 2 Samuel 12.

(9) Even the most prominent religious fanatics cannot feel biblical love, peace, or mercy when harming, punishing, torturing, or killing their alleged enemies. People can deceive themselves into believing they have irrational rights or duties but, as we will discuss in the fifth part of the book, no human being can falsify the biblical gifts of the Holy Spirit, nor can one genuinely experience them while flagrantly disobeying Jesus' law of love. Love, peace, joy, and mercy are mutually exclusive psychological aspects to the will to power, cruelty, and brutality. Ivan the Terrible must have realized that his life was hopelessly controversial; otherwise, he would not have behaved so terribly. Despite putting an enormous amount of effort into his religious behavior, he obviously could not feel close union with Jesus.

(10) How tragically unforgiving and merciless psychological self-judgment is in fanatic people is illustrated by the demise of another religious fanatic: Jim Jones. As a result of scrutinizing themselves and realizing their collective self-deception, Jones, a twentieth-century cult leader, and a number of his followers committed suicide en masse in a helpless rage and ultimate desperation. The pastoral judgment and healing of postmodern Ivan the Terrible-like religious fanatics ought to be much more Jesus-like: just and merciful.

The ultimate guide in assessing such leaders, recent or those despots chronicled by history, is Scripture. Jesus said, "A good tree cannot bear bad fruit, and a bad tree cannot bear good fruit" (Matthew 7:18). Zealotry or the desire for wealth and power, which are paranoid conditions of belief, can never masquerade for mercy, kindness, peace, mildness, gentleness, love, forgiveness, patience, and other gifts and fruits of the Holy Spirit. "By their fruit you will recognize them" (Matthew 7:16).

Notes

[1] Benedict J. Groeshel, "For Those Who Seek Spiritual Passages, The Spirituality of Spiritual Development" (New York NY: Crossroad), 121

[2] Vladimir Stanojevic, *Tragedija Genija* (Belgrade: Nolit, 1976) 85–95. See also Paul Ungar, *The Mystery of Christian Faith: A Tangible Union with the Invisible God* (Lanham, MD: University Press of America, 2008), 271.

[3] Benedict J. Groeshel, "For Those Who Seek Spiritual Passages, The Spirituality of Spiritual Development" (New York NY: Crossroad), 121

[4] Ibid.

CHAPTER THIRTY-SEVEN

IDOLATRY

Around 3,800 years ago, after God established his covenant with his elected people, the Hebrews, their fidelity was repeatedly tested. In Abraham's time, they had to choose between the idol of security in staying in the familiar territory of their homeland or living as nomadic strangers wandering through the stony desert toward the Promised Land as God intended. In Moses' time, they had to choose between slavery to Egyptian richness, abundance, and luxury or following Yahweh into the harshness of the desert. Once settled in the Promised Land, the Hebrews' corruption, greed, and ritual idolatry prompted Yahweh's punishment (the Babylonian exile), followed by a new revival of the Deuteronomium (the covenant). After this, the threat of idolatry appeared again in the form of Greco-Roman influence, and God intervened through the prophet Nathan and gave momentum to messianic expectations, which were eventually fulfilled by Jesus Christ. We recount the history of the elected people because it continues to repeat itself even in our day in the lives of the people of God, namely, his Church.

In the Catechism's definition, "Idolatry consists of divinizing what is not God."[1] For the purpose of pastoral healing, we define idolatry more broadly as worship or adoration of or attachment to objects, situations, or conditions that hinders the believer from seeking union with God. Psychologically, idolatry is anything that spoils one's commitment to Jesus. In biblical times, idols were commonly images of man-made gods, whereas today they tend to be objects that have Godlike importance or that give humans a feeling of Godlike omnipotence. Idolatry is false faith that John W. Whitehead[2] talks about, fuelling an overvalued attachment to success, money, luxury, power, popularity, prestige, and other man-made objects that jeopardize worship of God. In this context, Psalm 115:2–8 says:

Why do the nations say:
    "Where is their God?"
Our God is in heaven;
    he does whatever pleases him.
But their idols are silver and gold,
    made by the hands of men.
They have mouths, but cannot speak,
    eyes, but cannot see,
they have ears, but cannot hear,
    noses, but they cannot smell,
they have hands, but cannot feel,
    feet, but they cannot walk,
    nor can they utter a sound with their throats.
Those who made them will be like them,
    and so will all who trust in them.

The last verse (115:9) seems to perfectly describe our times. The current materialist-reductionist worldview reduces humankind from being created in the image and likeness of God to a worthless thing like idols themselves. Literally, "Those who made them will be like them, and so will all who trust in them."

Pastoral Considerations

(1) Worshipping, adoring, and being attached to objects that compromise union with God has always flourished. However, biblical forms of idolatry are today modernized and practiced universally as perhaps never before in history. In the sixth century, Pope Gregory the Great

classified seven behaviors as cardinal sins (pride, envy, gluttony, lust, anger, greed, and sloth), but in movies, advertisements, and daily social exchanges, Hodi observes, "For twenty-four hours a day citizens are repeatedly instructed to commit exactly these sins."[3] Idolatry has become a social sin and sickness of postmodern times. The digital age has had an addictive effect on culture in that people have not only become literal slaves to social media, but all that computers and digital media put at their fingertips: sex, alcohol, excess, materialism, commercialism, celebrities, and wealth.

(2) Let us next define the Christian's attitude toward the temptations of the contemporary world. As Frankl explains, "Primarily and normally, man does not seek pleasure. Or, for that matter, happiness—it is the side effect of self-transcending."[5] Therefore, psychologically speaking, Christians' approaching pleasure, happiness, or joy is the side effect of their transcendant movement toward Jesus. Achieving biblical joy is never Christians' purpose but rather a by-product of being like Christ. Nevertheless, this by-product is psychologically a paramount psychological-spiritual motivator in seeking union with Jesus.

(3) Pastoral healing focuses on helping Christians to abundantly receive the gifts that idolatry is unable to give. Nowhere are these gifts better formulated than in Matthew 5:1–12:

> "Blessed are the poor in spirit,
> for theirs is the kingdom of heaven.
> Blessed are those who mourn,
>   for they will be comforted.
> Blessed are the meek,
>   for they will inherit the earth.
> Blessed are those who hunger and thirst for righteousness,
>   for they will be filled.
> Blessed are the merciful,
>   for they will be shown mercy.
> Blessed are the pure in heart,
>   for they will see God.

Blessed are the peacemakers,

for they will be called children of God.

Blessed are those who are persecuted because of righteousness,

for theirs is the kingdom of heaven.

Blessed are you when people insult you, persecute you, and falsely say all kinds of evil against you because of me. Rejoice and be glad, because great is your reward in heaven, for in the same way they persecuted the prophets who were before you.

The pastoral healer's task is psychologically and empirically substantiating these biblical truths and debunking the lure of pleasure that the pursuit of worldly idols entails.

(4) How can pastoral healers demonstrate the primacy of biblical joy over worldly bliss? When a certain well-known businessman was asked how much more money it would take to satisfy him, he responded, "One dollar more." This is an answer indicative of a person practicing monetary idolatry, but ironically it illustrates why true satisfaction can never be obtained from idols. The human brain and mind are programmed to seek contentment, but psychological contentment is not a permanent state of mind. Lasting happiness requires not winning a single jackpot but winning a new and greater jackpot every day. Let us explore how this principle works in everyday life by examining the psychology of happiness, pleasure, and joy.

(5) For many, happiness is the result of attaining more—greater success, income, power, or luxury, for instance. The greatest enemy of happiness is permanency, having no unexpected increase of new gains. All objects that bring happiness eventually become accustomed and boring. For this reason, a permanent increase of happiness is psychologically impossible. The more success, income, power, and luxury one already has, the less possible it is to double, triple, or quadruple it. For example, a humble house brings a poor family significantly greater happiness than a palace does a billionaire. Despite endlessly seeking new sources of happiness the pattern repeats, and permanent pleasure from the possession of worldly idols becomes like a mirage, never achievable. Therefore, the "bliss balance" in idolatry (see

Section 10 of this chapter) is always negative. Seeking happiness in itself is not an idol, but it becomes an idol if worship of material possessions, power, or fame hinders the believer from seeking union with God, thus causing a negative bliss balance.

Fig. 37.1 The psychological dynamics in happiness

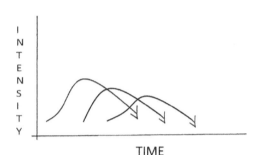

(6) Pleasure originates in satisfying our needs: food, drink, rest, work, and sex. However, fullness limits the pleasure of eating; drunkenness limits the pleasure of drinking; boredom sets the boundaries of leisure, travel, or extravagant holidays; bodily fatigue limits the time for which one can work; and satiation restricts the enjoyment of sex. Although the enjoyment of eating, drinking, sex, or resting is rechargeable in the sense that abstinence makes them pleasurable again, there are nevertheless natural boundaries that cannot be transgressed, and a lasting, steadily-improving state of permanent pleasure is unachievable. Seeking pleasure can become an idol if virtual worship or adoration of (or a sick and sinful attachment to) eating, drinking, sex, leisure, or extravagant pleasure-seeking attitudes prevents the believer from seeking union with God.

Fig. 37.2 The psychological dynamics in pleasure

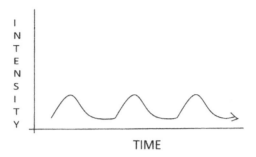

(7) Joy—and more exactly the biblical kind of permanent joy—originates from an ever-deepening relationship and union with God, at which the eight blessings of Jesus are directed. Such a blessed relationship has no psychological limits or boundaries. There is always the possibility of increasing one's biblical joy, peace, love, optimism, courage, and hope by steadily progressing in Christlike living. The more effort a believer puts into seeking union with Jesus, the more he experiences blessedness, the foretaste of the ultimate joy that surpasses all human understanding. In believers genuinely committed to Jesus, their bliss balance is truly positive.

Fig. 37.3 The psychological dynamics in biblical joy

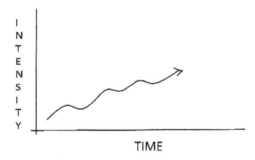

(8) Every Christian's life is an amalgamation of pleasure, happiness, and joy. These qualities are not equal, though. Discipleship involves a permanent progression of putting physical, emotional, intellectual, and all other dimensions of the personality on the Christlike side of the scale instead of on the side of worldly idols. Nevertheless, we are not yet entirely spiritual entities; we have bodies with a God-given need for happiness and pleasure. So where is the line drawn between a legitimate need for happiness and pleasure and sick or sinful slavery to hedonism? Likely, all Christians are challenged in delineating this boundary, in finding the right balance between focusing on biblical joy while also satisfying their physiological and psychological need for happiness and pleasure. Pastoral help with this effort consists of showing patients how they can integrate all three sources of bliss into a biblical context.

(9) As Packer notes, for people of faith, blissful events are not random, meaningless, natural occurrences; rather, they are theophanies, opportunities presented by Jesus for the joyful glorifying of God.[4] From this standpoint, the miracles of the Sabbath healing (Mark 3:1–6), the feeding of the 5,000 (John 6:1–15), and Jesus turning water to wine in Cana (John 2:1–10) were themselves less important than the fact that they were evidence of God's presence. Jesus' miracles were more important as signs of God's kingdom and of *zoe*, the possibility of everlasting life with Jesus, than as gifts of *bios*, worldly well-being. In a similar way, within the postmodern pleasantries of cars, houses, holidays, travel, and even enormous medical, technological, and scientific achievements, committed believers discern and celebrate God's glory. Holding *zoe* as more important than *bios* prevents slavery to idolatry and makes Jesus' presence and providence a permanent, reoccurring, and mystical theophany.

(10) Every Christian's life is an amalgamation of pleasure, happiness, joy, sadness, disappointment, and distress. Summing up all positive and negative inputs and calculating a typical equilibrium between these two groups of mutually exclusive experiences is what we call finding a bliss balance. A bliss balance can be more positive or more negative

depending in many ways upon how one distinguishes between worldly idols and biblical ideals and which of the two a person chooses to live for.

(11) Our worldly being serves to fulfil a Godly meaning. In a broad sense, idolatry emerges in the context of serving our worldly being more prominently than striving for biblical meaning. This behavioral pattern, which can also be summarized as disrespecting Jesus' basic commands given in Mark 12:29–31 is the most common form of social idolatry that has promoted abuse, conflict, war, and cruelty through history. The following is a noble example of how to resolve it.

In recent times, the European population has been sharply divided over the question of whether the immigration of many hundreds of thousands of unskilled immigrants without personal documents and work histories ought to be supported or prevented. Being mostly non-Christian, the immigrants' overwhelming numbers present a certain challenge for the very being of Christians in Europe. Nevertheless, Pope Francis opened the gates of the churches in Rome to feed and help immigrants and instructed other Christian communities to follow his example. Apparently, despite all the risks, fulfilling a biblical meaning was, for the Pope, more important than securing worldly well-being.

(12) Let us next discuss a case study of the healing of individual idolatry.

The M. family, originating from a very religious and well-situated Filipino background, emigrated from their country of origin despite bitter resistance from the wife's parents. The husband, Dr. N., had previously worked as an orthopaedist, but his efforts to continue his career in his new country failed. Nevertheless, the family lived in good financial conditions and, with other family members' help, purchased a four-bedroom house in a nice area. Dr. N. was working hard in a pyramid scheme, aiming to buy a second, even greater house for his mother- and father-in-law to stay in when visiting. When his in-laws finally came to visit, Dr. N. took out a huge bank loan and rented a limousine to pick up his guests from the airport. During their visit, though, the pyramid scheme he had invested all his hopes in collapsed. Yet he still attempted to impress them, taking out another bank loan and taking them on a Caribbean cruise. After the unsuspecting in-laws flew home to the Philippines, Dr. N. attempted suicide. His wife barely saved his life, which his idols very nearly took.

Pastoral healing in this and similar cases consists of first resolving basic conscious or unconscious conflicts (i.e., frustration, depression, competitiveness, jealousy, low self-esteem, anxiety, and fear) which push a subject toward compensating for distress and impairment with idolatry. These aetiological factors are often much deeper than those which simple rational persuasion can resolve. A professional healing is in such cases needed to resolve unresolved traumas, conflicts, and fixations, often originating in early childhood and facilitating escape to the opium of idolatry.

(13) The healing of idolatry is focused on the present as well as the future. Patients are coached in using cognitive-behavioral methods (like monitoring automatic thoughts and cognitions and using paradox intentions) to challenge, resist, ridicule, and eventually defeat their attraction to idolatry. For long-term solution, they discern biblical purposes and values to strive for, and these facilitate in genuine disciples a more steady progression toward joy than the pursuit of idols. In an angelic cycle, increasing biblical joy assists Christian commitment, and Christian commitment yields spiritual gifts of joy, optimism, hope, and courage.

(14) In fighting idolatry, no one can measure up to the ideals of the Sermon on the Mount. Christians ought not be discouraged but encouraged, though, as they are nevertheless decreasing the difference between themselves and the ideals noted in Matthew 5:1–12, the statutes of the kingdom of God. The criterion of success is permanent progression. To that end, the role of pastoral healing is most often only modest, encouraging patients to be closer to Jesus' ideals today than they were yesterday.

Notes

[1] Canadian Conference of the Catholic Bishops, *Catechism of the Catholic Church* (Ottawa: Publications Service, Canadian Conference of Catholic Bishops, 1994), 437.

[2] John W. Whitehead *True Christianity,* (Whestchester, IL, Crossway Books, 1989), 33.

[3] Sandor Hodi, *Kongresszus Abbaziaban, A Titokzatos EN nyomaban* (Ada, Serbia, Szechenyi Istvan Strategiakutato Tarsasag, 2014), 231.

[4] Viktor E. Frankl, *Man's Search for Ultimate Meaning* (New York: Basic Books, 2000), 85–9.

[5] J. I. Packer, *God's Plan for You* (Wheaton, IL: Crossway Books, 2001), 45.

CHAPTER THIRTY-EIGHT

BELIEVERS TORMENTED BY A
DARK NIGHT OF THE SOUL

F or Hebrews in biblical times, real poverty was not being struck by famine, slavery, or sickness, but feeling abandoned by God. Even Christians today may feel, if not a direct abandonment, an uneasiness, disquietude, or trepidation in not progressing sufficiently in closeness with God. An extreme and acute form of this concern is what was first described in the sixteenth century by Spanish poet and Carmelite mystic St. John of the Cross as a "dark night" in his poem "Ascent of Mount Carmel."[1] Starting out, the poem has an optimistic message. It describes the process of the purification of the soul which, although painful, ends in a blessed union with Jesus. St. Teresa of Avila gives the following similar report about encountering an angel of God:

> I saw in his hands a long dart of gold, and at the end the iron there seemed to be a little fire. This I thought he thrust through my heart several times, and it reached my very entrails. As he withdrew it, I thought it brought them with it, and left me burning with a great love of God. So great was the pain that it made me give those moans; and so utter the sweetness this sharpest of pains gave me that there was no wanting to stop, nor is there any contenting the soul with less than God. The pain is not physical but

spiritual, although the body does not fail to share in it somewhat, and indeed plenty. It is such delightful language of love that passes between the soul and God that I beg of His goodness that He gave the enjoyment of it to him who may think I die. The days that this lasted, I went about as if distracted: I did not wish to see or to speak, but to burn myself with my pain, which greater glory to me than anything there is in all creation.[2]

Such ecstatic experiences were preceded by painful periods of purification and spiritual dryness in the life of St. Teresa of Avila, as well. The expression "dark night of the soul" is used to indicate a spiritual crisis caused by the experience of apparent abandonment by God.

Probably the best-known modern case of suffering such a torment is that of St. Teresa of Kolkata. Emily Simpson Chapman recounts the following.

When the world looked at the face of Blessed Teresa of Kolkata, it saw pure, simple joy. Then, in 2007, ten years after Blessed Teresa's death, a collection of her private letters was published. Suddenly, the joy that the tiny sister from Albania once radiated seemed anything but simple. As the letters revealed, for the entirety of her public ministry, the founder of the Missionaries of Charity endured unceasing feelings of desolation and abandonment by God.[3]

From St. Teresa's letters it appears that for almost her whole life (except for the time close to her death) she often felt that her prayers were like "talking to a brick wall," and she suffered doubt, insecurity, misery, and frustration for decades. What are the pastoral reasons for such an almost dysphoric self-experience, and how should a healer deal with Christians suffering from it?

Pastoral Considerations

(1) Humans, as we have discussed, are psychological beings. We have no access to ideas, information, or knowledge not contained in our minds. Even our spiritual communication with God is registered psychologically.

Thus, the psychological components of our personalities also participate in our experiences and expressions of spiritual contents, including the dark night of the soul.

(2) Even persons deemed psychologically healthy experience oscillations of mood. Contrary to euthymia, meaning in the psychiatric vernacular a well-balanced feeling of contentment, the states of mind called in Greek "hyperthymia" are characterized by overly-dominant and overly-powerful emotions of joy or sadness. Strong emotional oscillations in one direction often follow oscillations in the opposite direction. For example, with so called "fulfilment melancholia," people slip into depression following an ecstatic experience. An experience of ecstatic transfections may also be followed by similarly extreme emotional oscillations in the directions of dryness, darkness, emptiness, loneliness, and, in the case of St. Teresa, a feeling of futilely praying to God as if he were a brick wall. These dry periods are not lasting, but are a psychological-spiritual preparation that herald new blissful experiences of a deeper union with Jesus. The purpose of pastoral healing is to convey this empirical truth for these suffering souls.

(3) Prominent Christians are sometimes impatient in their yearning to relive their previous ecstatic experiences. Such psychological cravings may seriously test affected believers' mental resilience—they genuinely suffer—so pastoral help is vitally needed.

(4) When addressing their concerns, we should first clarify a fundamental theological question: Does God ever really abandon people who genuinely seek a relationship with him? Christians can be warned or even chastised by God, but God is faithful. There is no biblical example of Jesus ever abandoning people who genuinely sought a relationship with him. So the feeling that he is being indifferent or unloving is not a reflection of his actions but of the believer's own functioning. Only two factors can truly prevent us from the feeling of living in a relationship with Jesus: sin and sickness.

(5) Sins are found in every human being, including exemplary Christians. As John of the Cross emphasized, the dark night of the soul is a process of self-scrutiny, cleansing, and repentance, an opportunity to grow in Christlikeness. He painted "a picture of extremely advanced souls

undergoing purification by periods of darkness and aridity, or plunged into utter darkness convinced that God has abandoned them forever."[4] Trusting in Jesus' ultimate love even in such dark periods is probably the strongest test of faith.

(6) The dark night of the soul cannot be simply erased or made less real by effort, prayer, or sacramental activities as it may be connected to underlying issues such as anxiety, fear, dysphoria, helplessness, anger, feelings of guilt, or jealousy connected to conscious or unconscious psychological problems which often disable communion with God. Furthermore, delicate clinical and subclinical forms of psychiatric disorders (endogenous, persistent, or reactive depression; and personality disorders with overvalued religious ideas) can manifest in symptoms that mimic the dark night of the soul.

(7) Pastoral healers need to be aware of the significant risk factors connected to this condition. The suffering involved in the dark night of the soul and the conditions mimicking it are unique to every individual. Not only do the duration, reoccurrence, and intensity differ, but so too the symptomatology of the affliction. The condition's gravity extends from feeling a transitory spiritual inefficiency to suicidal temptation. Accordingly, any concurrent disorders or psychological impairments, as in every other pastoral condition, ought to be taken care of before pastoral healing takes place.

(8) For otherwise mentally stable believers prone to ecstatic extroversion, there is no need for any pastoral intervention when they are in a state of limitless bliss and joy. However, in periods when their emotions swing to the opposite extreme and any small, meaningless personal imperfection "will burden and bewitch them,"[5] it helps such people to have a rational, logical, and theological understanding that they are not abandoned by God but rather that their emotions are polarized in a way that makes it seem so. The first measure for moving them toward that understanding usually consists of helping them to rationally exclude the possibility of being abandoned by God forever. Although their irrational feelings of abandonment may be strong, knowledge is a much more substantial tenant of Christian faith than pure emotionality. Applying what they know can amend what people in a dark night of the soul feel.

(9) People experiencing a dark night of the soul may appreciate the truth that the characteristic effects of closeness to God (such as spiritual gratification and joy) do not make or break one's relationship with him. Putting in effort, despite feelings of apathy, emptiness, meaninglessness, hopelessness, and abandonment, is more important to Jesus than reaping the benefits of doing so. When we admit our feelings of emptiness to God, he fills that void with his grace regardless of whether we perceive it or not. Putting forth rational effort to seek a relationship with Jesus is often the first sign of emotional healing.

(10) In discussing pastoral healing for depression (Ch. 12), we noted the case of a depressed orthodox priest using paradox intention (i.e., defeating his depression by paradoxically praying for depression). A similar approach may be used in healing the dark night of the soul. Contrary to patients' perceptions of abandonment, they may be encouraged to realize that Jesus is the closest to them exactly when they are suffering. Perceiving their sufferings as a call from God to deepen their relationship with Jesus may help committed Christians to discern a purpose in their sufferings. Such insight predisposes Christians to be less afraid of the dark night of the soul, to even seek and pray for it, which paradoxically may boost their hope for and factual experience of the shining of God's face in their lives once more.

(11) Suffering of at least minimal or subclinical signs of the dark night of the soul and conditions that mimic it are common to all people of faith. No person suffering from a dark night of the soul is alone. The sharing of experiences, church-related support groups, emotional and rational pastoral healing, and liturgical and sacramental activities may help such people to hear God's voice through the community of believers, which can sometimes help heal the dark night of the soul more efficiently than any individual therapist.

(12) The dark night of the soul in believers mimics life experience that atheists permanently suffer from. This kind of suffering in Christians is significantly greater, however, because they experience the loss of what they once had. They suffer from an acute "paradise lost" experience, while atheists are more accustomed to the painful experience of ultimate meaninglessness. Nevertheless, the micro episodes of the dark night of the soul that every Christian experiences enable insight into atheists' bleak state of mind.

Notes

[1] John of the Cross, *The Ascent of Mount Carmel* (New York: Magisterium Books, 2015).

[2] William Thomas Walsh, *Saint Teresa of Avila* (Rockford, IL: Tan Books, 1977), 147–9.

[3] Emily Simpson Chapman, *Understanding the Dark Night of the Soul*, OSW Newsweekly.

[4] Benedict J. Groeshel, "For Those Who Seek Spiritual Passages, The Spirituality of Spiritual Development" (New York NY: Crossroad), 185

[5] Ibid.

CHAPTER THIRTY-NINE

POSITIVISM AND HYPOCRISY

In this chapter, we will discuss positivism and hypocrisy together for the following reasons. Firstly, positivism (the assertion that every idea can be scientifically or rationally proven) and hypocrisy are individual but socially induced problems. Secondly, virtually no believer will seek pastoral healing solely because of them; nevertheless, topics connected to positivism, and especially hypocrisy, are concealed in most pastoral healings. Thirdly, positivism and hypocrisy need a special pastoral approach that combines philosophy and pastoral psychology. Fourthly, Christians are strongly against positivism but often have no well-prepared strategy for warding it off, and often they do not react as decisively against hypocrisy as Jesus did. And fifthly, positivism and hypocrisy cause more damage to faith than all other Luciferian temptations put together.

39.1 Positivism as a Spiritual Challenge

Let us start our overview of positivism by first placing it into its historical and social context.

The French philosopher August Comte (1798–1857), author of the *Cours de la Philosophie Positive*, described human scientific, philosophical, and social reasoning as having evolved through three stages: the theological, the metaphysical, and the positive stages. The theological stage was the age, in all Near Eastern cultures in Jesus' time, of religious beliefs. In the metaphysical stage, occurring during the Enlightenment, God was succeeded by the concept of an eternal, limitless, and omnipotent nature. The positive stage, which according to Comte we now live in, is characterized by interest only in the here and now—visible, touchable, and measurable facts—without seeking any further explanation about the past reasons for or future purposes of observed phenomena.[1]

Unfortunately, many aspects of Comte's predictions have materialized in our time. The postmodern collective mind ruled by positivism appreciates only positive facts. An invisible God, who introduced himself in Isaiah 40:25 by saying, "To whom will you compare me? Or who is my equal?" is hard to find a place for in such a world picture. Consequently, many forms of hesitation, distrust, and resistance that pastoral healing address are consciously or unconsciously conditioned by doubts about the existence of a sensorially invisible and positively unverifiable God.

Pastoral Considerations

(1) As noted in Chapter One, in their professional lives, postmodern believers need to think professionally, appreciating mostly positive facts. But on Sundays they are "sure of what [they] hope for and certain of what [they] do not see" (Hebrew's 11:1). Not every believer finds it easy to navigate his way between these conflicting viewpoints. Many make a compromise between empirical and spiritual information, believing one thing but knowing the opposite. How does pastoral healing approach this grave challenge impregnating Western culture?

(2) Besides doing nothing, sweeping problems under the carpet with a tragic optimism, there are two possible scenarios. The first is integrating biblical-theological and experiential-scientific truths, which we did in the first part of this book. The second option is to challenge irrational positivism through the pastoral healing of believers and nonbelievers affected by this epidemic. Is such an effort fruitful?

According an anecdotal story, when Joan of Arc was being put to death on a burning stake, an ant carrying a drop of water in its mouth approached.

An eagle flying overhead saw it and asked, "Do you think that with this drop of water in your mouth you can help her?" The ant looked up and replied, "At least I am doing what I can!" The individual believer is like the ant, perhaps not always effective in taking on great challenges. But ants can be profoundly effective when working together. Indeed, if we Christians act collectively, we will fulfil the call of Albert Camus.

> The world expects of Christians that they will raise their voices [such as against positivism and hypocrisy] so loudly and clearly and so formulate their protest that not even the simplest man can have the slightest doubt about what they are saying. Further, the world expects of Christians that they will eschew all fuzzy abstractions and plant themselves squarely in front of the bloody face of history. We stand in need of folk who have determined to speak directly and unmistakably and come what may, to stand by what they have said.[2]

So what is it we ought to do?

(3) The individual pastoral healing of positivism requires a strategic change. Healers must treat believers not like the world does in that patient seek the physician, but as Jesus did, in that they (along with pastors and priests) seek the patients (i.e., believers and nonbelievers fighting against positivism, scientism, relativism, and other "isms"). Jesus said, "I have not come to call the righteous, but sinners to repentance" (Luke 5:32). He himself sought out what was lost.

(4) In one-on-one sessions, the positivist's resistance may be emotionally softened, demonstrating that the Church has something to offer that the positivist world is unable to even ponder. Consciously or unconsciously, most positivist-inclined believers and nonbelievers need the spiritual gifts that no positive spiritless life, only faith, can give.

(5) All humans, including positivists, are wired to seek a purpose to live for and even, if necessary, to die for. Positivists are tormented by the perceived fundamental meaninglessness of their existence but pessimistically-apathetically conclude that they have no other choice but to accept, in Sienkiewicz's well-known formulation, their "coming from nowhere and

going to nothingness." Pastoral healing that appeals to the patients' emotions may awaken their interest in what is hidden from positive sciences and encourage them to search for ultimate truth that surpasses all human understanding. To paraphrase Frankl, the feelings of positivists may be more discerning than their reasoning can be sharp. Thus, the initial purpose in positivists' healing is giving reasons of the heart to seek God.

(6) There is a saying, "We believe because we love." In our case, the word "love" means a Jesus-like, positive, visible behavior as described in Matthew 5:43–48:

> You have heard it said that, "You shall love your neighbour and hate your enemy." But I say to you, love your enemies and pray for those who persecute you, so that you may be children of your Father in heaven; for he makes his sun to rise on the evil and on the good, and sends rain on the righteous and on the unrighteous. For if you love those who love you, what reward do you have? And if you greet only your brothers and sisters what more are you doing than others? Do not even the gentiles do the same? Be perfect, therefore, as your heavenly Father is perfect.

As Jesus explains, there is a unique "more" in Christian love, unknown to the world. Let me conceptualize it with an example.

The Trinitarian Order, established in 1198, was from the fifteenth century to the nineteenth century actively gathering money to pay the ransoms of prisoners captured by the Turks, who occupied large parts of the Balkans and Central Europe. If the Order had no money to pay for a prisoner, the friars went willingly into Turkish slavery to free the captives. Many thousands of Hungarian captives received their freedom this way.

Such displays of unselfishness are, in Frankl's terms, "value discerning"[3] motivators. They lend to the realization that there are nonpositive but nonetheless existent spiritual qualities that are impossible to explain with biological, psychological, or sociological laws. The realization that genuine Christians are so strongly motivated by a nonworldly but biblical love may then prompt even positivists to search beyond the visible, touchable, and measurable reality to discern the invisible spiritual truths they were previously ignorant of and perhaps even look for more of the same.

(7) Paradoxically, guilt, hopelessness, low self-esteem, and hesitation in acknowledging being the object of God's love disable positivist individuals from perceiving God's love. However, "[opening] the eyes that are blind, [freeing] captives from prison and [releasing] from the dungeon those who sit in darkness" (Isa. 42:7) and helping them to feel and understand that they are unaware of God's love often precipitates breakthroughs for such nonbelievers and gives believers a boost.

(8) Philosophy is a medicine for healing positivism. As pastoral healing progresses, philosophical questions come up and pastoral healers answer them according to their own judgment. For professionals and pastoral healers specialized in using philosophy as a medicine, let us formulate a possible philosophical approach for refuting a positivist worldview.

Plato (427–347 BC) realized that, in grasping sensorial reality, mathematicians use ideas (like squares, lines, or circles) that do not exist in nature but only in the human mind. He therefore concluded that truth is in ideas, not the senses.[4] Aristotle (384–22 BC), Plato's successor, then explored in his *Metaphysics* the reality "beyond-physics" (i.e., beyond the sensorial world).[5] Together, Plato and Aristotle "were teleologists in that they believed in a universal goal for all things, God, or the final cause."[6] With their influence, almost all Scholastic philosophy of the Middle Ages were engaged in exploring metaphysics. The Franciscans (like Bonaventure and Duns Scottus) explored God's interaction with the physical world from Plato's viewpoint, while the Dominicans (Thomas Aquinas or Albertus Magnus) did the same from Aristotle's perspective.

Then, however, came Enlightenment philosophy, which swing like a pendulum to the opposite extreme. The shift started with René Descartes (1596–1650), who introduced a dualistic body-spirit anthropological concept, practically disintegrating human nature. Next, Gottfried Wilhelm Leibniz described in his *Théodicée* of 1710 the concept of "prestabilized harmony," stating that God set up the body and spirit like two clocks showing the same time but functioning independently of each other. John Locke (1632–1704) then connected the intellect to the body in his *Essays Concerning Human*

Understanding, stating that there is nothing in the intellect that was not previously perceived by the senses—that is, all information comes from one source: experience.[7] Blaise Pascal (1623–62) rejected both Scholastic metaphysics and Locke's empiricism, proclaiming that "the heart has reasons of its own which the mind does not understand"[8] Immanuel Kant (1724–1804), challenged by David Hume's scepticism (asserting that we cannot even be sure that the sun will rise tomorrow without previously testing the idea), realized that there are facts we know independently of testing—for example, that the sum of external angles in every triangle must always equal 360 degrees or that the laws of mathematics or physics have a universal validity known *a priori* without any testing. In *The Critique of Pure Reason* (1781), he concluded, "There is something determinate in the mind that causes us to know what we know."[9] Thus, even physical laws "rest not on some constraining principle in the external world of nature, but in the fact that consciousness is so constituted that it cannot but so interpret the empirical data which it receives,"[10] so factually, "human understanding prescribed to nature her laws."[11]

Heroic attempts to revive metaphysics by great names like William James (1842–1910) and Charles. S. Pierce (1839–1914) did not succeed. Instead came countless contemporary, mutually-contradicting philosophies like pragmatism, empiriocriticism, logical-positivism, structuralism, existentialism, and constructivism. Such a deep sea of differing ideologies leads us to wonder how can we know what is philosophically true, reliable, plausible, and trustworthy for us today?

We do not recognize the world objectively as God does, and neither are we able to reason like the angels, cherubs, or seraphim. We can only perceive sensorial and transcendental reality as our human conditions permit. One may have the impression that we are approaching the boundaries that our human mental conditions permit us to know. With Max Planck's discovery of quantum physics, Freud's unearthing the subconscious, Einstein's Theory of Relativity, and the discoveries of the Big Bang, black holes, and antimatter, we have come to realize that the universe contradicts our accustomed, healthy, human, scientific and philosphical reasoning. As Hans Vaihinger's book *Die Philosophie Des "Als Ob"* (*The Philosophy of "As If"*)[12] puts it, we live in an "as if" (a sensorially or positively nonreal) reality which "cannot be as we perceive that it is." The effect of this scientific worldview, together with God's providence questioning psychological and social effects, will sooner or later precipitate a turnaround. Let me clarify what causes me to predict this.

To paraphrase Louis Bouyer's observation, history occurs in the form of a progressive spiral that causes not only the people of God but also the whole of humankind to go back periodically over analogous experiences, which are a part of gradually cleansing and deepening its relationship with God. This ensued for Hebrews during the Babylonian exile. The same phenomenon repeated when communist rulers attempted to turn away people from Jesus, but after the collapse of communism, a Christian revival occurred in Eastern Europe. Analogously, positivism turned substantial parts of the world away from God. But the more this happens, the more people perceive life as distanced from knowing the ultimate truth in scientific, social, and personal functioning. This awareness will sooner or later lead many people to acknowledge dependence on the "quite other" whom Christians call God.

Paradoxically, "What is really important is invisible to the eye; you only see properly with your heart."[13] It is a paramount task of Christians until the revival we are talking about happens to give the world "reasons of the heart" to discern that only living the ultimate truth, which is found in Jesus, brings meaning, peace, love, and a foretaste of ultimate joy that all humans fervently seek but are unable to find neither in the world nor in knowledge, science, or philosophy.

39.2 The Threat of Hypocrisy

The Greek word *hypokrisis* means enacting a role onstage. From this we get our English word *hypocrisy*, which the *Oxford American Dictionary* defines as "the simulation of virtue or goodness, insincerity."[14] This kind of behavior made even the meek, patient, and empathetic Jesus speak out in admonition. He said of hypocrites, "Everything they do is done for people to see: They make their phylacteries wide and the tassels of their prayer shawls long; they love the place of honor at banquets and the most important seats in the synagogues; they love to be greeted in the marketplaces and to have men call them 'Rabbi'" (Mt. 23:5–7). Hypocrisy frustrated him when he observed the temple (Lk. 19:45–48) and finally provoked him to use unusually harsh words in Matthew 23:15: "Woe to you, scribes and Pharisees, hypocrites...." However, *hypokrisis* is not reserved for Pharisees only; it is a common human problem. Even the best Christians often balance self-deceptive attempts to please their Christian consciences with their superego-type worldly consciences. Unfortunately, we are all tempted by the ideas that Niccolo Machiavelli (1469–1527) endorses in his famous and influential book *Il Principe* (*The Prince*).

As known, Machiavelli's book has a long history. It first circulated in manuscript form and was then published in 1532, five years after the author's death. In his book, Machiavelli gives practical advice to rulers, proclaiming:

> A good ruler must be a hypocrite, publicly projecting the image of honesty, modesty, and unselfishness, while using in secrecy deception, extortion, evil, cruelty—even murder—to protect the interests of the majority. Hypocrisy is not only permitted, but is the duty of a ruler, while compassion, empathy, or love of those in need is not only counterproductive but also unethical; it contradicts the interests of the republic.[15]

Machiavelli's *The Prince* is today not popular reading; however, its ideas imbue many aspects of society as it fits perfectly with fallen human nature.

Pastoral Considerations

(1) As with positivism, Christians seldom focus on the hypocrisy that was most harshly condemned by Jesus. Nevertheless, hypocrisy is still our worst enemy in building the kingdom of God. Let me illustrate this fact with a real historical situation.

Hypocrisy was an accepted behavior pattern in the Renaissance. It introduced a new kind of Christianity. Using poetic liberty, Renaissance hypocrites portrayed Jesus as an emperor, the Father as a pagan god, and the Holy Spirit as the inspirer of art, eroticism, and hedonism, which were regarded as a theophany. Discipleship was replaced with lavishness, extravagance, and splendour. The artistic ideals of sensual love as they appears from paintings of that period became synonymous with Christlikeness.[16] However, by killing the biblical God, the people also blotted out biblical hope, love, and joy, and in their place arose lingering anxiety, fear, and angst from suppressed feelings of meaninglessness, hopelessness, and guilt. The replacement of the Christian conscience with a Freud-Machiavellian superego removed the spiritual armour that protects from such conditions. Respectively, the foretaste of Judgment Day is documented in paintings like Durer's *Apocalypse* or Grunewald's *The Crucifixion*, which still provoke apocalyptic horror even in twenty-first century viewers.[17]

Hypocrisy is timeless. Postmodern societies suffer from it in often unrecognized forms.

(2) As Hans Vaihinger says in *The Philosophy of "As If,"* "People live by fictions (or views of how the world should be)."[18] Even our social lives are full of small, conventional deceptions. In this context, Guilmartin noted the response of a client to the usual question "How are you?"

> You really want to know how I am? I'll tell you how I am. I feel like I am losing it most of the time! I want to scream at my brother, scream at my doctors. I feel sad and empty. I've got to deal with medical policies, insurance, hospital administrators, my family, my mom, and somewhere in there my so-called normal life. So tell me, just how do I answer this question? Do I tell you how I really am? Or do I do what most of us do and smile and grimace a little and sigh, "Oh, I'm fine holding up."[19]

(3) Such seemingly conventional and innocent deceptions gradually multiply and consume many of our social interactions, conditioning us to live an "as if" lifestyle. People politely smile at each other on the streets as if they are happily greeting. They behave professionally in the office as if they are committed to serving their customers. They bear children as if multiplying life has a purpose. They purchase products as if they really need what they buy. They ask "How are you?" as if they are really interested in the answer. And they attend church as if they really try to live like Christ. Playing "as if" roles is most often a harmless social convention. Nevertheless, it often makes social behaviors insincere and inauthentic so

that "yes" does not always mean "yes" and "no" does not always mean "no." Hypocrites exaggerate and abuse such social "as if" patterns for Luciferian selfish and abusive purposes.

(4) As medicine heals disorders, helping patients not to be sick but to be healthy, so too should pastoral disciplines. In this effort, however, our purpose is not to close our eyes to reality, disregard problems, or escape into denial. On the contrary, we need to be radically open to acknowledging challenges, like that of hypocrisy, which is a danger not only for the world but also for the Church and for all Christians. In this context, let me illustrate the trap of hypocrisy that makes it hard to say whether it is more an intentional sin or a self-deceptive sickness by discussing a shocking historical event portrayed by the novelist Janos Erdody.

A group of horsemen arrived in the late hours of April 26, 1478, led by two high-ranking clerics: Roman Cardinal Raffaele Riario and the Bishop of Pisa, Francesco Salviati. They met secretly with a group of other assassins to synchronize their actions aiming to kill the rulers of Florence, the Medici brothers. The cardinal proposed a cunning plan to invite the Medicis to a solemn mass at the Santa Maria del Fiore church in Florence and there subsequently stab them to death. The signal for assassination would be given by Cardinal Riario by lifting the host at transubstantiation during the holy mass. Erdody reports Cardinal Riario's words justifying the plot: "It is a painful necessity that such a sad event must happen in God's house. But if this is the only way to serve the Church then assassination is a noble task, assisting the well-being of Florence, Europe, of the whole humankind." To eradicate a greater evil (the Medici brothers) for the Church and humankind, the Machiavellian assassins felt obliged to choose the smaller evil: eradicating the evil brothers. The plot occurred as proposed by the cardinal. When he lifted the holy host, the assassins attacked. One of the brothers, Giuliano, was killed, but Lorenzo Medici escaped and organized a bloody revenge.[20]

Pondering this scandalous event, we need to stop for a moment and make an apologetic digression. The incident gives us an opportunity to discuss a question pastoral healers are asked equally by Christians and atheists: How, in the Holy Body of Christ, could such unholy events happen, and how similarly outrageous events like child abuse happen today?

The Vatican II document *Lumen gentium* helps to answer this difficult question. It reads:

> Christ, "holy, innocent and undefiled" (Heb. 7:26), knew nothing of sin (2 Cor. 5:21), but came only to expiate the sins of the people (Heb. 2:17). The church, however, clasping sinners to her bosom, at once holy and always in need of purification, follows constantly the path of penance and renewal.[21]

The document "presents a twofold vision of the church, as 'holy in Christ' and 'sinful in its members.'"[22] Cardinal Hans Urs von Balthasar similarly states:

> There exists within the visible Church two opposing spirits, such as Augustine describes, following the Bible of the old and new covenant, as the battle between two civitates; and the Spiritual Exercises of Ignatius (more spiritually) as the opposition of the two casts of mind, one the Luciferian, the will to power; the other, the Christian, the will to poverty, abasement, and humility.[23]

Accordingly, there are two aspects of the visible Church. One aspect is biblical, "holy, innocent, and undefiled" as *Lumen gentium* defines it, while the other is caused by the Church's "clasping sinners to her bosom." Sinners bring with them their hypocritical behaviors, and von Balthazar therefore calls this aspect the "nonchurch." This is the answer to our question. Giuliano Medici's assassination happened not in the Church, which is "holy in Christ," but in the nonchurch, the Church's sinful members. The nonchurch's hypocrisy is the diametrical opposite of the biblical Church (i.e., the body of Christ's holiness). The two aspects can still, however, intersect because the body of Christ is not isolated by an iron curtain. We sinners behaviorally exit and reenter the metaphorical curtain separating the

Church from the nonchurch, sometimes unaware of our movements and other times aware and hypocritically disguising them.

(5) A Machiavellian self-deceptive hypocrisy can justify and explain away almost any selfishness, psychological problem, and sin. People putting on a mask of moral perfection eventually identify themselves by their masks. They become so accustomed to their hypocrisy that any sick or sinful behavior performed in their role-playing is for them (like for Cardinal Riario) almost justified, normal, necessary, and even ethical. The first step in helping hypocrites in such deep denial is to help them see themselves from a new perspective: that they are not only sinners but also sick sinners.

(6) The primary task of the healer in cases of hypocrisy is establishing an accepting, nonjudgmental, and compassionate therapeutic alliance with the patient. In this effort, it is often helpful to start communication with an exploration of the patient's background: his childhood and other formative experiences; his disappointments and frustrations; and other psychological promoters of hypocrisy, such as low self-esteem, hypomania, depression, anxiety, or irrational guilt, facilitating defensive two-faced attitudes. Also, borderline, schizoid, antisocial, paranoid, anxiety, and dissociative disorders, as well as personality traits ought to be addressed. In healing these ailments, professional help may be needed.

(7) We could summarize the pastoral healing of hypocritical believers in three steps. Since the self-esteem of hypocrites often oscillates between self-deceptive self-satisfaction and equally extreme but denied or suppressed guilt, healing often initially consists of encouraging not so much self-critical authenticity (what clients and patients are unable to exercise at this stage of healing) as "fighting the good fight of faith" (1. Tim. 6:12). This means striving, despite all imperfections, to be worthy of being known by God. Thus, the first step in healing may be increasing Christian self-esteem, provoking a longing for fullness of citizenship in the kingdom of God, and appreciating that Jesus died for hypocrites as well. The purpose of such a supportive approach is to decrease resistance to self-scrutiny.

(8) The second step in hypocrites' pastoral healing may be approached gradually by applying Matthew 7:20, recognizing bad trees (hypocrisy) by their bad fruits (a lack of receiving and reflecting biblical gifts sourcing

from union with Jesus). However, hypocrisy is always characterized by the use of countless defence mechanisms that prevent subjects from doing just that. So what can be done to resolve this seemingly unresolvable difficulty? How can hypocrites' denials, rationalizations, projections, and other self-deceptive defences be softened?

The Florentine assassins could deceive themselves in almost everything, but not in hearing positive feedback from their Christian consciences. It is impossible that the assassins felt the biblical gifts of the Spirit when plotting against their neighbours. It is also impossible that they were feeling biblical joy, empathy, peace, or love during their attempt to stab the Medici brothers to death. The admonition of Matthew 7:20 prevents hypocrites from experiencing good fruits from bad deeds. A cautious, gentle, Jesus-like confrontation with the bad fruits they bring is almost impossible for hypocrites to disregard.

In this self-scrutinizing process, what is needed is a long-lasting Socratic dialogue that helps subjects recognize when they are being "bad trees" and grasp that only a humble, repentant, and brokenhearted turning to Jesus and fulfilling of his main commands (Mark 12:29–31) can convert their living an ultimately meaningless life into a joyful foretaste of Jesus' forgiveness.

(9) As the third step, pastoral healing must focus, on the one hand, on curing the sick psychological causes of greed, jealousy, and the reckless seeking of success, power, luxury, prestige, and pomp and, on the other hand, positioning the patient to receive positive feedback from their Christian consciences, like the gifts of biblical peace, love, and joy. Committed Christian clients may also be coached in applying the biblical truth, "whenever I am weak, I am strong" (2 Cor. 12:10), which requires bringing them to appreciate exactly what they were previously resisting, like biblical humility, altruism, and love as summarized in the constitution of Gods' kingdom in Matthew 5:1–12 (Jesus' blessings). The blessedness that stems from such a biblical purpose far supersedes the mirage of worldly pleasure and happiness. The more clients receive biblical gifts in increasing abundance, the more they strive to live the ultimate truth of Jesus-like loving. This rationale seems, from a purely psychological perspective, unrealistic. However, similar patterns are observed regularly in virtually all successful pastoral healings since the Holy Spirit facilitates them.

(10) It is helpful for hypocritical believers to integrate themselves into the community of the people of God. As they do, pastoral healers may help them grasp what Jesus talks about in Matthew 20:16: "The last will be the first, and the first will be the last." Accepting and even intentionally trying to take on the position of the last and smallest in a community paradoxically gives them the authentic optimism, courage, and strength that they, as self-deceptive hypocrites, were missing. These biblical gifts then continually enforce their new Christlike lifestyle.

(11) The pastoral healing of Christian hypocrites is often difficult, with improvements and relapses. Not every intervention is as successful as healers hope for. Nevertheless, despite their intentionally-committed sins and unintentional sickness, hypocrites strive for ultimate joy like everyone else and even in their self-deceptive ways seek Jesus. So even resistant, stubborn, and seemingly unhealable hypocrites may also count on "God Whose Name Is Mercy."[24]

Notes

[1] Frederik Copleston, *A History of Philosophy* (Paramus, New York: Newman Press, 1975), 17.

[2] John W. Whitehead *True Christianity,* (Whestchester, IL, Crossway Books, 1989), 33

[3] Viktor E. Frankl, *Aerztliche Seelsorge* (Vienna: Franz Deuticke, 1965), 76.

[4] Louis P. Pojman, *Classics of Philosophy* (New York: Oxford University Press, 2003), 20.

[5] Will Durant, *The Story of Philosophy* (New York: Washington Square Press, 1953), 20–1.

[6] Pojman, *Classics of Philosophy*, 241.

[7] Ibid., 496.

[8] Copleston, *A History of Philosophy*, 164.

[9] Pojman, *Classics of Philosophy*, 566.

[10] Ibid., 820.

[11] F. L. Cross and E. A. Livingstone, *The Oxford Dictionary of the Christian Church* (New York: Oxford University Press, 1997), 919.

[12] Hans Vaihinger, *Die Philosphie Des Als Ob* (Berlin: Reuter & Reichard, 1921).

[13] Joseph Ratzinger, *Behold the Pierced One: An Approach to Spiritual Christology* (San Francisco, CA: Ignatius, 1986), 55.

[14] *Oxford American Dictionary*, Heald Colleges Edition, the most authoritative paperbound dictionary of American usage (New York: Oxford University Press, 1980).

[15] Erdody, *Requiem Firenzeert*, 150–2. See also Ungar, *Flawed Institution—Flawless Church*, 73-[16] Ibid., 71–2.

[17] Robert Fossier, *The Cambridge Illustrated History of the Middle Ages,* vol. III, 125–1520 (Cambridge: Cambridge University Press, 2006), 511–12. See also Ungar, *Flawed Institution—Flawless Church*, 98–9.

[18] Gerald Corey, *Theory and Practice of Counseling and Psychotherapy* (Thomson Brooks/Cole. Thomson Learning Academic Resource Center, 2005), 96.

[19] Nance Guilmartin, *Healing Conversations: What to Say When You Don't Know What to Say* (San Francisco: Jossey-Bass, 2002), 496.

[20] Erdody, *Requiem Firenzeert*, 61–2. See also Ungar, *Flawed Institution—Flawless Church*, 91–2.

[21] Luigi Accatoli, *When a Pope Asks Forgiveness: The Mea Culpa of John Paul II* (Boston: Pauline Books and Media, 1998), 30. See also Ungar, *Flawed Institution—Flawless Church*, 28.

[22] Accatoli, *When a Pope Asks Forgiveness*, 30. See also Ungar, *Flawed Institution—Flawless Church*, 28.

[23] Hans Urs von Balthasar, *Church and World* (Montreal: Palm Publishers, 1967), 14. See also Ungar, *Flawed Institution—Flawless Church*, 29.

[24] Pope Francis, *The Name of God Is Mercy* (New York: Random House, 2016).

PART FIVE

PASTORAL-PSYCHOLOGICAL ASPECTS OF EVANGELIZATION

So the question is evident: how can pastoral healers help in healing the psychological reasons facilitating the current spiritual crisis and help the postmodern evangelization of God-alienated people? To answer this question, we will start from the very basics and gradually progress to the most intensive topics, applicable even in evangelizing hardcore atheists. Self-evidently, the methods we discuss ought to be tailored to every evangelizer's personal gifts and fitted to the psychological and spiritual needs in the new evangelizing of already-baptized Christians and the evangelizing of non-Christians.

CHAPTER FORTY

THE ANATOMY OF BELIEVING

O ften, we experience ambivalence when choosing between scientific
knowledge and personal, subjective belief. The difficulty with belief
exclusive of knowledge, though, is articulated by the words of Karl S.
Lashley: "Everything existing can be scientifically examined; if we cannot
explore a phenomenon by science, the only reason is that it does not exist at
all."[1] At the same time, the substantial importance of belief is emphasized by
the Hungarian poet Petofi, who said, "Liberty and love, these two I need. I
would give my life for my love, and would give my love for liberty."[2] Neither
liberty nor love are scientific cognitions. However, some beliefs are apparently more important for humans than life itself. So which perspective is
correct? Do we rely upon knowledge to determine what is true, as Lashley
advocates, or belief, like Petofi?

40.1 Beliefs versus Knowledge (Revisited)

From a philosophical perspective, human perception of reality consists of two components, that of "being" and "meaning." Psychologically,
we recognize being (that something "is," that it exists) by what Lashley
described sensorial-scientifically. On the contrary, we perceive meaning
(like love, hope, or courage) by what Petofi talks about, introspectively,

meta-empirically—beyond sensorial-scientific experiences—as beliefs. We use these philosophical and psychological terms interchangeable.

Despite their differences, the two philosophical and psychological cognitions are not mutually exclusive. Detecting being helps correct recognition of meaning, and vice versa, discerning the meaning of whatever thing facilitates recognition of its being. Thus, we cannot arbitrarily believe whatever we choose not only because of the stringent psychological-spiritual criteria of our Christian consciences, but also because being, that what externally "is," limits wishful thinking. Reciprocally, in every area of human cognition, the discerned meaning facilitates interest, cognition, and realization of being. For example, their meaning (i.e., beliefs) motivate the realization of astronomical, medical, political, economic, artistic, and other enterprises. Therefore, knowledge is not a counterweight or an enemy to beliefs but one of the essential constituents that shapes them. Reciprocally, beliefs ought not to contravene reasoning, but should be confirmed by empirical validation. All mental functions, including knowing and experiencing, need to be united and corroborate genuine, trustworthy, and correct beliefs, and vice versa. But how does the theory work in practice?

It is well known that scientific information (like that of Galileo, Darwin, or Freud) often shapes belief systems and, equally, one's "will to believe"[3] shapes his knowledge about the external world. The latter can be illustrated by the story of an experiment executed by two groups of psychologists. Prior to the experiment, one group of psychologists believed that animals were able to think. The other group believed they could only learn based on trial and error. When the monkey they were observing used a stick placed inside of its cage as a tool to reach a banana placed outside of its cage, the first group indeed claimed that the monkey acted on insight, while the others resolutely proclaimed that the monkey only reached the banana after trial and error.[4] Psychologically, experience did not shape the psychologists' beliefs; their internal beliefs determined what they externally, objectively, and scientifically recognized.

Sometimes, beliefs dictating the perception of reality can produce quite bizarre results. I vividly remember a picture in my high school biology textbook. It portrayed a picture of a corncob about two feet long, held at one end by the Soviet biologist Michurin and at the other end by his disciple. The picture of the gigantic corncob was meant to vividly demonstrate the success of Soviet scientists. It was obviously impossible to do so, but those who decided to believe in the bright future of communism accepted it.

Something similar has happened concerning believers and nonbelievers. Their different beliefs have determined their information about the most essential aspect of reality: whether God exists. A similar process is occurring among Christians. For example, although it is a rule of exegesis that one's religious beliefs be shaped according to Scripture, unfortunately it is often the other way around: Scripture is interpreted according to one's belief system. Today, we have more than 20,000 Christian denominations interpreting the same Bible slightly or significantly differently according to their respective standards. Such practices have caused great social and religious catastrophes in Christian history. The following is one example.

In the sixteenth century, the Anabaptists established their New Zion—their perception of God's kingdom—in the German city of Munster. In response, the expelled bishop, Franz von Waldeck, mobilized his soldiers, and between 1534 and 1535 laid siege to the Anabaptists' fortifications, draining Munster of ammunition, food, and other vital supplies. Jan Matthys, one of the Anabaptists' leaders, believing he was the second Gideon, led a charge with twelve of his followers against the Catholic troops but was beheaded. The Anabaptists perceived these events as signs of the fulfilment of apocalyptic prophecies and legalized polygamy and cannibalism in the starving city. Some even stood at the city walls attempting to catch artillery shells fired against New Zion with their bare hands, all the while singing psalms and prayers. Finally, the city fell. Some of the Anabaptist leaders' dead bodies were put in cages and hanged from church steeples so that everyone could see that the right denomination triumphed. [5]

Only a short time later, the Thirty Years' War (1618–1648) engulfed all of Europe. Catholic and Protestant troops killed each other mercilessly in the name of Christ, interpreting their Bibles according to their distorted

Luciferian belief systems. Consequently, 40 percent of the European population perished, and a period of widespread doubt in the validity of Christian worldviews called the Enlightenment started.

These events illustrate the paramount power of perverted beliefs. They dictate behaviors that contradict not only a sound, rational, logical, discretional, and appreciative judgment, but above all, the Christian conscience, God's command of love, and all principles of Christlike living. This applies also to the contemporary mental climate whose irrational and nonsensical belief systems significantly contribute to postmodern people's collisions with the objective and stringent realities of life and thus cause countless psychological, social, religious, political, economic, and medical problems. We will later discuss in detail the psychological criteria of correct beliefs, correct interpretation of Scripture, correct discipleship, and correct evangelistic approaches to religious dilemmas. Let us first, however, look at where the immense power of belief stems from.

Humans perceive the most important things in life internally and subjectively, in their hearts, minds, and souls more so than externally, sensorially, and scientifically. Optimism, love, hope, beauty, freedom, meaning, ideals, tastes, hobbies, responsibility, preferences, patriotism, political attitudes, romantic attraction, faith, and connection with God, all of which contribute to making life worth living, are not facilitated by objective scientific observations alone but also by one's internal attitudes and belief systems. It is impossible, for instance, to scientifically, rationally, or logically convince people that they are loved by their spouses or that they love their spouses if they internally perceive the opposite. Love is an internal evidence immune to and stronger than scientific proof. Similarly, it is impossible to heal an obsessive, phobic, or scrupulous person by saying, "Oh, in reality this is nothing. It is only real in your subjective belief." The paramount power of subjective belief systems most often overwhelms all scientific, rational, or logical arguments. Even the proponents of Lashley need to seek answers where science stops giving solutions. Even for them, belief is the answer to the ultimate questions of the human being. This confirms our conclusion: the most crucial things in human life are experienced not externally, sensorially or scientifically, but by a strong internal and introspective evidence called belief systems.

The noted practical and historical examples demonstrate a mixed influence of beliefs. Genuine beliefs give purpose and ultimate value to human life that science is unable to consider or grasp, but dysfunctional beliefs have the power to overrule even the most obvious rational, logical, and moral facts. This makes belief systems in the positivist culture of the twenty-first century seem arbitrary, unreliable, and worthless.

40.2 Beliefs: Genuine Recognition or Private Delusion?

In his 1897 presentation "Will to Believe," William James said that "life would be greatly impoverished" without belief.[6] Gerald Corey even more poignantly notes that humans "can be fully understood only in the light of knowing the purpose and goals toward which we are striving."[7] The purpose of humans is to fulfil whatever they believe. They can be fully understood only by their intimate beliefs that act as powerful personal discernments. However, in the previous section we also observed a risk factor in belief convictions—the paramount power of perverted beliefs to dictate behaviors that contradict virtually all principles of Christlike loving and living. Thus, it is a crucial task to distinguish between our true and false beliefs. Let us take a look at this distinction first from a politically correct perspective.

Unlike the times of the Old Testament Hebrews, our times resemble Rome in the fourth century. During that time, the Greeks had their own gods, as did the Egyptians, Germans, Assyrians, Celts, Persians, and all other nations united under Pax Romana. The Romans, however, believed that none of these gods was genuine. In our times, people living in contemporary Western cultures have the right to believe whatever they want. Nevertheless, their religious beliefs, while socially tolerated, are regarded as egalitarian in their insignificance. Do we really, though, have the ability to convince ourselves of whatever we will or choose?

If we could believe whatever we choose, then a biblical sinner like Saul could have simply blotted out his guilty feelings when persecuting Christians and would have lived on happily as if nothing happened. Externally, all biblical and contemporary people could enact whatever they wanted to believe, but internally none could choose their beliefs or avoid bearing the consequences of their behaviors. As noted, our cultural climate propagates the opposite view, that people arbitrarily choose, believe, and trust whatever they want. Albert Ellis notes that "if a person experiences depression after a divorce, for example, it may not be the divorce itself that causes the depressive reaction, but the person's beliefs about being a failure, being rejected, or losing their mate. Thus, human beings are largely responsible for creating their own emotional reactions and disturbances."[8] Ellis hits the nail on the head in his second sentence—people are largely responsible for fabricating their own frustrations by accepting false beliefs as true. However, it is hard to agree with his first sentence. In my practice, I have never seen a divorce not caused by clear failure, rejection, or loss of a mate. Healthy humans are not self-deceptive. They are not like dissociated people, who escape from reality, and are even less like schizophrenics, who react with euphoria to sad events. If Ellis' proposal were possible, then beliefs would really be private delusions.

If we could arbitrarily believe whatever we choose, all marriage problems, all depression, all guilty feelings, all suicidal ideas, and all disorders and dysfunctional beliefs listed in the DSM-5 would be easy to heal. All humans would live in a self-chosen fantasy world, and nobody would be disappointed, divorced, disenchanted, sad, or frustrated. But we are all confronted with the stringent elemental forces of reality, and escaping into a happy kindergarten mindset is not possible. So what then are these stringent internal criteria that our beliefs adhere to as scientific recognitions that are adjusted to objective external criteria?

Virtually all disorders included in the DSM-5 have one commonality: dysfunctional beliefs facilitating the transgression of Jesus' basic commands in Mark 12:29–31. On the contrary, Adam and Eve's inheritance of being "like God, knowing good and evil" (Gen. 3:5) fuels all dysfunctional beliefs and motivates all unloving, unforgiving, and aggressive (unchristlike) behaviors. When sin and sickness of the mind are more powerful than Jesus' explicit command of love, such as Christians fighting each other in religious wars, a split personality similar to that of schizophrenia is produced.

461

With it, the sound, informed, rational, logical, discretional, and appreciative judgment of the Christian conscience is disregarded by selfishness and a Luciferian will to power," or being "like God, knowing good and evil" (Gen. 3:5).

With this information, let us ask: are beliefs a genuine recognition or a private delusion?

To paraphrase Karl Rahner, Jesus' law of love is the ultimate integrating factor in the history of all true human belief and behavioral systems.[9] Jesus' love is present in all true belief systems, or, to put it another way, all true beliefs, overtly or not, point toward Christianity and are true insofar as they carry the teaching of Christ hidden within them. Respectively, whether particular beliefs are delusional or a recognition of highest validity depends on whether they derive their validity from an inner connection with the ultimate truth of Jesus Christ. In the next section, let us test this seemingly overstated position.

40.3 A Reality Test of Beliefs

God has given us free will and entrusted us with using all the gifts in the world he created. While many things are available to us as Christians and can be misused, the fully-trained disciple can handle the temptations. This is analogous to the experience of Jesus' twelve apostles. To follow him, they abandoned family, homes, towns, professions—even their sins and former, nonproductive ways of living. In following Jesus, they were surely brought back to many of the very towns and situations they had abandoned. Nowhere do any of the four gospels record that the apostles were unable to deal with the reexposure to their previous ways of living; they were steadfastly committed to their new belief systems, called discipleship. Every individual believes that his beliefs are genuinely true. But what gave the apostles such strong evidence that their beliefs were true? Knowing as we do, how do we distinguish between true and false, right and wrong, and genuine or destructive beliefs? Let us start by illustrating the distinction with a profane example.

At the Battle of Waterloo, Napoleon hoped to first defeat the British and then the Prussian troops. The Prussians, however, reached the battlefield before the British were defeated. When it became obvious that the British and Prussian armies would unite against the much smaller French army, Napoleon allegedly cried out, "Futile hope!"

What really caused Napoleon's futile hope? Our first intuitive response would be that it was a mistake in his military or tactical judgment. From a pastoral perspective, however, the reasons are much deeper: his false hope was the effect of a spiritual-biblical cause.

According to Freud's anthropological model, the crucial role in forming Napoleon's false beliefs was played by his self. It had to satisfy his instinct's need to win but not collide with the superego (calculating if it would pay off) and adjust his behaviors to the conditions of the external reality (position him to achieve his chosen goals). However, would perfect satisfaction of instinct, obedience to the superego, and adjustment to external reality have freed Napoleon from false beliefs and their resulting disappointments?

No. The precondition for genuinely avoiding all false hopes and beliefs is Christian morality (i.e., resolving sick and sinful beliefs and behaviors). This requires not only a perfectly-functioning instinct, ego, and superego-type conscience, but obedience to a Holy Spirit-directed, biblically informed Christian conscience that enables saintlike behavior. The common reason for almost all dysfunctional moral beliefs and behaviors is, as the Catechism formulates, that "moral conscience remains in ignorance" when "errors of moral conscience" occur in the case of an "enslavement to one's passions." In other words, it is as if the moral conscience is blind, giving way to countless false discretional and appreciative judgments and self-deceptions. On the other hand, adhering to the Christian conscience is the precondition of discipleship. In this position, virtually all Christians are united.

The *Catechism of the Catholic Church* defines conscience as the "aboriginal vicar of Christ."[10] The Protestant version (for example, Luther's formulation) notes that conscience is a place "where we must live with God as man and wife."[11] In orthodox Christian understanding, even the Last Judgment, as St. Basil the Great predicted, will occur internally, in the conscience.[12] In this context, obeying the Christian conscience is of the highest epistemological value. It makes it possible to "believe the good news" (Mark 1:15), empirically corroborated by biblical love, joy, peace, and other spiritual gifts.

Respectively, a well-informed Christian conscience, like that adopted by the twelve apostles, is metaphorically like a "moral wildcard," able to correct all kinds of ethical mistakes and, accordingly, all the kinds of false purposes, beliefs, and behaviors we call sick and sinful. The conscience does not provide lexical knowledge or "know how" in accomplishing mathematical, scientific, or physical goals (such as how to win the Battle of Waterloo), but a wisdom of living in union with Jesus and building his kingdom of biblical love, peace, and joy. Thus, Christian conscience has a unique importance. It is a paramount internal criterion discerning reality from a biblical perspective. It helps shape meaningful beliefs, which facilitate right cognition of everyday reality, all verified by biblical gifts of the Spirit. Christian beliefs are adjusted to as stringent internal criteria as scientific recognitions are adjusted to objective external criteria.

Let us observe whether or not these formulations are confirmed by everyday reality. If Judas, the prodigal son, or King David had directed their behaviors according to their well-informed consciences, then they and their neighbours would not have had to pay bitter prices for their dysfunctional beliefs and behaviors. Adherence to a well-informed Christian conscience would also be the best guarantee of healing for the persistently-depressed Tammy (Preface), Daniel M'Naghten, Jeffrey Dahmer (Ch. 5), and all non-psychotic disorders listed by the DSM-5. In the case of Napoleon, if he had been striving to fulfil Jesus' main commands (Mark 12:29–31) independently of his military blunder, he could have escaped the tragedy of all his mistaken beliefs at Waterloo. In other words, if Napoleon, Tammy, Daniel M'Naghten, Jeffrey Dahmer, and those suffering from DSM-5 disorders had primarily focused on applying biblical directives in building God's kingdom, such as "Love the Lord your God with all your heart and all your strength," and "Love your neighbour as yourself," such commitment would surely have saved them (and millions of others) from limitless pain, suffering, and tragedy. Neither Jan Matthys, the Anabaptists rebelling in Munster, nor their opponents could have deceived themselves into biblical loving their neighbours as themselves while carrying out bloodthirsty murder against each other; they must have been aware that they were disregarding God's command of love, peace, and forgiveness. Napoleon deceived himself in many things, but it is quite impossible that he held Jesus-like love in his heart at Waterloo. So yes, the self, ego, I, and personality have the power to cheat, mislead, or deceive an individual in interpreting and respecting the Christian conscience, but such self-deception cannot be gratified by biblical hope, forgiveness, peace, joy, and love. Internally, as with Judas, the prodigal son, King David, M'Naghten, Dahmer, Tammy, and Napoleon, biblical gifts of faith cannot be experienced while transgressing the voice of the Christian conscience. If, though, sickness and sin can cause even the conscience to be erroneously interpreted, what is the psychological criterion of correct interpretation of the Christian conscience?

Everyone has the freedom to disobey his Christian conscience, but no one has the freedom to disregard the consequences of that choice. This makes the judgment of the Christian conscience (verified by receiving or losing biblical gifts) the supreme inspector of reality and religious beliefs. Receiving biblical optimism, peace, hope, love, and joy are exclusive consequences of progressing in fulfilling Jesus' commands and of Christlike living. This exclusivity constitutes an internal criterion, limiting erroneous, self-deceptive, or arbitrary interpretation of conscience, soul, and God's guidance. The most substantial common task in evangelization is helping to grasp the conscience's commands of the evangelizer and the evangelized person as a genuine expression of Mark 12:29–31: "Love the Lord your God with all your heart and all your strength" and "Love your neighbour as yourself." If this happens, then most private delusions will be resolved, and our task of evangelization will be completed, evangelized people having consciences analogous to that of Jesus' twelve apostles

Notes

[1] Lajos Kardos, *Behaviorismus* (Budapest: Gondolat Konyvkiado, 1970), 17.

[2] Sandor Petofi, *Petofi Sandor Osszes Koltemenyei* (Budapest: Oziris Kiado Kft, 2007), 217.

[3] Gerald Corey, *Theory and Practice of Counseling and Psychotherapy* (Thomson Brooks/Cole. Thomson Learning Academic Resource Center, 2005), 132.

[4] Lajos Kardos, *Behaviorizmus* (Budapest, Gondolat Konyvkiado, 1970), 147–9.

[5] August Franzen, *Kleine Kirchngeschihte* (Freiburg; Herder Bucherei, 1968), 23–34. See also Paul Ungar, *Flawed Institution—Flawless Church: A Response to Pope John Paul's Appeal for a Critical Self-Evaluation of the Church* (Newcastle Upon Tyne: Cambridge Scholars Publishing, 2013), 77–8.

[6] Corey, *Theory and Practice of Counseling and Psychotherapy*, 132.

[7] Ibid., 122.

[8] Ibid., 274.

[9] Joseph Ratzinger, *Truth and Tolerance; Christian Belief and World Religions* (San Francisco: Ignatius Press, 2004), 49–52.

[10] Canadian Conference of the Catholic Bishops, *Catechism of the Catholic Church* (Ottawa: Publications Service, Canadian Conference of Catholic Bishops, 1994), 377.

[11] Lindsay Jones (ed.), *Encyclopedia of Religion*, vol. 3 (Farmington Hills, MI: Thomson Gale, 2005), 1941.

[12] Mary Cuningham and Elizabeth Theokritoff. *The Cambridge Companion to the Orthodox Christian Faith* (New York: Cambridge University Press, 2008), 113.

CHAPTER FORTY-ONE

Why Does Being Human
Involve Seeking God?

Let us now focus on an even more unique human phenomenon than belief: religion. In everyday life, people who unswervingly and obstinately insist that they experience anything but physical reality are considered either seriously confused or delusional. Yet this is exactly how religious people are regarded. God is invisible, untouchable, immeasurable. He is virtually nonexistent, nothingness. So what psychologically motivates *Homo sapiens* to be *homo religious* and seek a basic relationship with a deity whose intrinsic quality is that he is completely ineffable?

Most Christians would respond: "We believe because we love God." Factually, reciprocating God's love is the last step in the evolution of faith. But what motivates us to make the first step and consider whether God exists? In other words, what prompted Stone Age people just as contemporary atheists to ponder whether a transcendental deity exists?

41.1 Angst, the Form of the Human Being

The little-known pagan Roman poet Albius Tibullus (55–19 BC) wrote, "First the gods created fear."[1] His observation was justified because fear is such a widespread phenomenon among non-Christians that it is as if it were the first and most universal creation of the pagan gods. It results in an array of unpleasant experiences and takes many nuanced forms, which are as follows.

(1) Fear itself is a biologically useful and necessary experience that helps protect life. It can be defined as an unpleasant feeling of existential threat, which is usually focused on a particular external cause that the subject is able to pinpoint and defend against. When functioning protectively, rational fear always has a beginning and an end in the sense that it lasts only as long as security is not reestablished, contrary to neverending irrational fear. For example, if an individual experiences fear because he is standing on the track of an oncoming train, stepping out of the danger zone puts an end to the fear.

(2) *Anxiety*, as defined by Sadock, Sadock, and Ruiz is a "feeling of apprehension caused by anticipation of a danger, which may be internal or external."[2] Anxiety signals a factually-existing challenge, threat, or danger, or the possibility of a no-win situation in the near future. The cause of anxiety is most often both external and internal. For example, anxiety prior to an exam may be the result of the risk of failing (external) and performance anxiety (internal). While externally-caused anxiety is generally useful, internally-caused anxiety is usually counterproductive, inhibiting and disabling appropriate functioning.

(3) *Angst* "is a Danish and German word whose meaning lies between the English words dread and anxiety."[3] It represents an invisible, untouchable, immeasurable, and nonexistent but nevertheless real future threat, like that of death. It is an omnipresent awareness, sadness, worry, concern, sorrow, torment, uneasiness, or apprehension. Protecting oneself from such an abstract and unknown future threat to life is hard. Martin Heidegger, in his book *Being and Time*, notes that while fear "discloses a particular aspect of the world as threatening, one does not feel angst about anything specific. 'Angst is oppressive and stifles one's breath—and yet it is nowhere.'" It relates to pure being—angst is "being in the world itself."[4] Therefore, as Eric summarizes, angst is the form of human being.[5]

(4) *Horror* is the experience of extreme fear that produces irrational instinctually-regulated defence reactions. For example, a lady fearful of

horses unexpectedly encountered a horse and rider while pedalling her bicycle. She covered both eyes with her hands and started to pedal as fast she could, falling from her bicycle in the process. In her case, the fear was so strong that it inhibited any meaningful defensive reaction. Horror can be expressed in the form of general inhibition or as a storm of useless, self-defeating movements, as in her case.

(5) *Panic* in a crowd is caused by realizing danger and amplified by the experience of personal helplessness and powerlessness. For example, a horrified cry of "Fire!" in a crowded movie theatre has a more terrifying effect than the actual observation of the threat of fire. In crowds, individual fear is exponentially multiplied by the horror of those nearby, provoking competition for personal survival that disregards the well-being of others.

Most variants of fear have a useful evolutionary role. Angst, however, is an exception as it does not help in the survival of the fittest. Therefore, the question of its purpose emerges. If it has no purpose in preserving life, why has it not disappeared in evolution?

41.2 Responses to Angst through History

Angst was first described by Robert Burton (1577–1640) in his work *The Anatomy of Melancholy*. He defines angst as a "fear without reason," for which we gave the example of the omnipresent threat of death. In human life, despite all insecurities, there exists one certainty: it ends with death. Death is factually a nothingness in the here and now, which means its threat cannot be resolved by rational means, and when death does approach, it is already too late to react to it. Angst regarding it is at the same time useless and hopeless. Since an efficient defence is not possible against an abstract threat in the present, the resolution of angst is also not possible.[6] Angst is a lifelong challenge—an ever-unfolding, virtually unsolvable, unpleasant experience. Blaise Pascal articulates this well in Section II of his *Thoughts* under the title "The Misery of Man without God." He writes, "Humans are similar to prisoners, waiting in chains to be executed while in the meantime watching the executions of others ... if there is greatness in man, this is 'in that he knows himself to be miserable.'"[7]

The Danish philosopher Soren Kierkegaard (1813–1855) distinguished "being" (like plants or animals) from "existing" (like an individual), characterized by making responsible choices. Neither of these forms of being is painless. The consequences of impersonal being for humans are "boredom, dread, and despair." Existing, on the contrary, evokes anguished dread in decision-making. It is like "standing at the edge of an abyss called 'decision'—whether to choose freedom or retreat back to the safety of the familiar." From anguished dread a "person can be rescued only by the act of choosing." The one who avoids the risk of choice "is avoiding life, and despair—the 'sickness unto death'—is the inevitable consequence." Kierkegaard pessimistically labels angst as the consequence of the freedom of choice and of the responsibility of undertaking actions despite unavoidably risking mistakes.[8] As his well-known statement from *Fear and Trembling* emphasizes, "If anyone on the verge of action should judge himself according to the outcome, he would never begin."

Kierkegaard's discouraging emotional pessimism echoes the thought of Georg Friedrich Wilhelm Hegel (1770–1831), who, in his *Science of Logic*, describes a paradox we use in every sentence with the word "is," meaning existence, or being. But what does the word "is" or "being" mean? The paradox he describes can be illustrated by the following example: Imagine a table. Subtract, one after the other, the table's properties, such as its shape, size, wood, colour, density, and every other property and consider only its bare existence. What do we have left? Mere "isness"—"existence." This is what the table has in common with every other thing in existence and what separates it from all nonexistent things. Therefore, pure being has in it no determinations or qualities whatsoever, for we have subtracted all these determinations from it. It is therefore completely indeterminate, vacant, and empty. It has no content whatsoever. It is simply nothing. The idea of being "therefore amounts for nothing." The pure "is" is pure nothingness.[9]

Thinkers of the twentieth century reacted to this self-defeating controversy in two different ways. Philosophers like Sartre, Heidegger, and Camus expressed nihilistic pessimism, while professionals like Yalom, Frankl, and May reacted with a meaningful optimism. Sartre (1905–1980), for example, in his seven-hundred-page book *Being and Nothingness* published in

1943, explained the reason for angst with an extrapolation of nothingness. Humans are "thrown into the world" but are consciously existing in it. Therefore, they are seeking reasons and purpose for our being. But we are "condemned to freedom," and live without being given a firm purpose to live for. We exist for nothing. The aimlessness of being human equals our all-permeating absurdity, estrangement, and angst "which accompany the consciousness of freedom."[10]

In contrast to Sartre, Frankl illustrated the tension between being and meaning with a biblical example. Exodus 14:19 describes Yahweh (the Angel of God) as a cloud leading the Hebrews through the Red Sea from Egyptian slavery to freedom in the Promised Land. The Hebrews could never reach the cloud; there was a constant gap between Yahweh and his people. If the Hebrews could have reached him, if the cloud would have been in the midst of the people, they would not have known which direction to move in. By remaining in front of his people, Yahweh showed them the direction in which to go. Indeed, the cloud's being always in front and unreachable created in the Hebrews a permanent divide between how they were and what they should become, between their being and the meaning they were to fulfil.[11]

Humans attempt to bridge the gap between being and meaning in many different ways. Freud described the "will to lust," Adler described the "will to power," and Frankl described, as his book titles reveal, the "will to meaning" and "will to ultimate meaning." He referenced Nietzsche's words: "The one who has a 'why' bears almost any 'how' in his life,"[12] implying that only one who has a strong purpose to live for can fully overcome pain, suffering, and disappointment.

41.3 Beating Angst: Responding to God's Calls

Frankl's teachings demonstrate that sceptics, agnostics, and atheists are metaphorically attempting to have being in the centre of their own existence. They determine what is morally good or evil, right or wrong, true or false, progressive or regressive, and healthy or sick, like the fictional Baron Munchausen (the baron of lies), who lifted himself by pulling his own hair.

Christians, on the contrary, follow the cloud in fulfilling their ultimate purpose—union with God. The life of sceptics is pure being without meaning. For them, in Eric's formulation, angst is genuinely the form of the human being, while for believers their form of being is trusting Jesus. This fact leads to a new, almost intuitive assumption: isn't it possible that as fear serves to protect biological life, so angst points human attention to everlasting life?

Seeking holiness contradicts all behavioral standards that the self, instinct, or the superego require. Faith is, from an atheist's worldly or materialist-evolutionist perspective, unnecessary and redundant. A Christlike lifestyle is counterproductive in the race for survival of the fittest. According to evolutionist principles, it should have disappeared from human behaviors a long time ago, but it did not. Billions of people of faith choose lifestyles that contradict all natural, biological, psychological, and sociological causes. Such an impressive effect of religious faith must have a cause. In the Christian understanding, it is believers responding positively to God's call. But how do people of faith hear God's call, while nonbelievers do not?

In all humans, action is a basic and imperative instinctual requirement to protect life. This paramount instinctual drive is challenged by the equally prominent awareness of unavoidable death, which evokes existential angst. Such angst emerges in both nonbelievers' and believers' lives. Their reactions to it, however, differ. Agnostic, sceptical, religiously indifferent, and apathetic people either wrestle like Sisyphus against existential threats or acknowledge their unavoidable aging and oncoming death. They either 1) perceive that, like Camus, "driven by the instinct for self-preservation, we never rest from having to face death,"[13] 2) escape into denial like Freud, who said, "The moment one inquires about the meaning of life, one is ill,"[14] or 3) resort to slander, like Richard Dawkins in his well-known book *The God Delusion*. Their beliefs prevented these protagonists from hearing God's calls.

While Camus, Freud, and Dawkins rely on their own (self-made) belief systems to answer the scientifically unanswerable ultimate questions of life facilitating their angst, Christians rely on biblical (Jesus-revealed) answers. Consequently, while Camus and Freud give pessimistic and nihilistic answers to ultimate questions of life, Christians discern bright and optimistic answers, they defeat angst by trusting Jesus. John 11:25–26 reads, "I [Jesus] am the resurrection and the life. He who believes in me will live, even though he dies; and whoever lives and believes in me will never die." This revelation is so real and evident to Christians that, as St. Paul described in Philippians 1:21 and 1:23, for them "to die is to gain," because in death they will "be with Christ, which is better by far." Thus, their beliefs enabled these protagonists to hear God's calls.

As noted, dysfunctional beliefs act like private delusions. They have the power to overrule even the most obvious, rational, logical, and moral facts. But how can we distinguish between true and false in this particular dispute? How can we distinguish which is more realistic: the pessimistic, nihilistic enslavement to a meaninglessness life of Camus, Freud, and Dawkins, or the Christian's triumphal victory over angst? How can we answer the crucial question of whether meaningless nature or a loving deity is raising in our minds these ultimate philosophical-theological questions that atheists and theists answer so differently?

Let me answer by sharing one of the saddest, most unsuccessful healing experiences of my whole career.

One of my first patients was a youngster who had attempted suicide. He was brought into the hospital's ICU and was unconscious. I fought for a few hours to save him. Finally, when he regained consciousness, I expected to hear him say, "Thank you for bringing me back from death!" But he shocked me by asking, "Why must I live? Why are you forcing me to live against my will?" My medical education taught me how to preserve human lives but nothing about the purpose someone ought to live for. I didn't know how I should respond, so I said very little. Following this, my patient was admitted to the psychiatric ward, but after few days he was discharged because he was neither psychotic nor depressed. Shortly after his discharge, he made a second suicide attempt. This time, he succeeded in killing himself.[15]

In the days that followed, I was tortured by the question of how I could have helped him and what I should have said to help him discern a purpose worth living for. I realized, though, that nothing in medicine, psychology, biology, philosophy, physics, or mathematics (that is, the whole natural world) could ask or give the answer he needed to hear; only God could. In other words, to answer ultimate questions of biological life biologically, humans could vegetate like intelligent animals or act like unprogrammed computers. But being living souls, they cannot. They must answer the question "Why do I live?" A satisfactory response to this question is not required and cannot be given by natural reality. But we are all called to see beyond natural reality and ask the ultimate questions of life that require the ultimate answer: the ultimate programmer who is God.

Thus, the element that was missing in my patient's life was a tangible—or at least mystical—sacred union with the almighty, eternal, and ultimate love of God. If he would have recognized the inquirer, God, he would have had everything in his life, but without giving the right response of faith and discipleship, he had nothing to live for. Although his psychological ailment occurred as a result of natural causes, it happened with a purpose—"so that the work of God might be displayed in his life" (Jn. 9:1–3).

Pope Benedict XVI made a similar observation: "Where there is no longer anything worth dying for, life is not worth living for."[16] Since existential angst, the feeling that life is not worth living for, is not healable by any worldly methods, this unavoidably points toward God, the only purpose worth dying for. Believers who experience the truth in Pope Benedict's words and the perpetual effects of God's love have no doubts about his existence; such genuine effects, such as as biblical optimism, peace, and joy, must have a genuine cause which they call God. In every area of human reasoning, facts that are perpetually proven true we call, not self-deceptions, illusions, or delusions, but correct recognitions. In the minds of Camus, Freud, or Dawkins, faith is the only exemption from this universal logical rule that we apply in every other area of sound reasoning.

Nevertheless, Frankl's creed is valid even in sceptics and lukewarm Christians, which is that even in an unknown form "behind the mask of disease, the spiritual person is always there."[17] The Spirit calls even skeptics not to be afraid (as people normally would be) of having to suffer or of being exploited. They can resist the Spirit's guidance but realize that what the world sees as a healthy fear of pain, poverty, unfairness, cruelty, sickness, and death is missing from disciples, who make a virtue of coping with their pain, and know that it is impossible to disregard. That committed Christians do not blame God for their misfortunes but rather perceive angst and anxiety as signs of their own failure to trust in God's loving providence is a form of witnessing that cannot be erased from atheists' hearts. The fact that real saints praised God for challenges in their lives because they were opportunities to grow in submission, faith, trust, and union with Jesus must have amazed Camus, Freud, or Dawkins by the mystery of faith. That with their lifestyle the disciples proved what Acts 5:41 describes—that overcoming sufferings grows faith, and that confronted with unavoidable sufferings the apostles were primarily concerned with conducting themselves "in a manner worthy of the gospel of Christ" (Phil. 1:21 and 1:30), proves that responding positively to God's calls is the greatest weapon against fear, pain, and despair—the forms of human being. Respectively, faith consists of two components. One is discerning God's call, and the other is behavioral (i.e., positively responding to it). Faith is God's action, which requires a positive human reaction. Even Christians are often mutually divided in attempting to grasp the mysterious interactions between supranatural and human components of faith. This illustrates the following supposition.

When you die, God will supposedly ask you: why do you think I should let you to enter the heaven? Some Christians would respond: because I was honest, I went to church every Sunday, I gave abundantly to charity, I prayed fervently, I tried to be unselfish, I genuinely attempted to live Christlike … and so on. For the other Christians all these answers are dead wrong. God would not let us into the heaven because of what we have done, but because of what Jesus has done for us. Can we resolve this controversy?

Evidently, *Jesus opened the gates of heaven for all humanity*, not human deeds. Therefore, being a recipient of God's love, of his calls, and of his grace is a human commonality. Christians include, while atheists exclude, themselves from this commonality. Thus, after Jesus enabled our justification, sanctification and salvation, a human choice and effort are also needed for discipleship. Our choice and efforts in accepting or rejecting faith, grace, and the Scriptures are substantial. Besides what Jesus has done for us, this basic choice all humans are confronted with constitutes faith, believing the Scriptures, and accepting God's grace.

All this, however, leads us to wonder that if God's call is as obvious and powerful as it seems to be to believers, what motivates countless atheists not to believe? Why are sceptics, agnostics, and religiously indifferent people so unsuccessful in hearing God's call and coming to know him? We will explore this in the next chapter.

Notes

1 Joseph Schwarz, *Durch Psychologie zum Gott, Argumente Fur Gottes Existenz* (Bishoofliches Ordinariat Eisenstadt, 1990), 26.

2 Benjamin James Sadock, Virginia Alcott Sadock, and Pedro Ruiz, *Kaplan and Sadock's Synopsis of Psychiatry: Behavioral Sciences/Clinical Psychiatry*, eleventh edition (Philadelphia, PA: Wolters Kluwer, 2015), *Behavior*274.

3 Gerald Corey, *Theory and Practice of Counseling and Psychotherapy* (Thomson Brooks/Cole. Thomson Learning Academic Resource Center, 2005), 132.

4 Adrian Tomer, Grafton T. Eliason, and Paul T. P. Wong (eds.), *Existential and Spiritual Issues in Death Attitudes* (New York: Lawrence Erlbaum Associates, 2008), 13.

5 Ljubomir Eric, *Strah, Anxioznost I Anxiozna Stanja* (Beograd Institut za Strucno Usavrsavanje I Specijalizaciju Zdravstvenih Radnika, 1972), 10.

6 Ibid., 11.

7 Tomer, Eliason, and Wong, *Existential and Spiritual Issues in Death Attitudes*, 13.

8 Ibid., 210–15.

9 Louis P. Pojman, *Classics of Philosophy* (New York: Oxford University Press, 2003), 914.

10 Ibid., 916.

[11] Maria Marshall and Edward Marshall, *Spiritual Psychotherapy: the Search for Lasting Meaning* (Canada, Ont.: Ottawa Institute of Logotherapy, 2015), 94–6.

[12] Ibid., 81.

[13] Joel Feinberg and Russ Shafer-Landau, *Reason and Responsibility: Readings in Some Basic Problems in Philosophy*, Tenth Edition (Belmont, CA: Wadsworth Publishing Company, 1999), 132.

[14] Maria Marshall and Edward Marshall, *Spiritual Psychotherapy: The Search for Lasting Meaning* (Canada, Ont.: Ottawa Institute of Logotherapy, 2015), 162

[15] Paul Ungar, *The Mystery of Christian Faith: A Tangible Union with the Invisible God* (Lanham, MD: University Press of America, 2008), 284–285

[16] Benedict XVI, *Benedictus, Day by Day with Pope Benedict XVI*, edited by Rev. Peter Cameron (New York: Magnificat, 2006), 79.

[17] Marshall and Marshall, *Spiritual Psychotherapy: The Search for Lasting Meaning*, 60

CHAPTER FORTY-TWO

THE ATHEIST'S FIASCO IN KNOWING GOD

The question raised at the end of the last chapter targets the psychology of approximately 3 percent of Americans who are genuine atheists, 5 percent of Americans who are agnostics, and 22 percent of Americans not affiliated with any religion.[1] Our question is "Why did they not succeed in establishing a fully fruitful relationship with God and the Church?"

Before we answer this question, let us discuss the obvious social reasons for atheism (such as how atheists interpret history and how they perceive Christianity) as well as individual reasons for denying God (i.e., to grasp what motivates atheists' resistance against Jesus).

42.1 The Collective Reasons for Atheism

A central topic of Jesus' ministry was proclaiming the kingdom of God. The New Testament mentions it more than 120 times. God's kingdom is not only a positive fact visible to everyone (Mk. 1:15), but "righteousness, peace and joy in the Holy Spirit" (Rom. 14:17). Jesus announced its closeness, but nevertheless we pray "your kingdom come, your will be done" (Mt. 6:10). Some elements of God's kingdom (like joy in the Holy Spirit) are already realized; others, like righteousness and peace, are not yet a full reality. God's kingdom is already among us but not yet realized. Why is this? If all Christians strive for it and if Jesus promised it, why are the substantial aspects of the kingdom of God (e.g., the universal unity, brotherhood, peace, and love depicted in Galatians 3:28—"we are all one in Christ Jesus") not yet a reality?

The tragic inheritance of Adam and Eve's fall is still affecting the kingdom's realization. As Samuel T. Coleridge wrote, the fall is "the fundamental postulate of the moral history of man. Without this hypothesis, man is unintelligible; with it every phenomenon is explicable." Adam and Eve's fall is therefore, in C. S. Lewis's words, "the key to history."[2] Adam and Eve's legacy of sin and sickness still powerfully influences our past and present. Respectively, in his influential book *God's City Against the Pagans*, St. Augustine suggests that there are two supernatural powers clashing on earth, God and Satan. St. Augustine imagined that God's love shaped the Church's history, while Satan's power shaped the world's.[3] To be able to reshape atheists' insights into a meaningful Christian context, evangelizers need to first know how atheists perceive the place and role of Christians in history. Let us for a moment divert from an Augustinian perspective and observe history as the people whom we are sent to evangelize perceive it.

As the very influential church historian St. Eusebius summarized, after AD 313, the year of Constantine's turnaround, "the emperor was perceived as an equivalent to the king of Israel, as the 'anointed one' of the Lord and therefore the truly messianic icon of Christ himself."[4] Consequently, it was widely believed that Constantine, the "King Messiah," had the full right to take all worldly and ecclesial powers into his hands and that he and God were partners in ruling all areas of life, people, countries, and every existing thing, even those far beyond the boundaries of the empire.[5] A quite similar tendency of enmeshing all sacral and worldly power in one hand occurred in the Western empires and the Church. Despite their competitive relationship and gradual mutual estrangement, for almost 700 years the Eastern and the Western ecclesial institutions coexisted and cooperated. However, in 1054 a fatal confrontation between the papal legate Cardinal Humbert Silva Candida and the Patriarch Michael Caerularius occurred when they mutually excommunicated each other's churches. Although on December 7,

1965, Pope Paul VI annulled this document,[6] the human-made fragmentation of the body of Christ could not be reversed. This first great schism was only the introduction to even greater religious conflicts. After 1650, when religious wars ended and the Enlightenment began, the memories of previous mutual bloody exterminations of people worshipping the same God evoked massive doubt in the validity of all mutually-excluding Christian affiliations. Religion has, in Western societies, become ever more replaced by "humanity," which has become the criterion of truth, justice, equality, compassion, and progress. This mentality, enforced by recent sexual abuse scandals, permeates the pores of our postmodern society and is uncritically generalized to the whole Church.

In the eyes of sceptics, the Luciferian nonchurch described by Cardinal Hans Urs von Balthazar still has such a prominent foothold in the institutional church that, in the eyes of ignorant atheists, replaces the holy body of Christ. Atheists, whom we are evangelizing, see only clericalism and the power-hunger hypocrisy of the nonchurch, but not the genuine Church, "the pillar and foundation of the truth" (1 Tim. 3:15). Atheists perceive that, among Christians, exactly the opposite of what Jesus prayed for in John 17:21–23 is still occurring; we Christians are not one as Christ is one with the Father, and the world does not believe. Did Jesus therefore proclaim God's kingdom in vain, and is reality disproving him?

No. God's kingdom is an external, visible, touchable, and measurable empire like the Byzantine. God's kingdom is "upon you" (Mt. 3:2; 12:28) and "within you" or "in the midst of you" (Lk. 17:21). Its realization, like the "history of salvation," as Louis Bouyer notes, "does not appear as a linear development. Rather, it is a progressive spiral which causes people of God to go back periodically over analogous (but not identical) experiences, which are only a gradual deepening of the content implied by the original experience."[7] The original experience in Bouyer's model is God. God's covenant with Noah, the Israelites' slavery in Egypt, their Babylonian exile, the upsurge of fascism, the downfall of communism—all these are part of the evolution of God's plan of salvation, which is not a straight path but a progressive spiral through collective and individual sickness and sin to renewed personal and collective awakenings and revivals. All Christians, hopefully together with all sceptical receivers of God's grace, are on that progressive spiral, unconsciously partaking in realizing God's kingdom.

42.2 The Individual Reasons for the Atheism of the "Best and Greatest Atheist"

If individuals are interested in knowing the genuine Christian way of living, they need to analyse Jesus' life and teaching. In a similar way, the best way to learn about the atheist lifestyle is from an atheist, one adored in his lifetime as the "best and greatest atheist": Joseph Stalin. In this we certainly do not insinuate that every atheist approves of or prefers a lifestyle like Stalin's, only that in every human being (believer or nonbeliever) there lives a "micro-Stalin" striving to see Adam and Eve's purpose of being "like God, knowing good and evil" (Gen. 3:5) through to completion.

Josif Visarionovic Dzugashvili, referred to as Stalin ("steel" in Russian), was born in 1878 in Gori, Georgia. His father was an alcoholic, so his mother, attempting to save him from an abusive home environment, sent him to the Orthodox theology seminary in Tbilisi. But Stalin, propagating Marxist ideology, was expelled from the seminary in 1899. He subsequently joined an underground Marxist organization as a "string boy" and there gradually climbed the hierarchical ladder. After Lenin's death in 1924 and his skilful purging of his political rivals, Stalin gained dictatorial power over the Soviet Union in 1930.[8] A typical pattern of his reign was maintaining a grip on power by organizing show trials, extorting irrational accusations and nonsensical confessions, and obtaining new fabricated accusations about the next victims by duress. In this way, he exterminated all possible rivals one by one. In his repeated *cistkas* (purges), his ex-comrades were blackmailed and given a chance to save their loved ones by admitting to crimes they could not possibly have committed. In a climate of fear and paranoia, anyone who wasn't unconditionally worshipping Stalin as a god was a potential enemy. Millions of Ukrainian peasants were intentionally starved to death, and some twenty million Russians were sent to gulags. Ninety-three of the 139 members of the Central Committee of the Communist Party, 81 of the 103 generals of the Red Army, and about one million Communist Party members were executed. Even Stalin's closest collaborators were not spared. Only very few inaugurated ambassadors died of natural causes; the rest were mercilessly jailed and executed. In the meantime, Stalin wrote and published his great ideas, and workers, peasants, scientists, the mass media, and artists glorified him. People thanked him for making the earth bring forth a harvest and decorated virtually every train, bus, house, ship, classroom, office, and street in every village and city with his portraits. A transfixed, ecstatic applause whenever his name was mentioned was a rule.[9] To understand his mental functioning, we need to know that Stalin was perceived as being "more than himself." His biographer, Simon Sebag Montefiore, noted that his son Vasily once praised himself, saying, "I am a Stalin as well." But Stalin responded with "No you are not, neither am I Stalin. Stalin is what the newspaper writes, what the TV shows, what people believe—Stalin is the power of the Soviet state."[10] The key to Stalin's popularity was, and still is, that he succeeded in achieving ultimate power not only for himself but also for masses of his followers. He embodied the atheist ideal of being like God like virtually no other human being.

However, Stalin had to pay a high price for his role. The more he behaved like God, the more he became aware of the temptation for countless other comrades to imitate his lifestyle and become a god like him. This caused intense and pervasive distrust, jealousy, and fear of assassination, as well as suspicion of being harmed, deceived, and persecuted. Doubting the loyalty of others, his fear of real and imagined enemies increased. Stalin spent all his life defending against the only unavoidable reality, death. His last years were occupied by frenetic drinking and a paranoid fear of his bodyguards, friends, and comrades. As he confessed to a general, "I am even afraid of my own shadow." He was especially mortified when his physicians attempted to protect him from death. When Dr. Vladimir Vinogradov dared to talk about his failing health, given two strokes in 1945 and 1949 and his extremely high blood pressure, Stalin reacted by purging "doctors, professors, murderers, and spies." He personally supervised the torturing of his primary physician, Dr. Sergej Preobrazenski, who had to be beaten "until he does not admit to being an English spy." Stalin was notoriously frightened of being poisoned in any of the prominent Moscow health institutions, so his bodyguards' duty was to supply him with medicines purchased anonymously from small, distant village pharmacies, thus reducing the potential for assassination by poison.[11] Despite all these efforts, though, on the morning of March 2, 1953, Stalin suffered a third stroke. Although he did not emerge all day, even his bodyguards lacked the courage to approach the soiled, wet, half-conscious Stalin lying paralyzed on the floor of his room. His death came after three days of agony on March 5, 1952 and was witnessed by his daughter Svetlana:

> His face was discolored, his features became unrecognizable.... He literary choked to death as we watched. The death agony was terrible ... at the last minute he opened his eyes. He looked either insane or raging and full of the horror of death. Suddenly, his left hand rose; he seemed either to be pointing upwards somewhere or threatening us all. Then the next moment, his spirit after one last effort tore itself from his body.[12]

However, Stalin's terror, as his biographer notes, was not "only an exemption, deviation, or aberration [from communist ideals] as some are attempting to rewrite history even today."[13] His uniqueness is in the fact that no other atheist in history had such misfortunes like him. All other prominent atheists have had to adapt their wish to be Godlike to a reality in which strong counterweights—their own consciences, the Church, the law, justice, and basic human rights—also exist. But Stalin was a dictator directed by pure instinct, ego, and a superego-like worldly conscience annihilating every opposition or counterbalance. Consequently, the atheist party and state propelled the "greatest atheist" to Godlike heights while dropping him to the depths of a living hell. In this perspective, he was indeed not an exemption, deviation, or aberration; he demonstrated what the absolute denying of God causes in all humans. No one of us is free of that temptation that even the "man of steel" could not resist. His example is a reminder even to Christians: a micro-Stalin exists in every one of us.

42.3 Is Atheism a Sickness or a Sinful Behavior?

As we have established throughout this book, there are two cardinal reasons for all possible behaviors that disregard God's law of love and/or ignore his existence. These are sin (i.e., the intentional and delibertae transgression Jesus' commands given in Mark 12:29–31), or sickness (i.e., dysfunctional psychological functioning causing the unintentional ignoring of God's laws). Both aspects of Adam and Eve's inheritance, also sin and sickness, have a common effect: they cause significant suffering, distress, and impairment. Which applies in the case of atheism? For example, was the failure of Stalin to respond to God's calls more sick or sinful? If confronted with a question like this, Stalin likely would have responded that his atheism was a free and responsible choice. He probably would have even given a plethora of reasons logically substantiating his fully conscious, reasonable, and intentional choosing to turn his back on Jesus. If we accept this hypothetical explanation, though, we would immediately be confronted with a tricky question: Would any rational human, fully aware of the real consequences of his decision, intentionally choose to estrange himself from God? It would be hard to assume such a possibility. However, in the tenth century, St. Anselm, when presenting his ontological proof of God's existence, implicitly spoke to this question by quoting Psalm 14:1: "The fool says in his heart, 'There is no God.'" In this verse, the inspired psalmist implies that atheism is not only sinful, but also a sick (i.e., foolish, irrational, or idiotic) condition.

As was stated in Chapter Five, the British court accepted in 1843 that "people are not guilty by reason of insanity if they have laboured under a mental disease such that they were unaware of the nature, the quality, and the consequences of their acts, or if they were incapable of realizing that their acts were wrong." It would be hard to imagine that the ultimately loving God would be less compassionate and just in judging sinners than the British court in judging M'Naghten. And indeed, the Catechism formulates, "Responsibility for an action can be diminished or even nullified by ignorance, inadvertence, duress, fear, habit, inordinate attachments, and other psychological or social factors."[14] Could then the hypothetical fool that Psalm 14:1 talks about at Judgment Day humbly beg for God's ultimate justice and mercy and hope in his heart for a "no responsibility" or "diminished responsibility" verdict using some sort of mental illness defence? That is, could millions of our contemporaries who unintentionally, or not completely intentionally, estrange themselves from God because of their deficient discretional or appreciative judgment? Could they be proclaimed by God as "incapable of fully realizing that their acts were wrong" and consequently receive lenient sentences?

Faced with the judgment of the ultimately just and merciful God, no human could hope to formulate any kind of defence. Even our own personal responsibility is an unknowable territory for us. C. S. Lewis explained the motives of atheists' behaviors by saying, "From the moment a created being becomes conscious of God as God and itself as self, it is faced with the terrible alternative of choosing God or the self for the centre."[15] Yet the psychological dynamics facilitating this terrible choice occurring in the hearts of atheists are a paramount mystery for everyone, even the subjects themselves. As previously noted, the relationship between sickness and sin is rarely an either/or category; it is most frequently an "also/as well as" category. Only Jesus knows how much any one of us is aware of the nature, quality, and consequences of our acts and capable of realizing that they are wrong.

On the other hand, it is a prominent task of every pastoral healer to help differentiate between sickness and sin in Christians and atheists alike. Pastoral healers, although aware that God's judgment is quite different from that of humans, often need to take a stand for the purpose of helping themselves and their clients understand their responsibility as much as possible. In this effort, it may help to remember our previous discussion visualizing the proportion of mental sickness and sin in non-Christian behaviors and apply this to the psychology of atheism, illustrated in Figure 42.1.

Fig. 42.1. Proportions of sin and sickness in atheism

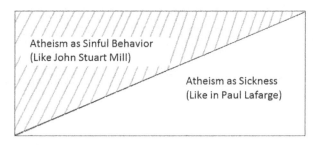

The figure above illustrates the variable distribution of sickness and sin in the dynamics of atheism. Atheism facilitated by sinful behavior in mentally healthy people making free and responsible choices could be placed at the left end of the diagram. Atheism facilitated more by sickness in people suffering from dysfunctional beliefs could be placed at the right end of the diagram. From left to right, the proportion of intentional, sinful estrangement from God decreases, while the proportion of sickness (i.e., dysfunctional beliefs) causing a particular form of atheism increases.

Let us test how this theoretical concept fits reality. We will in our case studies focus on the extremes. In the case study of a healthy atheist, John Stuart Mill (whom we have accordingly placed on the left end of the diagram), we will observe the significance of personal choice in denying God. In the case study of an apparently sick atheist, the suicidal Paul Lafargue (whom we have placed at the right end of the diagram), we will observe the contribution of sickness to denying God.

42.4 Atheism as Sin

Sin opens up a painful gap between God and sinner. To this divide, people in different moments of history have reacted in different ways. In ancient times, when the movement of the sun in the sky had a value of theophany, and God's presence was clear to everyone, people were inclined to sacrifice sinful behavior to preserve their relationship with God. Today, when God's presence is not perceived as a positive-sensory fact, atheists sacrifice their relationship with God to preserve the option of sinful living.

For example, King David (some 3,000 years ago) was an absolutist ruler. He could act not just similarly to God but as God himself and do with his subordinates whatever he wanted. His Luciferian selfishness directed his acting out with Bathsheba (described in 2 Sam. 11:2–12:17), subsequently covering one lie with another and eventually killing her husband, Uriah. However, when confronted with his sin by the prophet Nathan, he promptly gave up his lifestyle, repenting and turning back to God.

Atheists choose the opposite mindset. Just like King David, they are motivated by the dark sides of their personalities to behave "like God, knowing good and evil" (Gen. 3:5). However, they resolve the terrible alternative that C. S. Lewis spoke about by choosing the self as the centre of their lives instead of God. They do not repent like David but rather complete their turning away from God. This reality is observed in John Stuart Mill, a typical nineteenth-century utilitarian hedonist. Mill wrote:

> In everyday life I know what to call right or wrong, because I can plainly see its rightness or wrongness. Now if a god requires that what I ordinarily call wrong I must call right because he so calls it, even though I do not see the point of it and by refusing to do so he can sentence me to hell, to hell I will gladly go.[16]

In Freudian terms, Mill's personality was his instinct. When instinct dominates one's whole personality (ego and superego), a Christian conscience has no chance. In such people's minds, selfishness is acceptable as long as it "pays off." Contrary to King David, who sacrificed sinful living for a relationship with God, John Stuart Mill sacrificed his relationship with God for the continued illusion of being like God. We could illustrate John Stuart Mill's psychology by paraphrasing the well-known observation of Russian novelist Fyodor Dostoevsky: if there would be no God, everything would be permitted. Mill turned Dostoevsky's equation around: "For everything to be permitted, God must not be." God, for people like Mill, becomes unworthy of being known, a nothingness, while the personality becomes everything—the criteria of good and evil, right and wrong, true or false, and being or not being.

Mill's psychology is perhaps best explained by the words of existentialist Albert Camus (1913–1960).

> Traditionally in Western thought there are but two sources of criteria for making moral judgments: God and society ... man has been severed from both: the God image of religion is a figment, not a reality; and the absurd world has proven that as a source of moral criteria, it is worse than useless. Cut off from both these bases for moral judgment, the individual stands free and alone.... [So a person like Mill] can do whatever he wishes. All is permitted. He is free of guilt, for no one can make judgments.... The senses, not abstractions, will tell him unerringly what is good and what is evil.[17] Such people imagine that they do not need to be told by God how to live; their drives make this quite clear. But such form of living has also a backlash. Jean-Paul Sartre, as another example, described a feeling of nausea at the tragic "discovery of 'pure being' of a world for which there is no reason to exist, that is superfluous, but for which it was impossible not to exist. Such an experience is pure contingency and absolute absurdity."[18]

As previously established, people in denial, like Napoleon at Waterloo, *can choose beliefs but cannot choose the consequences of their beliefs.* By killing God, people like Mill and his followers also kill God's biblical gifts in their hearts. They lose the internal evidence of biblical meaning, joy, hope, love, and confidence, and in its place establish absurdity, meaninglessness, self-deception, and angst.

Unavoidably, this process accelerates a demonic cycle. Turning away from God causes the loss of biblical optimism, love, and joy, while seeing no purpose worth living and dying for deepens the internal evidence of living in a godless world. We can illustrate this demonic cycle with a figure borrowed from my book *The Mystery of Christian Faith; A Tangible Union with the Invisible God.*[19]

Fig. 42.2. The vicious circle occurring in atheists

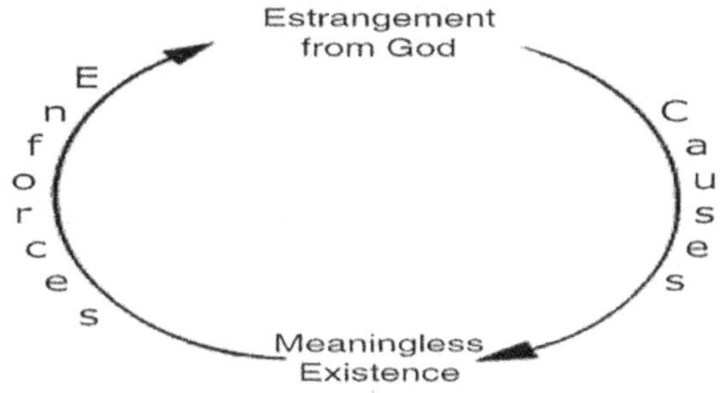

If, then, an atheist's self-experience is as grim as to provoke the nausea that Sartre described, why do they not convert instead of crying out "to hell I will gladly go"?

Genesis 3:6 answers this question: "When the woman saw that the fruit of the tree was good for food and pleasing to the eye, and also desirable for gaining wisdom she took some and ate it. She also gave some to her husband, who was with her, and he ate it. Then the eyes of both where opened; and they realized they were naked." Until consequences appear, becoming "like God, knowing good and evil" (Gen. 3:5) is attractive. Just like Eve, atheists are able to euphorically cry out "to hell I will gladly go" as long their illusion lasts.

42.5 Atheism as Sickness

In the DSM-5, the section "Other Problems That May Be a Focus of Clinical Attention" lists as "Religious or Spiritual Problems." They include, for example, "distressing experiences that involve loss or questioning of faith."[20] In this section, we are dissimilar to the DSM, focusing not only on the consequences of religious or spiritual problems (i.e., on distressing experiences), but also on their cause (the loss or questioning of faith). We will discuss the disordered, disregarding of God's existence (i.e., by a psychological ailment caused unintentionally or not deliberately) that causes a clinically significant suffering, distress, or impairment. Thus, *we are talking*

about atheism as a dysfunctional mental functioning causing, like other ail-
ments listed in the DSM-5, a significant suffering, distress, or impairment.

The Scriptures give a concise description of the threat of losing faith,
saying, "The man who loves his life will lose it, while the man who hates
his life in this world will keep it for eternal life" (Jn. 12:25). Do we have any
empirical proof that the biblical warning is realized in atheists?

As Tomer, Eliason, and Wong note, in the understanding of nineteenth
century atheists:

> the universe was nothing but matter-in-motion, and human beings, too, it
> appeared were nothing but matter-in-motion, mere cogs in a meaningless
> universe that could be nicely described by the physical sciences. Causal
> laws ruled the behavior of matter, and what we humans flippantly call
> 'free will' is little more than a hard-won illusion. Humans had thus been
> deprived of that wonderful feeling of being special, or having a secure
> place in the Sun, a little lower than the angels to be sure, but not by much.[21]

Respectively, there is a significant difference in the self-experience of
sceptics and believers. As beings created in God's image and likeness, people of God perceive their existence as infinitely worthy and themselves as
ultimately lovable and loved by God. Atheists—if they really are what they
say they are—seemingly have a very different self-experience; they must feel
unworthy, unloved, and unlovable, interpreting their being as a meaningless
event in the evolution of the universe. This significant difference in self-
experience is statistically not expressed in behaviors, though. Atheists are
not more destructive or prone to delinquency or evil than believers, nor do
they suffer from more psychoses or more instances of sadness and depression. They experience fun just as much as the people of God; are equally
healthy and successful in business; enjoy fashion, art, music, and social
events; are equally successful in politics, sciences, and philosophy; and
find just as much pleasure in luxuries, holidays, and merriment. They are
often popular and influential thinkers, able to intelligently, rationally, and
logically justify and prove the correctness of their beliefs. In other words,
atheists live life to the fullest and, in their view, even more so than people of

faith. There is, in reality, only one difference between believers and atheists, but it is a significant one. Let me illustrate it with a story of a genuine atheist, Paul Lafargue, the son-in-law of Karl Marx, who committed suicide in 1911 and left behind an interesting letter. Lafargue's letter read:

> I am giving up my life as a healthy seventy-year-old man, before old age—which has taken away from me, one after the other, many pleasures and joys—can paralyze my energy, break my will, and make me a burden to others. As a young couple, my wife and I promised each other that we would not live beyond my current age.... In good time I have prepared a hypodermic of cyanide acid.[22]

The Lafargue family likely had everything humans could possess at that time except the most important thing: trust in God. Accordingly, they perceived themselves as human machines that have no *zoe*, only *bios*, only a transitory, worthless, and meaningless worldly existence. People who do not escape into denial from such a reality perceive the absurdity, angst, and estrangement of such a life almost as a permanent self-Judgment Day. Let me explain what I mean.

Theologically, it is not the loving Jesus who will judge us on Judgment Day; rather, humans confronted with how they really lived will condemn themselves. Paul Lafargue's life was a kind of protracted self-condemnation to a gradual, meaningless end that Kierkegaard calls "sickness unto death." It proved Kierkegaard's other observation that "the alternative to faith is despair,"[23] or, in the DSM-5's terminology, helpless distress and impairment. Atheism is not listed in the DSM-5 as a disorder, but the atheists' despair and impairment is something that may be worse than the suffering caused by DSM-5 disorders. In Lafargue's case, the helpless frustration provoked by the mystery and misery of ultimately meaningless existence and loving no God or human worthy to live for acted as a permanent presuicidal syndrome, driving a continuous self-assessment and adjudication of "Is my life still worth living?" Few atheists end their lives like this, but every *Homo sapiens* without Jesus may be faced with the same distressing and unsolvable meaninglessness as the Lafargues. They lived in a compelling permanent self-Judgment Day, caused by transgressing against Jesus' main command, "Love the Lord your God with all your heart and all your strength" and "Love your neighbour as yourself" (Mark 12:29–31).

Traditionally, atheists (like Marx and Stalin) promote a utopia, the kingdom of God on earth, but without God. On the contrary, though, some of their contemporary followers deny even the value and merit of the human form of being. For them (as Frankl realized), if human life itself is meaningless, then *sustaining or multiplying such a form of being is also meaningless.*[24] They perceive human life as a worthless, almost shameful form of being that one is justified in terminating as soon as it does not pay off with comfort, enjoyment, and fun. Such devaluation of life in the form of an almost chronic presuicidal syndrome is unfortunately becoming a sign of the postmodern Western culture of euthanasia, abortion, and Russian roulette with drugs. We are left only to wonder whether it is more a form of worldly living or of spiritual dying.

42.6 Dealing with the Atheist's Resistance against Evangelization

The psychiatrist Viktor Frankl posed the philosophical question, "What is the meaning of life?" and responded to it by saying, "Man is not the one who poses the question, 'What is the meaning of life?' but who is asked this question, for it is life itself that poses it to him."[25] It is the lifelong task of all humans to define the meaning of life in a way that reflects their core beliefs about what is existent and nonexistent, true and false, sick and healthy, and (morally speaking) what is right and wrong, good and evil, holy and sinful. That explains why, as we have said, defending beliefs is often more important to humans than protecting life. Evangelization, though, requires a radical new birth from the Spirit (John 3:3), a wiping out of all previously established cognitive, emotional, and ethical concepts about life. Sceptics, agnostics, and atheists most often react to it like an ostrich that buries its head in the sand or exhibits extreme kinds of resistance. Managing resistance is therefore one of the most difficult but crucial aspects in traditional and new evangelization, and for its management evangelizers must be well prepared.

Some examples of the most unsuccessful forms of resistance are the following.

- Repression: involuntarily disposing of a painful memory, purpose, or duty into the subconscious
- Denial: closing one's eyes, half-consciously not wanting to realize unpleasant facts
- Reaction formation: actively expressing the impulse opposite of that which is being experienced (like concealing hate with enacted love)
- Projection: attributing to others one's unacceptable desires, impulses, or behaviors
- Displacement: shifting discharge impulses from a strong person to a soft target (like discharging anger felt toward one's boss to their children)
- Rationalization: artificially manufacturing good reasons to explain away one's sins
- Regression: returning to an earlier developmental stage (like adults behaving like children) to escape responsibility

In general, all of the defence mechanisms listed here are patients' attempts to decrease the anxiety, fear, and angst that comes with being forced to quickly or energetically give up their accustomed worldviews without receiving anything better in return. Resistance is a warning for the evangelizer to be more patient, slow down, be more empathetic or less directive, and allow (or even at times request) the subject's feedback, comments, and differing opinions or experiences that need to be appreciated, validated, and respected in order to further evangelization. Especially important is the humility, meekness, and self-criticism of the evangelizer. He or she, for example, should never state or enforce facts *ex cathedra*, but seek truth together with the evangelized person. In this context, a Socratic dialogue is often helpful as it involves not directly stating facts but asking questions and helping the evangelized person discern truth for himself. The most important dynamic in dealing with usual forms of resistance is not evoking fear of punishment but, on the contrary, fostering hope in the love of the all-forgiving and ultimately loving God.

Other useful defences which do not need specific healing regularly occur in healthy people. These include the following:

- Sublimation: diverting sexual and aggressive energy into socially-appreciated activities (like sports)
- Introjection: adopting the genuine values and standards of others (identifying with parental and biblical values)
- Identification: focusing on a worthy purpose (such as living with Christ) to decrease feelings of inferiority and to increase self-esteem
- Compensation: developing certain positive traits and noble efforts (self-sacrifice or charity) to make up for weaknesses.[26]

Besides these general forms of resistance, let us talk also about unique forms of defensive reactions occurring in evangelization. For example, when allegedly asked at his ninetieth birthday celebration "What if, when the time comes, you meet God and he asks, 'Why did you not believe?'" Bertrand Russell answered, "I would say, 'God, you gave us insufficient evidence.'" How could we characterize such a defence?

If the story is true, Russell revealed that he knew nothing about the evidence that believers have and by which they justify their reasons to believe. Indeed, factually, in discussions about God or faith, even very educated atheists are like very intelligent, well-informed toddlers attempting to talk about the sexuality of adults. Although the toddlers may be smart, even geniuses, adult sexuality is nevertheless a matter that they have never experienced and therefore are ignorant about. Similarly, even the greatest atheists like Russell, Freud, Ellis, and Dawkins have been surprisingly ignorant about the biblical God whom they talk about but cannot know since they have no experiential knowledge of him.

Healing this state, which we could classify as ignorant resistance (the least severe level of resistance), requires knowing the biblical God of love. But without faith, knowing God is impossible. Therefore, pastoral healers may use their own faith experience to help resistant sceptics grasp the loving nature of God. They may, in a humble way, explain where, when, how, and through which psychological functions they experience living in union with the loving God. Although imperfect, even secondhand information may help provide a foretaste of biblical hope and challenge self-imposed ignorance.

Beyond ignorance, the next levels of resistance counter behavioral and moral changes. Take, for example, the perspective of Louis Pojman, who says, "An absurd Godless tragedy, in which nature is omnipotent but blind, has brought forth rational, purposeful children who are superior to their mother and as such can discover moral ideals with which to sustain themselves in this ultimately meaningless existence. So, their ... morality doesn't need religion for legitimation."[27] John Stuart Mill's morality illustrates this mentality. He did not need God, as he himself was the legitimization of his morality. Sceptics like Mill perceive that "[God] requires that what I ordinarily call wrong I must call right because he so calls it, even though I do not see the point of it...." His inability to see the point of shaping his moral concepts to Jesus' commands, but proclaiming what is biblically good is bad and what is biblically bad is good, is a typical example of resistance in people desiring to be "like God, knowing good and evil" (Gen. 3:5). Nevertheless, such people worry "What if God exists after all? He could sentence me to hell!" They escape into helpless denial, which may be expressed in the irrational, verbal, and theatrical demonstration of being unafraid of hell as well as mystical defences (such as using swear-words against God) that express appropriate horror of hell, or both.

What were the psychological causes of Mill's resisting the ethical changes that faith requires?

As Pope Benedict XVI notes, "The human being does not trust God.... Tempted by the serpent, he harbors the suspicion that, in the end, God takes something away from his life, that God is a rival who curtails our freedom and that we will be fully human only when we have cast him aside."[28] What we may call "rivalry with God" is usually expressed in an overly-critical attitude toward evangelizers, the Church, and biblical teaching, especially on morality. At an early stage, such resistance is often resolvable by emotional means (giving reasons of the heart to believe), rational means (giving rational reasons to believe), and personal means (the pastoral healer's friendship and love).

However, there is one approach the evangelizer must specifically avoid. Since the atheist is a servant of instinct and master of conscience, painting a threatening image of God and provoking guilt or fear never help to decrease his resistance against biblical morality or increase trust in God. On the contrary, fear and horror evoke a Mill-like explosion, a Lafargue-like implosion, or a mixture of both reactions. Paradoxically, decreasing fear of hell increases striving for heaven.

At the next level, resistance may take intellectual forms. We have noted that even the very religious Carl Gustav Jung, in his book *Answer to Job*, described God as "suspicious," "jealous," "vengeful," "dangerous," and needing "propitiation."[29] Such a highly-intellectualized form of resistance against the biblical God may be classified as "philosophical resistance." It is expressed in the scientific, logical fight against a so-called judgmental, jealous, suspicious, vengeful, threatening, dangerous, and fear-evoking, or evil God. Its ultimate aim is to philosophically prove that God does not exist at all.

The first rule in approaching this form of resistance is to not engage in discussions with the patient but to demonstrate Jesus' compassion, mercy, and grace like we see in the stories of the adulterous woman (John 8:3–11) and the prodigal son (Luke 15:11–30). Healing fear in atheists like Ellis, Russell, or Dawkins by emotional means, by emphasizing a basic security with God, is paradoxically the method of choice in healing logical-philosophical resistance. If irrational fears of "God the enemy" are genuinely resolved, evangelists can then heal philosophical resistance relatively easily with rational and empirical approaches, which we will discus later.

An almost unsolvable form of resistance is known as *simple diversion,* attacking not the argument but the evangelizer's personality. An atheist using simple diversion, for example, might say, "You believe in God because you are old-fashioned, uneducated, or simply dull!"

Attacking one's personality (instead of their arguments) can be temporarily resolved by the healer's humility. A critical self-analysis of the alleged or real wrongdoings of the healer, other Christians, and the already mentioned nonchurch may help. However, if such an attitude does not help and the diversion cannot be stopped, the unproductive relationship should be stopped before further escalation occurs with insults or acting-out behaviors.

The most rare and most severe form of resistance is *autoaggressive resistance*. The discussion of pastoral issues seldom evokes an implosion as in the case of Paul Lafargue. However, if the signs of helpless rage and/or suicidal threats or behaviors appear, professional help needs to be sought.

As we see from this discussion, pastoral healing and evangelization are processes that move subjects from finding the courage to explore the possibility of God's existence to finding security in embracing God's love—from being horrified by "God the enemy" to being optimistically prepared to face and even pray "maranatha" (Come, O Lord) like members of the early Church did. The general form of pastoral healing for all noted types of resistance is a rational and emotional attitude of increasing optimism, trust, and hope in God's love and later motivation to persevere in racing toward him in the way that St. Paul talks about in 1 Cor. 9:24–27.

The final step in managing resistance entails giving biblical and experiential evidence that demonstrates to even committed atheists that they are the objects of God's forgiving love. Respectively, the purpose of every pastoral session is to enable a crescendo of biblical joy, peace, and love that supersedes hesitation, fear, and frustration in learning to know the unknown God. Although it is humanly hard to optimistically trust Jesus in life and death in the way that St. Paul describes in Philippians 1:21 and 1:23, it is precisely the purpose of pastoral healing to make the impossible happen with the help of the Holy Spirit.

Notes

[1] Michael Hout and Tom Smith, *Fewer Americans Affiliate with Organized Religions, Belief and Practice Unchanged: Key Findings from the 2014 General Social Survey* (Chicago: NORC, 2015), PDF.

[2] Samuel Taylor Coleridge, *Table Talk, May1 1830,* and C. S. Lewis,

Mere Christianity, book 11, 3. Quoted in the Roman Catholic Initiation of Adults, St. Jude's Parish (Vancouver, Canada, 2016–17), 27.

[3] Karl Heussi, *Kompendium der Kirchengeschihte* (Tubingen: Verlag von I.C.B. Mohr, 1998), 33.

[4] Louis Bouyer, *The Church of God, Body of Christ and Temple of the Spirit* (Chicago: Franciscan Herald Press, 1982), 31. See also Paul Ungar, *Flawed Institution—Flawless Church: A Response to Pope John Paul's Appeal for a Critical Self-Evaluation of the Church* (Newcastle Upon Tyne: Cambridge Scholars Publishing, 2013), 57.

[5] Ibid., 58.

[6] August Franzen *Kleine Kirchengenschihte* (Freiburg: Herder Bucherei, 1968), 87.

[7] Bouyer, *The Church of God, Body of Christ and Temple of the Spirit*, 517.

[8] Simon Sebag Montefiore, *Stalin, The Court of the Red Tsar* (London: Phoenix, 2004), 25–116.

[9] Ibid., 201–94.

[10] Ibid., 4.

[11] Ibid., 626–60.

[12] Ibid., 663–4.

[13] Ibid., 5.

[14] Canadian Conference of the Catholic Bishops, *Catechism of the Catholic Church* (Ottawa: Publications Service, Canadian Conference of Catholic Bishops, 1994), 371.

[15] C. S. Lewis, *The Problem of Pain*, chapter V, quoted from the Roman Catholic Initiation of Adults, St. Jude's Parish (Vancouver, Canada, 2016–17), 21.

[16] M. Petterson, W. Hasker, B. Reichenbach, and D. Basinger, *Reason and Religious Belief: An Introduction to the Philosophy of Religion* (New York, Oxford: Oxford University Press, 1991), 105. See also Paul Ungar, *The Mystery of Christian Faith: A Tangible Union with the Invisible God* (Lanham, MD: University Press of America, 2008), 279.

[17] Adrian Tomer, Grafton T. Eliason, and Paul T. P. Wong (eds.), *Existential and Spiritual Issues in Death Attitudes* (New York: Lawrence Erlbaum Associates, 2008), 457.

[18] Ibid., 462.

[19] Ungar, *The Mystery of Christian Faith*, 279.

[20] DSM-5. *Diagnostic and Statistical Manual of the American Psychiatric Association* (2013), 371.

[21] Tomer, Eliason, and Wong, *Existential and Spiritual Issues in Death Attitudes*, 424.

[22] Srboljub Stojiljkovic, *Psihijatrija sa Medicinskom Psihologijom* (Belgrade: Medicinska Knjiga, 1975), 122. See also Ungar, *The Mystery of Christian Faith*, 279.

[23] Tomer, Eliason, and Wong, *Existential and Spiritual Issues in Death Attitudes*, 13.

[24] Joseph Schwarz, *Durch Psychologie zum Gott, Argumente Fur Gottes Existenz* (Bishoofliches Ordinariat Eisenstadt, 1990), 32.

[25] Gerald Corey, *Theory and Practice of Counseling and Psychotherapy* (Thomson Brooks/Cole. Thomson Learning Academic Resource Center, 2005), 59.

[26] Viktor E. Frankl, *Man's Search for Ultimate Meaning* (New York: Basic Books, 2000), 29.

[27] Louis P. Pojman, *Classics of Philosophy* (New York: Oxford University Press, 2003), 1100.

[28] Pope Benedict XVI, Homily, December 8, 2005. Quoted from the Roman Catholic Initiation of Adults, St. Jude's Parish (Vancouver, Canada, 2016–17), 499.

[29] Don S. Browning and Terry D. Cooper, *Religious Thought and the Modern Psychologies* (Minneapolis: Augsburg Fortress Press, 2004), 171.

CHAPTER FORTY-THREE

BY WHICH PSYCHOLOGICAL FUNCTIONS DO BELIEVERS KNOW GOD?

In evangelizing, it is not only the message that is important but also the messenger. Christians need to be able to give credible reasons for their faith. This means explaining to sceptics how and by which psychological functions they experience and communicate with a sensorially invisible, untouchable, and immeasurable but nevertheless almighty, absolute, and eternal Lord as well as how they experience his ultimate providence, love, peace, and forgiveness.

43.1 The Christian Dualism as the Attitudinal Prerequisite of Knowing God

In the previous chapter, we established that which prevents atheists from knowing God. But what is different in Christians? Which personal attitudes enable them to recognize and respond positively to God's call?

As Cardinal John Henry Newman observed, most people do not perceive themselves as exemplary saints, but since they do not murder, rob, or harm their neighbours and they work hard, pay their taxes, and give to charity, they perceive themselves as morally proper. This is the morality of the superego-type pragmatic conscience and is the "religion of the natural man in every age and place; often very beautiful on the surface but worthless in God's sight; good as far as it goes but worthless and hopeless, because it does not go further, because it is based on self-sufficiency, and results in self-satisfaction...."[1] We understand from Newman's words why the world's criteria of moral uprightness are insufficient, but what about Christians? What explains their feeling unworthy and inadequate?

From the existential perspective, in the words of Kierkegaard, faith is the "inward certainty in anticipating infinity."[2] That inward certainty in anticipating infinity is rooted in the quality and depth of an individual's connection to God, and in this area all Christians feel inadequate. Although most do not flagrantly transgress the Ten Commandments very often, no one's past is without blemish held to the standards of the constitution of the kingdom of God proclaimed in the eight blessings of Matthew 5:1–12. For every Christian, St. Paul's warning is valid: "Let the one who boasts, boast in the Lord" (1 Cor. 1:31). However, none of us truly, constantly, and wholeheartedly boasts only in the Lord. Sin and sickness are powerful forces in our lives that often supersede our intentions, and even the best disciples and greatest saints may have experiences that cause them to say, "I do not understand what I do," as St. Paul does in Romans 7:15. Like St. Paul, we all feel responsible for sins but are unable to completely stop committing them. Despite this unsolvable dilemma, and despite being sick sinners, Christians are optimistic.

Disciples are aware that a repentant sinner can receive forgiveness, that the one who is forgiven is able to love Jesus, and that the one who loves Jesus can experience the gifts of faith. This biblical truth and psychological reality correlates with Jesus' parable about the Pharisee and the tax collector and its conclusion: "All who exult themselves will be humbled, but all who humble themselves will be exulted" (Lk. 18:10–14). The lack of such a mindset is what prevents atheists from knowing God, and the presence of it is what enables people of faith to recognize and respond positively to God's calls. Disciples intuitively and intentionally strive for a testimony like that of the woman of whom Jesus said, "Her sins, which were many, were forgiven;

hence she has shown great love. But the one whom little is forgiven, loves little" (Lk. 7: 47). Such an experience of being forgiven is the psychological prerequisite of knowing God. It gives Christians a quality of hope and perspective—the inward certainty in anticipating infinity—very different from the irrational self-confidence of John Stuart Mill and the self-defeating hopelessness of Paul Lafargue (Ch. 42).

The other great difference in Christians, though, is their noted courage to be optimists. My theology instructor illustrated Christians' courage with an anecdotal example. Two frogs fall into a jar of milk and are unable to crawl out. One frog gives up, sinks to the bottom, and dies. The other frog, however, is courageous. He hopes and fights. Fervently swimming in the milk, he makes butter from it and climbs out of the jar. Christians have the courage, hope, and determination to seek forgiveness as revealed by Jesus. Such complementing dualism of biblical optimism and courage paired with biblical humility and brokenheartedness are the psychological-spiritual prerequisites of knowing God; they are the personal attitudes that enable recognizing and responding positively to God's calls.

The previously noted truths shape the dynamics of evangelization. While a believer's communication with God is dialogic, evangelization is "trialogic." Its prerequisite is psychological-spiritual listening and responding to God's calls with humility and meekness on the part of both the evangelizer and the person being evangelized. The two help each other hear and respond to God and together become the "salt of the earth" (Lk. 14:34) and the "light of the world" (Mk. 4:21–24)—the means by which others also come to know God.

43.2 The Epistemology of Knowing God

Epistemology is the science of knowledge concerned with how we know that we know what we know. When using the term "knowing," we will not mean abstract philosophical knowing but concrete psychological, experiential knowledge. Christians not only speculatively know but passionately experience the transcendental God. This can be illustrated by an anecdotal story.

One evening John Wesley preached in a booming voice in his church, "Jesus is alive!" At once a member of the congregation called out, "But what makes you say this?" Wesley responded, "Because I talked to him for an hour this afternoon." For Wesley, his talking to Jesus was an evident personal experience, but it was not so for the sceptical person asking for proof. Was Wesley's experience nevertheless objectively trustworthy? If Wesley could prove his personal communication with Jesus by positive behavioral changes (like progressing in holiness), psychological tests, a polygraph test, or an EEG, would then the sceptic admit that, yes, Wesley was telling truth?

No, probably not. Despite the fact that all genuine Christians are likewise behaviorally demonstrating their "talking to Jesus," atheists do not believe them because their own personal experience of communicating with God is missing. But is it at least possible to clarify for them through which psychological functions Christians perceive their spiritual communication with an invisible, untouchable, and sensorially nonexistent person of Jesus?

Even most believers would say, "I do not know how, but I know that I know God." As St. Augustine (354–430) explains in his works *Teacher* and *On Free Will*, humans acknowledge reality not just with their physical eyes only, but also introspectively with their metaphorical inner eyes. In the case of discerning God, the inner eyes represent primarily the conscience. So "man gains knowledge of God and his soul by looking inward, not by examining the outside world."[3] Communication with God, similar to attraction or what is called "chemistry" in love, occurs introspectively, or meta-empirically.

As St. Augustine explains in his works *Teacher* and *On Free Will*, humans acknowledge reality not just with their actual physical eyes but also with their metaphorical inner eyes. The inner eyes, in the case of discerning God, represent the conscience. Therefore, "man gains knowledge of God and his soul by looking inward, not by examining the outside world."[3] Communication with God, similar to attraction or what is called chemistry in love, occurs mostly introspectively, or meta-empirically. It is a recognition that surpasses sole sensorial experiencing. But how does this take place?

Genuine love and faith are corroborated by internally, meta-empirically-evidenced lovable qualities of the beloved person and the ultimately lovable qualities of God. For lovers then, strong introspective evidence makes nothing more evident than that they love and are loved. This is similar to enabling believers to feel, know, and experience love for God and the reality that they are loved by him. In discussing belief systems, we noted that the most crucial things in human life, such as meaning, values, trust, joy, or peace, are experienced not externally, sensorially, or scientifically, but meta-empirically, by strong internally-experienced evidence. Among the strongest of such internal evidences belongs love (for people in love) and faith (for believers). The people of faith *communicate with the transcendental, quite-other God as plainly as communication with the sensorial, invisible, psychological-spiritual personalities of their loved ones.*

But one could say, "One may love a visible person, but how can an invisible person like God be known, loved, or trusted?" Let us address this question first from a theoretical perspective and then from an empirical perspective.

In Old Testament understanding, God was *quadosh*, meaning in Hebrew transcendental and nonsensorial. We know his personal characteristics, though, from what Hebrews called *kavod*, or God's glory. It is not easy to define this notion. God's glory is his almighty, eternal, and ultimate love; his creation of the earth and the creatures and humans on it; and his sustaining of all creation. It is Jesus' redemption, salvation, and sanctification of believers. In concrete terms, what perhaps best illustrates God's glory is Matthew 17:1–13, which describes Jesus' transfiguration. The picturesque metaphor that likens Jesus to the blinding sunshine—his "face shining like the sun" and his clothes a "dazzling white"—symbolizes his unimaginable glory.[4] If one receives the grace to internally experience the foretaste of the presence of God, then, as Pope Benedict XVI notes, it as though he is sensing what Peter, James, and John experienced as they witnessed the transfiguration.[5]

Let us translate biblical metaphors into concrete terms and observe this epistemological issue from a psychological perspective so that even a nonbeliever can follow it. We have noted that internal human experiences often shape our external perceptions. The one who is joyful will find thousands of external reasons to be joyful just as the one who is depressed will find thousands of external reasons to be depressed. Respectively, people of faith internally inspired by Jesus' love perceive and experience God's glory externally in the world. They discern countless signs of his glory, from the externally-displayed Big Bang that brought forth everything in existence to personal experiences that internally prove his presence, providence, and gifts. As the following example illustrates, the internal, personal experience of God is perhaps more important than knowing his external glory.

I once got an invitation from a Western university to give a presentation about the religious life in my home country, which is communist. Though giving such presentations abroad was not explicitly forbidden, it was very much frowned upon. Nevertheless, I gave the presentation. After my return, everything seemed quiet. However, some two months later I received a letter from a party examining committee ordering me to appear for a hearing to determine whether I was still fit to teach psychiatry at the faculty of medicine. The communists had immense power; they could humiliate anyone, fire anyone, or proclaim anyone incompetent. The examination was to take place on the seventh floor of the building, so I took the staircase to stall a little. I was tormented by fear, and it intensified with every step I ascended. When, however, I reached the third or fourth floor, I suddenly had a feeling of, "Okay, the communists are stronger. They can humiliate and fire me, and they can proclaim me insane. But still I have done the right thing. God is on my side. I have nothing to be afraid of. I will prevail." Because of these thoughts, my fears disappeared, and I entered the hearing room calmly. Seeing my demeanour, the examiners turned benevolent. They only warned me, "Don't do that anymore!" and released me. For me it was obvious that God intervened for me. He gave me courage, trust, and optimism in that stressful situation by allowing me to encounter his glory. Later, I questioned myself as to whether this encounter was a kind of illusion or a genuine detection of Jesus' glory. I answered with an analogy: as a key that opens a lock is not an illusion, so discerning the only right answer to a situation in which one is tested cannot be an illusion either, but rather a correct recognition.

For those who experience Jesus' glory, it is not essential to do so in a sensorial fashion. They psychologically perceive God's personality in the same way that we perceive others' personalities in our communications. Similar to how a loved one's personality (the "I") is invisible but expressed in his body language, so God's transcendental personality is expressed in his glory (in creation and the biblical gifts he extends to his people). In short, as a lover's joy is triggered by communicating with an invisible "you," so believers' biblical gifts are triggered by communicating with God's transcendental "Thee."

The reader might also ask if we have factual, empirically-validated proof that a being who is invisible to the senses can be loved or communicated with in a psychological-spiritual way? A couple of examples will help us answer this.

The famous poet Dante Alighieri (1265–1321) fell in love with the young and beautiful Lady Beatrice. Although she later married another man and he married another woman, Dante maintained a deep love and respect for her, as his collection of poems *La Vita Nuova* (*The New Life*) describes. In Dante's mind, Beatrice was the epitome of spiritual beauty and goodness, and her true home was not on earth but among God's angels in heaven. The angels, as Dante described in his love poem, were impatient, repeatedly begging God to bring Beatrice to heaven. So finally God gave in, and Lady Beatrice arrived in heaven at age twenty-four. In passing away, Beatrice's being as a person did not become invalid or cease to exist for Dante. His continued communication with her was, indeed, quite different from imagined communication with a nonexistent person only fantasized about. She continued to exist not as an "is" but as a "was," the safest form of being that nobody can erase from history. Dante continued to love and adore her and in some way communicate with her. The flame of love that Beatrice's memory lit in his heart brought fruit to his life, as the title of his text indicates. He forgave all the frustration, injustice, pain, humiliation, and insults he suffered and started to look at life from the point of view of Beatrice's soul—that is, from a Godly perspective. Although she no longer existed biologically, she was spiritually present for Dante, empowering his new life of Christian ideals.[6] For Dante, Beatrice's *zoe* soul, her spiritual form of being, was more real than the lack of her *bios*, her biological nonexistence.

Viktor Frankl reports a similar experience from his time in a concentration camp during the Second World War.

> Marching and stumbling in a crowd of inmates on an icy dawn, hiding his mouth behind his upturned collar, the man marching next to me whispered suddenly: "If our wives could see us now! I do hope they are better off in their camps and don't know what is happening to us!"
>
> That brought thoughts of his wife to Frankl's mind. As he describes, "Occasionally I looked at the sky, where the stars were fading and the pink light of dawn was beginning to spread behind a dark bank of clouds. But my mind clung to my wife's image, imagining it with an uncanny acuteness. I heard her answering me, saw her smile, her frank and encouraging look was more luminous than the sun which was beginning to rise."

He further describes, "My mind was still on the image of my wife. A thought crossed my mind: I did not even know if she was still alive. I knew only one thing—which I had learned well by now: love goes far beyond the physical person of the beloved. It finds its deepest meaning in its spiritual meaning, his and her inner self."

Was this an epistemologically correct recognition?

Frankl answers: "I did not know whether my wife was alive, and I had no means to finding out (during all my prison life there was no outgoing and no incoming mail); but at that moment it ceased to matter. There was no need for me to know; nothing could touch the strength of my love, my thoughts, and the image of my beloved. Had I known then that my wife was dead, I think that I would still have given myself, undisturbed by that knowledge, to the contemplation of her image, and that my mental conversation with her would have been just as vivid and just as satisfying. 'Set me like a seal upon thy heart, love is as strong as death'"[7]

Humans are created in God's image and likeness (Col. 1:15 and 2 Cor. 4:4) and are living souls (Gen 2:7); we are, as we have said, souls possessing bodies. As such, we perceive the world not only in a sensorial-psychological way but also in a spiritual-psychological way. We communicate with sensorially invisible personalities, the "you" of our loved ones in a spiritual-psychological language, similar to how we communicate in a spiritual-psychological language with God's transcendental "Thee." As love enabled Dante and Frankl to perceive the lovable personal qualities of their physically absent but spiritually present loved ones, so faith enables one to perceive the glory and love of the physically absent but spiritually present Jesus. Through these communications, God's presence is for Christians more real than his not being present in a visible, touchable, and measurable corporeal form.

43.3 Discussion

Let us briefly play devil's advocate and address the questions a sceptic might ask.

Q: Were the physically absent but spiritually present loved ones Dante and Frankl communicated with real or only their imaginations?

A: As noted (in Chapter Forty) we perceive reality as set up of being and meaning. The two recognitions are mutually inclusive. Discernment of being helps recognition of its meaning, and reciprocally, discernment of meaning facilitates interest for and cognition of being. Thus, the meaning Dante and Frankl discerned helped them to realize their loved ones as physically absent but spiritually present, or being. But for others not imbued by the same meaning (of love), the spiritual being of Dante and Frankl's loved ones remained imaginary. Whose cognition was right? The answer is self-evident: their strong meaning (love) facilitated the husband's cognition of their wife's or beloved's (nonsensorial) real being.

Q: But can we substantiate that love and faith are objectively-caused cognitions of objectively-existing realities?

A: For people in love, their reasons to love are neither subjective nor self-induced. On the contrary, they are objective in the sense that they exist independently of the subject's cognition. As Frankl noted, a lover discerns the real, objectively-existing qualities of their beloved. The lovable qualities in the beloved people exist objectively and independently of whether they are recognized by other people or not.[8] The same is true of God's personal characteristics. God and his love are objective categories existing independently of the observer's cognition. Just as being in love is the only possible way to realize the objectively-existing, lovable (psychological and spiritual) qualities of a human person (that for nonloving persons remain concealed), so faith is the only possible way to know the personality of the objectively-existing, transcendental God. Just as only people of faith were able to recognize the objectively-present, resurrected Jesus, many others saw him. Lacking faith, however, they did not recognize his. In the same way, today only disciples receive the spiritual gifts that enable them to discern their walking with God.

Q: If not a subjective imagination, isn't it then possible that faith is a delusion or a wishful thinking?

A: The philosopher William James would respond to such a question by saying that where there is a real effect, there must also be a real cause. If the reasons behind biblical love, peace, and joy are not biological, psychological, or sociological (i.e., naturally explicable), their reasons must be transcendental but nevertheless real. Since the gifts of faith have real effects, they must also have a real cause: a biblical God. Because of that, contrary to the distress and impairment that are a commonality of all delusions, genuine faith produces an unsurpassed joy. Believers who experience the perpetual effects of God's gifts have no doubts about his existence.

On the other hand, in wishful thinking, the perceived benefits must always outweigh the perceived costs. Striving to be Christlike means striving for a life of sacrifice that contradicts many biological, psychological, and sociological gains. Let us consider Jesus' blessings noted in Matthew 5:1–12. There is no worldly gain that could compensate for being poor in spirit, meek, hungry, merciful, mournful, pure in heart, persecuted, falsely accused, or sacrificial. Since the costs of Christian living outweigh worldly benefits, psychologically this excludes worldly wishful thinking but proves faith as a genuine recognition of the invisible God's genuine glory.

Q: The cognition of love and faith have similarities. But some 50 percent of marriages end in divorce. Is faith as equally untrustworthy as love?

A: We are not infallible in discerning being, meaning, or love. But high divorce rates do not mean that love is unreliable. On the contrary, if the success of marriages depended solely on self-deceptive perceptions or arbitrary choices, all marriages would be happy. That many marriages end in divorce exposes humans' incapability of self-deception. The same is valid in the epistemology of faith. Disappointment in a self-made or arbitrarily fabricated idol-god is inevitable. However, compulsory disillusionment with idols or nonbiblical concepts excludes the possibility of self-deception and proves the possibility of correctly recognizing God. As all genuine loves are verified by joy, trust, and peace, so a genuine relationship with Jesus is verified by biblical gifts of faith.

Q: Since we have noted that, without faith, knowing God is impossible, isn't it, conversely, impossible to grasp atheists' perspective without experiencing life as they do?

A: All Christians, like Peter, Thomas, and the disciples on the road to Emmaus, occasionally experience doubts, insecurities, and even what mystics call the dark night of the soul. We are sometimes acutely challenged with the same troubles that atheists chronically suffer from. Thus, unlike the way that atheists have never experienced what a genuine life with God is like, Christians do know what a life without God is like because they are repeatedly challenged by it. That means that we can, in fact, grasp why atheists experience so much difficulty in coming to know the God who is so evident to Christians.

Q: But couldn't faith be wishful thinking?

A: In wishful thinking, the perceived benefits must always outweigh the perceived costs. But striving to be Christlike means striving for a life of sacrifice that contradicts all biological, psychological, and sociological gains. Let us consider Jesus' blessings noted in Matthew 5:1–12. There is no worldly gain that could compensate for being poor in spirit, meek, hungry, merciful, mournful, pure in heart, persecuted, falsely accused, or sacrificial. The factual costs of Christian behavioral patterns outweigh all worldly benefits. Psychologically, this excludes worldly wishful thinking but proves faith as a genuine spiritual recognition.

Q: Aren't Jesus' messianic zeal and believers' faith socially learned behaviors?

A: St. Luke (2:41–52) records the story of Mary reprimanding the twelve-year-old Jesus for staying behind in Jerusalem. Jesus responded, "Didn't you know I had to be in my Father's house?" But his parents did not understand what he was saying to them. This demonstrates that Jesus was not conditioned or indoctrinated socially or solely by his earthly family; his real Father called him to his mission. The same is true with Christians. Faith is a personal response to God's call. It starts at the point where the influence of society stops. Only religious customs or traditions can be socially learned, not faith. As eyesight is not learned but is genetically, anatomically, and neurologically imprinted in our brains and minds, God's call or the universal human need to love and be loved by God are not matters of social learning but deeply imprinted needs in the human soul and conscience. Social learning may hinder or even prevent knowing God, but it can neither substantiate nor erase the human need for God, which is, to paraphrase Eric, the genuine form of the human being.

Notes

[1] John Henry Newman, "The Religion of Pharisee the Religion of Mankind." Quoted from the Roman Catholic Initiation of Adults, St. Jude's Parish (Vancouver, Canada, 2016–17), 499.

[2] Adrian Tomer, Grafton T. Eliason, and Paul T. P. Wong (eds.), *Existential and Spiritual Issues in Death Attitudes* (New York: Lawrence Erlbaum Associates, 2008), 13.

[3] Arthur Hyman and James Walsh, *Philosophy in the Middle Ages* (New York, Harper & Row Publishers, 1967), 16.

[4] Rudolph Schnackenburg, *The Gospel of Mathew* (Grand Rapids, MI, Cambridge: William B. Erdmans Publishing Company, 2002), 164.

[5] Benedict XVI, *Benedictus, Day by Day with Pope Benedict XVI*, edited by Rev. Peter Cameron (New York: Magnificat, 2006), 79.

[6] P. S. Kohan, *Istoria Zapadno Evropske Knjizevnosti* (Sarajevo: Veselin Maslesa, 1967), 48–51. See also Paul Ungar, *The Mystery of Christian Faith: A Tangible Union with the Invisible God* (Lanham, MD: University Press of America, 2008), 231.

[7] Viktor E. Frankl, *Man's Search for Ultimate Meaning* (New York: Basic Books, 2000), 48–51.

[8] Viktor E. Frankl, *Aerztliche Seelsorge* (Vienna: Franz Deuticke, 1965), 132.

CHAPTER FORTY-FOUR

EVANGELIZATION IN PRACTICE

W e have now laid the foundation for understanding the sceptic's unbelieving condition, but the crucial question remains: how we can help atheists dealing with a spiritual problem facilitated by psychological causes gain sufficient evidence of God's presence?

44.1 The Methodology

Luke 10:2 notes a basic problem in evangelization, which is that "the harvest is plentiful, but the workers are few." Therefore, evangelizers have designed new forms of massive public evangelizations. They all have specific advantages and disadvantages. The advantage (for example, that of mass televangelization) is that a great audience can be addressed, while the disadvantage is that the individual psychological-spiritual problems (for example, narcissism, sexual promiscuity, or idolatry) causing doubts and resistance against a Christlike living remain unresolved. The advantage of face-to-face evangelization is that individual problems causing resistance can be resolved. As noted in Luke 10:2, however, there are few workers. There are numerous attempts to find a compromise between public and individual forms of evangelization, such as establishing small groups of eight to ten evangelized people. Such arrangements have certain advantages for both public and individual forms, but they compromise the quantity and quality of the evangelization. Pastoral healing of the atheist's resistance against God can be adapted to and done in different forms, but the ideal solution is to evangelize such people individually while having sufficient workers for the plentiful harvest.

There are also significant differences, not only in form but also in methods between classical and new evangelization. A believer's first reaction to the scepticism of atheists, such as Russell's, would likely be to provide the evidence they say is missing, drawing perhaps from the apologetics of St. Anselm or St. Thomas.

St. Anselm (1033–1109), defined God in his well-known ontological proof as "that of which nothing greater can be thought." His intent was "to prove God's existence to everyone by using overwhelming theoretical proof independent of all previous experiences and superior to all other knowledge," implying that every reasonable person must be aware of the limits of thought and, respectively, the existence of God.[1] As Feinberg and Shafer-Landau say, "Perhaps no other argument in the history of thought has raised so many basic philosophical questions and stimulated so much hard thought. Even if it fails as a proof for the existence of God, it will remain as one of the high achievements of the human intellect."[2] Some contemporaries appreciate St. Anselm's ontological argument as valid, and others reject it.

Not all apologetic arguments require such effort to grasp as St. Anselm's logic. St. Thomas Aquinas presented proof that was easily understandable by everyone. In Part 1, Question 2, Article 3 of his *Summa Theologiae*, St. Thomas argues:

> Whatever is moved must be moved by another. If that by which it is moved be itself moved, then this also needs be moved by another, and that by another again. But this cannot go on to infinity, because then there would be no first mover, and consequently no other mover, seeing that subsequent movers move only inasmuch as they are moved by the first mover, as the staff moves only because it is moved by the hand. Therefore, it is necessary to arrive at the first mover, moved by no other, and this everyone understands to be God.[3]

How would sceptics react to arguments resting "on principles which can be known independently of our experience of the world just by reflecting on and understanding them"?[4]

They would probably immediately respond by quoting the materialist creed, which holds matter was never created, that it is eternally-existing and permanently moving without any need for a "first mover" even in initiating the Big Bang, as Richard Dawkins implied. Apologetic proof is excellent at demonstrating God's existence, but only to those who are already believers. Sceptics would probably look for counterarguments before considering the ideas of St. Anselm and St. Thomas. Faith is not a merely a rational-logical operation; it is a personal judgment. In other words, evangelization requires not only rational-logical judgment but also discretional judgment and, even more importantly, appreciative judgment. As noted, appreciative judgment refers to the application and realization of truths acquired by the conscience to all mental functions that help shape feelings, cognitions, will, and behavior. It also refers to the subordination and control of irrational reactions, impulses, drives, automatic thoughts, behavioral stereotypes, and all other forms of resistance to genuine discernment of a well-informed self and conscience. Therefore, the basic purpose of evangelization, besides sharing the Good News, is the facilitation of sound appreciative judgment that enables a person not only to know, *but to experience* the person of Jesus Christ.

Although Teresa of Avila "carefully defended the role of 'learned man' she gave priority to those who also 'had experience.'" As she stated, "This is a mistake we make: we think that with the years we shall come to understand what in no way can be comprehended without experience." [6] What kind of an experience, able to shape even the appreciative judgment of evangelized persons, is she talking about?

Knowing a person in an encyclopaedic way (knowing their age, height, weight, family status, or occupation) is very different from knowing them personally. A maximal personal knowledge originates from being in love with a person. As we have already observed, being in love enables the recognition of the hidden but real values in a person that only a lover perceives. Applied to God, Frank Sheed says (in an exaggerated way), "We realize that 'love of God is more important than knowledge of God.'" And similarly, before his execution, Thomas More said loosely, "Faith isn't a matter of reason, it is a matter of love."[5] So, as we said earlier, we believe because we love, and the knowledge of God sources less from reasoning and logic than from love. What is missing for atheists like Sigmund Freud, Richard Dawkins, and Bertrand Russell is the passionate experience of love from a loving God. Mirroring the love of God is the essence of evangelizing.

We noted that in evangelizing, the trustworthiness of the messenger is just as important as the message itself. Evangelizers should therefore be transparent and genuine in reflecting their passionate experience of the love of God. They may share their own reasons for believing as well as their personal experiences of Jesus' ultimate joy, love, peace, and forgiveness, but in doing so they must be painfully authentic and nonmanipulative. Consider the following story.

> Once, an Eastern ruler had a dream that he lost all his teeth in one night. The next day he called his fortuneteller and asked him, "What does this unusual dream mean?" The fortuneteller explained, "Oh, this is a very evil dream! It reveals that you will lose all your wives and suffer a long lonely and sad life." The ruler responded, "Ten lashes to this impostor!" He then called another fortuneteller and asked again, "What does this unusual dream mean?" This fortuneteller explained, "Oh, it is very good dream! It reveals that you will live longer than any of your wives and have a very long, happy life." The ruler responded, "Ten gold pieces to this good man!"[7]

In reality, both fortunetellers said the same thing, but their wording was different. The second fortuneteller knew how to manipulate the ruler to receive his ten gold pieces. He is an example of what evangelizers should not do. They need not manipulate or attempt to outsmart evangelized people to get the result they want; instead, they should formulate their message so that it genuinely reflects their beliefs and facilitates the hearer's citizenship in the kingdom of God. Listening is equally or more important than talking. Rather than instruction or therapy, a very empathetic ear is often required to listen to the pains, sufferings, and disappointments of those who are being evangelized. Therefore, evangelization never takes place within a subordinated, teacher-student relationship. The evangelizer ought never to presume "I know; you don't." The evangelizer is never "teaching" the evangelized person. We are all equally disciples, helping each other and learning from each other, together discerning the ultimate truth of Jesus Christ. Such considerations may help the evangelizer to get rid of his or her fears of inefficiency or talking too much or too less in length when presenting reasons to trust Jesus.

We will discuss the psychological basics of experience-based evangelization that we are talking about in three steps that may be successively applied and utilized as evangelization progresses.

44.2 The First Step: Finding Reasons of the Heart

Blaise Pascal (1623–1662) observed that after God's existence is irrefutably, philosophically proven, sceptics, despite being compelled to give in, still maintain that their convictions are correct and conclude that they were somehow misled by philosophical manipulations. Later, their previous doubts reemerge and their resistance is invigorated with new arguments. Pascal therefore realized that something much deeper than strong arguments is needed in evangelization. What is needed are "reasons of the heart."[8] But what do reasons of the heart look like in practice?

Pascal claimed that human reasoning is insufficient for knowing God. The problem, he says, is not in Christian doctrines or apologetics, but in pure, human, intellectual reasoning, which is insufficient for substantiating belief systems. Beliefs such as love, trust, meaning, and faith are more than only knowledge. Therefore, even the apologetic proofs of St. Anselm and St. Thomas Aquinas are not absolutely convincing for everyone. In every strictly theoretical argumentation, there is always some uncertainty that, in Pascal's impression, is enough to strengthen the faith of believers but provoke the resistance of nonbelievers, who feel outsmarted but not persuaded, much less converted. One can only completely accept a truth if he can submit to it.[9] In the context of evangelizing, this means that one can really know God only if he submits to him as confirmed by Jesus Christ in the Scriptures. Just as meaningful, trusting love requires a kind of joyful submission to the blissful truth of loving and being loved, so too does faith. Matthew 6:24 declares, "No one can serve two masters; for a slave will either hate the one and love the other, or be devoted to the one and despise the other." Submission is a precondition of following Jesus in discipleship (Matthew 10:37–38, 19:21–22; Luke 5:28, 9:59, 14:26–27; Mark 8:34; John 3:1–11, 12:25–26). Thus, as Pascal realized, discipleship is constituted not just of rational arguments but motivations much more profound that he summarized under the term reasons of the heart. Reasons of the heart refer to a complete commitment to Jesus and his revelation—holistic, intellectual, emotional, volitional, and experiential—or, metaphorically formulated, being a slave to Jesus. Such slavery is not oppressive slavery since Jesus says in John 15:15 "I do not call you servants any longer, because the servant does not know what the master is doing: but I have called you friends, because I have made known to you everything that I have heard from my Father."

Pascal was exactly correct. However, a total intellectual, wilful, experiential, passionate, conscientious, and conscious submission to Jesus Christ is not the beginning but the end and ultimate purpose of evangelization. Arriving at that ultimate purpose of submission to Jesus is a gradual process. It requires softening the ignorance, rivalry, philosophical resistance, and all other forms of resistance in people like Russell, Freud, and Dawkins by finding new reasons of the heart to attract them to Jesus.

Spotting such reasons of the heart fosters trust between the evangelized and the evangelizer. Rather than instruction or therapy, a very empathetic ear is often required to listen to the pains, sufferings, and disappointments of the evangelized, which may be at the root of their hardened animosity towards God (or the idea of God). Releasing such frustrations often helps the evangelized to emotionally see themselves from a different perspective. By so doing, their vision of God also changes. Finding such reasons of the heart is a process of self-reflection that reduces the angst toward "God the enemy" by awakening hope in the forgiving and merciful Jesus.

Evangelizing by finding reasons of the heart means many things. Above all, one reason is courage—the courage of sceptics to observe reality not only from their own accustomed standpoint, but also from one that acknowledges a deeply-implanted yearning for escape from the sufferings of meaningless existing. The reasons of the heart we are talking about also mean the following.

- The courage to consider a new anthropology and the possibility of being more than a worthless product of senseless evolution of eternal matter; to consider the biblical solution to the controversy between our instinctual need to protect life and the awareness of unavoidably passing away; and to ponder the possibility of eternal life
- The courage to acknowledge the slavery to angst, the "form of sceptics' being," and to consider the freedom, optimism, and hope that faith offers
- The courage to consider, in metaphorical terms, opening the eyes of the blind and releasing those who sit in darkness and ignorance, as prophesied by Isaiah 42:7
- The courage to consider resolving one's self-imposed confusion, ignorance, and denial regarding the biblical truth of the Messiah that contemporary atheists need no less than the Hebrews in biblical times
- The courage to seek forgiveness for one's imperfections, sickness, and sin
- The liberty from feeling lost and condemned and the recognition of being lovable and loved
- The hope that Jesus' judgment will be just and merciful
- The consideration that Jesus is counting not only sins but also weakness and sickness that facilitate the estrangement of believers and nonbelievers from God

As discussed earlier, in mentally healthy people, emotions are never independent from knowledge, and knowledge is never detached from emotions. Furthermore, the ultimate purpose of emotional considerations is awakening hope and ever-increasing courage to consider that, with Jesus' blood, our redemption, salvation, and sanctification become possible. As

Pope Benedict XVI describes, they increasingly attain in this process a special kind of knowledge—that of God's beauty.

> The beautiful is knowledge certainly, but, in a superior form, since it arouses man to the real greatness of the truth. True knowledge is being struck by the arrow of beauty that wounds man, moved by reality.... Being struck and overcome by the beauty of Christ is a more real, more profound knowledge than mere rational deduction.... The encounter with the beautiful can become the wound of the arrow that strikes the heart and in this way opens our eyes, so that later, from this experience, we take the criteria for judgment and can correctly evaluate ... [all other] arguments....[10]

No human words, not even Pope Benedict XVI's supremely sophisticated words, are able to imitate the Lord's evangelization described in biblical examples (as in Luke 15:11–30 and John 8:3–11). Nevertheless, there are countless planned and unplanned opportunities to resemble Jesus in building his kingdom. This is illustrated by a classical example.

> Victor Hugo, in his well-known novel *Les Misérables*, describes the ex-convict Jean Valjean stealing two expensive silver candleholders during his overnight stay in a retired bishop's house. When caught by the police and interrogated about the stolen treasures, the ex-convict explains that he received the candleholders as a gift from the old bishop. The investigators, finding his explanation suspicious, escort him back to the clergyman to corroborate the story. In a glance, the experienced priest grasps what has happened. However, he surprises everyone by crying out, "Oh, my dear friend, why didn't you take with you the other things I donated to you?" while quickly placing a few additional silver plates into Jean's bag. This unexpected example of Christlike love made Jean Valjean a new man. He used his skills in his future life to become worthy of the love he received through the example of Jesus' servant, the old retired bishop.[11]

It was not logic or argument that caused the miraculous change in the ex-convict's behavior; it was the feeling of a Christlike love and empathy that changed his life forever. Conjuring the foretaste of such love and empathy is the purpose of finding reasons of the heart for trusting Jesus. Let me illustrate this with another example.

At a workshop discussing whether Jesus' death on the cross factually has tangible effects, one lecturer told an unusual story. Two brothers lived in a Near Eastern city. One brother was good and spent all his time in prayer and hard work. The other brother was evil and he spent all his time drinking and womanizing. One night, as he usually did, the evil brother went partying. While the good brother was just completing his prayers, the evil brother suddenly ran into their home in a bloody shirt desperately crying out, "Brother, help me! The police are after me. I killed a man." The good brother took the bloody shirt from him and hid the evil brother in a closet. While the good brother was still holding the bloody shirt in his hands, the police arrived. Since he did not give any explanation or defend himself as he held the bloody shirt in his hands, the police arrested him. Soon he was tried and condemned. The night before his execution, the evil brother visited him. The good brother told him, "I will die, that you live." His sacrifice touched the heart of the bad brother, and from that time he lived an exemplary life. The lecturer asked us, "How do you comment on this story?"

I impulsively reacted, saying something like, "Your story is bizarre, absurd, and irrational." The lecturer, however, turned toward me and asked, "Let us suppose you are driving with your pregnant wife who, after a few drinks, hits a person on the crosswalk. Would you take the bloody shirt on yourself and say you were driving to spare her and your future offspring from incarceration?" I responded, "No way. She did not take care while driving. Why did she drink?" The lecturer, however, asked, "Are you really a good husband. Aren't you a bit selfish rejecting to take the bloody shirt instead of saving your wife? But let us turn to the reality," he said. "Aren't you also in your real, everyday life often unwilling to take on the bloody shirt?" Asking such questions, he gave us, his listeners, the reasons of heart to gain, not a logical, but an emotional insight into the factual and tangible moral effects of the mystery of Jesus' suffering for the whole of humankind, applying the fact that "the heart has reasons unknown to reasoning."[12]

44.3 The Second Step: Discerning Reasons of the Brain

Emotions are never independent from knowledge, and knowledge is never detached from emotions. The purpose of all previous emotional considerations is to awaken the desires, dreams, and imagination about "what if I could" be worthy, loved, and appreciated by Jesus. When these emotions emerge, evangelized people are open to appreciate reasons of the brain that rationally prove God's existence. Classically, it consists of giving proper proof of God's existence, which depends on the evangelized people's particular needs and preferences and also on the apologetic arsenal of the evangelizer. However, postmodern times also need postmodern approaches in substantiating reasons to believe in Jesus. For contemporaries, faith is not a matter of only scholastic, philosophical, theological, historical, biological, physical, astronomical, or logical proof, and neither is it a smart wagerlike choice that Pascal proposed in his *Thoughts* to the flamboyant Parisian aristocracy of his time.

Translated freely, Pascal's words are: "You must either believe or not believe that God is—which will you do? Your human reason cannot say. A game is going on between you and the nature of things which at the day of judgment will bring out either heads or tails. Weigh what your gains and your losses would be if you should stake all you have on heads or God's existence. If you win in such a case, you win eternal beatitude; if you lose, you lose nothing at all."[13] On the contrary, according to Pascal's wager, if tails comes up on Judgment Day and God exists, then one loses everything.

So then, what reasons for believing can a contemporary evangelizer communicate to people who have already found reasons of the heart and are seeking rational reasons to believe? Faith and the reality of God's presence ought not to be proven but must be discerned by evangelized people, or, in Frankl's words, "must be decided." Let me explain what Frankl's concept of "deciding" to trust God means in our context.

It helps subjects to see that their hesitations, doubts, dilemmas, and worldviews are understood and not *a priori* written off by the evangelizer as nonsensical. Indeed, the world pictures sceptics and believers are both, in Frankl's terms, "thinkable." Faith and scepticism are grasped in this context as two "thought possibilities" and not "thought necessities." So, "with respect to the decision we are called upon to make, there is no logical coercion; in no way are we logically forced, or logically obliged, to decide for one or the other." Evangelized people may feel less defensive if both interpretations—faith and distrust in God (and even their atheism)—are appreciated as having equal logical status. "Logically, there is as much which speaks for the one interpretation as for the other." Appreciating such virtual "logical egalitarianism" decreases resistance and forces responsibility upon the respondent. As Frankl explains, "He is not only faced with a question—he is faced with a decision. What he must perform is not an intelligent nor factual realization—but rather a personal commitment."[14] Initially, newly-evangelized persons often conceptualize that, although mutually exclusive, both views are thinkable and are able to in some way answer basic cosmological, astronomical, anthropological, and biological questions.

We could illustrate the human existential situation using a metaphorical scale. At one end of the scale is the ultimately loving, omnipotent God, creator and maintainer of everything. At the opposite end is the concept of the ultimately meaningless eternal matter directed by natural laws. The scale is in exact balance (the logic of both views having equal merit), so a choice must be made. And the choice between the two sides of the scale is inevitable as no one can avoid taking a stand in this eternal clash for or against Jesus (Lk. 12:49–53). People of faith place all their weight on one end of the metaphorical scale: God's side. They make a decision and throw all their mental energy, emotions, interests, thoughts, and efforts to the side they deem correct. There is no other way to experience love than by loving, and there is no other way to know God than through trusting, loving, and submitting to him in faith. Atheists are not invited to engage in logical or speculative arguments but to throw themselves onto the loving God's end of the scale. They must make that decision. The more complete such a commitment is, the more evident its consequences will be. Gradually receiving a foretaste of biblical peace, joy, love, purpose, optimism, and courage will be the criterion and proof of having made the right choice. Only if and when the evangelized person's heart (even unconsciously), with the Holy Spirit's help, decides to believe will the logical, rational, and scholastic arguments of St. Anselm and Thomas Aquinas (and all contemporary astronomical, physical, philosophical, biological, and historical arguments) for God's existence fall on fertile ground.

As Frankl summarizes, "After all [the pastoral healer] believes not only in God, but also in the unconscious belief on the part of the patient. And, at the same time, he believes that this unconscious God is one who has *not yet* become conscious to the patient."[15] Thus, evangelization is completed when the subject becomes fully conscious, emotionally and intellectually, of God's love, peace, and joy. When evangelized people make the free, responsible, and committed choice of faith, nothing can stop them from pursuing the last step: experiential evangelization.

44.4 The Third Step: Experiential Evangelization

In the early Christian centuries, and especially the Middle Ages, virtually all knowledge, science, and philosophy were "interpreted as the second channel of revelation for faith or as the development of truth already implicitly present in the original deposit of faith."[16] Plato and Aristotle had roles almost comparable to St. Peter and St. Paul in revealing faith.[17] Such an integrative relationship between faith and science lasted until 1632. After Galileo's Copernican revolution, however, science and theology parted ways. Galileo's discovery marked a turning point in human history, as if God stopped visibly, physically, and measurably demonstrating his existence.

The problem was that literal interpretation of the biblical verses of Joshua 10:12–14, which speak about God stopping the sun in the sky, made contemporaries believe that God placed the earth at the middle of the universe and that everything turned around us for our sake. The moving of the sun in the sky, which was believed to be the work of God's angels, was a daily epiphany, visible proof to everyone of God's providence and presence. However, Galileo's concepts turned this world picture upside down. A distraught Luther allegedly cried out, "The Bible does not say that God stopped the earth, but the sun!" And Cardinal Bellarmini, leading the trial against Galileo, foresaw the massive doubt that would later emerge. If the sun and stars were not turning around us, then we were not the centre of the universe, and so God did not create the universe for our sake. Perhaps a good and provident heavenly Father did not exist at all. Maybe only physical laws were moving the universe, and we humans were hopelessly lost in a senseless world.

As Lindsay Jones notes, "Galileo's trial in 1633 marked the beginning of what has since become a cliché—namely, the idea that science and religion must inevitably be in conflict."[18] Experiential evangelization aims to reverse this process. Its purpose is to bring God back to our everyday lives and bring everyday living back to God in order to help postmodern people realize and empirically experience God's presence as plainly as before Galileo's revelations. This effort looks much like what is described in Acts 5:12–16.

> The apostles performed many miraculous signs and wonders among the people, and all the believers used to meet together in Solomon's colonnade. No one else dared join them, even though they were highly regarded by the people. Nevertheless, more and more men and women believed in the Lord and added to their number. As a result, people brought the sick into the streets and laid them on beds and mats so that at least Peter's shadow might fall on them as he passed by. Crowds also gathered from the towns around Jerusalem, bringing their sick and those tormented by evil spirits, and all of them were healed.

In reading these verses today, one may have the impression that there is a gap between the reality we live in and what the Bible describes. As Jones says, "Religious faith and the act of prayer was seen, throughout much of antiquity, as at least as effective a cure as when medical and surgical interventions were largely futile"[19] In our times, believers' trust in prayer did not decrease, but their trust in the effectiveness of medicine radically increased. People in evangelization may therefore be tempted to feel as if they have to compromise between trusting God or professionals. But how do we resolve the seeming discrepancy between biblical reports and everyday mentality that require experiential facts? How do we help evangelized people gain empirical and practical firsthand evidence of God's presence and love equal to that described in Acts 5:16?

In John 14:12–13, Jesus himself hinted at the answer: "I tell you the truth, anyone who has faith in me will do what I have been doing. He will do even greater things than these because I am going to the Father. And I will do whatever you ask in my name so that the Son may bring glory to the Father." It is not easy to grasp what Jesus meant, so instead, let us determine what doing these "greater things" does *not* mean in a contemporary context.

D. A. Carson explains that the greater things Jesus talks about cannot mean more spectacular or more supernatural works because "it is hard to imagine works that are more spectacular or supernatural than the raising of Lazarus from the dead, the multiplication of bread, and the turning of water into wine."[20] Exegetes have suggested that Jesus was predicting that, after Pentecost, the disciples would do the same things he was doing (i.e., proclaiming the kingdom of God) and also greater things by spreading the gospels outside of Palestine and around the world to all humankind. However, as noted in Chapter Thirty-Five, for postmodern, Thomas-like cunctators, the greater things that Jesus promised are not merely spreading the signs of God's kingdom, such biblical love, peace, and joy "upon you" (Mt. 3:2; 12:28), "within you," or "in the midst of you" (Lk. 17:21) all around the world. For them, God's kingdom is observing grandiose and inexplicable miracles—visible and touchable proofs, or even theocratic empires and powers. What if with this fixation, however, miracle seekers fail to recognize the much less conspicuous miraculous signs and wonders that Jesus promised in John 14:12–13 occurring right before our eyes? Is it possible that we live in the same miraculous world today as our ancestors lived in biblical times?

The basic characteristic of biblical miracles is not grandiosity but their being a sign of God's acting through Jesus in proclaiming the kingdom of God. St. Matthew's Gospel (8:1–9:34) notes ten such miracles: the cleansing of the leper (8:1–4); the healing of the centurion's servant (8:5–13); the healing of many at Peter's house (8:14–17); the healing of the Nazarene demoniac (8:28–34); the healing of the paralytic (9:1–8); the healing of a woman (9:20–22); the restoration of a girl's life (9:23–26); the healing of two blind men (9:27–31); and the healing of a mute (9:32–34). Comparing these healings, it is hard not to see a parallel with contemporary pastoral healings.

As we substantiated in Chapter Two, every genuine healing of psychological and psychiatric ailments, like depression, anxiety, fear, aggression, jealousy, greed, envy, positivism, addiction, existential angst, and the feeling of meaninglessness in postmodern times points toward God. Psychiatric and psychological healing today would not be possible without fostering goodwill, forgiveness, love, trust, unselfishness, peace, and other Christian values in patients. Furthermore (as we discussed in detail in Part 2), no healing of DSM-5 disorders and psychological ailments is possible without explicitly or implicitly fulfilling Jesus' commands of "Love the Lord your God with all your heart and all your strength" and "Love your neighbour as yourself" (Mark 12:29–31).

We could continue listing further similarities. If we analyze the ten great public miracles noted in Matthew 8:1–9:34, we discern three commonalities: they are all marked with *visible signs, psychological changes, and spiritual effects. The visible signs* of the biblical miracles are Jesus' inexplicable and striking healings. The *psychological effects* of Jesus' miraculous interventions are the behavioral changes called "discipleship." The *spiritual effects* in all biblical miracles are the establishment of a new and close relationship with Jesus. There is a strong parallel between the biblical miracles and current pastoral healing. First, as Jesus' miracles were verified by striking and inexplicable healings, so also today pastoral counseling produces healing that no worldly science, psychology, or medicine can either grasp or replicate. Secondly, as biblical healings promoted discipleship psychologically, so pastoral healings today lead to behavioral changes in one's whole lifestyle. And thirdly, as Jesus' biblical healings always produced spiritual effects, so also contemporary pastoral healings help the client's sanctification and salvation. Thus, the parallel is obvious. Just as the healing of leprosy, paralysis or blindness in biblical times pointed toward the Messiah, so healing the sufferings associated with the sin and sickness continuum points toward Jesus today.

And so, exactly like St. Peter, contemporary healers also derive their ability to heal from an inner connection with truth, or more exactly, with some aspect of the ultimate truth of Jesus Christ. In this sense, although it may sound surprising to nonbelievers and is not apparent to everyone, all healings, professional and pastoral healings alike, are miracles. The form and manifestation of miracles changed; nevertheless, all healings, professional and pastoral healings alike, are signs of God's grace.

Let us note one more fact. The greatest miracles of Jesus are not his public healings. Jesus' spectacular public healings, witnessed by many, are minor compared to the miracles of his incarnation and resurrection, which were witnessed by no one. Jesus' incarnation and resurrection are the ultimate miracles which, despite occurring without any eyewitnesses, affect all Christians. Today, too, Jesus' greatest miracles occur invisibly. Though not witnessed publicly, his largest miracles are eminently and experientially verified today by the astounding, scientifically inexplicable psychological and spiritual healings of countless disciples. They occur invisibly in people's hearts, minds, and souls. Yes, it is a sign of the times that the appearance and phenomenology of miracles changed. Yes, Christians today do not bring their sick relatives to be healed by the shadows of Peter's successors. Yes, there is a decrease in the number of spectacular public miracles, but there is a growing number of invisible pastoral healings. With exponential multiplying of the suffering, impairment and distress linked to the sin and sickness continuum, foreseeably, the importance of the individual psychological-spiritual healings will also increase exponentially in the future. This will cause substantial changes. Already today, thanks to new pastoral approaches, the number of scientifically inexplicable and miraculous, psychological-spiritual healings is rising, heralding a new era in evangelizing, as well. The new evangelization tends to be personal, experiential, and it leads believers and non-believers on the path to becoming blessed.

In John 20:29, Jesus says to Thomas, "Do you believe because you see me? Blessed are those who believe without seeing." Because many saw miraculous Healings under Solomon's colonnade, they believed. However, in Jesus' words, blessed are those who have not seen such spectacular miracles and yet have believed—that is, blessed are the postmodern believers defeating with faith all kinds of sin and sickness. It is the Church's mission today to convey God's presence by methods that are different than those used in St. Peter's times. Experiential evangelization therefore means helping evangelized people to be blessed by biblical joy, peace, love, optimism, and meaning that only Jesus can give. It means appreciating that we live, no less than the early church, in a miraculous world in which literally everything is a sign pointing toward Jesus. It means discerning that the number of miracles has not decreased, but their kind and phenomenology changed, so that we are all called to do the "even greater things" Jesus spoke about. With the Holy Spirit's help, people experiencing this biblical-theological truth are well-evangelized.

44.5 After Conversion: Continuing Self-Scrutiny

While the life of nonbelievers is more or less static, an awakening in faith is the beginning of permanent growth. Progressing in discipleship requires a permanent self-scrutiny which entails becoming ever more Christlike, and this kind of scrutiny requires a different logic than what is used in any worldly reasoning. Since Christians' beliefs cannot be tested simply by discerning physical laws, most believers rely on God's revealed words. However, as Faw notes:

> Various believers interpret the Scripture quite differently…. There is no such thing as biblical fact that bypasses human interpretation. Although God's Word is absolute and infallible, our understanding of it clearly is not. The open discussion of ideas and thoughtful evaluation of differing viewpoints in the context of mutual trust and humble truth-seeking are vital. They help to counteract our ever-present human tendency to err.[21]

The open discussions Faw talks about are unquestionably helpful in controlling the human tendency to err, but as church history proves, they are not always a perfect guarantee. Note that our purpose is not to minimize the importance of the classical criteria of orthodoxy (such as exegesis, tradition, and ecclesial, doctrinal, or theological teachings), but to detect, develop, and engage a psychological-spiritual guard against errors in understanding the biblical message and knowing God. To discern it, let us turn to the Word of God, which gives the key to its own right understanding.

Psalm 16:11 reads, "You have made known to me the path of life; you will fill me with joy in your presence, with eternal pleasures at your right hand." In other words, knowing (and following) Yahweh's path of life leads to eternal pleasure at God's right-hand side. The gospels affirm the correlation between the ultimate truth (Jesus) and biblical joy even more categorically. Luke 24:32 says that the disciples' "hearts burning" helped them recognize the resurrected Jesus on the road to Emmaus. John 20:29 calls "blessed" those "who have not seen and yet have believed." And John 17:13 notes that recognition of the fullness of truth (Jesus) brings "fullness of joy." In sum, in the words of Xavier Leon Duffour, "Jesus' words brought the fruits: those who believed in him had the fullness of his joy."[22]

The ultimate truth (Jesus) is an ideal which never can be absolutely reached. In the same way, the fullness of his joy is never absolutely achievable. Nevertheless, the experience of believers always confirms a progression in these biblical truths. Even in everyday life, the Lord's disciples, though still on the way toward the ultimate truth of Jesus, were easy to recognize as living in the foretaste of the fullness of joy. This marked the the fulfilment of Jesus' prayer that his disciples "may have the full measure of my joy within them" (Jn. 17:13). Having Jesus' full measure of joy within them (i.e., receiving a foretaste of the fullness of joy) and its radiating from the disciples was so profound that it attracted their contemporaries to seek the ultimate truth, which is Jesus Christ. Thanks to their joy, the number of Christians quickly doubled, tripled, quadrupled, and quintupled. Therefore, since the earliest Christian centuries, the reception of biblical joy has played a crucial role in evangelizing and progressing in discipleship.

Could we apply this same logic to our self-scrutinizing today? If following the ultimate truth of Jesus produces ultimate joy, could we than reverse our point of view and assess our lives as to whether they reflect the ultimate truth of Jesus by the degree to which we experience a foretaste of the fullness of biblical joy?

As noted in *The Mystery of Christian Faith: A Tangible Union with the Invisible God*,[23] such an assessment occurs, consciously or unconsciously, in the everyday lives of all Christians, externally and internally. Externally, the world assesses Christians, their churches, and especially their leaders. To paraphrase Robert Barnes' words, they "look at the theorist first to see if he/

she knows how to live like Christ."[24] As Jesus was never shy in being questioned, tested, or assessed, neither should his disciples be uncomfortable with being scrutinized over whether they know how to live like Christ in bearing witness to biblical values. We consciously or unconsciously assess other Christians and their leaders, teachers, elders, bishops, and priests as to whether they know how to live like Christ, reflecting biblical truth, love, peace, and joy.

In internal self-assessment, Christians use the inner eyes of their consciences to examine whether they genuinely resemble Jesus in their lives. In addition to external adherence to tradition, canon law, Church teaching, and Scriptures, becoming Christlike is proven internally by reasons of the heart, or more precisely, by the foretaste of ultimate joy, which creates biblical peace, love, hope, optimism, power, and other spiritual-psychological gifts.

To be clear, we are speaking not about any kind of pleasure or happiness but explicitly about biblical joy. A growth in biblical love, peace, optimism, courage, and joy experienced by the disciple and reflected to neighbours is a psychological-spiritual indicator and criterion of progressing in Christlike living that is often more reliable than external criteria. As is well known, St. Pio was radically silenced and banned from priestly activities until 1933. Then, however, Pope Pius XI proclaimed, "I have not been badly disposed toward Padre Pio. I was badly informed." Trusting the judgment of the inner eyes of his conscience gave Padre Pio the resilience to persist in faith until his rehabilitation. But is such self-judgment reliable?

As historical examples prove, we can deceive others for a while, but we can never really deceive ourselves. Our positivist culture is suspicious about the reliability of our introspections; however, those who self-deceptively justify or deny their sin or sickness, who internally experience Luciferian hate, aggression, or murderous rage (like Judas, King David, Ivan the Terrible, Stalin, or proponents of religious wars) cannot falsify the experience of progressing in biblical love, peace, or joy while killing their opponents. We can only externally act as if we believe our lies. However, receiving the spiritual-psychological gifts of faith and staying on a sin-sick continuum are mutually exclusive. Thus, let us note that solely progressing toward Jesus' ultimate truth marks the fulfilment of his prayer, that his disciples "may have the full measure of my joy within them" (Jn. 17:13), and that it is impossible to gain internal evidence by any self-deception, cheating, or trickery.

Since the beginning of scientific reasoning, humankind's trust in the validity and reliability of logic has been so firm that we label as false everything contradicting its rules. Because receiving biblical joy exclusively correlates to Jesus' commands of "Love the Lord your God with all your heart and all your strength" and "Love your neighbour as yourself" (Mark 12:29–31), progression in the fulfilment of Jesus' commands is verified by receiving a foretaste of biblical joy. The experience of biblical hope, trust, courage, peace, love, joy, and other gifts of faith is as valid a measure for progressing in discipleship as logic is in scientific reasoning. A crescendo of biblical joy, in individual believers as well as those in contact with them, verifies one's interpretation of the Bible, theology, discipleship, denominational association, relationship with God, moral choices, and the appropriate role in building God's kingdom as much as it verifies a sound adherence to Church teachings. Inversely, belonging to the body of Christ verifies a daily, weekly, and monthly growth in biblical optimism, peace, and joy. Theologically and experientially, peace, forgiveness, compassion, and, above all, love have an epistemological-apologetical value since "whoever does not love does not know God, since God is love" (1 John 4:8).

Such continuous self-scrutiny has an effective role in fostering unity among believers as well. Since the great schism of 1054, theologians have had open, rational, logical, and scientific discussions about the right interpretation of the Scriptures, the right ecclesiology, and the right way of living Jesus' legacy. However, in denominational discussions, theological reasoning is not what most frequently determines beliefs; it is more often the mutual seeking of union with Jesus. The ecumenical toolset ought to include not only open discussions and scientific arguments but adherence to Jesus' command "that you love one another just as I loved you" (John 13:34), verified internally in the minds of proponents and also externally in their behaviors.

In practice, adherence to Jesus' command is less about theologically proving "I am right; you are wrong" and more about giving mutual support in seeking and spreading love, peace, forgiveness, joy, trust, and other spiritual gifts of Jesus' love. Believers' demonstrating Jesus-like love to each other can and will shape their beliefs and form a consensus in ecumenical exegesis, ecclesiology, and other theological disciplines much more efficiently than by open discussions. Maybe the focus ought to be less on proving "you were wrong in this" and more on self-assessment and admitting "I was mistaken in that." Let me illustrate the rationale of such ecumenical spirituality by paraphrasing Gotthold E. Lessing's play *Nathan the Wise*.

> It was a tradition in one Near Eastern family for the father to give a golden ring to his best son. So the ring travelled through time, from one generation to the next. But one father of many sons could not decide who among them was the best. He secretly bought many rings and gave a ring to each of his sons. After his death, the sons discovered his secret, but since every one of them believed his ring was the original, they got into a bitter fight. Unable to resolve it themselves, they asked a wise man, "Whose ring is the original?" After a long deliberation, the wise man responded, "By quarrelling you cannot decide which is the original ring. But he who, by his modesty, love, peace, and unselfishness, proves that he is the best amongst all of you is the one who has the original ring."[25]

As noted in the preface, and as is likely apparent to the reader, this book is written from a Catholic perspective. Nevertheless, for Catholics, Baptists, Lutherans, Presbyterians, Orthodox believers, and all other Christians dispersed among 20,000 denominations, proving that they possess the metaphorical original ring—the correct denomination—and proving their biblical, theological, and doctrinal orthodoxy is of paramount importance. Rational and scientific discussions are important, but Christians belonging to different theologies may prove more efficiently than any rational arguments that they belong to the right denomination by demonstrating biblical love, discipleship, and holiness. This was the most powerful proof of knowing God in the first Christian centuries, and it remains so today.

As St. Paul says in 1 Corinthians 13:4–8: "Love is patient; love is kind, love is not envious or boastful or arrogant or rude. It does not insist on its own way; it is not irritable or resentful; it does not rejoice in wrongdoing, but rejoices in the truth, It bears all things, believes all things, believes all things, hopes all things, endures all things." Such love enables God, whom we still so often disobey, to take a venerated place in our hearts, minds, and souls as well as in the hearts, minds, and souls of those who believe in the same Jesus but have different theologies, and facilitates the universal brotherhood envisioned in Galatians 3:28—"We are all one in Christ Jesus." As disciples striving for being one in Christ, we all pray for sainthood. In John 14:14, Jesus promised that we will receive whatever we ask in his name, and in Mark 11:24 he even more emphatically promised that when praying in his name we should perceive our petitions as already fulfilled. Despite being yet imperfect, all people of faith possess at least some minuscule, basic traits and elements of sainthood. All Christians, despite the fact that we have not yet completely achieved this goal, are on our way toward sainthood, manifest in our striving to be "all one in Christ Jesus."

Notes

[1] F. L. Cross and E. A. Livingstone, *The Oxford Dictionary of the Christian Church* (New York: Oxford University Press, 1997), 1035–7.

[2] Joel Feinberg and Russ Shafer-Landau, *Reason and Responsibility: Readings in Some Basic Problems in Philosophy* (Belmont, CA: Wadsworth Publishing Company, 1999), 12.

[3] Ibid., 19.

[4] Lindsay Jones (ed.), *Encyclopedia of Religion*, vol. 5 (Farmington Hills, MI: Thomson Gale, 2005), 2427.

[5] Quoted from the Roman Catholic Initiation of Adults, St. Jude's Parish (Vancouver, Canada, 2016–17), 427.

[6] Susan E. Schreiner: *Are You Alone Wise?: The Search for Certainty in the Early Modern Era* (New York: Oxford University Press, 2016), 307.

[7] Elizabeth S. Lukas, *A Life With Meaning: A Guide to the Fundamental Principles of Viktor E. Frankl's Logotherapy* (Berkley, CA: Institute of Logotherapy Press, 1998), 33.

[8] Ferenc Szabo, *Ember es Vilaga* (Rome: self-published, 1988), 78.

[9] Ibid., 80–3.

[10] Benedict XVI, *Benedictus, Day by Day with Pope Benedict XVI*, edited by Rev. Peter Cameron (New York: Magnificat, 2006), 240.

[11] Victor Hugo, *Les Misérables* (London: Penguin, 1967).

[12] Joseph Ratzinger, *Behold the Pierced One: An Approach to Spiritual Christology* (San Francisco, CA: Ignatius, 1986), 68.

[13] Feinberg and Shafer-Landau, *Reason and Responsibility*, 125.

[14] Viktor E. Frankl, *Man's Search for Ultimate Meaning* (New York: Basic Books, 2000), 48–51.

[15] Frankl, *Man's Search for Ultimate Meaning*, 77.

[16] Louis P. Pojman, *Classics of Philosophy* (New York: Oxford University Press, 2003), 368.

[17] Jones, *Encyclopedia of Religion*, vol. 5, 2958.

[18] Ibid., 3257.

[19] Ibid., 3428.

[20] D. A. Carson, *The Gospel According to John: Pillar New Testament Commentary* (Grand Rapids, MI: Eerdmans, 1991), 495.

[21] Benedict J. Groeschel, *For Those Who Seek Spiritual Passages: The Psychology of Spiritual Development* (New York: Crossroad Publishing Company, 1996), 74.

[22] Xavier Leon Duffour, *Rjecnik Biblijske Teologije* (Zagreb: Krscanska Sadasnjost 1988), 1376.

[23] Paul Ungar, *The Mystery of Christian Faith: A Tangible Union with the Invisible God* (Lanham, MD: University Press of America, 2008), 250–3.

[24] Robert Barnes, *Theories on Counseling* (Abilene, TX: Department

of Counseling and Human Development, Hardin Simons University, 1994), 2.

25 P. S. Kohan, *Istoroja Zapadnoeveropske Knjizevnosti* (Sarajevo: Veselin Maslesa, 1967), 285–90. See also Ungar, *The Mystery of Christian Faith*, 299.

CHAPTER FORTY-FIVE

CONCLUSION

There is no Protestant, Orthodox, or Catholic psychology or pathology, only a grave challenge affecting all Christians. Therefore, the purpose of this book is to transcend denominational boundaries and help all people of faith in dealing with our common trial: a psychological-spiritual pandemic of apocalyptic proportions. The suicide rate among youngsters in the last one hundred years has almost doubled, the statistic for depression has tripled, divorces have quadrupled, single-parent families have quintupled, and the rate of drug abuse in children has sextupled. I use a bit of poetic liberty, but the point is not overstated; psychiatric problems of every kind have skyrocketed. Mental disorders are multiplying so rapidly that, according to an anecdotal story, professionals have begun saying, "The DSM 5 has to be revised again as soon as possible, but no later than 2029. Why 2029? Because after that time there will be no normal people left to complete the job." How can Christians deal with this challenge that affects not only our relationship with God but even our human form of being?

Contemporary mass media are toppling the basic pillar of human dignity by disregarding the reality that we are a living soul and reducing us to "human animals," or even "human machines." In this perspective, Christian love is devalued; it seems unnecessary and redundant. So the sinful transgression of Jesus' commands "Love the Lord your God with all your heart and all your strength" and "Love your neighbour as yourself" Mark 12:

29-31, has almost become a standard in our times. Because sickness and sin are connected like a chicken and egg, humankind is caught in a vicious circle. *It is impossible to successfully heal the pandemic of mental illness without addressing sin, and it is equally impossible to tackle sinful behaviours without healing mental problems.*

Our contemporaries, just as people in biblical times, need a Jesus-like healing. In all Jesus' healings, the psychological and spiritual recovery occurred simultaneously. We also need to reconnect mental and spiritual healing. In numerous Christian counselling institutions, the light at the end of the tunnel is already visible, and professionals and clerics work together on a psychological-spiritual healing of the people of faith. Such professionals interested in theology, as well as clerics interested in healing practices, are the prophets of our times.

And we need not only prophetic clerics and pastoral healers, but Christian saints in all fields. There ought to be no such thing as Christian laity, but there already exists Christian saints who can verify in their areas of expertise that mankind's attempt to be "like God, knowing good and evil" (Gen. 3:5) causes all current spiritual-psychological crises. True Christians are striving for, and to some degree, are already possessing elements of sanctity. They should witness to the world that God is even closer to us than our own selves by reflecting biblical love, optimism, peace, and joy.

Is there any task given to us by God that is even more pressing than all those listed? Jesus gave the answer at the turning point of his ministry, just before his suffering. His high-priestly prayer that his disciples would be one as he is one with the Father "so that the world may believe" (Jn. 17:21–23) was his revelation of what we need to strive for even today. We may hope that when oneness of all disciples in Jesus occurs, atheists will echo the words of the third century pagans—"Look how Christians love each other"—and the world will believe in Jesus Christ. Then, empowered by the Father, united Christians will regain their spiritual, psychological, and biological resilience. With Jesus' help they will reclaim their biblical self-confidence, joy, optimism, and missionary purpose. And led by the Holy Spirit, they will be able to bring all people to appreciate the love of the invisible God, exponentially multiplying the number of believers as in the times of the original church and thus healing our culture, mortally wounded by sin and sickness.

Does all this represent an unrealistic utopia?

The whole of church history is a chronicle of mankind's being repeatedly tested. The tests Christians faced were different in the bloody persecutions of the early years. They were also different during the supremacy of the Church in the Middle Ages, and different again through the Renaissance, the Enlightenment, the French Revolution, secularism, modernism, fascism, and communism. The Church victoriously endured all these seemingly insurmountable tests. As the saying goes, "History is the teacher of life." It does not change, only repeats. Those who witnessed the sudden and unpredicted collapse of communism (widely and successfully touted as being the ultimate step in the evolution of human consciousness) know that the kind of turnaround we are talking about may occur, God willing, if Christians, inspired by the Holy Spirit, make it happen. They realize, like Hippocrates, the father of medicine, wrote, that "our way is long, the time is short, and our choice is urgent." If this book helped you to help others to make this choice, then it has fulfilled its purpose.

LITERATURE

Accatoli, Luigi. *When a Pope Asks Forgiveness, The Mea Culpa of John Paul II*: Boston, Pauline Books and Media, 1998, 30.

American College of Pediatricians. "Gender Identity Harms Children." Accessed September 2017. www.acpeds.org/the-college-speaks/position-statements/gender -ideology-harms- children.

Bailey, J. Michel and Rey Blanchard. *Suicide or transition: The only options for gender dysphoric kids?*. fourth Wave Web Publication. Accessed September 2017. www.fourthwavenow.com/tag/5michael-bailey/.

Balthasar, Hans Urs von. *Church and World*. Montreal: Palm Publishers, 1967.

Baird E. Forrest. *Philosophic Classics*. Vol. 3. Upper Saddle River: Prentice Hall, 2003.

Barlow H. David. *Clinical Handbook of Psychological Disorders, A Step-by-Step Treatment Manual*. Vol 4. The Guilford Press: New York, NY, 2003.

Barnes, Robert. *Theories in Counseling*. Abilene, TX: Departement of Counseling and Human Development, Hardin Simons University, 1994.

Bitter, Wilhelm. *Psychotherapie und Religioise Erfahrung.* Stuttgart: Ernst Klett, 1965.

Bouyer, Louis. *The Church of God, Body of Cjhrist and Temple of the Spirit.* Chicago: Franciscan Herald Press, 1982.

Bristow, Peter. *Christian Ethics and the Human Person.* Herefordshire, UK: Gracewing.

Brown, R. E., J. J. Castelot, J. A. Fitzmeyer, J. J. Kselman, J. J. McKenzie, D. D. Stanley, and A. Suelzer. *The Jerome Biblical Commentary.* Engelwood Cliffs, NJ: Prentice Hall, Inc., 1980.

Browning, S. Don and Terry D. Cooper. *Religious Thought and the Modern Psychologies,* 2nd ed. Mineapolis, MN: Augsburg Fortress Press, 2004.

Canadian Conference of the Catholic Bishops. *Catechism of the Catholic Church.* Ottawa: Publications Service, Canadian Conference of Catholic Bishops, 1994.

Carson, D.A. *The Gospel According to John, Pillar New Testament Commentary* (Grand Rapids, MI: Eerdmans, 1991), 495.

Chalmers, J. David. *Philosophy of Mind, Classical and Contemporary Readings.* New York, NY: Oxford University Press, 2002.

Colby, A. and L. Kohlberg. *The Measurement of Moral Judgment.* New York, NY: Cambridge University Press, 1987.

Coles Notes. *Total Study Edition Hamlet.* Missisauga, Ont. Canada: John Willey & Sons, 2012.

Copleston, Frederick. *A History of* Philosophy. Paramus, New York: Newman Press, 1975.

Corey, Gerald. *Theory and Practice of Counseling and Psychotherapy.* 7th ed. Thomson Brooks/Cole, Thomson Learning Academic Resource Center, 2005.

Cross, F. L. and E. A. Livingstone. *The Oxford Dictionary of the Christian Church*. New York, NY: Oxford University Press, 1997.

Cretella, Michelle. "Society Commentary: I'm a Pediatrician. How Transgender Ideology Has Infiltrated My Field and Produced Large Scale Child Abuse." The Daily Signal. Accessed July 3, 2017. www. DailySignal.com.

Cross, of the John. *The Ascent of Mount Carmel*. New York, NY: Magisterium Books, 2015.

Cuningham, Mary and Elizabeth Theokritoff. *The Cambridge Company to Orthodox Christian Faith*. New York, NY: Cambridge University Press, 2008.

DSM-5. *Diagnostic and Statistical Manual of the American Psychiatric Association*, Arlington, VA, 2013.

Dowd, E. Thomas and Steven Lars Nielsen. *The Psychologies in Religion, Working with the Religious Client*. New York, NY: Springer Publishing Company, 2006.

Durant, Will. *The Story of Philosophy*. New York, NY: Washington Square Press, 1953.

Erdody, Janos. *Requiem Firenzeert*. Budapest: Szepmuveszeti Kiado, 1977.

Eric, Ljubomir. *Strah, Anxioznost I Anxiozna Stanja*. Beograd Institut za Strucno Usavrsavanje I Specijalizaciju Zdravstvenih Radnika, 1972.

Erickson, Millar. *Christian Theology*. Grand Rapids, MI: Baker Book House, 1995.

Eugene, E., S. B. Flexner, G. Carruth, and J. M. Hawkins. *Oxford American Dictionary*, New York, NY: Avon Books, 1979.

Faw, W. Harold. *Psychology in Christian Perspective, An Analysis of Key Issues*. Grand Rapids, MI: Baker Book, 1995.

Feinberg, Joel and Russ Shafer-Landau. *Reason and Responsibility:*

Readings in Some Basic Problems in Philosophy. 10th ed. Belmont, CA: Wadsworth Publishing Company, 1999.

Groeschel, J. Benedict. *For Those Who Seek Spiritual Passages—The Psychology of Spiritual Development*. New York, NY: Crossroad Publishing Company, 1996.

Flanery, Austin. *Vatican Council II, Vol. 1: The Councilar and Postconcilar Documents*. Northport, NY: Costello Publishing Comp, 1992.

Flew, Anthony and Roy A Varghese. *There Is a God: How the World's Most Notorious Atheist Changed His Mind*. New York, NY: Harper Collins Publishers, 2007.

Guilmartin, Nancy. *Healing Conversations: What to Say When You Don't Know What to Say*. San Francisco, CA: Jossey-Bass, 2002.

Fenichel, Otto. *The Psychoanalytic Theory of Neurosis*. New York, NY: W.W. Norton & Company Inc., 1972.

Fossier, Robert. *The Cambridge Illustrated History of the Mioddle Ages*. Vol. 3. Cambridge, MA: Cambridge University Press, 2006.

Frame, Marsha Wiggins. *Integrating Religion and Spirituality in Counseling: A Comprehensive Approach*. Pacific Grove, CA: Thomson Brooks/Cole, 2003.

Frankl, Viktor E. *Anthropologische Grundlagen der Psychotherapie*. Bern, Stuttgart, Wien: Hans Huber, 1976.

Frankl, Viktor E. *Arztliche Seelsorge*. Wien: Franz Deuticke, 1965.

Frankl, Viktor E. *The Doctor and the Soul, From Psychotherapy to Logotherapy*. New York, NY: Vinatage Books, 1973.

Frankl, Viktor E. *The Unconscious God: Psychotherpay and Theology,* New York, NY: Simon Shuster, 1975.

Frankl, Viktor E. *Man's Search for Ultimate Meaning*. New York, NY: Basic Books, Member of the Perseus Book Group, 2000.

Franzen, August. *Kleine Kirchengenschihte*. Freiburg: Herder Bucherei, 1968.

Hauzer, Arnold. *Socijalna Istorija Umetnosti I Knjizevnosti*. Beograd: Kultura, 1966.

Havran, M. J. "The Church." In *New Catholic Encyclopedia*. 2nd ed. Vol. 3. Farmington Hills, MI: Thomson Gale in Association with the Catholic University of America, 2003.

Herman, Helen, Shekhar Saxena, and Rob Moodie. *Concepts, Emerging Evidence, Practice, Report of the World Health Organization Department of Mental Health and Substance Abuse in Collaboration with the Victorian Health Promotion Foundation and the University of Melbourne*. Geneva, Switzerland: Tushita Graphic Vision, 2005.

Heschl, Abraham. *Between God and Man*. New York, NY: The Free Press, 1959.

Heussi, Karl. *Kompendium der* Kirchengeschihte. Tubingen: Verlag von I.C.B. Mohr, 1998.

Hodi, Sandor. *Kongresszus Abbaziaban, A Titokzatos EN nyomaban*. Ada, Serbia: Szechenyi Istvan Strategiakutato Tarsasag, 2014.

Hugo, Viktor, *Les Miserables*. London: Penguin Books, 1976.

Hyman, Arthur and James Walsh. *Philosophy in the Middle Ages*. New York, NY: Harper & Row Publishers, 1967.

Jarosevski Mihail. *Istoria Psihologiei*. Moskva: Izdatelstvo Misl, 1966.

Jones, Lindsay. *Encyclopedia of Religion*. Detroit, MI: Thomson Gale, 2005.

Jung, Carl Gustav. *Man and His Symbols*. Aldus Books, 1964.

Jung, Carl Gustav. *Man and His Symbols*. New York, NY: Bantam, 1968.

Kardos, Lajos. *Behaviorismus*. Budapest: Gondolat Konyvkiado, 1970.

Kasper, Walter. *The God of Jesus Christ*. New York, NY: Crossroad, 1992.

Kohan, P. S. *Istoroja Zapadnoeveropske Knjizevnosti.* Sarajevo: Veselin Maslesa, 1967.

Koteesky, L. Ronald. *Psychology from a Christian Perspective.* 2nd ed. Langham, MD: University Press of America, 1991.

Leon-Duffour, Xavier. *Rijecnik Biblijske Teologije.* Edited by Josip Turcinovic. Zagreb: Krscanska Sadasnjost, 1988.

Lozano, Neal. *Resisting the Devil: A Catholic Perspective on Deliverance.* Huntington, IN: Our Sunday Visitor Publishing Division, Our Sunday Visitor Inc., 2010.

Lukas, S. Elizabeth. *A Life with Meaning: A Guide to Fundamental Principles of Viktor E. Frankl's Logotherapy.* Berkley, California: Institute of Logotherapy Press, 1998.

Marshall, Maria and Edward Marshall. *Spiritual Psychotherapy: The Search for Lasting Meaning.* Ontario, Canada: Ottawa Institute of Logotherapy, 2015.

Mendaglio, Sal. *Dabrowski's Theory of Positive of Positive Disintegration.* Scottsdale, AZ: Great Potential Press, 2008.

Mendez, Maria. *A Life with Meaning: Guide to Fundamental Principles of Viktor E. Frankl's Logotherapy.* Victoria, Trafford: 2004.

Montefiori, Sebag Simon. *Stalin: The Court of the Red Tsar.* Phoenix, AZ: Orion House, An imprint of Orion Books Ltd., 2004.

Mota, N. P., M. Burnett, and J. Sareen. "Associations Between Abortion, Mental Disorders and Suicidal Behavior in a Nationally Representative Sample." *The Canadian Journal of Psychiatry* 55(4). 2010.

Murphy, Nancy. *Bodies and Souls, or Spirited Bodies?* Cambridge: Cambridge University Press, 2006.

Nemeshegyi, Peter. *Egy Hit, Sokfele Teologia.* Budapest: Magyar Papi Egyseg, A Tavlatok Melleklete, 1998.

Newman, John Henry. "The Religion of the Pharisee, the Religion of Mankind." In *Sermons Preached to Various Occasions. Roman Catholic Initiation of Adults.*

Noonan, Moira and Anne Feaster. *Spiritual Dceptions in the Church and the Culture: A Comprehensive Guide to Discernment.* Niagara Falls, NY and Toronto, Canada: 2015.

Oxford American Dictionary, Heald Colleges Edition, New York, NY: Oxford University Press, 1980.

Packer, J. I. *God's Plan for You.* Wheaton, IL: Crossway Books, 2001.

Pegis, Anton C. *Basic Writings of Saint Thomas Aquinas.* New York, NY: Random House, 1945.

Petterson, M, W. Hasker, B. Reichenbach, and D. Basinger, *Reason and Religious Beleief, An Introduction to Philsophy of Religion.* New York, NY: Oxford University Press, 1991.

Pojman, P. Louis. *Classics of Philosphy.* 2nd ed. New York, NY: Oxford University Press, 2003.

Pojman, P. Louis and Lewis Vaughn. *Philosphy: The Quest for Truth.* 7th ed. New York, NY: Oxford University Press, 2009.

Pontifical Council for Pastoral Assistance to Healthcare Workers, The. *Charter for Health Care Workers.* Vatican City: 1995.

Pop Benedict XVI. "Blessed is the one who comes in the name of the Lord." *Day by Day with Pope Benedict XVI.* Edited by Fr. Peter John Cameron O.P. Yonkers, NY: Ignatius Press, 2006.

Pope Benedict XVI. "Christmas Adress to the Curia." Published on the Vativan's vebsite in official translation, 2003. Accessed September 2017. www.vatican.vaholyfather/benedictxvispeeches/2008/documents/hfben-xvispe20081222curia-romanaen.html.

Pope Francis. *Laudato Si.* Libreria Editrice Vatcano, 2016.

Pope Francis. *Gaudete et Exultate*. Libreria Editrice Vatcano, 2018.

Pope Francis. *The Name of God Is Mercy*. New York, NY: Random House, 2016.

Pope John Paul II. *Man and Woman He Created Them: A Theology of the Body*. Boston, MA: Pauline Books and Media, 2006.

Petofi, Sandor. *Petofi Sandor Osszes Koltemenyei*. Budapest: Oziris Kiado Kft, 2007.

Rape, M. Ronald and David H. Barlow. *Chronic Anxiety, Generalized Anxiety Disorder and Mixed Anxiety Disorder*. New York, NY: The Guilford Press, 1991.

Ratzinger, Joseph, *Behold the Pierced One: An Approach to Spiritual Christology*. San Francisco, CA: Ignatius, 1986.

Ratzinger, Joseph. *Called to Communion, Understanding the Church Today*. San Francisco, CA: Ignatius Press, 1996.

Ratzinger, Jospeh. *Truth and Tolerance: Christian Beleife and World Religions*. San Francisco, CA: Ignatius Press, 2004.

Rebic, Adalbert. *Biblijska Prapovjest*. Zagreb: Krscanska Sadasnjost, 1972. *Roman Catholic Innitation of Adults*.

Robinson, Pascal. "St. Francis of Assissi." *Catholic Encylopdia*. Accessed September 2017. www.robertappleton.com.

Szabo, Ferenc. *Ember es Vilaga*. Roma: 1988.

Sadock, Benjamin J., Virginia Alcott Sadock, and Pedro Ruiz. *Kaplan & Sadock's Synopsis of Psychiatry: Behavioral Sciences/Clinical Psychiatry*. 11th ed. Philadelphia, PA: Lippincott Williams & Wilkins, 2015.

Sadock, Benjamin J. and Virginia Alcott Sadock. *Kaplan & Sadock's Synopsis of Psychiatry: Behavioral Sciences/Clinical Psychiatry*. 10th ed. Philadelphia, PA: Lippincott Williams & Wilkins, 2007.

Sagi, Zoltan. *Kotelekeink, Massagunk Szorongasai*. Szabadka, Eletjel Konyvek, 2015.

Schnackenburg, Rudolf. *The Gospel According to St. John*. New York, NY: Herder and Herder, 1968.

Schnackenburg, Rudolf. *The Gospel of Matthew*. Grand Rapids, MI: William B. Erdmans Publishing Company, 2002.

Schreiner, E. Susan. *Are You Alone Wise? The Search for Certainty in the Early Modern Era*. New York, NY: Oxford University Press, 2016.

Schwarz, Joseph. *Durch Psychologie zum Gott: Argumente Fur Gottes Existenz*. Eisenstadt: 1988.

Seligman, Linda and Laurie W. Reichenberg. *Selecting Effective Treatments: A Comprehensive Systematic Guide to Treating Mental Disorders*. fourth ed. John Wiley & Sons, 2014.

Shakespeare, William. *Hamlet*. Coles Notes *Total Study Edition Hamlet,* (Missisauga, Ontario, John Willey & Sons, 2012) 93.

Stanojevic, Vladimir. *Tragedija Genija*. Beograd: Nolit, 1976.

Stefanics, Charlote and Rosemary Henrion. *The Power of the Human Spirit*. Kettering, OH: Joseph Publishing Company, 2002.

Stojiljkovic, Srboljub. *Psihijatrija sa Medicinskom Psihologijom*. Beograd: Medicinska Knjiga, 1975.

Tomer, Adrian, Grafton T. Eliason, and Paul T. P. Wong. *Existential and Spiritual Issues in Death Attitudes*. New York, NY: Lawrence Erlbaum Associates, Taylor & Francis Group, 2008.

Tomic, Celestin. *Prapovjet Spasenja*. Zagreb: Provincijalat Hrvatskih Franjevaca Konventualaca, 1977.

Trocquer, Rene Le. *What Is Man?*. London: Burns & Oates, 1961.

Tucker, Aviezer, "The Mind." In *New Dictionary of the History of Ideas*.

Vol 2. Edited by Maryanne Cline Horowitz. Farmington Hills, MI: Thomson Gale, 2005.

Ungar, Paul. *Flawed Institution-Flawless Church: A Response to Pope John Paul's Appeal for Critical Self-Evaluation of the Church*. Cambridge: Cambridge Scholars Publishing, 2013.

Ungar, Paul. *The Mystery of Christian Faith: A Tangible Union with the Invisible God*. Lanham, MD: University Press of America, 2008.

Vaihinger, Hans. *Die Philosphie Des Als Ob*. Berlin: Reuter & Reichard, 1921.

Vitz, C, Paul: Faith of Fatherless; The Psychology of Atheism, Dallas TX.: Spence Publsihing Company, 1999.

Walsh, Thomas Walsh. *Saint Teresa of Avila*. Rockford, IL: Tan Books, 1977.

Weir, Kirsten. "Is Pornography Addictive?" *The APA Handbook of Sexuality and Psychology* (Vol. 2) 45 (4) 2014

Weismayer, Joseph. *Dogmatik, VII Kapitel: Hofnung Auf Vollendung*. Wien: Fernkurs Fur Theologische Laienbildung, 1985.

Whitehead, John W. *True Christianity*. Whestchester, IL: Crossway Books, 1989.

About the Author

P aul Ungar is a psychologist who holds an MD, PhD, and a graduate degree in theology. He has taught psychiatry, theology, and psychology at various universities. Currently, he is a faculty member of the International Viktor Frankl Institute. He is also in private practice and active in the treatment of problems on the borderline of theology and psychology.

CPSIA information can be obtained
at www.ICGtesting.com
Printed in the USA
LVHW090903080320
649313LV00002B/3